P9-CFA-715

# Philosophy

# Philosophy
## The Power of Ideas

SIXTH EDITION

### Brooke Noel Moore

*California State University, Chico*

### Kenneth Bruder

*California State University, Chico*

Boston   Burr Ridge, IL   Dubuque, IA   Madison, WI   New York   San Francisco   St. Louis
Bangkok   Bogotá   Caracas   Kuala Lumpur   Lisbon   London   Madrid   Mexico City
Milan   Montreal   New Delhi   Santiago   Seoul   Singapore   Sydney   Taipei   Toronto

## Higher Education

PHILOSOPHY: THE POWER OF IDEAS, SIXTH EDITION

Published by McGraw-Hill, a business unit of The McGraw-Hill Companies, Inc., 1221 Avenue of the Americas, New York, NY 10020. Copyright © 2005, 2002, 1999, 1996, 1993, 1990 by The McGraw-Hill Companies, Inc. All rights reserved. No part of this publication may be reproduced or distributed in any form or by any means, or stored in a database or retrieval system, without the prior written consent of The McGraw-Hill Companies, Inc., including, but not limited to, any network or other electronic storage or transmission, or broadcast for distance learning. Some ancillaries, including electronic and print components, may not be available to customers outside the United States.

ISBN 0-07-287603-4

3 4 5 6 7 8 9 0 DOC/DOC 0 9 8 7 6 5

Editor-in-chief: *Emily Barrosse*
Publisher: *Lyn Uhl*
Sponsoring editor: *Jon-David Hague*
Marketing manager: *Zina Craft*
Production services manager: *Jennifer Mills*
Production service: *Matrix Productions, Inc.*
Manuscript editor: *Vicki Nelson*
Art director: *Jeanne M. Schreiber*
Design manager and cover designer: *Preston Thomas*
Interior designer: *Claire Seng-Niemoeller*
Art manager: *Robin Mouat*
Photo researcher: *Connie Gardner*
Illustrator: *Robin Mouat, Larry Daste/Evelyne Johnson Associates*
Production supervisor: *Randy Hurst*

The text was set in 10/12 Plantin Light by G&S Typesetters, Inc., and printed on acid-free, 45# New Era Matte by RR Donnelley, Crawfordsville.

Cover image: © Christian Michaels/Taxi/Getty Images

The credits for this book begin on page C-1, a continuation of the copyright page.

**Library of Congress Cataloging-in-Publication Data**

Moore, Brooke Noel.
    Philosophy : the power of ideas / Brooke Noel Moore, Kenneth Bruder.—6th ed.
        p.   cm.
    Includes bibliographical references and index.
    ISBN 0-07-287603-4
    1. Philosophy—Introductions.   2. Philosophy—History.   I. Bruder, Kenneth.   II. Title.

BD21.M66   2004
100—dc22
                                                              2004040302

www.mhhe.com

To Marianne Larson, Kathryn Dupier Bruder, and Albert Bruder

# Preface

What do you do with a philosophy degree? Well, of the twenty undergraduates selected to be on the *USA TODAY* 2004 All-USA College Academic First Team, four are philosophy majors. You could ask them.

Jon Novotny, from the University of Tulsa, credits philosophy with helping him see the bigger picture. Sara Shoener, of the University of Scranton, says majoring in philosophy "is the most practical thing I've ever done." Ryan Keller, of Brigham Young University, finds that philosophy opened his mind to different perspectives. And Cristina Bejan, of Northwestern University, used philosophy in writing two plays that were performed at Oxford's Burton Taylor Theatre during her junior year abroad. All four, in short, credit philosophy with broadening their horizons.[1]

We hope the changes in this edition will help broaden the horizons of anyone who reads the book. Here's what we've done:

Most important, we've added an appendix on aesthetics, written by Dominic McIver Lopes, of the University of British Columbia. We didn't write it, so we don't mind saying that this is one of the best short introductions to aesthetics you could hope to find.

We've also expanded our coverage by including new elements. The new materials added and subjects covered include:

- French feminism and psychoanalysis
- Hegel on the master-slave relationship
- Emmanuel Levinas
- Gilles Deleuze
- Alain Badiou
- Ayn Rand
- New reading excerpts from Plato's *Apology,* Plato's *Crito,* and Spinoza's *Ethics*
- New photographs
- Numerous new print and online references
- New profile and feature boxes

---

[1] *USA TODAY,* Feb. 12, 2004.

We have also done a bit of rearranging, consolidating the chapter titled "An Era of Suspicion" with the chapter "The Continental Tradition."

This book remains, however, the same straightforward, ungimmicky historical introduction to philosophy it has always been, one that contains separate treatments of the major branches of philosophy. Our presentation — a middle road between the historical approach and the "problems" approach — helps readers keep similar concepts together and helps instructors avoid leaving an impression that philosophy is a parade of unconnected speculations.

## Philosophy — Powerful Ideas

We concluded years ago that most people like philosophy if they understand it and that most understand it if it isn't presented to them in exhausting prose. In this text we strive above all else to make philosophy understandable while not oversimplifying.

We also concluded years ago that some people just aren't moved by the subject. Worse, we learned that among those who aren't are a few who are sane, intelligent, well informed, and reasonable and who generally have sound ideas about the world, vote for the right people, and are even worth having as friends. Philosophy is just not for everyone, and no text and no instructor can make it so.

So we do not expect that every student, or even every bright student, who comes in contact with philosophy will love the field. But we do hope every student who has had an introductory course in philosophy will learn that philosophy is more than inconsequential mental flexing. Philosophy contains powerful ideas, and it affects the lives of real people. Consequently, it must be handled with due care. The text makes this point clear.

## Philosophy: A Worldwide Search for Wisdom and Understanding

Until the middle of the twentieth century, most philosophers and historians of ideas in American and European universities thought philosophical reflection occurred only within the tradition of disciplined discourse that began with the ancient Greeks and has continued into the present. This conception of philosophy has been changing, however, first through the interest in Eastern thought, especially Zen Buddhism, in the fifties, then through the increasingly widespread publication of high-quality translations and commentaries of texts from outside the Western tradition in the following decades. Of course, the availability of such texts does not mean that unfamiliar ideas will receive a careful hearing or even that they will receive any hearing at all.

Among the most challenging threads of the worldwide philosophical conversation is what has come to be known in recent years as postcolonial thought. The lines defining this way of thinking are not always easy to draw — but the same could be said for existentialism, phenomenology, and a number of other schools of thought in philosophy. In any event, in many cultures and subcultures around the world, thinkers are asking searching questions about methodology and fundamental beliefs that are intended to have practical, political consequences. Because these thinkers frequently intend their work to be revolutionary, their ideas run a higher-than-usual risk of being lost to philosophy's traditional venues. We include in this book a small sample from such writers.

## Women in the History of Philosophy

Histories of philosophy make scant mention of women philosophers prior to the latter half of the twentieth century. For a long time it was assumed that lack of mention was due to a deficit of influential women philosophers. Scholarship such as that by Mary Ellen Waithe (*A History of Women Philosophers*) suggests that women have been more important in the history of philosophy than is often assumed. To date we lack full-length translations and modern editions of the works of many women philosophers. Until this situation changes, Waithe argues, it is difficult to reconstruct the history of the discipline with accuracy.

This text acknowledges the contributions of at least some women to the history of philosophy. We include women philosophers throughout the text in their historical context, and we also offer a chapter on feminist philosophy.

## Features

Among what we think are the nicer attributes of this book are these:

- Separate histories of metaphysics and epistemology; the continental, pragmatic, and analytic traditions; moral and political philosophy; feminist philosophy; and the philosophy of religion
- Coverage of postmodernism and multiculturalism
- A section titled "Other Voices," which contains chapters on Eastern influences, feminist philosophy, and postcolonial thought
- Recognition of specific contributions of women to philosophy
- A generous supply of easy original readings that don't overwhelm beginning students
- Boxes highlighting important concepts, principles, and distinctions or containing interesting anecdotes or historical asides
- Biographical profiles of many of the great philosophers
- End-of-chapter checklists of key philosophers and concepts, with mini-summaries of the philosophers' leading ideas
- End-of-chapter questions for review and reflection and lists of additional sources
- A pronunciation guide to the names of philosophers
- A brief subsection on American Constitutional theory
- A glossary/index that defines important concepts on the spot

- Teachable four-part organization: (1) Metaphysics and Epistemology, (2) Moral and Political Philosophy, (3) Philosophy of Religion, and (4) Other Voices
- A section on arguments and fallacies

## The Teaching Package

- An Online Learning Center available at www.mhhe.com/moore6e includes useful self-assessment quizzes to help students master chapter content. Students can also view and download a PDF file presenting detailed outlines of each chapter. A PowerPoint presentation, available for download by instructors, is designed as an in-class tool to help focus student attention and stimulate discussion using images of philosophers and creative graphics.
- *PowerWeb: Philosophy* is available through the Online Learning Center and contains more than 50 classical and contemporary readings from the most common topics taught in an introductory philosophy course. Students can log in using the access codes at the front of the *Philosophy* text.
- The Instructor's Resource CD-ROM by Dan Barnett, Butte College, contains point-by-point chapter summaries, lists of boxes, lists of reading selections (with brief descriptions of contents), titles of philosophers' main works, lecture ideas relating to questions asked at the ends of chapters, a complete bank of test questions available in Microsoft Word as well as a computerized test bank, and more than 90 PowerPoint slides that present the major topics and philosophers in the book.
- PageOut, www.pageout.net, McGraw-Hill's own course management system, is free with adoption and allows instructors to create powerful online resources and assessments. PageOut is perfect not only for instructors teaching online courses but also for instructors that want to make materials available to their students through the Web.

## Acknowledgments

For their help and support in various forms, we want to thank, first, friends and colleagues at California State University, Chico: Maryanne Bertram, Judy Collins-Hamer, Frank Ficarra, Jay Gallagher, Eric Gampel, Tony Graybosch, Ron Hirschbein, Tom Imhoff, Scott Mahood, Clifford Minor, Adrian Mirvish, Anne Morrissey, Jim Oates, Richard Parker, Michael Rich, Dennis Rothermel, Robert Stewart, Greg Tropea, and Alan Walworth.

Also, for their wise and helpful comments on the manuscript for earlier editions, we thank Ken King, previously Mayfield/McGraw-Hill; John Michael Atherton, Duquesne University; Stuart Barr, Pima Community College; Sherrill Begres, Indiana University of Pennsylvania; Gloria del Vecchio, Bucks County Community College; Mark A. Ehman, Edison Community College; Thomas Eshelman, East Stroudsburg University; Robert Ferrell, University of Texas at El Paso; James P. Finn, Jr., Westmoreland County Community College; Raul Garcia, Southwest Texas State University; Kenneth A. Long, Indiana University–Purdue University at Fort Wayne; Adrienne Lyles-Chockley, University of San Diego; Curtis H. Peters, Indiana University Southeast; Richard Rice, La Sierra University; Harry Settanni, Holy Family College; and William C. Sewell, Michigan Technological University.

For the sixth edition we are indebted to:

W. Mark Cobb, Pensacola Junior College
Ronald G. DesRosiers, Madonna College
Brenda S. Hines, Highland Community College
Chris Jackway, Kellogg Community College
Henry H. Liem, San José City College

And we wish to express our gratitude to the McGraw-Hill staff and freelancers—Jon-David Hague, Allison Rona, Jen Mills, Marty Granahan, Preston Thomas, Victoria Nelson, Connie Gardner, Diane Jones—as well as to Aaron Downey of Matrix Productions.

Special thanks are due to Anita Silvers for putting us in touch with Dominic McIver Lopes, to Ellen Fox for material on feminist philosophy, to Gregory Tropea for material on postcolonial thought, to Mary Ellen Waithe for explaining the thought of important women in the history of philosophy, to Emerine Glowienka for helping us with Aquinas' metaphysics, and to Dan Barnett for many things, including the Instructor's Resource CD-ROM, careful reading of the new manuscript, and contributing the discussion of creationism/evolutionism.

# Brief Contents

# Contents

*Part Two*
MORAL AND POLITICAL PHILOSOPHY   249

*Part Three*
# PHILOSOPHY OF RELIGION: REASON AND FAITH    393

*Part Four*
## OTHER VOICES    443

# 1

# Powerful Ideas

Beware when the great God lets loose a thinker on this planet. Then all
things are at risk.     — Emerson

I do not know how to teach philosophy without becoming a disturber
of the peace.     — Baruch Spinoza

There are two powers in the world, the sword and the mind. In the long run,
the sword is always beaten by the mind.     — Napoleon

What I understand by "philosopher": a terrible explosive in the presence
of which everything is in danger.     — Friedrich Nietzsche

Better to be on a runaway horse than to be a woman who does not reflect.
    — Theano of Crotona

For a revolution you need more than economic problems and guns; you need
a philosophy. Wars are founded on a philosophy, or on efforts to destroy one.
Communism, capitalism, fascism, atheism, humanism, Marxism — all are philosophies. Philosophies give birth to civilizations. They also end them.

The philosophy department works with high explosives, philosopher Van Meter Ames liked to say. It handles dangerous stuff. This book is an introduction to
philosophy. From it you will learn, among other things, why philosophy, as Ames
said, is dynamite.

## WHAT IS PHILOSOPHY?

The word **philosophy** comes from the two Greek words *philein,* which means "to love," and *sophia,* which means "knowledge" or "wisdom." Because knowledge can be discovered in many fields, the Greeks, who invented philosophy, thought of any person who sought knowledge in any area as a philosopher. Thus, philosophy once encompassed nearly everything that counted as human knowledge.

This view of philosophy persisted for over two thousand years. The full title of Sir Isaac Newton's *Principles,* in which Newton set forth his famous theories of mechanics, mathematics, and astronomy, is *Mathematical Principles of Natural Philosophy.* Even by the seventeenth century, then, physics was still thought of as a variety of philosophy. Likewise, nearly every subject currently listed in college catalogs at some point would have been considered philosophy. That's why the highest degree in psychology, mathematics, economics, sociology, history, biology, political science, and most other subjects is the Ph.D., the doctorate of philosophy.

However, philosophy can no longer claim those subject areas that have grown up and moved out of it. What, then, *is* philosophy today?

There is no simple answer to the question, but you can get a pretty good idea from a partial list of the issues that philosophers are concerned with. As you read this list, you may think that scholars in the existing intellectual disciplines tackle these questions as well. And they do. But when a thinker ponders these questions, he or she goes outside his or her discipline—unless the discipline is philosophy.

- Why is there something, rather than nothing at all?
- Does the universe have a purpose? Does life have a purpose?
- Is there order in the cosmos independent of what the mind puts there? Could the universe be radically different from how we conceive it?
- Is a person more than a physical body? What is the mind? What is thought?
- Do people really have free will?
- Is there a God?
- Does it make a difference if there is or isn't a God?
- What is art? What is beauty?
- What is truth?
- Is it possible to know anything with absolute certainty?
- What is moral obligation? What is the extent of our moral obligation to other people and other living things?
- What kind of person should I be?
- What are the ethically legitimate functions and scope of the state? What is its proper organization?

Yes, it is possible to go through life and never spend a minute wondering about such questions; but most of us have at least occasional moments of reflection about one or another of them.

In fact, it is pretty difficult not to think philosophically from time to time. Whenever we think or talk about a topic long enough, if our thinking or discussion is the least bit organized, we may become engaged in philosophy. For example, suppose your electric company undercharges you by mistake. Should you call their attention to it? You might think that if you don't, nobody will be the worse for it — if anyone at the company even notices the mistake in the first place. Yet you hesitate: Does someone have to *notice* that you underpaid the electric company for it to be wrong? What about the principle, you wonder? What you are doing is weighing principles against consequences — you are wondering, Which carries more weight? You are having a philosophical conversation with yourself. Unfortunately, when people get to this point in their thinking or conversation, they often just stop. They don't know what to think next, so they just drop the matter and go on about their business.

Or, perhaps later, when you are doing something on the Web, it may occur to you to wonder whether we might someday build a computer that could actually think. Perhaps your feeling is that computers can't possibly do this. Well, here again you are starting to think philosophically. *Why* can't computers think? Is it because they aren't made out of the right kind of organic stuff? Well, intelligent beings from other galaxies also might not be made out of our kind of stuff. So why not computers? Is it because computers don't have a soul? Because they aren't alive? Why don't they have souls? Why aren't they alive? What is it to be alive, anyway? All of these reflections are philosophical questions. The task of analyzing and trying to answer them is the task of philosophers.

One important feature of philosophical questions is that they cannot be answered, in any straightforward way, by the discovery of some fact or collection of facts. You can't just go out and observe whether computers can think or whether what makes an action okay is that it's not hurting anyone. Facts are often relevant to a philosophical question, but they cannot by themselves provide an answer.

This doesn't mean that philosophical questions are unanswerable. A common misconception about philosophy is that its questions cannot be answered. In fact, if a question truly were unanswerable, most philosophers would regard that as a good reason for not being interested in it.

Many philosophical questions concern norms. **Normative questions** ask about the value of something. The sciences are interested in finding out how things are, but they cannot tell us how things ought to be. When we decide that something is good or bad, right or wrong, beautiful or ugly, we are applying norms or standards. How can we establish whether or not it is okay to not call the electric company about the undercharge, or to drive faster than the speed limit, or to sacrifice a human being to please the gods? Do we just consult our conscience? A religious authority? Does what a majority of people think determine the issue? Is some *feature* of the action right or wrong, or what?

Often, too, philosophers ask questions about things that seem so obvious we might not wonder about them — for example, the nature of change. What is change? It's obvious what change is. If something changes, it becomes different — what's the problem? Well, for one thing, if we have a different thing, then aren't we considering *two* things, the original thing and the new and different thing?

## Which Came First, the Chicken or the Egg?

What comes to mind for many people when they think of philosophy and of philosophical questions is either or both of these inquiries: "Which came first, the chicken or the egg?" and "If there is nobody around, does a tree falling in a forest make a sound?"

The first question is not particularly philosophical and, in the light of evolution, is not even especially difficult: the egg came first.

The second question is often supposedly resolved by distinguishing between sound viewed as the mental experience of certain waves contacting certain sensory organs and sound as the waves themselves. If sensory organs are absent, it is said, there can be no sound-as-experience, but there can still be sound-as-waves. Philosophy, however, asks not simply whether a tree falling in the forest makes a sound if no one is there but, rather, *If nobody is there, is there even a forest?* Is there even a universe? In other words, the question, for philosophers, is whether things depend for their existence on being perceived and, if so, how we know that. A somewhat similar question (equally philosophical) is debated by contemporary astrophysicists, who wonder whether the universe and its laws require the presence of intelligent observers for their existence.

Shouldn't we therefore, strictly speaking, not say that something *changed* but, rather, that it was *replaced*? If, over the course of many years, you replaced every part in the Ford you bought—*every* part, the engine block, every door panel, every nut, bolt, and piece of steel, glass, rubber, vinyl, or whatever—would you still have the same Ford? Or if you gathered up all the original pieces and put them together again, would *that* be the original Ford?

Perhaps these questions seem to be questions of nomenclature or semantics and of no practical interest. But over the course of a lifetime every molecule in a person's body may possibly (or probably!) be replaced. Thus, we might wonder, say, whether an old man who has been in prison for forty years for a murder he committed as a young man is really the same person as the young man. Since (let us assume) not a single molecule of the young man is in the old man, wasn't the young man in fact replaced? If so, can his guilt possibly pertain to the old man, who is in fact a different man? What is at stake here is whether the old man did in fact commit murder, and it is hard to see how this might be simply a matter of semantics.

Other times philosophical questions come up when beliefs don't fit together the way we would like. We believe, for example, that anything that happens was caused to happen. We also believe that a cause *makes* its effect happen—if spoiled meat caused you to get sick, it *made* you sick. But we also believe that when we voluntarily decide to do something, nothing made us decide. And that belief seems to imply that our decision wasn't caused. So, which is it? Is every happening caused? Or are some happenings uncaused? Or is it perhaps that decisions aren't actually "happenings"? Do you see a way out of this dilemma? If so, congratulations. You are philosophizing.

Philosopher Nicholas Rescher compiled a list of contemporary American philosophical concerns. His list will give you an idea of some of the things philosophers currently are investigating.

- Ethical issues in the various professions (medicine, business, law, etc.)

- Computer-related issues: artificial intelligence, information processing, whether or not machines can think
- Rationality and its ramifications
- Social implications of medical technology (abortion, euthanasia, right to life, medical research issues, informed consent)
- Feminist issues
- Social and economic justice, policies that determine distribution of resources, equality of opportunity, human rights
- Truth and meaning in mathematics and formalized language
- Skepticism and relativism in knowledge and morals
- What it is to be a person; the rights and obligations of persons
- Issues in the history of philosophy

## MISCONCEPTIONS ABOUT PHILOSOPHY

A common misconception about philosophy, one that goes with the idea that philosophical questions are unanswerable, is expressed in the comment, "Philosophy never makes any progress." Now, progress comes in many forms. It doesn't happen only when questions are answered. Questions can be clarified, subdivided, and found to rest on confusions. They can be partially answered. These are all forms of progress. Even when a question is abandoned as unanswerable, that too is progress. Earlier answers to a question can be considered inadequate even if the final answer isn't in, and that's progress as well.

Another idea people have is that as soon as progress is made in a philosophical inquiry, the matter is turned over (or becomes) another field of learning. It is true, as we have already observed, that many disciplines that today are independent of philosophy had their origin within philosophy. But philosophy doesn't always relegate its subjects to other disciplines. To take the most obvious example, logic is still a branch of philosophy, despite an enormous expansion in scope, complexity, and explanatory power during the last hundred years.

A couple of other ideas people have about philosophy ought to be discussed here at the outset.

First is the idea that in philosophy one person's opinion is as correct as the next person's and that any opinion on a philosophical question is as good or valid or correct as any other opinion. This idea is especially widespread when it comes to opinions on normative questions, that is, questions of values. Let's say your opinion is that it's okay to underpay the electric company, and your roommate's opinion is that it isn't. Some people might hold that the two views are equally correct and that there is no way to settle the matter.

The first thing to notice is that, if your view that it is okay to underpay and your roommate's view that it isn't okay to underpay are equally correct, then it is both okay and not okay for you to underpay. That is just unintelligible nonsense.

People hardly ever *say* they want to philosophize. But whenever their thinking is at all organized, they may well be engaged in philosophy — though they are probably not aware of the fact.

Another thing to notice is that implied in your view is that you believe your view is *correct*. To see this, imagine saying to your roommate, "Well, I think it is okay for me to underpay the electric company, but I believe you are entirely correct when you say that it is not okay for me to underpay the electric company." That remark also is unintelligible nonsense. The moral: If *you* express the opinion that value judgments are all equally correct, then nobody will have the faintest notion of what you mean when *you* make a value judgment.

Despite these considerations, you may still suspect that in philosophy one opinion *is* as good as the next. But if you do, then you have to concede that the person who says that in philosophy one opinion is *not* as good as the next is expressing an opinion every bit as good as yours. In any event, most philosophers distinguish *philosophy* from mere opinion, the difference being that philosophy at the very least involves opinions *supported by good reasoning*. If you express your opinion without providing supporting reasoning, your teacher may think you have an interesting opinion, but he or she probably won't think you have produced good *philosophy*. Philosophy requires you to support your opinions, which, by the way, can be hard work.

Another idea people sometimes have when they first enter into philosophy is that "truth is relative." Now, there are numerous things a person might mean by that statement. If he or she means merely that people's beliefs are relative to their perspective or culture, then there is no problem. If, however, the person means that the same sentence might be both true and not true depending on one's perspective or culture, then he or she is mistaken. The same sentence cannot be both true and not true, and whatever a person wishes to convey by the remark "Truth is relative," it cannot be that. Of course, two different people from two different cultures or perspectives might *mean* something different by the same words, but that is a separate issue.

A different sort of misconception people have about philosophy is that it is light reading, something you relax with in the evening, after all the serious work of the day is done. In reality, philosophical writing generally takes time and effort to understand. Often it seems to be written in familiar, everyday language, but that can be deceiving. It is best to approach a work in philosophy with the kind of mental preparedness and alertness appropriate for a textbook in mathematics or science. You should expect to be able to read an entire novel in the time it takes you to understand just a few pages of philosophy. To understand philosophy, you have to reread a passage several times and think about it a lot. If your instructor assigns what seem to be short readings, don't celebrate. It takes much time to understand philosophy.

## THE TOOLS OF PHILOSOPHY: ARGUMENT AND LOGIC

So, then, philosophy is not light reading, and it is not mere expression of unsupported opinion. Philosophers *support* their views to make it plain why the reasonable person will accept what they say. Now, when someone supports a belief by giving a reason for accepting the belief, he or she has given an **argument.** Setting forth arguments is the most basic philosophical activity and is one of the activities that distinguishes philosophy from merely having opinions. (Incidentally, when you see a word or phrase in bold print in this book, it is defined in the glossary/ index at the back of the book.)

When you study other subjects, you are expected to remember what person A or person B believed or discovered or accomplished. When you study philosophy, you need to remember not just what the philosopher believed but also the arguments given. Unfortunately, in the case of some early philosophers about whose arguments we do not have much information, we have to make intelligent guesses. For an example of an argument, let's consider this one:

1. Whatever rights a man has, a woman should have too.
2. A man has the right to marry a woman.
3. Therefore, a woman should have the right to marry a woman.

The **conclusion** of an argument is the point the person is trying to establish (in this case, line 3). The reason the person gives for accepting the conclusion is stated in the **premises** (in this case, lines 1 and 2).

There are only two ways in which an argument—any argument—can fail or be "incorrect." First, one or more of the premises might be false or questionable. Second, the premises might fail to establish the conclusion. **Logic,** the theory of correct inference, is concerned with the second type of failure.

Common mistakes in reasoning of the second type are called **fallacies,** and one important contribution of logic has been the identification, classification, and analysis of fallacies. Anyone concerned with sound reasoning tries to avoid fallacies, but even philosophers aren't always successful in doing so. The following are frequently encountered fallacies, we hope more frequently encountered outside philosophy than within.

- ***Argumentum ad hominem*** (or in plain English, "argument to the person"). Frequently, people have the mistaken idea that they can successfully refute an opinion or view by criticizing the person who has that opinion or holds that view. One of the most important philosophers of the twentieth century, Martin Heidegger, supported the Nazis. You would be guilty of ad hominem reasoning if you thought that this fact about *Heidegger* refuted Heidegger's *views* on, say, technology. Except in very unusual circumstances, a person's views cannot be *refuted* by discrediting the person. Even if Martin Heidegger were a known pathological liar, pointing that out wouldn't entail that his views on technology were *false,* although it would be good reason for *suspending judgment* on the veracity of any factual claims he happened to make. (Suspending judgment is different from rejecting the claim as false.) Ad hominem arguments are surprisingly common, and it takes a special effort to evaluate a person's views on their merits and not on the merits of the person whose views they are.

- **Appeals to emotion.** Arguments that try to establish conclusions solely by attempting to arouse or play on the emotions of a listener or reader are known as appeals to emotion. Suppose we try to "prove" to you that God exists with the argument that "if you don't believe it you will burn in hell." We have not really given you a proof; we are just trying to scare you into agreeing with us.

- **Straw man.** Sometimes people (even philosophers) will "refute" someone's view by refuting what is actually a misrepresentation of that view. If we aren't careful, we may think the original view has been refuted rather than the "straw man" that actually has been attacked. When the Irish philosopher George Berkeley maintained that physical objects are really just clusters of sensations existing only in the mind, the English writer Samuel Johnson "refuted" Berkeley by noting that some physical objects are so hard that things just bounce off them. Johnson then kicked a rock, trying to demonstrate that rocks are too hard to be mere sensations. But Johnson had in fact misrepresented Berkeley, for Berkeley had never maintained that rocks are not hard. Johnson had set up a straw man that was easy to knock over.

- **Red herring.** This argument occurs when someone addresses a point other than the one actually at issue, that is, brings in something that is off the point. For example, suppose we wish to establish that people have free will— that is, that they could have acted otherwise than they did. Suppose, further, our "proof" is that people obviously do lots of things they do not like to do and that therefore people must be able to make choices. We have brought in a red herring. What we have proved is not that people could have acted otherwise than they did but, rather, that they can make choices. (The fact that you chose to act is not equivalent to the fact that you could have acted differently.)

As you can see, ad hominem arguments, appeals to emotion, and straw man arguments might all be said to be red herrings because they all seek to establish something that is not quite the issue. If you like, you can think of them as red herrings that have their own special names.

Why is there something, rather than nothing at all? Philosophy wonders.

- **Begging the question.** In this fallacy, one premise rests on an assumption that is more or less identical to the very thing you are trying to prove as your conclusion. For example, suppose what is at issue is whether you can know that your friends are really people (not zombies or robots controlled by Martians). Suppose someone then argues, "Of course your friends are really people, because they say they are and they would not lie to you." The problem with this "proof" is that one of its premises — that your friends would not lie to you — rests on the assumption that your friends really are people, which is the very thing at issue. Begging the question is also called *circular reasoning*.

- **Black-or-white fallacy.** Suppose someone says to you, "Either God exists, or there is no explanation for the universe. Therefore, because the universe must have some explanation, God exists." This argument offers just two options: either God exists or the universe has no explanation. This argument ignores a third possibility, namely, that there is an explanation for the universe that does not involve God. Arguments that limit us to two options when in fact more options exist commit the black-or-white fallacy. Other terms for this include *false dilemma, all-or-nothing fallacy,* and *either-or fallacy*.

If you are reading this book as part of a philosophy course, there could be lots of discussion in the class, and the discussion is apt to involve arguments — not in the sense of people fighting with each other using words but in the sense of people trying to support their views with reasons. It is possible that you will find examples of these fallacies among the arguments you hear. You may even find an example or two in the arguments you read about in this book.

An instructor we know once had her students make signs saying "straw man," "ad hominem," and the like and hold them up when someone in the class used one of these arguments. The problem, as we understand it, was that her students began taking the signs with them to other classes — and holding them up when the instructors spoke.

## THE DIVISIONS OF PHILOSOPHY

Most philosophical questions tend to fall into one of these four areas:

- *Questions related to being or existence.* **Metaphysics** is the branch of philosophy that is concerned with these questions. Two basic questions of metaphysics are: What is being? and What are its fundamental features and properties? Several of the questions listed at the beginning of this chapter are questions of metaphysics, including: Is there order in the cosmos independent of what the mind puts there? What is the mind? Do people have free will? Metaphysics, as you will see, has little to do with the occult or Tarot cards and the like.

- *Questions related to knowledge.* **Epistemology,** the theory of knowledge, is the branch of philosophy concerned with these questions. What is the nature of knowledge, and what are its criteria, sources, and limits? These are basic questions of epistemology, and thus it includes such questions from the list at the beginning of the chapter as: What is truth? and Is it possible to know anything with absolute certainty?

- *Questions related to values.* Included under this heading are primarily (1) **moral philosophy (ethics),** the philosophical study of moral judgments; (2) **social philosophy,** the philosophical study of society and its institutions; (3) **political philosophy,** which focuses on the state and seeks to determine its justification and ethically proper organization; and (4) **aesthetics,** the philosophical study of art and of value judgments about art.

- *Questions of logic, the theory of correct reasoning,* which seeks to investigate and establish the criteria of valid inference and demonstration.

Part One of this book is devoted to metaphysics and epistemology, which are closely related. Part Two is concerned with questions of values, especially moral and political values. We talked a bit about logic earlier in this chapter.

Although philosophy has four main branches, they do not each contain an equal number of theories or concepts or words. Your library probably has more holdings under political philosophy than under the other areas, and the fewest under epistemology or aesthetics.

There are other ways of dividing philosophy. Many universities offer philosophy courses that examine the fundamental assumptions and methods of other disciplines and areas of intellectual inquiry, such as science (philosophy of science), language (philosophy of language), and religion (philosophy of religion). Philosophy of science and philosophy of language are covered in Part One because most of the issues in these two areas are either metaphysical or epistemological issues. Part Three is devoted entirely to the philosophy of religion, especially to the question of whether God's existence can be proved.

The fourth and last part of this book is called "Other Voices," and in it we will consider various current themes in philosophy as well as influences and traditions beyond mainstream Western philosophy.

## THE BENEFITS OF PHILOSOPHY

We conclude this chapter with a few remarks on the benefits of studying philosophy.

The importance of some philosophical questions — Is there a God who is attentive, caring, and responsive to us? and Is abortion morally wrong? — is obvious and great. A justification would have to be given for *not* contemplating them. But some philosophical questions are of more or less obscure, and seemingly only academic or theoretical, consequence. Not everything philosophers consider is dynamite. The questions posed earlier about whether computers might be able to think someday would be perceived by many as pretty academic and theoretical.

But then, every field has its theoretical and nonpractical questions. Why do astronomers wonder about the distance and recessional velocity of quasars? Why are paleontologists interested in 135-million-year-old mammalian fossil remains in northern Malawi? Why do musicologists care whether Bach used parallel fifths? The answer is that some questions are inherently interesting to the people who pose them. An astronomer wonders about a quasar *just because it is there.* And some philosophical questions are like that too: the philosopher wants to know the answer simply to know the answer.

There are also side benefits in seeking answers to philosophical questions, even those that are difficult, abstruse, or seemingly remote from practical concerns. Seeing philosophical answers usually entails making careful distinctions in thought, words, and argument, and recognizing subtle distinctions among things and among facts. Philosophical solutions require logic and critical thinking skills, discussion, and exposition. Students of philosophy learn to look carefully for similarities and differences among things. They also develop an ability to spot logical difficulties in what others write or say and to avoid these pitfalls in their own thinking. In addition, they learn to recognize and critically assess the important unstated assumptions people make about the world and themselves and other people and life in general. These assumptions affect how people perceive the world and what they say and do, yet for the most part people are not aware of them and are disinclined

## Philosophers on Philosophy

Wonder is a feeling of a philosopher, and philosophy begins in wonder.  —*Plato*

All *definite* knowledge—so I should contend—belongs to science; all *dogma* as to what surpasses definite knowledge belongs to theology. But between theology and science there is a No Man's Land, exposed to attack from both sides; this No Man's Land is philosophy.  —*Bertrand Russell*

Without it [philosophy] no one can lead a life free of fear or worry.  —*Seneca*

Uncertainty, in the presence of vivid hopes and fears, is painful, but must be endured if we wish to live without the support of comforting fairy tales. . . . To teach how to live without certainty, and yet without being paralyzed by hesitation, is perhaps the chief thing that philosophy, in our age, can still do for those who study it.  —*Bertrand Russell*

The most important and interesting thing which philosophers have tried to do is no less than this; namely: To give a general description of the whole Universe, mentioning all of the most important kinds of things which we *know* to be in it, considering how far it is likely that there are in it important kinds of things which we do not absolutely *know* to be in it, and also considering the most important ways in which these various kinds of things are related to one another.  —*G. E. Moore*

The philosopher has to take into account the least philosophical things in the world.  —*C. Chincholle*

Life involves passions, faiths, doubts, and courage. The critical inquiry into what these things mean and imply is philosophy.  —*Josiah Royce*

What is philosophy but a continual battle against custom; an ever-renewed effort to transcend the sphere of blind custom?  —*Thomas Carlyle*

[Philosophy] consoles us for the small achievements in life, and the decline of strength and beauty; it arms us against poverty, old age, sickness and death, against fools and evil sneerers.  —*Jean de la Bruyère*

Not to care for philosophy is to be a true philosopher.  —*Blaise Pascal*

There is no statement so absurd that no philosopher will make it.  —*Cicero*

The most tragic problem of philosophy is to reconcile intellectual necessities with the necessities of the heart and the will.  —*Miguel de Unamuno*

Without philosophy we would be little above animals.  —*Voltaire*

Philosophy asks the simple question, What is it all about?  —*Alfred North Whitehead*

Philosophy limits the thinkable and therefore the unthinkable.  —*Ludwig Wittgenstein*

to consider them critically. These abilities are of great value in any field that requires clear thinking.

Thus, while few employers actively seek philosophy students as such to fill openings, many employers seek people with the skills that philosophy students tend to have in abundance, such as the abilities to think clearly and critically, to reason carefully, and to recognize subtle but important distinctions. Philosophy students tend to score above students in all other subjects on admissions tests for professional and graduate schools too. In fact, according to *The Economist,* "Philosophy students do better in examinations for business and management schools than anybody except mathematicians—better even than those who study economics, business or other vocational subjects." This helps explain why, according to *The Economist,* philosophy Ph.D.'s are less likely to be unemployed than even chemists or biologists. It is possible, of course, that philosophy attracts unusually capable students to begin with and that this accounts for results like these. But there is at least some reason to believe that the kind of training philosophy provides helps students to think, read, and write, and possibly to speak more critically, carefully, and cogently.

Finally, students who have learned their philosophical lessons well are not as likely as those who have not to become trapped by dogmatism. Such students have learned the value of open-mindedness and seeking solutions to problems that meet standards of coherence and reasonableness. These general attitudes, along with the critical-thinking skills that come with the practice of philosophical argumentation, can stand us in good stead when we are faced with many of the problems life generously provides for us.

## CHECKLIST

### Key Terms and Concepts

| | |
|---|---|
| philosophy | red herring |
| normative question | begging the question |
| argument | black-or-white fallacy |
| conclusion | metaphysics |
| premise | epistemology |
| logic | moral philosophy/ethics |
| fallacy | social philosophy |
| *argumentum ad hominem* | political philosophy |
| appeals to emotion | aesthetics |
| straw man | |

## QUESTIONS FOR DISCUSSION AND REVIEW

1. Why do you want to study philosophy?

2. Now that you've read this chapter, is philosophy what you expected it to be?

3. Why is it that the most advanced degree in so many fields is the doctor of philosophy?

4. Which of the questions on page 2 is the most interesting to you? What do you think the answer is?

5. If the electric company undercharges you, should you notify them? Why or why not?

6. If bit by bit you replace every part of your Ford, do you end up with the same Ford? If by the time you become an adult, every molecule in your body has been replaced with a different one, are you-the-adult the same person as you-the-child?

7. Are all philosophical questions unanswerable? How about the question you mentioned in question 4?

8. Is one person's opinion as correct as another's opinion when it comes to the question of whether murder is wrong? Why or why not?

9. Does what is true depend on what your society believes is true? Was the world flat when people believed it was flat?

10. Evaluate the argument on page 7. Does the conclusion follow from the premises? Are the premises true?

## SUGGESTED FURTHER READINGS

Here are some of the best reference books on philosophy in the English language.

Donald Abel, *Fifty Readings in Philosophy*, 2nd ed. (New York: McGraw-Hill, 2003). Readings by important philosophers on a broad range of subjects.

A. J. Ayer and Jane O'Grady, *A Dictionary of Philosophical Quotations* (Malden, Mass.: Blackwell, 1994). Essential quotations taken from the great Western philosophers.

Julian Baggini and Peter S. Fast, *The Philosopher's Toolkit* (Malden, Mass.: Blackwell, 2003). Provides the basic tools for argumentation, assessment, and conceptualization.

*The Bigview.com*, www.thebigview.com. A web page that gives a bird's-eye view of philosophy. Light but fun.

Simon Blackburn, *The Oxford Dictionary of Philosophy* (New York: Oxford University Press, 1995). Concise and readable.

Stuart Brown, Diane Collinson, and Robert Wilkinson, eds., *Biographical Dictionary of Twentieth-Century Philosophers* (New York: Routledge, 2002). Brief reviews of twentieth-century philosophers.

*A Buddhist Glossary,* http://www.chezpaul.org.uk/buddhism/books/glossary.htm. Brief definitions of Buddhist terms.

Steven M. Cahn, ed., *Exploring Philosophy* (New York: Oxford University Press, 2000). A new collection of contemporary essays on the basic questions posed by philosophy concerning knowledge, action, and the meaning of existence.

Clive Cazeaux, *The Continental Aesthetics Reader* (New York: Routledge, 2000). Readings in European aesthetics from the phenomenologist, poststructuralist, psychoanalyst, and feminist traditions.

Diane Collinson, *Fifty Major Philosophers* (London: Routledge, 1988). A relatively accessible and short reference book.

*Concise Routledge Encyclopedia of Philosophy* (New York: Routledge, 2003). Short entries on philosophical terms and philosophers.

F. C. Copleston, *History of Philosophy,* 9 vols. (New York: Doubleday, 1965). Still the most complete history of philosophy available to English-only readers.

Arthur C. Danto, *Connections to the World: The Basic Concepts of Philosophy* (New York: Harper & Row, 1989). An important contemporary philosopher summarizes some of the main problems.

Eliot Deutsch and Ron Bontekoe, *A Companion to World Philosophies.* (Malden, Mass.: Blackwell, 1999). Articles on philosophical issues concerning traditional ideas from around the world.

*Dictionary of Philosophy of Mind,* http://www.artsci.wustl.edu/~philos/MindDict/. Excellent resource in the philosophy of mind.

Paul Edwards, ed., *The Encyclopedia of Philosophy,* 8 vols. (New York: Macmillan, 1967). If you need to find out something about a philosopher or philosophical topic prior to 1967, begin here.

A. C. Ewing, *Fundamental Questions of Philosophy* (London: Routledge, 1985). Readable.

Albert Hakim, *Historical Introduction to Philosophy* (New York: Macmillan, 1987). An extensive collection of short original writings.

*History of Philosophy,* www.friesian.com/history.htm. Essays on many philosophical topics; the ones we have looked at seem pretty good and not too difficult.

Ted Honderich, *The Oxford Companion to Philosophy* (New York: Oxford University Press, 1995). A dictionary of short articles, definitions, and short biographies.

*The Internet Encyclopedia of Philosophy,* www.iep.utm.edu. Maintained by the University of Tennessee at Martin. A pretty good source of information on philosophical topics.

W. T. Jones, *History of Western Philosophy,* 2nd ed., 5 vols. (New York: Harper & Row, 1976). Shorter than Copleston and a tad more difficult to read, in our view.

Anthony Kenny, ed., *The Oxford History of Western Philosophy* (New York: Oxford University Press, 1994). An authoritative and beautifully illustrated history of Western philosophy, with articles by important contemporary philosophers.

E. D. Klemke, *The Meaning of Life* (New York: Oxford University Press, 1999). A group of contemporary essays by philosophers on this most basic of all issues.

Daniel Kolak, *Mayfield Anthology of Western Philosophy* (New York: McGraw-Hill, 1998). Twenty-five centuries of readings from Aristotle on Thales to Quine on empiricism.

John Lechte, *Fifty Key Contemporary Thinkers* (New York: Routledge, 1994). A brief survey of important figures in post-war thought.

Thomas Mautner, ed., *A Dictionary of Philosophy* (Cambridge, Mass.: Blackwell, 1996). Brief, up-to-date, and useful.

*Meta-Encyclopedia of Philosophy,* http://www.ditext.com/encyc/frame.html. Enables you to compare the entries in various philosophy encyclopedias on various topics. A good place to start research.

Thomas Nagel, *What Does It All Mean? A Very Short Introduction to Philosophy* (New York: Oxford University Press, 1987). Nagel is an influential contemporary American philosopher.

Alex Neill and Aaron Riley, *The Philosophy of Art: Readings Ancient and Modern* (New York: McGraw-Hill, 1995). Readings on aesthetics, starting with Plato.

Paul Oliver, *Teach Yourself 101 Key Ideas: Philosophy* (New York: McGraw-Hill, 2001). A guide to important people and ideas in the history of philosophy.

*Oxford Reference Online,* http://www.oxfordreference.com/pub/views/home.html. Go here to subscribe to this premier service.

G. H. R. Parkinson, *An Encyclopaedia of Philosophy* (London: Routledge, 1988). A nice one-volume set of essays on most of the important topics in Anglo-American philosophy.

G. H. R. Parkinson and S. G. Shanker, gen. eds., *The Routledge History of Philosophy,* 10 vols. (London and New York: Routledge, various dates). A detailed chronological survey of the history of Western philosophy, together with chronologies and glossaries.

*Philosophy News Service,* http://pns.hypermart.net. Just what the name implies: philosophy news.

*Philosophy Pages,* from Garth Kemerling, www.philosophypages.com. A dictionary of philosophical terms and names.

Louis P. Pojman, ed., *Classics of Philosophy* (New York: Oxford University Press, 1997). A relatively comprehensive selection of writings by Western philosophers from ancient times to the present.

*Readings in Modern Philosophy,* www.class.uidaho.edu/mickelsen/readings.htm. Writings of many modern philosophers from around 1500 to 1750. If you like the excerpts you read in this text, look here for more.

*Reference.allrefer.com,* http://reference.allrefer.com/encyclopedia/categories/philos.html. Another nice dictionary/encyclopedia that includes philosophy.

Bertrand Russell, *A History of Western Philosophy* (New York: Simon & Schuster, 1945). As readable as a novel, though critics find Russell brash and opinionated.

*Stanford Encyclopedia of Philosophy,* http://plato.stanford.edu/. Start here to access this authoritative source.

Leslie Stevenson, *Ten Theories of Human Nature* (New York: Oxford University Press, 1998). An expanded version of the popular *Seven Theories of Human Nature* considers the major worldviews determining present-day culture.

J. O. Urmson and Jonathan Rée, *The Concise Encyclopedia of Western Philosophy and Philosophers* (London: Routledge, 1995). A fine one-volume survey from a British viewpoint.

Mary Ellen Waithe, ed., *A History of Women Philosophers,* 4 vols. (Dordrecht: Martinus Nijhoff/Kluwer Press, 1987, 1989, 1991, 1995). Vol. 1: *Ancient Women Philosophers* (through A.D. 500); Vol. 2: *Medieval, Renaissance, and Enlightenment Women Philosophers* (500–1600); Vol. 3: *Modern Women Philosophers* (1600–1900); Vol. 4: *Contemporary* (twentieth century) *Women Philosophers.*

Nigel Warburton, *Philosophy: The Classics* (New York: Routledge, 1998). A quick tour of the great classic works of Western philosophy.

# Part One
# Metaphysics and Epistemology: Existence and Knowledge

# 2

# The Pre-Socratics

You cannot know what is not, nor can you express it. What can be thought
of and what can be — they are the same.      — Parmenides

It is wise to agree that all things are one.      — Heraclitus

You don't generally find metaphysics and epistemology very far apart.
**Metaphysics,** as you now know from reading Chapter 1, is the branch of
philosophy concerned with the nature and fundamental properties of being. **Epistemology** is the branch that explores the sources, nature, limits, and criteria of
knowledge. These days, when a philosopher makes a metaphysical assertion, he or
she will generally consider whether it is the kind of assertion that could possibly be
known; that's why metaphysics and epistemology go together. However, the first
philosophers were mainly metaphysicians, so we shall begin by discussing metaphysics. When we look at Plato, whose vast philosophy covered all subjects, we
shall take up epistemology.

In its popular usage, the word *metaphysics* has strange and forbidding associations. "Metaphysical bookstores," for example, specialize in all sorts of occult
subjects, from channeling, harmonic convergence, and pyramid power to past-life
hypnotic regression, psychic surgery, and spirit photography. However, the true
history of metaphysics is quite different. Given the way in which the term was originally coined, you may find its popular association with the occult somewhat amusing. Here is the true story.

Aristotle (384–322 B.C.E.) produced a series of works on a wide variety of
subjects, from biology to poetry. One set of his writings is known as the *Physics,*
from the Greek word *physika,* which means "the things of nature." Another set, to
which Aristotle never gave an official title but which he referred to occasionally as
"first philosophy" or "wisdom," was called simply "the books after the books on
nature" (*ta meta ta physika biblia*) by later writers and particularly by Andronicus

## The Nature of Being

When a philosopher asks, What is the nature of being? he or she may have in mind any number of things, including one or more of the following:

- Is being a *property* of things, or is it *some kind of thing* itself? Or is there some third alternative?

- Is being basically *one*, or are there *many* beings?

- Is being *fixed* and *changeless*, or is it *constantly changing*? What is the relationship between *being* and *becoming*?

- Does everything have the *same kind* of being?

- What are the fundamental *categories* into which all existing things may be divided?

- What are the fundamental *features* of reality?

- Is there a fundamental *substance* out of which all else is composed? If so, does it have any properties? Must it have properties?

- What is the world like *in itself*, independent of our perception of it?

- What manner of existence do *particular things* have, as distinct from *properties, relations,* and *classes*? What manner of existence do *events* have? What manner do *numbers, minds, matter, space,* and *time* have? What manner do *facts* have?

- That a particular thing has a certain characteristic—is that a fact about the *thing*? Or is it a fact about the *characteristic*?

Several narrower questions may also properly be regarded as questions of metaphysics, such as: Does God exist? Is what happens determined? Is there life after death? and Must events occur in space and time?

Some of these questions are none too clear, but they provide signposts for the directions a person might take in coming to answer the question, What is the nature of being? or in studying metaphysics. Because the possibilities are so numerous, we will have to make some choices about what topics to cover in the pages that follow. We cannot go on forever.

---

of Rhodes, who was the cataloger of Aristotle's works in the first century B.C.E. The word *metaphysics,* then, translates loosely as "after the *Physics.*"

The subjects Aristotle discussed in these works are more abstract and more difficult to understand than those he examined in the *Physics.* Hence, later authorities determined that their proper place was indeed "after the *Physics,*" and thus "*Metaphysics*" has stuck as the official title of Aristotle's originally untitled work and, by extension, as the general name for the study of the topics treated there—and related subjects. Aristotle's works are the source of the term *metaphysics,* but Aristotle was not the first metaphysician. As we'll show in this chapter, philosophers before Aristotle had also discussed some of these things.

The fundamental question treated in Aristotle's *Metaphysics,* and thus the fundamental metaphysical question, can be put this way: *What is the nature of being?* A number of different subjects might qualify as "related" to this question, and in contemporary philosophical usage metaphysics is a rather broad and inclusive field. However, for most philosophers it does not include such subjects as astral projection, psychic surgery, or UFOs. Instead, it includes such questions as those in the box "The Nature of Being."

*What is the nature of being?* One of the authors used to ask his introductory classes to answer that question in a brief essay. The most common response, along with "Huh?" "What?" "Are you serious?" and "How do you drop this class?" was "What do you *mean,* 'What is the nature of being?'" People are troubled by what the question means and are uncertain what sort of thing is expected for an answer. This is the way, incidentally, with a lot of philosophical questions — it is difficult to know exactly what is being asked or what an answer might look like.

In this chapter we will explore several different approaches that have been taken to this question.

The first philosophers, or first Western philosophers at any rate, lived in Ionia, on the coast of Asia Minor, during the sixth century B.C.E. They are known collectively as the **pre-Socratic philosophers,** a loose chronological term applied to the Greek philosophers who lived before Socrates (c. 470–399 B.C.E.). Most left little or nothing of their own writings, so scholars have had to reconstruct their views from what contemporaneous and later writers said about them.

Experience indicates that it is sometimes difficult to relate to people who lived so long ago. However, the thinking of these early philosophers has had a profound effect on our world today. During this period in Western history — ancient Greece before Socrates — a decisive change in perspective came about that ultimately made possible a deep understanding of the natural world. It was not *inevitable* that this change would occur, and there are societies that exist today whose members, for lack of this perspective, do not so much as understand why their seasons change. We are not arguing for the virtues of advanced technological civilization over primitive life in a state of nature, for advanced civilization is in some ways a mixed blessing. But advanced civilization is a fact, and that it is a fact is a direct consequence of two developments in thought. One of these, which we will not discuss, is the discovery by the Greeks of mathematics. The other, which we are about to discuss, is the invention by the Greeks of philosophy, specifically metaphysics.

## THE MILESIANS

Tradition accords to **Thales** [Thay-leez] (c. 640–546 B.C.E.), a citizen of the wealthy Ionian Greek seaport town of Miletus, the honor of being the first Western philosopher. And philosophy began when it occurred to Thales to consider whether there might be some *fundamental kind of stuff* out of which everything else is made. Today we are so accustomed to thinking of the complex world we experience as made up of a few basic substances (hydrogen, oxygen, carbon, and the other elements) that we are surprised there ever was a time when people did not think this. Thales deserves credit for helping to introduce a new and important idea into Western thought.

Thales also deserves credit for helping introduce a nonmythological way of looking at the world. The Greeks thought their gods were in charge of natural forces; Zeus, for example, the supreme god, was thought to sometimes alter the weather. Our own belief that nature runs itself according to fixed processes that govern underlying substances began to take shape about this time, and Thales' philosophizing contributed to this important change in outlook.

What is the basic substance, according to Thales? His answer was that *all is water,* and this turns out to be wrong. But it was not an especially silly answer

# PROFILE: Thales (c. 640–546 B.C.E.)

Thales was considered by many to be the wisest of the seven wise men of the ancient Greek world. But not by everyone. Once, when Thales was studying the stars, he stumbled into a well and was found by a Thracian maiden, who was inclined to think that Thales might know much about the heavens but was a bit dull when it came to what was right before his eyes.

But Thales was not dull. Aristotle called him the first philosopher, and he was also a valued political advisor. His prediction of an eclipse of the sun probably impressed even the Thracian maiden. Once, according to the twentieth-century philosopher Bertrand Russell, when an Egyptian king asked Thales to determine the height of a pyramid, Thales simply measured the height of the pyramid's shadow at the time of day when his own shadow equaled his own height.

When Thales took time away from his higher pursuits, he could be extremely practical. To counter the criticism of his fellow Milesians concerning his poverty, he used his knowledge of the heavens to foresee a bumper crop of olives. Then he hired all the olive presses in Miletus and Chios. When the crop came and the olives were harvested, Thales was able to rent the presses at his own price.

Philosophers, naturally, have said that this was Thales' way of showing that a philosopher could easily be wealthy—if he had an interest in money.

for him to have come up with. Imagine Thales looking about at the complicated world of nature and reasoning: "Well, if there is some underlying, more fundamental level than that of appearances, and some kind of substance exists at that level out of which everything else is made, then this basic substance would have to be something very flexible, something that could appear in many forms." And of the candidates Thales saw around him, the most flexible would have been water—something that can appear in three very different states. So we can imagine Thales thinking that if water can appear in these three very different forms that we know about, it may be that water can also appear in many other forms that we do not understand. For example, when a piece of wood burns, it goes up in smoke, which looks like a form of steam. Perhaps, Thales might have speculated, the original piece of wood was actually water in one of its more exotic forms.

We are guessing about Thales' reasoning, of course. And in any case Thales did come to the wrong conclusion with the water idea. But it was not Thales' *conclusion* that was important—it was what Thales was *up* to. Thales attempted to explain the complex world that we see in terms of a simpler underlying reality. This attempt marks the beginning of metaphysics and, for that matter, of science. Science is largely just an effort to finish off what Thales started.

Two other Milesians at about this time advanced alternatives to Thales' theory that the basic stuff is water. One of these was **Anaximander** [an-nex-im-AN-der] (610–c. 547 B.C.E.), a pupil of Thales, who maintained that the basic substance out of which everything comes must be even more elementary than water and every other substance of which we have knowledge. The basic substance, he thought, must be ageless, boundless, and indeterminate. From the basic stuff a nucleus of fire and dark mist formed; the mist solidified in its center, producing the world. The world is surrounded by fire, which we see as the stars and other heavenly bodies, through holes in the mist. The seasons change as powers of heat and cold and wetness and dryness alternate. Anaximander, as you can see, proposed a theory of the universe that explained things in terms of natural powers and processes.

The third great Milesian philosopher was **Anaximenes** [an-nex-IM-in-eez] (fl. c. 545 B.C.E.), who pronounced the basic substance to be air and said that air becomes different things through processes of condensation and rarefaction. When it is rarefied, air becomes fire; when it is condensed it becomes first wind, then (through additional condensation) clouds, water, earth, and, finally, stone. He said that the earth is flat and floats on air. It isn't hard to imagine why Anaximenes thought that air is the basic substance; after all, it is that which enables life to exist. Anaximenes attempted to explain natural occurrences with his theory, and his attempt to identify the basic principles of transformation of the underlying substance of the world continues to this day.

## PYTHAGORAS

Quite a different alternative was proposed by **Pythagoras** [puh-THAG-uh-rus] (c. 580 – c. 500 B.C.E.) and his followers, who lived in the Greek city of Crotona in southern Italy. The Pythagoreans kept their written doctrines pretty secret, and controversy remains over the exact content of these doctrines. Pythagoras is said to have maintained that things are numbers, and we can try to understand what this might mean. Two points make a line, three points define a surface, solids are made of surfaces, and bodies are made out of solids. Aristotle, a primary source of information about the early philosophers, reported in his *Metaphysics* that the Pythagoreans "construct natural bodies, things that have weight or lightness, out of numbers, things that don't have weight or lightness." However, Theano, the wife of Pythagoras, had this to say:

> Many of the Greeks believe Pythagoras said all things are generated from number. The very assertion poses a difficulty: How can things which do not exist even be conceived to generate? But he did not say that all things come to be from number; rather, in accordance *with* number — on the grounds that order in the primary sense is in number and it is by participation in order that a first and a second and the rest sequentially are assigned to things which are counted.

In other words, things are things — one thing ends and another thing begins — because they can be enumerated. If one thing can be distinguished from another thing, it is because things are countable. Also, in Theano's account, it would not matter whether a thing is a physical object or an idea. If we can delineate it from another of its type — if it can be enumerated — it is a thing; and if it is a thing, it can be enumerated.

## PROFILE: Pythagoras (c. 580–500 B.C.E.)

Pythagoras was born on the Greek island of Samos. You may safely disregard the reports that he descended from the god Apollo; he was the son of a prominent citizen named Mnesarchus.

Not much is known for certain about the life of Pythagoras, although it is known that eventually he traveled to southern Italy, where he founded a mystical-scientific school in the Greek-speaking city of Crotona. The Pythagoreans believed in the transmigration of the soul, shared their property, and followed a strict set of moral maxims that, among other things, forbade eating meat.

Unfortunately the Pythagorean community denied membership to a rich and powerful citizen of Crotona named Cylon. After Pythagoras retired to Metapontium to die, Cylon had his fellow Cro-

tonians attack the Pythagoreans and burn their buildings to the ground. Worse still, from the Pythagoreans' point of view, he had all the Pythagoreans killed, except for two.

The Pythagorean school was eventually restarted at Rhegium, where it developed mathematical theorems, a theory of the structure of sound, and a geometrical way of understanding astronomy and physics. To what degree these ideas actually stem from Pythagoras is a matter of conjecture.

Despite having written nothing, Pythagoras for many centuries was among the most famous of philosophers. Today, outside philosophy, he is remembered mainly for the Pythagorean theorem, which, in fact, the Babylonians had discovered much earlier.

So, according to Theano, Pythagoras meant there is an intimacy between things and numbers. Whatever the thing, whether it is physical or not, it participates in the universe of order and harmony: it can be sequenced, it can be counted, it can be ordered. And in the Pythagorean philosophy, the idea of orderliness and harmony applies to all things.

The Pythagorean combination of mathematics and philosophy helped promote an important concept in metaphysics, one we will encounter frequently. This is the idea that the fundamental reality is eternal, unchanging, and accessible only to reason. Sometimes this notion about fundamental reality is said to come from Plato, but it is fair to say it originated with the Pythagoreans.

## HERACLITUS AND PARMENIDES

Another important pre-Socratic philosopher was **Heraclitus** [hayr-uh-KLITE-us] (c. 535–475 B.C.E.), a Greek nobleman from Ephesus, who proposed yet another candidate as the basic element. According to Heraclitus, *all is fire*. In fixing fire as the basic element, Heraclitus was not just listing an alternative to Thales' water and Anaximenes' air. Heraclitus wished to call attention to what he thought was the essential feature of reality; namely, that it is *ceaselessly changing*. There is no reality, he maintained, save the reality of change: permanence is an illusion. Thus, fire, whose nature it is to ceaselessly change, is the root substance of the universe.

Parmenides favored logic over sense experience as the proper method for investigating things

Heraclitus did not believe that the process of change is random or haphazard. Instead, he saw all change as determined by a cosmic order that he called the **logos,** which is Greek for "word." He taught that each thing contains its opposite, just as, for example, we are simultaneously young and old and coming into and going out of existence. Through the *logos* there is a harmonious union of opposites, he thought.

Heraclitus is famous for the remark attributed to him, "You cannot step in the same river twice." The remark raises the important philosophical **problem of identity** or "sameness over change": Can today's river and yesterday's river be the *same,* since not a single drop of water in yesterday's river is in today's river? The question, obviously, applies not just to rivers, but to anything that changes over time: rivers, trees, chickens, and the World Wide Web. It also, significantly, applies to people, and this is the **problem of personal identity:** you are not *quite* the same person today as you were yesterday, and over a lifetime it begins to seem that we should just drop the qualifying word *quite.* The atoms in George Bush Senior are not the same atoms as in George Bush Junior, and so we have two different people there—but the atoms in George Bush Senior in 2005 likewise are not the same atoms as in George Bush Senior in 1959. So why do we count this as one person and not as two?

Change does seem to be an important feature of reality — or does it? A younger contemporary of Heraclitus, **Parmenides** [par-MEN-uh-deez], thought otherwise. Parmenides' exact dates are unknown, but he lived during the first quarter of the fifth century B.C.E.

Parmenides was not interested in discovering the fundamental *substance* that constitutes everything or in determining what the most important *feature* of reality is. His whole method of inquiry was quite unlike that of his predecessors. In all probability the Milesians, Heraclitus, and the Pythagoreans reached their conclusions by looking around at the world and considering possible candidates for its primary substance or fundamental constituents. Parmenides, by contrast, simply assumed some very basic principles and attempted to *deduce* from these what he thought *must be* the true nature of being. For Parmenides it would have been a complete waste of time to look to the world for information about how things really are.

## A Priori and A Posteriori Principles

To elaborate on a concept mentioned in the text, an a priori principle is one such that once we understand it, we don't require additional experience to confirm it. For example, if you understand English, you don't need additional sensory experience to know that anything that is red is colored or that if you have two apples in a bag and you put two more apples into it, you then will have four apples. Principles like this are called *a priori* because they are known as soon as they are understood and *prior* to additional experience.

By contrast, people understood the sentence "Smoking causes cancer" long before it was confirmed, and you probably understand the sen-

tence "A 10-pound object will fall to the earth just as quickly as a 100-pound object" even if you are unaware that it is true. (If you had a physics lab in high school, you no doubt confirmed the second sentence in an experiment.) Sentences like this express "a posteriori" principles.

In short, to understand some sentences is automatically to know they are true, and those sentences are said to be known a priori or to express a priori principles. To understand other sentences is not automatically to know they are true. Those sentences — if they are true — are said to be known a posteriori or to express a posteriori principles.

Principles like those Parmenides assumed are said in contemporary jargon to be **a priori principles,** or **principles of reason,** which just means that they are known *prior* to experience. It is not that we learn these principles first chronologically, but rather that our knowledge of them does not depend on our senses. (See the box "A Priori and A Posteriori Principles" for more details.)

For example, consider the principle "You can't make something out of nothing." If you wished to defend this principle, would you proceed by conducting an experiment in which you tried to make something out of nothing? In fact, you would not. You would base your defense on our inability to *conceive* of ever making something out of nothing.

Parmenides based his philosophy on principles like that. One of these principles was that if something changes, it becomes something different. Thus, he reasoned, if being itself were to change, then it would become something different. But what is different from being is non-being, and non-being just plain *isn't*. Thus, he concluded, being *does not change*.

What is more, being is *unitary*— it is a single thing. If there were anything else, it would not be being; hence, it would not be. (The principle assumed in this argument is similar to "a second thing is different from a first thing.")

Further, being is an *undifferentiated whole:* it does not have any parts. Parts are different from the whole, and if something is different from being, it would not be being. Hence, it would not be.

Further, being is *eternal:* it cannot come into existence because, first, something cannot come from nothing (remember?) and, second, even if it could, there would be no explanation why it came from nothing at one time and not at another. And because change is impossible, as already demonstrated, being cannot go out of existence.

By similar arguments Parmenides attempted to show that motion, generation, and degrees of being are all equally impossible. For examples of arguments demonstrating the impossibility of motion, see the box "On Rabbits and Motion."

## On Rabbits and Motion

Parmenides' most famous disciple, **Zeno** [ZEE-no] (c. 489–430 B.C.E.), devised a series of ingenious arguments to support Parmenides' theory that reality is one. Zeno's basic approach was to demonstrate that motion is impossible. Here are two of his anti-motion arguments:

1. For something, let's say a rabbit, to move from its own hole to another hole, it must first reach the midway point between the two holes. But to reach that point, it must first reach the quarter point. Unfortunately, to reach the quarter point, it must reach the point that is one-eighth the distance. But first, it must reach the point one-sixteenth the distance. And so on and so on. In short, a rabbit, or any other thing, must pass through an infinite number of points to go anywhere. Because some sliver of time is required to reach each of these points, a thing would require an infinite amount of time to move anywhere, and that effectively rules out the possibility of motion.

2. For a rabbit to move from one hole to a second hole, it must at each moment of its travel occupy a space equal to its length. But when a thing occupies a space equal to its length, it is at rest. Thus, because the rabbit—or any other thing—must occupy a space equal to its length at each moment, it must be at rest at each moment. Thus, it cannot move.

Zeno used logic to demonstrate that motion is an illusion

Well, yes, it seems obvious that things move. Which means either that there is a mistake in Zeno's logic or that rabbits, and just about every other thing, are not really the way they seem to be. Zeno favored the second alternative. You, probably, will favor the first alternative. So what is the mistake in Zeno's logic?

Heraclitus envisioned being as ceaselessly changing, whereas Parmenides argued that being is absolutely unchanging. Being is One, Parmenides maintained: it is permanent, unchanging, indivisible, and undifferentiated. Appearances to the contrary are just gross illusion.

## EMPEDOCLES AND ANAXAGORAS

The philosophies of Parmenides (being is unchanging) and Heraclitus (being is ceaselessly changing) seem to be irreconcilably opposed. The next major Greek philosopher, **Empedocles** [em-PED-uh-kleez] (c. 490–430 B.C.E.), thought that true reality is permanent and unchangeable, yet he *also* thought it absurd to dismiss the change we experience as mere illusion. Empedocles quite diplomatically sided in part with Parmenides and in part with Heraclitus. He was possibly the first philosopher to attempt to reconcile and combine the apparently conflicting metaphysics of those who came earlier. Additionally, Empedocles' attempt at reconciliation resulted in an understanding of reality that in many ways is very much like our own.

According to Empedocles, the objects of experience *do* change, but these objects are composed of basic particles of matter that *do not* change. These basic material particles themselves, Empedocles held, are of four kinds: earth, air, fire, and water. These basic elements mingle in different combinations to form the objects of experience as well as the apparent changes among these objects.

The idea that the objects of experience, and the apparent changes in their qualities, quantities, and relationships, are in reality changes in the positions of basic particles is very familiar to us and is a central idea of modern physics. Empedocles was one of the first to have this idea.

Empedocles also recognized that an account of reality must explain not merely *how* changes in the objects of experience occur but *why* they occur. That is, he attempted to provide an explanation of the forces that cause change. Specifically, he taught that the basic elements enter new combinations under two forces — love and strife — which are essentially forces of attraction and decomposition.

This portrayal of the universe as constituted by basic material particles moving under the action of impersonal forces seems very up to date and "scientific" to us today, and, yes, Empedocles was a competent scientist. He understood the mechanism of solar eclipses, for example, and determined experimentally that air and water are separate substances. He understood so much, in fact, that he proclaimed himself a god. Empedocles was not displeased when others said that he could foresee the future, control the winds, and perform other miracles.

A contemporary of Empedocles was **Anaxagoras** [an-ak-SAG-uh-rus] (c. 500–428 B.C.E.). Anaxagoras was not as convinced of his own importance as Empedocles was of his, but Anaxagoras was just as important historically. For one thing, it was Anaxagoras who introduced philosophy to Athens, where the discipline truly flourished. For another, he introduced into metaphysics an important distinction, that between *matter* and *mind*.

Anaxagoras accepted the principle that all changes in the objects of experience are in reality changes in the arrangements of underlying particles. But unlike Empedocles, he believed that everything is *infinitely* divisible. He also held that each different kind of substance has its own corresponding kind of particle and that each substance contains particles of every other kind. What distinguishes one substance from another is a preponderance of one kind of particle. Thus, fire, for example, contains more "fire particles" than, say, water, which presumably contains very few.

Whereas Empedocles believed that motion is caused by the action of two forces, Anaxagoras postulated that the source of all motion is something called **nous.** The Greek word *nous* is sometimes translated as "reason," sometimes as "mind," and what Anaxagoras meant by *nous* is apparently pretty much an equation between mind and reason. Mind, according to Anaxagoras, is sepa-

## The Olympics

Ancient Greece gave birth to more than philosophy. It also gave birth to the Olympics. This was around 776 B.C.E. in Olympia, near Athens. Thousands of spectators stopped doing whatever they were doing, including occasionally warring, and watched people compete in running, boxing, wrestling, the pentathalon, and other events (not including philosophizing). Actually, the competitors were all males: women couldn't participate, and married women couldn't even watch. This, at the time, was a pretty strict rule, and the penalty for violating it was . . . death.

The Olympics returned to Athens in 2004.

rate and distinct from matter in that it alone is unmixed. It is everywhere and animates all things but contains nothing material within it. It is "the finest of all things, and the purest, and it has all knowledge about everything, as well as the greatest power."

Before mind acted on matter, Anaxagoras believed, the universe was an infinite, undifferentiated mass. The formation of the world as we know it was the result of a rotary motion produced in this mass by mind. In this process gradually the sun and stars and moon and air were separated off, and then gradually too the configurations of particles that we recognize in the other objects of experience.

According to Anaxagoras, mind did not *create* matter but only acted on it. Notice also that Anaxagoras' mind did not act on matter for some *purpose* or *objective*. These are strong differences between Anaxagoras' mind and the Judaeo-Christian God, although in other respects the concepts are not dissimilar. And, although Anaxagoras was the first to find a place for mind in the universe, Aristotle and Plato both criticized him for conceiving of mind as merely a mechanical cause of the existing order.

Finally, Anaxagoras' particles are not physical particles like modern-day atoms. If every particle is made of smaller particles, as Anaxagoras held, then there are no smallest particles, except as abstractions, as infinitesimals, as idealized "limits" on an infinite process. For the idea that the world is composed of actual physical atoms, we must turn to the last of the pre-Socratic philosophers, the Atomists.

## Mythology

Western philosophy was born on the back of Greek **myths** and not merely in the sense that early philosophers were seeking an alternative, more observationally based, systematic understanding. Thales spoke of all things being full of gods. Xenophanes objected to anthropomorphizing gods within Greek mythology. Heraclitus disliked Homer and Hesiod for using myths that led to misunderstandings about the true nature of things. Conversely, Plato made frequent and fruitful use of myths. The allegory of the cave in the *Republic* (see Chapter 3) provides a key for understanding both his metaphysics and his epistemology. In the *Symposium*, heavenly and earthly love are different, just like the two Aphrodites. Plato's own creation theory in the *Timaeus* is couched in mythical terms.

In the *Principles of a New Science Concerning the Common Nature of All Nations* (1725), Italian philosopher Giambattista Vico placed myths at the early stages of civilization in what he called the "age of the gods." A more scientific approach to the interpretation of myths began in the middle of the nineteenth century and continues to the present day. Western thinking is constantly being renewed by the discovery of new and hidden meanings in the Greek myths. Recent examples include the founding of psychoanalysis by Sigmund Freud, which to no small degree is based on his unique interpretation of the Oedipus myth. In the United States, the writings on mythology by Mircea Eliade and Joseph Campbell have found a significant following.

## THE ATOMISTS

The Atomists were **Leucippus** [loo-SIP-us or loo-KIP-us] and **Democritus** [dee-MOK-rut-us]. Not much is known of Leucippus, although he is said to have lived in Miletus during the mid-fifth century B.C.E., and the basic idea of **Atomism** is attributed to him. Democritus (460–370 B.C.E.) is better known today, and the detailed working out of Atomism is considered to be the result of his efforts. He was also a brilliant mathematician.

The Atomists held that all things are composed of physical atoms — tiny, imperceptible, indestructible, indivisible, eternal, and uncreated particles composed of exactly the same matter but different in size, shape, and (though there is controversy about this) weight. Atoms, they believed, are infinitely numerous and eternally in motion. By combining with one another in various ways, atoms compose the objects of experience. They are continuously in motion, and thus the various combinations come and go. We, of course, experience their combining and disassembling and recombining as the generation, decay, erosion, or burning of everyday objects.

Some qualities of everyday objects, such as their color and taste, are not really "in" the objects, said the Atomists, although other qualities, such as their weight and hardness, are. This is a distinction that to this day remains embodied in common sense; yet, as we will discuss in Chapter 6, it is totally beset with philosophical difficulties.

Anyway, the Atomists, unlike Anaxagoras, believed that there is a smallest physical unit beyond which further division is impossible. And also unlike Anaxagoras, they saw no reason to suppose that the original motion of atoms resulted

## PROFILE: Democritus (460–370 B.C.E.)

Democritus was the most widely traveled of the early philosophers. On the death of his father, he took his inheritance and left his home in Abdera, Thrace, to learn from the Chaldean Magi of Persia, the priest-geometers of Egypt, and the Gymnosophists of India. He may also have gone to Ethiopia. But he came to Athens as an unknown, for Democritus despised fame and glory.

Democritus thought that most humans waste their lives pursuing foolish desires and pleasures. He himself was far more interested in pursuing wisdom and truth than riches, and he spent his life in relative poverty. He found the cemetery a congenial place in which to cogitate.

from the activity of mind; indeed, they did not believe it necessary in the first place to explain the origin of that motion. As far as we can tell, they said in effect that atoms have been around forever, and they have been moving for as long as they have been around. This Atomist depiction of the world is quite modern. It is not such an extravagant exaggeration to say that, until the convertibility of matter and energy was understood in our own century, the common scientific view of the universe was basically a version of atomism. But the Atomist theory did run up against one problem that is worth looking at briefly.

The Greek philosophers generally believed that for motion of any sort to occur, there must be a void, or empty space, in which a moving thing may change position. But Parmenides had argued pretty convincingly that a void is not possible. Empty space would be nothingness — that is, non-being — and therefore does not exist.

The Atomists' way of circumventing this problem was essentially to ignore it (although this point, too, is controversial). That things move is apparent to sense perception and is just indisputable, they maintained, and because things move, empty space must be real — otherwise, motion would be impossible.

One final point about the Atomist philosophy must be mentioned. The Atomists are sometimes accused of maintaining that chance collisions of atoms cause them to come together to form this or that set of objects and not some other. But even though the Atomists believed that the motion of the atoms fulfills no purpose, they also believed that atoms operate in strict accordance with physical laws. Future motions would be completely predictable, they said, for anyone with sufficient information about the shapes, sizes, locations, direction, and velocities of the atoms. In this sense, then, the Atomists left nothing to chance; according to them, purely random events, in the sense of just "happening," do not occur.

The view that future states and events are completely determined by preceding states and events is called **determinism.** When you read the box "Free Will versus Determinism," you will see that determinism seems to contradict the belief in free will.

# Free Will versus Determinism

Here are two beliefs that are both dear to common sense. We hold the first belief thanks (in part) to the Atomists.

1. The behavior of atoms is governed entirely by physical law.

2. Humans have free will.

Do you accept both (1) and (2)? We are willing to wager that you do.

Unfortunately, (1) and (2) do not get along comfortably with each other. Here is why. It seems to follow from (1) that whatever an atom does, it has to do, given the existing circumstances, because physical laws determine what each atom does in the existing circumstances. Thus, if the laws determine that an atom does X in circumstance C, then, given circumstance C, the atom has to do X.

But anything that happened as a result of free will presumably did not have to happen. For ex-ample, suppose that I, of my own free will, move my arm. Whatever the circumstances were in which I chose to move my arm, I could always have chosen otherwise and not moved my arm. Therefore, when I moved my arm of my own free will, my arm, and thus the atoms in my arm, did not have to move, even given the existing circumstances. Thus, if (2) holds, it is *not true* that an atom must have done what it did, given the existing circumstances. But if (1) holds, then it *is true*.

As the famous twentieth-century physicist Arthur Eddington said, "What significance is there in my struggle tonight whether I shall give up smoking, if the laws that govern matter already preordain for tomorrow a configuration of matter consisting of pipe, tobacco, and smoke connected with my lips?"

To sum up this chapter, despite the alternative theories the pre-Socratics advanced, an important common thread runs through their speculation, and it is this:

All believed that the world we experience is merely a manifestation of a more fundamental, underlying reality.

That this thought occurred to people represents a turning point in the history of the species and may have been more important than the invention of the wheel. Had it not occurred, any scientific understanding of the natural world would have proved to be quite impossible.

The desire to comprehend the reality that underlies appearances did not, however, lead the various pre-Socratic philosophers in the same direction. It led the Milesians to consider possible basic substances and the Pythagoreans to try to determine the fundamental principle on which all else depends. It led Heraclitus to try to determine the essential feature of reality, Parmenides to consider the true nature of being, and Empedocles to try to understand the basic principles of causation. Finally, it led Anaxagoras to consider the original source of motion and the Atomists to consider the construction of the natural world. Broadly speaking, these various paths of inquiry eventually came to define the scope of scientific inquiry. But that was not until science and metaphysics parted ways about two thousand years later.

## CHECKLIST

To help you review, here is a checklist of the key philosophers and terms and concepts of this chapter. The brief descriptive sentences summarize the philosophers' leading ideas. Keep in mind that some of these summary statements are oversimplifications of complex positions.

### Philosophers

- **Thales**   held that the basic stuff out of which all else is composed is water.

- **Anaximander**   held that the original source of all things is a boundless, indeterminate element.

- **Anaximenes**   said that the underlying principle of all things is air.

- **Pythagoras**   maintained that enumerability constitutes the true nature of things.

- **Heraclitus**   held that the only reality is ceaseless change and that the underlying substance of the universe is fire.

- **Parmenides**   said that the only reality is permanent, unchanging, indivisible, and undifferentiated being and that change and motion are illusions of the senses.

- **Zeno**   devised clever paradoxes seeming to show that motion is impossible.

- **Empedocles**   held that apparent changes in things are in fact changes in the positions of basic particles, of which there are four types: earth, air, fire, and water. Two forces cause these basic changes: love and strife.

- **Anaxagoras**   maintained that all things are composed of infinitely divisible particles; the universe was caused by mind (*nous*) acting on matter.

- **The Atomists**   (especially **Leucippus** and **Democritus**) said that all things are composed of imperceptible, indestructible, indivisible, eternal, and uncreated atoms. Motion needs no explanation.

### Key Terms and Concepts

| | |
|---|---|
| metaphysics | problem of identity |
| epistemology | problem of |
| pre-Socratic | personal identity |
|   philosophers | a priori principle/ |
| *logos* |   a posteriori principle |
| myths | determinism |
| *nous* | free will versus |
| Atomism |   determinism |

## QUESTIONS FOR DISCUSSION AND REVIEW

1. Explain the derivation of the word *meta-physics*.

2. Provide some possible interpretations of the question, What is the nature of being?

3. Compare and contrast the metaphysics of the three Milesians. Whose metaphysics seems most plausible to you, and why?

4. The Pythagoreans theorized that all things come to be in accordance with number. What does this theory mean?

5. Compare and contrast the metaphysics of Heraclitus and Parmenides.

6. Explain and critically evaluate Parmenides' arguments that being is unitary, undifferentiated, and eternal.

7. Compare and contrast the metaphysics of Empedocles, Anaxagoras, and the Atomists. Whose views are the most plausible, and why?

8. "The behavior of atoms is governed entirely by physical law." "Humans have free will." Are these statements incompatible? Explain.

9. Is it true that something cannot come from nothing?

10. Defend this claim: The way things seem cannot be the way they are.

## SUGGESTED FURTHER READINGS

Julia Annas, ed., *Voices of Ancient Philosophy* (New York: Oxford University Press, 2000). An introductory reader in ancient philosophy including such themes as fate and freedom, reason and emotion, knowledge and belief.

Forrest E. Baird, ed., *Ancient Philosophy* (Upper Saddle River, N.J.: Prentice-Hall, 1997). An anthology of the philosophical classics from the ancient world.

John Burnet, *Early Greek Philosophy*, 4th ed. (London: Macmillan, originally published in 1930). This is generally considered the standard work on the subject.

Marc Cohen, Patricia Curd, and C. D. C. Reeve, eds., *Readings in Ancient Greek Philosophy* (Indianapolis: Hackett, 2000). A good selection of the important readings in ancient Greek philosophy.

Patricia Curd, *The Legacy of Parmenides, Eleatic Monism, and Later Presocratic Thought* (Princeton, N.J.: Princeton University Press, 1998). An interpretation of Parmenides' thought and an analysis of his relation to other philosophers.

Terence Irwin, *Classical Philosophy* (New York: Oxford University Press, 1999). A good anthology of the writings of ancient Greek and Roman philosophers on the basic questions of philosophy.

G. S. Kirk, J. E. Raven, and M. Schofield, *The Presocratic Philosophers: A Critical History with a Selection of Texts,* 2nd ed. (Cambridge: Cambridge University Press, 1983). This is a comprehensive treatment of the pre-Socratics.

A. A. Long, *The Cambridge Companion to Early Greek Philosophy* (New York: Cambridge University, 1999).

A consideration of some of the pre-Socratic philosophers and the problems they faced.

Alexander P. D. Mourelatos, ed., *The Pre-Socratics: A Collection of Critical Essays* (Princeton, N.J.: Princeton University Press, 1993). A series of essays on the pre-Socratics.

Merrill Ring, *Beginning with the Pre-Socratics,* 2nd ed. (Mountain View, Calif.: Mayfield, 2000). An introductory-level text about the beginnings of philosophy in ancient Greece.

Mary Ellen Waithe, ed., *A History of Women Philosophers,* vol. 1 (Dordrecht, Boston, and London: Kluwer Academic Press, 1991). The first of a four-volume series on the history of women philosophers.

Eduard Zeller, *Outlines of the History of Greek Philosophy* (New York: Dover 1980). Perhaps the best survey of Greek philosophy from the pre-Socratics to Neoplatonism in the Roman Empire.

# 3

# Socrates, Plato

Love [is] between the mortal and the immortal. . . . [It is] a grand spirit
which brings together the sensible world and the eternal world and merges
them into one great whole.  — Diotima in Plato's *Symposium*, 202e

I [Socrates] affirm that the good is the beautiful.  — Plato's *Lysis*, 216d

If you have heard of only one philosopher, it is probably one of the big three: Socrates, Plato, or Aristotle. These three were the most important philosophers of ancient Greece and in some respects the most important, period. Plato was the pupil of Socrates, and Aristotle was the pupil of Plato. This chapter covers Socrates and Plato and the following chapter, Aristotle.

## SOCRATES

In the fifth century B.C.E., the center of Western civilization was Athens, a city-state and a democracy. This period of time was some three centuries after the first Olympic Games and the start of alphabetic writing, and approximately one century before Alexander the Great demonstrated that it is possible to conquer the world, or what passed for it then. Fifty thousand citizens of Athens governed the city and the city's empire. Athenians did not settle disputes by brawling but, rather, by discussion and debate. Power was not achieved through wealth or physical strength or skill with weapons; it was achieved through words. Rhetoricians, men and women with sublime skill in debate, created plausible arguments for almost any assertion and, for a fee, taught others to do it too.

These rhetoricians, the Western world's first professors, were the **Sophists.** They were interested in practical things, and few had patience with metaphysical speculation. They demonstrated their rhetorical abilities by "proving" the seemingly unprovable—that is, by attacking commonly held views. The net effect was an examination and a critique of accepted standards of behavior within Athenian society. In this way, moral philosophy began. We will return to this topic in Chapter 10.

At the same time in the fifth century B.C.E., there also lived a stonemason with a muscular build and a keen mind, **Socrates** [SOK-ruh-teez] (470–399 B.C.E.). He wrote nothing, but we know quite a bit about him from Plato's famous "dialogues," in which Socrates almost always stars. (Plato's later dialogues reflect Plato's own views, even though "Socrates" is doing the speaking in them. But we are able to extract a reasonably detailed picture of Socrates from the earlier dialogues.)

Given the spirit of the times, it is not surprising that Socrates shared some of the philosophical interests and practices of the Sophists. We must imagine him wandering about the city, engaging citizens in discussion and argument. He was a brilliant debater, and he was idolized by many young Athenians.

But Socrates did not merely engage in sophistry—he was not interested in arguing simply for the sake of arguing—he wanted to discover something important, namely, the *essential nature* of knowledge, justice, beauty, goodness, and, especially, traits of good character such as courage. The method of discovery he followed bears his name, the "Socratic method." To this day, more than twenty centuries after his death, many philosophers equate proficiency within their own field with skill in the **Socratic** (or **dialectic**) **method.**

The method goes like this: Suppose you and Socrates wish to find out what knowledge is. You propose, tentatively, that knowledge is strong belief. Socrates then asks if that means that people who have a strong belief in, say, fairies must be said to *know* there are fairies. Seeing your mistake, you reconsider and offer a revised thesis: knowledge is not belief that is *strong* but belief that is *true.*

Socrates then says, "Suppose the true belief, which you say is knowledge, is based on a lucky guess. For instance, suppose I, Socrates, ask you to guess what kind of car I own, and you guess a Volvo. Even if your guess turns out to be right, would you call that knowledge?"

By saying this, Socrates has made you see that knowledge cannot be equated with true belief either. You must therefore attempt a better analysis. Eventually you may find a definition of knowledge that Socrates cannot refute.

So the Socratic/dialectic method is a search for the proper definition of a thing, a definition that will not permit refutation under Socratic questioning. The method does not imply that the questioner knows the essential nature of knowledge. It only demonstrates that the questioner is skilled at detecting misconceptions and at revealing them by asking the right questions. In many cases the process may not actually disclose the essence of the thing in question, and if Plato's dialogues are an indication, Socrates himself did not have at hand many final, satisfactory definitions. Still, the technique will bring those who practice it closer to this final understanding.

The **Delphi Oracle** is said to have pronounced Socrates the wisest of people. (An oracle is a shrine where a priest delivers a god's response to a human question. The most famous oracle of all time was the Delphi Oracle, which was housed in the great temple to Apollo in ancient and Hellenistic Greece.) Socrates thought the pronouncement referred to the fact that he, unlike most people, was *aware* of his

Socrates' prison—or what is left of it

ignorance. Applying the Socratic method, one gets good at seeing misconceptions and learning to recognize one's own ignorance.

Socrates was not a pest who went around trapping people in argument and making them look idiotic. He was famous not only for his dialectical skill but also for his courage and stamina in battle. He staunchly opposed injustice, even at considerable risk to himself. His trial and subsequent death by drinking hemlock after his conviction (for "corrupting" young men and not believing in the city's gods) are reported by Plato in the gripping dialogues *Apology, Crito,* and *Phaedo.* These dialogues portray Socrates as an individual of impressive character and true grit. Although it would have been easy for him to escape from prison, he did not do so because, according to Plato, by having chosen to live in Athens, he had implicitly promised to obey the laws of the city.

Richard Robinson summarizes the greatest value of Socrates, as we perceive him through Plato, as lying in Socrates' clear conception of the demands placed on us by reason:

> [Socrates] impresses us, more than any other figure in literature, with the supreme importance of thinking as well as possible and making our actions conform to our thoughts. To this end he preaches the knowledge of one's own starting-points, the hypothetical entertainment of opinions, the exploration of their consequences and connections, the willingness to follow the argument

wherever it leads, the public confession of one's thoughts, the invitation to others to criticize, the readiness to reconsider, and at the same time firm action in accordance with one's present beliefs. Plato's *Apology* has in fact made Socrates the chief martyr of reason as the gospels have made Jesus the chief martyr of faith.

## PLATO

When we pause to consider the great minds of Western history, those rare individuals whose insight elevates the human intellect by a prodigious leap, we think immediately of Socrates' most famous student, **Plato** (c. 427–347 B.C.E.), and Plato's student, Aristotle (384–322 B.C.E.). Both Plato and Aristotle were interested in practically every subject, and each spoke intelligently on philosophical topics and problems. Platonic metaphysics formed the model for Christian theology for fifteen centuries. This model was superseded only when translations of Aristotle's works were rediscovered by European philosophers and theologians in the thirteenth century A.D. After this rediscovery, Aristotle's metaphysics came to predominate in Christian thinking, although Christianity is still Platonic in many, many ways.

### Plato's Metaphysics: The Theory of Forms

Plato's metaphysics is known as the **Theory of Forms,** and it is discussed in several of the two dozen compositions we have referred to as **Plato's dialogues.** The most famous dialogue is the *Republic,* from the so-called middle period of Plato's writings, during which Plato reached the peak of genius. The *Republic* also gives Plato's best-known account of the Theory of Forms.

According to Plato's Theory of Forms, what is truly real is not the objects we encounter in sensory experience but, rather, **Forms,** and these can only be grasped intellectually. Therefore, once you know what Plato's Forms are, you will understand the Theory of Forms and the essentials of Platonic metaphysics. Unfortunately, it is not safe to assume Plato had *exactly* the same thing in mind throughout his life when he spoke of the Forms. Nevertheless, Plato's concept is pretty clear and can be illustrated with an example or two.

The Greeks were excellent geometers, which is not surprising because they invented the subject as a systematic science. Now, when a Greek geometer demonstrated some property of, say, *circularity,* he was not demonstrating the property of something that could actually be found in the physical world. After all, you do not find circularity in the physical world: what you find are *things*—various round objects—that approach perfect circularity but are not *perfectly* circular. Even if you are drawing circles with an excellent compass and are paying close attention to what you are drawing, your "circle" is not perfectly circular. Thus, when a geometer discovered a property of circularity, for example, he was discovering something about an *ideal* thing. Circularity does not exist in the physical world. Circularity, then, is an example of a Form.

## PROFILE: Aristocles, a.k.a. "Plato" (c. 427–347 B.C.E.)

"Plato" was the nickname of an Athenian whose true name was Aristocles. The nickname, which means "broad shoulders," stuck, and so did this man's philosophy. Few individuals, if any, have had more influence on Western thought than Plato.

Plato initially studied with Cratylus, who was a follower of Heraclitus, and then with Socrates. He was also influenced by the Pythagoreans, from whom he may have derived his great respect for mathematics. Plato thought that the study of mathematics was a necessary introduction to philosophy, and it is said that he expelled from his Academy students who had difficulty with mathematical concepts.

Plato founded his Academy in 387, and it was the first multisubject, multiteacher institution of higher learning in Western civilization. The Academy survived for nine centuries, until the emperor Justinian closed it to protect Christian truth.

Plato's dialogues are divided into three groups. According to recent respected scholarship, the earliest include most important the *Apology,* which depicts and philosophically examines Socrates' trial and execution; the *Meno,* which is concerned with whether virtue can be taught; the *Gorgias,* which concerns the nature of right and wrong; and the first book of the *Republic.* The dialogues from the middle period include the remaining books of the *Republic, Phaedo, Symposium, Phaedrus, Cratylus, Parmenides,* and *Theaetetus.* In the most famous of these, the *Republic,* Plato explains and interrelates his conceptions of justice, the ideal state, and the Theory of Forms. Plato's later dialogues include most notably the *Timaeus,* which is Plato's account of the creation of the universe; the *Sophist,* which examines the nature of nonbeing; and the *Laws,* which is concerned with what laws a good constitution should contain. The *Laws* is Plato's longest dialogue and the only dialogue in which Socrates is not present.

Here is another example. Consider two beautiful objects: a beautiful statue and a beautiful house. These are two very different objects, but they have *something* in common — they both qualify as beautiful. Beauty is another example of a Form. Notice that beauty, like circularity, is not something you encounter directly in the physical world. What you encounter in the physical world is always some object or other, a house or a statue or whatever, which may or may not be beautiful. But beauty itself is not something you meet up with; rather, you meet up with *objects* that to varying degrees *possess* beauty or, as Plato said, "participate" in the Form *beauty.* Beauty, like circularity, is an ideal thing, not a concrete thing.

You may be tempted to suppose that the Forms are just ideas or concepts in someone's mind. But this might be a mistake. Before any people were around, there were circular things, logs and round stones and so on — that is, things that came close in varying degrees to being perfectly circular. If there were circular things when there were no people around, or people-heads to have people-ideas in, it would seem that circularity is not just an idea in people's heads. It may be more difficult to suppose that there were beautiful things before there were people to think of things as beautiful, but this difficulty might only be due to assuming that "beauty is in the eyes of the beholder." Whether that assumption truly is justified is actually an unsettled question. (It is a question that belongs to the aesthetics branch of philosophy.)

Sometimes Plato's Forms are referred to as *Ideas,* and the Theory of Forms is also said to be the Theory of Ideas. But *Idea* is misleading because, as you can see, Plato's Forms are not the sort of ideas that exist in people. We will stick with the word *Forms.*

Forms have certain important and unusual features. We will begin by asking: How *old* is circularity? Immediately on hearing the question, you will realize that circularity is not any age. Circular things, sand dollars and bridge abutments and so on, are some age or other. But circularity itself has no age. The same thing is true of beauty, the Form. So we can see that the Forms are ageless, that is, *eternal.*

They are also *unchanging.* A beautiful house may change due to alterations or aging, but that couldn't happen to beauty itself. And you, having learned that the circumference of the circle is equal to $\pi$ times twice the radius distance, aren't apt to worry that someday the circle may change and, when it does, the circumference will no longer equal $2\pi r$. (Mathematics teachers did not have to revise what they knew about circularity when New Math came in.)

Finally, the Forms are *unmoving* and *indivisible.* Indeed, what sense would it make even to suppose that they might move or be physically divided?

When you think of these various characteristics of Forms and remember as well that Plato equated the Forms with true reality, you may begin to see why we stated that Plato's metaphysics formed the model for Christian theology. You may also be reminded, we hope, of what Parmenides said about true being (i.e., that it is eternal, unmoving, unchanging, and indivisible). Of course, you should also remember that for Parmenides there is only one being, but for Plato there are many Forms.

But why did Plato say that only the Forms are truly real? A thing is beautiful only to the extent it participates in the Form *beauty,* just as it is circular only if it participates in the Form *circularity.* Likewise, a thing is large only if it participates in the Form *largeness,* and the same principle would hold for all of a thing's properties. Thus, a large, beautiful, round thing—a beautiful, large, round oak table, for instance—couldn't be beautiful, large, or round if the Forms *beauty, largeness,* and *circularity* did not exist. Indeed, if the Forms *oak* and *table* did not exist, "it" wouldn't even be an oak table. Sensible objects—that is, the things we encounter in sensory experience—are what they are only if they sufficiently participate in their corresponding Forms. Sensible objects owe their reality to the Forms, so the ultimate reality belongs to the Forms.

Many people scold philosophers, mathematicians, and other thinkers for being concerned with abstractions and concepts. "That's all very interesting," they say about some philosophical or mathematical theory, "but I'm more interested in the *real* world." By "real world" they mean the world you experience with your senses. On the face of it, at least, Plato makes out a convincing case that that world is *not* the real world at all.

Plato was aware that there is a sense in which the objects we see and touch are real. Even appearances are *real* appearances. But Plato's position is that the objects

## The Cave

In the *Republic*, Plato uses a vivid allegory to explain his two-realms philosophy. He invites us to imagine a cave in which some prisoners are bound so that they can look only at the wall in front of them. Behind them is a fire whose light casts shadows of various objects on the wall in front of the prisoners. Because the prisoners cannot see the objects themselves, they regard the shadows they see as the true reality. One of the prisoners eventually escapes from the cave and, in the light of the sun, sees real objects for the first time, becoming aware of the big difference between them and the shadow images he had always taken for reality.

The cave, obviously, represents the world we see and experience with our senses, and the world of sunlight represents the realm of Forms. The prisoners represent ordinary people, who, in taking the sensible world to be the real world, are condemned to darkness, error, ignorance, and illusion. The escaped prisoner represents the philosopher, who has seen light, truth, beauty, knowledge, and true reality.

Of course, if the philosopher returns to the cave to tell the prisoners how things really are, they will think his brain has been addled. This difficulty is sometimes faced by those who have seen the truth and decide to tell others about it.

we see and touch have a *lesser* reality because they can only approximate their Form and thus are always to some extent flawed. Any particular beautiful thing will always be deficient in beauty compared with the Form *beauty*. And, as any particular beautiful thing owes whatever degree of beauty it has to the Form *beauty,* the Form is the source of what limited reality as a beautiful thing the thing has.

Thus, Plato introduced into Western thought a *two-realms* concept. On one hand, there is the realm of particular, changing, sense-perceptible or "sensible" things. This realm Plato likened to a cave (see the box "The Cave"). It is the realm of flawed and lesser entities. Consequently, it is also, for those who concern themselves with sensible things, a source of error, illusion, and ignorance. On the other hand, there is the realm of Forms — eternal, fixed, and perfect — the source of all reality and of all true knowledge. This **Platonic dualism** was incorporated into Christianity and transmitted through the ages to our thought today, where it lingers still and affects our views on virtually every subject.

Now, Plato believed that some forms, especially the Forms *truth, beauty,* and *goodness,* are of a higher order than other Forms. For example, you can say of the Form *circularity* that it is beautiful, but you cannot say of the Form *beauty* that it is circular. So the Form *beauty* is higher than the Form *circularity*. This fact will turn out to be very important when we consider Plato's ethics in the second part of this book. Also, as we shall see in Part Two, Plato connected his Theory of Forms with a theory of the ideal state (see the box "What Is Beauty?").

### Plato's Theory of Knowledge

The first comprehensive theory of knowledge in philosophy was Plato's. Certainly many of his predecessors had implicit theories of knowledge, and some of them spoke explicitly on epistemological subjects. Some were quite skeptical. A **skeptic**

## What Is Beauty?

The Hope Diamond and a Lamborghini Countach share a common property: both are beautiful. But what, exactly, is *beauty?* It is an abstract thing, an example of a Platonic Form. However, the beauty possessed by a diamond and an automobile is physical beauty, which is not identical with Absolute Beauty, which Plato equated with the Form *goodness.*

is a doubter, a person who doubts that knowledge is possible. Xenophanes (c. 570 – 480 B.C.E.) declared that even if truth were stated it would not be known. Heraclitus (c. 535 – 475 B.C.E.), whom we talked about earlier, was a contemporary of Xenophanes. He had the idea that, just as you cannot step into the same river twice, everything is in flux; this theory suggests it is impossible to discover any fixed truth beyond what is expressed in the theory itself. (Heraclitus, however, apparently did not himself deduce skeptical conclusions from his metaphysical theory.) Cratylus, a younger contemporary of Socrates (470 – 399 B.C.E.), carried this flux theory even further, arguing that you cannot step even once into the same river because both you and the river are continually changing. And, as if that were not enough, he said that our words themselves change in their meaning as we speak them, and therefore true communication is impossible. Likewise impossible, one would think, would be knowledge. Cratylus, it is said, largely abstained from conversation and merely wiggled his finger when someone spoke to him, figuring that his understanding of words he heard must necessarily be different from the meaning the speaker intended.

Skeptical themes are also found in the pronouncements of the Sophists. If you were a citizen of Athens and wanted to be influential, you needed to be trained by a Sophist, who could devise an argument to back up any claim. Because the Sophists could make a plausible case for any position, they seemed to show that one idea is as valid as the next, a theory that supports skepticism.

Gorgias (c. 485 – 380 B.C.E.), one particularly famous Sophist, said: "There is no reality, and if there were, we could not know of it, and even if we could, we could not communicate our knowledge." This statement parallels that of Xenophanes, just mentioned.

In Plato's Myth of the Cave a group of prisoners is placed so they can see, on the wall of the cave, only reflections of objects carried back and forth in front of a fire behind them. Because the reflections are all they see, the prisoners assume the reflections to be reality.

The best-known Sophist philosopher of all, Protagoras (c. 490–421 B.C.E.), said that "man is the measure of all things." This can be interpreted—and was interpreted by Plato—as meaning that there is no absolute knowledge: one person's views about the world are as valid as the next person's. Plato argued strenuously against this theory. In his dialogue *Theaetetus,* Plato pointed out that if Protagoras is correct, and one person's views really are as valid as the next person's, then the person who views Protagoras's theory as false has a valid view. To this day beginning philosophy students subscribe to Protagoras's theory (without knowing it is Protagoras's theory), and to this day philosophy instructors use Plato's argument against it.

In the *Theaetetus,* Plato also tried to show that another popular idea about knowledge is mistaken. This is the idea that knowledge may be equated with sense perception. Plato had several reasons for thinking this equation is false.

One reason for thinking that knowledge is not just sense perception is the fact that knowledge clearly involves more than sense perception. For example, sense perception by itself tells us a straight stick stuck in water is bent—*thinking* is required for us to know the stick is actually straight. Further, just to know the stick *exists* or is of a certain *length* involves thought. Visual sensations give you colored expanses, auditory sensations give you sounds, but existence itself is a concept that cuts across several senses simultaneously and is supplied by thought. Judgments of length, for example, involve making comparisons with rulers or tape measures, and comparing is a mental activity.

Another reason knowledge is not just sense perception is that you can retain knowledge even *after* you are no longer sensing a thing. Finally, and even more important, in Plato's view true knowledge is knowledge of what *is*. Because the objects of sense perception are always changing (remember Heraclitus?), sense perception and knowledge cannot be one and the same.

True knowledge, Plato was positive, must be concerned with what is *truly real*. This means, of course, that the objects of true knowledge are the Forms because the objects of sense perception are real only to the extent that they "participate" in the Forms.

This, then, is essentially Plato's theory of knowledge, and he elaborated on it in the *Republic*—especially in a passage known as the **Theory of the Divided Line** and in the **Myth of the Cave.**

The Theory of the Divided Line is used by Plato to contrast knowledge, on one hand, with mere belief or opinion, on the other. Plato illustrates his theory by dividing a line in two parts. The upper part of the line stands for knowledge, and the lower part stands for belief (opinion). Knowledge is concerned with absolutes—absolute beauty, absolute good, and so forth—in short, with the Forms. And this is not unreasonable of Plato. If your "knowledge" of beauty or goodness or circularity or the like is limited to this or that beautiful car or good deed or round plate, then you really do not have knowledge of *absolute* beauty, goodness, or circularity. At best you have a bunch of opinions that, as they are as likely as not to be riddled with error, come closer to *ignorance* than to true knowledge.

In Plato's Divided Line, the upper part of the line represents knowledge and the lower part represents opinion. Plato also subdivided the knowledge section of the line into two parts, and did the same for the opinion section. (How these further subdivisions are to be understood is a matter of controversy.) What is essential to remember is that, according to Plato, the highest form of knowledge is that obtained through the *use of reason* because perfect beauty or absolute goodness or the ideal triangle cannot be perceived.

## Plato's Theory of Love and Becoming

As mentioned earlier, knowledge is true ultimately because it is knowledge of what is. Plato believed that it is not enough to know the truth; rather, a person must also become that truth. This is where Plato's epistemology, or theory of truth, becomes a metaphysics, or theory of being. To know for Plato is to be. The more you know, the more you are and the better you are.

Plato began, as we saw, with the Myth of the Cave that shows how and why human beings are in the dark about the truth of things. And this ignorance is almost universal—even Socrates admits that he has no knowledge. What allows humans eventually to come into the light of day regarding the truth of things is the Forms.

Each individual has in his or her immortal soul a perfect set of Forms that can be remembered (*anamnesis*), and only this constitutes true knowledge. To remember the Forms is to know the absolute truth and simultaneously to become just and wise. Through the Forms, all skeptical doubts are laid to rest and the individual becomes good in the process. This way of thinking is so powerful and compelling that twentieth-century philosopher Martin Heidegger suggested that all Western philosophy since Plato is but a variety of Platonism.

Plato believed in two radically separate spheres: the realm of shadows or imperfect, changing beings and the realm of perfect, eternal, unchanging Forms. The problem is, how do we get out of the cave to the perfect world of Forms? In his dialogue *The Symposium,* Plato postulated the notion of love as the way in which a person can go from the state of imperfection and ignorance to the state of perfection and true knowledge. He defined love as a longing for and a striving to attain the object of longing. Love is that which seeks to possess the beautiful and to recreate in beauty. Human beings love to love: they truly come alive only in seeking a beloved, whether that beloved is another human being or an idea or health or money.

For Plato, love is meant to be the force that brings all things together and makes them beautiful. It is the way by which all beings, but especially human beings, can ascend to higher stages of self-realization and perfection. Plato's love begins as an experience of lacking something. Love provokes both thought and effort in the pursuit of what is lacking. The deeper the thought, the greater the love.

Plato initially mirrored the Athenian view that the deepest human relationships were between two men, usually an older man and a younger one. Women were not only considered the weaker sex but were also thought to be superficial, excitable, and superstitious. Marriage had as its purpose the reproduction and raising of children, and physical lovemaking was considered a low form of love. Plato's love does not exclude physical beauty, but "Platonic love" begins at a higher stage of development, namely, with the sharing of beautiful thoughts with a beautiful person. Plato believed that this kind of love should be experienced while a person is young. It is this intellectual or spiritual love that begins the ascent of love, which may eventually lead to the permanent possession of Absolute Beauty or Goodness.

The love for just one other human, even if that person is as noble as a Socrates, remains a limited form of intellectual eros. It is but the first step in the ascent of philosophical love to Absolute Beauty. To reach the higher stages of love means entering what is called the *mysteries.* Plato has Socrates recount a theory of love given to him by a woman named Diotima. Socrates implies that few may be able to follow this line of reasoning, which he himself has difficulty comprehending, but Diotima's theory of love was this: The higher forms of love express the will to immortality and the will to produce immortal "children," not merely physical children. All love seeks to possess beauty and to reproduce in beauty, but the creation of immortal children (like the writings of Homer) can grant the author immortality. A first step beyond merely loving a beautiful person and begetting beautiful thoughts lies in the realization that beauty in all things is one and the same and that all love is one. A further step involves the recognition of the superiority of intellectual or spiritual beauty over physical beauty. Then love must expand beyond preoccupations with a particular person to an appreciation of the beauty of moral practices and laws. An individual is part of larger social groupings, each with accompanying obligations. Love here takes the form of appreciating and aptly participating in organizations such as a city-state like Athens. Yet no matter how wide a person's involvement is in the moral and social spheres of love, this still does not represent the highest and most inclusive love. A person begins to glimpse the all-inclusive, all-uniting kind of love by first seeing the beauty of knowledge as a whole or at least many of the different forms of knowledge. This leads to an appreciation and love of the whole realm of beauty or the integrated beauty of everything there is. In the happiness of viewing such vast beauty, a person will have beautiful thoughts and be able to speak beautiful words. Eventually such a person may be able to make the final leap to the beauty and truth, which is beyond all mortal things.

The last and highest stage of love lies in the discovery of the ultimate mystery, Absolute Beauty itself. The beauty of this being contains no change of any kind. It was never born and will never die, nor will it increase or decrease. It is not good in one part and bad in another. It is perfect and one with itself forever. All imperfect things participate in this Beauty, thereby receiving a modicum of fulfillment and self-realization. Plato indicated that once a person has seen Absolute Beauty, then such a fortunate person would no longer be dazzled by mere physical beauty or the other rubbish of mortality. This, for human beings, is the ultimate kind of immortality, he thought.

Thus, love for Plato is the ultimate way of knowing and realizing truth. For mortals, love is a process of seeking higher stages of being: physical love begets mortal children; intellectual or spiritual love begets immortal children. The greater the love, the more it will contain an intellectual component. The lifelong longing and pursuit seeks ever higher stages of love so that it can eventually lead to the possession of Absolute Beauty. This is the pursuit that motivates the highest sorts of human beings and that transforms entire civilizations. To love the highest is to become the best.

SELECTION 3.1
# Apology*

*Plato*

[*In 399 B.C.E., Socrates was sentenced to death by an Athenian court for impiety and corrupting the youth of Athens. This excerpt is from Plato's dialogue* Apology, *in which Socrates is seen defending himself.*]

I will make my defense, and I will try in the short time allowed to do away with this evil opinion of me which you have held for such a long time. I hope I

may succeed, if this be well for you and me, and that my words may find favor with you. But I know to accomplish this is not easy—I see the nature of the task. Let the event be as the gods will; in obedience to the law I make my defense.

I will begin at the beginning and ask what the accusation is which has given rise to this slander of me and which has encouraged Meletus to proceed against me. What do the slanderers say? They shall be my prosecutors and I will sum up their words in

*From Christopher Biffle, *A Guided Tour of Five Works by Plato*, 3rd Edition, Mountain View, CA: Mayfield, 2001, pp. 36–40. Based on the nineteenth century translation by

Benjamin Jowett. Reprinted with permission from The McGraw-Hill Companies.

an affidavit. "Socrates is an evil-doer and a curious person, who searches into things under the earth and in the heavens. He makes the weaker argument defeat the stronger and he teaches these doctrines to others." That is the nature of the accusation and that is what you have seen in the comedy of Aristophanes. He introduced a man whom he calls Socrates, going about and saying he can walk in the air and talking a lot of nonsense concerning matters which I do not pretend to know anything about—however, I mean to say nothing disparaging of anyone who is a student of such knowledge. I should be very sorry if Meletus could add that to my charge. But the simple truth is, O Athenians, I have nothing to do with these studies. Very many of those here are witnesses to the truth of this and to them I appeal. Speak then, you who have heard me, and tell your neighbors whether any of you ever heard me hold forth in few words or in many upon matters of this sort. . . . You hear their answer. And from what they say you will be able to judge the truth of the rest.

There is the same foundation for the report I am a teacher and take money; that is no more true than the other. Although, if a man is able to teach, I honor him for being paid. There are Gorgias of Leontium, Prodicus of Ceos, and Hippias of Elis,[2] who go round the cities and are able to persuade young men to leave their own citizens, by whom they might be taught for nothing, and come to them, whom they not only pay but are also thankful if they may be allowed to pay them.

There is actually a Parian philosopher residing in Athens who charges fees. I came to hear of him in this way: I met a man who spent a world of money on the sophists, Callias, the son of Hipponicus, and knowing he had sons, I asked him: "Callias," I said, "if your two sons were foals or calves, there would be no difficulty in finding someone to raise them. We would hire a trainer of horses, or a farmer probably, who would improve and perfect them in their own proper virtue and excellence. But, as they are human beings, whom are you thinking of placing over them? Is there anyone who understands human and political virtue? You must have thought about this because you have sons. Is there anyone?"

"There is," he said.

"Who is he?" said I. "And of what country? And what does he charge?"

"Evenus the Parian,"[3] he replied. "He is the man and his charge is five minae."

Happy is Evenus, I said to myself, if he really has this wisdom and teaches at such a modest charge. Had I the same, I would have been very proud and conceited; but the truth is I have no knowledge like this, O Athenians.

I am sure someone will ask the question, "Why is this, Socrates, and what is the origin of these accusations of you; for there must have been something strange which you have been doing? All this great fame and talk about you would never have come up if you had been like other men. Tell us then, why this is, as we should be sorry to judge you too quickly."

I regard this as a fair challenge, and I will try to explain to you the origin of this name of "wise" and of this evil fame. Please attend then and although some of you may think I am joking, I declare I will tell you the entire truth. Men of Athens, this reputation of mine has come from a certain kind of wisdom which I possess. If you ask me what kind of wisdom, I reply, such wisdom as is attainable by man, for to that extent I am inclined to believe I am wise. Whereas the persons of whom I was speaking have a superhuman wisdom which I may fail to describe, because I do not have it. He who says I have, speaks false and slanders me.

O men of Athens, I must beg you not to interrupt me, even if I seem to say something extravagant. For the word which I will speak is not mine. I will refer you to a wisdom which is worthy of credit and will tell you about my wisdom—whether I have any and of what sort—and that witness shall be the god of Delphi.[4] You must have known Chaerephon. He was a friend of mine and also a friend of yours, for he shared in the exile of the people and returned with you. Well, Chaerephon, as you know, was very impetuous in all his doings, and he went to Delphi and boldly asked the oracle to tell him whether—as I said, I must beg you not to interrupt—he asked the oracle to tell him whether there was anyone wiser than I was. The Pythian prophetess answered, there was no man wiser. Chaerephon is dead himself but his brother, who is in court, will confirm the truth of this story.

Why do I mention this? Because I am going to explain to you why I have such an evil name. When I heard the answer, I said to myself, "What can the god mean and what is the interpretation of this riddle? I know I have no wisdom, great or small. What can he mean when he says I am the wisest of men? And yet he is a god and cannot lie; that would be against his nature." After long consideration, I at last thought of a method of answering the question.

I reflected if I could only find a man wiser than myself, then I might go to the god with a refutation in my hand. I would say to him, "Here is a man who is wiser than I am, but you said I was the wisest." Accordingly I went to one who had the reputation of wisdom and observed him—his name I need not mention; he was a politician whom I selected for examination. When I began to talk with him I could not help thinking he was not really wise, although he was thought wise by many and wiser still by himself. I tried to explain to him that he thought himself wise but was not really wise. The result was he hated me, and his hatred was shared by several who were present and heard me. So I left him, saying to myself, as I went away: "Well, although I do not suppose either of us knows anything really beautiful and good, I am better off than he is—for he knows nothing and thinks that he knows. I neither know nor think that I know. In this latter, then, I seem to have an advantage over him." Then I went to another who had still higher philosophical pretensions, and my conclusion was exactly the same. I made another enemy of him and of many others besides him.

After this I went to one man after another, being aware of the anger that I provoked; and I lamented and feared this, but necessity was laid upon me. The word of the god, I thought, ought to be considered first. And I said to myself, "I must go to all who appear to know and find out the meaning of the oracle." And I swear to you Athenians, by the dog, I swear,[5] the result of my mission was this: I found the men with the highest reputations were all nearly the most foolish and some inferior men were really wiser and better.

I will tell you the tale of my wanderings and of the Herculean labors,[6] as I may call them, which I endured only to find at last the oracle was right. When I left the politicians, I went to the poets: tragic, dithyrambic, and all sorts. There, I said to myself, you will be detected. Now you will find out you are more ignorant than they are. Accordingly, I took them some of the most elaborate passages in their own writings and asked what was the meaning of them—thinking the poets would teach me something. Will you believe me? I am almost ashamed to say this, but I must say there is hardly a person present who would not have talked better about their poetry than the poets did themselves. That quickly

showed me poets do not write poetry by wisdom, but by a sort of inspiration. They are like soothsayers who also say many fine things, but do not understand the meaning of what they say. The poets appeared to me to be much the same, and I further observed that upon the strength of their poetry they believed themselves to be the wisest of men in other things in which they were not wise. So I departed, conceiving myself to be superior to them for the same reason I was superior to the politicians.

At last I went to the artisans, because I was conscious I knew nothing at all, and I was sure they knew many fine things. In this I was not mistaken, for they did know many things of which I was ignorant, and in this they certainly were wiser than I was. But I observed even the good artisans fell into the same error as the poets. Because they were good workmen, they thought they also knew all sorts of high matters, and this defect in them overshadowed their wisdom. Therefore, I asked myself on behalf of the oracle whether I would like to be as I was, having neither their knowledge nor their ignorance, or like them in both. I answered myself and the oracle that I was better off as I was.

This investigation led to my having many enemies of the worst and most dangerous kind and has given rise also to many falsehoods. I am called wise because my listeners always imagine I possess the wisdom which I do not find in others. The truth is, O men of Athens, the gods only are wise and in this oracle they mean to say wisdom of men is little or nothing. They are not speaking of Socrates, only using my name as an illustration, as if they said, "He, O men, is the wisest who, like Socrates, knows his wisdom is in truth worth nothing." And so I go my way, obedient to the gods, and seek wisdom of anyone, whether citizen or stranger, who appears to be wise. If he is not wise, then in support of the oracle I show him he is not wise. This occupation quite absorbs me, and I have no time to give either to any public matter of interest or to any concern of my own, but I am in utter poverty by reason of my devotion to the gods.

There is another thing. Young men of the richer classes, who have little to do, gather around me of their own accord. They like to hear the pretenders examined. They often imitate me and examine others themselves. There are plenty of persons, as they soon enough discover, who think they know something, but really know little or nothing. Then those who are examined by the young men, instead of being angry with themselves, are angry with me. "This confounded Socrates," they say, "this villainous misleader of youth!" Then if somebody asks them, "Why, what evil does he practice or teach?," they do not know and cannot tell. But so they may not appear ignorant, they repeat the ready-made charges which are used against all philosophers about teaching things up in the clouds and under the earth, and having no gods, and making the worse argument defeat the stronger. They do not like to confess their pretense to knowledge has been detected, which it has. They are numerous, ambitious, energetic and are all in battle array and have persuasive tongues. They have filled your ears with their loud and determined slanders. This is the reason why my three accusers, Meletus and Anytus and Lycon, have set upon me. Meletus has a quarrel with me on behalf of the poets, Anytus, on behalf of the craftsmen, Lycon, on behalf of the orators. As I said at the beginning, I cannot expect to get rid of this mass of slander all in a moment.

This, O men of Athens, is the truth and the whole truth. I have concealed nothing. And yet I know this plainness of speech makes my accusers hate me, and what is their hatred but a proof that I am speaking the truth? This is the reason for their slander of me, as you will find out either in this or in any future inquiry.

---

## SELECTION 3.2
# Republic*

*Plato*

---

[*After the Bible, Plato's dialogue* Republic *is perhaps the most widely read Western book of all time. In this selection, Plato compares Goodness (or the Good) to the sun, sets forth his famous Theory of the Divided Line, and explains the Myth of the Cave.*]

*Glaucon:* But, Socrates, what is your own account of the Good? Is it knowledge, or pleasure, or something else?

*Socrates:* There you are! I exclaimed; I could see all along that you were not going to be content with what other people think.

*G:* Well, Socrates, it does not seem fair that you should be ready to repeat other people's opinions but not to state your own, when you have given so much thought to this subject.

*S:* And do you think it fair of anyone to speak as if he knew what he does not know?

*G:* No, not as if he knew, but he might give his opinion for what it is worth.

*S:* Why, have you never noticed that opinion without knowledge is always a shabby sort of thing? At the best it is blind. One who holds a true belief without intelligence is just like a blind man who happens to take the right road, isn't he?

*G:* No doubt.

*S:* Well, then, do you want me to produce one of these poor blind cripples, when others could discourse to you with illuminating eloquence?

*G:* No, really, Socrates, you must not give up within sight of the goal. We should be quite content with an account of the Good like the one you gave us of justice and temperance and the other virtues.

*S:* So should I be, my dear Glaucon, much more than content! But I am afraid it is beyond my powers; with the best will in the world I should only disgrace myself and be laughed at. No, for the moment let us leave the question of the real meaning of good; to arrive at what I at any rate believe it to be would call for an effort too ambitious for an inquiry like ours. However, I will tell you, though only if you wish it, what I pic-

---

*From *The Republic of Plato,* translated by Francis McDonald Cornford (Oxford: Clarendon Press, 1941). By permission of Oxford University Press.

ture to myself as the offspring of the Good and the thing most nearly resembling it.

*G:* Well, tell us about the offspring, and you shall remain in our debt for an account of the parent.

*S:* I only wish it were within my power to offer, and within yours to receive, a settlement of the whole account. But you must be content now with the interest only; and you must see to it that, in describing this offspring of the Good, I do not inadvertently cheat you with false coin.

*G:* We will keep a good eye on you. Go on.

*S:* First we must come to an understanding. Let me remind you of the distinction we drew earlier and have often drawn on other occasions, between the multiplicity of things that we call good or beautiful or whatever it may be and, on the other hand, Goodness itself or Beauty itself and so on. Corresponding to each of these sets of many things, we postulate a single Form or real essence, as we call it.

*G:* Yes, that is so.

*S:* Further, the many things, we say, can be seen, but are not objects of rational thought; whereas the Forms are objects of thought, but invisible.

*G:* Yes, certainly.

*S:* And we see things with our eyesight, just as we hear sounds with our ears and, to speak generally, perceive any sensible thing with our sense-faculties.

*G:* Of course.

*S:* Have you noticed, then, that the artificer who designed the senses has been exceptionally lavish of his materials in making the eyes able to see and their objects visible?

*G:* That never occurred to me.

*S:* Well, look at it in this way. Hearing and sound do not stand in need of any third thing, without which the ear will not hear nor sound be heard; and I think the same is true of most, not to say all, of the other senses. Can you think of one that does require anything of the sort?

*G:* No, I cannot.

*S:* But there is this need in the case of sight and its objects. You may have the power of vision in your eyes and try to use it, and colour may be there in the objects; but sight will see nothing and the colours will remain invisible in the absence of a third thing peculiarly constituted to serve this very purpose.

*G:* By which you mean——?

*S:* Naturally I mean what you call light; and if light is a thing of value, the sense of sight and the power of being visible are linked together by a very precious bond, such as unites no other sense with its object.

*G:* No one could say that light is not a precious thing.

*S:* And of all the divinities in the skies is there one whose light, above all the rest, is responsible for making our eyes see perfectly and making objects perfectly visible?

*G:* There can be no two opinions: of course you mean the Sun.

*S:* And how is sight related to this deity? Neither sight nor the eye which contains it is the Sun, but of all the sense-organs it is the most sun-like; and further, the power it possesses is dispensed by the Sun, like a stream flooding the eye. And again, the Sun is not vision, but it is the cause of vision and also is seen by the vision it causes.

*G:* Yes.

*S:* It was the Sun, then, that I meant when I spoke of that offspring which the Good has created in the visible world, to stand there in the same relation to vision and visible things as that which the Good itself bears in the intelligible world to intelligence and to intelligible objects.

*G:* How is that? You must explain further.

*S:* You know what happens when the colours of things are no longer irradiated by the daylight, but only by the fainter luminaries of the night: when you look at them, the eyes are dim and seem almost blind, as if there were no unclouded vision in them. But when you look at things on which the Sun is shining, the same eyes see distinctly and it becomes evident that they do contain the power of vision.

*G:* Certainly.

*S:* Apply this comparison, then, to the soul. When its gaze is fixed upon an object irradiated by truth and reality, the soul gains understanding and knowledge and is manifestly in possession of intelligence. But when it looks towards that twilight world of things that come into existence and pass away, its sight is dim and it has only opinions and beliefs which shift to and fro, and now it seems like a thing that has no intelligence.

*G:* That is true.

*S:* This, then, which gives to the objects of knowledge their truth and to him who knows them his power of knowing, is the Form or essential nature of Goodness. It is the cause of knowledge and truth; and so, while you may think of it as an object of knowledge, you will do well to regard it as something beyond truth and knowledge and, precious as these both are, of still higher worth. And, just as in our analogy light and vision were to be thought of as like the Sun, but not identical with it, so here both knowledge and truth are to be regarded as like the Good, but to identify either with the Good is wrong. The Good must hold a yet higher place of honour.

*G:* You are giving it a position of extraordinary splendour, if it is the source of knowledge and truth and itself surpasses them in worth. You surely cannot mean that it is pleasure.

*S:* Heaven forbid. But I want to follow up our analogy still further. You will agree that the Sun not only makes the things we see visible, but also brings them into existence and gives them growth and nourishment; yet he is not the same thing as existence. And so with the objects of knowledge: these derive from the Good not only their power of being known, but their very being and reality; and Goodness is not the same thing as being, but even beyond being, surpassing it in dignity and power.

(Glaucon exclaimed with some amusement at my exalting Goodness in such extravagant terms.)

It is your fault; you forced me to say what I think.

*G:* Yes, and you must not stop there. At any rate, complete your comparison with the Sun, if there is any more to be said.

*S:* There is a great deal more.

*G:* Let us hear it, then; don't leave anything out.

*S:* I am afraid much must be left unspoken. However, I will not, if I can help it, leave out anything that can be said on this occasion.

*G:* Please do not.

*S:* Conceive, then, that there are these two powers I speak of, the Good reigning over the domain of all that is intelligible, the Sun over the visible world — or the heaven as I might call it; only you would think I was showing off my skill in etymology. At any rate you have these two orders of things clearly before your mind: the visible and the intelligible?

*G:* I have.

*S:* Now take a line divided into two unequal parts, one to represent the visible order, the other the intelligible; and divide each part again in the same proportion, symbolizing degrees of comparative clearness or obscurity. Then (A) one of the two sections in the visible world will stand for images. By images I mean first shadows, and then reflections in water or in close-grained, polished surfaces, and everything of that kind, if you understand.

*G:* Yes, I understand.

*S:* Let the second section (B) stand for the actual things of which the first are likenesses, the living creatures about us and all the works of nature or of human hands.

*G:* So be it.

*S:* Will you also take the proportion in which the visible world has been divided as corresponding to degrees of reality and truth, so that the likeness shall stand to the original in the same ratio as the sphere of appearances and belief to the sphere of knowledge?

*G:* Certainly.

*S:* Now consider how we are to divide the part which stands for the intelligible world. There are two sections. In the first (C) the mind uses as images those actual things which themselves had images in the visible world; and it is compelled to pursue its inquiry by starting from assumptions and travelling, not up to a principle,

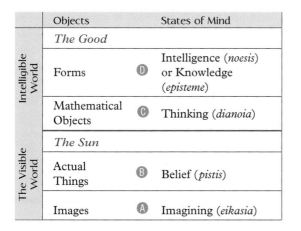

| Objects | | States of Mind |
|---|---|---|
| *The Good* | | |
| Forms | D | Intelligence (*noesis*) or Knowledge (*episteme*) |
| Mathematical Objects | C | Thinking (*dianoia*) |
| *The Sun* | | |
| Actual Things | B | Belief (*pistis*) |
| Images | A | Imagining (*eikasia*) |

(Intelligible World spans the top rows: The Good, Forms, Mathematical Objects. The Visible World spans: The Sun, Actual Things, Images.)

but down to a conclusion. In the second (D) the mind moves in the other direction, from an assumption up towards a principle which is not hypothetical; and it makes no use of the images employed in the other section, but only of Forms, and conducts its inquiry solely by their means.

*G:* I don't quite understand what you mean.

*S:* Then we will try again; what I have just said will help you to understand. (C) You know, of course, how students of subjects like geometry and arithmetic begin by postulating odd and even numbers, or the various figures and the three kinds of angle, and other such data in each subject. These data they take as known; and, having adopted them as assumptions, they do not feel called upon to give any account of them to themselves or to anyone else, but treat them as self-evident. Then, starting from these assumptions, they go on until they arrive, by a series of consistent steps, at all the conclusions they set out to investigate.

*G:* Yes, I know that.

*S:* You also know how they make use of visible figures and discourse about them, though what they really have in mind is the originals of which these figures are images: they are not reasoning, for instance, about this particular square and diagonal which they have drawn, but about *the* Square and *the* Diagonal; and so in all cases. The diagrams they draw and the models they make are actual things, which may

have their shadows or images in water; but now they serve in their turn as images, while the student is seeking to behold those realities which only thought can apprehend.

*G:* True.

*S:* This, then, is the class of things that I spoke of as intelligible, but with two qualifications: first, that the mind, in studying them, is compelled to employ assumptions, and, because it cannot rise above these, does not travel upwards to a first principle; and second, that it uses as images those actual things which have images of their own in the section below them and which, in comparison with those shadows and reflections, are reputed to be more palpable and valued accordingly.

*G:* I understand: you mean the subject-matter of geometry and of the kindred arts.

*S:* (D) Then by the second section of the intelligible world you may understand me to mean all that unaided reasoning apprehends by the power of dialectic, when it treats its assumptions, not as first principles, but as *hypotheses* in the literal sense, things 'laid down' like a flight of steps up which it may mount all the way to something that is not hypothetical, the first principle of all; and having grasped this, may turn back and, holding on to the consequences which depend upon it, descend at last to a conclusion, never making use of any sensible object, but only of Forms, moving through Forms from one to another, and ending with Forms.

*G:* I understand, though not perfectly; for the procedure you describe sounds like an enormous undertaking. But I see that you mean to distinguish the field of intelligible reality studied by dialectic as having a greater certainty and truth than the subject-matter of the 'arts,' as they are called, which treat their assumptions as first principles. The students of these arts are, it is true, compelled to exercise thought in contemplating objects which the senses cannot perceive, but because they start from assumptions without going back to a first principle, you do not regard them as gaining true understanding about those objects, although the objects themselves, when connected with a first principle, are intelligible. And I think you would call the state of mind of the students of geometry and other such arts, not intelligence, but thinking, as being something between intelligence and mere acceptance of appearances.

S: You have understood me quite well enough. And now you may take, as corresponding to the four sections, these four states of mind: *intelligence* for the highest, *thinking* for the second, *belief* for the third, and for the last *imagining*. These you may arrange as the terms in a proportion, assigning to each a degree of clearness and certainty corresponding to the measure in which their objects possess truth and reality.

G: I understand and agree with you. I will arrange them as you say.

S: Next, here is a parable to illustrate the degrees in which our nature may be enlightened or unenlightened. Imagine the condition of men living in a sort of cavernous chamber underground, with an entrance open to the light and a long passage all down the cave. Here they have been from childhood, chained by the leg and also by the neck, so that they cannot move and can see only what is in front of them, because the chains will not let them turn their heads. At some distance higher up is the light of a fire burning behind them; and between the prisoners and the fire is a track with a parapet built along it, like the screen at a puppet-show, which hides the performers while they show their puppets over the top.

G: I see.

S: Now behind this parapet imagine persons carrying along various artificial objects, including figures of men and animals in wood or stone or other materials, which project above the parapet. Naturally, some of these persons will be talking, others silent.

G: It is a strange picture, and a strange sort of prisoners.

S: Like ourselves; for in the first place prisoners so confined would have seen nothing of themselves or of one another, except the shadows thrown by the fire-light on the wall of the Cave facing them, would they?

G: Not if all their lives they had been prevented from moving their heads.

S: And they would have seen as little of the objects carried past.

G: Of course.

S: Now, if they could talk to one another, would they not suppose that their words referred only to those passing shadows which they saw?

G: Necessarily.

S: And suppose their prison had an echo from the wall facing them? When one of the people crossing behind them spoke, they could only suppose that the sound came from the shadow passing before their eyes.

G: No doubt.

S: In every way, then, such prisoners would recognize as reality nothing but the shadows of those artificial objects.

G: Inevitably.

S: Now consider what would happen if their release from the chains and the healing of their unwisdom should come about in this way. Suppose one of them set free and forced suddenly to stand up, turn his head, and walk with eyes lifted to the light; all these movements would be painful, and he would be too dazzled to make out the objects whose shadows he had been used to see. What do you think he would say, if someone told him that what he had formerly seen was meaningless illusion, but now, being somewhat nearer to reality and turned towards more real objects, he was getting a truer view? Suppose further that he were shown the various objects being carried by and were made to say, in reply to questions, what each of them was. Would he not be perplexed and believe the objects now shown him to be not so real as what he formerly saw?

G: Yes, not nearly so real.

S: And if he were forced to look at the fire-light itself, would not his eyes ache, so that he would try to escape and turn back to the things which he could see distinctly, convinced that they really were clearer than these other objects now being shown to him?

G: Yes.

*S:* And suppose someone were to drag him away forcibly up the steep and rugged ascent and not let him go until he had hauled him out into the sunlight, would he not suffer pain and vexation at such treatment, and, when he had come out into the light, find his eyes so full of its radiance that he could not see a single one of the things that he was now told were real?

*G:* Certainly he would not see them all at once.

*S:* He would need, then, to grow accustomed before he could see things in that upper world. At first it would be easiest to make out shadows, and then the images of men and things reflected in water, and later on the things themselves. After that, it would be easier to watch the heavenly bodies and the sky itself by night, looking at the light of the moon and stars rather than the Sun and the Sun's light in the day-time.

*G:* Yes, surely.

*S:* Last of all, he would be able to look at the Sun and contemplate its nature, not as it appears when reflected in water or any alien medium, but as it is in itself in its own domain.

*G:* No doubt.

*S:* And now he would begin to draw the conclusion that it is the Sun that produces the seasons and the course of the year and controls everything in the visible world, and moreover is in a way the cause of all that he and his companions used to see.

*G:* Clearly he would come at last to that conclusion.

*S:* Then if he called to mind his fellow prisoners and what passed for wisdom in his former dwelling-place, he would surely think himself happy in the change and be sorry for them. They may have had a practice of honouring and commending one another, with prizes for the man who had the keenest eye for the passing shadows and the best memory for the order in which they followed or accompanied one another, so that he could make a good guess as to which was going to come next. Would our released prisoner be likely to covet those prizes or to envy the men exalted to honour and power in the Cave? Would he not feel like Homer's Achilles, that he would far sooner 'be on earth

as a hired servant in the house of a landless man' or endure anything rather than go back to his old beliefs and live in the old way?

*G:* Yes, he would prefer any fate to such a life.

*S:* Now imagine what would happen if he went down again to take his former seat in the Cave. Coming suddenly out of the sunlight, his eyes would be filled with darkness. He might be required once more to deliver his opinion on those shadows, in competition with the prisoners who had never been released, while his eyesight was still dim and unsteady; and it might take some time to become used to the darkness. They would laugh at him and say that he had gone up only to come back with his sight ruined; it was worth no one's while even to attempt the ascent. If they could lay hands on the man who was trying to set them free and lead them up, they would kill him.

*G:* Yes, they would.

*S:* Every feature in this parable, my dear Glaucon, is meant to fit our earlier analysis. The prison dwelling corresponds to the region revealed to us through the sense of sight, and the fire-light within it to the power of the Sun. The ascent to see the things in the upper world you may take as standing for the upward journey of the soul into the region of the intelligible; then you will be in possession of what I surmise, since that is what you wish to be told. Heaven knows whether it is true; but this, at any rate, is how it appears to me. In the world of knowledge, the last thing to be perceived and only with great difficulty is the essential Form of Goodness. Once it is perceived, the conclusion must follow that, for all things, this is the cause of whatever is right and good; in the visible world it gives birth to light and to the lord of light, while it is itself sovereign in the intelligible world and the parent of intelligence and truth. Without having had a vision of this Form no one can act with wisdom, either in his own life or in matters of state.

*G:* So far as I can understand, I share your belief.

*S:* Then you may also agree that it is no wonder if those who have reached this height are reluctant to manage the affairs of men. Their souls long to spend all their time in that upper world—

naturally enough, if here once more our parable holds true. Nor, again, is it at all strange that one who comes from the contemplation of divine things to the miseries of human life should appear awkward and ridiculous when, with eyes still dazed and not yet accustomed to the darkness, he is compelled, in a law-court or elsewhere, to dispute about the shadows of justice or the images that cast those shadows, and to wrangle over the notions of what is right in the minds of men who have never beheld Justice itself.

*G:* It is not at all strange.

*S:* No; a sensible man will remember that the eyes may be confused in two ways — by a change from light to darkness or from darkness to light; and he will recognize that the same thing happens to the soul. When he sees it troubled and unable to discern anything clearly, instead of laughing thoughtlessly, he will ask whether, coming from a brighter existence, its unaccustomed vision is obscured by the darkness, in which case he will think its condition enviable and its life a happy one; or whether, emerging from the depths of ignorance, it is dazzled by excess of light. If so, he will rather feel sorry for it; or, if he were inclined to laugh, that would be less ridiculous than to laugh at the soul which has come down from the light.

*G:* That is a fair statement.

*S:* If this is true, then, we must conclude that education is not what it is said to be by some, who profess to put knowledge into a soul which does not possess it, as if they could put sight into blind eyes. On the contrary, our own account signifies that the soul of every man does possess the power of learning the truth and the organ to see it with; and that, just as one might have to turn the whole body round in order that the eye should see light instead of darkness, so the entire soul must be turned away from this changing world, until its eye can bear to contemplate reality and that supreme splendour which we have called the Good. Hence there may well be an art whose aim would be to effect this very thing, the conversion of the soul, in the readiest way; not to put the power of sight into the soul's eye, which already has it, but to ensure

that, instead of looking in the wrong direction, it is turned the way it ought to be.

*G:* Yes, it may well be so.

*S:* It looks, then, as though wisdom were different from those ordinary virtues, as they are called, which are not far removed from bodily qualities, in that they can be produced by habituation and exercise in a soul which has not possessed them from the first. Wisdom, it seems, is certainly the virtue of some diviner faculty, which never loses its power, though its use for good or harm depends on the direction towards which it is turned. You must have noticed in dishonest men with a reputation for sagacity the shrewd glance of a narrow intelligence piercing the objects to which it is directed. There is nothing wrong with their power of vision, but it has been forced into the service of evil, so that the keener its sight, the more harm it works.

*G:* Quite true.

*S:* And yet if the growth of a nature like this had been pruned from earliest childhood, cleared of those clinging overgrowths which come of gluttony and all luxurious pleasure and, like leaden weights charged with affinity to this mortal world, hang upon the soul, bending its vision downwards; if, freed from these, the soul were turned round towards true reality, then this same power in these very men would see the truth as keenly as the objects it is turned to now.

*G:* Yes, very likely.

*S:* Is it not also likely, or indeed certain after what has been said, that a state can never be properly governed either by the uneducated who know nothing of truth or by men who are allowed to spend all their days in the pursuit of culture? The ignorant have no single mark before their eyes at which they must aim in all the conduct of their own lives and of affairs of state; and the others will not engage in action if they can help it, dreaming that while still alive, they have been translated to the Islands of the Blest.

*G:* Quite true.

*S:* It is for us, then, as founders of a commonwealth, to bring compulsion to bear on the noblest natures. They must be made to climb the ascent to the vision of Goodness, which we called the highest object of knowledge; and, when they have looked upon it long enough, they must not be allowed, as they now are, to remain on the heights, refusing to come down again to the prisoners or to take any part in their labours and rewards, however much or little these may be worth.

*G:* Shall we not be doing them an injustice, if we force on them a worse life than they might have?

*S:* You have forgotten again, my friend, that the law is not concerned to make any one class specially happy, but to ensure the welfare of the commonwealth as a whole. By persuasion or constraint it will unite the citizens in harmony, making them share whatever benefits each class can contribute to the common good; and its purpose in forming men of that spirit was not that each should be left to go his own way, but that they should be instrumental in binding the community into one.

*G:* True, I had forgotten.

*S:* You will see, then, Glaucon, that there will be no real injustice in compelling our philosophers to watch over and care for the other citizens. We can fairly tell them that their compeers in other states may quite reasonably refuse to collaborate: there they have sprung up, like a self-sown plant, in despite of their country's institutions; no one has fostered their growth, and they cannot be expected to show gratitude for a care they have never received. 'But,' we shall say, 'it is not so with you. We have brought you into existence for your country's sake as well as for your own, to be like leaders and king-bees in a hive; you have been better and more thoroughly educated than those others and hence you are more capable of playing your part both as men of thought and as men of action. You must go down, then, each in his turn, to live with the rest and let your eyes grow accustomed to the darkness. You will then see a thousand times better than those who live there always; you will recognize every image for what

it is and know what it represents, because you have seen justice, beauty, and goodness in their reality; and so you and we shall find life in our commonwealth no mere dream, as it is in most existing states, where men live fighting one another about shadows and quarrelling for power, as if that were a great prize; whereas in truth government can be at its best and free from dissension only where the destined rulers are least desirous of holding office.'

*G:* Quite true.

*S:* Then will our pupils refuse to listen and to take their turns at sharing in the work of the community, though they may live together for most of their time in a purer air?

*G:* No; it is a fair demand, and they are fair-minded men. No doubt, unlike any ruler of the present day, they will think of holding power as an unavoidable necessity.

*S:* Yes, my friend; for the truth is that you can have a well-governed society only if you can discover for your future rulers a better way of life than being in office; then only will power be in the hands of men who are rich, not in gold, but in the wealth that brings happiness, a good and wise life. All goes wrong when, starved for lack of anything good in their own lives, men turn to public affairs hoping to snatch from thence the happiness they hunger for. They set about fighting for power, and this internecine conflict ruins them and their country. The life of true philosophy is the only one that looks down upon offices of state; and access to power must be confined to men who are not in love with it; otherwise rivals will start fighting. So whom else can you compel to undertake the guardianship of the commonwealth, if not those who, besides understanding best the principles of government, enjoy a nobler life than the politician's and look for rewards of a different kind?

*G:* There is indeed no other choice. One who holds a true belief without intelligence is just like a blind man who happens to take the right road, isn't he?

### SELECTION 3.3

# Meno*

*Plato*

[*In this selection from the dialogue* Meno, *"Socrates" explains another of Plato's theories about knowledge: Knowledge about reality comes from within the soul through a form of "recollection" rather than from without through being taught. The passage also serves to show that, in Plato's opinion, the soul is immortal. In the dialogue, Socrates has a boy who knows nothing of geometry construct a square twice the size of a given square. After one or two failed attempts, the boy succeeds without having been taught how to do it by Socrates. How could he succeed unless knowledge of geometry was not already within his soul?*]

*Meno:* But how will you look for something when you don't in the least know what it is? How on earth are you going to set up something you don't know as the object of your search? To put it another way, even if you come right up against it, how will you know that what you have found is the thing you didn't know?

*Socrates:* I know what you mean. Do you realize that what you are bringing up is the trick argument that a man cannot try to discover either what he knows or what he does not know? He would not seek what he knows, for since he knows it there is no need of the inquiry, nor what he does not know, for in that case he does not even know what he is to look for.

*M:* Well, do you think it a good argument?

*S:* No.

*M:* Can you explain how it fails?

*S:* I can. I have heard from men and women who understand the truths of religion—
(*Here he presumably pauses to emphasize the solemn change of tone the dialogue undergoes at this point.*)

*M:* What did they say?

*S:* Something true, I thought, and fine.

*M:* What was it, and who were they?

*S:* Those who tell it are priests and priestesses of the sort who make it their business to be able to account for the functions which they perform. Pindar speaks of it too, and many another of the poets who are divinely inspired. What they say is this—see whether you think they are speaking the truth. They say that the soul of man is immortal: at one time it comes to an end—that which is called death—and at another is born again, but is never finally exterminated. . . .

Thus the soul, since it is immortal and has been born many times, and has seen all things both here and in the other world, has learned everything that is. So we need not be surprised if it can recall the knowledge of virtue or anything else which, as we see, it once possessed. All nature is akin, and the soul has learned everything, so that when a man has recalled a single piece of knowledge—*learned* it, in ordinary language—there is no reason why he should not find out all the rest, if he keeps a stout heart and does not grow weary of the search; for seeking and learning are in fact nothing but recollection.

We ought not then to be led astray by the contentious argument you quoted. It would make us lazy, and is music in the ears of weaklings. The other doctrine produces energetic seekers after knowledge; and being convinced of its truth, I am ready, with your help, to inquire into the nature of virtue.

*M:* I see, Socrates. But what do you mean when you say that we don't learn anything, but that what we call learning is recollection? Can you teach me that it is so?

*S:* I have just said that you're a rascal, and now you ask me if I can teach you, when I say there

*From *Plato, Protagoras and Meno,* translated by W. K. C. Guthrie (London: Penguin Press, 1956). Translation copyright © 1956 W. K. C. Guthrie. Reproduced by permission of Penguin Books Ltd.

is no such thing as teaching, only recollection. Evidently you want to catch me contradicting myself straight away.

*M:* No, honestly, Socrates, I wasn't thinking of that. It was just habit. If you can in any way make clear to me that what you say is true, please do.

*S:* It isn't an easy thing, but still I should like to do what I can since you ask me. I see you have a large number of retainers here. Call one of them, anyone you like, and I will use him to demonstrate it to you.

*M:* Certainly. (*To a slave-boy.*) Come here.

*S:* He is a Greek and speaks our language?

*M:* Indeed yes—born and bred in the house.

*S:* Listen carefully then, and see whether it seems to you that he is learning from me or simply being reminded.

*M:* I will.

*S:* Now boy, you know that a square is a figure like this?
(*Socrates begins to draw figures in the sand at his feet. He points to the square* ABCD.)

*Boy:* Yes.

*S:* It has all these four sides equal?

*Boy:* Yes.

*S:* And these lines which go through the middle of it are also equal? (*The lines* EF, GH.)

*Boy:* Yes.

*S:* Such a figure could be either larger or smaller, could it not?

*Boy:* Yes.

*S:* Now if this side is two feet long, and this side the same, how many feet will the whole be? Put it this way. If it were two feet in this direction and only one in that, must not the area be two feet taken once?

*Boy:* Yes.

*S:* But since it is two feet this way also, does it not become twice two feet?

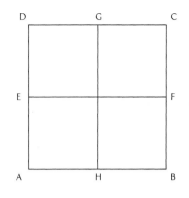

*Boy:* Yes.

*S:* And how many feet is twice two? Work it out and tell me.

*Boy:* Four.

*S:* Now could one draw another figure double the size of this, but similar, that is, with all its sides equal like this one?

*Boy:* Yes.

*S:* How many feet will its area be?

*Boy:* Eight.

*S:* Now then, try to tell me how long each of its sides will be. The present figure has a side of two feet. What will be the side of the double-sized one?

*Boy:* It will be double, Socrates, obviously.

*S:* You see, Meno, that I am not teaching him anything, only asking. Now he thinks he knows the length of the side of the eight-feet square.

*M:* Yes.

*S:* But does he?

*M:* Certainly not.

*S:* He thinks it is twice the length of the other.

*M:* Yes.

*S:* Now watch how he recollects things in order—the proper way to recollect.

You say that the side of double length produces the double-sized figure? Like this I mean, not long this way and short that. It must be equal on all sides like the first figure, only twice its size, that is eight feet. Think a moment whether you still expect to get it from doubling the side.

*Boy:* Yes, I do.

*S:* Well now, shall we have a line double the length of this (AB) if we add another the same length at this end (BJ)?

*Boy:* Yes.

*S:* It is on this line then, according to you, that we shall make the eight-feet square, by taking four of the same length?

*Boy:* Yes.

*S:* Let us draw in four equal lines (*i.e., counting* AJ, *and adding* JK, KL, *and* LA *made complete by drawing in its second half* LD), using the first as a base. Does this not give us what you call the eight-feet figure?

*Boy:* Certainly.

*S:* But does it contain these four squares, each equal to the original four-feet one?
(*Socrates has drawn in the lines* CM, CN *to complete the squares that he wishes to point out.*)

*Boy:* Yes.

*S:* How big is it then? Won't it be four times as big?

*Boy:* Of course.

*S:* And is four times the same as twice?

*Boy:* Of course not.

*S:* So doubling the side has given us not a double but a fourfold figure?

*Boy:* True.

*S:* And four times four are sixteen, are they not?

*Boy:* Yes.

*S:* Then how big is the side of the eight-feet figure? This one has given us four times the original area, hasn't it?

*Boy:* Yes.

*S:* And a side half the length gave us a square of four feet?

*Boy:* Yes.

*S:* Good. And isn't a square of eight feet double this one and half that?

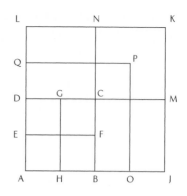

*Boy:* Yes.

*S:* Will it not have a side greater than this one but less than that?

*Boy:* I think it will.

*S:* Right. Always answer what you think. Now tell me: was not this side two feet long, and this one four?

*Boy:* Yes.

*S:* Then the side of the eight-feet figure must be longer than two feet but shorter than four?

*Boy:* It must.

*S:* Try to say how long you think it is.

*Boy:* Three feet.

*S:* If so, shall we add half of this bit (BO, *half of* BJ) and make it three feet? Here are two, and this is one, and on this side similarly we have two plus one; and here is the figure you want.
(*Socrates completes the square* AOPQ.)

*Boy:* Yes.

*S:* If it is three feet this way and three that, will the whole area be three times three feet?

*Boy:* It looks like it.

*S:* And that is how many?

*Boy:* Nine.

*S:* Whereas the square double our first square had to be how many?

*Boy:* Eight.

*S:* But we haven't yet got the square of eight feet even from a three-feet side?

*Boy:* No.

*S:* Then what length will we give it? Try to tell us exactly. If you don't want to count it up, just show us on the diagram.

*Boy:* It's no use, Socrates, I just don't know.

*S:* Observe, Meno, the stage he has reached on the path of recollection. At the beginning he did not know the side of the square of eight feet. Nor indeed does he know it now, but then he thought he knew it and answered boldly, as was appropriate — he felt no perplexity. Now however he does feel perplexed. Not only does he not know the answer; he doesn't even think he knows.

*M:* Quite true.

*S:* Isn't he in a better position now in relation to what he didn't know?

*M:* I admit that too.

*S:* So in perplexing him and numbing him like the sting-ray, have we done him any harm?

*M:* I think not.

*S:* In fact we have helped him to some extent towards finding out the right answer, for now not only is he ignorant of it but he will be quite glad to look for it. Up to now, he thought he could speak well and fluently, on many occasions and before large audiences, on the subject of a square double the size of a given square, maintaining that it must have a side of double the length.

*M:* No doubt.

*S:* Do you suppose then that he would have attempted to look for, or learn, what he thought he knew (though he did not), before he was thrown into perplexity, became aware of his ignorance, and felt a desire to know?

*M:* No.

*S:* Then the numbing process was good for him?

*M:* I agree.

*S:* Now notice what, starting from this state of perplexity, he will discover by seeking the truth in company with me, though I simply ask him questions without teaching him. Be ready to catch me if I give him any instruction or expla-nation instead of simply interrogating him on his own opinions.

(*Socrates here rubs out the previous figures and starts again.*)

Tell me, boy, is not this our square of four feet? (ABCD.) You understand?

*Boy:* Yes.

*S:* Now we can add another equal to it like this? (BCEF.)

*Boy:* Yes.

*S:* And a third here, equal to each of the others? (CEGH.)

*Boy:* Yes.

*S:* And then we can fill in this one in the corner? (DCHJ.)

*Boy:* Yes.

*S:* Then here we have four equal squares?

*Boy:* Yes.

*S:* And how many times the size of the first square is the whole?

*Boy:* Four times.

*S:* And we want one double the size. You remember?

*Boy:* Yes.

*S:* Now does this line going from corner to corner cut each of these squares in half?

*Boy:* Yes.

*S:* And these are four equal lines enclosing this area? (BEHD.)

*Boy:* They are.

*S:* Now think. How big is this area?

*Boy:* I don't understand.

*S:* Here are four squares. Has not each line cut off the inner half of each of them?

*Boy:* Yes.

*S:* And how many such halves are there in this figure? (BEHD.)

*Boy:* Four.

*S:* And how many in this one? (ABCD.)

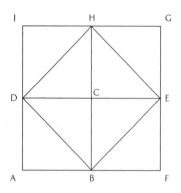

*Boy:* Two.

*S:* And what is the relation of four to two?

*Boy:* Double.

*S:* How big is this figure then?

*Boy:* Eight feet.

*S:* On what base?

*Boy:* This one.

*S:* The line which goes from corner to corner of the square of four feet?

*Boy:* Yes.

*S:* The technical name for it is 'diagonal'; so if we use that name, it is your personal opinion that the square on the diagonal of the original square is double its area.

*Boy:* That is so, Socrates.

*S:* What do you think, Meno? Has he answered with any opinions that were not his own?

*M:* No, they were all his.

*S:* Yet he did not know, as we agreed a few minutes ago.

*M:* True.

*S:* But these opinions were somewhere in him, were they not?

*M:* Yes.

*S:* So a man who does not know has in himself true opinions on a subject without having knowledge.

*M:* It would appear so.

*S:* At present these opinions, being newly aroused, have a dream-like quality. But if the same questions are put to him on many occasions and in different ways, you can see that in the end he will have a knowledge on the subject as accurate as anybody's.

*M:* Probably.

*S:* This knowledge will not come from teaching but from questioning. He will recover it for himself.

*M:* Yes.

*S:* And the spontaneous recovery of knowledge that is in him is recollection, isn't it?

*M:* Yes.

*S:* Either then he has at some time acquired the knowledge which he now has, or he has always possessed it. If he always possessed it, he must always have known; if on the other hand he acquired it at some previous time, it cannot have been in this life, unless somebody has taught him geometry. He will behave in the same way with all geometrical knowledge, and every other subject. Has anyone taught him all these? You ought to know, especially as he has been brought up in your household.

*M:* Yes, I know that no one ever taught him.

*S:* And has he these opinions, or hasn't he?

*M:* It seems we can't deny it.

*S:* Then if he did not acquire them in this life, isn't it immediately clear that he possessed and had learned them during some other period?

*M:* It seems so.

*S:* When he was not in human shape?

*M:* Yes.

*S:* If then there are going to exist in him, both while he is and while he is not a man, true opinions which can be aroused by questioning and turned into knowledge, may we say that his soul has been for ever in a state of knowledge? Clearly he always either is or is not a man.

*M:* Clearly.

*S:* And if the truth about reality is always in our soul, the soul must be immortal, and one must take courage and try to discover — that is, to recollect—what one doesn't happen to know, or (more correctly) remember, at the moment.

*M:* Somehow or other I believe you are right.

*S:* I think I am. I shouldn't like to take my oath on the whole story, but one thing I am ready to fight for as long as I can, in word and act: that

is, that we shall be better, braver and more active men if we believe it right to look for what we don't know than if we believe there is no point in looking because what we don't know we can never discover.

*M:* There too I am sure you are right.

---

## CHECKLIST

To help you review, here is a checklist of the key philosophers and terms and concepts of this chapter. The brief descriptive sentences summarize the philosophers' leading ideas. Keep in mind that some of these summary statements are oversimplifications of complex positions.

### *Philosophers*

- **Sophists**   were ancient Greek teachers of rhetoric. Through them and Socrates, moral philosophy began.

- **Socrates**   was Plato's mentor and philosophy's most illustrious practitioner of the Socratic/ dialectic method.

- **Plato**   was most famous for his Theory of Forms and his two-realm doctrine: two separate worlds with two types of knowledge.

### *Key Terms and Concepts*

| | |
|---|---|
| Socratic/dialectic method | skeptic |
| Delphi Oracle | knowledge not identical to sense perception |
| Forms/Theory of Forms | Theory of the Divided Line |
| Plato's dialogues | Myth of the Cave |
| Platonic dualism | |

## QUESTIONS FOR DISCUSSION AND REVIEW

1. Can you step into the same river twice? once?

2. Plato's metaphysics incorporates ideas from some of the earlier philosophers mentioned in Chapter 2. Identify those philosophers and their ideas.

3. Give an example of a Platonic Form not mentioned in the text. Explain whether it really exists, and why.

4. Does a world of Forms exist separately from the world of concrete, individual things? Explain.

5. What is the Myth of the Cave?

6. Is sense perception knowledge?

7. Can beauty be in more than one object at one time? Explain.

8. Are appearances real for Plato? Are they real in fact?

## SUGGESTED FURTHER READINGS

J. L. Ackrill, *Essays on Plato and Aristotle* (New York: Oxford University Press, 1997). Selected essays by a famous classics scholar.

Julia Annas, *Ancient Philosophy: A Very Short Introduction* (New York: Oxford University Press, 2000). A brief look at some of the problems faced by the ancient Greeks and Romans.

Jonathan Barnes, R. M. Hare, and C. C. W. Taylor, *Greek Philosophers* (New York: Oxford University Press, 1999). Essays by three eminent scholars on Socrates, Plato, and Aristotle.

Christopher Biffle, *A Guided Tour of Five Works by Plato: Euthyphro, Apology, Crito, Phaedo (Death Scene), Allegory [Myth] of the Cave,* 2nd ed. (Mountain View, Calif.: Mayfield, 1995). The best introduction there is to these five dialogues.

Alan Bloom, trans., *The Republic of Plato,* 2nd ed. (New York: Basic Books, 1991). The famous translation by one of America's best-known intellectuals.

Thomas C. Brickhouse and Nicholas D. Smith, *Plato's Socrates* (New York: Oxford University Press, 1994). An analysis of the Socratic philosophy.

Scott Buchanan, ed., *Portable Plato* (New York: Viking Penguin, 1980). A selection of Plato's writings, suitable for the introductory reader.

Ronna Burger, *The Phaedo, A Platonic Labyrinth* (South Bend, Ind.: St. Augustine's Press, 1999). A comprehensive study of Plato's *Phaedo,* which contains the Theory of Forms and Plato's ideas on the immortality of the soul.

David Gallop, trans., *Defence of Socrates, Euthyphro, Crito* (New York: Oxford University Press, 1999). This book gives access to the character of Socrates and the nature of his final trial.

E. Hamilton and H. Cairns, eds., *The Collected Dialogues of Plato* (New York: Bollingen Foundation, 1961). This is what you need to acquaint yourself firsthand with Plato's dialogues. Be sure to read the *Republic,* if you haven't already.

Richard Kraut, ed., *The Cambridge Companion to Plato* (New York: Cambridge University Press, 1996). A modern, convenient, accessible guide to Plato's thought.

Alexander Nehamas, *Virtues of Authenticity: Essays on Plato and Socrates* (Princeton, N.J.: Princeton University Press, 1998). A collection of important essays on Plato and Socrates by a noted American scholar.

Plato, *Symposium,* Paul Woodruff, trans. (Indianapolis: Hackett, 1989). An English translation of Plato's dialogue on love.

Plato, *The Last Days of Socrates.* Hugh Tredennick and Harold Tarrant, trans. (New York: Penguin, 2003). Selections from Platonic dialogues concerning the trial and death of Socrates.

Daryl H. Rice, *A Guide to Plato's Republic* (New York: Oxford University Press, 1997). A comprehensive interpretation of Plato's classic.

Stanley Rosen, *Plato's Symposium* (South Bend, Ind.: St. Augustine's Press, 1999). The first full-length study of Plato's *Symposium* published in English.

Nicholas D. Smith, *The Philosophy of Socrates* (Boulder, Colo.: Westview Press, 1999). A comprehensive introduction to the life and thought of Socrates.

Harold Tarrant, *Plato's First Interpreters* (Ithaca, N.Y.: Cornell University Press, 2000). An exploration of ancient interpretations of Plato's writings.

A. E. Taylor, *Plato: The Man and His Works* (New York: Methuen, 1960). A standard introduction to Plato's philosophy.

C. C. W. Taylor, ed., *Oxford Studies in Ancient Philosophy* (New York: Oxford University Press, annually). Original articles by contemporary scholars on Aristotle, Plato, the Atomists, and others.

Irwin Terence, *Classical Philosophy* (New York: Oxford University Press, 1999). A wide-ranging collection of brief readings from classical antiquity.

Gregory Vlastos, *Socrates: Ironist and Moral Philosopher* (Ithaca, N.Y.: Cornell University Press, 1991).

Robin Waterfield, *Plato's Republic* (New York: Oxford University Press, 1993). A recent translation of the *Republic,* available in paperback.

# 4

# Aristotle

Motion being eternal, the first mover, if there is but one, will be eternal also.

— Aristotle

Plato's most distinguished pupil was **Aristotle** (384–322 B.C.E.), on whom Plato had a tremendous influence. Aristotle was eventually hired to be a teacher of Alexander the Great, and Alexander attributed his happiness to his teacher, Aristotle. Nevertheless, it is a good bet that Alexander, who conquered the world, was not preoccupied with philosophy.

We noted earlier that we owe the term *metaphysics* to Aristotle, or at least to those who catalogued his works. But metaphysics formed just a part of Aristotle's interests. Aristotle was interested in every subject that came along, and he had something reasonably intelligent to say about all of them, from poetry to physics, from biology to friendship.

Aristotle's books are more systematic than are Plato's, providing evidence of his more painstaking attention to nature. It should tell you something, however, that although Plato is a main staple of any decent literature program, Aristotle is not. Cicero did praise Aristotle for his "copious and golden eloquence," but many find Aristotle a bit tedious. Maybe that is because what we have from Aristotle is mainly lecture notes edited by some of his students.

Nevertheless, Aristotle was a careful observer and a brilliant theorizer, and his thought influenced philosophy in the future. Some fifteen centuries after his death, he was considered the definitive authority on all subjects outside religion, a fact that may have impeded more than it helped scientific progress because science, to get anywhere, cannot assume that something is so solely because some authority says that it is so, even if that authority is Aristotle.

What we call metaphysics Aristotle called "first philosophy." First philosophy, in Aristotle's view, is in some sense more abstract and general than are the specific sciences, and it considers the most basic questions of existence. The most basic question of existence is, What is it to be? so we will begin there.

# PROFILE: Aristotle (384–322 B.C.E.)

Aristotle was not correct about every-thing. He thought the brain is a minor organ compared with the heart and that eels are spontaneously generated from mud. He also thought that pars-nips cause erections and that women are an inferior product.

But he did know a great deal. In fact, Aristotle systematized all that was then known, and, as if that were not sufficient, he extended the limits of knowledge in virtually every existing subject, in-cluding biology, psychology, zoology, physics, and astronomy as well as in those areas that today are deemed the province of philosophy, including ethics, politics, aesthetics, metaphysics, and logic. His work was of enormous and lasting significance.

Aristotle was born in Stagira, a Greek colony along the Macedonian coast. His father, Nico-machus, was the physician of the king of Macedo-nia, Amyntas II. When he was eighteen, Aristotle went to Athens, where he studied under Plato at Plato's Academy for some twenty years. Plato may ultimately have come to resent Aristotle, and Aris-totle eventually discovered that he disagreed with important Platonic doctrines, but Aristotle always retained a great respect for his teacher.

In 342 Aristotle was hired by Philip of Macedo-nia to tutor his son, Alexander, who was thirteen at the time. Alexander, of course, went on to conquer most of the then civilized world, but we suspect that

none of this was the result of anything Aristotle taught him. Whatever Alex-ander learned from Aristotle, he re-paid by sending Aristotle zoological specimens from his many travels and by funding his studies.

In 335 Aristotle formed his own school at the Lyceum, in Athens, and some of the sharper members of the Academy joined up with Aristotle. Be-cause of his practice of lecturing in the Lyceum's walking place, or *peripatos,* Aristotle's followers became known as the peripatetics, the "walkers."

Aristotle emphasized the importance of direct observation of nature and believed that you must obtain factual data before you can begin to theorize. He also maintained that knowledge of things re-quires description, classification, and causal expla-nation. This is, of course, the modern scientific view, although (as was explained in the text) Aris-totle emphasized a different aspect of causation from that stressed in modern science.

Aristotle's works are often classified under five headings: the *Organum,* which consisted of six trea-tises on logic; the *Rhetoric* and the *Poetics;* his works on natural science, including most important the *Physics* and *De Anima* (On the Soul); *Metaphysics;* and the works on ethics and politics, which in-clude the *Nicomachean Ethics, Eudemian Ethics,* and *Politics.*

## WHAT IS IT TO BE?

In Aristotle's opinion, to be is to be a particular thing. And each thing, Aristotle maintained, is a combination of *matter* and *form.* A statue, for example, is a chunk of marble with a certain form. It is the same with other things too. There is some stuff out of which each thing is made, and there is the particular form this bit of stuff takes. Without the stuff, the thing would not exist, because you cannot have a thing made out of nothing. Likewise, without form, the thing would not exist. With-out form, the stuff would not be some *particular kind of thing;* it would just be *stuff.* The form determines what the thing is; it is the essential nature of the thing.

For example, the marble of the statue is the same marble as it was when it was cut into a block at the quarry. But now it has a new form, and that form is what dis-

## Aristotle and the Deaf

Aristotle had the idea that hearing is more important than sight in acquiring knowledge, and he believed that the blind are more intelligent than the deaf. Probably at least in part because of Aristotle's authority, it was not generally believed that the deaf were educable. In fact, during the Middle Ages, priests barred the deaf from churches on the ground that they could not have faith. Schools for the deaf are only a relatively recent phenomenon.

tinguishes the marble now from the marble in the block in the quarry. Yes, the marble has always had *some* form or other, but its transformation to this particular form is what makes it a statue. Thus, the form is what determines what a thing is, and for this reason Aristotle equated a thing's form with its essence.

According to Aristotle, you need both form and matter to have a thing, and, with the exception of god (discussed later), neither form nor matter is ever found in isolation from the other.

Things do change, of course: they become something new. Thus, another basic question is, What produces a change? In Aristotle's opinion each change must be directed toward some end, so just four basic questions can be asked of anything:

1. *What is the thing?* In other words, what is its form? Aristotle called this the **formal cause** of the thing. We do not use the word *cause* that way, but Aristotle did, and we just have to accept that.
2. *What is it made of?* Aristotle called this the **material cause.**
3. *What made it?* This Aristotle called the **efficient cause,** and this is what today we often mean by "cause."
4. *What purpose does it serve?* That is, for what end was it made? This Aristotle called the **final cause.**

Consider again a statue, Michelangelo's *David,* for example. What it is, (1), is a statue. What it is made of, (2), is marble. What made it, (3), is Michelangelo (or Michelangelo's chisel on the marble). And (4), it was made for the purpose of creating a beautiful object. Of course, natural objects were not made by humans for their purposes, but they still do have "ends." The end of an acorn, for instance, is to be a tree.

But consider the acorn example more closely. The acorn is not actually a tree, only potentially so, correct? Change can therefore be viewed, according to Aristotle, as movement from potentiality to actuality. Because actuality is the source of change, *pure actuality* is the *ultimate* source of change. Pure actuality is the unchanged changer or unmoved mover or, in short, god. It should be noted that the pure actuality that Aristotle equated with god is not God, the personal deity of the Jewish or Christian religions.

It sometimes is difficult to perceive the ancient Greek metaphysicians as all being concerned with the same thing. But Aristotle explained that his predecessors were all concerned with *causation.* Thales, for example, was concerned with the stuff from which all is made: the material cause of things. Empedocles and Anaxagoras were concerned with why there is change, with efficient causation. In his Theory of Forms, Plato considered formal causation. It remained for Aristotle himself, Aristotle thought, to present an adequate explanation of final causation. So Aristotle gave us a handy way of integrating (and remembering) ancient Greek metaphysics.

## ACTUALITY AND POSSIBILITY

Aristotle delineated the different kinds of imperfect, changing beings in terms of possibility and actuality. At one extreme is matter, which consists only of possibility. Matter, as we saw, is that which must be moved because it cannot move or form itself. At the other extreme is god as pure actuality, which can only move things without god being moved or changed in any way. God is the unmoved mover. Any movement on god's part would imply imperfection and is therefore impossible. Nature (*physis*) and all the things of the universe exist between these two poles. Things move and are moved as a process of actualizing some of their potentialities. There is a penchant in each being to take on ever-higher forms of being in an effort to approach the unmoving perfection of god. It is things' love of and longing for perfection or god that moves the universe. God remains the unmoved mover.

Aristotle maintained that the stars, having the most perfect of all shapes, were beings with superhuman intelligence. Being much closer to god in the hierarchy of beings, they are incarnated gods unto themselves. Because their actions are much more rational and purposeful than those of the lower order beings on the earth, stars exercise a benevolent influence on earthly matters. Today many people read their astrology charts in the newspaper every day, and some political leaders even organize their programs around them. In this regard, Aristotle has not been the only one seeing stars.

To Aristotle, the earth is a mortal sphere. Things on it come to be and then cease to be. Earthly things are in a constant, unsettled state of becoming. As a consequence, earthly things and earthly matters long for the fixity and quietude that perfection allows. And although they strive mightily to become as perfect and godlike as possible, they never exhaust their own potentiality. Since god alone is pure act and perfect actualization, changes in the natural world go on without ceasing.

## ESSENCE AND EXISTENCE

Aristotle was the first philosopher to discuss being in terms of **existence and essence** or, more exactly, in terms of existence and **substance (*ousia*)**. The first judgment to be made regarding a thing is whether or not it exists. Then, further judgments need to be made. Therefore, a judgment regarding existence is but a first step. Further judgments need to be made regarding a thing's substance and its characteristics. If a thing is, what is it? Aristotle gives the term "substance" a double meaning. "Substance" refers first of all to the individual, particular thing. For example, humans are given proper names, which mark them out as singular. Aris-

Athens today. Ancient Greece gave us Plato and Aristotle, systematic mathematics, the Olympics, and (last but not least) democracy.

totle called this quality of uniqueness "this-thereness" (*tode ti*). "Substance" secondarily refers to what a thing is in common with other things. In English, this is known as the thing's essence, or that in virtue of which it is the sort of thing it is. Each thing has an essence or definition, which it often shares with other like things. We, for example, share the essence of human beings or rational animals as Aristotle defined us. Aristotle believed these essences to be fixed species, which can be determined and hierarchically ordered. For example, the physical world can be divided into mineral, vegetable, and animal genera. To be a specific thing is to have a set potential that is more or less realized at any given time and is in a continuous process of actualization. This forming process constitutes a thing's being and allows it to become a whole individual. Happiness, for example, is one way of measuring to what degree a human is succeeding at fulfilling his or her potential. Other key ways of measuring fulfillment of potential include truth, beauty, oneness, and justice.

## TEN BASIC CATEGORIES

Aristotle thought that there are yet other ways that humans use to think about things. These are the ten basic categories of being, which he developed. Besides substance itself, humans make judgments regarding things in terms of their quantity, quality, relationships, place, time, posture, constitution, passivity, and activity. Aristotle thought that all possible predicates, or what we can attribute to things, could be subsumed under these basic categories or classifications. These categories allow us to comprehend various aspects of any thing's being. Not only do we want to know that a thing is; we want to know what it is and how it functions. Aristotle, like his teacher Plato, believed that the more we know about things, the better off we will be.

Aristotle defined human beings as rational animals. The soul (**psyche**) is the form of the body and that which prevents humans from falling apart. The human soul also provides the purposes and the ultimate end that human beings pursue. Part of this is the natural penchant humans have to try to fulfill as much of their potential as possible. Curiously, Aristotle thought that the principal organ of the soul was the heart, whereas the brain, he thought, was concerned with cooling the overheated blood.

## THE THREE SOULS

In fact, Aristotle believed that humans have three souls, which form a single unity. The first is the vegetative soul, the source of nourishment and reproduction. The second, the animal soul, is the basis of sensation as well as the ability to move. It is the animal soul that gives humans the ability to experience feelings of pleasure and pain. It also allows humans to avoid or to pursue pleasure and/or pain. The third soul is the *nous,* or the intelligent or spiritual soul. This soul is pure and immortal. It does not share the mortality of the body but is much more akin to the gods. Certain psychic processes are common to animals and humans and have their root in the animal soul. But there is likewise a higher speculative way of thinking that is unique to the human soul and gives rise to the human interest in ethics, epistemology, and metaphysics. The human soul alone can know the nature of being-as-a-whole and can intimate what God's nature must be.

## ARISTOTLE AND THE THEORY OF FORMS

It is an important fact that Aristotle took great issue with Plato's Theory of Forms. For Plato, two or more items, coins, let's say, can both be said to be circular if they participate in a third thing, the Form *circularity*. According to Plato, the Form *circularity* exists apart or separately from individual coins and other circular things, and they are dependent on it for their existence as circular things, as explained earlier. But according to Aristotle, this talk of participating is metaphorical and meaningless. Further, he thought that Plato was mistaken in holding that, although individual circular things depend for their existence as circular things on the Form *circularity,* the reverse does not hold true. For in fact (believed Aristotle), the re-

## Aristotle and Plato on Forms

These coins are all circular. Plato thought they are all circular because they "partake" in *circularity*, which, Plato said, existed apart and separately from particular coins. Aristotle thought that Plato's theory was metaphorical and meaningless. He held that universals like circularity have no independent existence apart from particular things.

verse does hold true: if there were not individual circular things, there would be no such thing as the Form *circularity*.

One of Aristotle's most compelling arguments against the Theory of Forms is known as the **Third Man argument.** It goes like this. Plato said that what ties two circular coins together, what they have in common, is the Form *circularity*. But what, Aristotle asked, ties the coins together *with* the Form *circularity*? Some *further* form? Well, what ties this further Form together with the first Form, yet *another* Form? You can see the problem.

Aristotle's own view is that the Forms are **universals**—something that more than one individual can be. Many different individual things can be beautiful or circular or large or green; so beauty, circularity, largeness, and greenness are universals. But only one thing can be you, and only one thing can be Aristotle; so you and Aristotle are not universals, but particulars. Universals, Aristotle insisted, do not exist separately or apart from particulars. Circularity and greenness, for example, have no independent existence apart from particular round things and particular green things (see the box "Aristotle and Plato on Forms").

Aristotle is fairly convincing when he tells us what is wrong with Plato's Theory of Forms, but he is less helpful in explaining just what universals are. The apparent failure of Aristotle (or Plato or their contemporaries) to produce a satisfactory theory of universals and their relationship to particulars resulted in an obsession with the problem through many centuries.

Now, a short summary statement of the differences between Plato's and Aristotle's metaphysics is bound to be a grotesque oversimplification, unless the sentences are very complicated. Nevertheless, the oversimplified difference comes to this: according to Plato, there are two realms. One is the realm of particular, changing, sensible things, and the other is a separate and superior realm of eternal, fixed, and unchanging Forms to which the particular things owe their reality. According to Aristotle, forms are found only within particular things, which are an embodiment of both form and matter. Aristotle did not disdain having knowledge of particular, sensible things, and because these things are always changing, Aristotle was much concerned with change itself. This concern led him to his theory of the four causes that underlie change.

## ARISTOTLE'S THEORY OF KNOWLEDGE

Most things for Aristotle are known through sense experience and are thought about using discursive reasoning, or reasoning from one thing or aspect to another. For example, Aristotle sought to define things by determining how a thing is similar to other things (**genus**) and how it is specifically different (species, or **specific difference**). Such discursive reasoning defines things by way of their limitations, sameness, and differences. Chains of related things can build up a composite picture of things based on cause and effect, on subject and object, on possibility and actuality. This kind of thinking works well in the changing, imperfect world of which we humans are so much a part. Discursive reasoning is the basis of the natural sciences but also provides a way of understanding ourselves and our everyday lives. But Aristotle believed that there is an entirely different kind of thinking that is at times necessary, namely, intuition. Intuition is an immediate, direct seeing of a certain truth. For example, that which is absolutely simple, namely god, needs ultimately to be known via intuition. God's existence and nature can be roughly intimated as the cause of the natural world. But a deeper, more compelling comprehension of god requires intuition. Also, the highest principles of knowing must be known intuitively as they can never be adequately known or proven via discursive reasoning. This includes the most fundamental of all logical and epistemological principles, the principle of contradiction, which states that a thing cannot both be and not be at the same time and in the same respect. Without this fundamental principle, no discursive reasoning is even possible.

## LOGIC

Before we end this chapter, one other aspect of Aristotle's philosophy needs to be mentioned. Aristotle made a great contribution to the history of logic. To be specific, it was Aristotle who first *made a study of the principles of sound reasoning,* especially those involved in one of the most important forms of inference — the syllogism.

What is inference? To *infer* one proposition from other propositions is to see that the first one *follows from* the others. For example, the proposition "Some philosophers are Greeks" follows from (and thus may be inferred from) the propositions "Some philosophers were born in Greece" and "All philosophers who were born in Greece are Greeks."

This particular inference is a syllogism, which means that in it one proposition is inferred from two others. The syllogism is an absolutely fundamental form of inference, and Aristotle made the first complete analysis of the syllogism. His analysis was so brilliant and thorough it is still taught in universities throughout the world, just as Euclid's examination of the fundamentals of geometry still serves as the basis for beginning courses in that subject. Aristotle's treatment of the syllogism is the basis for beginning courses in logic, and Aristotle is known as the father of logic.

Aristotle examined other important areas of logic as well, and he attempted to define the *forms of thought,* or ways in which we think about reality. Because Aristotle assumed that the ways in which we think about reality represent the way reality is, there is tight linkage between Aristotle's logic and his metaphysics — but Aristotelian logic is a subject for another book.

SELECTION 4.1
# Metaphysics★

*Aristotle*

[*This selection will enable you to understand why, for Aristotle, metaphysics is the examination of the most general features of being. In the selection, Aristotle is not trying to prove some overall thesis but, rather, is only describing various important and interesting aspects of the process of change. Included are the relation of form to matter, the nature of forms, the types of generation (i.e., the ways things come into existence), "opposed" forms or essences (e.g., the essence of healthiness is the absence of diseases, its opposite), and the role of contemplation in "artificial" generation (generation resulting from human activity).*]

## The Process of Change

Everything which comes into being is brought about by something, that is, by a source from which its generation comes. And it is composed of something. Now this latter is best described not as the absence of the thing but as the matter from which it comes. And it becomes a particular thing, as a sphere or a circle or some other thing. Now one does not "make" the material — as the bronze — of which a thing is composed; so one does not make the sphere, except in a secondary sense, in so far as

the bronze circle is a circle and one makes it. For the act of making a particular thing is a process of making it out of some material in general. I mean that to make the bronze round is not to make the "round" or the "sphere," but quite a different thing — that of putting this form into what did not have it previously. If one made the "form," one would make it out of something else, for this would underlie it, as when one makes a sphere out of bronze. This is done by making of a particular kind of substance, namely bronze, a special sort of thing, namely a sphere. And if one makes this "sphere" also in the same way, it is evident that he will make it in the same manner, and the process of origination will go on to infinity. It is evident therefore that the form, or whatever one ought to call the shape of the perceived object, is not "made." It does not "become," nor does it have an origin. Nor is there any for the essential conception of a thing. For this is what is implanted in another entity, either by training or by nature or by force. But one does cause the "bronze sphere" to *be.* For one makes it out of bronze and the form of "sphere." One puts the form into this matter, and it is then a bronze sphere. But if there is an origin for "the idea of sphere in general" it will be something generated from something else. That which is generated will have to be analyzed again in turn, and each reduced to something further, then that to something else; I mean in one aspect into matter, in another into form. A sphere is a figure whose surface is everywhere equally distant from a center. One aspect of it is the material into which the form is to be put; the other the form which is to be put into it. The whole is what results, namely, the bronze sphere.

It is evident from what we have said that the part which is spoken of as the form or the essence does not originate; but the combination which derives its name from this does; and in everything which originates there is matter, and it is now this thing, now that. Is there then a "sphere" beside the particular spheres? Or is there a "house" beside the houses of brick? Or would there never be any particular things if this were so? The genus gives the general character, but is not a definite particular thing. But one makes and produces such and such a thing out of "this" particular substance. And when it has been produced it is "this thing of such and such a kind." This concrete existing thing is "Kallias" or "Socrates," just as the other was "this bronze sphere," but it is man and animal in general just as the other was a bronze sphere in general. It is evident then that the formal principle, as some are accustomed to speak of forms, if they are something aside from the particulars and beside the acts of generation and the essences, is of no use. For not by virtue of them would there be particular instances of them. In some cases indeed it is evident that that which causes is the same sort of thing as that which is caused, yet not identically the same, nor one numerically, but in form—as in the case of the products of nature. Man begets man, (and so it is), except where something arises of different nature, as when a horse begets a mule. Yet these cases also are really similar to the others; but what is common to a horse and an ass has not been given a name as a "proximate genus"; perhaps it would be "mule."

So it is evident that it is not at all necessary to supply forms as patterns, (for they would have to be found in these cases especially, since these are certainly substances). The begetter is adequate to the production of the effect and to the embodiment of the form in the matter. And the compound—such and such a form in this flesh and these bones—is Kallias or Socrates. They differ because of their matter, for it is different, but they are the same in form. For the form is indivisible.

Of things which come into existence some are generated by nature, some by art, some by chance. And all things which are generated are generated by something and from something and as some particular thing. Some particular thing, I mean with respect to each category, such as substance, quantity, quality or place. Origination by nature occurs in the case of those things whose origin is through the processes of nature. The substance of which they are formed we call matter; the source from which they arise is some thing in nature; the kind of thing which they become is "man" or "plant" or some other thing of the kind which we are especially accustomed to call "substances." All things which have an origin, whether by nature or by art, have a material part. Each of them might exist or not exist; and the seat of this double possibility is the material part of them. In general that out of which and in accordance with which they arise is some natural thing. For that which comes into being has some natural character as that of a plant or an animal. And that under the influence of which it arises is a natural object which with reference to its form may be said to be homogeneous. And this form is found in another individual; as one man begets another man. In this way arise the things which come about by nature; but other originations are called artificial creations.

Artificial creations result from acquired skill, or external power, or deliberate planning. Some of these also come about spontaneously and by chance, in nearly the same manner as some things are generated by nature. For there some kind of things arise in some instances from seed, in other instances without seed. Into these things we shall have to look later; but those things arise by art, the forms of which are in some one's mind. And by form I mean the essential conception of the thing and its fundamental essence. And indeed in a certain sense opposites have the same form. The opposed essence is that of the absence of the given thing, as health is the absence of disease. For by the absence of the former, disease becomes manifest. But health is the determining principle, in the soul and in knowledge. The healthy condition of one who has been ill comes about as follows: Since such and such a condition is health, it is necessary, if there is to be health, that some other condition exist, as uniform temperature, and if there is to be uniform temperature then warmth. And in this manner one continues one's analysis until one arrives at a certain thing which one can do as the first step. The activity which comes from this is an artificial productivity, in this case the production of health. So in this sense it is true that health comes from health, and a house from a house, that which has material content from that which does not. The essence of the physician's art and of the builder's art is the form of health and the form of the house. And the essence without matter I call the essential conception.

One aspect of the process of production and of action is called the intellectual contemplation, the other the practical effecting of them. The one which has to do with the principle and the form is intellectual contemplation. That which refers to the aim of the intellectual contemplation is the practical application. And each of the intermediate steps has the like phases. For instance, if one will be healthy it is necessary to have an even temperature. What does the maintenance of an even temperature involve? This: it will result if one is kept warm. And what will do this? The following; but this exists only as a possibility. Yet it is in one's power. So then the action and the source from which the development of the healthy state springs, if it is from an artificial source, is the "form" in one's mind; but if from chance, still it results from something which at sometime or other is the source of activity used by him who acts with conscious skill. In the case of medical treatment perhaps the source is in causing warmth, and one produces this by rubbing. So the warmth in the body is either a part of health or there follows it something of a kind which is a part of health, or is so after some intermediate stages. And this last step is what causes the essential part and what is thus a part is to health as the stones are to a house; and likewise with other things.

As we have said, nothing can arise unless something preexists. Therefore that some part necessarily exists is evident. For the material part is a part. And it enters into a thing and pervades its changes.

And so it is also with the things mentioned in our statement. We tell what bronze circles are by distinguishing two phases; saying of the material that it is bronze; and of the form that it is such and such a shape. And this is the genus under which it is placed first. The brazen circle includes matter in its notion. Some things receive names from the matter out of which they come when they arise, being said, of course, to be not "that substance" but "of that substance," as the image of a man is said to be not "stone" but "of stone." But a healthy man is not designated from that out of which he has come. The reason for this is that he has come from a condition opposite to his present one, as well as out of a substance which we call his material being. Thus it is both a man and a sick man who becomes well. But the statement is made rather with reference to the negative state; one becomes healthy from being ill rather than from being a man. Consequently the well person is not said to be ill, but a man and a healthy man. But in those things to which there is no evident opposite, or none with a name, as of any kind of form in bronze, or the bricks or boards of a building, generation is said to be out of these, as in the other case it was out of the condition of illness. Wherefore, as in that case that from which this comes is not used in the name, so here the image of the man is not called "wood" but is styled "wooden," or "brazen" not "bronze," or "stony" not "stone"; and a house is said to be "of brick" not "bricks." Nor does the image come from wood, nor the house from bricks, if one looks at the matter exactly; and one could not say this without qualification, for it is necessary that generation come through the changing of a source — through its not remaining permanent. For these reasons then we use such modes of expression.

---

## CHECKLIST

### *Key Terms and Concepts*

| | |
|---|---|
| formal, material, efficient, and final causes | *nous* |
| | Third Man argument |
| existence and essence | universals |
| substance (*ousia*) | definition by genus |
| psyche | and species-specific difference |

## QUESTIONS FOR DISCUSSION AND REVIEW

1. What are the four Aristotelian causes of a baseball?

2. Aristotle believed that if individual horses did not exist, there would be no such thing as the Form *horse*. Is this correct?

3. Are universals real? In what sense?

4. Can there be essences without existence?

5. What are the two kinds of substance?

6. How can human beings have three souls: vegetable, animal, and rational (*nous*)?

7. Explain what Aristotle means by "intuition." Do humans have intuition?

8. Do you agree with Aristotle that every change is directed toward some end?

9. Explain why pure actuality is the ultimate source of change, for Aristotle.

10. Why is god the unmoved mover, according to Aristotle?

11. Review Aristotle's ten categories of being. Could alien intelligences think about things in terms of different categories?

## SUGGESTED FURTHER READINGS

J. L. Ackrill, *Essays on Plato and Aristotle* (New York: Oxford University Press, 1997). Selected essays by a famous classics scholar.

Aristotle, *Metaphysics,* in J. Barnes, ed., *The Complete Works of Aristotle,* vol. 2 (Princeton: Princeton University Press, 1984). Aristotle's *Metaphysics* is not always easy to read and understand, but it is entertaining. It contains useful information on Aristotle's predecessors, too.

Jonathan Barnes, *Aristotle: A Very Short Introduction* (New York: Oxford University Press, 2000). Only 110 pages, this introduction by a capable writer is very suitable for beginners.

Jonathan Barnes, ed., *The Cambridge Companion to Aristotle* (New York: Cambridge University Press, 1995). A modern, convenient guide to Aristotle's thought.

Jonathan Barnes, ed., *Complete Works of Aristotle,* Revised Oxford Translation (Princeton: Princeton University Press, 1983). For the price of a single textbook, you can buy the complete 2,500-page works of Aristotle.

Jonathan Barnes, R. M. Hare, and C. C. W. Taylor, *Greek Philosophers* (New York: Oxford University Press, 1999). Essays by three eminent scholars on Socrates, Plato, and Aristotle.

David Bostock, ed., Robin Waterfield, trans., *Aristotle's Physics* (New York: Oxford University Press, 1996). A recent translation of the *Physics.*

Alan D. Code, *Aristotle* (Boulder, Colo.: Westview Press, 2001). An analysis of the main concepts and doctrines of Aristotle's logic, natural science, metaphysics, ethics, and political science.

Cynthia A. Freeland, *Feminist Interpretation of Aristotle* (University Park, Pa.: Pennsylvania State University, 1993). Readings from a feminist perspective on various aspects of Aristotle's philosophy.

Justin E. Kaplan, *The Pocket Aristotle* (New York: Pocket Books, 1983). A selection of Aristotle's writings suitable for the introductory reader.

Richard McKeon, ed., *The Basic Works of Aristotle* (New York: Random House, 1941). A readable translation of Aristotle's principal works.

Ted Sadler, *Heidegger and Aristotle: The Question of Being* (Athlone Press, 1996, distributed by Transaction Press, Somerset, N.J.). A presentation of the two great philosophers of being, one ancient and one modern.

T. Scaltsas, E. Charles, and M. L. Gill, eds., *Unity, Identity, and Explanation in Aristotle's Metaphysics* (New York: Oxford University Press, 1994). Fourteen essays by contemporary experts discussing Aristotle's theory of unity and identity of substances.

A. E. Taylor, *Aristotle* (New York: Dover Publications, 1955). A popularly written introduction to Aristotle's ideas.

C. C. W. Taylor, ed., *Oxford Studies in Ancient Philosophy* (New York: Oxford University Press, annually). Original articles by contemporary scholars on Aristotle, Plato, the Atomists, and others.

# 5

# Philosophers of the Hellenistic and Christian Eras

*Though philosophers disagree on the nature of things, and the mode of investigating truth, and of the good to which all our actions ought to tend, yet on these three great general questions, all their intellectual energy is spent.*

—St. Augustine

Before he died in 323 B.C.E. at age thirty-two, Aristotle's student Alexander the Great, son of the Macedonian king Philip II, had conquered the entire civilized Western world, pulverizing all opposition and naming a score of cities after himself to ensure that everyone got the message. The Macedonian domination of the Greek-speaking world, known as the **Hellenistic age** (*Hellene* means "Greek"), was a period of major achievements in mathematics and science.

Having started with Alexander around 335 B.C.E., Macedonian hegemony was carried forth by the families of three of Alexander's generals and lasted about a century and a half, until Philip V of Macedon and Antiochus III of Syria were each defeated (around 190 B.C.E.) by a new ascending power: Rome. From that time on for approximately the next seven hundred years, the Western world *was* the Roman Empire, built on plunder and the power of the sword.

For two centuries, beginning in 27 B.C.E. with the reign of Julius Caesar's grand-nephew Octavian, who was known as "Augustus, the first Roman emperor and savior of the world," the Roman Empire enjoyed peace, security, and political stability. But eventually, after the reign of Marcus Aurelius (161–180 C.E.), conditions deteriorated into chaos. Nevertheless, the ultimate fall of the empire was postponed by Diocletian, who divided the empire into eastern (Byzantine) and western (Roman) halves, and by Constantine I, who granted universal religious tolerance, thus in effect recognizing Christianity. Finally, however, internal anarchy opened

A Roman aqueduct today. Perhaps great, great, great grandparents of contemporary Italians swam here.

the Roman frontiers to the barbarians. Although the Eastern empire survived until the fifteenth century, in 476 the last emperor of the West was deposed by the Goths. The Dark Ages followed.

If the Romans were anything, they were practical. They built aqueducts and underground sewers and had glass windows. Wealthy Romans lived in lavish town houses equipped with central heating and running water. Roman highways were built on a road base four feet thick and were paved with concrete and squared stone. Roman roads and bridges are still used today, and some may outlive the interstates.

But although they were masters of the applied arts and of practical disciplines such as military science and law (Roman law provided the basis for modern civil law), the Romans had little use for art for art's sake or for literature or science. From the Roman perspective, no form of entertainment was quite so satisfying as watching men fight other men to the death, although seeing humans fight animals came in a close second. Witnessing public torture was a popular entertainment, much like the movies are today.

## METAPHYSICS IN THE ROMAN EMPIRE

In philosophy the contributions of the Romans were minimal and almost entirely unoriginal. During Hellenistic and Roman periods there were four main traditions or "schools" of philosophy; three of these arose around the time of Alexander and were in fact products of Greek culture, not Roman. Two of these—Stoicism and Epicureanism—were concerned mainly with the question of how individuals should best conduct their affairs. If there had been supermarkets at the time, Stoic and Epicurean advice would have been available in paperbacks for sale at the checkout counters. These schools of philosophy are discussed in Chapter 10. The third school—**Skepticism**—(to which we will turn shortly) was concerned with the possibility of knowledge. The remaining school, unlike these other three, did arise during Roman times, but this school was for all intents and purposes a revision of Plato's philosophy. It is known as **Neoplatonism,** and it had considerable influence on the metaphysics of Christianity.

## Plotinus

The great philosopher of Neoplatonism was **Plotinus** [pluh-TIE-nus] (c. 205– 270 C.E.). During Plotinus's lifetime, the Roman Empire was in a most dismal state, suffering plague, marauding barbarian hordes, and an army incompetent to do anything but assassinate its own leaders. Civilization was tottering dangerously near the abyss. Plotinus, however, was inclined to ignore these earthly trifles, for he had discovered that by turning his attention inward, he could achieve union with god.

Now think back for a moment to Plato. According to Plato's metaphysics, there are two worlds. On one hand, there is the cave, that is, the world of changing appearances: the world of sensation, ignorance, error, illusion, and darkness. On the other hand, there is the light, that is, the world of Forms: the world of intellect, knowledge, truth, reality, and brightness whose ultimate source of existence and essence is the Form *the Good*. Plotinus further specified this ultimate source or reality as god or the One. For Plotinus, god is above and beyond everything else— utterly transcendent.

But Plotinus's god, like Plato's Good, and unlike the Christian God, is not a personal god. God, according to Plotinus, is indefinable and indescribable, because to define or describe god would be to place limitations on what has no limits. About god it can be said only that god is. And god can be apprehended only through a coming together of the soul and god in a mystical experience. This mystical "touching" of god, this moment in which we have the "vision," is the highest moment of life.

## The Rise of Christianity

As mentioned in the accompanying Profile, Plotinus's thought was very influential on the last of the great ancient philosophers, Augustine, who also happens to be one of the two or three most important Christian theologians of all time. Eventually, the predominance of Christianity in Europe came to define the framework within which most Western philosophizing took place. Not long after Plotinus, the great philosophers of the western part of the Roman Empire, or what became of the western part, were almost without exception Christians.

## PROFILE: Plotinus (c. 205–270 c.e.)

Plotinus's interest in philosophy began when he was twenty-eight in Alexandria (the most famous Alexandria, the one in Egypt). His first teacher was Ammonius, the "Sack Carrier," who was so called because he earned his living as a gardener.

About 244, Plotinus traveled to Rome and founded what came to be a renowned school of Neoplatonic philosophy. Even the emperor Gallienus and his wife, Salonina, patronized the school. Plotinus tried to get his students to ask questions for themselves; consequently the discussions were lively and sometimes almost violent. On one occasion, Plotinus had to stop a particularly ugly confrontation between a senator and a rich man; he urged both parties to calm themselves and think rather only of the One (about which see the text).

Plotinus himself was a quiet, modest, and selfless human being. He was thought to possess an uncanny ability to penetrate into the human char-

acter and its motives, and so he was sought out for all manner of practical advice.

He would not, however, acknowledge his birthday. This is because, at least according to Porphyry, who wrote a biography of Plotinus, Plotinus was ashamed that his immortal soul was contained in a mortal body, and the event of his soul entering his body was therefore something to be regretted. He also would not allow his face to be painted or his body to be sculpted. In fact, his long disregard of his body eventually caused him to lose his voice, and his hands and feet festered with abscesses and pus. Because Plotinus greeted his students with an embrace, the net result was a falling off in enrollment.

Plotinus's philosophy had a great influence on St. Augustine and other doctors and fathers of the Church. Christian theology is unthinkable without the mystical depth that comes from Plotinus.

The original Christians, including Jesus and his followers, were Jews. Christianity gradually evolved from a Jewish sect to a separate religion. Now, the Romans were generally pretty tolerant of the religious ideas and practices of the various peoples under their subjugation, but the Jews, including members of the Christian splinter sect, were not willing to pay even token homage to the Roman emperor-deities. The Christians, moreover, were unusually active in trying to make converts. Thus, to Roman thinking, the Christians were not only atheists who ridiculed the Roman deities but also, unlike more orthodox Jews, fanatical rabble-rousers who attempted to impose on others what to the Romans counted as gross superstition. As a result, for a couple of centuries or so the Christians were persecuted from time to time by assorted Roman emperors, sometimes rather vigorously.

Nevertheless, of the numerous cults that existed during the first couple of centuries of the Common Era (c.e.), Christianity eventually became the most popular. Its followers became so numerous and, thanks to the administrative efforts of Paul of Tarsus (later St. Paul), so well organized that by the early part of the fourth century, the emperor Constantine announced its official toleration.

Specifics of Christian doctrine need not concern us, and its central beliefs are well known: Jesus is the son of God, and Jesus' life, crucifixion, and resurrection are proof of God's love for humans and forgiveness of human sin; in addition, those who have faith in Christ will be saved and have life everlasting. The God of Chris-

## PROFILE: St. Augustine (354–430 C.E.)

Augustine grew up in northern Africa. His father was a successful man of the world, and Augustine was expected to follow a similar path. Accordingly, he studied rhetoric in Carthage. While there, however, he fell in with a group of students known as the "rebels," who found amusement in such pastimes as attacking innocent passersby at night. Augustine, to his credit, did not participate in these episodes, though he did steal fruit from a neighbor's tree for the sheer perversity of doing so.

As a young man, Augustine also indulged in many love affairs. He took a concubine, and the union produced a son. He came to have doubts about his lifestyle, however, and eventually these doubts began to take the upper hand. With the encouragement of his family, he became engaged to a young woman of a prominent family. But

Augustine grew impatient and took a new lover.

In the meanwhile, Augustine's studies had taken him to Rome and to Milan, where he became a professor of rhetoric. His mother, Monica, had already become a Christian. Through her encouragement and through Augustine's exposure to St. Ambrose, the celebrated preacher, Augustine was baptized into Christianity at the age of thirty-three. He returned to northern Africa and soon thereafter was called on to serve as Bishop of Hippo.

As bishop, Augustine used his rhetorical abilities to the full in fiercely attacking what he perceived to be the many heresies of the time. His thinking was dominated by two themes, the sinfulness of human beings and the inscrutability of God. At the age of seventy-two, he withdrew from the world and died in self-chosen solitude.

tianity is thought (by Christians) to be the creator of all; and he is also thought to be distinct from his creation.

### St. Augustine

**St. Augustine** [AUG-us-teen] (354–430 C.E.), who came from the town of Tagaste, near what is today the Algerian city of Annaba, transferred Platonic and Neoplatonic themes to Christianity. Transported down through the ages to us today, these themes affect the thought of both Christian and non-Christian.

"Whenever Augustine," Thomas Aquinas later wrote, "who was saturated with the teachings of the Platonists, found in their writings anything consistent with the faith, he adopted it; and whatever he found contrary to the faith, he amended." Through Augustine, Christianity became so permanently interwoven with elements of Platonic thought that today, as the English prelate William Inge said, it is impossible to remove Platonism from Christianity "without tearing Christianity to pieces."

St. Augustine regarded Plotinus and Plato as having *prepared* him for Christianity by exposing him to important Christian principles before he encountered them in Scripture. (But neither Plato nor Plotinus was Christian.) Augustine had a very strong inclination toward skepticism and was tempted to believe that

## Augustine on God and Time

The *ex nihilo* theory (God created the world out of nothing) invites a troublesome question for Christian theology: Why did God choose to create the world at the time he did and not at some other? Thanks to Plato and Plotinus, Augustine was able to provide a potentially reasonable answer to this question.

According to Augustine, the question rests on a false assumption, that God (and his actions) exist *within* time. On the contrary, Augustine maintained, God does not exist in time; instead, time began with the creation by God of the world. God is *beyond* time. In this way the timeless attribute of Plato's Good and Plotinus's One was transferred by Augustine to the Christian God.

But what exactly, Augustine wondered, is time? Here Augustine broke new philosophical ground by coming forth with a very tempting answer to this question.

"What, then, is time?" he asked. "If no one asks of me, I know; if I wish to explain to him who asks, I know not." On one hand only the present exists, for the past is no more, and the future is not yet. But on the other hand certain things did happen in the past, and other things will happen in the future, and thus past and future are quite real. How can the past and the future be both real and nonexistent?

Augustine's answer to this almost hopelessly baffling question is that past and future exist only in the human mind. "The present of things past is memory; the present of things present is sight; and the present of things future is expectation."

Augustine's analysis of time is that it is a subjective phenomenon. It exists "only in the mind." (Thus, before God created us, there was no time.) As will be discussed in Chapter 7, the idea that time is subjective was later developed by the eighteenth-century philosopher Immanuel Kant into the theory that time, space, causation, and other basic "categories" of being are all subjective impositions of the mind on the world. The same idea was then carried to its ultimate conclusion by the Absolute Idealists, who said that the world *is* mind.

Augustine's views on time can be found in the eleventh book of his *Confessions*.

"nothing can be known." Plato and Plotinus enabled Augustine to overcome this inclination.

Today we take for granted the concept of a separate, immaterial reality known as the transcendent God. Even those who do not believe in God are familiar with this concept of God's immateriality and are not inclined to dismiss it as blatant nonsense (though some, of course, do). But careful reflection reveals that there is not much within experience that gives rise to this concept, for we seem to experience only concrete, physical things. Through the influence of Plato and Plotinus, St. Augustine perceived that belief in a distinct immaterial reality was not the blindly superstitious thing that it might seem. And through Augustine's thought, the Christian belief in a nonmaterial God received a philosophical justification, a justification without which (it is arguable) this religion would not have sustained the belief of thoughtful people through the ages. (Other explanations of the durability of the Christian belief in God are, of course, possible.)

Augustine accepted the Platonic view that "there are two realms, an intelligible realm where truth itself dwells, and this sensible world which we perceive by sight and touch." Like Plato before him, St. Augustine thought that the capacity of the human mind to grasp eternal truths implies the existence of something infinite and eternal apart from the world of sensible objects, an essence that in some sense represents the source or ground of all reality and of all truth. This ultimate ground and highest being Augustine identified with God rather than with Platonic Forms.

Augustine, however, accepted the Old Testament idea that God created the world out of nothing. This idea of **creation *ex nihilo,*** creation out of nothing, is really quite a startling concept when you think about it, and Greek thinkers had had trouble with it. Their view had been that getting something from nothing is impossible. (The box "Augustine on God and Time" describes Augustine's thinking about creation.)

Augustine also accepted the Gospel story of the life, death, and resurrection of Jesus Christ and believed that God took on human form in the person of Jesus. Thus, Augustinian theology gives God a human aspect that would have been unthinkable for Neoplatonists, who thought that the immaterial realm could not be tainted with the imperfection of mere gross matter.

It is sometimes said that St. Augustine is the founder of Christian *theology.* Certainly his influence on Christian thought was second to none, with the exception of St. Paul, who formulated a great deal of Christian doctrine. One very important aspect of St. Augustine's thought was his concept of evil, in which the influence of Plato and Plotinus is again evident. (We will say something about this Chapter 10.)

## Augustine and Skepticism

**Total skeptics** maintain that nothing can be known or, alternatively, profess to suspend judgment in all matters. **Modified skeptics** do not doubt that at least some things are known, but they deny or suspend judgment on the possibility of knowledge about particular things, such as God, or within some subject matter, such as history or ethics. In the Hellenistic and Roman periods after Plato, two schools of skepticism developed, and they were something like rivals: the **Academics** (who flourished during the third and second centuries B.C. in what had earlier been Plato's Academy) and the **Pyrrhonists** (the disciples of **Pyrrho** [PEER-row] of Elis, c. 360–270 B.C.E.). The Academics and Pyrrhonists were both total skeptics; the main difference between them seems to be one of phrasing. The Academics held that "all things are inapprehensible"—that is, nothing can be known. The Pyrrhonists said, in effect, "I suspend judgment in the matter, and I suspend judgment on all other issues I have examined too." In short, Pyrrhonists maintained that they did not know whether knowledge is possible.

The most famous skeptic of all time was the last great Pyrrhonist skeptic, **Sextus Empiricus** [SEX-tus em-PEER-uh-kus], who lived in the second to third centuries C.E. Although Sextus' writings are extensive and constitute the definitive firsthand report on Greek skepticism, little is known about Sextus himself. We do not know where he was born or died or even where he lived. We do know, however, that he was a physician.

In Sextus' writings may be found virtually every skeptical argument that has ever been devised. Sextus set forth the **Ten Tropes,** a collection of ten arguments by the ancient skeptics against the possibility of knowledge. The idea behind the Ten Tropes was this. Knowledge is possible only if we have good grounds for

## PROFILE: Pyrrho (c. 360–270 B.C.E.)

Not a great deal is known about Pyrrho, after whom the Pyrrhonist tradition is named, for he left no writings. Diogenes Laertiús, a third-century Greek biographer (whose tales about the ancient philosophers, despite their gossipy and sometimes unreliable nature, are an invaluable source of history), reported that Pyrrho was totally indifferent to and unaware of things going on around him. A well-known story told by Diogenes Laertiús is that once, when Pyrrho's dear old teacher was stuck in a ditch, Pyrrho passed him by without a word. (Or perhaps this story indicates that Pyrrho was quite aware of things around him.) According to other reports, however, Pyrrho was a moderate, sensible, and quite level-headed person.

It is at any rate true that Pyrrho held that nothing can be known about the hidden essence or true nature of things. He held this because he thought every theory can be opposed by an equally sound contradictory theory. Hence, we must neither accept nor reject any of these theories but, rather, must suspend judgment on all issues. The suspension of judgment, *epoche,* was said by Pyrrho to lead to *ataraxia,* tranquility or unperturbedness. Pyrrho's fame was apparently primarily a result of his exemplary *agoge* (way of living), though there are differences of opinion about what that way of life actually was.

## Sextus' Asterisk

In a seventeenth-century play by the great French comic playwright Molière called *The Forced Marriage,* a skeptic is beaten in one scene. While he is being beaten, the skeptic is reminded that skeptics cannot be sure that they are being beaten or feel pain. Molière, evidently, did not view skepticism as a serious philosophy.

In defense of Sextus, we might mention that Sextus placed a small asterisk beside his skepticism.

He said that he did not "deny those things which, in accordance with the passivity of our sense impressions, lead us involuntarily to give our assent to them." That I am in pain is an *involuntary* judgment on my part and therefore does not count, Sextus would say.

We leave it to you to determine if this tactic enables Sextus to escape Molière's criticism.

believing that what is, is exactly as we think it is or perceive it to be. But we do not have good grounds for believing that what is, is exactly as we think it is or perceive it to be. For one thing, we never are aware of any object as it is independent of us but only as it stands in relationship to us. Therefore, we cannot know how any object really is in itself.

For example, think of a wooden stick. The qualities we think it has are those we perceive by sense — but not so fast! Does the stick have *only* those qualities that it appears to us to have? Or does it have *additional* qualities that are unknown to us? Or does it have *fewer* qualities than appear to us? The senses themselves cannot tell us which of these options is correct, and Sextus argues that because the senses cannot tell us, the mind cannot either. (The seventeenth-century French comic playwright Molière famously made fun of this theory, as you can see in the box "Sextus' Asterisk.")

Now, back to St. Augustine. During the Christianization of the Roman Empire skepticism waned, but St. Augustine was familiar with Academic Skepticism through the description by the Roman historian Cicero. Augustine concluded that total skepticism is refuted in at least three ways.

First, skepticism is refuted by the **principle of noncontradiction,** which states that a proposition and its contradiction cannot *both* be true—one *or* the other must be true. The propositions "The stick is straight" and "It is false that the stick is straight" cannot both be true. Thus, we at least know that the stick cannot be both straight and not straight. However, not all contemporary philosophers are convinced by this argument of St. Augustine's, and it does not exactly confront the line of reasoning employed by Sextus Empiricus.

Second, Augustine held that the act of doubting discloses one's *existence* as something that is absolutely certain: from the fact *I am doubting,* it follows automatically that *I am.* (The famous French philosopher René Descartes elaborated on a similar refutation of skepticism, which will be described in Chapter 6.) Some contemporary philosophers, however, are unconvinced by this maneuver as it too does not quite address the specific line of reasoning employed by Sextus.

Finally, Augustine also held that sense perception itself gives a rudimentary kind of knowledge. Deception in sense perception occurs, he said, only when we "give assent to more than the fact of appearance." For example, the stick appears bent at the point it enters the water. If we assent only to the appearance of the oar and say merely that it *looks* bent, we make no mistake. It is only if we judge that the oar actually *is* bent that we fall into error.

Augustine saw these three insights as a refutation of skepticism and regarded this refutation as highly important, but he did not try to derive anything else of great importance from them. The most important truths for Augustine are received by revelation and held on faith, and this doctrine was assumed throughout the Christian Middle Ages.

## Hypatia

Another important figure of this period was **Hypatia** [hy-PAY-sha] (c. 370–415). Recent scholarship discloses that Hypatia's influence on Western thought was significant, especially through her teaching and her work on astronomy in what was at the time a center of culture and learning, Alexandria.

Hypatia and her father, Theon, a famous mathematician and astronomer, taught the astronomy of Ptolemy. Claudius Ptolemy was a second-century scholar whose work was the definitive treatment of astronomy (and would remain so for well over a thousand years, until the sixteenth century, when the Ptolemaic system was overthrown by Nicholas Copernicus). Hypatia was the last major commentator on Ptolemy's work.

Hypatia was hardly a skeptic. She and her father prepared an updated edition of Ptolemy that included thousands of astronomical observations that had been recorded in the centuries after Ptolemy's death. Ptolemy's theory, which postulated the earth as the center of the universe and the sun going around the earth, gave pretty accurate predictions of celestial events, but not one hundred percent accurate predictions, and the further away in time an observer was from Ptolemy, the less accurate were the predictions. Hypatia improved the theories, extending computations to many additional place values (using an abacus!). This greater accuracy improved the predictability of astronomical calculations. She tinkered with Ptolemy's theory, using more sophisticated algebra and geometry than he had, to make astronomical facts a better fit with his theory and with theories of mathematics and geometry that he had relied on to develop his theory of astronomy. She tried to improve the rigor of theorems by finding and filling gaps to achieve greater completeness. Sometimes she improved the soundness of proofs by devising direct proofs where only indirect proofs existed before.

Especially important, Hypatia found errors in the part of Ptolemy's theory that showed how the sun revolved around the earth. (This was important from both the Christian and the pagan standpoint — Hypatia was a pagan — because from either standpoint philosophically the earth must be the center of the universe.) Equally important philosophically, she tried to demonstrate the *completeness* of Ptolemy's astronomy and Diophantus's theory of algebra (Diophantus was an important Greek mathematician). A theory is "complete" when it explains everything within its scope. There are difficulties in proving completeness, but mostly they have not been understood until this century. In Hypatia's time nobody knew how to show that a theory is complete. Hypatia's approach was to introduce as many refutations and counterexamples to a theory as she could think up.

For Hypatia, mathematics and astronomy were ways of checking metaphysical and epistemological features of Plato's, Aristotle's, and Plotinus's philosophies against the physical universe. For example, Aristotle held that the circle is the most perfect shape. If the circle is the most perfect shape, then its ideal Form, in Plato's sense of Form, must be that which is reflected by God's perfect creation, the universe. Plato's and Aristotle's thought could be checked against astronomical theories and findings about the shape of the universe.

Philosophically, Hypatia was sympathetic to Plotinus's metaphysics and to stoicism (see Chapter 10). She, and all good Plotinians, believed that the solution to

## PROFILE: Hypatia of Alexandria (c. 370–415)

Hypatia taught in Alexandria, Egypt, at what was called the Museum. Back then, philosophy was still a pretty wide field, and philosophers like Plotinus and Hypatia were not about to impose distinctions (as we now do) among such subjects as religion, mathematics, astronomy, and the slice of philosophy known as metaphysics.

Hypatia became famous when she was very young. By 390, students were coming to her from throughout northern Africa. (Europe was still an uncivilized place, but Alexandria was late antiquity's equivalent of Silicon Valley.) Every decent scientist and philosopher passed through Alexandria.

Hypatia was a pagan, but she had a lot of students who were Christians and maybe even a few Jewish students. Considering that by 410 relationships among different religious groups were so bad that there were frequent riots, Hypatia must have made sense to lots of people with very different orientations. One came from Cyrene (in Libya) to become her student and went on to convert to Christianity, becoming first a priest and then a bishop.

Over the past thousand or so years, when anybody has bothered to write about Hypatia, the chronicler has invariably told the story of how she dealt with sexual harassment by one of her male students. She supposedly threw the fifth-century equivalent of a used sanitary napkin at him—and never heard from him again. (Apparently, the Museum did not have procedures for dealing with sexual harassment.)

Until this century, it was thought that Hypatia wrote only three books and that all of them were lost. Can you imagine your copy of this book being found fifteen centuries from now, and its being discovered to contain the last surviving fragment of Descartes's *Meditations*? That is what happened to all of Hypatia's works! From what we know now, it looks as if Hypatia prepared about half a dozen scholarly writings of various lengths. Some of those writings have only recently been identified by scholars as being by her. Her works were copied, edited, translated, retranslated, incorporated into other people's writings, bought, sold, and traded by scholars from Rome to Baghdad to Britain for more than a thousand years. Versions of her different works exist in Greek, Latin, Hebrew, and Arabic—but not in English. Writings by Hypatia include an edition of Diophantus's *Arithmetica*, a work based on Archimedes' *Sphere and Cylinder*; an anonymous work on one-sided figures; a commentary on Archimedes' *Dimension of the Circle*; a commentary on Apollonius Pergaeus's *Conics* that formed the basis for later commentaries, including one by the astronomer Edmund Halley (of Halley's Comet fame); and a commentary on part of Ptolemy's *Syntaxis Mathematica*.

In 415, Hypatia was savagely murdered, allegedly by a gang of monks. Her corpse was then hacked into pieces and burned.

---

the mystery of the One, the ultimate source of reality, would explain everything. It would explain the nature of God, the nature of the universe, and our place in it.

For Hypatia philosophy was more than an abstract intellectual exercise: it implied personal ethical and religious knowledge, a way of living. Hypatia introduced beginning students to Plato's metaphysics and to Plotinus's interpretations of Plato to make a difference in their daily lives. Mathematics and astronomy were considered essential ingredients in preparation for a study of metaphysics. Consequently, she prepared careful, symmetrical expositions of elements of mathematical and astronomical proofs for her students.

We are not sure which later astronomers noticed Hypatia's commentary on Ptolemy, because apparently only two copies of it have survived. Both were obtained during the Renaissance by the Lorenzo di Medici library. Thus, her work could have been seen over a thousand years later by the young graduate student Nicholas Copernicus, who was traveling around Italy trying to read all the Ptolemy he could find. But we don't know whether Copernicus actually saw Hypatia's work or whether it influenced him to rethink the geocentric model of the universe.

## THE MIDDLE AGES AND AQUINAS

Augustine died in 430, some forty-six years before the date usually assigned as the end of the (Western) Roman Empire. The final centuries of the empire had witnessed the spread of Christianity through all classes of society and eventually an alliance between the Church and the state. They also had seen a growing belief in demons, magic, astrology, and other dark superstitions. After the abdication of the last Roman emperor in 476, the light of reason was all but extinguished in Europe. These Dark Ages lasted to about 1000. Compared with the shining cultures of the East at the same time, Europe barely qualified as a civilization.

Precipitating the fall of the empire were barbarian invasions, and after the fall the invading hordes arrived in waves. In the first wave, a group of Germanic kingdoms replaced the empire. In the next century (i.e., the sixth), Justinian, the Byzantine emperor, partially reconquered the Western empire; but shortly after his death Italy was invaded by the ferocious Lombards, and Syria, Egypt, and Spain were conquered by the Muslims. The Carolingian Franks under Charlemagne restored stability for a brief time, bringing into existence (on Christmas Day, 800) what later was called the Holy Roman Empire, although subsequent invasions by the Vikings and Muslims again spread chaos and destruction. During this period Slavic conquests of the Balkans separated Greek and Latin cultures, and the Greek and Latin churches also gradually drew apart.

Original philosophy was virtually nonexistent during the Dark Ages, though the two most capable and learned thinkers of this grim and lightless period, Boethius in the sixth century (who was executed for treason) and John Scotus in the ninth (whose work was posthumously condemned), were both philosophers of remarkable ability. The thought of both men, though basically Neoplatonic, was original and profound.

By about 1000, the age of invasions was substantially over. The assorted northern invaders had been Christianized, a series of comparatively stable states was spread over Europe, and a relationship of rough interdependence and equality existed between the pope and the various secular authorities.

During the high Middle Ages, as the next few centuries are called, the pope became the most powerful leader in Europe. The Church was the unifying institution of European civilization, and monarchs were averse to defying it. After all, the Church stood at the gateway to heaven.

In the growing security and prosperity that followed the Dark Ages, urban centers grew and intellectual life, centered in the great universities that arose under the

During the high Middle Ages, several universities were founded, including, famously, the University of Paris. This is a photograph of the Sorbonne, one of the most famous colleges making up the original university. It was founded in 1247 by a French theologian, Robert de Sorbon.

auspices of the Church, was stimulated through commercial and military contact with Greek, Arabian, Jewish, and (more indirectly) Indian cultures.

Still, independent or unorthodox thinking was not without its hazards, especially if it laid any foundation for what Church authorities perceived to be a heretical viewpoint. During the medieval Inquisition, those accused of heresy were brought to trial. The trials, however, were secret, and there was no such thing as the right to counsel. One's accusers were not named, and torture was used in service of the truth. An interesting practice was that of torturing not only the accused but also those speaking on behalf of the accused. As might be imagined, one was apt to find few witnesses on one's behalf. It was not unusual for heretics to recant their sins.

Nevertheless, despite all this, the high Middle Ages was a period of growing personal liberty, spreading literacy, and increasing intellectual vigor. One philosophical problem important to thinkers of the time—as it had been to Aristotle (see Chapter 4)—was the problem of **universals,** which is described in the box "Universals."

Contact with the Arabian world during the high Middle Ages led to a rekindling of interest among European church leaders in the philosophy of Aristotle. Through the centuries the Muslim world had enjoyed greater access to ancient Greek philosophy than had the Christian, and many Christian thinkers first

# Universals

The three main philosophical problems from around 1000 to 1200 were these: (1) rationally proving the existence of God, (2) understanding the relationship between reason and faith, and (3) solving the "problem of universals." Herewith, more about (3).

Some words name a single thing, for example, "Aristotle," "Bill Gates," and "Billy the Kid." Other words are general or "universal" and apply to more than one thing, for example, "tree," "philosopher," "horse," or "beautiful." The so-called problem of universals concerns how these universal words could have meaning.

Pretty clearly, names for single things, such as "Billy the Kid," get their meaning by designating things that exist in the world outside the mind. But what about universal words? Do the words "tree," "philosopher," and "beautiful" denote things that exist in the world outside the mind? Those who believe they do subscribe to the theory of **realism.** Those who believe universal words correspond only to concepts in the mind agree with the theory of **conceptualism.** And those who think you can account for universal words without invoking universals as real things out there in the world or as concepts in the mind subscribe to the theory of **nominalism.**

Why is this issue important? For one thing, Christian belief held that the Father, the Son, and the Holy Spirit — three individual things — are the selfsame thing, God. The word "God," therefore, applies to more than a single thing and in this respect is a universal word. Furthermore, when Adam and Eve ate the apple, thereby committing "original sin," the sin tainted *humankind*, and that is why all people need baptism. "Humankind," of course, is a universal word.

Thus, the status of universals is important from a Christian standpoint. If only individual things exist, as nominalists maintain, then the three individuals of the Trinity must be three separate individuals — that is, three gods rather than one. If only individual things exist, then only the *individuals* Adam and Eve sinned. Thus, humankind is not tainted by original sin because there is no universal humankind.

Plato was the first to raise the question of universals. Plato's Forms are universal things existing outside the mind (if they really exist).

encountered Aristotle's philosophy through Arabian commentaries on Aristotle and through Latin translations of Arab translations of Greek texts. Because Aristotle's repudiation of Plato's realm of Forms seemed at odds with Christian philosophy, which was Augustinian and Platonic in outlook, some Church thinkers (notably one named Bonaventura, 1221–1274) thought it necessary to reject Aristotle. Others (notably one called Albert the Great, 1193–1280) came to regard Aristotle as the greatest of all philosophers and concluded that there must be an underlying accord between Christian principles and Aristotle's philosophy.

The most important of those who belonged to the second group was **St. Thomas Aquinas** [uh-QUYNE-nuss] (1225–1274), whose philosophy was deemed by Pope Leo XIII in 1879 to be the official Catholic philosophy. To this day Aquinas' system is taught in Catholic schools as the correct philosophy, and so Aquinas' thought continues to affect living people directly.

Aquinas had access to translations of Aristotle's works that were directly from the Greek (not Latin translations of Arab translations), and his knowledge of Aristotle was considerable and profound. In a manner similar to that in which Augustine had mixed Platonic philosophy with Christianity, Aquinas blended Christianity with the philosophy of Aristotle, in effect grafting the principles and distinctions of the Greek philosopher to Christian revealed truth. The result was a complete Christian philosophy, with a theory of knowledge, a metaphysics, ethical and political philosophies, and a philosophy of law. Expect to encounter Aquinas again in this book.

Another way in which Aquinas is important is this. In Aquinas' time a distinction was finally beginning to be made between *philosophy* and *theology*. No person was more concerned with tracing the boundaries of the two fields than was Aquinas. His main idea was that philosophy is based on precepts of reason and theology on truths of revelation held on faith.

Aquinas was convinced that there is a real external world ordered by law and that human beings truly can have knowledge of that world. He did not believe that reality was a product of the human mind, nor was he sympathetic to attacks on the value of the sciences. However, Aquinas held that even though we can have true knowledge of the natural world, such knowledge is insufficient. It does not take into account the other realm — namely, the realm of supernatural truth. Large portions of this realm are inaccessible by human reason, Aquinas held, including the most profound aspects of Christian belief: the Trinity, God's taking on human form, and Christ's resurrection. Such mysteries are beyond our ability to adequately comprehend through reason.

Although such mysteries were beyond human reason, Aquinas believed they were not contrary to human reason. He held that there can be only one truth, part of which is accessible to human reason and part of which requires faith. Human reason, for Aquinas, could know of the existence of God and also that there can be but one God. However, other aspects of God's being are less available to human reason. In the end, philosophy serves as a handmaiden for theology — and reason as an instrument of faith.

Some of the main points of Aquinas' metaphysics may be summarized as follows. *Change,* Aquinas thought, can be explained using the Aristotelian four-cause theory: the efficient cause is that which produces the change; the material cause is the stuff that changes; the formal cause is the form the stuff takes; and the final cause is what explains why there was a change.

All physical things are composed of matter and form, he said, following Aristotle. Matter, which remains constant throughout a change, is that which a thing is made out of, and form is that which determines what sort of thing it is. By virtue of being separate clumps of matter, these two rocks are different, and by virtue of having the same form, these two rocks are both rocks and thus are the same. Contrary to the Platonic-Augustinian tradition, Aquinas held that the form of a thing cannot exist apart from matter.

But Aquinas went beyond Aristotle to point out that, besides the composition of matter and form in things, there is also a composition of its essence (matter plus form) and its existence. *What* something is (its essence) is not the same as *that* it is (its existence); otherwise, it would always exist, which is contrary to fact. Further, if existing were identical with any one kind of thing, everything existing would be only that one kind — again, contrary to fact. Aquinas made a unique contribution to metaphysics by highlighting that existence is the most important actuality in anything, without which even form (essence) cannot be actual.

Moreover, Aquinas also emphasized that nothing could cause its own existence, because it would already need to exist (as cause) before it existed (as effect),

According to the philosophy of Aquinas, these rocks are separate and distinct clumps of *matter*, but they all have the same *form* and thus are all rocks. Likewise, all physical things are composed of *matter* and *form*. Further, *what* something is (its *essence*: matter plus form) is distinct from the fact *that* it is (its *existence*).

which is a contradiction. So anything that begins to exist is caused to exist by something already existing and, ultimately, by an Uncaused Cause of Existence, God. Thus, Aquinas went beyond Aristotle's concept of God as Pure Act (because God is changeless, without beginning or end) to an understanding of God as Pure Act of Existence.

Some aspects of God's nature can be known. We can know that God is the perfect being that exists in himself yet is the source of the known universe. It is only through the Scriptures, however, that humans can know how creation represents the realization of the Divine Ideas (Plato in substantially changed form).

Thomistic *cosmology* (theory of the universe as an ordered whole) is based on a geocentric view of the universe, and this is also true of Aquinas' psychology. The earth is the center of the universe, and the human being is the center of the earth's existence. Remember that Aristotle believed that matter is passive and that the form is the effective, active principle of a thing. For Aquinas, the "essential form" of the human body is the soul. The soul, of course, is nothing physical; it is a pure form without matter. As a pure form, the soul is indestructible and immortal. It is, indeed, the principle of activity and life of the person. In addition, the soul is immortal in its individual form: each person's soul, unique to her or him, is immortal. Each soul is a direct creation of God and does not come from human parents. It stands in a relationship of mutual interdependency relative to the body. A human being is a *unity* of body and soul. Aquinas taught that without the soul the body

## Why Do Humans Stand Upright?

For four reasons, said Aquinas:

1. Animals use their sense organs for seeking food. Because the sense organs are located mostly in the face, their faces are turned to the ground. Humans, by contrast, also use the senses to pursue truth, and for this purpose it is better that they are able to look up and about.

2. The brain functions better when it is above the other parts of the body.

3. If we walked on all fours, our hands would not be available for other purposes.

4. If we walked on all fours, we would have to take hold of food with our mouths, which would re-quire our lips and tongue to be thick and hard, hindering speech.

In short, we walk erect because certain purposes (communicating, seeking truth, using our hands and brain) are best served by doing so. This is a **teleological explanation,** the type of explanation that we mentioned in connection with Aristotle in Chapter 4. Explanations like this, which refer to a "final cause," imply a designing intelligence that determines the purpose served by the characteristics of a species.

---

would be formless and that without a body the soul would have no access to knowledge derived from sensation.

Aquinas' epistemology was built on Aristotle's notion of three powers of the soul, namely, the vegetative (e.g., reproduction), animal (e.g., sensation), and human (e.g., the understanding). Aquinas also agreed with Aristotle's idea that human knowing is relatively passive and receptive. Knowledge is reached when the picture in the understanding agrees with what is present in reality (*adaequatio rei et intellectus*). Such knowledge is empirical in that it has its source in experience and is based on sense perceptions rather than on participation in the Divine Ideas. However, sense experience always accesses individually existing things; what leads to knowledge is the discovery of the essence of things that represents their definition. The discovery of essences requires imagination and human intelligence.

A final consideration of Aquinas' thinking concerns his proofs for the existence of God. We will examine them in detail in Chapter 13 but mention here that the proofs are variations on the idea that things must have an ultimate cause, creator, designer, source of being, or source of goodness: namely, God. Our knowledge of God's *nature,* however, is in terms of what God is *not*. For example, because God is unmoved and unchangeable, God is eternal. Because he is not material and is without parts, he is utterly simple. And because he is not a composite, he is not a composite of essence and existence: his essence is his existence.

Aquinas believed that the task of the wise person is to find both order and reason in the natural world. It is in the systematic ordering of the complexities of reality that human greatness can be found. Aquinas created a philosophical/theological system during the zenith hour in the power of the Church and of the pope, and interest in it experienced a strong revival in the nineteenth and twentieth centuries. These ideas continue to play a vital role in the Church as an institution and in religion as a governing factor in daily life.

## SELECTION 5.1

# Confessions*

*St. Augustine*

[*When you think about it, neither the past nor the future exists, and the present has no duration. What, then, is left of time? In this famous selection from his* Confessions, *Augustine presents his thoughts on these and related puzzles—and offers a solution to them.*]

### Book XI—Time and Eternity

What is time? Who can explain this easily and briefly? Who can comprehend this even in thought so as to articulate the answer in words? Yet what do we speak of, in our familiar everyday conversation, more than of time? We surely know what we mean when we speak of it. We also know what is meant when we hear someone else talking about it. What then is time? Provided that no one asks me, I know. If I want to explain it to an inquirer, I do not know. But I confidently affirm myself to know that if nothing passes away, there is no past time, and if nothing arrives, there is no future time, and if nothing existed there would be no present time. Take the two tenses, past and future. How can they "be" when the past is not now present and the future is not yet present? Yet if the present were always present, it would not pass into the past: it would not be time but eternity. If then, in order to be time at all, the present is so made that it passes into the past, how can we say that this present also "is"? The cause of its being is that it will cease to be. So indeed we cannot truly say that time exists except in the sense that it tends towards non-existence.

xv (18) Nevertheless we speak of "a long time" and "a short time," and it is only of the past or the future that we say this. Of the past we speak of "a long time," when, for example, it is more than a hundred years ago. "A long time" in the future may mean a hundred years ahead. By "a short time ago" we would mean, say, ten days back, and "a short time ahead" might mean "in ten days' time." But how can something be long or short which does not

exist? For the past now has no existence and the future is not yet. So we ought not to say of the past "it is long," but "it was long," and of the future "it will be long." My Lord, my light, does not your truth mock humanity at this point? This time past which was long, was it long when it was past or when it was still present? It could be long only when it existed to be long. Once past, it no longer was. Therefore it could not be long if it had entirely ceased to exist.

Therefore let us not say "The time past was long." For we cannot discover anything to be long when, after it has become past, it has ceased to be. But let us say "That time once present was long" because it was long at the time when it was present. For it had not yet passed away into non-existence. It existed so as to be able to be long. But after it had passed away, it simultaneously ceased to be long because it ceased to be.

(19) Human soul, let us see whether present time can be long. To you the power is granted to be aware of intervals of time, and to measure them. What answer will you give me? Are a hundred years in the present a long time? Consider first whether a hundred years can be present. For if the first year of the series is current, it is present, but ninety-nine are future, and so do not yet exist. If the second year is current, one is already past, the second is present, the remainder lie in the future. And so between the extremes, whatever year of this century we assume to be present, there will be some years before it which lie in the past, some in the future to come after it. It follows that a century could never be present.

Consider then whether if a single year is current, that can be present. If in this year the first month is current, the others lie in the future: if the second, then the first lies in the past and the rest do not yet exist. Therefore even a current year is not entirely present; and if it is not entirely present, it is not a year which is present. A year is twelve months, of which any month which is current is present; the others are either past or future. Moreover, not even a month which is current is present, but one day. If

---

*From *St. Augustine: Confessions,* translated by Henry Chadwick. Copyright © 1991, Henry Chadwick. By permission of Oxford University Press.

the first day, the others are future; if the last day, the others are past; any intermediary day falls between past and future.

(2) See—present time, which alone we find capable of being called long, is contracted to the space of hardly a single day. But let us examine that also: for not even one day is entirely present. All the hours of night and day add up to twenty-four. The first of them has the others in the future, the last has them in the past. Any hour between these has past hours before it, future hours after it. One hour is itself constituted of fugitive moments. Whatever part of it has flown away is past. What remains to it is future. If we can think of some bit of time which cannot be divided into even the smallest instantaneous moments, that alone is what we can call "present." And this time flies so quickly from future into past that it is an interval with no duration. If it has duration, it is divisible into past and future. But the present occupies no space.

Where then is the time which we call long? Is it future? We do not really mean "It is long," since it does not yet exist to be long, but we mean it will be long. When will it be long? If it will then still lie in the future, it will not be long, since it will not yet exist to be long. But if it will be long at the time when, out of the future which does not yet exist, it begins to have being and will become present fact, so that it has the potentiality to be long, the present cries out in words already used that it cannot be long.

xvi (21) Nevertheless, Lord, we are conscious of intervals of time, and compare them with each other, and call some longer, others shorter. We also measure how much longer or shorter one period is than another, and answer that the one is twice or three times as much as the other, or that the two periods are equal. Moreover, we are measuring times which are past when our perception is the basis of measurement. But who can measure the past which does not now exist or the future which does not yet exist, unless perhaps someone dares to assert that he can measure what has no existence? At the moment when time is passing, it can be perceived and measured. But when it has passed and is not present, it cannot be.

xvii (22) I am investigating, Father, not making assertions. My God, protect me and rule me (Ps. 22:1; 27:9). Who will tell me that there are not three times, past, present, and future, as we learnt when children and as we have taught children, but only the present, because the other two have no existence? Or do they exist in the sense that, when the present emerges from the future, time comes out of some secret store, and then recedes into some secret place when the past comes out of the present? Where did those who sang prophecies see these events if they do not yet exist? To see what has no existence is impossible. And those who narrate past history would surely not be telling a true story if they did not discern events by their soul's insight. If the past were non-existent, it could not be discerned at all. Therefore both future and past events exist.

xviii (23) Allow me, Lord, to take my investigation further. My hope, let not my attention be distracted. If future and past events exist, I want to know where they are. If I have not the strength to discover the answer, at least I know that wherever they are, they are not there as future or past, but as present. For if there also they are future, they will not yet be there. If there also they are past, they are no longer there. Therefore, wherever they are, whatever they are, they do not exist except in the present. When a true narrative of the past is related, the memory produces not the actual events which have passed away but words conceived from images of them, which they fixed in the mind like imprints as they passed through the senses. Thus my boyhood, which is no longer, lies in past time which is no longer. But when I am recollecting and telling my story, I am looking on its image in present time, since it is still in my memory. Whether a similar cause is operative in predictions of the future, in the sense that images of realities which do not yet exist are presented as already in existence, I confess, my God, I do not know. At least I know this much: we frequently think out in advance our future actions, and that premeditation is in the present; but the action which we premeditate is not yet in being because it lies in the future. But when we have embarked on the action and what we were premeditating begins to be put into effect, then that action will have existence, since then it will be not future but present.

(24) Whatever may be the way in which the hidden presentiment of the future is known, nothing can be seen if it does not exist. Now that which already exists is not future but present. When therefore people speak of knowing the future, what is seen is not events which do not yet exist (that is, they really are future), but perhaps their causes or signs which already exist. In this way, to those who

see them they are not future but present, and that is the basis on which the future can be conceived in the mind and made the subject of prediction.

Again, these concepts already exist, and those who predict the future see these concepts as if already present to their minds.

Among a great mass of examples, let me mention one instance. I look at the dawn. I forecast that the sun will rise. What I am looking at is present, what I am forecasting is future. It is not the sun which lies in the future (it already exists) but its rise, which has not yet arrived. Yet unless I were mentally imagining its rise, as now when I am speaking about it, I could not predict it. But the dawn glow which I see in the sky is not sunrise, which it precedes, nor is the imagining of sunrise in my mind the actuality. These are both discerned as present so that the coming sunrise may be foretold.

So future events do not yet exist, and if they are not yet present, they do not exist; and if they have no being, they cannot be seen at all. But they can be predicted from present events which are already present and can be seen. . . .

xx (26) What is by now evident and clear is that neither future nor past exists, and it is inexact language to speak of three times—past, present, and future. Perhaps it would be exact to say: there are three times, a present of things past, a present of things present, a present of things to come. In the soul there are these three aspects of time, and I do not see them anywhere else. The present considering the past is the memory, the present considering the present is immediate awareness, the present considering the future is expectation. If we are allowed to use such language, I see three times, and I admit they are three. Moreover, we may say, There are three times, past, present, and future. This customary way of speaking is incorrect, but it is common usage. Let us accept the usage. I do not object and offer no opposition or criticism, as long as what is said is being understood, namely that neither the future nor the past is now present. There are few usages of everyday speech which are exact, and most of our language is inexact. Yet what we mean is communicated.

xxi (27) A little earlier I observed that we measure past periods of time so that we can say that one period is twice as long as another or equal to it, and likewise of other periods of time which we are capable of measuring and reporting. Therefore, as I was saying, we measure periods of time as they are passing, and if anyone says to me "How do you know?" I reply: I know it because we do measure time and cannot measure what has no being; and past and future have none. But how do we measure present time when it has no extension? It is measured when it passes, but not when it has passed, because then there will be nothing there to measure.

When time is measured, where does it come from, by what route does it pass, and where does it go? It must come out of the future, pass by the present, and go into the past; so it comes from what as yet does not exist, passes through that which lacks extension, and goes into that which is now nonexistent. Yet what do we measure but time over some extension? When we speak of lengths of time as single, duple, triple, and equal, or any other temporal relation of this kind, we must be speaking of periods of time possessing extension. In what extension then do we measure time as it is passing? Is it in the future out of which it comes to pass by? No, for we do not measure what does not yet exist. Is it in the present through which it passes? No, for we cannot measure that which has no extension. Is it in the past into which it is moving? No, for we cannot measure what now does not exist. . . .

xxiv (31) Do you command me to concur if someone says time is the movement of a physical entity? You do not. For I learn that no body can be moved except in time. You tell me so, but I do not learn that the actual movement of a body constitutes time. That is not what you tell me. For when a body is moved, it is by time that I measure the duration of the movement, from the moment it begins until it ends. Unless I have observed the point when it begins, and if its movement is continuous so that I cannot observe when it ceases, I am unable to measure except for the period from the beginning to the end of my observation. If my observing lasts for a considerable time, I can only report that a long time passed, but not precisely how much. When we say how much, we are making a comparison—as, for example, "This period was of the same length as that," or "This period was twice as long as that," or some such relationship.

If, however, we have been able to note the points in space from which and to which a moving body passes, or the parts of a body when it is spinning on its axis, then we can say how much time the movement of the body or its parts required to move from one point to another. It follows that a body's movement is one thing, the period by which we measure is another. It is self-evident which of these is to be described as time. Moreover, a body may at one point be moving, at another point at rest. We measure by time and say "It was standing still for the same time that it was in movement," or "It was still for two or three times as long as it was in movement," or any other measurement we may make, either by precise observation or by a rough estimate (we customarily say "more or less"). Therefore time is not the movement of a body. . . .

xxvii (34) Stand firm, my mind, concentrate with resolution. "God is our help, he has made us and not we ourselves" (Ps. 61:9; 99:3). Concentrate on the point where truth is beginning to dawn. For example, a physical voice begins to sound. It sounds. It continues to sound, and then ceases. Silence has now come, and the voice is past. There is now no sound. Before it sounded it lay in the future. It could not be measured because it did not exist; and now it cannot be measured because it has ceased to be. At the time when it was sounding, it was possible because at that time it existed to be measured. Yet even then it had no permanence. It came and went. Did this make it more possible to measure? In process of passing away it was extended through a certain space of time by which it could be measured, since the present occupies no length of time. Therefore during that transient process it could be measured. But take, for example, another voice. It begins to sound and continues to do so unflaggingly without any interruption. Let us measure it while it is sounding; when it has ceased to sound, it will be past and will not exist to be measurable. Evidently we may at that stage measure it by saying how long it lasted. But if it is still sounding, it cannot be measured except from the starting moment when it began to sound to the finish when it ceased. What we measure is the actual interval from the beginning to the end. That is why a sound which has not yet ended cannot be measured: one cannot say how long or how short it is, nor that it is equal to some other length of time or that in relation to another it is single or double or any such proportion. But when it has come to an end, then it will already have ceased to be. By what method then can it be measured?

Nevertheless we do measure periods of time. And yet the times we measure are not those which do not yet exist, nor those which already have no existence, nor those which extend over no interval of time, nor those which reach no conclusions. So the times we measure are not future nor past nor present nor those in process of passing away. Yet we measure periods of time.

(35) "God, Creator of all things"—*Deus Creator omnium*—the line consists of eight syllables, in which short and long syllables alternate. So the four which are short (the first, third, fifth, and seventh) are single in relation to the four long syllables (the second, fourth, sixth, and eighth). Each of the long syllables has twice the time of the short. As I recite the words, I also observe that this is so, for it is evident to sense-perception. To the degree that the sense-perception is unambiguous, I measure the long syllable by the short one, and perceive it to be twice the length. But when one syllable sounds after another, the short first, the long after it, how shall I keep my hold on the short, and how use it to apply a measure to the long, so as to verify that the long is twice as much? The long does not begin to sound unless the short has ceased to sound. I can hardly measure the long during the presence of its sound, as measuring becomes possible only after it has ended. When it is finished, it has gone into the past. What then is it which I measure? Where is the short syllable with which I am making my measurement? Where is the long which I am measuring? Both have sounded; they have flown away; they belong to the past. They now do not exist. And I offer my measurement and declare as confidently as a practised sense-perception will allow, that the short is single, the long double—I mean in the time they occupy. I can do this only because they are past and gone. Therefore it is not the syllables which I am measuring, but something in my memory which stays fixed there.

(36) So it is in you, my mind, that I measure periods of time. Do not distract me; that is, do not allow yourself to be distracted by the hubbub of the impressions being made upon you. In you, I affirm, I measure periods of time. The impression which passing events make upon you abides when they are gone. That present consciousness is what I am measuring, not the stream of past events which have caused it. When I measure periods of time, that is what I am actually measuring. Therefore, either this is what time is, or time is not what I am measuring.

What happens when we measure silences and say that a given period of silence lasted as long as a given sound? Do we direct our attention to measuring it as if a sound occurred, so that we are enabled to judge the intervals of the silences within the space of time concerned? For without any sound or utterance we mentally recite poems and lines and speeches, and we assess the lengths of their movements and the relative amounts of time they occupy, no differently from the way we would speak if we were actually making sounds. Suppose someone wished to utter a sound lasting a long time, and decided in advance how long that was going to be. He would have planned that space of time in silence. Entrusting that to his memory he would begin to utter the sound which continues until it has reached the intended end. It would be more accurate to say the utterance has sounded and will sound. For the part of it which is complete has sounded, but what remains will sound, and so the action is being accomplished as present attention transfers the future into the past. The future diminishes as the past grows, until the future has completely gone and everything is in the past.

xxviii (37) But how does this future, which does not yet exist, diminish or become consumed? Or how does the past, which now has no being, grow, unless there are three processes in the mind which in this is the active agent? For the mind expects and attends and remembers, so that what it expects passes through what has its attention to what it remembers. Who therefore can deny that the future does not yet exist? Yet already in the mind there is an expectation of the future. Who can deny that the past does not now exist? Yet there is still in the mind a memory of the past. None can deny that present time lacks any extension because it passes in a flash. Yet attention is continuous, and it is through this that what will be present progresses towards being absent. So the future, which does not exist, is not a long period of time. A long future is a long expectation of the future. And the past, which has no existence, is not a long period of time. A long past is a long memory of the past.

## CHECKLIST

To help you review, here is a checklist of the key philosophers and terms and concepts of this chapter. The brief descriptive sentences summarize the philosophers' leading ideas. Keep in mind that some of these summary statements are oversimplifications of complex positions.

### *Philosophers*

- **Plotinus**   held that reality emanates from the One.

- **St. Augustine**   provided Platonic philosophical justification for the Christian belief in a nonmaterial God, rejected skepticism, and diagnosed the cause of error in sense perception.

- **Pyrrho**   held that every theory can be opposed by an equally valid contradictory theory; we must suspend judgment on all issues.

- **Sextus Empiricus**   was the most famous total skeptic. He held the position "I do not know whether knowledge is possible."

- **Hypatia**   instructed students in Plato, Aristotle, Plotinus, and Ptolemy and improved the mathematical rigor of Ptolemy's astronomical

theories, stressing the importance of philosophy and mathematics to life.

- **St. Thomas Aquinas**   blended Christianity with the philosophy of Aristotle, delineating the boundary between philosophy and theology.

### *Key Terms and Concepts*

| | |
|---|---|
| Hellenistic age | *ataraxia* |
| Skepticism | *agoge* |
| Neoplatonism | principle of |
| creation *ex nihilo* | noncontradiction |
| total versus modified | universals |
| skeptic | realism |
| Academics | conceptualism |
| Pyrrhonists | nominalism |
| Ten Tropes | teleological explanation |
| *epoche* | |

## QUESTIONS FOR DISCUSSION AND REVIEW

1. Compare and contrast the views of the Academics and the Pyrrhonists.

2. "Nothing can be known." What is a powerful objection to this claim?

3. "I do not know whether knowledge is possible." Defend or attack this claim.

4. Defend some version of total skepticism.

5. What is creation *ex nihilo*? State a reason for thinking that creation *ex nihilo* is impossible.

6. Explain the difference between realism, conceptualism, and nominalism. Which theory is the most plausible, and why?

7. Billy the Kid cannot be in more than one place at a given time. Can Billy the Kid's *height* (five feet four inches) be in more than one place? Explain.

8. Can we say only what God is not?

9. Give a teleological explanation of why polar bears have white fur.

## SUGGESTED FURTHER READINGS

Julia Annas and Jonathan Barnes, *The Modes of Scepticism: Ancient Texts and Modern Interpretations* (Cambridge: Cambridge University Press, 1985). Reflects the revival of interest in ancient skepticism. Excellent.

Augustine, *Against the Academics,* vol. 3, Sister Mary Patricia Garvey, trans. (Milwaukee: Marquette University Press, 1957). Contains easy-to-understand arguments against skepticism.

Augustine, *Confessions, The,* Maria Boulding, trans. (New York: New City Press, 1998). Much in this is not purely philosophical, but most of it is interesting.

Augustine, *Confessions,* Henry Chadwick, trans. (New York: Oxford University Press, 1998). A new translation with an introduction by the translator.

Marcus Aurelius, *Meditations,* Gregory Hays, trans. (London: Weidenfeld and Nicolson, 2003). A new, readable translation of the writings of the Stoic Roman emperor.

Robert Black, ed., *Renaissance Thought: A Reader.* (New York: Routledge, 2001). Essays by modern writers on Renaissance humanism, philosophy, and political thought.

John Burnet, *Early Greek Philosophy,* 4th ed. (London: Macmillan, originally published in 1930). This is a standard work on early Greek philosophy.

William Carter, *The Way Things Are: Basic Readings in Metaphysical Philosophy* (New York: McGraw-Hill, 1998). Readings from the Anglo-American approach to key metaphysical problems.

Henry Chadwick, *Augustine: A Very Short Introduction* (New York: Oxford University Press, 2001). Said by reviewers to be the best brief introduction to Augustine's context and thought.

M. T. Clark, ed., *An Aquinas Reader* (New York: Image Books, 1955). Aquinas wrote too much to read it all; a reader like this one may prove useful.

Brian Davies, *The Thought of Thomas Aquinas* (New York: Oxford University Press, 1992). An introduction, but demanding.

Lloyd P. Gerson, *Plotinus* (London: Routledge, 1994). A major treatise on the philosophy of Plotinus.

E. Gilson, *History of Christian Philosophy in the Middle Ages* (New York: Random House, 1955). A work by one of the foremost medieval authorities. See also Gilson's *The Christian Philosophy of Saint Augustine,* L. Lynch, trans. (New York: Random House, 1960), and *The Christian Philosophy of St. Thomas Aquinas,* L. Shook, trans. (New York: Random House, 1956).

Philip P. Hallie, ed., *Scepticism, Man, and God: Selections from the Major Writings of Sextus Empiricus* (Middletown, Conn.: Wesleyan University Press, 1964). Clear, readable, authoritative.

R. J. Hankinson, *The Sceptics* (New York: Routledge, 1995). An up-to-date consideration of the philosophical issues within the Greek skeptical tradition.

Christopher Hookway, *Scepticism* (New York: Routledge, 1990). A review of the historical development of skepticism and its consequences for present-day thought and action.

Brad Inwood and L. P. Gerson, trans., *Hellenistic Philosophy, Introductory Readings* (Indianapolis: Hackett, 1988). A well-chosen selection of readings from Stoicism, Epicureanism, and Skepticism.

G. S. Kirk, J. E. Raven, and M. Schofield, *The Presocratic Philosophers: A Critical History with a Selection of Texts,* 2nd ed. (Cambridge: Cambridge University Press, 1983). This is a comprehensive treatment of the pre-Socratics.

Charles Landesmann and Robin Meeks, *Philosophical Skepticism* (Malden, Mass.: Blackwell, 2003). A useful collection of writings on traditional skeptics and their opponents.

Benson Mates, ed. and trans., *The Skeptic Way: Sextus Empiricus's Outlines of Pyrrhonism* (New York: Oxford University Press, 1996). A recent translation, with commentary and an introduction.

Dominic J. O'Meara, *Plotinus, An Introduction to the Enneads* (New York: Oxford University Press, 1993). Suitable for beginners.

Mark Morford, *The Roman Philosophers* (New York: Routledge, 2002). A review of the Roman thinkers who are still very much influencing our time.

Jason L. Saunders, ed., *Greek and Roman Philosophy after Aristotle* (New York: The Free Press, 1994). A useful and accessible collection of texts of Hellenistic philosophers.

R. W. Sharples, *Stoics, Epicureans and Sceptics* (New York: Routledge, 2002). A basic account of the Stoic, Epicurean, and skeptic philosophies from 323 B.C.E. to 200 C.E.

Mary Ellen Waithe, "Finding Bits and Pieces of Hypatia," in Linda Lopez McAlister, ed., *Hypatia's Daughters* (Indianapolis: Indiana University Press, 1995).

Julius R. Weinberg, *A Short History of Medieval Philosophy* (Princeton: Princeton University Press, 1991). A survey of the main philosophers from Augustine to William of Ockham.

# 6

# The Rise of
# Modern Metaphysics
# and Epistemology

Every part of the universe is body, and that which is not body is not part of
the universe.     —Thomas Hobbes

Wood, stone, fire, water, flesh . . . are things perceived by my senses;
and things perceived by the senses are immediately perceived; and things
immediately perceived are ideas; and ideas cannot exist outside the mind.
    — George Berkeley

The transitional period between medieval and modern times was the Renaissance (fourteenth through sixteenth centuries). Through its emphasis on worldly experience and reverence for classical culture, the Renaissance helped emancipate Europe from the intellectual authority of the Church. The modern period in history (and philosophy) that followed lasted through the nineteenth century. Its interesting cultural and social developments include, among other things, the rise of nation-states, the spread of capitalism and industrialization, the exploration and settlement of the New World, the decline of religion, and the eventual domination of science as the most revered source of knowledge. The last development is the most important to a history of metaphysics and epistemology and is briefly described in the box "The Scientific Revolution."

To most educated Westerners today, it is a matter of plain fact that there exists a universe of physical objects related to one another spatiotemporally. These objects are composed, we are inclined to believe, of minute atoms and subatomic particles that interact with one another in mathematically describable ways.

## The Scientific Revolution

Science, as you and we too think of it, began with the Scientific Revolution, which itself commenced when Copernicus (1473–1543) broke with long tradition and proposed (mid-sixteenth century) that the earth is not the center of the universe but in fact revolves, with the other planets, around the sun. The essence of the revolution lies in several ideas: (1) it is *important* to understand how the world works; (2) to do that, you have to *examine the world itself* rather than read Aristotle or consult scripture; (3) a fruitful way to examine the world is through *experimentation*—this is an idea expressed most clearly by Francis Bacon (1561–1626); and (4) the world is a *mechanical system* that can be *described mathematically*—this is an idea expressed most clearly by René Descartes (1596–1650). The details of the mechanistic Cartesian picture of the universe were filled in (to a degree) by the observations and findings of (among others) Tycho Brahe (1546–1601), Johannes Kepler (1571–1630), Galileo Galilei (1564–1642), and, most important, Sir Isaac Newton (1642–1727), who combined the various discoveries into a unified description of the universe based on the concept of gravitation.

Certain newly invented instruments aided the early scientists in their study of the world, including, most famously, the telescope, the microscope, the vacuum pump, and the mechanical clock. And by no means were the findings of the new science limited to astronomy and the dynamics of moving bodies. There were, for example, William Harvey's (1578–1657) discovery of the circulation of the blood, William Gilbert's (1540–1603) investigations of electricity and magnetism, and the various discoveries of Robert Boyle (1627–1691)—the father of chemistry—concerning gases, metals, combustion, acids and bases, and the nature of colors.

Another important idea that came to be characteristic of the Scientific Revolution was that the fundamental constituents of the natural world are basically corpuscular or atomistic—things are made out of tiny particles. The modern scientists (in effect) declared that Democritus had gotten things right.

We are also accustomed to think that in addition to the spatiotemporal *physical* universe there exist human (and perhaps other) observers who are able to perceive their corner of the universe and, within certain limits, to understand it. The *understanding,* we are inclined to suppose, and the *minds* in which this understanding exists, are not themselves physical entities, though we also tend to think that understanding and minds depend in some sense on the functioning of physical entities such as the brain and central nervous system. They, the understanding itself and the minds that have it—unlike physical things such as brains and atoms and nerve impulses and energy fields—exist in time but not space. They, unlike physical things, are not bound by the laws of physics and are not made up of parts.

Thus, today it seems to be a matter of plain common sense that reality has a dual nature. The world or the universe, we believe, consists of physical objects on one hand and minds on the other. In a normal living person, mind and matter are intertwined in such a way that what happens to the body can affect the mind and what happens in the mind can affect the body. The clearest examples of mind–body interaction occur when the mind, through an act of will, causes the body to perform some action or when something that happens to the body triggers a new thought in the mind.

Galileo being tried for heresy before a papal tribunal.

So this *commonsense metaphysics*, as we have been describing it, is dualistic. It supposes that two different kinds of phenomena exist: physical and mental (often called "spiritual"). **Dualism** is essentially the "two-realms view" invented by Plato, incorporated with changes into Christianity by Augustine and others, and transmitted to us in its contemporary form by early modern philosophers.

Although our commonsense metaphysics is dualistic, it did not have to be that way; we might have adopted an alternative metaphysical perspective. Here are the main possibilities:

- **Dualism.** This view holds that what exists is either physical or mental ("spiritual"); some things, such as a human person, have both a physical component (a physical body) and a mental component (a mind).

- **Materialism,** or physicalism. This view holds that only the physical exists. Accordingly, so-called mental things are in some sense manifestations of an underlying physical reality. (Do not confuse metaphysical materialism with the doctrine that the most important thing is to live comfortably and acquire wealth.)

- **Idealism.** This view holds that only the mental (or "spiritual") exists. Accordingly, so-called physical things are in some sense manifestations of the mind or of thought. (Do not confuse metaphysical idealism with the views of the dreamer who places ideals above practical considerations.)

## Chronology of Postmedieval History

Here, for easy reference, are the dates of the major periods in postmedieval history mentioned in the text:

*The Renaissance:* the fourteenth through sixteenth centuries

*The Reformation and Counter-Reformation:* the sixteenth century

*The Scientific Revolution:* the seventeenth century (though that revolution still continues)

*The Enlightenment* or *Age of Reason:* the eighteenth century

*The Industrial Revolution:* the mid-eighteenth to mid-nineteenth centuries

*The Romantic Period:* the late eighteenth to very early nineteenth centuries

*The Age of Technology:* the twentieth century to the present

- **"Alternative views."** Some theorists have held that what exists is ultimately neither mental nor spiritual; still others have believed that what exists is ultimately both mental and physical. How could it be both mental and physical? According to this view, often called **double aspect theory,** the mental and physical are just different *ways of looking at* the same things — things that in themselves are neutral between the two categories.

Thanks to the legacy of Greek and Christian influences on Western civilization, dualism continues to command the assent of common sense. Increasingly, however, the march of science seems philosophically to undermine metaphysical dualism in favor of materialism. At stake here are three important questions:

1. Does an immaterial God exist?
2. Do humans have free will?
3. Is there life after death?

Unfortunately for those who would prefer the answer to one or another of the questions to be "yes," a scientific understanding of the world tends to imply the materialist view that all that exists is matter. This is one major reason why modern metaphysics may be said to be concerned with powerful stuff: riding on the outcome of the competition among the perspectives just listed (dualism, materialism, idealism, and alternative views) is the reasonableness of believing in God, free will, and the hereafter.

Let us therefore consider each of these perspectives as it arose during the modern period of philosophy.

## DESCARTES AND DUALISM

Many European thinkers of the sixteenth century began to question established precepts and above all to question the accepted authorities as arbiters of truth. That so-and-so said that something is true was no longer automatically accepted as proof of that something, no matter who said it or what the something was. This tendency to question authority effectively set the stage for the Scientific Revolution and modern philosophy, both of which are products of the seventeenth century. (For a chronology of postmedieval history, see the box on page 102.)

Modern philosophy is usually said to have begun with **René Descartes** [day-KART] (1596–1650), mathematician, scientist, and, of course, philosopher. Descartes's importance to Western intellectual history cannot be overestimated. Other thinkers we have mentioned may have equaled him in significance, but none surpassed him. He made important contributions to physiology, psychology, optics, and especially mathematics, in which he originated the Cartesian★ coordinates and Cartesian curves. It is thanks to Descartes that students now study analytic geometry; he introduced it to the world.

Descartes was a Catholic, but he also believed there are important truths that cannot be ascertained through the authority of the Church. These include those truths that pertain to the ultimate nature of existing things.

But what, then, he wondered, is to be the *criterion* of truth and knowledge in such matters? What is to be the criterion by which one might separate *certain knowledge* about matters of fact from inferior products such as *mere belief*?

Such questions were not new to philosophy, of course. During the Renaissance, the classical skeptical works, notably those by Sextus, were "rediscovered," published, and taken quite seriously — even contributing to the controversies during the Protestant Reformation about the knowability of religious beliefs. In addition, in the sixteenth and seventeenth centuries, various new skeptical writings appeared. Especially noteworthy in this resurgent skeptical tradition were Pierre Gassendi (1592–1655) and Marin Mersenne (1588–1648), who separately used a variety of skeptical arguments (which we do not have the space to discuss) to

---

★ *Cartesian* is the adjective form of *Descartes*.

## PROFILE: René Descartes (1596–1650)

Descartes had the great fortune to be able to transform his inheritance into a comfortable annual income from which he lived. And he did not waste his time. Before he died, he had made important advances in science, mathematics, and philosophy. Descartes founded analytic geometry and contributed to the understanding of negative roots. He wrote a text in physiology and did work in psychology. His work in optics was significant. His contributions in philosophy are of enormous importance.

As a youth, Descartes attended the Jesuit College at La Flèche and the University of Poitiers. When he was twenty-one, he joined the Dutch army and, two years later, the Bavarian army. His military experience allowed him to be a spectator of the human drama at first hand and granted him free time to think. In 1628 he retired to Holland, where he lived for twenty years in a tolerant country in which he was free from religious persecution.

Descartes was a careful philosopher and a cautious person. Although he took great issue with the medievalist thinking of his teachers, he did not make them aware of his reactions. Later, when he heard that the Church had condemned Galileo for his writings, he decided that he would have his works published only one hundred years after his death. He subsequently changed his mind, though he came to wish that he had not. For when he did publish some of his ideas, they were bitterly attacked by Protestant theologians; Catholic denunciations came later. This caused Descartes to say that had he been smarter he would not have written anything so he would have had more peace and quiet to think.

Two unconnected incidents in Descartes's life are always mentioned in philosophy texts. One is that the insights that underlay his philosophy came to him in dreams after spending a winter day relaxing in a well-heated room while in the army in Bavaria. The other is that he accepted an invitation, with some reluctance, to tutor Queen Christina of Sweden in 1649. This was a big mistake, for the cold weather and early hour of his duties literally killed him. We can only speculate what the queen learned from the episode.

Descartes's principal philosophical works are *Discourse on Method* (1637), *Meditations on First Philosophy* (1641), and *Principles of Philosophy* (1644).

establish the unknowability of the true nature of things. Both believed, however, that a study of the appearances of things could yield information useful for living in this world.

Descartes was vitally concerned with skeptical questions as to the possibility of knowledge, but he was no skeptic. His interest in mathematics strongly affected his philosophical reflections, and it was his more-or-less lifelong intention to formulate a unified science of nature that was as fully certain as arithmetic.

He did, however, employ skepticism as a method of achieving certainty. His idea was simple enough: I will doubt everything that can possibly be doubted, he reasoned, and if anything is left, then it will be absolutely certain. Then I will consider what it is about this certainty (if there is one) that places it beyond doubt, and that will provide me with a *criterion* of truth and knowledge, a yardstick against which I can measure all other purported truths to see if they, too, are beyond doubt.

## Skepticism as the Key to Certainty

Let's see how Descartes's *doubting methodology* worked.

To doubt every proposition that he possibly could, Descartes employed two famous conjectures, the **dream conjecture** and the **evil demon conjecture.** For all I know, Descartes said, I might now be dreaming—that is Descartes's dream conjecture. And further, he said, for all I know, some malevolent demon devotes himself to deceiving me at every turn so that I regard as true and certain propositions that are in fact false. That supposition is Descartes's evil demon conjecture.

Yes, these two conjectures are totally bizarre, and Descartes was as aware of that as you are. But that is just the point. What Descartes was looking for was a measure of certainty that escapes even the most incredible and bizarre possibilities of falsehood.

And what he discovered, when he considered everything he thought he knew in the light of one or the other of these two bizarre possibilities, is that he could doubt *absolutely everything, save one indubitable truth:* "I think, therefore I am"— **cogito, ergo sum.** Remember this phrase, which is from Descartes's *Discourse on Method.*

What Descartes meant is that any attempt to doubt one's existence as a thinking being is impossible because to doubt is to think and to exist. Try for a moment to doubt your own existence, and you will see what Descartes meant. The self that doubts its own existence must surely exist to be able to doubt in the first place. (For further description of this line of reasoning, see the box "Descartes's Conjectures.") Like Augustine, Descartes had found certain truth in his inability to doubt his own existence.

## The "Clear and Distinct" Litmus Test

Descartes went much further than Augustine. Having supposedly found certain knowledge in his own existence as a thing that thinks, he reasoned as follows:

> I am certain that I am a thing that thinks; but do I not then likewise know what is required to make me certain of a truth? In this knowledge of my existence as a thinking thing there is nothing that assures me of its truth, excepting the clear and distinct perception of that which I state, which would not indeed suffice to assure me that what I say is true, if it could ever happen that a thing that I conceived so clearly and distinctly could be false. And accordingly it seems to me that already I can establish as a general rule that all things that I perceive very clearly and very distinctly are true.

In other words, Descartes examined his single indubitable truth to see what guaranteed its certainty and saw that any other proposition he apprehended with identical "clarity and distinctness" must likewise be immune to doubt. In short, he had discovered in the certainty of his own existence an essential characteristic of certain truth: anything that was as clear and distinct as his own existence would pass the litmus test and would also have to be certain.

## Descartes's Conjectures

*For all I know, I might now be dreaming.* This is Descartes's dream conjecture, and it is easy enough to disprove, correct? I just pinch myself. But then again . . . am I just dreaming that I pinched myself? Might not any evidence I have that I am now awake just be dream evidence? Can I really be certain that I won't find myself in a few moments waking up, realizing that I have been dreaming? And thus can I really be sure that the things I see around me, this desk and book, these arms and legs, have any existence outside my mind?

Well, you may say, even if I am dreaming, there are still many things I cannot doubt; even if I am dreaming, I cannot doubt, for instance, that two and three are five or that a square has four sides.

But then again — and this is where Descartes's evil demon conjecture comes in — of course, it

*seems* absolutely certain to me that two and three make five and that a square has four sides. But *some* propositions that have seemed absolutely certain to me have turned out to be false. So how can I be sure that *these* propositions (that two and three make five and that a square has four sides), or any other proposition that seems certain to me, are not likewise false? For all I know, a deceitful and all-powerful intelligence has so programmed me that I find myself regarding as absolute certainties propositions that in fact are not true at all.

Descartes thought that these two conjectures combined in this way to force him "to avow that there is nothing at all that I formerly believed to be true of which it is impossible to doubt."

I think, therefore
I am, I think. . .

Using this **clear and distinct criterion,** Descartes found to his own satisfaction that he could regard as certain much of what he had initially had cause to doubt. This doubting methodology was like geometry, in which a theorem whose truth initially only *seems* true is demonstrated as absolutely certain by deducing it from basic axioms by means of rules of logic. Descartes's axiom was, in effect, "I think, therefore I am," and his rule of logic was "Whatever I perceive clearly and distinctly is certain."

## Oliva Sabuco de Nantes and the Body–Soul Connection

Descartes speculated that the mind interacts with the body in the pineal gland. Sixty or so years before Descartes, **Oliva Sabuco de Nantes** [sah-BOO-ko] (1562–?) proposed that, as the properties of the mind (or "soul," as she called it) are not physical properties, they cannot be physically located in some specific spot. Thus, she reasoned, the connection between body and soul occurs *throughout* the brain. The brain and the rest of the body "serve the soul like house servants serve the house," she maintained. She argued that a person is a microcosm (a miniature version) of the world, and this discloses that, in the same way as God activates, rules, and governs the world, the soul governs the "affects, movements, and actions of humans."

It is worth mentioning that Sabuco also believed that the intimate connection between soul and brain means there is a close relationship between psychological and physical health and between morality and medicine. For example, as soon as a negative emotion such as *sorrow* begins to affect our body, she said, we must control it before it becomes unmanageable *despair*. Virtuous passions promote good health, she said; immoral passions cause sickness and disease. As an illustration, she cited ex-

cessive sexual activity, which causes (she believed) excessive loss of an essential brain fluid, resulting in brainstem dehydration and the insanity found in advanced cases of syphilis and gonorrhea. There exists, she reasoned, a natural, medical basis for moral sanctions against sexual promiscuity. (It is pretty easy to think of a modern illustration of this thesis.)

Sabuco, born in Alcaraz, Spain, published her important book, *New Philosophy of Human Nature,* when she was only twenty-five years old. This was at the tail end of the Spanish Inquisition — not the most congenial of times for objective scholarship — and Sabuco was taking something of a risk as a woman writer of philosophy. Nevertheless, she was highly knowledgeable about ancient and medieval thinkers, and her book was cleared by the Church with only a few changes. It became quite influential and was published several times during her lifetime and in every century after her death.

Certainly, Sabuco did not solve the problem of mind–body interaction, but she anticipated by several hundred years today's holistic medicine with its emphasis on the intimate connection between mental and physical well-being.

And so Descartes, having armed himself with an absolutely reliable litmus test of truth, discovers first that he has certain knowledge that God exists. (We shall go over the details of Descartes's proof of God's existence in Part Three.) Also, Descartes finds that he knows for certain, and that therefore it is the case, that God would not deceive the thinking mind with perceptions of an external world — a world of objects outside the mind — if such did not exist. Thus, for Descartes, there are, beyond God, two separate and distinct substances, and reality has a dual nature. On one hand is *material substance,* whose essential attribute is **extension** (occupancy of space), and on the other hand is *mind,* whose essential attribute is **thought.** Because a substance, according to Descartes, "requires nothing other than itself to exist," it follows that mind and matter are totally independent of each other. Still, he thought that in a living person the mind and the material body interact, the motion of the body being sometimes affected by the mind and the thoughts of the mind being influenced by physical sensations.

This is, of course, familiar stuff. Our commonsense metaphysics is pretty much the dualistic metaphysics of Descartes. (However, see the box on Oliva Sabuco.) Unfortunately, there are unpleasant difficulties in the Cartesian dualistic

## Variations on a Theme

I feel, therefore I exist.          — *Thomas Jefferson*

I rebel, therefore I am.          — *Albert Camus*

I ought, therefore I can.          — *Immanuel Kant*

I want, therefore I am.          — *Leo Tolstoy*

Sometimes I think: and sometimes I am.
                              — *Paul Valéry*

Only the first word of the Cartesian philosophy is true: it was not possible for Descartes to say *cogito, ergo sum*, but only *cogito*.          — *Moses Hess*

I labor, therefore I am a man.          — *Max Stirner*

There is, of course, the *cogito, ergo sum* principle — perhaps the most famous of all philosophical theories . . . which, incidentally, is fallacious.
                              — *Barrows Dunham*

*Cogito, ergo sum* . . . can only mean, "I think, therefore I am a thinker." The truth is, *sum ergo cogito*.
                              — *Miguel de Unamuno*

metaphysics. These difficulties vexed Descartes and have yet to be plausibly resolved. In Chapter 9 we explain these difficulties in some detail.

To anticipate what is said there, Descartes thought:

1. Material things, including one's own body, are completely subject to physical laws.

But he also thought:

2. The immaterial mind can move one's body.

The difficulty is that if the immaterial mind can do this, then one's body evidently is *not* completely subject to physical laws after all. It seems contradictory to hold both (1) and (2). Do *you* hold both (1) and (2)?

Descartes also found it difficult to understand just how something immaterial *could* affect the movement of something material. He said that the mind interacts with the body through "vital spirits" in the brain, but he recognized that this explanation was quite obscure and almost wholly metaphorical. It was, in short, a dodge.

Some of Descartes's followers proposed a solution to the problem of how the immaterial mind interacts with the material body, given that the body is supposed to be subject to physical laws. The solution is called **parallelism.** The mind, they argued, does not *really* cause the body to move. When I will that my hand should move, my act of willing only *appears* to cause my hand to move.

What actually happens is two parallel and coordinated series of events: one a series of mental happenings, and the other a series that involves happenings to material things. Thus, my act of willing my hand to move does not cause my hand to move, but the act of willing and the movement of the hand *coincide*. Hence, it *appears* that the willing causes the moving.

Why do these events just happen to coincide? To account for the coinciding of the mental happenings with the physical happenings, Descartes's followers invoked God. God, they said, is the divine coordinator between the series of mental happenings and the series of material happenings. (In a variant of parallelism known as **occasionalism,** when I will my hand to move, that is the occasion on which God causes my hand to move.)

This theory of parallelism seems farfetched, true. But perhaps that only illustrates how serious a difficulty it is to suppose both that material things, including one's body, are completely subject to physical laws and that the immaterial mind can move one's body.

To date, a satisfactory explanation of the problem of interaction still has not been found.

Despite these problems, Descartes thought he had succeeded in establishing metaphysical dualism as absolutely certain. He also thought he had shown that the mind, because it is not in space and hence does not move, is not in any sense subject to physical laws and therefore is "free." The metaphysical dualism that survives today as mere "common sense," though it originated with Plato and was incorporated into Christianity by Augustine, survives in the form developed by Descartes. Yesterday's philosophy became today's common sense.

Notice Descartes's overall approach to metaphysical issues. Instead of asking "What is the basic stuff?" or "Of what does reality consist?" Descartes took an indirect approach and asked, in effect, "What do I know is the basic stuff?" and "Of what can I be certain about the nature of reality?" Descartes tried to discover *metaphysical* truth about what *is* through epistemological inquiry about *what can be known*.

We will call this approach to metaphysical truth the **epistemological detour.** After Descartes, and largely because of him, modern philosophy has attached considerable importance to epistemology, and metaphysical inquiry is often conducted via the epistemological detour.

Unfortunately, maybe the least debatable part of Descartes's overall reasoning is the two skeptical arguments (the dream conjecture and the evil demon conjecture) he advanced at the outset, which seem to make it a live issue whether what passes for knowledge genuinely is knowledge. After Descartes, the philosophers of the seventeenth century became divided about the power of reason in overcoming skepticism. This division is summarized in the box later in this chapter titled "Rationalism and Empiricism."

## HOBBES AND MATERIALISM

**Thomas Hobbes** (1588–1679) read Descartes's *Meditations* before their publication and raised several criticisms, which, together with Descartes's rejoinders, were published by Descartes. About ten years later, in 1651, Hobbes published his own major work, *Leviathan.*

Hobbes was on close terms with many of the best scientists and mathematicians of the period, including most significantly Galileo, and their discoveries seemed to him to imply clearly that all things are made of material particles and that all change reduces to motion. Accordingly, the basic premise of Hobbes's metaphysics is that *all that exists is bodies in motion,* motion being a continual relinquishing of one place and acquiring of another. Because, according to Hobbes, there are two main types of bodies, physical bodies and political bodies, there are two divisions of philosophy, natural and civil. Here we are concerned with Hobbes's natural philosophy. Later we will examine his "civil," or political, philosophy, which was enormously important.

Now, this business that all that exists is bodies in motion might sound plausible, until you consider such things as thoughts or acts of volition or emotion. Can it really be held that *thought* is just matter in motion? that *emotions* are? that *hatred* is? "Yes," said Hobbes.

## Perception

Hobbes's strategy was to show that there is a basic mental activity, **perception,** or, as he called it, "sense," from which all other mental phenomena are derived and that perception itself reduces to matter in motion.

Perception, he maintained, occurs as follows: Motion in the external world causes motion within us. This motion within (which Hobbes called a "phantasm") is experienced by us as an external object (or group of objects) having certain properties. The properties do not *really* exist in the objects, Hobbes said; they are just the way the objects *seem* to us:

> The things that really are in the world outside us are those motions by which these seemings are caused.

So motion outside us causes motion within us, which is a perception. If the internal motion remains for a while even after the external object is no longer present, it is then *imagination* or *memory*. And *thinking*, he said, is merely a sequence of these perceptions. (There are subtleties in his account of thinking we won't now bother with.)

Now humans, unlike animals (Hobbes said), are able to form signs or names (words) to designate perceptions, and it is this ability that allows humans to reason. In Hobbes's view, *reasoning* is nothing but "adding and subtracting of the consequences of general names." Reasoning occurs, for example, when you see that the consequences of the name *circle* are, among other things, that if a straight line is drawn through the center of a circle, the circle has been divided into two equal parts.

As for *decisions* and other voluntary actions, such as walking or speaking or moving our arms, these are all movements of the body that begin internally as "endeavors," caused by perceptions. When the endeavor is toward something that causes it, this is *desire;* when away from it, it is *aversion.* Love is merely desire, and hate merely aversion. We call a thing "good" when it is an object of desire, and "bad" when it is an object of aversion. *Deliberation* is simply an alternation of desires and aversions, and *will* is nothing but the last desire or aversion remaining in a deliberation.

We've left out the finer details of Hobbes's account, but this should show you how Hobbes tried to establish that every aspect of human psychology is a derivative of perception and that perception itself reduces to matter in motion.

This theory that all is matter in motion may well strike you as implausible, maybe even ridiculous. Nevertheless, as you will see in Chapter 9, it expresses in a rudimentary form a view that is quite attractive to many contemporary philosophers and brain scientists, namely, that every mental activity is a brain process of one sort or another. So let us try to focus on the difficulties in this theory that make it seem somewhat implausible.

## Difficulties in Hobbes's Theory

The most serious difficulty in Hobbes's theory is probably this: all psychological states, according to Hobbes, are derivatives of perception. Therefore, if there is anything wrong with his account of perception, there is something wrong with his entire account of mental states.

Now, according to Hobbes, perception is merely a movement of particles within the person, a movement of particles within that is caused by a movement of particles without. Thus, when I perceive a lawn (for instance), a movement of particles takes place within me that is the perception of a soft, green lawn, and this internal motion of particles is caused by the motion of particles outside me.

But here is the difficulty: when I look at the lawn, the internal movement (i.e., the perception) is not *itself* green and soft. Neither, according to Hobbes, is the lawn. So how is it that the internal movement of particles is experienced as a soft, green lawn? And, further, *what is it* that *experiences* the internal movement? The internal movement is, after all, just movement. In other words, *how* do the qualities of softness and greenness become apparent, and *to what* do they become apparent? Later, in Chapter 9, we will go into this difficulty in more detail, and we will see that it is still a problem even for the most up-to-date versions of materialism.

Hobbes's philosophy aroused considerable antagonism — the charge was that Hobbes was an atheist — and in his later years his work had to be printed outside his own country, in Amsterdam. Still, in the long run, and despite the entrenchment of Cartesian dualism in common sense, variations of Hobbes's materialist philosophy were and are accepted by some of the keenest intellects of philosophy and science. Many philosophers and scientists really do not believe that anything exists except matter.

## THE ALTERNATIVE VIEWS OF CONWAY, SPINOZA, AND LEIBNIZ

So much, then, for Descartes and dualism and Hobbes and materialism. We still need to discuss the remaining two perspectives listed at the beginning of this chapter, idealism and "alternative views." Since historically idealism was introduced last, we turn now to these alternative views — the three alternative metaphysical systems of Anne Conway, Benedictus de Spinoza, and Gottfried Wilhelm, Baron von Leibniz. It must be said that Spinoza and Leibniz had the greatest influence on subsequent developments, but we shall treat the three in chronological order.

# PROFILE: Anne Finch, The Viscountess Conway (1631–1679)

Like most women of the seventeenth century, Anne Conway, as she is usually called, had no formal education. Her father, who was Speaker of the House of Commons, died a week before Anne was born. But her family remained influential, her half-brother becoming Lord High Chancellor in England. So Anne Finch grew up knowing some of the most important and influential English intellectuals of her time. At home, she somehow managed to learn French, Latin, Hebrew, and Greek. She also studied mathematics and philosophy. She was critical of the work of Descartes (or "Cartes," as he was sometimes called), Hobbes, and Spinoza. And she discussed philosophy with some fairly well-known philosophers who lived in or visited England during her lifetime. The philosophical community was a small one there, and everybody in it seemed to know everybody else. She worked closely with some influential philosophers known as the Cambridge Platonists.

Anne Conway suffered from migraine headaches, and that is supposed to account for the un-

readable scrawl with which she penciled her book, *The Principles of the Most Ancient and Modern Philosophy*. Depending on which scholar you read, she wrote it either between 1671 and 1674 or between 1677 and 1679. She died without having a chance to correct or revise it. Her husband was away in Ireland at the time; and Francis Mercury von Helmont, her friend and one of the colleagues with whom she often discussed philosophy and religion, preserved her body in wine until her husband could return for the funeral.

Von Helmont had Conway's work translated into Latin and published in 1690. Two years later, it was translated back into English by somebody whose initials were J. C. Now, von Helmont was a good friend of Leibniz and showed him Conway's book. Scholars who have studied Conway's philosophy consider her to have been a forerunner of Leibniz in many ways.

## The Metaphysics of Anne Conway

The metaphysical system that **Anne Conway** (1631–1679) developed is a *monadology:* a view that all things are reducible to a single substance that is itself irreducible. (This is roughly what atomic theory was until the discovery of subatomic particles in the twentieth century.) The most famous monadology in the history of philosophy is that of Leibniz. Leibniz was familiar with Conway's metaphysics, and scholars believe Conway's philosophy was a forerunner of Leibniz's.

In Conway's view, there is a kind of continuum between the most material and the most mental or "spiritual" substances. All created substances ("Creatures," Conway called them) are both mental and physical to some degree or other. Conway also argued that all created substances are dependent on God's decision to create them. Moreover, she said that all such Creatures have both an individual essence (what makes one thing different from another) and an essence that is common to all. This essence in common is what later came to be known as *de re* modality. The idea of *de re* essentially means that a property (in this case, the property of being both mental and physical) must be a property of anything that is created by God; otherwise, it ceases to be what it is. It could not exist except that it is necessarily both mental and physical. Everything — persons, animals, plants, inanimate objects (furniture) — is a substance. And everything is partly physical and partly mental, and could not be otherwise.

God, of course, is another matter, Conway believed. God is nonmaterial, non-physical; God is also all-perfect. Therefore, the one thing God cannot do is change his mind about being spiritual. To change his mind and be physical one moment, spiritual the next, and maybe back again, would imply that one state or the other was less than perfect. What possible reason could God have to want to change? What's not to like? Now, that does not mean that God cannot be physical; he just does not *want* to be and never would want to be because that would suggest that he was not perfect before the change. And we all know that if God is anything, he is perfect. God created Christ (making God older than Christ), and Christ, God's first physical manifestation of himself (his first Creature), always had some degree of physical essence and some degree of mental or spiritual essence.

Because God is perfect, Conway held, he is changeless and therefore exists outside the dimension of time. Conway's concept of time is less technical than, but philosophically much like, that articulated recently by the great contemporary physicist Stephen Hawking in his book *A Brief History of Time,* according to whom (roughly) time is the succession of events. Conway called events "motions" and "operations" of created objects (Creatures). Understood this way, time is the measure of changes in things. Because creating (making Creatures) is part of God's primary essence (a necessary property — the way God defines himself, as creator), Conway's God is an eternal creator. The universe is therefore not something that was made at some specific time: it always existed because God always existed and he was always creating. Past and future are all God's present.

## Spinoza

God also played an important role in the philosophy of **Benedictus de Spinoza** [spin-O-zuh] (1632–1677), even though Spinoza was considered an atheist. About the time Hobbes was sending his work to Amsterdam for publication, Spinoza was completing his major work, *Ethics,* in that city. Holland, during this period of history, was the most intellectually tolerant of all European countries, sort of a seventeenth-century Berkeley, California. It was probably also the only country in which the government would have tolerated Spinoza's opinions, which, like Hobbes's, were considered atheistic and repulsive.

Spinoza's *Ethics* consists of some 250 "theorems," each of which he attempted to derive by rigorous deductive logic from a set of eight basic definitions and seven self-evident axioms. Given his axioms and definition of substance (that which depends on nothing else for its conception; i.e., that which is self-subsistent), Spinoza is able to prove that there are no multiple substances, as Descartes thought, but only one infinite substance. Spinoza equated this substance with God, but we must not be misled by his proof of God. Spinoza's "God" is simply *basic substance:* it is not the personal Judaeo-Christian God; rather, it is simply the sum total of everything that is. It is reality, nature. Although Spinoza was considered an atheist, he was not. On the contrary, he was a pantheist: God is all.

## PROFILE: Benedictus de Spinoza (1632–1677)

The gentle Spinoza was among the most ethical men ever to have lived. "As a natural consequence," twentieth-century philosopher Bertrand Russell observed, "he was considered, during his lifetime and for a century after his death, a man of appalling wickedness."

Spinoza's family was one of many Jewish families that fled Portugal for Holland to escape the terrors of the Inquisition. His serious nature and love of learning were appreciated by all until he pointed out that the Old Testament and biblical tradition were full of inconsistencies. This produced a venomous wrath in the Jewish community. At first Spinoza was offered an annual pension for concealing his doubts. When this failed, the logical next step was taken: an attempt was made to murder him. He was finally, of course, excommunicated from the synagogue.

For a time, Spinoza lived in the house of his Latin teacher, though he later rented a room in a tiny house in Rhynsburg, now a suburb of Leyden, where he earned a sparse living by grinding glass lenses. He lived a modest and frugal existence and preferred to work on his philosophy than to do anything else.

Spinoza became known despite his quiet and retiring existence, and at one point he was offered a professorship at Heidelberg. He declined the appointment, realizing that there would be restrictions on his academic freedom and fearing that his philosophy might draw sharp reactions in German society. In that suspicion he was probably correct, if the fact that many German professors referred to him as "that wretched monster" is any indication.

Still, after his death, some of the greatest thinkers eventually came to appreciate his depth. Hegel went so far as to say that all subsequent philosophy would be a kind of Spinozism.

Spinoza died when he was forty-four, from tuberculosis. His condition was aggravated by the glass dust that he was forced to breathe in his profession. Today, the society for out-of-work American philosophers is called "The Lensgrinders."

Because there is only one substance, according to Spinoza, thought and extension are not the attributes of two separate and distinct substances, mind and matter, as Descartes had thought. What they are, in Spinoza's system, are different attributes of the one basic substance—they are alternative ways of conceiving of it.

So a living person, from Spinoza's point of view, is not a composite of two different things. The living person is a single unit or "modification" of substance that can be conceived either as extension or as thought. Your "body" is a unit of substance conceived as extension; your "mind" is the selfsame unit of substance conceived as thought.

Because, according to Spinoza, the infinite substance is infinite in all respects, it necessarily has infinite attributes. Therefore, thought and extension are not the only attributes of substance. They are just the only attributes we know—they are the only ways available to us of characterizing or conceiving substance. They are, so to speak, the only "languages" in terms of which we can speak and think about reality or substance.

Accordingly, for Spinoza there is no problem in explaining how the mind interacts with the body, for they are one and the same thing. Wondering how the mind and the body interact is like wondering how your last glass of *wine* and your last glass of *vino* could mix with each other. The mind and the body are the same thing, conceptualized from different viewpoints.

In Spinoza's system, there is no personal immortality after death. Further, free will is an illusion; whatever happens is caused by the nature of substance. Material bodies are governed by the laws of physics, and what happens to them is completely determined by what happened before. Because the mental and the material are one and the same, what happens in minds is as inevitable as what happens in bodies. Everything was, is, and will be exactly as it must be.

There is certainly more to Spinoza's philosophy than this, but this is enough for our purposes here. Where Descartes had postulated two separate substances, both Hobbes and Spinoza postulated only one. For Hobbes, however, what exists is only material; a nonmaterial mental realm does not exist. For Spinoza, what exists is both material and mental, depending on how it is conceptualized. Thus, although neither Hobbes nor Spinoza is faced with Descartes's problem of explaining how two realms, the mental and the material, interact, Hobbes is faced with a different problem, that of *explaining away* the mental realm. We are inclined to ask Hobbes just how and why this illusory mental realm seems so clearly to be real when in fact it is not. For Spinoza, the mental realm is real, and there is nothing that he needs to explain away.

Before leaving Spinoza, we should mention that his philosophy is interesting not merely for its content but for its form as well. Spinoza attempted to geometrize philosophy to an extent unequaled by any other major philosopher.

Euclid began his *Elements* with a set of basic definitions and unproved postulates, and from them he logically derived a set of geometric theorems. Likewise, Spinoza began with definitions and seemingly self-evident axioms and proceeded to derive theorems or "propositions" from them.

For example, Spinoza's Proposition III states, "Things which have nothing in common cannot be one the cause of the other." And under that proposition Spinoza gives a proof that refers back to two of his axioms. Thus, giving Spinoza his definitions, and assuming his axioms are beyond doubt and that he made no mistakes in logic, every one of Spinoza's propositions — his *entire* philosophy — is beyond doubt! Spinoza, unlike Descartes, did not take the epistemological detour by explicitly asking, "What can be known?" But by geometrizing his philosophy, Spinoza attempted to provide a metaphysical system that could be known with certainty to be true.

## Leibniz

Many recent scholars qualified to make such a judgment think that **Gottfried Wilhelm, Baron von Leibniz** [LIBE-nits] (1646–1716), was the most brilliant intellect of his age. This judgment is made specifically with the fact in mind that Leibniz was the contemporary of a very bright light, Sir Isaac Newton (1642–1727). Leibniz and Newton, independently of each other, developed the calculus — and at the time, there was bitter controversy over who did so first. Leibniz's calculus was published in 1684, a few years before Newton's, but Newton had been

## Newtonians, Metaphysicians, and Émilie du Châtelet

One of the important intellectual controversies of the eighteenth century was whether there could be such a thing as action at a distance. On one hand were the Cartesians (followers of Descartes), who said that, if an object is to move, another object must *come up against it and push it.* On the other hand were the Newtonians (followers of Sir Isaac Newton), who believed in action at a distance—for example, two objects will attract one another through the force of gravity, even though they are separated by space. Cartesians generally viewed the concept of action at a distance, and the forces postulated to explain such action, as mystical and bizarre.

This controversy was just a minor skirmish in a broader conceptual battle, that between Newtonian empirical physics, which was based on observation and experimentation, and speculative metaphysics, which was grounded to a large extent purely on reason and was represented by the Cartesians and, most important, the brilliant Leibniz. According to the metaphysicians, even if Newtonian science described *how* the universe operates, it did not show *why* the universe must operate in that way. The metaphysicians felt that Newtonian physics lacked the rational grounding or certainty found in the systems of a Descartes or a Leibniz.

The metaphysical group had other problems with Newtonianism, too, such as how God fit into the Newtonian picture of the universe. If the universe is a vast physical machine, couldn't God change his mind and destroy it—maybe make a different machine? How could there be human free will if the Newtonians were right and humans are just small parts in God's big machine? Do humans have free will, can they do what they choose, or are they nothing more than bodies, moving in reaction to immaterial forces?

A major participant in the disputes between science and metaphysics was **Émilie du Châtelet** [SHA-ta-lay] (1707–1749). Du Châtelet, a colleague (and lover) of Voltaire, was both a scientist and a philosopher, and her writings were respected by both camps. Her two-volume annotated translation of Newton's *Mathematical Principles of Natural Philosophy* (1759) remains to this day *the* French translation of Newton.

In her three-volume work, *Institutions de Physique* (1740), du Châtelet sought to answer some of the metaphysicians' complaints about Newtonianism. She did this essentially by adapting Leibniz's metaphysical principles (for example, the principle of sufficient reason and the principle of the identity of indiscernibles) to Newtonian science in such a way as to provide, she hoped, a vigorous metaphysical foundation for it and to allay fears that Newtonianism required abandoning important theological tenets. Although du Châtelet perhaps did not resolve all the problems, it is safe to say that she did as much as anyone to bring to focus exactly what the bones of contention were.

slow in publishing his work. (Another controversy between the followers of both thinkers is discussed in the box "Newtonians, Metaphysicians, and Émilie du Châtelet.)

Because Leibniz's philosophy is highly technical and difficult to characterize or summarize in a brief passage, we won't go into it in detail. Basically, it is a complicated metaphysical system according to which the ultimate constituents of reality are indivisible atoms. But Leibniz's atoms are not indivisible units of matter, for, because matter is extended, a piece of matter, however tiny, is always further divisible. Instead, Leibniz's atoms are what he called **monads,** which are indivisible units of force or energy or activity. Here, Leibniz anticipated by a couple of centuries the views of contemporary physics, according to which material particles are a form of energy. Leibniz, however, believed the monads to be entirely *nonphysical* and often referred to them as "souls," though he distinguished them from souls in the ordinary sense.

Leibniz's philosophy is not just haphazard or idle speculation. His entire metaphysical system seems to follow from a few basic and plausible assumptions, or basic principles. One of these principles, for example, the **principle of the identity of indiscernibles,** says that if two beings have exactly the same set of properties, then they are identical with one another. Another principle, known as the **principle of sufficient reason,** says that there is a sufficient reason why things are exactly as they are and are not otherwise. Leibniz also used this principle as a proof of God, as we shall see in Chapter 13.

Leibniz's most famous work is the *Monadology.*

## THE IDEALISM OF LOCKE AND BERKELEY

Descartes, Hobbes, Conway, and Spinoza all belonged to the lively seventeenth century, the century that produced not only great philosophy but also some of the most important scientific discoveries of all time. The seventeenth century, you may recall from your history books, was also the century of the Thirty Years' War (1618–1648), which was the most brutal European war before this century and the English Civil War. It also witnessed the Sun King (Louis XIV of France), the opening of Harvard, the founding of Pennsylvania, and the popularization of smoking.

In England the most important philosopher of the time was **John Locke** (1632–1704). In his great work, *An Essay Concerning Human Understanding,* Locke wished to inquire into the origin, certainty, and extent of human knowledge. Many of his views will almost certainly be shared by most readers of this book. Locke's epistemology is indeed so widely accepted that much of it is now thought to be so much common sense. You should be prepared, however — terrible philosophical difficulties attend Locke's basic position, as commonsensical as it will probably seem.

### John Locke and Representative Realism

Locke's fundamental thesis is that all our ideas come from experience. The human mind at birth, he wrote (echoing Aristotle), is essentially a *tabula rasa,* or blank slate. On this blank slate, experience makes its imprint. External objects impinge on our senses, which convey into the mind ideas, or, as we might prefer to say today, perceptions, of these objects and their various qualities. In short, sensation furnishes the mind with all its contents. ***Nihil in intellectu quod prius non fuerit in sensu*** — nothing exists in the mind that was not first in the senses. This, of course, is familiar and plausible.

These ideas or perceptions of some of the qualities of external objects are accurate copies of qualities that actually reside in the objects, Locke said. This is what he means. Think of a basketball. It has a certain size, shape, and weight, and when we look at and handle the ball, our sensory apparatus provides us with accurate pictures or images or ideas or perceptions of these "primary" qualities, as Locke called them.

*Locke's Theory:* According to Locke, when we say we are looking at an external object, what we are really doing is attending to the perceptions or "ideas" of the object in our mind. Some of these perceptions, such as those of a basketball's size and shape, accurately represent qualities in the object itself. Other perceptions, such as those of the basketball's color and odor, do not represent anything in the object.

The basketball also has the power to produce in us ideas of "secondary" qualities, such as the brown color, the leathery smell, the coolness we feel when we hold it, and so forth. Are these qualities really in the basketball? Well, of course, you will say. And that is exactly what Locke said. These secondary qualities do not exist in the basketball except as the powers of the basketball to produce in us ideas of color and taste and so forth — but the color and taste are purely subjective and exist in us merely as ideas. In other words, in Locke's view — and we will bet that this is your view as well — if all sentient creatures were removed from the proximity of the basketball, there would not *be* any brownness, leathery odor, or coolness, but only an object of a certain size and shape and weight, composed of minute particles that collectively would smell leathery and feel cool and look brown if any creatures with sense organs then came into existence and held and looked at and sniffed the ball.

This theory that Locke accepted is often called **representative realism.** In a sentence, it is the theory that we perceive objects *indirectly* by means of our "representations" or ideas or perceptions of them, some of which are accurate copies or representations or reflections of the real properties of "external" objects, of objects "outside the mind." This theory is widely held and is probably regarded by most people as self-evident. Open almost any introductory psychology text, and you will behold implicit in its discussion of perception Locke's theory of representative realism.

Now, we said a moment ago that terrible philosophical difficulties attend to this very nice, down-to-earth, commonsense theory known as representative realism, and it is time for us to explain ourselves. As justifiable as Locke's theory may seem, it is subject to a powerful objection, stated most eloquently by the Irish bishop and philosopher George Berkeley.

## George Berkeley and Idealism

If Locke is correct, then we experience sensible things, things like basketballs and garden rakes, *indirectly* — that is, through the intermediary of our ideas or perceptions. But if that is true, **George Berkeley** [BAR-klee] (1685–1753) said, then we

## PROFILE: George Berkeley (1685–1753)

Berkeley was born in Ireland and studied at Trinity College, Dublin. He was made a Fellow of the College in 1707. His *Treatise Concerning the Principles of Human Knowledge* (1709) was a great success and gave Berkeley a lasting reputation, though few accepted his theory that nothing exists outside the mind.

Berkeley eventually obtained a post that included a lucrative stipend. But he gave up the post in what proved to be a futile attempt to establish a college in the Bermudas to convert the Indians in North America. He was made Bishop of Cloyne in 1734.

Berkeley was known for his generosity of heart and mind, and also for his enthusiasm for tar water (water made from pine tar). He especially liked the fact that tar water did not have the same effects as alcohol. His writings about the health benefits of drinking tar water actually caused it to become a fad in English society for a time.

Berkeley's main works, in addition to the one already mentioned, are *Essay Towards a New Theory of Vision* (1709) and *Three Dialogues between Hylas and Philonous* (1713).

cannot know that *any* of our ideas or perceptions accurately represent the qualities of these sensible things. Why can't we know this? Because, Berkeley argued, if Locke is correct, we do not directly experience the basketball (or any other object) itself. Instead, what we directly experience is our *perceptions* and *ideas* of the basketball. And if we do not have direct experience of the basketball itself, then we cannot compare our perceptions or ideas of the basketball with the basketball itself to see if they "accurately represent" the basketball's qualities.

Indeed, given Locke's position, Berkeley said, we cannot really know that a thing like a basketball or a garden rake even *exists*. For according to Locke's theory, it is not the *object* we experience but, rather, our *perceptions* or *ideas* of it.

This, then, is Berkeley's criticism of Locke's theory. As satisfying as it might seem to common sense, Locke's position is the short road to skepticism. If we accept Locke's theory, then we cannot know that "sensible things," things like basketballs and rakes and even our own hands and feet, actually exist.

Berkeley began his criticism of Locke's theory by noting that the objects of human knowledge consist of "ideas" (1) conveyed to the mind through the senses (sense perceptions), (2) perceived by the mind when the mind reflects on its own operations, or (3) compounded or divided by the mind with the help of memory and imagination. "Light and colors, heat and cold, extension (length) and figures (shapes)—in a word the things we see and feel—what are they but so many sensations, notions, ideas, or impressions on the sense?"

There exist, therefore, Berkeley said, ideas and the minds that have them. However, Berkeley observed, people have the strange opinion that houses, mountains, rivers, and all sensible objects have an existence outside the mind. But that is a contradictory opinion, Berkeley suggested. "For what are the forementioned objects but the things we perceive by sense? And what do we perceive besides our own

## Rationalism and Empiricism

A doctrine that St. Thomas Aquinas (see Chapter 5) accepted and attributed to Aristotle, and that John Locke also accepted, is *nihil in intellectu quod prius non fuerit in sensu;* that is, there is nothing in the intellect that was not first in the senses. This doctrine is called **empiricism.** Another doctrine, known as **rationalism,** holds that the intellect contains important truths that were not placed there by sensory experience. "Something never comes from nothing," for example, might count as one of these truths, because experience can tell you only that something has never come from nothing so far, not that it can never, ever happen (or so a rationalist might argue). Sometimes rationalists believe in a *theory of innate ideas,* according to which these truths are "innate" to the mind — that is, they are part of the original dispositions of the intellect.

The empiricist is, in effect, a type of modified skeptic — he or she denies that there is any knowledge that does not stem from sensory experience. Most rationalists, by contrast, do not deny that *some* knowledge about the world can be obtained through experience. But other rationalists, such as Parmenides (see Chapter 2), deny that experience can deliver up any sort of true knowledge. This type of rationalist is also a type of modified skeptic.

Classical rationalism and empiricism in modern philosophy were mainly a product of the seventeenth and eighteenth centuries. Rationalism is associated most significantly during that time period with Descartes (1596–1650), Spinoza (1632–1677), and Leibniz (1646–1716). These three are often called the *Continental rationalists* and are contrasted with Locke (1632–1704), Berkeley (1685–1753), and Hume (1711–1776), the *British empiricists.* (We discuss Hume in the next chapter.) Philosophers from other periods, however, are sometimes classified as rationalists or empiricists depending on whether they emphasized the importance of reason or experience in knowledge of the world. Those earlier philosophers treated in this book who are usually listed as rationalists are, among others, Pythagoras, Parmenides, and Plato. Those who are often listed as empiricists are Aristotle, Epicurus, and Aquinas. Immanuel Kant (1724–1804), also discussed in the next chapter, is said to have synthesized rationalism and empiricism because he believed that all knowledge *begins* with experience (a thesis empiricists agree with) but also believed that knowledge is not limited to what has been found in experience (a thesis rationalists agree with).

Modern epistemology, as you will see, has been predominantly empiricist. This is because the Continental rationalists, and later rationalists too, were primarily metaphysicians. That is to say, they were generally less concerned with discussing the possibility of knowledge and related issues than with actually coming to propose some philosophically important theory about reality. The great exception is Descartes, a rationalist who concerned himself explicitly with the possibility of knowledge.

ideas or sensations? And is it not plainly contradictory that any one of these, or any combination of them, should exist unperceived?"

At this point, John Locke's theory kicks in and says that our ideas of *primary* qualities (extension, figure, motion, and so on) *represent* to us or *resemble* properties that exist outside the mind in an inert, senseless substance called matter. "But it is evident," Berkeley wrote, "that extension, figure, and motion are only ideas existing in the mind and consequently cannot exist in an unperceiving substance."

Common sense, of course, tells us that the so-called secondary qualities such as tastes, odors, and colors, exist only in the mind because, after all, what tastes sweet or smells good or seems red to one person will taste bitter or smell bad or seem green to another person. But, Berkeley argued, "let anyone consider those ar-

## Berkeley's Argument Analyzed

Berkeley obviously did not just assert dogmatically, without reason, that sensible things are in fact groups of ideas. He had *arguments* for his view, as set forth in the selections. His main arguments may be analytically summarized as follows:

1. What we experience are sensations or ideas.

2. Among the things we experience are size and shape.

3. Therefore, size and shape are sensations or ideas.

4. Hence, it is self-contradictory to say that objects do not have sensations or ideas but do have size and shape. [For size and shape are sensations or ideas.]

5. Hence objects, conceived of as things that do not have sensations or ideas but do have size and shape, cannot exist.

6. Thus, because objects, conceived in this way, cannot exist, they must just *be* clusters of ideas or sensations. To be, Berkeley wrote, is to be perceived: *esse est percipi*.

In this argument, (6) follows from (5), and (5) follows from (4), which follows from (3), which follows from (2) and (1). Because (2) seems indisputable, the entire argument rests on (1).

Can (1) be challenged? Well, try to do so. You might contend (a) that we never experience sensations or ideas. (But is this silly?) Or you might contend (b) that some of the items we experience are sensations or ideas but that others are not. (But then how would we distinguish one from the other?) Or finally, you might contend (c) that although the only things we experience are sensations or ideas, at least some of these *warrant the inference* that external bodies exist. Option (c), of course, is John Locke's representative realism, which leaves it entirely mysterious how our sensations do warrant such an inference, if, according to (c), we experience only sensations, never objects.

If you are not wholly satisfied with any of the options (a), (b), or (c), *or* with Berkeley's argument, you have company, including the next great philosopher after Berkeley, David Hume.

guments which are thought to prove that colors and tastes exist only in the mind, and he shall find they may with equal force prove the same thing of extention, figure, and motion." In other words, extension, figure, and motion are relative to the observer, too. A cookie, for example, might taste sweet to one taster and bitter to another; but its shape will be elliptical to an observer viewing it from the side and round to an observer viewing it straight on, and its size will be smaller to an observer farther away.

Of course, our inclination is to distinguish the *perceived* size and shape of a cookie from the size and shape that are the cookie's "true" size and shape. But Berkeley pointed out that size and shape (and the other qualities) *are* perceived qualities. Talking about an *unperceived* size or shape is nonsense. It is like talking about unfelt pain. And thus sensible objects, because they are nothing more than their qualities, are themselves only ideas and exist only in the mind.

But, you may still insist (in frustration?), surely there are material things "out there" that have their own size, shape, texture, and the like! Well, Berkeley has already responded to this line of thought: it is contradictory to suppose that size, shape, texture, and so on could exist in unthinking things. Size, shape, texture, and so on are *ideas,* and it is silly to suppose that ideas could exist in unthinking things.

Berkeley's main argument is paraphrased in the box "Berkeley's Argument Analyzed."

Telegraph Avenue on Berkeley, California. Berkeley was named after George Berkeley because of his line of poetry, "Westward the course of empire takes its way."

## Material Things as Clusters of Ideas

This theory of Berkeley's is idealism, the last of the four metaphysical philosophies. There are other versions of idealism, but in Berkeley's version, sensible things such as tables, chairs, trees, books, and frogs, are not material things that exist outside the mind. They are, in fact, groups of ideas and as such are perceived directly and exist only within the mind. Because they are ideas, we can no more doubt their existence than we can doubt our own aches and pains (which also, indeed, are ideas).

Berkeley's idealism does not mean, however, that the physical world is a mere dream or that it is imaginary or intangible or ephemeral. Dr. Samuel Johnson (1709–1784), the famous English literary critic and scholar, believed that he had refuted Berkeley by kicking a stone, evidently thinking that the solidity of the stone was solid disproof of Berkeley. In fact, Johnson succeeded only in hurting his foot and demonstrating that he did not understand Berkeley. A stone is just as hard an object in Berkeley's philosophy as it is to common sense, for the fact that a stone exists only in the mind does not make its hardness disappear.

As for the stones found in dreams, Berkeley distinguished unreal dream stones from real stones just the way you and we do. Stones found in dreams behave in an irregular and chaotic manner — they can float around or change into birds or whatever — compared with those found in waking life. And Berkeley distinguished stones that we conjure up in our imagination from real stones by their lack of vividness and also by the fact that they, unlike real stones, can be brought into existence by an act of our will.

## Berkeley and Atheism

So Berkeley's position is that sensible things cannot exist independent of perception — to be is to be perceived (***esse est percipi***). What, then, happens to this desk when everyone leaves the room? What happens to the forest when all the people go away? What happens to sensible things when no one perceives them?

Berkeley's answer is that the perceiving mind of God makes possible the continued existence of sensible things when neither you nor any other people are perceiving them. Because sensible things do not depend on the perception of humans and exist independently of them, Berkeley wrote, "There must be some other mind wherein they exist." This other mind, according to Berkeley, is God.

Berkeley believed that the greatest virtue of his idealist system was that it alone did not invite skepticism about God. Dualism, he thought, by postulating the existence of objects outside the mind, made these objects unknowable and was just an open invitation to skepticism about their existence; skepticism about the existence of sensible objects, he thought, would inevitably extend itself to skepticism about their creator, God. Materialism, he believed, made sensible objects independent of God; and thus it, too, led to skepticism about God. His own system, he thought, by contrast made the existence of sensible objects undeniable (they are as undeniable as your own ideas). This meant for Berkeley that the existence of the divine mind, in which sensible objects are sustained, was equally undeniable.

So, for Berkeley, the fact that sensible things continue to exist when we do not perceive them is a short and simple proof of God's existence. Another similar proof, in Berkeley's view, can be derived from the fact that we do not ourselves cause our ideas of tables, chairs, mountains, and other sensible things. "There is therefore," he reasoned, "some other will or spirit that produced them" — God.

Berkeley was aware that his theory that what we call material things are ideas both in God's mind and in our own raises peculiar questions about the relationship between our minds and the mind of God. For example, if a mountain is an idea in God's mind and we perceive the mountain, does that mean we perceive or have God's ideas?

With Berkeley, Hobbes, Descartes, and Spinoza, the four basic metaphysical perspectives of modern philosophy were set out: reality is entirely physical (Hobbes), *or* it is entirely nonphysical or "mental" (Berkeley), *or* it is an even split (Descartes), *or* "matter" and "mind" are just alternative ways of looking at one and the same stuff (Spinoza).

An alternative, epistemological classification of these philosophers was given in the box "Rationalism and Empiricism."

## SELECTION 6.1

# Meditations on First Philosophy*

*René Descartes*

[*Descartes's* Meditations on First Philosophy *is among the most widely read books of all time—right up there, almost, with Plato's* Republic. *In this selection, Descartes is trying to doubt everything that can be doubted and finds that almost everything that he previously thought he knew for certain is actually open to question.*]

Reason persuades me that I ought no less carefully to withhold my assent from matters which are not entirely certain and indubitable than from those which appear to me manifestly to be false. . . .

All that up to the present time I have accepted as most true and certain I have learned either from the senses or through the senses; [and], although the senses sometimes deceive us concerning things which are hardly perceptible, or very far away, there are yet many others to be met with as to which we cannot reasonably have any doubt. . . .

For example, there is the fact that I am here, seated by the fire, attired in a dressing gown, having this paper in my hands and other similar matters. And how could I deny that these hands and this body are "mine[?] . . ."

At the same time I must remember that . . . I am in the habit of sleeping and in my dreams representing to myself the same things. . . . How often has it happened to me that in the night I dreamt that I found myself in this particular place, that I was dressed and seated near the fire, while in reality I was lying undressed in bed! At this moment it does indeed seem to me that it is with eyes awake that I am looking at this paper. . . . But in thinking over this I remind myself that on many occasions I have in sleep been deceived by similar illusions, and in dwelling carefully on this reflection I see . . . that there are no certain indications by which we may clearly distinguish wakefulness from sleep. . . .

*Rene Descartes, "Meditations on First Philosophy" from *The Philosophical Works of Descartes,* translated by Elizabeth S. Haldane and G. R. T. Ross, Vol. 1 (Cambridge: The University Press, 1911).

At the same time we must at least confess that . . . whether I am awake or asleep, two and three together always form five, and the square can never have more than four sides, and it does not seem possible that truths so clear and apparent can be suspected of any falsity.

Nevertheless . . . how do I know that I am not deceived every time that I add two and three, or count the sides of a square, or judge of things yet simpler, if anything simpler can be imagined? . . . Possibly God has not desired that I should be thus deceived, for He is said to be supremely good. . . . But let us . . . grant that all that is here said of a God is a fable. . . . I shall then suppose, not that God who is supremely good and the fountain of truth, but some evil genius not less powerful than deceitful, has employed his whole energies in deceiving me; I shall consider that the heavens, the earth, colors, figures, sound, and all other external things are nought but the illusions and dreams of which this genius has availed himself in order to lay traps for my credulity; I shall consider myself as having no hands, no eyes, no flesh, no blood, nor any senses, yet falsely believing myself to possess all these things. . . .

[Yet even if] there is some deceiver or other, very powerful and very cunning, who ever employs his ingenuity in deceiving me[,] then without a doubt I exist also if he deceives me, and let him deceive me as much as he will, he can never cause me to be nothing so long as I think that I am something. So that after having reflected well and carefully examined all things, we must come to the definite conclusion that this proposition: I am, I exist, is necessarily true each time that I pronounce it, or that I mentally conceive it.

But what am I, now that I suppose that there is a certain genius which is extremely powerful, and, if I may say so, malicious, who employs all his powers in deceiving me? Can I affirm that I possess the least of all those things which I have just said pertain to the nature of body? I pause to consider, I revolve all these things in my mind, and I find none of which I can say that it pertains to me. It would be tedious to stop to enumerate them. Let us pass to the attributes of soul and see if there is any one which is in me? What of nutrition or walking [the first mentioned]? But if it is so that I have no body it is also true that I can neither walk nor take nourishment. Another attribute is sensation. But one cannot feel without body, and besides I have thought I perceived many things during sleep that I recognised in my waking moments as not having been experienced at all. What of thinking? I find here that thought is an attribute that belongs to me; it alone cannot be separated from me. I am, I exist, that is certain. But how often? Just when I think; for it might possibly be the case if I ceased entirely to think, that I should likewise cease altogether to exist. I do not now admit anything which is not necessarily true: to speak accurately I am not more than a thing which thinks, that is to say a mind or a soul, or an understanding, or a reason, which are terms whose significance was formerly unknown to me. I am, however, a real thing and really exist; but what thing? I have answered: a thing which thinks. . . . What is a thing which thinks? It is a thing which doubts, understands, [conceives], affirms, denies, wills, refuses, which also imagines and feels. . . .

. . . [I]n the little that I have just said, I think I have summed up all that I really know, or at least all that hitherto I was aware that I knew. In order to try to extend my knowledge further, I shall now look around more carefully and see whether I cannot still discover in myself some other things which I have not hitherto perceived. I am certain that I am a thing which thinks; but do I not then likewise know what is requisite to render me certain of a truth? Certainly in this first knowledge there is nothing that assures me of its truth, excepting the clear and distinct perception of that which I state, which would not indeed suffice to assure me that what I say is true, if it could ever happen that a thing which I conceived so clearly and distinctly could be false; and accordingly it seems to me that already I can establish as a general rule that all things which I perceive very clearly and very distinctly are true.

[*At this point in the* Meditations, *Descartes proves to his own satisfaction that he perceives clearly and distinctly that God exists and that God would never permit Descartes to be deceived as long as Descartes forms no judgment except on matters clearly and distinctly represented to Descartes by his understanding. He then continues:*]

Because I know that all things which I apprehend clearly and distinctly can be created by God as I apprehend them, it suffices that I am able to apprehend one thing apart from another clearly and distinctly in order to be certain that the one is different from the other, since they may be made to exist in separation at least by the omnipotence of God . . . and therefore, just because I know certainly that I exist, and that meanwhile I do not remark that any other thing necessarily pertains to my nature of essence, excepting that I am a thinking thing, I rightly conclude that my essence consists solely in the fact that I am a thinking thing . . . [and as] I possess a distinct idea of body, inasmuch as it is only an extended and unthinking thing, it is certain that this I is entirely and absolutely distinct from my body, and can exist without it. . . .

There is certainly further in me a certain passive faculty of perception, that is, of receiving and recognising the ideas of sensible things, but this would be useless to me, if there were not either in me or in some other thing another active faculty capable of forming and producing these ideas. . . . [A]nd since God is no deceiver, [and since] He has given me . . . a very great inclination to believe that [these ideas] are conveyed to me by corporeal objects, I do not see how He could be defended from the accusation of deceit if these ideas were produced by causes other than corporeal objects. Hence we must allow that corporeal things exist. . . . [And] we must at least admit that all things which I conceive in them clearly and distinctly, that is to say, all things which, speaking generally, are comprehended in the object of pure mathematics, are truly to be recognised as external objects. . . .

[O]n the sole Ground that God is not a deceiver . . . there is no doubt that in all things which nature teaches me there is some truth contained. . . . But there is nothing which this nature teaches me more expressly than that I have a body which is adversely affected when I feel pain, which has need of food or drink when I experience the feelings of hunger and thirst, and so on; nor can I doubt there being some truth in all this.

Nature also teaches me by these sensations of pain, hunger, thirst, etc., that I am not only lodged in my body as a pilot in a vessel, but that I am very closely united to it, and so to speak so intermingled with it that I seem to compose with it one whole. For if that were not the case, when my body is hurt, I, who am merely a thinking thing, would not feel pain, for I should perceive this wound by the understanding only, just as the sailor perceives by sight when something is damaged in his vessel. . . .

[T]here is a great difference between mind and body, inasmuch as body is by nature always divisible, and the mind is entirely indivisible. For, as a matter of fact, when I consider the mind, that is to say, myself inasmuch as I am only a thinking thing, I cannot distinguish in myself any parts, but apprehend myself to be clearly one and entire; and although the whole mind seems to be united to the whole body, yet if a foot, or an arm, or some other part, is separated from my body, I am aware that nothing has been taken away from my mind. And the faculties of willing, feeling, conceiving, etc.,

cannot be properly speaking said to be its parts, for it is one and the same mind which employs itself in willing and in feeling and understanding. But it is quite otherwise with corporeal or extended objects, for there is not one of these imaginable by me which my mind cannot easily divide into parts, and which consequently I do not recognise as being divisible. [T]his would be sufficient to teach me that the mind or soul of man is entirely different from the body, if I had not already learned it from other sources.

I further notice that the mind does not receive the impressions from all parts of the body immediately, but only from the brain, or perhaps even from one of its smallest parts, to wit, from that in which the common sense is said to reside.

## SELECTION 6.2
# Ethics
*Benedictus de Spinoza*

[*This excerpt will give you a good idea of Spinoza's geometric method in which metaphysical certainties ("Proportions") are deduced from a short list of "Definitions" and self-evident "axioms."*]

## Definitions and Axioms

*Definitions*   I. By that which is *self-caused,* I mean that of which the essence involves existence, or that of which the nature is only conceivable as existent.

II. A thing is called *finite after its kind,* when it can be limited by another thing of the same nature; for instance, a body is called finite because we always conceive another greater body. So, also, a thought is limited by another thought, but a body is not limited by thought, nor a thought by body

III. By *substance,* I mean that which is in itself, and is conceived through itself: in other words, that of which a conception can be formed independently of any other conception.

IV. By *attribute,* I mean that which the intellect perceives as constituting the essence of substance.

V. By *mode,* I mean the modifications of substance, or that which exists in, and is conceived through, something other than itself.

VI. By *God,* I mean a being absolutely infinite — that is, a substance consisting in infinite attributes, of which each expresses eternal and infinite essentiality.

*Explanation.*—I say absolutely infinite, not infinite after its kind: for, of a thing infinite only after its kind, infinite attributes may be denied; but that which is absolutely infinite, contains in its essence whatever expresses reality, and involves no negation.

VII. That thing is called free, which exists solely by the necessity of its own nature, and of which the action is determined by itself alone. On the other hand, that thing is necessary, or rather constrained, which is determined by something external to itself to a fixed and definite method of existence or action.

VIII. By *eternity,* I mean existence itself, in so far as it is conceived necessarily to follow solely from the definition of that which is eternal.

*Explanation.*—Existence of this kind is conceived as an eternal truth, like the essence of a thing, and, therefore, cannot be explained by means of contin-

*From *The Chief Works of Benedictus de Spinoza,* Vol 2, revised edition, translated by R. H. M. Elwes (London: George Bell & Sons, 1901), 45–48.

uance or time, though continuance may be conceived without a beginning or end.

*Axioms* I. Everything which exists, exists either in itself or in something else.

II. That which cannot be conceived through anything else must be conceived through itself.

III. From a given definite cause an effect necessarily follows; and, on the other hand, if no definite cause be granted, it is impossible that an effect can follow.

IV. The knowledge of an effect depends on and involves the knowledge of a cause.

V. Things which have nothing in common cannot be understood, the one by means of the other; the conception of one does not involve the conception of the other.

VI. A true idea must correspond with its ideate or object.

VII. If a thing can be conceived as non-existing, its essence does not involve existence.

## Seven Propositions on Substance

*Propositions* PROP. I. *Substance is by nature prior to its modifications.*

*Proof.*—This is clear from Defs. iii. and v.

PROP. II. *Two substances, whose attributes are different, have nothing in common.*

*Proof.*—Also evident from Def. iii. For each must exist in itself, and be conceived through itself; in other words, the conception of one does not imply the conception of the other.

PROP. III. *Things which have nothing in common cannot be one the cause of the other.*

*Proof.*—If they have nothing in common, it follows that one cannot be apprehended by means of the other (Ax. v.), and, therefore, one cannot be the cause of the other (Ax. iv.). *Q.E.D.*

PROP. IV. *Two or more distinct things are distinguished one from the other, either by the difference of the attributes of the substances or by the difference of their modifications.*

*Proof.*—Everything which exists, exists either in itself or in something else (Ax. i.),—that is (by Defs. iii. and v.), nothing is granted in addition to the understanding, except substance and its modifications. Nothing is, therefore, given besides the understanding, by which several things may be dis-

tinguished one from the other, except the substances, or, in other words (see Ax. iv.), their attributes and modifications. *Q.E.D.*

PROP. V. *There cannot exist in the universe two or more substances having the same nature or attribute.*

*Proof.*—If several distinct substances be granted, they must be distinguished one from the other, either by the difference of their attributes, or by the difference of their modifications (Prop. iv.): If only by the difference of their attributes, it will be granted that there cannot be more than one with an identical attribute. If by the difference of their modifications—as substance is naturally prior to its modifications (Prop. i.),—it follows that setting the modifications aside, and considering substance in itself, that is truly (Defs. iii. and vi.), there cannot be conceived one substance different from another,—that is (by Prop. iv.), there cannot be granted several substances, but one substance only. *Q.E.D.*

PROP. VI. *One substance cannot be produced by another substance.*

*Proof.*—It is impossible that there should be in the universe two substances with an identical attribute, i.e., which have anything common to them both (Prop. ii.), and, therefore (Prop. iii.), one cannot be the cause of another, neither can one be produced by the other. *Q.E.D.*

*Corollary.*—Hence it follows that a substance cannot be produced by anything external to itself. For in the universe nothing is granted, save substances and their modifications (as appears from Ax. i. and Defs. iii. and v.). Now (by she last Prop.) substance cannot be produced by another substance, therefore it cannot be produced by anything external to itself. *Q.E.D.* This is shown still more readily by the absurdity of the contradictory. For, if substance be produced by an external cause, the knowledge of it would depend on the knowledge of its cause (Ax. iv.), and (by Def. iii.) it would itself not be substance.

PROP. VII. *Existence belongs to the nature of substance.*

*Proof.*—Substance cannot be produced by anything external (Corollary Prop. vi.), it must, therefore, be its own cause—that is, its essence necessarily involves existence, or existence belongs to its nature.

## SELECTION 6.3

# Treatise Concerning the Principles of Human Knowledge

*George Berkeley*

[*Berkeley's philosophy—that what we call material objects are really just ideas in the mind—strikes newcomers to philosophy as bizarre and preposterous. In this selection, Berkeley defends his view through a series of arguments and rebuttals to those who would disagree with him. Enjoy Berkeley's direct and powerful and elegant English.*]

It is evident to anyone who takes a survey of the objects of human knowledge, that they are either ideas (1) actually imprinted on the senses, or else such as are (2) perceived by attending to the passions and operations of the mind, or lastly (3) ideas formed by help of memory and imagination, either compounding, dividing, or barely representing those originally perceived in the aforesaid ways. By sight I have the ideas of lights and colors, with their several degrees and variations. By touch I perceive hard and soft, heat and cold, motion and resistance, and of all these more and less either as to quantity or degree. Smelling furnishes me with odors, the palate with tastes, and hearing conveys sounds to the mind in all their variety of tone and composition. And as several of these are observed to accompany each other, they come to be marked by one name, and so to be reputed as one thing. Thus, for example, a certain color, taste, smell, figure, and consistence, having been observed to go together, are accounted one distinct thing, signified by the name "apple." Other collections of ideas constitute a stone, a tree, a book, and the like sensible things. . . .

2. But besides all that endless variety of ideas or objects of knowledge, there is likewise something which knows or perceives them, and exercises divers operations, as willing, imagining, remembering, about them. This perceiving, active being is what I call mind, spirit, soul, or myself. By which words I do not denote any one of my ideas, but a thing entirely distinct from them wherein they exist, or, which is the same thing, whereby they are perceived; for the existence of an idea consists in being perceived.

3. That neither our thoughts, nor passions, nor ideas formed by the imagination, exist without the mind, is what everybody will allow. And it seems no less evident that the various sensations or ideas imprinted on the sense, however blended or combined together (that is, whatever objects they compose), cannot exist otherwise than in a mind perceiving them. . . .

4. It is indeed an opinion strangely prevailing amongst men, that houses, mountains, rivers, and in a word all sensible objects, have an existence, natural or real, distinct from their being perceived by the understanding. But with how great an assurance and acquiescence soever this principle may be entertained in the world, yet whoever shall find in his heart to call it in question may, if I mistake not, perceive it to involve a manifest contradiction. For what are the forementioned objects but the things we perceive by sense? and what do we perceive besides our own ideas or sensations? and is it not plainly repugnant that any one of these, or any combination of them, should exist unperceived?

5. Light and colors, heat and cold, extension and figures—in a word the things we see and feel—what are they but so many sensations, notions, ideas, or impressions on the sense? And is it possible to separate, even in thought, any of these from perception? . . .

8. But, say you, though the ideas themselves do not exist without the mind, yet there may be things like them, whereof they are copies or resemblances, which things exist without the mind in an unthinking substance. I answer, an idea can be like nothing but an idea; a color or figure can be like nothing but another color or figure. . . . Again, I ask whether those supposed originals or external things, of which our ideas are the pictures or representations, be themselves perceivable or no? If they are, then they are ideas and we have gained our point; but if you say they are not, I appeal to anyone whether it be sense to assert a color is like something which is in-

visible; hard or soft, like something which is intangible; and so of the rest.

9. Some there are who make a distinction betwixt primary and secondary qualities. By the former they mean extension, figure, motion, test, solidity or impenetrability, and number; by the latter they denote all other sensible qualities, as colors, sounds, tastes, and so forth. The ideas we have of these they acknowledge not to be the resemblances of anything existing without the mind, or unperceived, but they will have our ideas of the primary qualities to be patterns or images of things which exist without the mind, in an unthinking substance which they call matter. By matter, therefore, we are to understand an inert, senseless substance, in which extension, figure, and motion do actually subsist. But it is evident from what we have already shown, that extension, figure, and motion are only ideas existing in the mind, and that an idea can be like nothing but another idea, and that consequently neither they nor their archetypes can exist in an unperceiving substance. Hence, it is plain that the very notion of what is called matter, or corporeal substance, involves a contradiction in it.

10. They who assert that figure, motion, and the rest of the primary or original qualities do exist without the mind in unthinking substances, do at the same time acknowledge that color, sounds, heat, cold, and such-like secondary qualities, do not; which they tell us are sensations existing in the mind alone. . . . Now, if it be certain that those original qualities are inseparably united with the other sensible qualities, and not, even in thought, capable of being abstracted from them, it plainly follows that they exist only in the mind. But I desire anyone to reflect and try whether he can, by any abstraction of thought, conceive the extension and motion of a body without all other sensible qualities. For my own part, I see evidently that it is not in my power to frame an idea of a body extended and moving, but I must withal give it some color or other sensible quality which is acknowledged to exist only in the mind. In short, extension, figure, and motion, abstracted from all other qualities, are inconceivable. Where therefore the other sensible qualities are, there must these be also, to wit, in the mind and nowhere else.

11. Again, great and small, swift and slow, are allowed to exist nowhere without the mind, being entirely relative, and changing as the frame or position of the organs of sense varies. The extension therefore which exists without the mind is neither great nor small, the motion neither swift nor slow, that is, they are nothing at all. . . .

12. That number is entirely the creature of the mind, even though the other qualities be allowed to exist without, will be evident to whoever considers that the same thing bears a different denomination of number as the mind views it with different respects. Thus, the same extension is one, or three, or thirty-six, according as the mind considers it with reference to a yard, a foot, or an inch. Number is so visibly relative, and dependent on men's understanding, that it is strange to think how anyone should give it an absolute existence without the mind. . . .

14. It is said that heat and cold are affections only of the mind, and not at all patterns of real beings, existing in the corporeal substances which excite them, for that the same body which appears cold to one hand seems warm to another. Now, why may we not as well argue that figure and extension are not patterns or resemblances of qualities existing in matter, because to the same eye at different stations, or eyes of a different texture at the same station, they appear various, and cannot therefore be the images of anything settled and determinate without the mind? Again, it is proved that sweetness is not really in the sapid (i.e. flavorful) thing, because the thing remaining unaltered the sweetness is changed into bitter, as in case of a fever or otherwise vitiated palate. Is it not as reasonable to say that motion is not without the mind, since if the succession of ideas in the mind become swifter, the motion, it is acknowledged, shall appear slower without any alteration in any external object?

15. In short, let anyone consider those arguments which are thought manifestly to prove that colors and tastes exist only in the mind, and he shall find they may with equal force be brought to prove the same thing of extension, figure, and motion. . . . the arguments foregoing plainly show it to be impossible that any color or extension at all, or other sensible quality whatsoever, should exist in an unthinking subject without the mind, or in truth, that there should be any such thing as an outward object. . . .

18. But though it were possible that solid, figured, movable substances may exist without the mind, corresponding to the ideas we have of bodies, yet how is it possible for us to know this? Either we must know it by sense or by reason. As for our senses, by them we have the knowledge only of our sensations, ideas, or those things that are immediately perceived by sense, call them what you will; but they do not inform us that things exist without the mind. . . . It remains therefore that if we have any knowledge at all of external things, it must be by reason, inferring their existence from what is immediately perceived by sense. But what reason can induce us to believe the existence of bodies without the mind, from what we perceive. . . . it is granted on all hands (and what happens in dreams, frenzies, and the like, puts it beyond dispute) that it is possible we might be affected with all the ideas we have now, though there were no bodies existing without, resembling them. Hence, it is evident the supposition of external bodies is not necessary for the producing of our ideas; since it is granted that they are produced sometimes, and might possibly be produced always in the same order we see them in at present, without their concurrence. . . .

20. In short, if there were external bodies, it is impossible we should ever come to know it; and if there were not, we might have the very same reasons to think there were that we have now. Suppose (what no one can deny possible) an intelligence without the help of external bodies, to be affected with the same train of sensations or ideas that you are, imprinted in the same order and with like vividness in his mind. I ask whether that intelligence hath not all the reason to believe the existence of corporeal substances, represented by his ideas, and exciting them in his mind, that you can possibly have for believing the same thing?

22. I am content to put the whole upon this issue: if you can but conceive it possible for one extended movable substance, or, in general, for any one idea, or anything like an idea, to exist otherwise than in a mind perceiving it, I shall readily give up the cause. . . .

23. But, say you, surely there is nothing easier than for me to imagine trees, for instance, in a park, or books existing in a closet, and nobody by to perceive them. I answer, you may so, there is no difficulty in it; but what is all this, I beseech you, more than framing in your mind certain ideas which you call books and trees, and the same time omitting to frame the idea of anyone that may perceive them? But do not you yourself perceive or think of them all the while? . . . When we do our utmost to conceive the existence of external bodies, we are all the while only contemplating our own ideas.

---

## CHECKLIST

To help you review, here is a checklist of the key philosophers and terms and concepts of this chapter. The brief descriptive sentences summarize the philosophers' leading ideas. Keep in mind that some of these summary statements are oversimplifications of complex positions.

### Philosophers

- **René Descartes**   was the "father" of modern philosophy, a Continental rationalist, and a dualist. He said there are two separate and distinct substances: material substance and mind.

- **Oliva Sabuco de Nantes**   proposed that the connection between body and soul occurs throughout the brain.

- **Thomas Hobbes**   was the first great modern materialist. He held that all that exists is bodies in motion.

- **Anne Conway**   argued against parts of the philosophies of Descartes, Hobbes, and Spinoza. An essentialist who argued that everything other than God has both physical and mental essences — God is totally mental — she had a big influence on Leibniz's monadology.

- **Benedictus de Spinoza**   was a neutralist and Continental rationalist. He maintained that thought and extension are attributes of a single substance.

- **Gottfried Wilhelm Leibniz**   was a Continental rationalist who held that the ultimate constituents of reality are monads, which are nonmaterial, indivisible units of force.

- **Émilie du Châtelet** adapted Leibniz's metaphysical principles to Newtonian science.

- **John Locke** was a British empiricist who held that we perceive objects indirectly by means of our perceptions of them, some of which he believed were accurate copies of the real properties of objects.

- **George Berkeley** was a British empiricist and idealist who denied the existence of material substance and held that sensible objects exist only in the mind.

## Key Terms and Concepts

dualism
materialism
idealism
double aspect theory
dream conjecture
evil demon conjecture
*cogito, ergo sum*
clear and distinct
  criterion
extension (as the
  essential attribute
  of material
  substance)
thought (as the
  essential attribute
  of mind)
parallelism

occasionalism
epistemological detour
perception
monads
principle of the
  identity of
  indiscernibles
principle of sufficient
  reason
*tabula rasa*
*nihil in intellectu quod*
  *prius non fuerit in sensu*
representative realism
empiricism
rationalism
*esse est percipi*

## QUESTIONS FOR DISCUSSION AND REVIEW

1. Define or explain dualism, materialism, and idealism.

2. Explain and critically evaluate either Descartes's dream conjecture or his evil demon conjecture.

3. Since Descartes tried to question everything, should he have questioned whether there could be thinking without an "I" that does the thinking?

4. "We can think. This proves we are not just mere matter." Does it?

5. "Material things, including one's own body, are completely subject to physical laws." "The immaterial mind can move one's body." Are these two claims incompatible? Explain.

6. What is parallelism?

7. Explain Hobbes's idea that all mental activity reduces to matter in motion.

8. What does Spinoza claim is the relationship of the mind to the body?

9. Explain Anne Conway's concept of time and its relationship to her view of God and creatures.

10. Why does Berkeley say that sensible objects exist only in the mind?

11. Are the qualities of sensible objects (e.g., size, color, taste) all equally relative to the observer?

12. Does Berkeley's philosophy make everything into a dream?

13. If all our knowledge comes from experience, why might it be difficult to maintain that we have knowledge of external objects?

14. *Do* we have knowledge of external objects? Explain.

15. Why did Berkeley maintain that it is a contradiction to hold that sensible objects exist outside the mind?

16. Is there really a difference between primary and secondary qualities?

17. Is your brain your mind? Explain.

18. What difficulties do you see with supposing that a nonmaterial mind could make things happen in a brain?

19. Psychokinesis is the mental power by which psychics claim to make changes in the external physical world — to bend spoons, to cause balls to roll, and so on. Is there any difference between using your mind to bend a spoon and using your mind to bend your arm? Explain.

## SUGGESTED FURTHER READINGS

Margaret Atherton, *Women Philosophers of the Early Modern Period* (Indianapolis: Hackett, 1994). Anthology of excerpts from Princess Elisabeth of Bohemia, Margaret Cavendish, Mary Astell, Damaris Cudworth Masham, Anne Conway, Catharine Trotter Cockburn, and Lady Mary Shepherd.

George Berkeley, *Principles of Human Knowledge, Three Dialogues,* Howard Robinson, ed. (New York: Oxford University Press, 1999). Contains a useful introduction.

Christopher Biffle, *A Guided Tour of René Descartes' Meditations on First Philosophy* (New York:

McGraw-Hill, 2000). Accessible translation of Descartes's *Meditations* I–VI with a guide to thinking about them critically.

Robert Black, ed., *Renaissance Thought: A Reader* (New York: Routledge, 2001). Essays by modern writers on Renaissance humanism, philosophy, and political thought.

E. O. Burtt, *The English Philosophers from Bacon to Mill* (New York: Modern Library, 1939). A general book on modern philosophy.

William Carter, *The Way Things Are: Basic Readings in Metaphysical Philosophy* (New York: McGraw-Hill, 1998). Readings from the Anglo-American approach to key metaphysical problems.

Anne Conway, *The Principles of the Most Ancient and Modern Philosophy* (Cambridge: Cambridge University Press, 1996). At last, an affordable paperback edition of Conway.

David E. Cooper, ed., *Epistemology, The Classic Readings* (New York: Blackwell, 1999). Essential readings from Plato to Bertrand Russell on the theory of knowledge.

John Cottingham, *The Rationalists* (New York: Oxford University Press, 1988). A brief introduction to the philosophies of the rationalists.

John Cottingham, ed., *The Cambridge Companion to Descartes* (New York: Cambridge University Press, 1995). Essays on Descartes that reveal his pivotal position in the history of philosophy.

Michael Della Rocca, *Representation and the Mind-Body Problem in Spinoza* (New York: Oxford University Press, 1996). An examination of Spinoza's thought on mind and knowledge.

René Descartes, *Philosophical Works,* in two volumes, E. S. Haldane and G. R. T. Ross, trans. (Cambridge: The University Press, 1968). This is what you need to read Descartes.

C. J. Ducasse, *A Critical Examination of the Belief in Life after Death* (Springfield, Ill.: Charles C Thomas, 1974). The first part of the book contains an excellent elementary discussion of the various theories of mind.

Stephen Gaukroger, *Descartes: An Intellectual Biography* (Oxford: Clarendon Press, 1997). A first biography tracing Descartes's intellectual development and philosophical ideas.

Errol E. Harris, *Spinoza's Philosophy: An Outline* (Atlantic Highlands, N.J.: Humanities Press, 1992). The title says it all.

Nicholas Jolley, ed., *The Cambridge Companion to Leibniz* (New York: Cambridge University Press, 1995). A collection of essays on all aspects of Leibniz's philosophy.

S. Lamprecht, ed., *Locke Selections* (New York: Scrib-

ner's, 1928). If you want to read more than "Selections," you must turn to his *Essay Concerning Human Understanding,* in two volumes, A. C. Fraser, ed. (New York: Dover, 1959). This (the Fraser edition) is a heavily annotated work.

John Locke, *An Essay Concerning Human Understanding* (New York: Oxford University Press, 1979).

Benson Mates, *The Philosophy of Leibniz* (New York: Oxford University Press, 1986). An excellent exposition of the metaphysics of Leibniz.

G. H. R. Parkinson, ed., *Routledge History of Philosophy,* vol. 4, *The Renaissance and Seventeenth Century Rationalism* (London: Routledge, 1994). A collection of fairly readable essays.

Stephen Priest, *The British Empiricists* (London: Penguin Books, 1990). A useful introduction to the British empiricist tradition extending from Hobbes through to Russell and Ayer.

Anthony Savile, *Routledge Philosophy Guidebook to Leibniz and the Monadology* (New York: Routledge, 2000). A brief exposition of Leibniz's idealism.

Roger Scruton, *A Short History of Modern Philosophy* (London: Routledge, 1984). From Descartes to Wittgenstein.

Tom Sorell, *Descartes: A Very Short Introduction.* (New York: Oxford University Press, 2000). A short but accessible introduction to Descartes's life and thinking.

Tom Sorell, ed., *The Cambridge Companion to Hobbes* (Cambridge: Cambridge University Press, 1996). A review of Hobbes's life and the full range of his philosophical concerns.

Richard Tuck, *Hobbes: A Very Short Introduction* (New York: Oxford University Press, 1989). A quick look at Hobbes's life and key ideas.

J. O. Urmson and A. J. Ayer, *The British Empiricists* (New York: Oxford University Press, 1992). A set of introductory readings on the lives and thoughts of Locke, Berkeley, and Hume.

Mary Ellen Waithe, ed., *A History of Women Philosophers,* vol. 3, *Modern Women Philosophers: 1600–1900* (Dordrecht: Kluwer Academic Press, 1991). Chapters about thirty-one women philosophers of the period.

J. Wild, ed., *Spinoza Selections* (New York: Scribner's, 1930). This volume contains enough original material for the introductory student.

F. J. E. Woodbridge, ed., *Hobbes Selections* (New York: Scribner's, 1930). Here, too, we think that the selected original material will be sufficient for the introductory student.

R. S. Woolhouse, *The Empiricists* (New York: Oxford University Press, 1988). A short introduction to the British empiricists.

# 7

# The Eighteenth and Nineteenth Centuries

The mind has never anything present to it but . . . perceptions, and cannot possibly reach any experience of their connection with [external] objects.
— David Hume

Though all our knowledge begins with experience, it does not follow that it all arises out of experience.     — Immanuel Kant

The eighteenth century ushered in the Enlightenment, and despite the French and American revolutions, the century was marked by comparative peace and stability, an improved standard of living, and an increase in personal freedom. Fewer witches were prosecuted, and burning heretics became rare. Religion continued to decline in importance politically, socially, and intellectually. Commerce expanded. Money grew. In short, all was well. Handel composed *The Messiah*.

After George Berkeley, the two most important philosophers of the eighteenth century were David Hume (1711–1776) and Immanuel Kant (1724–1804). Hume and Kant were both very reluctant to allow even the possibility of metaphysical knowledge. Hume believed that all our knowledge is limited to what we experience, namely, sensory impressions (although he was not willing to agree with Berkeley and say that sensible objects are just clusters of sensory impressions). Kant was more generous about what we can know, as we shall see.

## DAVID HUME

The epistemology of **David Hume** (1711–1776), like that of George Berkeley (see previous chapter), is a development of the empiricist thesis that all our ideas come from experience — that is, from sensation or inner feelings. In some passages Hume displays total skepticism, but mostly he appears as a modified skeptic who focuses his attention on certain narrower issues that have continued to dominate epistemological inquiry since Hume's time.

Much of Hume's epistemology rests on four assumptions. To see whether you agree with them or not, mark "T" or "F" in front of each of these four statements:

1. **T or F**   Every claim that something exists is a factual claim. (That is, when you claim that something exists, you are expressing what you think is a fact.)
2. **T or F**   Factual claims can be established only by observation or by causal inference from what is observed. (For example, you can tell if an engine is knocking just by listening to it, but to know that it has worn bearings, you have to make an inference as to the cause of the knocking.)
3. **T or F**   Thought, knowledge, belief, conception, and judgment each consist in having ideas.
4. **T or F**   All ideas are derived from, and are copies of, impressions of sense or inner feelings, that is, perceptions.

If you marked "T" to each of these four statements, you agree with Hume. But what do these four assumptions entail?

### The Quarter Experiment

Let's begin with (1) and (2). First, put a quarter in front of you next to this book. The quarter exists, correct? This claim, according to principle (2), can be established — that is, proved or justified — only by observation or by inference from what you observe.

But what is it you observe? The quarter? Well, no, as a matter of fact that does not seem quite right. Look at what you call the quarter. Leave it on your desk, and get up and move around the room a bit, looking at the quarter all the while. What you *observe*, as you move about, is a silverish object that constantly changes its size and shape as you move. Right now, for example, what you observe is probably elliptical in shape. But a quarter is not the sort of thing that constantly changes its size and shape, and a quarter is never elliptical (unless someone did something illegal to it). *So what you observe changes its size and shape, but the quarter does not change its size and shape. It follows that what you observe is not the quarter.*

Here you might object. "What I am seeing is a silverish object from various distances and angles," you might say.

# PROFILE: David Hume (1711–1776)

David Hume died of cancer at the age of sixty-five. In the face of his own death, he retained his composure and cheerfulness, having achieved the goal of the ancient skeptics, *ataraxia* (unperturbedness). It may be questioned, though, whether his calm good nature resulted from his skepticism, for apparently he exhibited this trait of personality throughout his life.

Born in Edinburgh, Scotland, of a "good family," as he said in his autobiography, Hume was encouraged to study law but "found insurmountable aversion to everything but the pursuits of philosophy and general learning." Before he was thirty, he published *A Treatise of Human Nature,* one of the most important philosophical works ever written. Yet, at the time, Hume's *Treatise* "fell dead-born from the press," as he put it, "without reaching such distinction as even to excite a murmur among the zealots." Convinced that the failure of the work was due more to form than content, he recast parts of it anew in *An Enquiry Concerning Human Understanding* and *An Enquiry Concerning the Principles of Morals.* The latter work, in Hume's opinion, was incomparably his best. Hume's last philosophical work, *Dialogues Concerning Natural Religion,* was published posthumously in 1779. There are differences between Hume's *Treatise* and *An Enquiry Concerning Human Understanding,* his two works in epistemology, and philosophers disagree about the merits of each. Although during his lifetime Hume was primarily known as a historian rather than as a philosopher, his impact on subsequent philosophy, especially in Great Britain and other English-speaking countries, and on Kant, was significant.

In the passage that follows, Hume's friend economist Adam Smith quotes a letter from Hume's physician at the time of Hume's death and then adds a few thoughts of his own. The passage discloses a great deal about Hume's soul, and we quote at length.

*Dear Sir,*

*Yesterday, about four o'clock, afternoon, Mr. Hume expired. The near approach of his death became evident in the night between Thursday and Friday, when his disease became excessive, and soon weakened him so much,* *that he could no longer rise out of his bed. He continued to the last perfectly sensible, and free from much pain or feelings of distress. He never dropped the smallest expression of impatience; but when he had occasion to speak to the people about him, always did it with affection and tenderness. . . . When he became very weak, it cost him an effort to speak; and he died in such a happy composure of mind, that nothing could exceed it.*

*Thus died our most excellent and never to be forgotten friend; concerning whose philosophical opinions men will, no doubt, judge variously . . . but concerning whose character and conduct there can scarce be a difference of opinion. His temper, indeed, seemed to be more happily balanced, if I may be allowed such an expression, than that perhaps of any other man I have ever known. Even in the lowest state of his fortune, his great and necessary frugality never hindered him from exercising, upon proper occasions, acts both of charity and generosity. It was a frugality bounded not upon avarice, but upon the love of independency. The extreme gentleness of his nature never weakened either the firmness of his mind or the steadiness of his resolutions. His constant pleasantry was the genuine effusion of good nature and good humor, tempered with delicacy and modesty, and without even the slightest tincture of malignity, so frequently the disagreeable source of what is called wit in other men. It never was the meaning of his raillery to mortify; and therefore, far from offending, it seldom failed to please and delight, even those who were frequently the objects of it; there was not perhaps any one of all his great and amiable qualities which contributed more to endear his conversation. And that gayety of temper, so agreeable in society, but which is so often accompanied with frivolous and superficial qualities, was in him certainly attended with the most severe application, the most extensive learning, the greatest depth of thought, and a capacity in every respect the most comprehensive. Upon the whole, I have always considered him, both in his lifetime and since his death, as approaching as nearly to the ideal of a perfectly wise and virtuous man as perhaps the nature of human frailty will permit.*

*I ever am, dear sir,*

*Most affectionally yours, Adam Smith*

But, in fact, if you consider carefully what you are observing, it is a silverish object that changes its size and shape. You do not see a silverish disk that looks the same from every vantage point. What you see does change. Thus, it still follows, because the quarter does not change, that what you see is not the quarter.

What is it, then, that you observe? According to Hume, it is your *sense impressions* of the quarter. Thus, if your belief that the quarter exists is to be justified, that belief must be a causal inference from what you observe — that is, from your impressions — to something that is distinct from your impressions and causes them, namely, the quarter. But there is a major problem here: you never experience or are in any way in contact with anything that is distinct from your impressions. Thus, you never observe a connection between your perceptions and the quarter. So how could you possibly establish that the quarter *causes* your impressions? And if you cannot establish that, then, according to Hume, you cannot regard your belief in the existence of the quarter as justified.

Of course, the same considerations apply to a belief in the existence of any external object whatsoever. Here is Hume expressing these considerations in his own words:

> The only existences, of which we are certain, are perceptions. . . . The only conclusion we can draw from the existence of one thing to that of another, is by means of the relation of cause and effect, which shews, that there is a connection betwixt them. . . . But as no things are ever present to the mind but perceptions; it follows that we may observe a conjunction or a relation of cause and effect between different perceptions, but can never observe it between perceptions and objects. 'Tis impossible, therefore, that from the existence of any of the qualities of the former, we can ever form any conclusion concerning the existence of the latter.

Now, go back to assumptions (3) and (4). Notice that it follows directly from these two assumptions that there is no knowledge, belief, conception, judgment, thought, or even idea of external objects (things distinct from our sense impressions of them). Here again Hume explains:

> Now, since nothing is ever present to the mind but perceptions, and since all ideas are derived from something antecedently present to the mind; it follows, that 'tis impossible for us so much as to conceive or form an idea of anything specifically different from ideas and impressions. Let us fix our attention out of ourselves as much as possible: Let us chase our imagination to the heavens, or to the utmost limits of the universe; we never really advance a step beyond ourselves, nor can conceive any kind of existence, but those perceptions, which have appeared in that narrow compass.

## Hume on the Self

According to Hume, similar careful scrutiny of the notion of the self or mind, supposedly an unchanging nonmaterial substance within us, discloses that we have no knowledge of such a thing. Indeed, we do not really have even an *idea* of the mind, if the mind is defined as an unchanging nonmaterial substance within, Hume holds. Our ideas cannot go beyond our sense impressions, and we have no impressions of the mind, except perhaps as a bundle of impressions.

## A Lot of Destruction

Hume noted that Berkeley's reasons for denying the existence of material substance "admit of no answer, and produce no conviction." The same has in effect been said about much of Hume's own philosophy. The wit Sydney Smith once remarked, "Bishop Berkeley destroyed the world in one volume octavo, and nothing remained after his time but mind—which experienced a similar fate from the hand of Mr. Hume in 1737; so that with all the tendency to destroy there remains nothing left for destruction."

---

Some philosophers, said Hume, imagine we are conscious of what we call our "self" or "mind" and that we feel its existence and are certain of its "perfect identity and simplicity." But, he asked, "From what impression could this idea be derived?"

> It must be some one impression that gives rise to every real idea. But self is not any one impression, but that to which our several impressions and ideas are supposed to have a reference. If any impression gives rise to the idea of self, that impression must continue invariably the same through the whole course of our lives, since self is supposed to exist after that manner. But there is no impression constant and invariable. . . . There is no such idea. . . .
>
> For my part, when I enter most intimately into what I call *myself,* I always stumble on some particular perception or other, of heat or cold, light or shade, love or hatred, pain or pleasure. I never can catch myself at any time without a perception, and never can observe any thing but the perception. . . . The mind is a kind of theatre, where several perceptions successively make their appearance; pass, re-pass, glide away, and mingle in an infinite variety of postures and situations. There is properly no *simplicity* in it at one time, nor *identity* in different. . . . The comparison of the theatre must not mislead us. They are the successive perceptions only, that constitute the mind.

### Hume on Cause and Effect

Because any inference from the existence of one thing to that of another is founded, according to Hume, on the relation of cause and effect (statement 2 on page 134), Hume analyzed that relation carefully. He discovered that experience reveals no necessary connection between a cause and an effect.

At first this thesis—that we experience no necessary connection between a cause and its effect—seems straightforwardly false. The car going by *makes* the noise you hear, doesn't it? The impact of the golf club *drives* the ball down the fairway. Disconnecting a spark plug *forces* the engine to idle roughly. The cue ball *moves* the eight ball when it hits it. What could be plainer than that in each case the cause *necessitates* the effect?

Yet by paying attention to what he actually experienced in an instance of so-called causation, Hume discovered that he did not experience the cause actually *producing* the effect. Instead, he discovered one event simply being conjoined with a second event. He saw the cue ball hitting the eight ball, and he saw the eight ball rolling away, but he did not see the cue ball *making* the eight ball move.

Do we see the pin *making* the balloon pop? Hume maintained that all he saw was just (1) the pin coming into spatial contact with the balloon and (2) the balloon popping. He did not see the pin *making* the balloon pop.

If you consider an instance of causation, you may find you agree with Hume. Do you really perceive the car *making* the noise you hear? Or do you, instead, just see the car *and* hear the noise? Do you perceive the flame *producing* heat? Or do you just see the flame *and* feel the heat? Consider the matter carefully. Which is it? Do you perceive X *causing* Y? Or do you just perceive X *and* Y? Hume found that in every single instance in which he experienced an event X supposedly causing another event Y, he didn't really experience X *causing* Y, but only X *and* Y. He concluded that it is really just the **constant conjunction** of X and Y that we take for causation. We experience a constant conjunction of flame and heat, and the causation we suppose is in flame is really only in our minds.

Not only that, because so-called causation really boils down to just a constant conjunction of a so-called cause with a so-called effect, there is no real justification for supposing that the so-called cause will always be accompanied by the so-called effect. For example, you have experienced a constant conjunction between flame and heat. Are you not then justified in supposing that future experience will show a similar conjunction between flame and heat?

Well, Hume's answer is that you are *not* justified. If you say that the next flame you encounter will be accompanied by heat, it is because you assume that **the future will resemble the past.** Indeed, all reasoning based on present and past experience assumes that the future will be like the past. But that means, Hume saw in a flash, that the assumption itself cannot be proved by an appeal to experience. To attempt to prove the assumption by appealing to experience, he observed, "must evidently be going in a circle."

It is hard to exaggerate the significance of this finding, as a moment's thought will show. The fact that all inference from past and present experience rests on an apparently unprovable assumption (that the future will resemble the past) leads to skeptical conclusions even more sweeping than Hume for the most part was willing to countenance. It means, for instance, that much of what we think we know we do not really know. Will food and water nourish you the next time you eat and drink? Will our names be the same this evening as they are now? Will the words at the beginning of this sentence have changed meaning by the time you get to the end of the sentence? Evidently the answers to these questions, though seemingly obvious, *are mere assumptions that we cannot really know.*

Perhaps you can now understand why, in the conclusion to Book I of *A Treatise of Human Nature,* Hume reflects that what he has written shows that

> the understanding, when it acts alone, and according to its most general principles, entirely subverts itself, and leaves not the lowest degree of evidence in any proposition, either in philosophy or common life.

Thus, Hume says, he is "ready to reject all belief and reasoning, and can look upon no opinion even as more probable or likely than another." This skepticism is not modified: it is uncompromisingly total. Hume said, though, that a true skeptic "will be diffident in his philosophical doubts, as well as of his philosophical conviction." In other words, a true (total) skeptic will doubt his doubts too.

Now that you have looked at the philosophy of David Hume, you will perhaps see why we have given this book the title it has. If Hume's ideas are correct, then must we not in the end despair, as Cratylus did (Chapter 3), and watch the world from a distance, merely wiggling our fingers?

## IMMANUEL KANT

It is time now to turn to **Immanuel Kant** [kahnt] (1724–1804). Most scholars regard Kant as one of the most brilliant intellects of all time. Unfortunately, they also consider him one of the most difficult of all philosophers to read. Difficult or not, Kant provided a significant and ingenious response to Hume's skepticism. In a sentence, Kant believed that certain knowledge does indeed exist, and he set about to show how this could be possible, given Hume's various arguments that pointed in the opposite direction.

### The Ordering Principles of the Mind

Think back for a second to Descartes. Descartes believed he could prove to himself that objects like tables and harpsichords and planets and so forth exist outside the mind. But his "proof" of these "external" objects was circuitous. First, Descartes had to prove to himself that he existed. Then he had to prove that God existed. Then he had to argue that God would not deceive him on such an important thing as the existence of tables and harpsichords and other external objects. Perhaps it is not surprising that this "proof" did not win many adherents.

John Locke, as we saw, believed knowledge comes from the sensations or "ideas" furnished to the mind by experience. The problem with this theory, George Berkeley was quick to see, is that it limits our knowledge to our sensations or ideas—which means we cannot know anything exists except our sensations or ideas. Berkeley essentially accepted this and maintained that tables and harpsichords must just *be* clusters of sensations or ideas. David Hume, too, agreed that

# PROFILE: Immanuel Kant (1724–1804)

Kant was one of the first modern philosophers to earn his living as a professor of philosophy. Though he hardly ever left Königsberg, his birthplace, his ideas traveled far, and he is considered by many as the greatest philosopher, ever.

Kant's first works were in natural science and secured for him a substantial reputation before his appointment as professor of logic and metaphysics at Königsberg in 1770. After his appointment, he wrote nothing for ten years as he contemplated the issues that eventually appeared in his most important work, the *Critique of Pure Reason* (1781, 2nd ed. 1787). The actual writing of the book took "four or five months," he said, and was done "with the utmost attention to the contents, but with less concern for the presentation or for making things easy for the reader." Readers universally understand what he meant.

The reaction to the work was primarily one of confusion, and this led Kant to publish a shorter, more accessible version of his major work, titled *Prolegomena to Any Future Metaphysics* (1783). This is an excellent book with which to begin the study of Kant's epistemology and metaphysics. To fix dates a bit, Kant's *Prolegomena* came out in the same year the American War of Independence ended and, incidentally, the first successful hot-air balloon flight was made.

Two years after publication of the *Prolegomena,* Kant's first major treatise on ethics, the *Foundations of the Metaphysics of Morals,* appeared. A comparatively brief work, it is nevertheless one of the most important books ever written on ethics.

Kant's second and third critiques, the *Critique of Practical Reason* (1788) and *Critique of Judgment* (1790), were concerned with morality and aesthetics, respectively. In addition to the three *Critiques,* the *Prolegomena,* and the *Foundations,* Kant wrote many other lesser works.

In his last years he suffered the indignity of hearing younger German philosophers say that he had not really understood what he had written, an unusually stupid idea that history has long since laid to rest.

our knowledge is limited to our sensations or ideas, though he didn't think that tables and harpsichords and the like just *are* sensations/ideas. Hume thought "'tis vain to ask whether there be bodies [external objects] or not"—and tried to figure out what caused us to believe in bodies.

It was scandalous, Immanuel Kant thought, that philosophy was reduced to either the idealism of Berkeley or the skepticism of Hume. Accordingly, Kant offered his own (complicated) proof of external objects. The usual way to try to prove the existence of external objects had been to argue from sensations outward to objects. Kant tried a different approach. His strategy, roughly, was to argue that a stream of sensations could not qualify as experience unless the stream was unified and conceptualized by the mind as the experience of external objects. (Arguments of this sort, which attempt to establish something as a necessary precondition of the possibility of experience, are called "transcendental arguments," and there is much current controversy as to what, if anything, they really prove.)

Kant compared himself to Copernicus (1473–1542), who developed the heliocentric theory of planetary motion, which eventually replaced the old view that the sun and planets circle the earth. Before Copernicus, people assumed that the apparent motion of the sun was its real motion. Copernicus realized that the apparent motion of the sun was due to *our* motion, not the sun's motion. Kant had a very similar idea, known sometimes as the **Copernican revolution in philosophy.** According to this idea, the fundamental properties or characteristics of objects in the world outside the mind are due to our *minds,* not to the objects themselves.

What Kant meant is perhaps best illustrated by thinking of a person wearing blue glasses. The person sees everything in blue. Why? Because the glasses "impose" blueness on the person's sensations. Likewise, all of us experience the world as consisting of external objects. Not only that, we see the objects as existing in space and time and as related to one another causally. Why? Because, Kant theorized, our minds impose these forms on our sensations. Our sense-data are processed by the mind in such a way that we have the sort of experience we do, just as the sense-data of Mr. Blue Glasses are processed by his glasses in such a way that he has the sort of blue experience he does.

Kant's revolutionary theory — that sense-data are processed by the mind in such a way that we have the sort of experience we do have — explains how we can be sure of many of the things we are sure of. For example, according to Hume, we *cannot* be absolutely certain that the next flame we encounter will be accompanied by heat (maybe the flaming stuff will be some odd, new synthetic substance). Nevertheless, we *can* be certain that the flame certainly will at least be in space and time. This knowledge could not be derived from experience because experience informs us only of the way things have been so far, not of the way they must be. We can be certain that any flame we encounter will be in space and time, Kant said, only if space and time are "imposed" on our sensory data by the perceiving component of the mind.

Just think of an electric door or a TV camera. Data enters into the device, but it doesn't *experience* anything. The device is sensitive to light — it has "sensations" — but no experience. Likewise, for our sensations to qualify as experience, they must be processed in certain specific ways. First of all, these sensations must be subject to spatial-temporal shaping. That is, the perceiving part of the mind must perceive them as objects existing outside us in space and time. Second, they must also be **conceptualized** — brought under concepts. For raw sensory stimulation to qualify as experience, it must be organized and recognized as a *person* or *car* or *strawberry* or whatever. Sensory stimulation that isn't conceptualized is "blind," Kant said.

Further, Kant held, to qualify as experience, sensory stimulation must be **unified** in a single connected consciousness. If it weren't unified, it could never qualify as experience. In addition, he said, unification and conceptualization must conform to rules of cognition, just as perception must conform to spatial-temporal shaping. Thus, sensory stimulation must be organized as the experience of objects in space and time; but, likewise, it must be organized as the experience of objects that conform to cause-and-effect and other relationships. Change, for example, must be experienced as the change of a permanent substance whose quantity in nature remains constant.

This theory explains nicely, Kant said, how we know that we will *never* experience uncaused change. The only way to explain such certain knowledge is to assume that the mind "imposes" causation on experienced change. To *qualify* as experienced, a change *must* be subject to causation —just as to qualify as seen a thing must be blue to the person who is forced to wear blue glasses.

## Things-in-Themselves

In substance, then, this was Kant's response to the challenge David Hume put to epistemology. Hume was partially correct. He was correct in thinking that knowledge *begins* with experience. But he was not correct in thinking that knowledge is derived from experience. It is better to say that the mind is *awakened* by experience. But once awakened, it doesn't simply receive and store stimulation as would a camera. It actively processes it according to underlying principles and categories, which can be disclosed by careful examination.

However — and this is a big "however" — according to Kant, our knowledge is limited to **phenomena,** or *experienceable* objects — things that could be the subject of experience. For only things that are experienced are subject to the categorizing and unifying activity of the mind. To be experienced, objects must be in space and time, be related to one another by cause and effect, and otherwise be subject to the principles of cognition; but we cannot apply these categories and principles to things "as they are in themselves"—**noumena,** or things that exist outside experience. Concerning this "noumenal" world beyond experience, the world of the thing-in-itself, ***das Ding-an-sich*** (as it is said in German), skepticism is unavoidable, for Kant. When rules that apply to the world of experience are applied to a reality-beyond-experience, contradictions and mistakes result. Kant was willing to say that three "ideas of reason"— God, world, self — at least point to *possibilities* in the noumenal realm, but we can have no knowledge of the realm. Kant's epistemology limits legitimate metaphysical reasoning to this world.

So, relative to the world of experience, Kant was not a skeptic. But relative to things-in-themselves, he was. This doesn't mean he made no headway relative to Hume. On Hume's theory, we simply cannot be certain that the future will resemble the past — because Hume assumed all knowledge is derived from experience. But this seems wrong: we can be certain that, in some respects, the future will resemble the past. We can be certain that we will never *experience* an uncaused event (despite the fact that contemporary physicists speak of uncaused events on the subatomic level). We can be certain that we will never experience an object that isn't in space or time. We can be certain that we will never experience an object that has no properties. Kant's theory seems better able than Hume's to explain these and similar facts.

## THE NINETEENTH CENTURY

Kant died in 1804, at the beginning of the nineteenth century. The first part of the nineteenth century was the Romantic era in European arts and letters, which arose in revolt against the rationalism of the preceding century. This was the period that emphasized adventure and spiritual vision in literature, produced huge and noisy symphonies, and stressed exotic themes in the visual arts. Careful reasoning was out; emotional spontaneity was in.

In philosophy, although Kant's successors did not exactly repudiate what he had written, they certainly did stand it on its ear. This dramatic response to Kant was German **Absolute Idealism,** the philosophies of Johann Gottlieb Fichte (1762–1814), Friedrich Wilhelm Joseph von Schelling (1775–1854), and **Georg Wilhelm Friedrich Hegel** [HAY-gul] (1770–1831).

Kant had argued that the mind imposes certain categories on the objects of experience and that this is what makes it possible to have knowledge of the world of experience. His epistemological thesis, as we have seen, is that we can have knowledge *only* of the world of experience and can have no knowledge of things "as they are in themselves." The Absolute Idealists, however, transformed this epistemological skepticism into metaphysical idealism. What could there be such that the mind could not know it? they asked. If it is not knowable, they reasoned, then it is unthinkable; and if it is unthinkable, why, it just plain isn't. So thought, or consciousness, does not merely categorize reality: its categories *are* reality. There cannot be unknowable things-in-themselves, they said, for everything that is, is a product of the knowing mind.

Reality is not, however, the expression of your thought or ours or any other particular person's, they said, for neither you nor any other person created the world of independent external things that exists around us. Rather, reality is the expression of *infinite* or *absolute* thought or consciousness. And when we think or philosophize about reality, this is consciousness becoming aware of itself, that is, becoming infinite.

So, from the perspective of Hegel, the cosmos and its history are the concrete expression of thought. Thus, everything that happens and every field of human inquiry are the proper domain of the philosopher, who alone can understand and interpret the true relationship of each aspect of reality to the whole. Absolute Idealism, as this philosophy is called, attempted to achieve a complete and unified conception of all reality, a conception that gave meaning to each and every aspect in relationship to the sum total. It was the towering pinnacle of metaphysical speculation, and virtually everything that happened subsequently in metaphysics and epistemology happened in reaction to it, as you are about to see.

## Main Themes of Hegel

Hegel's philosophy is difficult, but the main themes are these:

1. "Everything depends on grasping the truth not merely as Substance but as Subject as well." This means that what is true, what is real, is not merely that which is thought *of*, but that which *thinks*. Thus, what is most real—the Absolute—is thought thinking of itself.
2. Hegel's idealism is different from Berkeley's. For Berkeley, the objective world in fact exists in the minds of individuals. For Hegel, the objective world is an unfolding or expression of infinite thought, and the individual mind is the vehicle of infinite thought reflecting on itself.

## PROFILE: Georg Hegel (1770–1831)

There was a sort of incredible solemnness about Hegel that earned him the nickname "the old man" while he was still a university student at Tübingen, Germany. He was serious about everything he did and was even somber when he drank. In high school he devoted his time to collecting copious notes concerning what he thought were the ultimate questions of life, a sure sign that he would wind up as a philosopher.

Hegel's fellow university student Friedrich Schelling gained renown in philosophy early in life. But for Hegel it was a struggle. After having served as a private tutor, newspaper editor, and director of a high school, he was given a professorship at Heidelberg and then at Berlin, where, finally, he became famous. His lectures drew large audiences despite his tendency to stop and start and break off in midsentence to page furiously through his notes. His listeners could

sense that something deep and important was happening. Hegel was quite handsome and became popular with the society women of Berlin. All this satisfied him enormously.

Not everyone admired Hegel, however. Arthur Schopenhauer, another famous philosopher we will discuss a bit later, described Hegel as an unimaginative, unintelligent, disgusting, revolting charlatan who ruined the entire generation of intellectuals who followed him. You should bear in mind, though, that poor Schopenhauer attempted to schedule his lectures at Berlin at the same hour as Hegel's — and found himself lecturing to an empty hall.

Hegel's main works are *Phenomenology of Mind* (1807), in which he first presented his metaphysical system, *Science of Logic* (1812–1816), *Encyclopedia of the Philosophical Sciences* (1817), and *Philosophy of Right* (1821).

3. Reality, the Absolute, for Hegel, is not a group of independent particulars or states of affairs, but rather like a coherent thought system such as mathematics it is an integrated whole in which each proposition (each state of affairs) is logically connected with all the rest. Thus, an *isolated* state of affairs is not wholly real; likewise, a proposition about this or that aspect or feature of reality is only partially true. The only thing that is totally true (or totally real, because these amount to the same thing) is the complete system.

4. **The Absolute,** the sum total of reality, is a system of conceptual triads. To formalize Hegel's system somewhat artificially: for proposition or concept *A* there is a negation, *not-A;* and within the two there is a synthetic unity, or synthesis, *B. B,* however, has a negation, *not-B,* and within *B* and *not-B* there is a synthesis, *C.* And so on. Thus, the higher levels of the system are implicit in the lower levels — for example, *C* and *B* are both implicit in *A.* In this way the entire system of thought and reality that is the Absolute is an integrated whole in which each proposition is logically interconnected with the rest.

Note that for Hegel this triadic structure is not a method by means of which we discover truth. Instead, it is the way things are: it is the actual structure of

## Ludwig van Beethoven

As you can see, the great German composer Ludwig van Beethoven (1770–1827) lived at almost exactly the same time as Hegel. Beethoven was the link between the controlled and formal Classical era in music and the passionate and tempestuous Romantic era. Hegel's philosophy, for some reason, perhaps because of its grandness and scope, reminds one much more of the music of the Romantic era.

thought. Thus, for example, the most basic or fundamental category or concept is *being*. But being is nothing without *not-being*, its opposite. And the synthesis of these opposites is *becoming*; hence, the Absolute is becoming. In similar fashion, at each stage of his exposition Hegel posits a *thesis*, to which there belongs an *antithesis*, and the thesis and antithesis are a unity in a higher *synthesis*. The higher levels of the system are always implicit in the lower levels.

Ultimately, therefore, we come to the apex, or highest triad, of Hegel's system: the synthesis of "Idea" and "Nature" in "Spirit." And Idea and Nature are each, in turn, the synthesis of two lower opposing concepts. Thus, Idea is the synthesis of subjectivity (that which thinks) and objectivity (that which is thought of). What Hegel means by "Idea" is self-conscious thought, which is exactly what you would expect to be the synthesis of that which thinks and that which is thought of. "The absolute Idea," Hegel wrote, "alone is being, eternal life, self-knowing truth, and it is all truth."

The antithesis of Idea is Nature. In other words, on one hand there is self-knowing or self-conscious thought ("Idea"), and on the other there is what we might call the independent world (Nature), the external expression of Idea, or Idea outside itself. (It is in his philosophy of Nature that Hegel attempted to integrate the various concepts of science into his system.)

So Nature and Idea, as thesis and antithesis, have their own synthesis. As we said, this is the synthesis of the main triad of Hegel's entire system and is what Hegel called "Spirit." We might translate "Spirit" as "thought knowing itself both as thought and as object" or as "the Idea returning into itself." We did not say that Hegel is easy.

The philosophy of Spirit also has three main subdivisions: subjective spirit and its antithesis, objective spirit, with the synthesis as Absolute Spirit. Subjective spirit is the realm of the human mind; objective spirit is the mind in its external manifestation in social institutions. Hegel's analysis of objective spirit contains his social and political philosophy, in which he attempts to display the relationships (always more or less triadic) among such various concepts as property, contract, crime, punishment, right, personality, family, society, and the state.

In the end, therefore, we come to know the part played by every aspect of reality in the whole, and we are led to understand that the highest conception of the Absolute is as Spirit.

So Hegel's system is really a grandiose vision of the history of the universe and the history of human consciousness as a necessary unfolding of infinite reason. It purports to be a complete conceptual framework for each aspect of reality and for every component of human thought and history. This system represents the towering summit of metaphysical speculation.

## Arthur Schopenhauer

Reactions to Hegel's Absolute Idealism were swift and strong. Karl Marx (1818–1883) tried to turn Hegel on his head by interpreting the evolutionary progress of the species as being due to economic factors. (We cover the details of Marx's theory in Chapter 11.) Søren Kierkegaard (1813–1855) poured scorn on Hegel's grandiose scheme. Friedrich Nietzsche (1844–1900) rejected Hegel's idealism and all similar metaphysics. (We cover Kierkegaard and Nietzsche in the next chapter.) However, the most famous attacks on Hegel's exuberant rationalism came from **Arthur Schopenhauer** [SHOW-pun-owr] (1788–1860). Schopenhauer regarded Hegel personally as an opportunistic charlatan and viewed him philosophically as a dud. For Schopenhauer, Hegel's "reason" was an exercise in philistine self-deception; his attempt to paint the world in rational terms, pathetic and misguided. Schopenhauer didn't stop with Hegel: science and the humanities as a whole have been mustered, he believed, to picture the universe as reasonable, governed by laws under the master of the rational human intellect. Reality, he maintained, is very different.

Specifically, for Schopenhauer human beings are rarely rational in their actions. On the contrary, they are blindly driven by will to pursue selfish desires. Reason is invoked after the fact as a way of rationalizing what has been done from impulse, he held. Schopenhauer's world is peopled with vicious little men who commit atrocities in pursuit of trifling objects. It is a world in which no one can be trusted and security requires sleeping with a loaded pistol under the pillow. Their willfulness makes humans a violent part of a grotesque scenario that has neither sense nor reason, in Schopenhauer's view.

Believe it or not, Schopenhauer took his philosophical departure to be Kant, who had argued that the phenomenal world is structured by the understanding. However, according to Schopenhauer, it is the *will* that does the structuring. This, very roughly, is his theory.

How do you come to know yourself? You come to know your character through your decisions and choices, correct? Well, these are the result of willing. Further, from the perspective of the will, the act of willing and the bodily act that we ordinarily say is *caused* by that act are one and the same thing: "The action of the will

Arthur Schopenhauer (1788–1860)

is nothing but the act of will objectified, i.e., translated into perception," Schopenhauer wrote.

Certainly this theory is plausible enough, and it enabled Schopenhauer to regard not just one's body but *all* phenomena as the objectification of will. Further, according to Schopenhauer, the will is the force that makes plants grow, forms crystals, turns magnets toward the North Pole — in short, does everything.

Schopenhauer's theory is difficult as this point because he, like Kant, made a distinction between phenomena and noumena. Schopenhauer distinguished between cosmic, impersonal, will-in-itself and its manifestation in the phenomenal world. Will-in-itself is the originating source of everything that happens and, as such, is not determined by anything else. It is, one might say, blind and purposeless. Each person is a manifestation of will-in-itself and subject to unceasing striving. Accordingly, the world is in disarray and is a sorry sight, because we are witless lackeys of this errant, cosmic will. One can achieve a measure of peace and happiness, according to Schopenhauer, only to the degree one escapes the tyranny of will. This can be done by moving beyond knowledge of one's own will to objectivity and understanding of will-in-itself, in which state the world of phenomena becomes a kind of nothingness. He spoke of this detached state as one of ecstasy and rapture and thought it could be glimpsed through art, music, and aesthetic experience.

Sigmund Freud (1856–1939), who read Schopenhauer, based psychoanalysis on the concept that human actions stem not from rationality but from unconscious drives and instincts in what he called the *id,* or "it" part of the self. The influence of Schopenhauer is evident.

Friedrich Nietzsche also read Schopenhauer and became convinced that the world is driven by cosmic will, not by reason. However, that is a story for our next chapter.

SELECTION 7.1

# An Enquiry Concerning Human Understanding*

*David Hume*

[*In this selection from* An Enquiry Concerning Human Understanding, *David Hume argues that the contents of the mind fall into two and only two categories. One category includes thoughts or ideas, and the other contains "impressions"— the material given to us by our senses and experience. The difference between ideas and impressions, he says, is solely that thoughts and ideas are less vivid or forceful than sensory impressions. He then argues that all the creative power of the mind amounts to nothing more than the power to compound and transpose the material given to us by the senses and experience. Hence, he writes, when we suspect a word is employed without any meaning or idea, we only have to ask from what impressions the supposed idea comes. If we cannot discover any impressions, that confirms our suspicions. Contrast these views with those of Kant in the following selection.*]

## Section II. Of the Origin of Ideas

Every one will readily allow, that there is a considerable difference between the perceptions of the mind, when a man feels the pain of excessive heat, or the pleasure of moderate warmth, and when he afterwards recalls to his memory this sensation, or anticipates it by his imagination. These faculties may mimic or copy the perceptions of the senses; but they never can entirely reach the force and vivacity of the original sentiment. The utmost we say of them, even when they operate with greatest vigour, is, that they represent their object in so lively a manner, that we could almost say we feel or see it. But, except the mind be disordered by disease or madness, they never can arrive at such a pitch of vivacity, as to render these perceptions altogether undistinguishable. All the colours of poetry, however splendid, can never paint natural objects in such a manner as to make the description be taken for a real landscape. The most lively thought is still inferior to the dullest sensation.

We may observe a like distinction to run through all the other perceptions of the mind. A man in a fit of anger, is actuated in a very different manner from one who only thinks of that emotion. If you tell me, that any person is in love, I easily understand your meaning, and form a just conception of his situation; but never can mistake that conception for the real disorders and agitations of the passion. When we reflect on our past sentiments and affections, our thought is a faithful mirror, and copies its objects truly; but the colours which it employs are faint and dull, in comparison of those in which our original perceptions were clothed. It requires no nice discernment or metaphysical head to mark the distinction between them.

Here therefore we may divide all the perceptions of the mind into two classes or species, which are distinguished by their different degrees of force and vivacity. The less forcible and lively are commonly denominated *Thoughts* or *Ideas.* The other species want a name in our language, and in most others; I suppose, because it was not requisite for any, but philosophical purposes, to rank them under a general term or appellation. Let us, therefore, use a little freedom, and call them *Impressions;* employing that word in a sense somewhat different from the usual. By the term impression, then, I mean all our more lively perceptions, when we hear, or see, or feel, or love, or hate, or desire, or will. And *impressions* are distinguished from ideas which are the less lively perceptions, of which we are conscious, when we reflect on any of those sensations or movements above mentioned.

Nothing, at first view, may seem more unbounded than the thought of man, which not only escapes all human power and authority, but is not even restrained within the limits of nature and reality. To form monsters, and join incongruous shapes and appearances, costs the imagination no more trouble than to conceive the most natural and familiar objects. And while the body is confined to one planet, along which it creeps with pain and difficulty; the thought can in an instant transport us into the most distant regions of the universe;

---

*David Hume, "An Enquiry Concerning Human Understanding," in *Philosophic Classics: From Plato to Nietzsche,* Walter Kaufmann and Forrest E. Baird, eds. (Englewood Cliffs, NJ: Prentice-Hall, 1994).

or even beyond the universe, into the unbounded chaos, where nature is supposed to lie in total confusion. What never was seen, or heard of, may yet be conceived; nor is any thing beyond the power of thought, except what implies an absolute contradiction.

But though our thought seems to possess this unbounded liberty, we shall find, upon a nearer examination, that it is really confined within very narrow limits, and that all this creative power of the mind amounts to no more than the faculty of compounding, transposing, augmenting, or diminishing the materials afforded us by the senses and experience. When we think of a golden mountain, we only join two consistent ideas, *gold* and *mountain,* with which we were formerly acquainted. A virtuous horse we can conceive; because, from our own feeling, we can conceive virtue; and this we may unite to the figure and shape of a horse, which is an animal familiar to us. In short, all the materials of thinking are derived either from our outward or inward sentiment: the mixture and composition of these belongs alone to the mind and will. Or, to express myself in philosophical language, all our ideas or more feeble perceptions are copies of our impressions or more lively ones.

To prove this, the two following arguments will, I hope, be sufficient. First, when we analyze our thoughts or ideas, however compounded or sublime, we always find that they resolve themselves into such simple ideas as were copied from a precedent feeling or sentiment. Even those ideas, which, at first view, seem the most wide of this origin, are found, upon a nearer scrutiny, to be derived from it. The idea of God, as meaning an infinitely intelligent, wise, and good Being, arises from reflecting on the operations of our own mind, and augmenting, without limit, those qualities of goodness and wisdom. We may prosecute this enquiry to what length we please; where we shall always find, that every idea which we examine is copied from a similar impression. Those who would assert that this position is not universally true nor without exception, have only one, and that an easy method of refuting it; by producing that idea, which, in their opinion, is not derived from this source. It will then be incumbent on us, if we would maintain our doctrine, to produce the impression, or lively perception, which corresponds to it.

Secondly, if it happens, from a defect of the organ, that a man is not susceptible of any species of sensation, we always find that he is as little suscep-

tible of the correspondent ideas. A blind man can form no notion of colours; a deaf man of sounds. Restore either of them that sense in which he is deficient; by opening this new inlet for his sensations, you also open an inlet for the ideas; and he finds no difficulty in conceiving these objects. The case is the same, if the object, proper for exciting any sensation, has never been applied to the organ. A Laplander or Negro has no notion of the relish of wine. And though there are few or no instances of a like deficiency in the mind, where a person has never felt or is wholly incapable of a sentiment or passion that belongs to his species; yet we find the same observation to take place in a less degree. A man of mild manners can form no idea of inveterate revenge or cruelty; nor can a selfish heart easily conceive the heights of friendship and generosity. It is readily allowed, that other beings may possess many senses of which we can have no conception, because the ideas of them have never been introduced to us in the only manner by which an idea can have access to the mind, to wit, by the actual feeling and sensation.

There is, however, one contradictory phenomenon, which may prove that it is not absolutely impossible for ideas to arise, independent of their correspondent impressions. I believe it will readily be allowed, that the several distinct ideas of colour, which enter by the eye, or those of sound, which are conveyed by the ear, are really different from each other; though, at the same time, resembling. Now if this be true of different colours, it must be no less so of the different shades of the same colour; and each shade produces a distinct idea, independent of the rest. For if this should be denied, it is possible, by the continual gradation of shades, to run a colour insensibly into what is most remote from it; and if you will not allow any of the means to be different, you cannot, without absurdity, deny the extremes to be the same. Suppose, therefore, a person to have enjoyed his sight for thirty years, and to have become perfectly acquainted with colours of all kinds except one particular shade of blue, for instance, which it never has been his fortune to meet with. Let all the different shades of that colour, except that single one, be placed before him, descending gradually from the deepest to lightest; it is plain that he will perceive a blank, where that shade is wanting, and will be sensible that there is a greater distance in that place between the contiguous colours than in any other. Now I ask, whether it be possible for him, from his own imagination, to supply this deficiency, and raise up to himself the idea of that particular shade, though it had never been conveyed to him by his senses? I believe there are few but will be of opinion that he can; and this may serve as a proof that the simple ideas are not always, in every instance, derived from the correspondent impressions; though this instance is so singular, that it is scarcely worth our observing, and does not merit that for it alone we should alter our general maxim.

Here, therefore, is a proposition, which not only seems, in itself, simple and intelligible; but, if a proper use were made of it, might render every dispute equally intelligible, and banish all that jargon, which has so long taken possession of metaphysical reasonings, and drawn disgrace upon them. All ideas, especially abstract ones, are naturally faint and obscure; the mind has but a slender hold of them: they are apt to be confounded with other resembling ideas; and when we have often employed any term, though without a distinct meaning, we are apt to imagine it has a determinate idea annexed to it. On the contrary, all impressions, that is, all sensations, either outward or inward, are strong and vivid: the limits between them are more exactly determined: nor is it easy to fall into any error or mistake with regard to them. When we entertain, therefore, any suspicion that a philosophical term is employed without any meaning or idea (as is but too frequent), we need but enquire, *from what impressions is that supposed idea derived?* And if it be impossible to assign any, this will serve to confirm our suspicion.★ By bringing ideas into so clear a light we may reasonably hope to remove all dispute, which may arise, concerning their nature and reality.

---

★It is probable that no more was meant by those, who denied innate ideas, than that all ideas were copies of our impressions; though it must be confessed, that the terms, which they employed, were not chosen with such caution, nor so exactly defined, as to prevent all mistakes about their doctrine. For what is meant by *innate*? If innate be equivalent to natural, then all the perceptions and ideas of the mind must be allowed to be innate or natural, in whatever sense we take the latter word, whether in opposition to what is uncommon, artificial, or miraculous. If by innate be meant, contemporary to our birth, the dispute seems to be frivolous; nor is it worth while to enquire at what time thinking begins, whether before, at, or after our birth. Again, the word idea, seems to be commonly taken in a very loose sense, by LOCKE and others; as standing for any of our perceptions, our sensations and passions, as well as thoughts. Now in this sense, I should desire to know, what can be meant by asserting, that self-love, or resentment of injuries, or the passion between the sexes is not innate?

---

SELECTION 7.2

## Critique of Pure Reason ★

*Immanuel Kant*

---

[*In the previous selection, you saw that Hume thought all concepts are derived from sensory "impressions." To put this point in Kant's language, Hume thought that all concepts are "empirical" and none are "a priori" (these phrases mean the same). In this difficult selection, Kant argues that time is not empirical (i.e., that time is a priori). In other words, according to Kant, time is not derived from sensory impressions or what Kant calls "intuitions." He also explains what time is.*]

---

★From Immanuel Kant's *Critique of Pure Reason,* translated by Norman Kemp Smith (London: Macmillan and Company, 1929). Reprinted by permission of Macmillan, London, UK.

### Transcendental Aesthetic Section II, Time

*§4, Metaphysical Exposition of the Concept of Time*

1. Time is not an empirical concept that has been derived from any experience. For neither coexistence nor succession would ever come without our perception, if the representation of time were not presupposed as underlying them *a priori*. . . .

2. Time is a necessary representation that underlies all intuitions. We cannot, in respect of appearances in general, remove time itself, though we can quite well think time as void of appearances. Time is, therefore, given *a priori*. In it alone is

actuality of appearances possible at all. Appearances may, one and all, vanish; but time (as the universal condition of their possibility) cannot itself be removed.

3. . . . Time has only one dimension; different times are not simultaneous but successive (just as different spaces are not successive but simultaneous). These principles cannot be derived from experience, for experience would give neither strict universality nor apodeictic certainty. We should only be able to say that common experience teaches us that it is so; not that it must be so. These principles are valid as rules under which alone experiences are possible; and they instruct us in regard to the experiences, not by means of them.

4. Time is not a discursive, or what is called a general concept, but a pure form of sensible intuition. Different times are but parts of one and the same time. . . . Moreover, the proposition that different times cannot be simultaneous is not to be derived from a general concept. . . .

§6, *Conclusions from These Concepts*

(a) Time is not something which exists of itself, or which inheres in things as an objective determination, and it does not, therefore, remain when abstraction is made of all subjective conditions of its intuition. Were it self-subsistent, it would be something which would be actual and yet not an actual object. Were it a determination or order inhering in things themselves, it could not precede the objects as their condition. . . .

(b) Time is nothing but the form of inner sense, that is, of the intuition of ourselves and of our inner state. It cannot be a determination of outer appearances; it has to do neither with shape nor position, but with the relation of representations in our inner state. . . .

(c) Time is the formal *a priori* condition of all appearances whatsoever. Space, as the pure form of all *outer* intuition, is so far limited; it serves as the *a priori* condition only of outer appearances. But since all representations, whether they have for their objects outer things or not, belong, in themselves, as determinations of the mind, to our inner state; and since this inner state stands under the formal condition of inner intuition, and so belongs to time, time is an *a priori* condition of all appearance whatsoever. It is the immediate condition of inner appearances (of our souls), and thereby the mediate condition of outer appearances. Just as I can say *a priori* that all outer appearances are in space, and are determined *a priori* in conformity with the relations of space, I can also say, from the principle of inner sense, that all appearances whatsoever, that is, all objects of the senses, are in time, and necessarily stand in time-relations.

If we abstract from *our* mode of inwardly intuiting ourselves — the mode of intuition in terms of which we likewise take up into our faculty of representation all outer intuitions — and so take objects as they may be in themselves, then time is nothing. It has objective validity only in respect of appearances, these being things which we take *as objects of our senses.* . . .

Time is therefore a purely subjective condition of our (human) intuition (which is always sensible, that is, so far as we are affected by objects), and in itself, apart from the subject, is nothing.

### SELECTION 7.3

# The Philosophy of History*

*Georg Hegel*

[*In the previous selection, you saw that Kant thought that time is really a construct of the mind. In this selection, Hegel goes Kant one further: everything, Hegel says, is a construct of Reason. Hegel doesn't argue for this thesis in this selection but only asserts that it has been "proved."*]

The only Thought which Philosophy brings with it to the contemplation of History, is the simple conception of *Reason;* that Reason is the Sovereign of the World; that the history of the world, therefore, presents us with a rational process. This conviction and intuition is a hypothesis in the domain of history as such. In that of Philosophy it is no hypothesis. It is there provided by speculative cognition, that Reason—and this term may here suffice us, without investigation the relation sustained by the Universe to the Divine Being—is *Substance,* as well as *Infinite Power;* its own *Infinite Material* underlying all the natural and spiritual life which it originates, as also the *Infinite Form*—that which sets this Material in motion. On the one hand, Reason is the

*From Georg Hegel, *The Philosophy of History,* translated by J. Sibree (New York: The Colonial Press, 1900).

substance of the Universe; viz., that by which and in which all reality has its being and subsistence. On the other hand, it is the *Infinite Energy* of the Universe; since Reason is not so powerless as to be incapable of producing anything but a mere ideal, a mere intention—having its place outside reality, nobody knows where; something separate and abstract, in the heads of certain human beings. It is *the Infinite complex of things,* their entire Essence and Truth. It is its own material which it commits to its own Active Energy to work up; not needing, as finite action does, the conditions of an external material of given means from which it may obtain its support, and the objects of its activity. It supplies its own nourishment, and is the object of its own operations. While it is exclusively its own basis of existence, and absolute final aim, it is also the energizing power realizing this aim; developing in it not only the phenomena of the Natural, but also of the Spiritual Universe—the History of the World. That this "Idea" or "Reason" is the *True,* the *Eternal,* the absolutely *powerful* essence; that it reveals itself in the World, and that in that World nothing else is revealed but this and its honor and glory—is the thesis which, as we have said, has been proved in Philosophy, and is here regarded as demonstrated.

### SELECTION 7.4

# The World As Will and Representation*

*Arthur Schopenhauer*

[*Some terminology: By "empirical" Schopenhauer means "capable of being verified by observation and experiment, capable of being encountered in space and time."*

*From Arthur Schopenhauer, *The World As Will and Representation,* translated by E. F. J. Payne, Vol. II (New York: Dover, 1966). Copyright © 1958 (renewed 1986) by the Falcon's Wing Press. Reprinted by permission of Dover Publications, Inc.

*By "ideality" he means the property of existing in consciousness or thought.*

*By "phenomenon" he means an object of experience in space and time. By "phenomenon of the brain" he means an experience produced by the brain.*]

### On the Fundamental View of Idealism

In endless space countless luminous spheres, round each of which some dozen smaller illuminated ones revolve, hot at the core and covered over with a hard cold crust; on this crust a mouldy film has produced living and knowing beings: this is empirical truth, the real, the world. Yet for a being who thinks, it is a precarious position to stand on one of those numberless spheres freely floating in boundless space, without knowing whence or whither, and to be only one of innumerable similar beings that throng, press, and toil, restlessly and rapidly arising and passing away in beginningless and endless time. Here there is nothing permanent but matter alone, and the recurrence of the same varied organic forms by means of certain ways and channels that inevitably exist as they do. All that empirical science can teach is only the more precise nature and rule of these events. But at last the philosophy of modern times, especially through Berkeley and Kant, has called to mind that all this in the first instance is only *phenomenon of the brain,* and is encumbered by so many great and different *subjective* conditions that its supposed absolute reality vanishes, and leaves room for an entirely different world-order that lies at the root of that phenomenon, in other words, is related to it as is the thing-in-itself to the mere appearance.

"The world is my representation" is, like the axioms of Euclid, a proposition which everyone must recognize as true as soon as he understands it, although it is not a proposition that everyone understands as soon as he hears it. To have brought this proposition to consciousness and to have connected it with the problem of the relation of the ideal to the real, in other words, of the world in the head to the world outside the head, constitutes, together with the problem of moral freedom, the distinctive characteristic of the philosophy of the moderns. For only after men had tried their hand for thousands of years at merely *objective* philosophizing did they discover that, among the many things that make the world so puzzling and precarious, the first and foremost is that, however immeasurable and massive it may be, its existence hangs nevertheless on a single thread; and this thread is the actual consciousness in which it exists. This condition, with which the existence of the world is irrevocably encumbered, marks it with the stamp of *ideality,* in spite of all *empirical* reality, and consequently with the stamp of the mere *phenomenon.* Thus the world must be recognized, from one aspect at least, as akin to a dream, indeed as capable of being put in the same class with a dream. For the same brain-function that conjures up during sleep a perfectly objective, per-ceptible, and indeed palpable world must have just as large a share in the presentation of the objective world of wakefulness. Though different as regards their matter, the two worlds are nevertheless obviously moulded from one form. This form is the intellect, the brain-function. Descartes was probably the first to attain the degree of reflection demanded by that fundamental truth; consequently, he made that truth the starting-point of his philosophy, although provisionally only in the form of sceptical doubt. By his taking *cogito ergo sum* as the only thing certain, and provisionally regarding the existence of the world as problematical, the essential and only correct starting-point, and at the same time the true point of support, of all philosophy was really found. This point, indeed, is essentially and of necessity *the subjective, our own consciousness.* For this alone is and remains that which is immediate; everything else, be it what it may, is first mediated and conditioned by consciousness, and therefore dependent on it. It is thus rightly considered that the philosophy of the moderns starts from Descartes as its father. Not long afterwards, Berkeley went farther along this path, and arrived at *idealism* proper; in other words, at the knowledge that what is extended in space, and hence the objective, material world in general, exists as such simply and solely in our *representation,* and that it is false and indeed absurd to attribute to it, *as such,* an existence outside all representation and independent of the knowing subject, and so to assume a matter positively and absolutely existing in itself. But this very correct and deep insight really constitutes the whole of Berkeley's philosophy; in it he had exhausted himself.

Accordingly, true philosophy must at all costs be *idealistic;* indeed, it must be so merely to be honest. For nothing is more certain than that no one ever came out of himself in order to identify himself immediately with things different from him; but everything of which he has certain, sure, and hence immediate knowledge, lies within his consciousness. Beyond this consciousness, therefore, there can be no *immediate* certainty; but the first principles of a science must have such a certainty. It is quite appropriate to the empirical standpoint of all the other sciences to assume the objective world as positively and actually existing; it is not appropriate to the standpoint of philosophy, which has to go back to what is primary and original. *Consciousness* alone is immediately given, hence the basis of philosophy is limited to the facts of consciousness; in other words, philosophy is essentially *idealistic*. Realism, which commends itself to the crude understanding by appearing to be founded on fact, starts precisely from an arbitrary assumption, and is in consequence an empty castle in the air, since it skips or denies the first fact of all, namely that all that we know lies within consciousness. For that the *objective existence* of things is conditioned by a representer of them, and that consequently the objective world exists only *as representation,* is no hypothesis, still less a peremptory pronouncement, or even a paradox put forward for the sake of debate or argument. On the contrary, it is the surest and simplest truth, and a knowledge of it is rendered more difficult only by the fact that it is indeed too simple, and that not everyone has sufficient power of reflection to go back to the first elements of his consciousness of things. There can never be an existence that is objective absolutely and in itself; such an existence, indeed, is positively inconceivable. For the objective, as such, always and essentially has its existence in the consciousness of a subject; it is therefore the representation of this subject, and consequently is conditioned by the subject, and moreover by the subject's forms of representation, which belong to the subject and not to the object.

That the *objective world would exist* even if there existed no knowing being at all, naturally seems at the first onset to be sure and certain, because it can be thought in the abstract, without the contradiction that it carries within itself coming to light. But if we try to *realize* this abstract thought, in other words, to reduce it to representations of perception, from which alone (like everything abstract) it can have content and truth; and if accordingly we attempt to *imagine an objective world without a knowing subject,* then we become aware that what we are imagining at that moment is in truth the opposite of what we intended, namely nothing but just the process in the intellect of a knowing being who perceives an objective world, that is to say, precisely that which we had sought to exclude. For this perceptible and real world is obviously a phenomenon of the brain; and so in the assumption that the world as such might exist independently of all brains there lies a contradiction. . . .

True idealism, on the other hand, is not the empirical, but the transcendental. It leaves the *empirical* reality of the world untouched, but adheres to the fact that all *object,* and hence the empirically real in general, is conditioned by the *subject* in a twofold manner. In the first place it is conditioned *materially,* or as *object* in general, since an objective existence is conceivable only in face of a subject and as the representation of this subject. In the second place, it is conditioned *formally,* since the *mode and manner* of the object's existence, in other words, of its being represented (space, time, causality), proceed from the subject, and are predisposed in the subject. Therefore immediately connected with simple or *Berkeleian* idealism, which concerns the *object in general,* is *Kantian* idealism, which concerns the specially given *mode and manner* of objective existence. This proves that the whole of the material world with its bodies in space, extended and, by means of time, having causal relations with one another, and everything attached to this—all this is not something existing *independently* of our mind, but something that has its fundamental presuppositions in our brain-functions, *by means of* which and *in* which alone is *such* an objective order of things possible. For time, space, and causality, on which all those real and objective events rest, are themselves nothing more than functions of the brain; so that, therefore, this unchangeable *order* of things, affording the criterion and the clue to their empirical *reality,* itself comes first from the brain, and has its credentials from that alone. Kant has discussed this thoroughly and in detail; though he does not mention the brain, but says "the faculty of knowledge." He has even attempted to prove that that objective order in time, space, causality, matter, and so on, on which all the events of the real world ultimately rest, cannot even be *conceived,* when closely considered, as a self-existing order, i.e., an order of things-in-themselves, or as something absolutely objective and positively existing; for if we attempt to think it out to the end, it leads to contradictions. . . .

But even apart from the deep insight and discernment revealed only by the Kantian philosophy, the inadmissible character of the assumption of absolute *realism,* clung to so obstinately, can indeed be directly demonstrated, or at any rate felt, by the mere elucidation of its meaning through considerations such as the following. According to realism, the world is supposed to exist, as we know it, independently of this knowledge. Now let us once remove from it all knowing beings, and thus leave behind only inorganic and vegetable nature. Rock, tree, and brook are there, and the blue sky; sun, moon, and stars illuminate this world, as before, only of course to no purpose, since there exists no eye to see such things. But then let us subsequently put into the world a knowing being. That world then presents itself *once more* in his brain, and repeats itself inside that brain exactly as it was previously outside it. Thus to the *first* world a *second* has been added, which, although completely separated from the first, resembles it to a nicety. Now the *subjective* world of this perception is constituted in *subjective,* known space exactly as the *objective* world is in *objective,* infinite space. But the subjective world still has an advantage over the objective, namely the knowledge that that external space is infinite; in fact, it can state beforehand most minutely and accurately the full conformity to law of all the relations in that space which are possible and not yet actual, and it does not need to examine them first. It can state just as much about the course of time, as also about the relation of cause and effect which governs the changes in outer space. I think that, on closer consideration, all this proves absurd enough, and thus leads to the conviction that that absolutely *objective* world outside the head, independent of it and *prior* to all knowledge, which we at first imagined we had conceived, was really no other than the second world already known *subjectively,* the world of the representation, and that it is this alone which we are actually capable of conceiving. Accordingly the assumption is automatically forced on us that the world, as we know it, exists only for our knowledge, and consequently in the *representation* alone, and not once again outside that representation. In keeping with this assumption, then, the thing-in-itself, in other words, that which exists independently of our knowledge and of all knowledge, is to be regarded as something quite different from the *representation* and all its attributes, and hence from objectivity in general. What this is, will afterwards be the theme of our second book.

On the other hand, the controversy about the reality of the external world, considered in §5 of our first volume, rests on the assumption, just criticized, of an objective and a subjective world both in *space,* and on the impossibility, arising in the case of this presupposition, of a transition, a bridge, between the two. On this controversy I have to make the following remarks.

Subjective and objective do not form a continuum. That of which we are immediately conscious is bounded by the skin, or rather by the extreme ends of the nerves proceeding from the cerebral system. Beyond this lies a world of which we have not

other knowledge than that gained through pictures in our mind. Now the question is whether and to what extent a world existing independently of us corresponds to these pictures. The relation between the two could be brought about only by means of the law of causality, for this law alone leads from something given to something quite different from it. This law itself, however, has first of all to substantiate its validity. Now it must be either of *objective* or of *subjective* origin; but in either case it lies on one bank or the other, and therefore cannot serve as a bridge. If, as Locke and Hume assumed, it is *a posteriori,* and hence drawn from experience, it is of *objective* origin; it then itself belongs to the external world in question, and therefore cannot vouch for the reality of that world. For then, according to Locke's method, the law of causality would be demonstrated from experience, and the reality of experience from the law of causality. If, on the other hand, it is given *a priori,* as Kant more correctly taught, then it is of *subjective* origin; and so it is clear that with it we always remain in the *subjective.* For the only thing actually given *empirically* in the case of perception is the occurrence of a sensation in the organ of sense. The assumption that this sensation, even only in general, must have a *cause* rests on a law that is rooted in the form of our knowledge, in other words, in the functions of our brain. The origin of this law is therefore just as subjective as is that sensation itself. The *cause* of the given sensation, assumed as a result of this law, immediately manifests itself in perception as *object,* having space and time as the form of its appearance. But again, even *these* forms themselves are of entirely subjective origin, for they are the mode and manner of our faculty of perception. That transition from the sensation to its cause, which, as I have repeatedly shown, lies at the foundation of all sense-perception, is certainly sufficient for indicating to us the empirical presence in space and time of an empirical object, and is therefore fully satisfactory for practical life. But it is by no means sufficient for giving us information about the existence and real inner nature of the phenomena that arise for us in such a way, or rather of their intelligible substratum. Therefore, the fact that, on the occasion of certain sensations occurring in my organs of sense, there arises in my head a *perception* of things extended in space, permanent in time, and causally operative, by no means justifies me in assuming that such things also exist in themselves, in other words, that they exist with such properties absolutely belonging to them, independently of my head and outside it. This is the correct conclusion of the *Kantian* philosophy. It is connected with an earlier result of Locke which is just as correct, and very much easier to understand. Thus, although, as is allowed by Locke's teaching, external things are positively assumed to be the causes of the sensations, there cannot be any *resemblance* at all between the *sensation,* in which the *effect* consists, and the objective *nature* or *quality* of the *cause* that gives rise to this sensation. For the sensation, as organic function, is above all determined by the very artificial and complicated nature of our sense-organs; thus it is merely stimulated by the external cause, but is then perfected entirely in accordance with its own laws, and hence is wholly subjective. Locke's philosophy was the criticism of the functions of sense; but Kant has furnished the criticism of the functions of the brain. But to all this we still have to add the result of Berkeley, which has been revised by me, namely that every *object,* whatever its origin, is, *as object,* already conditioned by the subject, and thus is essentially only the subject's *representation.* The aim of realism is just the object without subject but it is impossible even to conceive such an object clearly. . . .

. . . [T]he proposition that "the subject would nevertheless be a knowing being, even if it had no object, in other words, no representation at all" is just as false as is the proposition of the crude understanding to the effect that "the world, the object, would still exist, even if there were no subject." A consciousness without object is no consciousness at all. A thinking subject has *concepts* for its object; a sensuously perceiving subject has objects with the qualities corresponding to its organization. Now if we deprive the *subject* of all the particular determinations and forms of its knowing, all the properties in the *object* also disappear, and nothing but *matter without form and quality* is left. This matter can occur in experience as little as can the subject without the forms of its knowledge, yet it remains opposed to the bare subject as such, as its reflex, which can only disappear simultaneously with it. Although materialism imagines that it postulates nothing

more than this matter — atoms for instance — yet it unconsciously adds not only the subject, but also space, time, and causality, which depend on special determinations of the subject.

The world as representation, the objective world, has thus, so to speak, two poles, namely the knowing subject plain and simple without the forms of its knowing, and crude matter without form and quality. Both are absolutely unknowable; the subject, because it is that which knows; matter, because without form and quality it cannot be perceived. Yet both are the fundamental conditions of all empirical perception. Thus the knowing subject, merely as such, which is likewise a presupposition of all experience, stands in opposition, as its clear counterpart, to crude, formless, quite dead (i.e., will-less) matter. This matter is not given in any experience, but is presupposed in every experience. This subject is not in time, for time is only the more direct form of all its representing. Matter, standing in opposition to the subject, is accordingly eternal, imperishable, endures through all time; but properly speaking it is not extended, since extension gives form, and hence it is not spatial. Everything else is involved in a constant arising and passing away, whereas these two constitute the static poles of the world as representation. We can therefore regard the permanence of matter as the reflex of the timelessness of the pure subject, that is simply taken to be the condition of every object. Both belong to the phenomenon, not to the thing-in-itself; but they are the framework of the phenomenon. Both are discovered only through abstraction; they are not given immediately, pure and by themselves.

The fundamental mistake of all systems is the failure to recognize this truth, namely that *the intellect and matter are correlatives,* in other words, the one exists only for the other; both stand and fall together; the one is only the other's reflex. They are in fact really one and the same thing, considered from two opposite points of view; and this one thing — here I am anticipating — is the phenomenon of the will or of the thing-in-itself. Consequently, both are secondary, and therefore the origin of the world is not to be looked for in either of them.

## CHECKLIST

To help you review, here is a checklist of the key philosophers and terms and concepts of this chapter. The brief descriptive sentences summarize the philosophers' leading ideas. Keep in mind that some of these summary statements are oversimplifications of complex positions.

### Philosophers

- **David Hume** held that there is no metaphysical knowledge and maintained that knowledge is limited to what we experience. He summoned powerful arguments to question our supposed knowledge of the self, causality, God, and the external world.
- **Immanuel Kant** believed the mind imposes a certain form and order on experienceable objects. He held that there can be no knowledge of things "as they are in themselves," independent of experience.
- **Georg Hegel** was the premier exponent of Absolute Idealism. He rejected the concept of the "thing-in-itself" and held that all reality is the expression of thought or reason.
- **Arthur Schopenhauer** held that the world is structured and driven by will.

### Key Terms and Concepts

| | |
|---|---|
| constant conjunction | phenomena |
| "The future will resemble the past." | noumena |
| | *Ding-an-sich* |
| Copernican revolution in philosophy | Absolute Idealism |
| | the Absolute |
| principle that perceptions must be conceptualized and unified to qualify as experience | |

## QUESTIONS FOR DISCUSSION AND REVIEW

1. Do you ever experience anything other than your own perceptions? Explain.
2. Explain Hume's reasons for questioning the idea of the mind/self.
3. "Necessity is something in the mind, not in the objects." Explain what this means and what Hume's reasons were for holding it.
4. Will the future resemble the past? Can you *know* that it will, or must you merely *assume* that it will?
5. If knowledge begins with experience, must it also rise from experience? Explain.
6. Is it possible that we may someday experience an event that is in neither space nor time? If not, why not?
7. Is it possible for extraterrestrial aliens to experience things that are not in space or time?
8. Do infants have *experience*, or do they just have sensations? Do cats? Do fish? Explain.
9. Can we have knowledge of things-in-themselves? Be sure to clarify what you mean by "things-in-themselves."
10. "Everything depends on grasping the truth not merely as Substance but as Subject as well." Who said this, and what does it mean?

## SUGGESTED FURTHER READINGS

A. J. Ayer, *Hume: A Very Short Introduction* (New York: Oxford University Press, 2001). One of the twentieth century's most important philosophers introduces readers to his own philosophical predecessor.

Frederick C. Beiser, ed., *The Cambridge Companion to Hegel* (New York: Cambridge University Press, 1993). A collection of essays.

E. O. Burtt, *The English Philosophers from Bacon to Mill* (New York: Modern Library, 1939). A general book on modern philosophy.

Arthur Collins, *Possible Experience: Understanding Kant's Critique of Pure Reason* (Berkeley: University of California Press, 1999). An interpretation of Kant as a realist rather than as an idealist.

J. N. Findlay, *Hegel: A Re-examination* (New York: Humanities Press, 1970). A readable presentation of Hegel's principal works.

Richard M. Gale, *The Blackwell Guide to Metaphysics* (Malden, Mass.: Blackwell, 2002). Introduction to the core issue in metaphysics.

Paul Guyer, ed., *The Cambridge Companion to Kant* (New York: Cambridge University Press, 1992). A collection of essays.

G. W. F. Hegel, *The Phenomenology of Mind* (New York: Harper & Row, 1967). Hegel's first major work and a brilliant reinterpretation of Western philosophy through the eyes of an Absolute Idealist. Not light reading, though.

Stephen Houlgate, ed., *The Hegel Reader* (Malden, Mass.: Blackwell, 1998). Presumably the most comprehensive collection of Hegel's writings available in English.

David Hume, *A Treatise of Human Nature*, 2nd ed., L. A. Selby-Bigge, ed., with second edition revisions and variant readings by P. H. Nidditch (New York: Oxford University Press, 1978).

Christopher Janaway, *Schopenhauer* (New York: Oxford University Press, 1994). A short exposition of Schopenhauer's metaphysics.

W. T. Jones, *Kant and the Nineteenth Century*, 2nd ed. (New York: Harcourt Brace Jovanovich, 1975). Jones's section on Hegel contains enough original material for the introductory student and explains it all very nicely too.

Immanuel Kant, *Prolegomena to Any Future Metaphysics*, P. Carus, trans. (Indianapolis: Hackett, 1977). This is Kant's own (relatively) simplified introduction to his thinking about metaphysics and epistemology. If you want to have a look at the *Critique of Pure Reason* itself, the Norman Kemp Smith translation is published by St. Martin's in New York (1965). If you need help with this difficult work, you cannot do better than H. J. Paton's *Kant's Metaphysics of Experience*, in two volumes (London, 1936). Paton's work covers only the first half of the *Critique*, but it explains it, sentence by difficult sentence, in clear English.

Jaegwon Kim and Ernest Sosa, eds., *A Companion to Metaphysics* (Malden, Mass.: Blackwell, 2002). Reference work on major topics and philosophers concerning metaphysics.

Daniel Kolak, *The Mayfield Anthology of Western Philosophy* (Mountain View, Calif.: Mayfield, 1998). Important selections from major philosophers.

Isaac Krannuck, ed., *The Portable Enlightenment Reader* (New York: Penguin Books, 1995). A collection of important texts of the most significant philosophers of the time.

Manfred Kuehn, *Kant* (New York: Cambridge University Press, 2001). A biography of dealing with Kant's life and thought.

J. Loewenberg, ed., *Hegel Selections* (New York: Scribner's, 1929). Hegel is very, very difficult.

Michael J. Loux, ed., *Metaphysics, Contemporary Readings* (New York: Routledge, 2001). Selections from contemporary authors on metaphysical topics.

Bryan Magee, *The Philosophy of Schopenhauer* (New York: Oxford University Press, 1997). An important exposition of the thought of Schopenhauer.

David Fate Norton, ed., *The Cambridge Guide to Hume* (New York: Cambridge University Press, 1993). Review of the philosophical ideas of one of the most important philosophers to have written in the English language.

David Pears, *Hume's System, An Examination of the First Book of His Treatise* (New York: Oxford University Press, 1991). An important examination.

Terry Pinkard, *Hegel* (New York: Cambridge University Press, 2000). The key ideas of Hegel are presented in the context of a recent biography.

Stephen Priest, *The British Empiricists* (London: Penguin Books, 1990). A useful introduction to the British empiricist tradition extending from Hobbes through to Russell and Ayer.

Rudiger Safranski, *Schopenhauer and the Wild Years of Philosophy* (Cambridge, Mass.: Harvard University Press, 1991). Fascinating account of the powerful thinker's life and work.

Arthur Schopenhauer, *Essays and Aphorisms*, R. J. Hollingdale, trans. (New York: Penguin, 1973). A nice introduction to the psychological insights of Schopenhauer.

Roger Scruton, Peter Singer, Christopher Janaway, and Michael Tanner, *German Philosophers: Kant, Hegel, Schopenhauer, Nietzsche* (New York: Oxford University Press, 2001). Studies of four of the most important German philosophers, by leading contemporary scholars.

Robert C. Solomon and Kathleen M. Higgins, eds., *Routledge History of Philosophy*, vol. 7, *Age of German Idealism* (London: Routledge, 1994). Introductory essays covering from Kant through the first half of the nineteenth century.

Robert Stern, *Hegel and the Phenomenology of Spirit* (New York: Routledge, 2002). A helpful introduction to one of the most difficult books in Western philosophy.

James Van Cleve, *Problems From Kant* (New York: Oxford University Press, 1999). A comprehensive new analysis of Kant's *Critique of Pure Reason*.

# 8

# The Continental Tradition

Experience, it is said, makes a man wise. That is very silly talk. If there were nothing beyond experience, it would simply drive him mad.
  —Søren Kierkegaard

Man is a rope, tied between beast and Superman—a rope over an abyss.
  —Friedrich Nietzsche

The existentialist says at once that man is anguish.    —Jean-Paul Sartre

Absolute Idealism left distinct marks on many facets of Western culture. True, science was indifferent to it, and common sense was perhaps stupefied by it, but the greatest political movement of the nineteenth and twentieth centuries— Marxism—was to a significant degree an outgrowth of Absolute Idealism. (Bertrand Russell remarked someplace that Marx was nothing more than Hegel mixed with British economic theory.) Nineteenth- and twentieth-century literature, theology, and even art felt an influence. The great Romantic composers of the nineteenth century, for example, with their fondness for expanded form, vast orchestras, complex scores, and soaring melodies, searched for the all-encompassing musical statement. In doing so they mirrored the efforts of the metaphysicians, whose vast and imposing systems were sources of inspiration to many artists and composers.

As we have said, much of what happened in philosophy after Hegel was in response to Hegel. This response took different forms in English-speaking countries and on the European continent—so different that philosophy in the twentieth century was split into two traditions or, as we might say nowadays, two "conversations." So-called analytic philosophy and its offshoots became the predominant tradition of philosophy in England and eventually in the United States. The response to Hegelian idealism on the European continent was quite different, however, and is known (at least in English-speaking countries) as **Continental**

**philosophy.** Meanwhile, the United States developed its own brand of philosophy — called *pragmatism* — but ultimately analytic philosophy became firmly entrenched in the United States as well.

In this chapter we will concentrate on Continental philosophy; Chapter 9 will cover analytic philosophy and pragmatism.

Within Continental philosophy may be found various identifiable schools of philosophical thought: existentialism, phenomenology, hermeneutics, deconstruction, and critical theory. Two influential schools were existentialism and phenomenology, and we will begin this chapter with them.

Both existentialism and phenomenology have their roots in the nineteenth century, and many of their themes can be traced back to Socrates and even to the pre-Socratics. Each school of thought has influenced the other to such an extent that two of the most famous and influential Continental philosophers of this century, Martin Heidegger (1889–1976) and Jean-Paul Sartre (1905–1980), are important figures in both movements, although Heidegger is primarily a phenomenologist and Sartre primarily an existentialist.

## EXISTENTIALISM

Some of the main themes of existentialism are the following:

- Traditional and academic philosophy is sterile and remote from the concerns of real life.
- Philosophy must focus on the individual in her or his confrontation with the world.
- The world is irrational (or, in any event, beyond total comprehending or accurate conceptualizing through philosophy).
- The world is absurd, in the sense that no ultimate explanation can be given for why it is the way it is.
- Senselessness, emptiness, triviality, separation, and inability to communicate pervade human existence, giving birth to anxiety, dread, self-doubt, and despair.
- The individual confronts, as the most important fact of human existence, the necessity to choose how he or she is to live within this absurd and irrational world.

The existentialists do not guarantee that this **existential predicament,** as it might be called, can be solved. What they do say is that without utter honesty in confronting the assorted problems of human existence, life can only deteriorate — that without struggling doggedly with these problems, the individual will find no meaning or value in life.

Now, many of these themes had already been introduced by those brooding thinkers of the nineteenth century, Arthur Schopenhauer (see previous chapter), Søren Kierkegaard, and Friedrich Nietzsche. All three had a strong distaste for the optimistic idealism of Hegel—and for metaphysical systems in general. Such philosophy, they thought, ignored the human predicament. For all three the universe, including its human inhabitants, is seldom rational, and philosophical systems that seek to make everything seem rational are just futile attempts to overcome pessimism and despair.

**Søren Kierkegaard** [KEER-kuh-gard] (1813–1855) scorned Hegel's system, in which the individual dissolves into a kind of abstract unreality. By contrast, Kierkegaard emphasized the individual and especially the individual's will and need to make important choices. Where Hegel was abstract to a degree rarely found outside, say, mathematics, Kierkegaard was almost entirely concerned with how and what the individual actually chooses in the face of doubt and uncertainty.

For Kierkegaard, existence in this earthly realm must lead a sensitive person to despair. Despair, Kierkegaard held, is the inevitable result of the individual's having to confront momentous concrete ethical and religious dilemmas *as an individual*. It is the result of the individual's having to make, *for himself and alone,* choices of lasting significance.

According to Kierkegaard, despair is the *sickness-unto-death* and is the central philosophical problem. Is there anything in this world or outside it to which the individual can cling to keep from being swept away by the dark tides of despair? This, for Kierkegaard, is the fundamental question. His eventual conclusion was that nothing earthly can save a person from despair. Only a subjective commitment to the infinite and to God, not based on abstract intellectualizing or theoretical reasoning, can grant relief.

Kierkegaard emphasized the theme of the irrationality of the world in opposition to Hegel's belief in its utter rationality. The earth, Kierkegaard thought, is a place of suffering, fear, and dread. Of these three, dread, according to Kierkegaard, is the worst because it has no identifiable object or specifiable cause. Dread renders us almost helpless to resist it. Kierkegaard regarded the idea that philosophy should be concerned with general or ideal "truths" and abstract metaphysical principles with disdain. Philosophy must speak to the anguished existence of the individual who lives in an irrational world and who must make important decisions in that world.

**Friedrich Nietzsche** [NEE-cheh] (1844–1900) read Arthur Schopenhauer (1788–1860) and became convinced that the world is driven by cosmic will, not by reason. Nietzsche rejected Hegel's idealism and all similar rationalist metaphysics. However, he disagreed with Schopenhauer as to the nature of the cosmic will. For Nietzsche, the world is driven and determined by the **will-to-power.** However, according to Nietzsche, Western society had become increasingly decadent. People had come to lead lives largely devoid of joy and grandeur. They were enslaved by a morality that says "no" to life and to all the affirms it. They had become part of a herd, part of a mass that is only too willing to do what it is told. The herd animal, he held, is cowardly, reactionary, fearful, desultory, and vengeful. The mediocrity of Western civilization, he believed, was a reflection of these qualities. Only the rare and isolated individual, the Superman, or *Übermensch*—a famous concept in Nietzsche's philosophy—can escape the triviality of society.

The Superman, according to Nietzsche, embraces the will-to-power and overthrows the submissive and mediocre "slàve" mentality that permeates society and

## PROFILE: Søren Kierkegaard (1813–1855)

Søren Kierkegaard, Danish philosopher and religious thinker, was virtually unknown outside Denmark until the twentieth century. Ultimately, however, his thought had a profound impact on existentialist philosophy and Protestant theology.

Kierkegaard's life was outwardly unexciting. He attended the universities of Copenhagen and Berlin and was much influenced by German culture, though he made polemical attacks on Hegel, whose metaphysics he regarded as totally inapplicable to the individual.

As for his inward life, Kierkegaard professed himself to have been, since childhood, "under the sway of a prodigious melancholy," and his grim outlook was made even gloomier by the confession of his father—himself no carefree spirit—that he had sinned and had even cursed God. Finding himself without moorings, Kierkegaard regarded dread and despair as the central problems of his life, and he learned that he could escape their grasp only through a passionate commitment of faith to God and the infinite.

Although Kierkegaard became engaged to marry, he found it necessary to break off the engagement, apparently because God occupied the "first place" in his life, though his own writing about the subject is murky. The episode, at any rate, was so momentous that even the sketchiest biography of Kierkegaard is obliged to mention the woman's name: Regine Olsen. The agony of choosing between God and Regine, a choice Kierkegaard felt he had to make, affected him profoundly.

Kierkegaard defined three types of life: the aesthetic, the ethical, and the religious. These correspond to what English philosophy professor Ray Billington has called the life of the observer, the life of the follower, and the life of the initiator. The "aesthetic" life is dominated by impulse, emotions, and sensual pleasures and does not truly involve making choices. The "ethical" life does involve making choices, but those who live this life make choices on the basis of some kind of moral code, which they in effect fall back on as a sort of crutch. But at a higher and much more difficult plane, that of the "religious," individuals realize that they must decide all issues for themselves. They face the agony of having to rely on their own judgment while never knowing whether this judgment is correct. The despair one faces at this level is overcome only by a "leap of faith," that total and infinite commitment to God.

Some of Kierkegaard's most important philosophical works, *Either/Or* (1843), *Philosophical Fragments* (1844), and *The Concluding Unscientific Postscript* (1846), were published under pseudonyms.

dominates religion. In his embrace of the will-to-power, the *Übermensch* not only lives a full and exciting life but creates a new, life-affirming morality as well. He creates rather than discovers values. God, whom the meek and compassionate worship as the source of values, is just simply "dead."

Nietzsche also believed we have no access to absolute truths—such things as Plato's Forms and Kant's a priori principles of knowing. Indeed, he believed there are no facts, only interpretations. We will discuss a recent development of this idea in a later chapter when we encounter Jacques Derrida, a "deconstructionist."

Metaphysics is difficult for those who believe there are no facts, and Nietzsche's philosophy is consciously antimetaphysical. Nevertheless, Nietzsche did subscribe to one metaphysical concept, "the eternal recurrence of the same." This

## PROFILE: Friedrich Wilhelm Nietzsche (1844–1900)

Nietzsche was the son of a Lutheran minister. His father died of insanity when Nietzsche was four, and Nietzsche was raised until he was fourteen in a household of women, consisting of his mother, sister, grandmother, and two maiden aunts.

After studying at the universities of Bonn and Leipzig, Nietzsche, whose genius was evident from the beginning, was appointed associate professor of classical philology at the University of Basel at the unheard-of young age of twenty-four without even having written a doctoral thesis. Within two years he had become a full professor. In 1879, however, he was forced by ill health to resign his chair, and by 1889, he, like his father earlier, had become irretrievably insane. Nietzsche's insanity, however, may have been caused by medication.

Two of the principal intellectual influences on Nietzsche's life were the writings of Schopenhauer and the music of Richard Wagner, which Nietzsche compared to hashish in its ability to relieve mental pressure. For a period Nietzsche and Wagner — one of the century's most brilliant philosophers and one of its most brilliant composers — were friends, though this friendship did not last.

Nietzsche's writings have been enormously influential in Continental philosophy. Nietzsche saw himself as an active nihilist whose role was to tear down the old "slave morality" of Christian civilization. He looked to the *Übermensch*, whose will-to-power would set him beyond conventional standards of morality, a line of thought that later was seized upon, misinterpreted, and misused by defenders of Nazism.

Nietzsche's widespread popularity outside philosophical circles owes much to the power of thought expressed in numerous infamous quotations. "Which is it," Nietzsche asked in one of these, "is man one of God's blunders or is God one of man's?"

---

is the theory that what happens recurs, exactly the same, again and again. Those with the slave mentality despise their lives and have a deep resentment for most everything that happens. They long to escape this life and hope that some afterlife will provide a modicum of happiness and fulfillment. They would look on the idea that what happens recurs again and again with horror and regret. The *Übermensch*, by contrast, affirms and celebrates life and bends it to his will. Having no regrets, he would relish the idea that life would happen again and again in exactly the same way.

Nietzsche, Kierkegaard, and Schopenhauer signaled that the smug self-satisfaction of nineteenth-century European philosophy — and culture — camouflaged emptiness and decadence. Their concern for the situation of the individual person; their disdain for abstract, remote, and (in their view) meaningless systems of thought; their denial of the rationality of the world and the people within it; their awareness of a vacuity, triviality, and pettiness within human existence; their efforts to find a reason for not despairing entirely — these themes spread rapidly into *belles lettres* (literature) as a whole in the late nineteenth and early twentieth centuries.

Sigmund Freud, for example, regarded the human being as a sexual animal from birth, one moved by unconscious and irrational drives over which there is little intelligent control. Art movements like Dadaism, Surrealism, and Expressionism expressed disenchantment with the established life of the bourgeoisie and its culture and values and sought to break out of the straitjacket of worn-out ideas and safe lifestyles. A sense that life is meaningless and empty, that the individual is alone and isolated and unable to communicate with others except on the most trivial of levels, permeated the thinking of the intellectuals and literati of the time and has persisted in art, literature, and philosophy until today.

Another persistent theme in twentieth-century literature pertains to the horror of coping in an absurd world—a world in which there is no apparent reason why things happen one way and not another. The characters in the stories and novels of Franz Kafka (1883–1924), a Czech whose mother tongue and the language in which he wrote was German (a fact itself suggestive of human dislocation), invariably find themselves thrust into a situation they do not comprehend but in which they must nevertheless act and be judged for their actions. Nor are they certain that the situation in which they find themselves is not one of their own making. Kafka's parable "The Metamorphosis," for example, tells of an ordinary salesman who supports his sister and aging parents. One day the salesman awakens at home to find that his body has been changed into that of a giant insect. He does not know why this has happened, and he will die without finding out. At first he is treated compassionately by the other family members, on whom he is of course dependent, but soon they resent his not supporting them and eventually come to regard him as a nuisance as well as an unwelcome family secret. At one point, pieces of fruit thrown by a frustrated and irate family member become embedded in his body and grow infected. Slowly but inevitably, the metamorphosized man loses heart and dies. Kafka presumably thought the story represented to some extent the fate of all human beings.

## TWO EXISTENTIALISTS

Existentialism as a philosophical movement was something of a direct reaction to perceived social ills and was embraced by artists and writers as much as by philosophers per se. So it is not surprising that two of the greatest existentialist philosophers, Albert Camus and Jean-Paul Sartre, wrote drama, novels, and political tracts as well as philosophical works. Both also thought it important to disseminate their ideas into society as a whole in the hope of having some direct influence. Both were involved in the French Resistance during World War II against the terror of German fascism. Both thought—despite their belief in the absurdity of life—that responsible social action is necessary, as is an understanding of the sociopolitical forces at work in the world.

Camus and Sartre are by no means the only existentialist philosophers. Other famous existentialists include Gabriel Marcel and Simone de Beauvoir in France (discussed in Chapter 14), Karl Jaspers in Switzerland, Martin Heidegger in Germany (whose work in phenomenology is discussed later in this chapter), Miguel de Unamuno and José Ortega y Gasset in Spain, and Nicola Abbagnano in Italy.

# Literature and Philosophy

There is a big difference between a novel or a poem and a philosophical essay. Still, themes and ideas that might loosely be described as "philosophical" are encountered throughout the world's great literature. Literature, after all, personifies human perspectives, thoughts, aspirations, values, and concerns. Often it is an immediate response to the current human situation and human needs. For example, beginning in the late nineteenth century, various European writers began to challenge the values of their culture and emphasized the idea that the individual is alone and isolated. Existentialism began this way, and the main themes of the movement, such as absurdity and meaninglessness, were only later thematized and delineated by writer-philosophers such as Camus, Sartre, and de Beauvoir.

The extent to which literature is or contains philosophy is itself a philosophical issue of controversy and substance. However, we can mention several literary approaches or viewpoints or "takes" on life that qualify in obvious ways as philosophical. The first might be described as a viewpoint based on absence. This way of thinking is based on the idea that the world is radically defective in that it is incapable of providing human beings what they truly need to be satisfied and/or happy. Examples of such writers include Franz Kafka, Fyodor Dostoyevsky, Albert Camus, Jean-Paul Sartre, and Samuel Beckett. Such writers take a position on human nature and needs, though they do so implicitly rather than explicitly.

A second basic literary approach is based on fullness. This viewpoint sees life as immeasurably rich and bountiful. Life is to be lived all out and every moment intensified and enjoyed. This is the traditional bailiwick of Romantics such as Goethe, Nietzsche, and Lord Byron. Goethe wrote: "If you want to create something, you must be something." American examples of this approach to life and literature include the poetry of Walt Whitman and the writings of Ralph Waldo Emerson and Henry David Thoreau. More contemporary examples would be Henry Miller and Anais Nin.

A third literary approach is the tragic stance. Here, life for whatever reason is tragic at its best and pathetic at its worst. The underlying pessimism in the plays of Sophocles and William Shakespeare are considered by many the very height of Western literature and culture. *Oedipus Rex, Hamlet,* and *King Lear* have not been surpassed for their dramatic power and truth telling. Shakespeare powerfully suggests this stance in Hamlet: "To be or not to be, that is the question." Strindberg and the films of Ingmar Bergman are powerful contemporary variations of the tragic stance. Two examples by American writers of this approach are Arthur Miller's *The Death of a Salesman* (1949) and Eugene O'Neill's *Long Day's Journey into Night* (1956). The tragic stance is related to the first viewpoint: the fundamental philosophical question, Camus asserted, is whether there is any reason not to commit suicide.

A fourth literary approach to life is the comic vision. Life here is seen as a comedy, a kind of cosmic joke. It is better to laugh at life rather than to cry. As Erasmus wrote in the fifteenth century: "The highest form of bliss is living with a certain degree of folly." Erasmus thought that folly is not difficult to find but surrounds us everywhere in our everyday lives. A more modern writer who recognized the absurdity of life yet refused to be defeated by it was Eugene Ionesco. He wrote: "To become conscious of what is atrocious and to laugh at it is to become master of what is atrocious." A potent example in American literature of this attitude can be found in Joseph Heller's *Catch-22.* There are similarities here with Stoicism, covered in Chapter 10.

A fifth approach to life through literature is developed by Martin Heidegger in his interpretations of poets like Hölderlin, Rainer Maria Rilke, and Georg Trakl. This literature, in the view of Heidegger, is the pursuit of the unknown, the unthought, and the unsaid. The poetic thinker's task is to go out into the darkness and experience the human condition in the deepest way possible. Herman Melville wrote "I love all men who *dive.* Any fish can swim near the surface, but it takes a great whale to go downstairs five miles or more; and if he doesn't attain the bottom, why, all the lead in Galena can't fashion the plummet that will. I'm not talking of Mr. Emerson now — but of that whole crop of thought-divers, that have been diving and coming up again with bloodshot eyes since the world began."

A sixth literary approach uses the medium to provide rules, maxims, and suggestions as to how

*(continued)*

## Literature and Philosophy *(continued)*

life ought to be lived. There is the whole genre of coming-to-maturity or growing-up novels in literature which provide lessons for the young and not so young. Actually, almost all significant literature includes drawing the consequences of actions and moral lessons. The examples of such writers are rife. We will mention only two of the greatest. The writings of Cervantes are a veritable storehouse of proverbs and wise sayings, such as, "Never stand begging for that which you have the power to earn." Another writer known for his didactic potency is Charles Dickens. He wrote for example: "Reflect on your present blessings, of which every man has many, not on your past misfortunes, of which all men have some." Literature can provide the average reader with an initial access to philosophy and

deeper questions in life. Heinrich Heine's *Siddhartha* is a classic example of a novel about how to become a noble, even heroic, person. For a while there, Robert M. Pirsig's *Zen and the Art of Motorcycle Maintenance* was something of a cult novel and continues after twenty-five years to be read by young people who are interested in knowing how Zen, and Eastern philosophy generally, can provide a model for living well in the present. Another fictional work that has been widely read and that has introduced many to the history of philosophy is Josten Gaarder's *Sophie's World*. Here whole swaths of Western philosophy are presented in an approachable and readable way that also relates them to contemporary life and its problems.

But Camus and Sartre are especially representative of the movement, and we will focus on them. Camus, we might note, was reluctant to be classified as an existentialist because that lumped him together with Sartre, with whom Camus quarreled.

### Albert Camus

**Albert Camus** [kah-MOO] (1913–1960) grew up in poverty in Algeria and fought in the French Resistance against the Nazis. He saw much suffering, waste, and death even before the war, and, perhaps not surprisingly, the principal philosophical question for him was *Is there any reason not to commit suicide?* Camus believed that this question arises when a person stops deceiving himself or herself and begins seeing the world without preconceived illusions (see the box "Life Is Absurd").

Many people, Camus believed, live their whole lives and die without ever seeing things as they really are. More specifically, instead of seeing the "tragic nature of life," they waste their lives in "stupid self-confidence." That is, although they in fact spend their lives in or near despair in an absurd world that continually frustrates true human needs, they mask the fact with a forced optimism. And the more "profitable" such false optimism is, the more entrenched it becomes. In Camus's view, for many of us self-deception has become a dominant mode of being. This implies as well that often we are strangers to ourselves and to our own inability to meet our fundamental needs.

What are these basic needs? According to Camus, there are two: the need for clarity or understanding and the need for social warmth and contact. Unfortunately, however, we live in an absurd world, a world in which these basic human

# Existentialism in European Literature

As we said in the preceding box, starting in the late nineteenth century, some European artists began to challenge the culture and values of their society. In various ways, their works expressed their sense that life is meaningless and empty and that the individual is alone and isolated. A sampling of literature from the late nineteenth through the mid-twentieth centuries shows some of the ways in which those themes were presented.

- "Notes from the Underground" (1864), a story by Fyodor Dostoyevsky, tells how an imperfect society can waste the lives of its best members. The "underground man" lives in a society that prefers and rewards mediocrity. Hence his intelligence, sensitivity, and strength of character are neither needed nor wanted. He is condemned to watch second-rate compatriots surpass him and achieve success while his own superior talents languish unused. He is left with a life of bitterness, hopelessness, and shame. His sole pleasure consists in acts of spite and revenge, more imaginary than real.

- "The Death of Ivan Ilyich" (1884), a story by Leo Tolstoy, provides a powerful and moving example of the meaninglessness and futility of life. Ivan Ilyich had led what he thought was a successful, busy, ambitious life. But when he learns that, though still in the prime of life, he has an incurable and fatal disease, he begins noticing that his wife and family members are really only concerned about the inheritance and that his fellow workers have already begun jockeying to replace him. He sees that no one really cares about him or has any genuine sympathy for his situation. He cannot understand the insincerity and cruelty of others, including that of his own family, and he cannot understand God's cruelty and His absence in time of need.

Above all, Ivan cannot understand why he is so *alone*, abandoned to suffer and die. Has he done something deserving of such punishment? Ivan exclaims, "I am not guilty," but Tolstoy adds that Ivan "is not certain it is so."

- *The Trial* (1925), a novel by Franz Kafka, explores the idea that we can feel responsible — or even *be* responsible — for the situations in which we find ourselves (and whose causes we certainly do not understand). A man, Joseph K., is arrested, convicted, and executed without ever being able to find out what crime he was supposed to have committed. Nor is he conscious of having committed any crime. Yet such is his sense of self-doubt that he is never sure he does not deserve to be condemned.

- *The Bald Soprano* (1950), a play by Eugène Ionesco, is in the dramatic tradition known as "theater of the absurd." Two strangers meet at a dinner party and enter into conversation. Slowly they discover that they had sat in the same train compartment five weeks earlier, live in the same city and house, and both have a daughter with one red eye and one white eye. Ultimately, to their delight, they discover that they are husband and wife.

- *Waiting for Godot* (1953), a play by Samuel Beckett, explores the inability of humans to communicate with one another. Two tramps, Didi and Gogo, wait in a desertlike environment for someone named Godot to arrive, who will tell them what to do. They talk only to pass the time, not because they have anything to say. They seem often to be talking at the same time on entirely different subjects without either one noticing. And it does not matter, for it does not interrupt the emptiness of the words.

needs are unmet. The need for clear understanding of the world founders on the "opaqueness and density of the world"; indeed, it founders on the very fact that the world is absurd and consequently provides no sufficient reason for why things happen one way and not another.

The second essential need, the need for human warmth and contact, also remains unfulfilled, Camus thought. Humans in this violent age tend to remain

# PROFILE: Albert Camus (1913–1960)

Camus was born in Mondovi, Algeria, on November 7, 1913. His French father was a farmworker and his Spanish mother, a maid. His father died in the war soon after Camus's birth, forcing Camus's mother to move into the impoverished quarter of Algiers at the end of the Casbah. Camus later considered the poverty in which he grew up the great source of his deepest insights. His Spanish pride and intensity as well as his intellectual acumen were noticed by a teacher, Louis Germain, who made sure that Camus could attend a first-rate high school, one normally accessible only to the rich.

Camus was athletic and played goalie for the Racing Universitaire. After one game, he left the playing field in a sweat, which developed into a cold and then into tuberculosis. This meant that he would not be able to become a teacher after he passed his state examination in philosophy. Instead, he turned to journalism, working at first for the *Algeria Republican*. By the age of twenty he was already married and separated and had both joined and quit the Communist Party. He had also formed his own theater group, l'Équipe.

Camus was eventually thrown out of Algeria for writing articles concerning the poverty and backwardness in its provincial areas. During World War II, he was the lead article writer for the French Resistance newspaper *Combat*. After the war, he wrote such major works as *The Stranger*, *The Rebel*, and *The Plague* and also maintained his involvement with theater groups. In 1957 he received the Nobel Prize for literature. He was killed in an automobile accident in 1960.

Camus was a straightforward, unpretentious person who always had time for his friends, for actors, and for young people starting out. Many looked upon him as a kind of big brother. He was proud to be a human being and dedicated himself to the love and enjoyment of this world. He believed that the secret of the art of living lies in the sun, the sea, and a youthful heart.

## Life Is Absurd

One of Camus's principal theses is that life as we find it is absurd. The notion of absurdity implies that there is no ultimate reason that things are the way they are. It also implies that life is unjust and frustrates human needs. Most important, perhaps, that the world is absurd seems to mean, for Camus, that it provides no absolute or necessary basis of value. That we must make choices and decide how to act in a valueless and absurd world is often called the "existential predicament."

strangers to one another (as well as to themselves); they live solitary existences in which relationships are matters of convention rather than of mutual sharing and understanding. The absurdity of life in frustrating essential human needs means that hoped-for happiness often turns to misery and despair — even though many hide this tragedy from themselves behind a facade of baseless hopes.

Camus likened life to the fate of Sisyphus in the myth of the same name. Sisyphus had provoked the wrath of the gods and was condemned to roll a huge stone up a hill, only to see it roll back down again. This act repeated itself forever. Human beings, according to Camus, are similarly condemned to lives of "futile and hopeless labor," without reasonable hope of fulfilling their true needs. No matter how hard we try to live a just and meaningful existence, it is unlikely that our efforts will lead to lasting results.

In this context it may easily be understood why Camus considered the question of suicide to be a primary philosophical issue. *Why indeed* should one wish to continue living under such circumstances as Camus has depicted? Nevertheless, Camus regarded suicide as unacceptable. Suicide, he thought, is a kind of weakminded acquiescence to an unjust destiny. Camus believed, perhaps paradoxically, that by struggling against the Sisyphean fate to the end, by rebelling against the absurdity and tragedy of life, it is possible to give life meaning and value. His position indeed is that *only* through this struggle with an absurd world can the individual achieve fulfillment, solidarity with others, and "a brief love of this earth."

Increasingly, Camus focused his concern on the grotesque inhumanity and hideous cruelty of a world torn asunder by war and Nazism. Civilization, he thought, certainly with some justification, is suffering from a "plague" of epidemic proportions, a plague that kills many and sickens all. (Perhaps Camus's most famous work was *The Plague*, 1947.) In such an unjust world, one finds oneself committing violent acts *merely to survive*. Camus viewed the world as, in effect, sponsoring an ongoing competition in murder, as a place in which it is difficult to raise a finger without killing somebody. Capital punishment, he thought, is just one example of how the "decent citizen" is reduced to the level of a murderer. And in outright warfare the morality of violence exceeds control and comes into the open.

Camus wrote that "one cannot always live on murders and violence." By living out the values of the lowest animals, the individual is delivered up to the merciless power of despair and cynicism. Camus loathed the "absolute cynicism" of modern society that, he implied, drove humans to desperation and prevented them "from taking responsibility for their own life."

Thus, Camus came increasingly to insist that each individual must spend his or her life fighting the plague — that is, the degeneracy of the world. Each must resist the temptations offered by cunning and violence; what is called for, he thought, is a "revolt" against the existing "order." Perhaps as a way of fighting the plague, Camus's thinking after the war became increasingly concerned with social and political issues. This represents a shift from his early works, which are focused much more strictly on the concerns of the individual.

But Camus thought that the revolt against a revolting world must be "measured" and limited. What Camus means is made clearer in his play *Caligula* (1944), in which the Roman emperor Caligula is presented as an example of a man who discovers the implicit cruelty and viciousness of human existence. In order not to fall victim to this evil, Caligula revolts against it in an unmeasured way, through his own acts of cruelty and viciousness. Such an unmeasured reaction was unacceptable to Camus; it meant becoming more bestial than the other beasts. In short, for Camus, the violence of the world does not excuse or justify violence in response (also see, in this respect, the box "*The Just*").

Thus, the best that is possible for the individual, Camus implied, is a measured revolt wherein he or she spends life resisting violence and injustice. The effort, he maintained, must be predicated on the assumption that "any mutilation of mankind is irrevocable." The individual must fight for justice and liberty and against

## The Just

In his play *The Just* (1950), Camus expresses approval of a Russian terrorist who murders the Grand Duke and then insists on paying for his deed with his own life, the point being that there can be no justification for taking another's life. Ca-mus is sometimes described as a "courageous humanist." His emphasis on the necessity of brave and unceasing struggle against violence and inhumanity discloses an implicit hope that human goodness ultimately will reign victorious.

all forms of tyranny: "Let us die resisting," he wrote. Yet we must have no illusions or false optimism about the possible results of our action. For it may well be that nothing will improve: in an absurd world, nothing is guaranteed.

### Jean-Paul Sartre

Albert Camus was agnostic, maintaining that he did not know whether or not there is a God. **Jean-Paul Sartre** [sartr] (1905–1980) was atheistic. Man, Sartre said, is *abandoned,* by which "we mean that God does not exist." And according to Sartre, the abandonment of man—that is, the nonexistence of God—has drastic philosophical implications. Basically, there are four (and after you read about them you might read the box "Is Sartre Only for Atheists?").

First, because there is no God, there is no maker of man and no such thing as a divine conception of man in accordance with which man was created. This means, Sartre thought, that there is no such thing as a human nature that is common to all humans; no such thing as a specific essence that defines what it is to be human. Past philosophers had maintained that each thing in existence has a definite, specific essence; Aristotle, for example, believed that the essence of being human is being rational. But for Sartre, the person must produce her or his own essence, because no God created human beings in accordance with a divine concept. Thus, in the case of human beings, Sartre wrote, "**existence precedes essence,**" by which he meant very simply that you are what you make of yourself. You are what *you* make of yourself.

The second implication of the nonexistence of God is this. Because there is no God, there is no ultimate reason why anything has happened or why things are the way they are and not some other way. This means that the individual in effect has been *thrown* into existence without any real reason for being. But this does not mean that the individual is like a rock or a flea, which also (because there is no God) have no ultimate reason or explanation. Rocks and fleas, Sartre would say, only have what he calls "being-in-itself" (in French, *être-en-soi*), or mere existence. But a human being, according to Sartre, not only exists, that is, has being-in-itself, but also has "being-for-itself" (*être-pour-soi*), which means that a human being, unlike an inanimate object or a vegetable, is a self-aware or conscious subject that creates its own future. We will return to this point momentarily.

## PROFILE: Jean-Paul Sartre (1905–1980)

Jean-Paul Sartre studied philosophy at the École Normale Supèrieure. He also studied the philosophies of Husserl and Heidegger, and spent one year in Berlin. While still a graduate student, he met Simone de Beauvoir, who later played a key role in the early phases of the women's liberation movement, especially with her famous book, *The Second Sex* (1948). Their friendship and mutual support lasted until Sartre's death, though in the opinion of historian Paul Johnson, "In the annals of literature, there are few worse cases of a man exploiting a woman." (Sartre never wrote anything about their relationship.)

During World War II, Sartre served in the French army, became a German prisoner of war, escaped, and worked in the Resistance movement. Throughout his life he supported political causes and movements, including the French Communist Party. In 1951, he tried unsuccessfully to found a new political party, radically leftist but noncommunist in orientation.

Sartre's most famous works include the novel *Nausea* (1939), the play *No Exit* (1944), and the philosophical treatise *Being and Nothingness* (1943). In 1964 Sartre declined the Nobel Prize in literature, citing "personal reasons."

When Sartre died, fifty thousand people marched behind his coffin through the streets of Paris. He was indeed a national treasure.

### Is Sartre Only for Atheists?

If God does exist, then technically speaking we are not "abandoned." But some of the main problems that arise from abandonment seem also to arise merely if we cannot *know* whether God exists. For if we do not know whether God exists, then we do not know whether there is any ultimate reason why things happen the way they do, and we do not know whether those values we believe are grounded in God really do have objective validity.

In fact, even if we do know that God exists and also know that values are grounded in God, we still may not know which values are grounded in God: we may still not know what the absolute criteria and standards of right and wrong are. And even if we know what the standards and criteria are, just what they mean will still be a matter for subjective interpretation. And so the human dilemma that results may be very much the same as if there were no God.

Nonatheists should not dismiss Sartre too hastily.

Third, because there is no God and hence no divine plan that determines what must happen, "there is no determinism." Thus, "man is free," Sartre wrote, "man is freedom"; in fact, he is **condemned to be free.** Nothing forces us to do what we do. Thus, he said, "we are alone, without excuses," by which he meant simply that we cannot excuse our actions by saying that we were forced by circumstances or moved by passion or otherwise determined to do what we did.

Fourth, because there is no God, there is no objective standard of values: "It is very troubling that God does not exist," Sartre wrote, "for with him disappears every possibility of finding values . . . there can no longer be any good a priori."

Consequently, because a Godless world has no objective values, we must establish or invent our own values.

Consider briefly what these various consequences of our **abandonment** entail. That we find ourselves in this world without a God-given "human nature" or "essence"; that we are active, conscious, and self-aware subjects; that we are totally free and unconstrained (and unexcused) by any form of determinism; and that we must create our own values—these facts mean that each individual has an awesome responsibility. According to Sartre, first of all, we are responsible for what we are. "Abandonment implies that we ourselves choose our being." Second, we must *invent* our own values. And third and finally, because "nothing can be good for us without [also] being [good] for all," in inventing our own values we also function as *universal legislators* of right and wrong, good and evil. In choosing for ourselves, we choose for all. "Thus, our responsibility is much greater than we had supposed it, for it involves all mankind."

This responsibility for oneself and thus for all humankind, Sartre thought, we experience as anguish, and it is clear why he maintained that this is so: our responsibility is total and profound and *absolutely inescapable*. You might perhaps object that many people, perhaps even most, certainly do not seem to be particularly anxious, let alone anguished. It is true, Sartre admitted, that many people are not consciously or visibly anxious. But this merely is because they are hiding or fleeing from their responsibility: they act and live in self-deception or inauthenticity, what Sartre called "**bad faith.**" Further, he said, they are ill at ease with their conscience, for "even when it conceals itself, anguish appears."

It is not difficult to understand why one might seek to avoid shouldering one's responsibility to oneself and thus to others, for as Sartre depicted it, this responsibility is overwhelming. But in Sartre's view something else also contributes to the difficulty of this task: one does not know *what* to choose because the world is experienced as absurd. It is experienced as absurd, Sartre maintains, because, since God does not exist, it lacks necessity—it lacks an ultimate rhyme or reason for being this way and not that way. The world, therefore, is experienced as fundamentally senseless, unreasonable, illogical, and, therefore, "nauseating." It calls forth both revulsion and boredom. It is "perfectly gratuitous" (*gratuitá parfaite*) and often just simply too much (*de trop*).

Nevertheless, according to Sartre, it is only through acceptance of our responsibility that we may live in **authenticity.** To be responsible, to live authentically, means intentionally to make choices about one's life and one's future. These choices are made most efficaciously, Sartre maintained, by becoming "engaged" in the world and by selecting a **fundamental project,** a project that can mobilize and direct all of one's life energies and permit one to make spontaneous choices. Through this project, in short, the individual creates a world that does not yet exist and thus gives meaning to his or her life.

So Sartre's metaphysics (or antimetaphysics), which stood opposed to the belief in God, determinism, necessity, and the objectivity of values, in effect leaves the human individual in what may plausibly be called an absurd situation. There is nothing that one must do; there is nothing that must be done. To find meaning in life, the individual must create his or her world and its values by making authentic choices. These choices first take the form of intentions directed toward future events. Then they become actions of an engaged being in a world of people, a political (and politically troubled) world. The choices that we make are made for all humankind and are, therefore, in this limited sense "absolute" ethical principles. Although we initially find ourselves in an absurd world not of our choosing, we can remake that world through our choices and actions, and we must do so, as difficult as that may be.

## Sartre and Kant on Ethics

"I choose myself perpetually," Sartre wrote. By this he meant that we each are in a continual process of constructing ourselves and our values or ethics. And Sartre believed that when a person determines something to be right for himself or herself, that person is also determining it to be good for all.

This universalization of individual choices is reminiscent of Immanuel Kant's supreme precept of morality, the categorical imperative, according to which you must only act in such a way that the principle on which you act could be a universal law. Kant, however, as we will see in Part Two, grounded the categorical imperative and hence all morality in reason, which he thought determines a priori what is right and wrong. Sartre, however, maintains that there is no a priori moral law and that Kant's formal law is inadequate as a guide for concrete action in everyday life. It is rather what a person does that in fact determines his morality. "In choosing myself, I choose man," Sartre said.

It is perhaps arguable, however, that *this* principle ("in choosing myself, I choose man") is for Sartre a universal principle underlying morality.

## You Are What You Do

According to Sartre, you create yourself through your choices. But be aware that for Sartre these self-creating choices are not found in mere "philosophical" abstractions or speculations. The choices that count, for Sartre, are those that issue forth in actions. "There is reality only in action," he wrote, "man is nothing other than the whole of his actions."

This means that, according to Sartre, no hidden self or true you lies behind your deeds. If, for example, in your actions you are impatient and unforgiving, it is a fiction for you to think, "Well, if others could see into my heart they would know that in reality I am patient and understanding." If you are cowardly in your deeds, you deceive yourself if you believe that "in truth" or "deep, down inside" you are courageous. If you have not written great poetry, then it is an illusion for you to believe that you nevertheless have the soul of a great poet.

It is easy to see why Sartre believed that his doctrine horrified many people. Many people think of their behavior as but poorly reflecting their true character, which they believe is in some way superior to the character that displays itself in their actions. Those who think this deceive themselves, according to Sartre.

This exposition of Sartre's thought focuses on his understanding of what might be called the existential predicament. His thinking evolved over time, and he became increasingly concerned—like Camus—with social and political issues. These interests and his fascination with Marxist philosophy led to a modification of his existentialist stance, but we can do no more in this book than mention this. We have also not dealt with his epistemology, his aesthetics, or his views on psychoanalysis.

## PHENOMENOLOGY

This impressive-sounding word denotes the philosophy that grew out of the work of Edmund Husserl (1859–1938). In brief, **phenomenology** interests itself in the essential structures found within the stream of conscious experience — the stream of phenomena — as these structures manifest themselves independently of the assumptions and presuppositions of science.

Phenomenology, much more than existentialism, has been a product of philosophers rather than of artists and writers. But like existentialism, phenomenology has had enormous impact outside philosophical circles. It has been especially influential in theology, the social and political sciences, and psychology and psychoanalysis. Phenomenology is a movement of thinkers who have a variety of interests and points of view; phenomenology itself finds its antecedents in Kant and Hegel (though the movement regarded itself as anything but Hegelian). Kant, in the *Critique of Pure Reason,* argued that all objective knowledge is based on phenomena, the data received in sensory experience. In Hegel's *Phenomenology of Mind,* beings are treated as phenomena or objects for a consciousness.

What are **phenomena**? It is difficult to convey precisely what is meant by the term, but it may help for you to consider the distinction between the way something is immediately experienced and the way it "is." Place a penny on the table before you, look at it, and concentrate on your experience as you look. The penny-in-experience changes its shape and size as you move your head. Of course you are accustomed to assuming that there is a second penny "beyond" this changing penny-in-experience, the so-called "real" penny. You must ignore this assumption. Forget about the "real" penny, and focus on the penny-in-experience. Indeed, don't restrict your attention to the *penny*-in-experience. Contemplate the table-in-experience, the room-in-experience. Consider your *entire* experience at the moment. And when you do this, ignore your inclination to suppose that there is a second world (the "real" world) lying beyond the world-in-experience. Congratulations: you are now practicing the phenomenological method. Notice that, as long as you limit your attention to the world-in-experience, you can have certain knowledge. The world beyond experience, the "real" world assumed by natural science, is a world concerning which much is unknown and doubtful. But the world-in-experience, the world of pure phenomena, can be explored without the same limitations or uncertainties.

### Edmund Husserl

The first great phenomenologist, **Edmund Husserl** [HOO-surl] (1859–1938), attempted to rekindle Europe's waning faith in the possibility of certainty by proposing a universal phenomenology of consciousness, a "science" that studies the structures that are the same for every consciousness. Accordingly, he developed **transcendental phenomenology,** whose purpose it was to investigate phenomena without making any assumptions about the world. To investigate phenomena in this way is to "bracket" or "exclude" one's presupposition about the existence or nature of an "external" or "physical" or "objective" world. Husserl called this process **phenomenological reduction,** and you just did it above. Its purpose is to examine the meaning produced by pure impersonal consciousness and to describe the human "life-world" in terms of those essences (which all human beings share) found within conscious experience.

This sounds a bit like psychology, but Husserl distinguished transcendental phenomenology from regular psychology, which approaches the mind with the assumptions and methods of the other natural sciences in their study of the "objective" world. It (Husserl's phenomenology) also sounds a bit like traditional idealistic metaphysics, in which everything is reduced to thought. But that tradition at least invokes the dualistic world view of the natural sciences in order to deny it. Phenomenology, in theory, simply explores conscious experience without making any metaphysical assumptions.

## Martin Heidegger

In any event, Husserl believed phenomenology opens up for scrutiny a realm that escapes the uncertainty and conditional status of the empirical world, and he called for a "return to the things themselves" (i.e., phenomena). **Martin Heidegger** [Hy-dig-ger] (1889–1976) was stimulated by Husserl's call to return to the things themselves and by Husserl's major work, *Logical Investigations* (1900). Heidegger, too, was convinced that it was necessary to look at things with fresh eyes, unshrouded by the presuppositions of the present and past. He, too, wanted rigorously to ground things in a deeper source of certainty. But for Heidegger, this source is not phenomena, as it was for Husserl, or anything subjective at all. On the contrary, for Heidegger, the ultimate source is *Being* itself.

Although Being is continuously manifesting itself in things, according to Heidegger, Being itself has been forgotten. Humans have been caught up in their own ideas. Being has been reduced to a world of "objects" that are manipulated and dominated by human "subjects" through a series of human-made logics. Logic is equated with truth when in fact, according to Heidegger, it is only a means to control and use things after human designs; that is, logic is logistics.

Heidegger believed that it is both arrogant and destructive to assume that humans are the masters of nature or to follow Protagoras's dictum that man is the measure of all things. This assumption of the absolute power of humanity was for Heidegger the real cause of the cultural destitution and social dissolution within the twentieth century. Heidegger thought that we live in an intellectually impoverished (*dürftig*) time, and that it is likely to become worse until we abandon our presumptuousness and return to the wisdom inherent in Being itself. The return must involve *listening* to Being instead of toying with things arbitrarily.

According to Heidegger, we are basically ignorant about the thing that matters most: the true nature of Being. Our lives are a kind of Socratic search for this lost

## PROFILE: Martin Heidegger (1889–1976)

Heidegger was born in the small town of Messkirch near the Black Forest of Germany. Originally he went to the University of Freiburg to study theology, but he soon after began studying philosophy. Heidegger studied Husserl's philosophy closely and became personally acquainted with Husserl after the latter took a chair at Freiburg in 1916.

Almost from the beginning Heidegger stood out — not merely because of his countrified mode of dress but also because of his profound thought. Over the years Heidegger grew increasingly critical of Husserl's philosophy, and, though he was named to Husserl's chair in philosophy at Freiburg in 1928, their friendship came to an end.

Initially Heidegger was quite taken with the National Socialist (Nazi) party in post–World War I

Germany and remained a party member until the end of World War II. This was a prestigious gain for the Nazis, especially when Heidegger was made rector of the University of Freiburg. During Heidegger's brief term as rector (he withdrew after ten months), he made speeches and was otherwise active in support of Hitler and his movement. After the war, Heidegger did not speak out to condemn Nazi atrocities. There is controversy as to what his true sentiments were, however.

Although Heidegger did not teach formally after the war, he remained in Freiburg until his death. His works are in the process of being published — in eighty volumes.

and unknown source of all things. Consciousness of the priority of Being would mean a new beginning for philosophy as well as for Western civilization, he held.

Heidegger, therefore, initially sought to establish a scientific study of Being as the root of all meaning and necessity in things. This effort broadened out later and became a quest for an even more direct approach to Being itself. Early on — for example, in his first major work, *Being and Time* (1927) — Heidegger's ideas still contained much that is Husserlian and Kantian in approach. He still sought true knowledge in a priori structures found in the human mind. It is only in his later thinking — after he had what he called a fundamental "turning about" — that he sought to uncover Being directly, beyond the a priori categories or structures of human perception and thought. He did so without assurance that any absolute certainty about Being itself is even possible.

It is usually with reference to his earlier work that Heidegger is sometimes called an existentialist. Heidegger himself resisted this appellation. Yet he was very much influenced by Kierkegaard and Nietzsche, and the concern expressed in his early works with such existentialist themes as fear, dread, meaninglessness, and death is quite evident. Sartre studied in Germany for a brief time in the 1930s and was influenced by Heidegger. Sartre attributed the concept of abandonment to Heidegger, and Sartre and Heidegger both were concerned with the concepts of bad faith, authenticity, a life's project, and others.

Still, in decisive ways, Heideggerian and Sartrian philosophies are dissimilar. Heidegger never did abandon his belief in Being as the basic principle of philosophy, whereas for Sartre individual existence was of paramount importance. Sartre believed that as a consequence of the nonexistence of God nothing about Being is necessary; Heidegger believed that Being is absolutely necessary. Politically, Sartre considered himself a Marxist and accepted much of the Marxist view of historical events, whereas Heidegger was not in any sense sympathetic to the Marxist world-view. All in all, Heidegger and Sartre philosophically are quite different, despite the superficial resemblance.

At the heart of Heidegger's *Being and Time* is the notion of **Sinn** (sense, meaning), the absence of which in life was said to be the problem of human existence. For Heidegger, the human being is **thrown into the world** and soon experiences both fear and dread when confronted with forces beyond understanding. The better part of human life, he maintains, needs to be used in *"headbreaking,"* that is, in attempting to discover what the appearances mean—what they suggest and hide.

Further, humans are "beings-in-the-world," which means that they can be open only to what is within the horizons of their world. They exist and are conscious within a world with other beings, but the meaning of human relationships is at first but dimly perceived and poorly understood. As a consequence of their lack of insight and understanding, many humans live ungenuine and inauthentic lives. They do not make adequate or appropriate choices for themselves because they do not understand who they are or what they are confronting. And although they may experience unease living in a world beyond their comprehension, they make too little effort to extend their comprehension. They suffer from a kind of "primitive" being, which Heidegger refers to as **everydayness,** and fail to fulfill their real potential. Thus, Heidegger invoked the concept of everydayness to explain why human beings continue to lead unthinking lives.

Another typical existential theme connected by Heidegger with an everyday existence is an inauthentic mode of communication, namely, *chatter.* Speech is reduced to a meaningless flood of words that camouflages fear, prevents understanding, and precludes any meaningful communication. Nothing truly meaningful is ever said or allowed to be said.

An authentic existence can be found, according to Heidegger, only if one can understand oneself as a totality. And seeing oneself as a whole can happen only by facing the hard fact that one is mortal. We are, Heidegger said, "beings-unto-death." By facing death, we can see and delineate the limits of our being. We begin to see the limited amount of time yet available and begin to realize we must not waste it.

The innermost nature of the human being, according to Heidegger, is caring— a concern for beings in the world. This caring takes place over time. And thinking must do so as well. Thus, for Heidegger, we are essentially *temporal* beings.

According to Heidegger, human thinking is "ecstatic," which means it is directed toward an anticipated future. The most effective way of embracing one's future, he thought, is by throwing oneself open into Being. This project (*Entwurf*) opens the person to the fundamental truth of Being that has been forgotten. Therefore, the individual who has been thrown into the world finds her or his ground and truth in the openness and light of the truth of Being itself.

As noted earlier, Heidegger thought that the cultural and intellectual poverty of the twentieth century was a direct result of the pervasive assumption that the value of things is solely determined by human intelligence and human will (the assumption that man is the measure of all things). This assumption or metaphysical stance, he thought, has led not only to individual loneliness, alienation, and un-fulfillment but to social destructiveness as well. For Heidegger, this metaphysical point of view, which he perceived as having been entrenched in Western civiliza-tion since Plato, assumed the superiority of Ideas over any physical reality existing "outside" the mind. In Heidegger's opinion, Nietzsche's will-to-power, whereby the will becomes the absolute determiner of the value of things and of oneself, rep-resented the philosophical culmination of this Platonic metaphysics.

*Poetry*    According to the later Heidegger, instead of imposing our thought on things, we must think in a quiet, nonimpositional way so that we can catch a glimpse of Being as it shows itself. In contrast to others in the phenomenological tradition, Heidegger believed that thought cannot impose itself on Being because Being makes thought possible. What is required, therefore, he said (in contrast to the existentialists), is a new kind of thinking in which humans look to Being itself for enlightenment and not merely to themselves. This kind of thinking occurs, ac-cording to Heidegger, in the best poetry. Poetic thinking can uncover the as-yet un-seen, unthought, and unspoken. Therefore, he said, systematic philosophy, with its grandiose schemes, with its mind–body and other dualistic splits, with its meta-physics and metaphysical traditions, must give way to this more original kind of thinking. Through this deeper way of thinking, Heidegger said, we may at long last rediscover the depth of what has been forgotten—Being itself.

Heidegger wrote essays about many poets, including Hölderlin, Rilke, Trakl, and others. But he also wrote poems that suggest how the poet might bring a glim-mer of light to the darkness within existence. For example:

> When the early morning light quietly grows
>     above the mountains. . . .
>
> The world's darkening never reaches to the
>     light of Being.
>
> We are too late for the gods and too early for
>     Being. Being's poem, just begun, is man.
>
> To head toward a star—this only.
>
> To think is to confine yourself to a single
>     thought that one day stands still like a star
>     in the world's sky.

But to enter into the abyss of Being, for Heidegger, is a difficult, long, and soli-tary undertaking. It requires patience and courage, too. He wrote:

> All our heart's courage is the echoing response
>     to the first call of Being which gathers our
>     thinking into the play of the world.*

---

*Martin Heidegger, from *Poetry, Language, Thought,* translated by Albert Hofstadter, New York: HarperCollins, 1971. Copyright © 1971 Martin Heidegger. Reprinted by permission of HarperCollins Publishers, Inc.

It is the poet, for Heidegger, who ventures out into the unknown to find the "unique thought" that will bring the necessary light for the coming time.

***Eastern Philosophy*** Especially later in his life, Heidegger grew interested in Eastern philosophy and especially the philosophy of Lao Tzu (see Chapter 16). Perhaps Heidegger's new way of thinking — listening to Being — represents a coming together of Eastern and Western philosophizing. Certainly there are common currents and themes. Both believed that "nature is not human-hearted" (Lao Tzu) and that what is called human "knowledge" is mostly ignorance. Both felt that "those who care will be cared for" (Lao Tzu). What is necessary, according to both, is to take nature [Being] as a "guide." And it is as Lao Tzu suggested: "In the clarity of a still and open mind, the truth will be revealed."

## Emmanuel Levinas

Born in Kaunas, Lithuania, Emmanuel Levinas (1906–1995) was the son of a bookstore manager. Levinas, understandably, became an avid reader, especially of classic Russian literature and the Hebraic *Bible*. In 1923 he went to Strasburg (Germany) to study philosophy and focused on the philosophy of Husserl and Heidegger. Levinas was mainly responsible for introducing phenomenology into France. During World War II his parents were killed by the Nazis and he himself was interned in a prisoner of war camp. After the war, he took up a number of academic posts, culminating in a professorship at the Sorbonne. His principal writings center around two areas of concern: Talmudic commentaries and ethics, understood in the broader sense of being aware of what and how we humans exist in the world.

Martin Heidegger, as you know from what we have written already, had made a radical critique of the whole history of Western metaphysics interpreted as a form of Platonism. Western metaphysics represented for Heidegger a devolutionary process that ended in Nietzsche's nihilism and the complete forgetting of Being itself. Heidegger not only declared the end of metaphysics but also attempted to establish a new way of thinking about Being that he initially called ontology.

Levinas based his critique of Heidegger mainly on Heidegger's major early work, *Being and Time* (1927). In stark contrast with Heidegger, Levinas wanted philosophy to break out of the stranglehold of Being. Levinas tried to establish a philosophy rooted in the notions of radical otherness and unbridgeable separateness. Philosophy begins, he believed, with the horrible experiences of our otherness (*alterity*). Other people exist as unovercomable alterity. Time, language, and even existence itself is experienced as other. And God, for Levinas, exists as Absolute Otherness, a separateness never to be breached. True meaning and understanding of ourselves for Levinas can only be reached by a meeting with this radical Other in all its strangeness. The attempt to meet with the Other represents an act of transcendence and is the key human event. The Other exists "prior to any act" whatsoever.

Thus, for Levinas, ontology (the study of Being) represented the wrong-headed attempt to reduce this irreducible otherness to sameness, to reduce the Other to a mere object for consciousness. The project is doomed because the Other exists prior to ontology. Instead of starting with Being and trying to explain beings, we must begin with beings in their separateness and otherness. In particular, we must confront other humans in their invisibility and incomprehensibility. The Other remains a puzzle but a puzzle that can nevertheless reveal secrets.

The secrets of the Other both reveal and hide themselves in the human face (*le visage*). The face for Levinas is our epiphany into the Other. First of all, the face of the Other throws into question the "I" that we have constructed in our alienation from the Other. To know ourselves, we must know the Other. We are therefore "hostage" to the Other for our being and for our understanding of ourselves.

The Other, for Levinas, is the infinite in the individual self. As encountered in the form of the face, it solicits us to posit ourselves for this Other. It is that which makes communication possible. It opens us up to the transcendent, to the Absolutely Other, to the infinite, to God and to His Law. This takes us to the realm of Levinas's transcendental ethical philosophy. For Levinas, ethics is prior to ontology. The responsibility of thinking is always in response to an unfulfilled and ultimately unfulfillable obligation to the Other.

The Good, for Levinas, is therefore prior to the true. Our primary responsibility is for the Other, and that responsibility trumps even our obligation to ourselves and to the world of things. It is an obligation of self-sacrifice to the Other, an obligation to the infinite. In meeting the Other, we find our own meaning, the "answer" that we are.

This vigilance toward the Other grounds our being and represents the original form of openness to the world. The concomitant forgetting of self leads to real communication and justice. Levinas offers the Hebraic *Bible* as a model of ethical transcendental philosophy. The Absolute Other to which we are responsible is God or the Most High. By studying the written Law, our obedience to God ruptures our egoism as we respond to God's commandments. This allows us to attain true freedom.

Levinas had a profound influence on French thinkers such as Jean-Paul Sartre (discussed earlier in this chapter) and, as we will see, Jacques Derrida.

## AN ERA OF SUSPICION

"My experiences," wrote Friedrich Nietzsche in his posthumously published confessional called *Ecce Homo*, "entitle me to be quite generally suspicious of the so-called 'selfless' drives, of all 'neighbor love' that is ready to give advice and go into action." In the last third of the twentieth century, diverse Continental voices were raised against what they saw as suspicious assumptions about the meaning of right and wrong, the nature of language, and the very possibility of human self-understanding. Some Continental philosophers have been suspicious about Western metaphysical systems that they claim lead to the manipulation of nature or that set up a certain ethnic or cultural perspective as absolute truth. Some voices have raised suspicions about the common assumption that language in some way represents external reality. Still others claim to find deep ideological biases in even the most "neutral" philosophical observations.

Philosopher and sociologist Jürgen Habermas has challenged the legitimacy of some of the rational principles assumed by the human sciences. French philosopher Michel Foucault explored the deeply ingrained social power systems that shape how social institutions deal with the sexuality of their members and with those who are sick, criminal, or insane. Jacques Derrida developed the technique of deconstruction in literary and philosophical criticism to show, he said, that language meanings cannot be "tied down" and that as a result claims that certain passages express the "truth" become suspicious indeed. Finally, American philosopher Richard Rorty, deeply influenced by Continental philosophy and the American pragmatism of William James and John Dewey, proposed a new task for philosophy. Because the discipline could never find "the truth," it must be used in the service of human beings to extend one's horizons, one's possibilities.

## Jürgen Habermas

**Jürgen Habermas** [HAHB-ur-mahs] (1929–    ), a professor at the University of Frankfurt, is one of many thinkers influenced by the critical approach of the Frankfurt School (see box). In this context "critical" does not necessarily mean "negative" but, rather, "reflective" or "thoughtful." This goes far beyond the reflection a physicist might bring to the results of a failed experiment ("What went wrong? Is there a hidden variable I have not accounted for? Is my theory faulty?"). The kind of reflection critical theory emphasizes is reflection on the assumptions of science or philosophy. For instance, empirical science approaches the world with a view to finding lawlike regularities in the things it examines; the measure of knowledge thus becomes the predictive power of the experimental method. Underlying the practice of empirical science is the assumption that its findings are independent of the observer (or, if not, then the presence of the observer can be corrected for). When the experimental method is used on the human being, it is no surprise that what emerges is a picture of a thing (a human thing) that also follows lawlike regularities and for which more or less sophisticated predictions can be made.

The tendency in modern technocratic society, Habermas says, is for this description of experimental science to become definitional of all knowledge. Although logical positivism (as we will see in Chapter 9) has been sharply criticized, its influence is still felt in the normal, ongoing scientific enterprise. But Habermas points out that "positivistic science" is only one way of looking at the world, and it is no surprise that such a perspective would claim to find "objective facts" that would make it possible for human beings to exert control over nature. Yet such a perspective, says Habermas, is inappropriate for the investigation of mutually shared meanings we experience in the everyday human world in which we live. Positivistic science treats human beings as objective things; what is needed is an approach to knowledge that treats the human being as a subject, one not isolated from other subjects but, on the contrary, interacting with them. This interaction takes

Can empirical science investigate subjectivity?

place in a domain that allows the sharing of intersubjective experiences and that provides contexts of history, art, literature, and language itself that enable us to understand one another. (Imagine a visitor who begins putting asphalt in his mouth after you suggest, "Let's eat up the street." He does not understand that you mean that fast-food restaurant a block away, but it is likely he will learn fast.)

This "practical" interest each of us has in understanding one another, Habermas says, is the realm of a science he calls historical/hermeneutical. (**Hermeneutics** deals with the principles of interpretation — of the Bible, of other texts, and of the language of human interactions.) He emphasizes that in this "practical" science, the individual cannot be treated as an objective unit; on the contrary, my human identity is to a greater or lesser extent the creation of human language and of the society into which I am born. Through this society and language, I gain a "pre-understanding" of others in my quest for mutual self-understanding; that is, I cannot understand myself if I cannot understand the words and actions of others. The meanings of those words and actions give me a context for making sense of myself in the human world.

But for Habermas there is a second kind of knowledge that is also inappropriate for the positivistic sciences. Habermas calls this "emancipatory knowledge," and it is the concern of **critical theory.** It is the work of critical theory to make explicit the controlling ideology of a political or social order. "Ideology" misrepresents and distorts the truth about the existence and use of arbitrary power throughout a society. The roots of ideology go deep into the heart of what a society takes to be knowledge. For example, a social order may be blind to its own fundamental belief that the method of positivistic science, which reduces the human being to the status of a thing for purposes of study, is the surest road to truth. In the realm of the practical, such a reductionistic ideology can be seen, say, in the treatment of a

## PROFILE: Jürgen Habermas (1929–    )

Habermas was born in Düsseldorf, Germany. He was raised in Gummersbach, where his father was the director of a seminary. When World War II ended, he was sixteen years old. He studied at the University of Bonn and was especially interested in Hegel, Marx, and modern Marxist thinkers. After receiving his Ph.D. in 1954, he became an assistant to Theodor Adorno at the University of Frankfurt. Adorno and Max Horkheimer were the leading figures in the Frankfurt School, renowned for the attempts its followers made to integrate the disciplines of philosophy, psychoanalysis, social science, and literary criticism. Habermas would make his own substantial contribution to the School's thought. The subject matter of his books varies greatly, but his overall concern has been to free people and thinking from unnecessary and unhelpful rules, categories, and other constraints. He achieved widespread recognition relatively early on with books such as *Theory and Practice* (1962), *The Logic of the Social Sciences* (1967), *Toward a Rational Society* (1971), *Knowledge and Human Interest* (1981), *The Theory of Communicative Action* (1981), and *Theory of Social Action* (1984).

## Frankfurt School

The Institute for Social Research was founded in 1923, affiliated with the University of Frankfurt, and, after exile in New York during the Nazi era, returned to Frankfurt in 1949. Those associated with the school were loosely united in the task of developing from Marxism a critical theory approach to art and the human sciences that would, on one hand, reject crude materialist determinism as an ideology and, on the other hand, reject positivism and any possibility of a value-free social science. Those associated with the school include Herbert Marcuse (1878–1979), Theodor Adorno (1903–1969), and Jürgen Habermas.

poem as a single object, independent of the society that produced it, to be studied just for itself. Habermas would agree with Marx that ideology produces reification; that is, reification takes human acts or properties, objectifies them, and then treats them as independent of the human world. In a capitalist society, for example, money is the reification of human labor and is in the end used against the laborer. But Habermas is critical of Marx's own reduction of human art and literature — Marx called them the "superstructure" — to the "base" of strict materialism. Thus, Habermas's own critical theorizing is Marxian — in the critical spirit of Marx — but not Marxist.

For Habermas, critical theory can bring a kind of freedom or emancipation from the chains of ideology as those who practice the method come to reflect on their own most deeply held assumptions and come to see that they are false. Ultimately, such emancipation would change society and the way human beings communicate one with another. Habermas proposed a theory of communicative competence in which what he called the **ideal speech situation** supplies the basis for rational (that is, nonideological) communication. The ideal speech situation, in which persons are free to speak their minds and listen to reason without fear of being blocked, is a norm of language itself, he said, and is presupposed in every

## Philosophical Anthropology

When he was a tender undergraduate, one of the authors traveled to the University of Tübingen in Germany to study. He signed up for a course called "Philosophische Anthropologie." He had no idea what the course might be about, but he could at least translate its name, which is the main reason he signed up for it. It was the first course in philosophy he had ever taken.

On the first day of class, he sat in the middle of a huge lecture hall—more German students were in that one class than were in all the courses in philosophy he took after that, back in America, combined. The Herr Professor walked to the lectern, shuffled through some notes, ripped off his glasses and sucked on them like a pipe, and gazed heavenward for several minutes, deep in thought. "*Was,*" he asked the ceiling, "*ist der Mensch?*"—What is man? This struck your author as a fairly interesting question—at least to get things started—and he waited for the answer.

What is man? What is a human being? This is the fundamental question of philosophical anthropology, which, along with beer, is important in German universities.

The term *anthropology* goes back to the Greeks and has been used ever since to denote the study of humans (*anthropos*) and their society. Early Church fathers used the term to distinguish the study of humans from the study of God; over the centuries—and especially during the sixteenth to eighteenth centuries—anthropology became increasingly divorced from theology, metaphysics, and the natural sciences. Kant, for example, held that to be worldly wise, we must go beyond the natural sciences and acquire an extensive knowledge of human nature through biographies, histories, travel books, plays, and so forth. For Kant, such an anthropology, though not a science, provided a practical study of what a free and self-determined human being is.

In the nineteenth century, German Romantics ("Romantic" here does not mean "lover"; it denotes a member of the important nineteenth-century movement that emphasized imagination and emotions in literature and art) sought a vision of the total human being. Hegel, however, distinguished between anthropology, which considers humans as they are *potentially*, and philosophy of history, which considers humans as they are *actually*. The Hegelian attack on anthropology and its lack of historical grounding has been carried on by selected German philosophers up to the present, where we find it lingering in Martin Heidegger and the Frankfurt School of social philosophy, both mentioned in this chapter. Today, "philosophical anthropology," as the philosophical study of human nature and existence is called, is moving away from the philosophy of history and seeks to establish itself as an independent discipline. It includes semiotics and structuralism.

*Was ist der Mensch?* Unfortunately, the professor's answer lasted the entire semester. Unfortunately, too, your author did not understand the answer. In fact, that single question, *Was ist der Mensch?*, was the *only* thing your author understood in the entire course, for his knowledge of German was none too good. (Later, when he read an English translation of the professor's lectures, he found he still was not sure of the answer.)

---

discourse. The person who lies, for example, does so with the assumption that there is such a thing as speaking the truth (otherwise, the concept of a lie would be meaningless). In a paper published in 1970, Habermas declared that "insofar as we master the means for the construction of an ideal speech situation, we can conceive the ideas of truth, freedom, and justice, which interpret each other—although of course only as ideas. On the strength of communicative competence alone, however, . . . we are quite unable to realize the ideal speech situation; we can only anticipate it." Recent work by Habermas has focused on the rise of countercultural groups, feminism, and various liberation movements and whether they constitute the beginnings of the kind of free society he envisions.

## Michel Foucault

**Michel Foucault** [foo-KO] (1926–1984) was intensely suspicious of philosophic or scientific truth claims, especially claims by the human sciences (such as psychology and sociology) to have discovered something true — that is, objectively true — about the human being. At first, Foucault thought of himself as an archaeologist, digging through historical strata to lay bare the discourses that shaped societies (and shape our own). *Discourse* here is a word that describes how people talk, the shape they give to the multitude of interactions within a society, and how they act as a result. It is Foucault's point that a study of such discourse reveals not the steady march of science in its smashing of superstition (that image itself is a kind of superstition) but, rather, the substitution of one invented reality for another, neither more nor less "true."

For example, the old view of disease as an outside "evil power" that attempted to kill the body was replaced in the late eighteenth century by the discourse of professionalized medicine, in which disease was spoken of as internal to the body. The proper role of medicine was not to cast out invading evil spirits but physically to cut out diseased flesh. But the "success" of such surgery has come at the price of turning ourselves into mere objects in need of fixing up. Medical technology can sustain the human body for a long time if in our discourse it is seen as some complex machine, but the image of a machine, which permeates our thinking, effectively reduces the human being to a mere mechanism, an object. The meaning (or lack of meaning) this image gives to human existence is not truer than the ancient view, just other. The dominant view of death (or of insanity, or criminality) is part of a discourse that — lo and behold! — finds (that is, creates) a never-ending parade of sick people, the insane, the criminal.

In his **archaeological** period, Foucault's work seemed to owe something to the structuralist movement in France, although he would disavow any connection. Foucault claimed to have found in his archaeological method a series of discontinuous "created realities," or **epistemes,** that serve in each era as the ground of the true and the false. But since these epistemes are a social given, there can be no appeal to any absolute truth of things (unless "absolute truth" is part of the particular episteme, but that would mean such a concept is merely a construct of social discourse and not "absolute" at all). Though the nature of the epistemes cannot be spelled out here, suffice it to say that Foucault's program is decidedly anti-Hegelian. Where Hegel saw the working out of history as the Absolute Reason becoming self-conscious, Foucault saw history as a series of discontinuities, one following the next but with no hint of true progress.

Yet Foucault's own project was brought into question by the implications of the archaeological method. It assumes a kind of objectivity on the part of the researcher and his "findings," but such objectivity, Foucault came to believe, was mere illusion. After all, if Foucault was himself working from within a particular episteme, no objective history of other epistemes would even be possible. Rather than abandon his relativistic stance, Foucault abandoned archaeology. Instead, beginning in the 1970s, he devoted himself to what Friedrich Nietzsche had earlier called **genealogy.**

For Foucault, genealogy did not commit one to a universal theory or to a particular view of the human subject. The emphasis in genealogy was not knowledge

## PROFILE: Michel Foucault (1926–1984)

Foucault told a group of American philosophers in Berkeley, California, in April 1983 that when Jürgen Habermas had visited him in Paris, Foucault "was quite struck by his observation of the extent to which the problem of Heidegger and of the political implications of Heidegger's thought was quite a pressing and important one for him." Habermas interpreted Heidegger as a German neoconservative and Heidegger's Nazism as somehow connected with Heidegger's own philosophical positions.

Foucault told the interviewers that he believed there was "a very tenuous 'analytic' link between a philosophical conception and the concrete political attitude of someone who is appealing to it; the 'best' theories do not constitute a very effective protection against disastrous political choices." But, Foucault added, "I don't conclude from this that one may say just anything within the order of theory, but, on the contrary, that a demanding, prudent, 'experimental' attitude is necessary; at every moment, step by step, one must confront what one is thinking and saying with what one is doing, with what one is."

Before he died on June 25, 1984, of toxoplasmosis-produced lesions on the brain as a result of AIDS, Foucault was engaged during most of his academic career in a project that attempted to chart the power relations by which societies exclude, lock up, or institutionalize the insane, the prisoner, the homosexual—those persons society defines as "other." Unlike Habermas, Foucault denied that societies could ever free themselves from such exclusionary forces; no "ideal speech situation" was possible.

Foucault himself was something of a scandal to "polite" French society. One biographer writes of the philosopher's sadomasochistic erotic practices, his appearance in public wearing leather clothes, his open affection for men, and his fondness of the gay bathhouses of San Francisco.

Born in Poitiers, France, on October 15, 1926, Foucault was the firstborn son of a surgeon. He was a professor of the Collège de France from 1970. Foucault's major works include *Madness and Civilization* (English translation 1965), *The Birth of the Clinic: An Archaeology of Medical Perception* (1973), *Discipline and Punish: The Birth of the Prison* (1977), *The Order of Things: An Archaeology of the Human Sciences* (1970), and *The History of Sexuality* (3 volumes, English translation 1978–1986).

(as it had been in archaeology) but power. In his later books Foucault was less concerned with the language-worlds created by various societies than with the "micropractices" of the body within a given society. This is not simply the physical body but the lived body, an embodied consciousness. For example, one of the features of the embodied person is ability to dominate others; therefore, it is possible to trace the development (the genealogy) of various laws against assault. A court sets up its own rules and acts on them and calls it justice; the practice of the court is just what justice is, but justice is really an illusion for a reordering of power relationships. Genealogy does not provide any theories to explain what is going on; it simply evokes the small practices and social habits that constitute you and us, illuminating how such practices express the working of the power of the body. Genealogy is not prescriptive, but descriptive.

## Structuralism versus Deconstruction

**Structuralism** is a methodology that seeks to find the underlying rules and conventions governing large social systems such as language or cultural mythology. It hearkens back to Swiss linguist **Ferdinand de Saussure** [so-SIWR] (1857–1913), who emphasized the study of the language system itself (*langue*) rather than particular speech (*parole*). Saussure was concerned with the "deep structures" of language common to all speakers. He saw linguistics as the study of signs, which he defined as a combination of the *signifier* (the physical thing that signifies) and the *signified* (that which is signified). A sentence is a sequence of signs the meaning of which depends not only on the order of the signs ("I can go" vs. "Can I go?") but also on the contrast of each sign with other signs in the language that are not present. Thus, the "I" in "I can go" contrasts with other possible subjects: she, he, you, and so on. It is the relationship between the "I" and these other signs not present that gives the "I" its meaning because our understanding of "I" takes place with the linguistic system and its interrelationships as background. How the "I" differs from other subjects gives the sign its meaning. Notice here that the emphasis Saussure makes is on the internal linguistic system and its infrastructure; it is of little concern to him whether a given sentence expresses something true about the outside world.

French anthropologist **Claude Lévi-Strauss** [LAY-vee-STROWSS] (1908– ) adapted Saussure's methods and applied them to his ethnographic research. Lévi-Strauss was interested in finding the underlying structures of thought in the myths of nonindustrial societies and in human communities generally. Characteristic of Lévi-Strauss's structuralist approach, as shown, for example, in *The Savage Mind* (1962; English translation 1966), is the search for a group of rules or "laws" that accounts for the social complexities of even so-called primitive cultures. Cultures (and literary works) were seen as systems of signs the meaning of which could be found in the particular relationships of signs with other signs in the system itself. The implication is that the individual person is very much a construct of the underlying, impersonal rules of the system.

## Jacques Derrida

The analysis of sign systems of various types, from advertising slogans to animal communication, is now called **semiotics** (from the Greek word *semeion,* meaning "sign"); most of the structuralist methodology fits within this "science of signs." But is such a science really possible? That is, are meanings within language or cultural systems stable enough to provide a definitive interpretation of texts or rituals arising from those systems? In the late 1960s, French philosopher and literary theorist **Jacques Derrida** [day-ree-DAH] (1930– ) said the answers were "no." He maintained that no such stable meanings were possible and that no definitive meaning of a text could ever be established. In fact, the very notion of a "definitive meaning" implied certain unproven (and unprovable) assumptions about texts and language.

Derrida's **deconstructive method** is to lay bare those assumptions about language, to "question" the text about possible multiple meanings, and in so doing to

## PROFILE: Jacques Derrida (1930 –    )

Derrida was born into a lower-middle-class Sephardic Jewish family in El Biar, Algiers. Early on, he was interested in sports and even had the notion of becoming a soccer player. He experienced considerable difficulty with anti-Semitism at the lycée where he studied. While in his teens, he published some poetry in North African journals. After a couple of unsuccessful attempts, he was eventually admitted at the age of nineteen to the prestigious École Normale Supérieure in Paris. He married in 1957. During the sixties, he was part of the political foment in Paris. His fame began to spread during his memorable participation in a colloquium at Johns Hopkins University. He has taught there and at Yale University in recent years and has published over twenty books.

One curious episode in Derrida's life occurred when he was nominated for an honorary degree at Cambridge University. In a very unusual way, four Cambridge dons expressed their displeasure and disagreement with such an award. A great hullabaloo followed with nineteen academics publishing a letter in *The Times* decrying his writings as incomprehensible and full of French verbal tricks and gimmicks. The implication was that he was a charlatan. After much furor, a vote was taken, which Derrida won, and he showed up to claim his title. But the row continues, with many in the Anglo-American philosophical world looking on his writings with grave suspicions.

show what he calls the **free play of signifiers.** By this Derrida means that the writer of a word "privileges" that word for a moment; this "privileging" becomes the medium for the play of the signifier—*différence*—rather than any background of a fixed linguistic system (which, according to Derrida, does not exist): This is reminiscent of the Heraclitean tradition that "you cannot step into the same river twice"; only now it means "you cannot step into the same language twice." Because meaning can occur only as experience, our experiences are constantly overriding ("overwriting") the dictionary definitions of words, effacing those definitions, which in turn are also in flux. A printed dictionary gives the false impression that language has stable meanings, whereas those meanings are continuously "at play" and changing. The use of a word not only goes beyond the dictionary definition but also "effaces" those forces at work that act just beyond the horizon of consciousness. These "forces" are no more available to us than Kant's *Ding-an-sich,* or thing-in-itself (see Chapter 7). From the perspective of deconstruction, then, there are no extralinguistic connections available to anchor meanings within language. The use of a word at one moment implies at least a slightly different background context than the use of the word at another time, and thus a difference in meaning. But precisely what this difference is can never be pinned down because even to ask a question about a change in meaning is to change a meaning. Derrida put it this way in a speech in 1966 at Johns Hopkins University in Baltimore, Maryland: "The concept of centered structure is in fact the concept of a play based on a fundamental ground, a play constituted on the basis of a fundamental immobility and a reassuring certitude, which is itself beyond the reach of play. And on the basis of this certitude anxiety can be mastered, for anxiety is invariably the result of a certain mode of being implicated in the game, of being caught by the game, of being as it were at stake in the game from the outset." But now, says Derrida, there has come (in deconstruction) a rupture of the metaphysical center (whether it be Plato's unchanging Forms or some other metaphysical conception that has no "play," no give). "This [rupture] was the moment when language invaded the universal problematic, the moment when, in the absence of a center or origin, everything became discourse . . . that is to say, a system in which the central signified, the original or transcendental signified, is never absolutely present outside a system of differences. The absence of the transcendental signified extends the domain and the play of signification infinitely."★

Derrida's comments recall Saussure's system of "differences," but Derrida takes Saussure's observation to its logical extreme: because all things intelligible to human beings must pass through their language system to be understood, they inevitably become "texts." Thus, the meaning of, say, the transcendental Forms can be found only through an exploration of the continual play of signifiers as Plato is interpreted and interpreted again. No ultimate meaning can be found—what Plato really meant, what a Form really is—because if all human understanding comes through textuality, there is no ultimate meaning to be found.

Thus, Derrida is suspicious of any claim to final interpretation (he calls such claims absolutely ridiculous). He wants to break down the binary thinking of the structuralists (and others), who tend to privilege the first term in each dyad: male/female, white/black, mind/body, master/slave, and so on. Derrida suggests that the first term has significance only in relation to, and only because of, the second term. That is, a master can be a master only if there are slaves; the existence of the master is dependent on the existence of the slave. Derrida's method seeks to bring to the foreground the less privileged terms and thus the implicit assumptions embedded within language systems.

Derrida did not use his deconstructive method only to throw into question the assumptions of structural linguists like Saussure and linguistic analysts like some of those found in the analytic tradition. He also used it to attack the structural anthropology of Claude Lévi-Strauss. Derrida tried to show that Lévi-Strauss failed to see history as a gradually evolving process. Derrida also believed that there is no basis for making myths into a fixed, coherent system; therefore, the philosopher cannot be an "engineer" who finds unifying elements within myths. Myths have no single unitary source; hence, interpretation of them is not scientific but, rather, a product of the imagination. Myths have no authors and no single source and cannot give rise to scientific knowledge.

Derrida also criticizes Lévi-Strauss's preference for the past and its presumed natural innocence. New structures of development are seen as catastrophes by Lévi-Strauss. Play, which is a positive element of change for Derrida, is seen by Lévi-Strauss as a disruptive force that is ruinous of origins and archaic forms within society. Derrida is much closer to Nietzsche in not being attached to origins in

---

★Jacques Derrida, "Structure, Sign and Play," in *Writing and Difference* (Chicago: University of Chicago Press, 1978), pp. 279, 280.

actively interpreting society. It is much more important to think what has yet to be and what has yet to be imagined. Thinking must enter the realm of the unknown, the monstrous, the terrifying, the as yet unformed and unformulated.

Derrida's critique of linguistic structuralism and of structural anthropology represents but a part of his thinking. His deepest forays into philosophy concern the metaphysical. Here his thinking is most influenced by Hegel, Husserl, and Heidegger. He most tellingly used his deconstructive method to attack Husserl's transcendental idealism.

Derrida started his critique by agreeing with Heidegger that metaphysics had been reduced to onto-theology, or a metaphysics according to which all beings stem from a divine logos. *Onto-theology* is a term used by Heidegger to describe the development of metaphysics since Plato. Metaphysics has increasingly come to reduce being into beings and the highest and first being or God. Since Nietzsche's declaration that "God is dead," modern metaphysics has sought to find structures of absolute certainty in human subjectivity and logic. For Heidegger, this has meant that metaphysics is at an end because it has forgotten being entirely and replaced it with a sterile logic and human hubris. Derrida sees this artificial reduction of metaphysics to a supposed transcendental, absolutely certain logic. You may recall the word *transcendental* as referring back to Immanuel Kant and meaning the a priori structures within human consciousness before we perceive anything that allows us to organize sense-data into objects understandable to ourselves and others. Husserl attempted to ground human knowing in a transcendental science of logic or on a universal phenomenology of consciousness (see earlier in this chapter). Derrida elaborated on this development as a logocentrism, and this term is meant to apply to Heidegger's thinking as well. The logocentric worldview is based on a nostalgia for an original state of full being or presence that is now lost. Beings are held to derive their structure and meaning from a divine logos similar to the *logos* Heraclitus first posited in the sixth century B.C.E. *Logos* has many meanings in Greek, such as word, speech, thought, reason, but for Heraclitus and later thinkers it is the principle and source of order, necessity, and rationality in the universe. Logocentrism is based on a preference for a stable, hierarchical world of necessary being. The necessity and transcendence of such a world is available only to a few rare persons who are capable of thinking transcendentally. Derrida used the deconstructive method to uncover unfounded assumptions and the artificial oppositions on which logocentric thinking is based.

Much of Derrida's critique of Western thinking concentrates on the transcendental phenomenology of Edmund Husserl. Husserl had sought a purer and more authentic science of metaphysics. To achieve purity and absolute certainty in knowing, Husserl sought a transcendental consciousness that is beyond any particular, individual consciousness. Phenomenology was to be based on eidetic structures, or ideal objects that had the same kind of certainty and clarity as geometrical concepts. The word *eidetic* stems from the Greek word *eidos*, which refers back among other things to Plato's Ideas or Forms, which are taken to be true, perfect, permanent, and nonphysical. These essences, or eidetic, transcendental structures, must be distinguished from empirical structures available through sense-experience.

Husserl sought to find a nonempirical, transcendental form of consciousness. He wanted language to have an ideality of meaning as well as a pure logical grammar. Truths do not need to be represented using empirical content; they can be directly intuited. But for Derrida, there is no direct intuition of these truths; there is only mediated, representational knowledge that is dependent on linguistic structures. He further claimed that truth does not take place prior to language but, rather, depends on language and on temporality for its existence. Idealization of language as well as idealization of original content means the death of existent things. Transcendental philosophy such as Husserl's leaves out and cannot deal with human finitude and with historical change. Such things as death, metaphor, and imaginative creativity cannot be taken into account. Derrida develops contingent or historically changeable concepts and ways of dealing with aspects of language and thinking that Husserl left undeveloped. Derrida thought that these changing, uncertain aspects of things are not on the periphery of language use and metaphysics but, rather, constitute their very core. Only through the playful use of language will the interaction between the presence and absence of things as well as between their certainty and uncertainty enter consciousness.

Thinking and language can never be closed systems of absolutely certain, transcendental concepts. Rather, they should be open ended, if temporally limited. They must in some way be capable of dealing with things' uniqueness — their changeability, uncertainty, and incompleteness. The claims of deconstruction are much more modest, but they can affect reality in a more positive way. Derrida's philosophy is a plea for reason to be used in the realms of metaphysics, anthropology, and linguistics. He furthers extends this procedure to the realms of politics, ethics, and psychology. In a way, he was the Socrates for the twentieth century, forcing a recognition that most claims of absolute knowledge are full of contradictions and untenable.

Derrida's books include *Of Grammatology* (1967; English translation 1976) and *Writing and Difference* (1967; English translation 1978).

## Gilles Deleuze

Gilles Deleuze [jeel duh LOOZ] (1925–1995), one of the important figures in contemporary Continental philosophy, wrote on so many different topics —film, literature, logic, politics—that it is difficult to summarize his philosophy. We shall focus on the one thing that stands out most, though: the notion of *multiplicity,* and the affirmation of multiplicity in whatever field Deleuze was studying. Deleuze made study of multiplicity the centerpiece of his thought. Specifically, he claimed that any unified or singular entity, any "one," is abstracted from an original multiplicity. This view of the "one" in relation to the "multiple" led Deleuze to be suspicious of any claim that anything, any "one," is transcendent or beyond the multiple (we will explain what this means in a second). Transcendence in general is one of the great enemies of Deleuze's philosophy, so it is no wonder that Deleuze was generally critical of Plato. Plato, you will remember, in effect claimed that the world we perceive is an illusion, the shadows in the cave (see Chapter 3). The real world, according to Plato, is found in a transcendent realm of Forms (an ideal realm of things beyond the appearances we sense directly). Now Deleuze thought this was exactly 180 degrees backward. Plato should have said the multiplicity of

# PROFILE: Gilles Deleuze (1925–1995)

Born in Paris, Deleuze had a typical academic career, and, although as a philosopher he advocated difference and change, he rarely traveled and seemed to lead a very sedate life. He is often characterized as a philosophical outsider, and for several reasons. His interests were not typical of his day: for example, he was always interested in British empiricism (which has never been too popular in France), and he preferred writing about the "minor" thinkers in the philosophical tradition, thinkers who tend to be overlooked: like the Stoics, Spinoza, and Henri Bergson. (Bergson [1859–1941] was another important French philosopher, most famous for tracing the relationship between free will and the subjective experience of time.) Deleuze was also never an adherent of any of the major philosophical movements in twentieth-century France: existentialism, phenomenology, structuralism, and postmodernism. This makes his philosophy idiosyncratic, but few would deny its influence. Indeed, Michel Foucault once wrote: "Perhaps one day, this century will be known as Deleuzian."

Deleuze wrote some of his most famous books with a colleague, Félix Guattari. While the books Deleuze wrote on his own tended to be studies of single philosophers, the books he wrote with Guattari were much more political in orientation and more sweeping in scope. The most famous of these is *Anti-Oedipus*, which was very influential on the young, politically oriented generation of French students in the early 1970s. *Anti-Oedipus* argues that desire should not be seen as something that lacks what it desires (as has been argued since Plato). Desire is instead something like a "machine"—it links up with things that are outside it. Deleuze and Guattari study the kinds of things desire links up with. Sometimes these are things that restrain desire, such as social institutions, the family, the church, or the military. One of the most important claims in *Anti-Oedipus* is that desire can actively seek its own repression. But desire can also link up with things that take it into uncharted territories. Deleuze and Guattari prefer to see desire doing this and try to find ways in which desire can be helped to make such new and transgressive links.

Deleuze is considered one of the major players in postmodernism. His books include: *Nietzsche and Philosophy* (1962), *Difference and Repetition* (1968), and *The Fold: Leibniz and the Baroque* (1988).

---

appearances is the real thing, and the Forms?—there are no Forms. This view is very close to Nietzsche's, to whom Deleuze was greatly indebted. Consider, for instance, the chair on which you are seated. For Plato, the chair's reality lies in the fact that it participates in an ideal Form. Deleuze thought of the chair as essentially interconnected with the room, its function, its role in human lives and society, and so forth.

Also like Nietzsche, Deleuze thought that the philosophical method—the way philosophy goes about doing things—ought to be changed. To criticize traditional philosophy, Deleuze used the model of a tree. Often, he claimed, philosophers study things as if they were trees. How so? Well, many times philosophers presume that what they are thinking about is something that is clear, distinct, and well organized. However, Deleuze would claim that this is an idealized view that neglects how things really are. This approach to things is not able to consider multiplicity correctly. To correct this approach, Deleuze proposed thinking of things in terms of *rhizomes* rather than trees. Rhizomes are plants that tend to grow horizontally rather than vertically. Rather than sending their roots deep into the ground, and rather than being clearly unified and distinct entities, rhizomes spread out, growing up and all over things that are in their way, getting tangled up with other rhizomes. Think of grass, or of ivy climbing up and over whatever it comes across. If philosophers approach things as rhizomes, they will come up with a very different picture of how things are.

Consider how a tree-based approach to a study of *language* would differ from a rhizome-based approach. A tree-based approach would study language the way you probably studied it in high school. You break language down into categories (nouns, verbs, adjectives), and you study the rules for forming grammatically correct sentences. While this way of studying language may help you speak a language correctly, does it accurately reflect the way you speak? A rhizomatic approach to language would point out how "proper English" is only one way in which English is spoken—and a very rare one at that! We rarely speak clearly and in a grammatically correct way (even if we should). We stutter, mumble, leave sentences incomplete; our subjects and our verbs don't agree. Indeed, with Deleuze's rhizomatic approach to language, you might be led to ask whether English is even *one* language (an assumption that a tree-based approach would make). Is there really *one* "English"? Who speaks it? The Queen of England?

Deleuze's rhizomatic approach to language would point out that English is really a multiplicity of dialects, and so-called "proper English" is merely one dialect — one little part of a larger rhizome — one that tries to achieve dominance over other dialects. Furthermore, each of us speaks any number of different versions of English. We speak one way with our friends, another way with our family, another way at school, and yet another way at work. While the rules we use for speaking may be similar in each case, there are important differences in the kinds of words we use, the tone of voice we employ, and perhaps even in the way we hold our bodies when we speak. These kinds of things a rhizomatic approach to language would focus on: it would consider not only language itself, but also such things as the voice and the body that are intertwined with our use of language.

This rhizomatic approach to language illustrates Deleuze's main philosophical concern. We are always tempted to turn things into "ones," into discrete entities, and to consider them in abstraction from their relations with other things. Philosophy should instead address multiplicity and difference. Deleuze applied this approach to literature, film, politics, psychoanalysis, and other things. The details are often difficult, but this should give you an idea of one of the most important aspects of the underlying perspective.

## Alain Badiou

Alain Badiou [uh LANE Buh DEEW] (1937–  ), once a troublemaker in some of Deleuze's courses, is, like Deleuze, primarily interested in thinking about multiplicity. Like Deleuze, he claims that there is no transcendent "one": infinite difference is all there is. However, Badiou raises an objection to Deleuze's approach to the multiple and accuses Deleuze of being a closet monist (*monist* means "one-ist"). Even though Deleuze did not want to say that "all is one," Badiou charges that

Deleuze's philosophy treats the multiple as if it is a singularity-totality: something like a "one-all," which is a term Deleuze sometimes uses.

Badiou argues that it is impossible to totalize everything that exists. In fact, what exists is "infinite": indeed, it is "infinitely infinite." The topic of infinity is something that sets Badiou apart from most contemporary Continental philosophers, who believe that infinity is something abstract, something that we cannot imagine and cannot even think about. For a long time, and since Heidegger especially, an emphasis in Continental philosophy has been on finitude: considering how knowledge is finite and limited, and arguing in some cases that the finitude of our knowledge is based on our own mortality. Badiou points out that despite the fact we are mortal and cannot ever have any experience of infinity, mathematicians have been thinking about and working with infinity (especially in set theory) for over a century. Philosophers have fallen way behind them. Badiou suggests that philosophers should again start looking at what mathematicians are doing, as they did in Plato's day. This may lead philosophers to think very differently about being.

Another important topic in Badiou's philosophy, as well as Deleuze's, is the notion of the event. In ordinary language, an event is just a term for anything that happens, but in Deleuze and Badiou's philosophies *event* takes on special meaning. It refers to those rare moments at which one is led to question the concepts and beliefs one has always relied on. Events, according to Badiou, come in four varieties: events in science, politics, art, and love. For example, in science Einstein's development of the theory of relativity was a scientific event that forced scientists to think differently. Love, which arises from an encounter with another person, can also be seen as an event that forces one to change one's habits, one's usual attitudes and beliefs. Badiou attempts to come up with a philosophy of the event that studies how people in different walks of life struggle to remain faithful to an event that has changed them.

## Richard Rorty

American philosopher **Richard Rorty** (1931–   ) is suspicious of the traditional claims of philosophy itself to have the methods best suited to finding "truth." He has adopted the way of American pragmatism exemplified by William James and John Dewey (see Chapter 9) and has applied it to the role of literature in society. The "best" literature, Rorty says, can open to its readers new possibilities for constructing a meaningful life. Some philosophical writing falls into this category (Rorty offers the example of Derrida), but philosophy has no corner in helping a person extend the possibilities of life. Rorty would characterize himself as a liberal ironist, adhering to the tradition of political liberalism in the public square (which offers us the freedom to pursue private projects) and irony in the private sphere (in which our "absolute" values are human constructs and in which we must live with meanings we have ourselves created).

In the last few years, Rorty has sought to combine American liberalism with Continental literature and philosophy, and to do so through the medium of pragmatism. Heidegger, he says, was a brilliant thinker, but chance events played a great

## PROFILE: Richard Rorty (1931– )

Rorty was born in New York City to political parents who were followers of Leon Trotsky. He was admitted to the University of Chicago at the age of fifteen and received his Ph.D. from Yale University in 1956. He taught at Wellesley for three years and then at Princeton University until 1982. Initially, he was caught up in the tide of analytic philosophy and was especially interested in the efforts to assimilate the thought of the later Wittgenstein. During this period, he published *The Linguistic Turn* (1967). In the 1970s, Rorty gave up the search for the certain foundations in epistemology and ethics. He turned toward the more contingent thinking of John Dewey and Martin Heidegger. Instead of pursuing absolute truth and its foundations, he sought to understand historical change and linguistic usage as a matter of erstwhile human practice. Philosophy was to be a hermeneutical interpretation of culture, thought, and history or an attempt to understand events in their temporal, spatial, and open-ended context. To the Greeks, Hermes was the son of Zeus and a messenger of the gods. The Greek word *hermeneuein* means to lay out or explain. This phase of Rorty's thought is marked by the publication of *Philosophy and the Mirror of Nature* (1979).

Rorty has increasingly seen himself as a pragmatist, one who, not unlike John Dewey before him, is concerned with contingency, liberalism, and self-creation of the individual. Philosophy is contingent in that its conclusions are never absolutely true, certain, and fixed. For Rorty, liberal democracy, especially the American version, represents the best form of social organization presently available. He also has come to believe in the importance of community, including the function of advocacy wherein viewpoints and political positions are advanced and argued vigorously as an important part of the social process. In 1989 he published *Contingency, Irony, and Solidarity*.

role in Heidegger's personal choices and commitments. If it had been otherwise, Heidegger might have come to the United States before investing in Nazi ideology and might thus have lived a wholly honorable life. As it was, says Rorty, Heidegger was "a coward, a liar and the greatest philosopher of the century." What is important now is that Heidegger can function as an example: "What binds early to late Heidegger," writes Rorty, "is the hope of finding a vocabulary which will keep him authentic—one which will block any attempt to affiliate oneself with a higher power, . . . to escape from time into eternity. . . . He wants a self-consuming and continually self-renewing final vocabulary. . . . Reading Heidegger has become one of the experiences with which we have to come to terms, to redescribe and make mesh with the rest of our experiences, in order to succeed in our own projects of self-creation. But Heidegger has no general public utility." That is, says Rorty, Heidegger fails as a public philosopher because in part he succumbs to a tendency to claim that those words that are meaningful to him ought to be meaningful to others. But in the private sphere, Heidegger offers an example of a philosophy professor who quested after authenticity—an example that Rorty, for one, can take to heart.

However, let's get back to Rorty himself and consider exactly what his "pragmatism" amounts to. Rorty's main thesis seems to be this.

We tend to think of evolution or God or nature as having made us into something like machines that accurately photocopy the world around us, provided we are objective and approach the world with "an unclouded mental eye or a rigorous method." In other words, we tend to think that, provided we are objective, the "truth" will force itself on us. In Rorty's language, we tend to think inquiry is "constrained" by the world out there. Rorty, however, thinks that objectivity is but a fiction and the idea of the truth is a myth. Why? Because "there is no method for knowing *when* one has reached the truth, or when one is closer than before."

We might think of it this way. Culture A has its standards of what counts as evidence, reasonableness, knowledge, and truth. Rorty refers to cultures as "conversations" and refers to the standards of evidence, reasonableness, knowledge, truth, and so forth as "constraints on inquiry." If people from culture (or "conversation") A think they have arrived at the truth, they have done so only vis-à-vis their own culture's constraints on inquiry. But have they reached the truth? Only if their "constraints"—that is, standards or evidence and so forth—are correct. Unfortunately, there is no way people can step outside their perspective to evaluate their constraints/standards. And the question "Are the constraints/standards of culture A correct?" is meaningless from within culture A. It is something like asking, "Is the Constitution constitutional?" So people in culture A cannot know when they have reached the truth, if knowing the truth requires an objective viewpoint beyond their own.

Likewise, it is meaningless for the people in culture B to wonder if culture B's constraints/standards are correct. Of course, people in either A or B can evaluate the constraints/standards of the *other* culture. But that still does not tell them whether *their own* constraints/standards are correct. This means, ultimately, that nobody can say whether she or he has reached the truth, except in the sense of truth held in one's own culture. Truth, then, is whatever "survives all objections within one's culture." Thus, Rorty writes, "the only sense in which we are constrained to truth is that we can make no sense of the notion that the view which can survive all objections might be false."

Rorty also refers to the standards of evidence, reasonableness, knowledge, and truth as "starting points" and describes his pragmatic view that standards are relative to one's culture by saying that the starting points are "contingent." Philosophically, Rorty says, our choice is "between accepting the contingent character of starting-points, and attempting to evade that contingency. To accept the contingency of starting-points (i.e., to accept the relativity of evidence, reasonableness, truth, etc.) is to accept our inheritance from, and our conversation with, our fellow-humans as our only source of guidance." This is Rorty's way of saying we are bound by the standards of our culture.

Those who have tried to evade this contingency, according to Rorty, must maintain that we are copy machines (our word, not Rorty's) that, when functioning rightly, photocopy or apprehend the truth. Plato thought we apprehend the truth at the top of the divided line (see Chapter 3), Christians when we tune into the voice of God in the heart, and Descartes and his followers when we empty the mind and seek the indubitable (see Chapter 6). After Kant, Rorty says, philosophers have hoped to find absolute truth by exploring the a priori structure of experience (see Chapter 7).

If we give up trying to evade the "contingency of starting points," then "we shall lose what Nietzsche called 'metaphysical comfort.'" However, "we may gain a renewed sense of community." Further, "our identification with our community — our society, our political tradition, our intellectual heritage — is heightened when we see this community as ours rather than nature's, shaped rather than found, one among many which men have made."

Thus, Rorty concludes, "what matters is our loyalty to other human beings clinging together against the dark, not our hope of getting things right." These views can be found in Rorty's *Consequences of Pragmatism* (1982).

## SELECTION 8.1
# Existentialism and Humanism*

*Jean-Paul Sartre*

[*This is a pretty clear and straightforward explanation of what existentialism is, followed by examples and illustrations.*]

What is this that we call existentialism? . . . Actually it is the least shocking doctrine, and the most austere; it is intended strictly for technicians, and philosophers. However, it can easily be defined. What makes the matter complicated is that there are two kinds of existentialists: the first who are Christian, and among whom I will include Jaspers and Gabriel Marcel, of the Catholic faith; and also, the atheistic existentialists among whom we must include Heidegger, and also the French existentialists, and myself. What they have in common is simply the fact that they think that existence precedes essence, or, if you wish, that we must start from subjectivity. . . .

What does it mean here that existence precedes essence? It means that man exists first, experiences himself, springs up in the world, and that he defines himself afterwards. If man, as the existentialist conceives him, is not definable, it is because he is nothing at first. He will only be [something] afterwards, and he will be as he will have made himself. So, there is no human nature, since there is no God to think it. Man simply is, not only as he conceives himself, but as he determines himself, and as he conceives himself after existing, as he determines himself after this impulse toward existence; man is

nothing other than what he makes himself. This is the first principle of existentialism. It is also what we call subjectivity. . . . Man is at first a project which lives subjectively, instead of being a moss, a decaying thing, or a cauliflower; nothing exists prior to this project; nothing is intelligible in the heavens, and man will at first be what he has planned to be. Not what he may wish to be. . . . If existence really precedes essence, man is responsible for what he is. Thus, the first step of existentialism is to show every man [to be] in control of what he is and to make him assume total responsibility for his existence. And, when we say that man is responsible for himself, we do not [only] mean that man is responsible for his precise individuality, but that he is responsible for all men. . . . When we say that man determines himself, we understand that each of us chooses himself, but by that we mean also that in choosing himself he chooses all men. Indeed, there is not one of our actions which, in creating the man we wish to be, does not [also] create at the same time an image of the man we think we ought to be. To choose to be this or that, is to affirm at the same time the value of what we choose, for we can never choose evil; what we choose is always the good, and nothing can be good for us without [also] being [good] for all. . . .

This enables us to understand what some rather lofty words, like anguish, abandonment, despair mean. As you will see, it is quite simple. First, what do we mean by anguish? The existentialist readily declares that man is [in] anguish. That means this: the man who commits himself and who realizes that it is not only himself that he chooses, but [that] he is

---

*From Jean-Paul Sartre, *L'Existentialisme est un humanisme* (Paris: Editions Nagel, 1946), translated by Deanna Stein McMahon.

also a lawgiver choosing at the same time [for] all mankind, would not know how to escape the feeling of his total and profound responsibility. Certainly, many men are not anxious; but we claim that they are hiding their anguish, that they are fleeing from it; certainly, many men believe [that] in acting [they] commit only themselves, and when one says to them: "what if everyone acted like that?" they shrug their shoulders and reply: "everyone does not act like that." But really, one should always ask himself: "what would happen if everyone did the same?" and we cannot escape this troubling thought except by a kind of bad faith. The man who lies and who excuses himself by declaring: "everyone does not act like that," is someone who is ill at ease with his conscience, because the act of lying implies a universal value attributed to the lie. Even when it conceals itself, anguish appears. . . .

And when we speak of abandonment, an expression dear to Heidegger, we mean only that God does not exist, and that we must draw out the consequences of this to the very end. . . . The existentialist, on the contrary, thinks that it is very troubling that God does not exist, for with him disappears every possibility of finding values in an intelligible heaven; there can no longer be any good a priori, since there is no infinite and perfect consciousness to think it; it is not written anywhere that the good exists, that we must be honest, that we must not lie, since precisely we exist in a context where there are only men. Dostoyevsky has written, "If God did not exist, everything would be allowed." This is the point of departure for existentialism. Indeed, everything is allowed if God does not exist, and consequently man is abandoned, because neither in himself nor beyond himself does he find any possibility of clinging on [to something]. At the start, he finds no excuses. If, indeed, existence precedes essence, we will never be able to give an explanation by reference to a human nature [which is] given and fixed; in other words, there is no determinism, man is free, man is freedom. Moreover, if God does not exist, we do not find before us any values or orders which will justify our conduct. So, we have neither behind us nor before us, in the luminous realm of values, any justifications or excuses. We are alone, without excuses. It is what I will express by saying that man is condemned to be free. Condemned, because he has not created himself, and nevertheless, in other respects [he is] free, because once [he is] cast into the world, he is responsible for everything that he does. . . .

To give you an example which [will] allow [you] to understand abandonment better, I will cite the case of one of my students who came to see me in the following circumstances. His father was on bad terms with his mother, and moreover, was inclined to be a collaborator. His older brother had been killed in the German offensive of 1940, and this young man, with feelings somewhat primitive but generous, wanted to avenge him. His mother lived alone with him, quite distressed by the semi-betrayal of his father and by the death of her eldest son, and found consolation only in him. This young man had the choice, at that time, between leaving for England and enlisting in the Free French Forces—that is to say, to forsake his mother—or to stay near his mother and to help her [to] live. He fully realized that this woman lived only for him and that his disappearance—and perhaps his death—would cast her into despair. He also realized that, in reality, [and] concretely, each action that he performed with regard to his mother had its surety in the sense that he was helping her to live, whereas each action that he might perform in order to leave and fight was an ambiguous action which could be lost in the sands, to answer no purpose. For example, leaving for England, he might remain indefinitely in a Spanish camp, while passing through Spain; he might arrive in England or in Algiers and be placed in an office to keep records. Consequently, he found himself facing two very different kinds of action: one concrete, immediate, but applying only to one individual; or else an action which applied to a whole [group] infinitely vaster, a national community but which was by that reason ambiguous, and which could be interrupted on the way. And, at the same time, he hesitated between two kinds of ethics. On the one hand, an ethic of sympathy, of individual devotion; and on the other hand a wider ethic but whose effectiveness was more questionable. He had to choose between the two. Who could help him to choose? Christian doctrine? No. Christian doctrine says: "be charitable, love your neighbor, devote yourself to others, choose the hardest way, etc. . . ." But which is the hardest way? Whom must we love as our brother, the soldier or the mother? Which has the greatest utility, the one [which is] definite, to help a definite individual to live? Who can decide it *a priori*? No one. No written ethic can tell him. The Kantian ethic says: "never treat others as [a] means, but as [an] end." Very well; if I remain near [with] my mother I will treat her as an end and not as means, but by this same action, I risk treating those who fight around me as a means; and conversely if I go to rejoin those who are fighting I will treat them as an end, and by this action I risk treating my mother as a means.

If these values are vague, and if they are still too broad for the specific and concrete case that we are considering, it remains for us only to rely on our instincts. This is what this young man tried to do; and when I saw him, he said: "basically, what counts is the sentiment; I ought to choose that which actually pushes me in a certain direction. If I feel that I love my mother enough to sacrifice everything else for her — my desire for vengeance, my desire for action, my desire for adventures — I [will] stay near her. If, on the contrary, I feel that my love for my mother is not sufficient, I [will] leave." But how [do we] judge the weight of a feeling? What constituted the worth of his feeling for his mother? Precisely the fact that he stayed for her. I may say, I love this friend enough to sacrifice such a [a certain] sum of money for him; I can say it, only if I have done it. I may say: I love my mother enough to remain with her, if I have remained with her. I can determine the worth of this affection only if, precisely, I have performed an action which confirms and defines it. Now, as I require this affection to justify my action, I find myself caught in a vicious circle.

Further, Gide has said very well, that a feeling which is acting and a feeling which is real are two nearly indiscernible things: to decide that I love my mother by remaining near her, or to act a part which will make me stay for my mother, is nearly the same thing. In other words, the feeling is constituted by the actions that we perform: I cannot then consult it in order to guide myself according to it. What that means is that I can neither seek for in myself the authentic state which will push me to act, nor demand from an ethic the concepts which will allow me to act. At least, you say, he went to see a professor to ask his advice. But, if you seek advice from a priest, for example, you have chosen this priest, you already knew, after all, more or less, what he was going to advise you. In other words, to choose the adviser is still to commit yourself. The proof of it is what you will say, if you are a Christian: consult a priest. But there are priests who are collaborators, priests who wait for the tide to turn, priests who belong to the resistance. Which [should you] choose? And if the young man chooses a priest who is a member of the resistance, or a priest who is a collaborator, he has already decided [on] the kind of

advice he will receive. Thus, in coming to see me, he knew the reply that I was going to make to him, and I had only one reply to make: you are free, choose, that is to say, invent. No general ethic can show you what there is to do; there is no sign in the world. The Catholics will reply: "but there are signs." Let's admit it; it is myself in any case who chooses the meaning that they have. . . .

Abandonment implies that we ourselves choose our being. Abandonment goes with anguish. As for despair, this expression has a very simple meaning. It means that we will restrict ourselves to a reliance upon that which depends on our will, or on the set of the probabilities which make our action possible. . . . From the moment when the possibilities that I am considering are not strictly involved by my action, I must take no further interest in them, because no God, no design can adjust the world and its possibilities to my will. . . . Quietism is the attitude of men who say: "others can do what I cannot do." The doctrine that I am presenting to you is exactly opposite to quietism, since it claims: "there is reality only in action." It goes further [than this] besides, since it adds: "man is nothing other than his project, he exists only in so far as he realizes himself, thus he is nothing other than whole of his actions, nothing other than his life." According to this, we can understand why our doctrine horrifies a good many men. Because often they have only one way of enduring their misery. It is to think: "circumstances have been against me, I was worth much more than what I have been; to be sure, I have not had a great love, or a great friendship, but it is because I have not met a man or a woman who was worthy of it. I have not written very good books because I have not had the leisure to do it. I have not had children to whom to devote myself because I did not find a person with whom I could have made my life. [There] remains, then, in me, unused and wholly feasible a multitude of dispositions, inclinations, possibilities which give me a worth that the simple set of my actions does not allow [one] to infer." Now, in reality, for the existentialist there is no love other than that which is made, there is no possibility of love other than that which manifests itself in a love; there is no genius other than that which expresses itself in works of art. The genius of Proust is the totality of Proust's works; the genius of Racine is the set of his tragedies, beyond that there is nothing. Why [should we] attribute to Racine the possibility of writing a new tragedy, since precisely he did not write it? In his life a man commits himself, draws his own figure, and beyond this figure there is nothing. Obviously, this thought may seem harsh to someone who has not had a successful life. But, on the other hand, it prepares men to understand that only reality counts, that the dreams, the expectations, the hopes allow [us] only to define a man as [a] disappointed dream, as miscarried hopes, as useless expectations; that is to say that that defines them negatively and not positively. However, when we say "you are nothing other than your life," that does not imply that the artist will be judged only by his artworks, for a thousand other things also contribute to define him. What we mean is that man is nothing other than a set of undertakings, that he is the sum, the organization, the whole of the relations which make up these undertakings.

---

## SELECTION 8.2
# The Myth of Sisyphus*

*Albert Camus*

---

[*Camus begins by asserting that I know only that I and the world outside me exist; the rest of supposed knowledge is mere "construction." (Especially interesting is his view that trying to define or understand himself is nothing but water slipping through his fingers.) He ends with observing how absurd it is that the heart longs for clear understanding, given the irrationality of everything.*]

Of whom and of what indeed can I say: "I know that!" This heart within me I can feel, and I judge that it exists. This world I can touch, and I likewise judge that it exists. There ends all my knowledge, and the rest is construction. For if I try to seize this self of which I feel sure, if I try to define and to summarize it, it is nothing but water slipping through my fingers. I can sketch one by one all the aspects it is able to assume, all those likewise that have been attributed to it, this upbringing, this origin, this ardor or these silences, this nobility or this vileness. But aspects cannot be added up. This very heart which is mine will forever remain indefinable to me. Between the certainty I have of my existence and the content I try to give to that assurance, the gap will never be filled. Forever I shall be a stranger to myself. In psychology as in logic, there are truths but no truth. Socrates' "Know thyself" has as much

value as the "Be virtuous" of our confessionals. They reveal a nostalgia at the same time as an ignorance. They are sterile exercises on great subjects. They are legitimate only in precisely so far as they are approximate.

And here are trees and I know their gnarled surface, water and I feel its taste. These scents of grass and stars at night, certain evenings when the heart relaxes—how shall I negate this world whose power and strength I feel? Yet all the knowledge on earth will give me nothing to assure me that this world is mine. You describe it to me and you teach me to classify it. You enumerate its laws and in my thirst for knowledge I admit that they are true. You take apart its mechanism and my hope increases. At the final stage you teach me that this wondrous and multicolored universe can be reduced to the atom and that the atom itself can be reduced to the electron. All this is good and I wait for you to continue. But you tell me of an invisible planetary system in which electrons gravitate around a nucleus. You explain this world to me with an image. I realize then that you have been reduced to poetry: I shall never know. Have I the time to become indignant? You have already changed theories. So that science that was to teach me everything ends up in a hypothesis, that lucidity founders in metaphor, that uncertainty is resolved in a work of art. What need had I of so many efforts? The soft lines of these hills and the hand of evening on this troubled heart teach me much more. I have returned to my beginning. I realize that if through science I can seize phenomena and enumerate them, I cannot, for all that, appre-

---

*From *The Myth of Sisyphus* by Albert Camus, translated by Justin O'Brien, copyright © 1955, 1983 by Alfred A. Knopf. Used by permission of Alfred A. Knopf, a division of Random House, Inc.

hend the world. Were I to trace its entire relief with my finger, I should not know any more. And you give me the choice between a description that is sure but that teaches me nothing and hypotheses that claim to teach me but that are not sure. A stranger to myself and to the world, armed solely with a thought that negates itself as soon as it asserts, what is this condition in which I can have peace only by refusing to know and to live, in which the appetite for conquest bumps into walls that defy its assaults? To will is to stir up paradoxes. Everything is ordered in such a way as to bring into being that poisoned peace produced by thoughtlessness, lack of heart, or fatal renunciations.

Hence the intelligence, too, tells me in its way that this world is absurd. Its contrary, blind reason, may well claim that all is clear; I was waiting for proof and longing for it to be right. But despite so many pretentious centuries and over the heads of so many eloquent and persuasive men, I know that is false. On this plane, at least, there is no happiness if

I cannot know. That universal reason, practical or ethical, that determinism, those categories that explain everything are enough to make a decent man laugh. They have nothing to do with the mind. They negate its profound truth, which is to be enchained. In this unintelligible and limited universe, man's fate henceforth assumes its meaning. A horde of irrationals has sprung up and surrounds him until his ultimate end. In his recovered and now studied lucidity, the feeling of the absurd becomes clear and definite. I said that the world is absurd, but I was too hasty. This world in itself is not reasonable, that is all that can be said. But what is absurd is the confrontation of this irrational and the wild longing for clarity whose call echoes in the human heart. The absurd depends as much on man as on the world. For the moment it is all that links them together. It binds them one to the other as only hatred can weld two creatures together. This is all I can discern clearly in this measureless universe where my adventure takes place.

SELECTION 8.3

## The History of Sexuality★

*Michel Foucault*

[*Foucault examines the increasing medicalization of sexuality as part of an institutional spiraling of power and pleasure.*]

The medicalization of the sexually peculiar was both the effect and the instrument of this [power]. Embedded in bodies, becoming deeply characteristic of individuals, the oddities of sex relied on a technology of health and pathology. And conversely, since sexuality was a medical and a medicalizable object, one had to try and detect it — as a lesion, a dysfunction, or a symptom — in the depths of the organism, or on the surface of the skin, or

among all the signs of behavior. The power which thus took charge of sexuality set about contacting bodies, caressing them with its eyes, intensifying areas, electrifying surfaces, dramatizing troubled moments. It wrapped the sexual body in its embrace. There was undoubtedly an increase in effectiveness and an extension of the domain controlled; but also a sensualization of power and a gain of pleasure. This produced a twofold effect: an impetus was given to power through its very exercise; an emotion rewarded the overseeing control and carried it further; the intensity of the confession renewed the questioner's curiosity; the pleasure discovered fed back to the power that encircled it. . . .

The medical examination, the psychiatric investigation, the pedagogical report, and family controls may have the overall and apparent objective of saying no to all wayward or unproductive sexualities, but the fact is that they function as mechanisms with a double impetus: pleasure and power. The pleasure that comes of exercising a power that questions, monitors, watches, spies, searches out, palpates, brings to light; and on the other hand, the pleasure that kindles at having to evade this power, flee from it, fool it, or travesty it. The power that lets itself be invaded by the pleasure it is pursuing; and opposite it, power asserting itself in the pleasure of showing off, scandalizing, or resisting. Capture and seduction, confrontation and mutual reinforcement: parents and children, adults and adolescents, educators and students, doctors and patients, the psychiatrist with his hysteric and his perverts, all have played this game continually since the nineteenth century. These attractions, these evasions, these circular incitements have traced around bodies and sexes, not boundaries not to be crossed, but *perpetual spirals of power and pleasure*. . . .

We must therefore abandon the hypothesis that modern industrial societies ushered in an age of increased sexual repression. . . . It is said that no society has been more prudish; never have the agencies of power taken such care to feign ignorance of the thing they prohibited, as if they were determined to have nothing to do with it. But it is the opposite that has become apparent, at least after a general review of the facts: never have there existed more centers of power; never more attention manifested and verbalized; never more circular contacts and linkages; never more sites where the intensity of pleasures and the persistency of power catch hold, only to spread elsewhere.

---

SELECTION 8.4

# Madness and Civilization*

*Michel Foucault*

---

[*Foucault seeks to relate reason and madness and to understand the way they interact in determining civilization.*]

We have yet to write the history of that other form of madness, by which men, in an act of sovereign reason, confine their neighbors, and communicate and recognize each other through the merciless language of non-madness; to define the moment of this conspiracy before it was permanently established in the realm of truth, before it was revived by the lyricism of protest. We must try to return, in history, to that zero point in the course of madness at which madness is an undifferentiated experience, a not yet divided experience of division itself. We must describe, from the start of its trajectory, that "other

form" which relegates Reason and Madness to one side or the other of its action as things henceforth external, deaf to all exchange, and as though dead to one another.

This is doubtless an uncomfortable region. To explore it we must renounce the convenience of terminal truths, and never let ourselves be guided by what we may know of madness. None of the concepts of psychopathology, even and especially in the implicit process of retrospections, can play an organizing role. What is constitutive is the action that divides madness, and not the science elaborated once this division is made and calm restored. What is originative is the caesura that establishes the distance between reason and non-reason; *reason's subjugation of non-reason*, wresting from it its truth as madness, crime, or disease, derives explicitly from this point. Hence we must speak of that initial dispute without assuming a victory, or the right to a victory; we must speak of those actions re-examined in history, leaving in abeyance all that may figure as a conclusion, as a refuge in truth; we shall have to speak *of this act of scission, of this distance set, of this void instituted between reason and what is not reason,* without ever relying upon the fulfillment of what it claims to be.

## Madness, Civilization, and Sensibility

Civilization, in a general way, constitutes a milieu favorable to the development of madness. If the progress of knowledge dissipates error, it also has the effect of propagating a taste and even a mania for study; the life of the library, abstract speculations, the perpetual agitation of the mind without the exercise of the body, can have the most disastrous effects. Tissot explains that in the human body it is those parts subject to frequent work which are first strengthened and hardened; among laborers, the muscles and fibers of the arms harden, giving them their physical strength and the good health they enjoy until an advanced age; "among men of letters, the brain hardens; often they become incapable of connecting their ideas," and so are doomed to dementia. The more abstract or complex knowledge becomes, the greater the risk of madness. A body of knowledge still close to what is most immediate in the senses, requiring, according to Pressavin, only a little work on the part of the inner sense and organs of the brain, provokes only a sort of physiological happiness: "The sciences whose objects are easily perceived by our senses, which offer the soul agreeable relations because of the harmony of their consonance . . . perform throughout the entire bodily machine a light activity which is beneficial to all the functions." On the contrary, a knowledge too poor in these sensuous relations, too free with regard to the immediate, provokes a tension of the brain alone which disequilibrates the whole body; sciences "of things whose relationships are difficult to grasp because they are not readily available to our senses, or because their too complicated relations oblige us to expend great application in their study, present the soul with an exercise that greatly fatigues the inner sense by a too continuous tension upon that organ." Knowledge thus forms around feeling a milieu of abstract relationships where man risks losing the physical happiness in which his relation to the world is usually established. Knowledge multiplies, no doubt, but its cost increases too. Is it certain that there are more wise men today? One thing, at least, is certain: "there are more people who have the infirmities of wisdom." The milieu of knowledge grows faster than knowledge itself.

But it is not only knowledge that detaches man from feeling; it is sensibility itself: a sensibility that is no longer controlled by the movements of nature, but by all the habits, all the demands of social life.

SELECTION 8.5

# Toward a Rational Society★

*Jürgen Habermas*

[*Habermas seeks to understand the dialectical relationship between technology and decision making in the social and political world, especially in democracies.*]

The relation of technical progress and social lifeworld and the translation of scientific information into practical consciousness is not an affair of private cultivation.

I should like to reformulate this problem with reference to political decision-making. In what follows we shall understand "technology" to mean scientifically rationalized control of objectified processes. It refers to the system in which research and technology are coupled with feedback from the economy and administration. We shall understand "democracy" to mean the institutionally secured forms of general and public communication that deal with the practical question of how men can and want to live under the objective conditions of their ever-expanding power of control. Our problem can then be stated as one of the relation of technology and democracy: how can the power of technical control be brought within the range of the consensus of acting and transacting citizens?

I should like first to discuss two antithetical answers. The first, stated in rough outline, is that of Marxian theory. Marx criticizes the system of capitalist production as a power that has taken on its own life in opposition to the interests of productive freedom, of the producers. Through the private form of appropriating socially produced goods, the technical process of producing use values falls under the alien law of an economic process that produces exchange values. Once we trace this self-regulating character of the accumulation of capital back to its origins in private property in the means of production, it becomes possible for mankind to comprehend economic compulsion as an alienated result of its own free productive activity and then abolish it. Finally, the reproduction of social life can be rationally planned as a process of producing use values; society places this process under its technical control. The latter is exercised democratically in accordance with the will and insight of the associated individuals. Here Marx equates the practical insight of a political public with successful technical control. Meanwhile we have learned that even a well-functioning planning bureaucracy with scientific control of the production of goods and services is not a sufficient condition for realizing the associated material and intellectual productive forces in the interest of the enjoyment and freedom of an emancipated society. For Marx did not reckon with the possible emergence at every level of a discrepancy between scientific control of the material conditions of life and a democratic decision-making process. This is the philosophical reason why socialists never anticipated the authoritarian welfare state, where social wealth is relatively guaranteed while political freedom is excluded.

Even if technical control of physical and social conditions for preserving life and making it less burdensome had attained the level that Marx expected would characterize a communist stage of development, it does not follow that they would be linked automatically with social emancipation of the sort intended by the thinkers of the Enlightenment in the eighteenth century and the Young Hegelians in the nineteenth. For the techniques with which the development of a highly industrialized society could be brought under control can no longer be interpreted according to an instrumental model, as

though appropriate means were being organized for the realization of goals that are either presupposed without discussion or clarified through communication.

Hans Freyer and Helmut Schelsky have outlined a counter-model which recognizes technology as an independent force. In contrast to the primitive state of technical development, the relation of the organization of means to given or preestablished goals today seems to have been reversed. The process of research and technology—which obeys immanent laws—precipitates in an unplanned fashion new methods for which we then have to find purposeful application. Through progress that has become automatic, Freyer argues, abstract potential continually accrues to us in renewed thrusts. Subsequently, both life interests and fantasy that generates meaning have to take this potential in hand and expend it on concrete goals. Schelsky refines and simplifies this thesis to the point of asserting that technical progress produces not only unforeseen methods but the unplanned goals and applications themselves: technical potentialities command their own practical realization. In particular, he puts forth this thesis with regard to the highly complicated objective exigencies that in political situations allegedly prescribe solutions without alternatives.

> Political norms and laws are replaced by objective exigencies of scientific-technical civilization, which are not posited as political decisions and cannot be understood as norms of conviction or Weltanschauung. Hence, the idea of democracy loses its classical substance, so to speak. In place of the political will of the people emerges an objective exigency, which man himself produces as science and labor.

In the face of research, technology, the economy, and administration—integrated as a system that has become autonomous—the question prompted by the neohumanistic ideal of culture, namely, how can society possibly exercise sovereignty over the technical conditions of life and integrate them into the practice of the life-world, seems hopelessly obsolete. In the technical state such ideas are suited at best for "the manipulation of motives to help bring about what must happen anyway from the point of view of objective necessity."

It is clear that this thesis of the autonomous character of technical development is not correct. The pace and *direction* of technical development today depend to a great extent on public investments: in the United States the defense and space administrations are the largest sources of research contracts. I suspect that the situation is similar in the Soviet Union. The assertion that politically consequential decisions are reduced to carrying out the immanent exigencies of disposable techniques and that therefore they can no longer be made the theme of practical considerations, serves in the end merely to conceal preexisting, unreflected social interests and prescientific decisions. As little as we can accept the optimistic convergence of technology and democracy, the pessimistic assertion that technology excludes democracy is just as untenable.

These two answers to the question of how the force of technical control can be made subject to the consensus of acting and transacting citizens are inadequate. Neither of them can deal appropriately with the problem with which we are objectively confronted in the West and East, namely, how we can actually bring under control the preexisting, unplanned relations of technical progress and the social life-world. The tensions between productive forces and social intentions that Marx diagnosed and whose explosive character has intensified in an unforeseen manner in the age of thermonuclear weapons are the consequence of an ironic relation of theory to practice. The direction of technical progress is still largely determined today by social interests that arise autochthonously out of the compulsion of the reproduction of social life without being reflected upon and confronted with the declared political self-understanding of social groups. In consequence, new technical capacities erupt without preparation into existing forms of life-activity and conduct. New potentials for expanded power of technical control make obvious the disproportion between the results of the most organized rationality and unreflected goals, rigidified value systems, and obsolete ideologies.

Today, in the industrially most advanced systems, an energetic attempt must be made consciously to take in hand the mediation between technical progress and the conduct of life in the major industrial societies, a mediation that has previously taken place without direction, as a mere continuation of natural history. This is not the place to discuss the social, economic, and political conditions on which a long-term central research policy would have to depend. It is not enough for a social

system to fulfill the conditions of technical rationality. Even if the cybernetic dream of a virtually instinctive self-stabilization could be realized, the value system would have contracted in the meantime to a set of rules for the maximation of power and comfort; it would be equivalent to the biological base value of survival at any cost, that is, ultrastability. Through the unplanned sociocultural consequences of technological progress, the human species has challenged itself to learn not merely to affect its social destiny, but to control it. This challenge of technology cannot be met with technology alone. It is rather a question of setting into motion a politically effective discussion that rationally brings the social potential constituted by technical knowledge and ability into a defined and controlled relation to our practical knowledge and will. On the one hand, such discussion could enlighten those who act politically about the tradition-bound self-understanding of their interests in relation to what is technically possible and feasible. On the other hand, they would be able to judge practically, in the light of their now articulated and newly interpreted needs, the direction and the extent to which they want to develop technical knowledge for the future.

This *dialectic of potential and will* takes place today without reflection in accordance with interests for which public justification is neither demanded nor permitted. Only if we could elaborate this dialectic with political consciousness could we succeed in directing the mediation of technical progress and the conduct of social life, which until now has occurred as an extension of natural history; its conditions being left outside the framework of discussion and planning. The fact that this is a matter for reflection means that it does not belong to the professional competence of specialists. The substance of domination is not dissolved by the power of technical control. To the contrary, the former can simply hide behind the latter. The irrationality of domination, which today has become a collective peril to life, could be mastered only by the development of a political decision-making process tied to the principle of general discussion free from domination. Our only hope for the rationalization of the power structure lies in conditions that favor political power for thought developing through dialogue. The redeeming power of reflection cannot be supplanted by the extension of technically exploitable knowledge.

SELECTION 8.6

# Philosophy and
# Social Hope*

*Richard Rorty*

[*Rorty considers the possible future of pragmatism and pluralism in determining social hopes and changes in contemporary society.*]

We have learned quite a lot, in the course of the past two centuries, about how races and religions can live in comity with one another. If we forget these lessons, we can reasonably be called irrational. It makes good pragmatic and pluralist sense to say that the nations of the world are being irrational in not creating a world government to which they should surrender their sovereignty and their nuclear warheads, that the Germans were being irrational in accepting Hitler's suggestion that they expropriate their Jewish neighbours, and that Serbian peasants were being irrational in accepting Milosevic's suggestion that they loot and rape neighbours with whom they had been living peacefully for 50 years.

Insofar as 'postmodern' philosophical thinking is identified with a mindless and stupid cultural relativism — with the idea that any fool thing that calls itself culture is worthy of respect — then I have no use for such thinking. But I do not see that what I have called 'philosophical pluralism' entails any such stupidity. The reason to try persuasion rather than force, to do our best to come to terms with people whose convictions are archaic and ingenerate, is simply that using force, or mockery, or insult, is likely to decrease human happiness.

We do not need to supplement this wise utilitarian counsel with the idea that every culture has some sort of intrinsic worth. We have learned the futility of trying to assign all cultures and persons places on a hierarchical scale, but this realization does not impugn the obvious fact that there are lots of cultures we would be better off without, just as there are lots of people we would be better off without. To

say that there is no such scale, and that we are simply clever animals trying to increase our happiness by continually reinventing ourselves, has no relativistic consequences. The difference between pluralism and cultural relativism is the difference between pragmatically justified tolerance and mindless irresponsibility.

So much for my suggestion that the popularity of the meaningless term 'postmodernism' is the result of an inability to resist the claims of philosophical pluralism combined with a quite reasonable fear that history is about to turn against us. But I want to toss in a concluding word about the *un*popularity of the term — about the rhetoric of those who use this word as a term of abuse.

Many of my fellow philosophers use the term 'postmodernist relativism' as if it were a pleonasm, and as if utilitarians, pragmatists and philosophical pluralists generally had committed a sort of 'treason of the clerks,' as Julien Benda puts it. They often suggest that if philosophers had united behind the good old theologicometaphysical verities — or if James and Nietzsche had been strangled in their cradles — the fate of mankind might have been different. Just as Christian fundamentalists tell us that tolerance of homosexuality leads to the collapse of civilization, so those who would have us return to Plato and Kant believe that utilitarianism and pragmatism may weaken our intellectual and moral fibre. The triumph of European democratic ideals, they suggest, would have been much more likely had we philosophical pluralists kept our mouths shut.

But the reasons, such as the three I listed earlier, for thinking that those ideals will not triumph have nothing to do with changes in philosophical outlook. Neither the ratio of population to resources, nor the power which modern technology has put in the hands of kleptocrats, nor the provincial intransigence of national governments, has anything to do with such changes. Only the archaic and ingenerate belief that an offended nonhuman power will punish those who do not worship it makes it possible to see a connection between the intellectual shift from unity to plurality and these various concrete reasons for historical pessimism. This shift leaves us nothing with which to boost our social hopes, but that does not mean there is anything wrong with those hopes. The utopian social hope which sprang up in nineteenth-century Europe is still the noblest imaginative creation of which we have record.

## CHECKLIST

To help you review, here is a checklist of the key philosophers and terms and concepts of this chapter. The brief descriptive sentences summarize the philosophers' leading ideas. Keep in mind that some of these summary statements are oversimplifications of complex positions.

### Philosophers

- **Søren Kierkegaard,** a nineteenth-century philosopher, rejected the Hegelian idea of a rational universe and anticipated some of the themes of existentialism.

- **Friedrich Nietzsche** also reacted strongly against Hegelian idealism; he anticipated important themes of existentialism.

- **Albert Camus,** a French existentialist writer, emphasized the absurdity of the world and the inability of the individual to meet genuine human needs within it.

- **Jean-Paul Sartre,** a French existentialist writer, emphasized the significance of abandonment and its implications.

- **Edmund Husserl** was the first great phenomenologist.

- **Martin Heidegger** emphasized the importance of returning to Being itself independent of the mental categories we assign to it.

- **Emmanuel Levinas** was a transcendental ethicist who sought to establish the primordiality of ethics over metaphysics and ontology.

- **Jürgen Habermas** was one of the major German contributors to critical theory.

- **Michel Foucault** was a French philosopher who provided a critique of conventional social attitudes regarding madness and sexuality.

- **Ferdinand de Saussure** was a Swiss thinker who laid the foundations for modern linguistics.

- **Claude Lévi-Strauss** was a French anthropologist who adapted and applied Saussure's structuralist approach to ethnographic research.

- **Jacques Derrida** was an influential French deconstructionist.

- **Gilles Deleuze** believed that multiplicity, rather than identiy or oneness, is the basic principle of philosophy.

- **Alain Badiou** agreed with Deleuze that infinite difference is all there is; charged Deleuze with treating multiplicity as a single totality.

- **Richard Rorty** is an American philosopher who interprets Continental philosophy through a pragmatic perspective.

### Key Terms and Concepts

Continental philosophy
existential predicament
will-to-power
"existence precedes essence"
*condemned* to be free
abandonment
bad faith
authenticity
fundamental project
phenomenology
phenomena
transcendental phenomenology

phenomenological reduction
*Sinn*
thrown into the world
everydayness
hermeneutics
critical theory
ideal speech situation
epistemes
archaeology and geneaology
structuralism
semiotics
deconstructive method
free play of signifiers

## QUESTIONS FOR DISCUSSION AND REVIEW

1. To what extent are we responsible for the situations in which we find ourselves? Does responsibility begin at birth or at some other time?

2. To what extent are we responsible for the situations in which others find themselves? If we cannot hold others to blame for our troubles, does it make sense for us to hold ourselves to blame for theirs?

3. Can humans communicate with one another? (Do not assume that communicating is the same as talking.) Are people ever really *not* strangers? Explain.

4. If there is no objective right and wrong, good and bad, then how should we determine how to live?

5. Suppose you set a goal for yourself and then achieve it. What do you do then — set other goals and achieve them? Why bother?

6. Are any goals inherently better than others? Why or why not?

7. What is "bad faith," and how do we recognize whether we have it?

8. What does it mean to say that we live in an absurd world? *Do* we live in an absurd world?

9. Explain the myth of Sisyphus. To what extent is this situation an accurate depiction of life?

10. What does it mean to say that we are abandoned?

11. What does it mean to say that existence precedes essence?

12. Does a belief in God rescue us from the existential predicament?

13. What does Sartre mean by saying that we are condemned to be free? What does he mean by saying, "I choose myself perpetually"? And what does he mean by saying, "In choosing myself, I choose man"?

14. Do you think it is true that most humans live inauthentic lives?

15. Is most human conversation really "chatter"? Is most of *your* conversation really chatter?

16. Can having a "fundamental project" save us from a "lost life"? Explain.

17. Is it possible to detect one's own ideological biases?

18. What attitudes do we harbor today concerning madness and sexuality?

19. Do human beings use language, or does language "use" human beings? Discuss.

20. Must a technocratic society also be a dehumanizing society?

21. Do all oppressed groups suffer? Are all groups that suffer oppressed?

22. How much do you think the metaphors we use influence the way we look at the world? What reasons can you give for your view?

## SUGGESTED FURTHER READINGS

Forrest E. Baird and Walter Kaufmann, *Twentieth Century Philosophy* (Upper Saddle River, N.J.: Prentice-Hall, 1997). Critical texts of contemporary philosophy from Edmund Husserl to Charles Taylor.

Samuel Beckett, *Waiting for Godot* (New York: Grove, 1954). In its way, this play is the ultimate expression of the predicaments faced by human beings in an absurd world.

Roy Boyne, *Foucault and Derrida, the Other Side of Reason* (Boston: Unwin Hyman, 1990). An accessible review of the contrasting viewpoints of Derrida and Foucault.

Robert B. Brandom, ed., *Rorty and His Critics* (Malden, Mass.: Blackwell, 2000). Some of the world's greatest living philosophers comment on Rorty's thought. His replies are included.

Albert Camus, *Myth of Sisyphus and Other Essays* (New York: Random House, 1959). Camus's thematic rendering of the absurdity of the world and possible reactions to it.

Jane Chamberlain and Jonathan Rée, *The Kierkegaard Reader* (Malden, Mass.: Blackwell, 2001). A selection of Kierkegaard's writings which provides a rounded picture of his thought.

Randall Collins, *The Sociology of Philosophies* (Cambridge, Mass.: Harvard University Press, 2002). A social theory of intellectual change east and west.

Peter Dews, *Habermas: A Critical Reader* (Malden: Mass.: Blackwell, 1999). An introduction, but difficult.

Fyodor Dostoyevsky, *Notes from the Underground with The Grand Inquisitor* (New York: E. P. Dutton, 1960). A presentation of life's suffering, irrationality, and absurdity — themes that were to become hallmarks of existentialism in the twentieth century.

Hubert L. Dreyfus, *Being-in-the-World: A Commentary on Heidegger's "Being and Time," Division 1* (Cambridge, Mass.: Bradford, 1990). A famous commentary on Heidegger's difficult and most famous work.

Elizabeth Fallaize, ed., *Simone de Beauvoir, A Critical Reader* (New York: Routledge, 1998). Essays evaluating the thought of the great French thinker.

Karen S. Feldman and William McNeill, eds., *Continental Philosophy* (Malden, Mass.: Blackwell, 1998). Essential writings of fifty important thinkers in modern European philosophy.

Michael Freeden, *Ideology* (New York: Oxford University Press, 2003). A brief guide to the place of ideology in the modern day world.

Paul Gorner, *Twentieth Century German Philosophy* (New York: Oxford University Press, 2000). A discussion of some of the important twentieth-century philosophers, including Husserl and Heidegger.

Michael Hammond, Jane Howarth, and Russell Keat, *Understanding Phenomenology* (Cambridge, Mass.: Basil Blackwell, 1991). An introduction to phenomenology via the thought of Husserl, Sartre, and Merleau-Ponty.

Séan Hand, *The Levinas Reader* (Cambridge, Mass.: Blackwell, 1994). Selections of Levinas's writings concerning ethics, phenomenology, aesthetics, and politics.

Martin Heidegger, *Basic Writings* (New York: Harper & Row, 1977). A sampling of Heidegger's writings from his earlier and later periods of thought, covering his most important themes.

David Couzens Hoy, ed., *Foucault: A Critical Reader* (Cambridge, Mass.: Basil Blackwell, 1991). Critical essays on Foucault by leading contemporary figures such as Rorty and Habermas.

Edmund Husserl, *Ideas Pertaining to a Pure Phenomenology and to a Phenomenological Philosophy,* in Edmund Husserl, *Collected Works,* F. Kersten, trans. (The Hague: Martinus Nijhoff Publishers, 1982). An introduction to Husserl's transcendental phenomenology.

Michael Inwood, *Heidegger* (New York: Oxford University Press, 1997). A useful introduction to the earlier and later thought of Martin Heidegger, including such themes as truth, being-in-the-world, time, and authenticity.

Franz Kafka, *The Metamorphosis, The Penal Colony, and Other Stories* (New York: Schocken, 1988). A good collection of Kafka's stories.

Peggy Kamuf, ed., *A Derrida Reader, between the Blinds* (New York: Harvester Wheatsheaf, 1991). A representative collection of Derrida's writings.

Richard Kearney, ed., *Continental Philosophy in the Twentieth Century* (New York: Blackwell, 1994). Survey of key contemporary European philosophers.

Richard Kearney, ed., *Routledge History of Philosophy,* vol. 8, *Twentieth Century Continental Philosophy* (London: Routledge, 1994). An excellent overview of Continental philosophy. Contains a useful timeline.

Richard Kearney and Mara Rainwater, *The Continental Philosophy Reader* (New York: Routledge, 1996). A useful anthology of writings of modern European philosophers.

Søren Kierkegaard, *Fear and Trembling* (New York: Penguin, 1986). An excellent introduction to some of the themes developed later by the existentialists.

John Lecte, *Fifty Key Contemporary Thinkers* (London: Routledge, 1994). Covers Continental philosophers from structuralism to postmodernity, as well as other thinkers.

Stephen T. Leonard, *Critical Theory in Political Practice* (Princeton, N.J.: Princeton University Press, 1990). An attempt to evaluate critical social theory in terms of its practical application. Thinkers criticized include Marx, Habermas, and Foucault.

Eric Matthews, *Twentieth-Century French Philosophy* (New York: Oxford University Press, 1996). An historical account of the major twentieth-century French thinkers.

David McLellan, *Ideology,* 2nd ed. (Minneapolis: University of Minnesota Press, 1995). A discussion of the nature of ideology and its development within Marxist and non-Marxist traditions.

Dermot Moran and Timothy Mooney, *The Phenomenology Reader* (New York: Routledge, 2002). A fairly comprehensive collection of first source texts from the phenomenological tradition.

Friedrich Nietzsche, *A Nietzsche Reader,* R. J. Hollingdale, trans. (New York: Penguin, 1978). A good contemporary translation of selections that provide a broad overview of Nietzsche's concerns.

George Patterson, *Routledge Philosophy Guidebook to the Later Heidegger* (New York: Routledge, 2000). A review of Heidegger's all important later thinking.

Herman Philipse, *Heidegger's Philosophy of Being, A Critical Interpretation* (Princeton, N.J.: Princeton University Press, 1999). An exhaustive examination of Heidegger's metaphysical thought.

Richard Polt, *Heidegger, An Introduction* (Ithaca, N.Y.: Cornell University Press, 1999). A highly regarded recent introduction to a difficult philosopher.

Paul Rabinow, ed., *The Foucault Reader* (New York: Penguin Books, 1991). A good introduction to one of the seminal thinkers of our time.

Rudiger Safranski, *Martin Heidegger: Between Good and Evil,* Ewald Osers, trans. (Cambridge, Mass.: Harvard

University Press, 1998). An excellent biography and review of Heidegger's thought.

Rudiger Safranski, *Nietzsche: A Philosophical Biography* (London: Granta Books, 2002). A beautifully written presentation that brings alive Nietzsche's life and thought.

Jean-Paul Sartre, *Being and Nothingness*, Hazel Barnes, trans. (London: Routledge, 1969). Sartre's most important work in philosophy. Not light reading.

Jean-Paul Sartre, *Existentialism and Humanism* (London: Methuen, 1987). A clear, nontechnical depiction of some of the principal concepts of existentialism, including essence, existence, freedom, and responsibility.

Roger Scruton, Peter Singer, Christopher Janaway, and Michael Tanner, *German Philosophers: Kant, Hegel, Schopenhauer, Nietzsche* (New York: Oxford University Press, 2001). Studies of four of the most important German philosophers, by leading contemporary scholars.

Hugh J. Silverman, ed., *Derrida and Deconstruction* (New York: Routledge, 1989). A compilation of essays studying Derrida's interpretation of philosophers from Plato to Foucault and including Freud, Heidegger, and Sartre.

Robert C. Solomon, *Continental Philosophy Since 1750, The Rise and Fall of the Self* (New York: Oxford University Press, 1988). Brief and readable.

Robert Solomon and Kathleen M. Higgins, *Reading Nietzsche* (New York: Oxford University Press, 1989). Helpful.

Michael Tanner, *Nietzsche: A Very Short Introduction* (New York: Oxford University Press, 2001). Succinct, accessible.

Stephen K. White, ed., *The Cambridge Companion to Habermas* (New York: Cambridge University Press, 1999). Essays by leading scholars on Habermas's thinking and his relationship to the Frankfurt School of critical theory.

Rolf Wiggershaus, *The Frankfurt School*, Michael Robertson, trans. (Cambridge, Mass.: Bradford, 1994). A massive book on the history and accomplishments of the Frankfurt School.

Richard Wolin, *Heidegger's Children* (Princeton: Princeton University Press, 2001). The book traces Heidegger's influence on the United States via emigré philosophers like Herbert Marcuse, treated in Chapter 12.

# 9

# The Pragmatic and Analytic Traditions

It is no truer that "atoms are what they are because we use 'atom' as we do" than that "we use 'atom' as we do because atoms are as they are." Both of these claims . . . are entirely empty.     — Richard Rorty

We have no way of identifying truths except to posit that the statements that are currently rationally accepted (by our lights) are true.
— Hilary Putnam

As the twenty-first century begins, we might reflect briefly on all the last one brought us: air travel, Einstein, nuclear weapons, television and computers, clones, photographs of sunsets on Mars, war on civilian populations, genocide, AIDS, the rise and fall of the Soviet Union, racial integration in the United States, and rock and roll. In art and literature, traditional structures and approaches were cast aside with abandon. Schoenberg and Stravinsky brought the world music that lacked fixed tonal centers; Cage brought it music that lacked sound. In Europe existentialist philosophers proclaimed the absurdity of the human predicament. In Russia the followers of Marx declared an end to the then existing order; still later the followers of the followers declared an end to Marx.

In philosophy, on the continent of Europe in the twentieth century the assault on idealism was begun by the nihilistic attacks of Schopenhauer and Nietzsche (nihilism is the rejection of values and beliefs) and by the religious anti-idealism of Søren Kierkegaard. Anti-Hegelianism reached its summit in existentialism, according to which life is not only not perfectly rational, it is fundamentally irrational and absurd. Meanwhile, in Britain and the United States philosophers were busy with other things, as we explain in this chapter.

## PRAGMATISM

The United States's distinctive contribution to philosophy is known as **pragmatism** or, sometimes, American pragmatism. The brightest lights of pragmatism were the "classic" pragmatists **C. S. Peirce** (1839–1914), **William James** (1842–1910), and **John Dewey** (1859–1952). In general, pragmatists rejected the idea that there is such a thing as fixed, absolute truth. Instead, they held that truth is relative to a time and place and purpose and is thus ever-changing in light of new data.

To fine-tune this a bit, Peirce and James created a philosophy club in Cambridge, Massachusetts, in the 1870s, from whose discussions pragmatism sprang. James credited Peirce with inventing pragmatism, however. For himself, Peirce, one of America's foremost logicians, regarded pragmatism as a rule for determining the meaning of ideas: "In order to ascertain the meaning of an intellectual conception one should consider what practical consequences might conceivably result by necessity from the truth of that conception, and the sum of these consequences will constitute the entire meaning of the conception." The method would show, among other things, according to Peirce, "that almost every proposition of ontological metaphysics is either meaningless . . . or else . . . absurd."

As for truth, Peirce advanced a famous formulation: "The opinion which is fated to be ultimately agreed to by all who investigate, is what we mean by the truth." This conception foreshadows that of contemporary pragmatists who are discussed later in this chapter.

Despite Peirce's historical right to be viewed as the founder of American pragmatism, it was James who pushed pragmatism most forcefully and with whom the concept generally came to be associated. James was one of the more readable and entertaining writers in the history of ideas. From James's point of view, "The whole function of philosophy ought to be to find out what definite difference it will make to you and us, at definite instants of our life, if this world-formula or that world-formula be the true one." To determine either the meaning or the truth of an idea, you must evaluate its usefulness or workability — an idea's meaning and truth lies in its cash value, according to James. This is because the purpose of thought is to help us obtain satisfactory relations with our surroundings. For James, an idea is a roadmap; its value, meaning, and truth lie in its ability to carry us "from any one part of our experience to any other part, linking things satisfactorily, working securely, simplifying, saving labor."

James was also famous for the related theory that in some cases it is justifiable to choose or *will* to hold a belief because of the "vital good" or "vital benefit" holding it provides to you. This does *not* mean you should believe smoking is good for your health on the grounds that the thought makes you feel good. The belief that smoking is good for your health really *won't* work for you in the long run. Ideas that have been verified or falsified by the community of scientific investigators enable us to make the most accurate predictions about the future and therefore may be counted on to possess the highest degree of workability. However, *if* a person *must* either accept or reject a belief *and* the evidence for and against the belief weighs in equally, then choose as your "vital good" dictates, said James. For example, "On pragmatic principles, if the hypothesis of God works satisfactorily in the

## PROFILE: John Dewey (1859–1952)

John Dewey lived almost a century. He was born before the American Civil War, and he died during the Korean War. His influence on American life was profound.

Dewey was the third of four children in his family. His father owned a grocery business and then a tobacco business in Burlington, Vermont, where Dewey was raised. Dewey was not considered a brilliant mind as a high school student, but his discovery of philosophy as a junior at the University of Vermont awakened slumbering genius. He received his Ph.D. at Johns Hopkins and taught at Michigan, Minnesota, Chicago, and Columbia. He continued to write, publish, and lecture long after his retirement from Columbia in 1930.

Dewey exerted his greatest influence on society by virtue of his educational theories. He was an effective proponent of progressive education, which opposed formal, authoritarian methods of instruction in favor of having students learn by performing tasks that are related to their own interests. Today, educational practice throughout the United States and in many areas across the world generally follows the fundamental postulates of Dewey's educational philosophy, although his belief that the school is the central institution of a democratic society is not always shared by American taxpayers.

A kind, generous, and modest man, Dewey was also an effective social critic and an influential participant in reform movements. He was utterly fear-less in advocating democratic causes, even those, like women's suffrage, that were deeply unpopular. Despite having unreconcilable philosophical differences with philosopher Bertrand Russell (discussed later in this chapter), Dewey was active on Russell's behalf when Russell was denied permission to teach at the City College of New York in 1941 (see the profile on Russell). He was also one of the original founders of the American Civil Liberties Union.

Dewey was not the world's most inspiring public speaker, and one of his students said that you could understand his lectures only by reading your notes afterwards. Maybe the popularity of these lectures of his throughout the world despite the stylistic drawbacks is sound indication of the power of Dewey's ideas.

The bibliography of Dewey's works runs over one hundred fifty pages, and his writings touch on virtually every philosophical subject. All told, he wrote forty books and seven hundred articles. His thought dominated American philosophy throughout the first part of the twentieth century. He was and still is America's most famous philosopher.

Among the most famous of Dewey's works are *Reconstruction in Philosophy* (1920), *Human Nature and Conduct* (1922), *Experience and Nature* (1925), *The Quest for Certainty* (1929), *Art As Experience* (1934), *Freedom and Culture* (1939), and *Problems of Men* (1946).

widest sense of the word, it is 'true.'" We will consider this theory more carefully in Part Three, a discussion of the philosophy of religion.

For Peirce, what is true is what investigators agree to; the *sum* of its consequences is what a conception means. James, by contrast, has a much more individualistic concept of meaning and truth: roughly, what is true is what "works" for the individual. Of course, for James, what the community of scientific investigators agree to is what ultimately does work for the individual. So, as a practical matter, for both James and Peirce the same scientific findings will count as true.

John Dewey's brand of pragmatism is known as **instrumentalism,** according to which, roughly, the forms of human activity, including thought, are instruments used by people to solve practical problems. In Dewey's view, thinking is not a search for "truth" but, rather, an activity aimed at solving individual and social problems, a means by which humans strive to achieve a satisfactory relationship with their environment.

From Dewey's perspective, metaphysics, like religious rites and cults, has been a means of "escape from the vicissitudes of existence." Instead of facing the uncertainties of a constantly changing world, metaphysicians have sought security by searching for fixed, universal, and immutable truth.

From Dewey's point of view, nature is experience. This is what he means. Objects are not fixed substances but individual things ("existences" or "events," he called them) that are imbued with meanings. A piece of paper, for instance, means one thing to a novelist, another to someone who wants to start a fire, still another to an attorney who uses it to draw up a contract, still another to children making paper airplanes, and so on. A piece of paper is an instrument for solving a problem within a given context. What a piece of paper *is* is what it means within the context of some activity or other.

But when he held that an object is what it means within an activity, Dewey did not mean to equate the object with the thought about it. That was the mistake made by idealism, in Dewey's view. Idealism equated objects with thought about them and thus left out of the reckoning the particular, individual thing. Objects are not reducible to thought about objects, according to Dewey. Things have an aspect of particularity that idealism entirely neglects, he held.

But this does not mean that Dewey thought that there are fixed, immutable substances or things. The doctrine that "independent" objects exist "out there" outside the mind — realism — is called by Dewey the **spectator theory of knowledge.** It is no more acceptable to Dewey than is idealism. On the contrary, his view was that, as the uses to which a thing is put change, the thing itself changes. To refer to the earlier example, a piece of paper is *both* (1) a particular item and (2) what is thought about it within the various and forever-changing contexts in which it is used.

Given this metaphysical perspective, from which abstract speculation about so-called eternal truths is mere escapism, it is easy to understand why Dewey was primarily interested in practical problems and actively participated in movements of social, political, and educational reform. He was effective as a social activist, too. Few individuals have had more impact on American educational, judicial, or legislative institutions than did Dewey. The educational system in which you most probably were raised, which emphasized experimentation and practice rather than abstract learning and authoritarian instructional techniques, is the result of his influence.

Recent U.S. philosophy has been much influenced by Dewey and the pragmatists. However, to understand what happened, we have to back up to the end of the nineteenth century and to what transpired at that time in Britain. What transpired there — analytic philosophy — eventually overwhelmed and replaced pragmatism in American philosophy departments. Only in the past twenty or so years has pragmatism been making a modest comeback.

## ANALYTIC PHILOSOPHY

To understand analytic philosophy, we first of all have to understand what analysis is.

## What Analysis Is

Just what is **analysis,** anyway? Quite simply put, philosophical analysis resolves complex propositions or concepts into simpler ones. Let's take an elementary example. The proposition

Square circles are nonexistent things.

might be resolved by analysis into the simpler proposition

No squares are circular.

This second proposition is "simpler" philosophically because it refers only to squares and their lack of circularity, whereas the first proposition refers to two distinct classes of entities, square circles and nonexistent things.

Moreover, the first proposition is very troubling philosophically. It is certainly an intelligible proposition. Hence, it would seem that square circles and nonexistent things must (somehow and amazingly) exist in some sense or another. If they did not exist, the proposition would be about nothing and thus would not be intelligible. (It is precisely this reasoning that has led some philosophers to conclude that every object of thought must exist "in some sense," or "subsist.")

The second sentence contains the same information as the first but does not have the puzzling implications of the first. Not only is it simpler than the second, it is also clearer. Once the first sentence is recast or analyzed in this way, we can accept what the first sentence says without having to concede that square circles and nonexistent things exist "in some sense."

This very simple example of analysis will perhaps help make it clear why many analytic philosophers have regarded analysis as having great importance for the field of metaphysics. Be sure that you understand the example and everything we have said about it before you read any further.

## A Brief Overview of Analytic Philosophy

To understand how analysis became so important as a method of philosophy, think back to Kant (Chapter 7). Kant thought that knowledge is possible if we limit our inquiries to things as they are experienceable, because the mind imposes categories on experienceable objects. The Absolute Idealists, Hegel being the prime example, then expanded on Kant's theory and held that the categories of thought *are* the categories of being. Absolute Idealism quickly caught hold in Western philosophy, and even in England clever versions of it flourished in the late nineteenth century. We say "even in England" because prior to this time English philosophy had been firmly rooted in empiricism and common sense.

One Englishman who subscribed to idealist metaphysical principles was **Bertrand Russell** [RUSS-ul] (1872–1970). Russell, however, had taken an interest in philosophy in the first place because he studied mathematics and wanted to find a satisfactory account of numbers and mathematics. He began to think that Absolute Idealist philosophies involve a couple of very dubious and interrelated assumptions: first, that propositions all have the subject/predicate form, and second, that an object's relationships to other objects are part of the essential nature of

## PROFILE: Bertrand Russell (1872–1970)

Bertrand Russell came from a distinguished background. His grandfather, Lord John Russell, was twice prime minister; his godfather was John Stuart Mill, of whom much mention is made in later chapters; and his parents were prominent freethinkers. Because his parents died when he was young, Russell was brought up in the household of Lord Russell. This side of the family was austerely Protestant, and Russell's childhood was solitary and lonely. As a teenager, he had the intuition that God did not exist and found this to be a great relief.

In the fall of 1890, at a time when several other brilliant philosophers were also there, Russell went to Cambridge to study mathematics and philosophy. Many of Russell's important works in philosophy and mathematics were written during his association with Cambridge, first as a student, then as a fellow and lecturer. His association with Cambridge ended in 1916, when he was dismissed for pacifist activities during World War I. He was restored as a fellow at Cambridge in 1944.

Russell was dismayed by the enthusiasm among ordinary people for the war, and his own pacifism created much resentment. After he was dismissed from Cambridge, he was imprisoned for six months for his pacifism; thereafter, he held no academic position again until he began to teach in the United States in 1938.

Russell thought that without a proper education a person is caught in the prison of prejudices that make up common sense. He wanted to create a kind of education that would be not only philosophically

sound but also nonthreatening, enjoyable, and stimulating. To this end he and his wife, Dora, founded the Beacon Hill School in 1927, which was influential in the founding of similar schools in England and America.

In addition to writing books on education during the period between the wars, Russell wrote extensively on social and political philosophy. His most infamous popular work, *Marriage and Morals* (1929), was very liberal in its attitude toward sexual practices and caused the cancellation of his appointment to City College of New York in 1940. He was taken to court by the mother of a CCNY student, and the court revoked Russell's appointment "for the sake of public health, safety, and morals." Apparently the most damaging part of the evidence against Russell was his recommendation in the book that a child caught masturbating should not be physically punished.

World War II and the Nazi onslaught caused Russell to abandon his pacifism. In 1961, however, he was again imprisoned, this time for activity in demonstrations against nuclear weapons, and in 1967 he organized the so-called war crimes tribunal directed against American activities in Vietnam.

Russell received the Nobel Prize for literature in 1950, one of many honors bestowed on him. In his autobiography he said that three passions had governed his life: the longing for love, the search for knowledge, and unbearable pity for the suffering of humankind. Throughout his life Russell exhibited intellectual brilliance and extraordinary personal courage.

that object. Russell felt that these assumptions were incompatible with there being more than one thing (which was why Absolute Idealist theories all maintained there is but one thing, the Absolute) and thus that they were incompatible with mathematics. Further, when Russell read what Hegel had to say about mathematics, he was horrified, finding it both ignorant and stupid. So Russell abandoned Absolute Idealism.

What Russell had in mind by saying he wished to find a satisfactory account of numbers and mathematics was this. Basically he wanted to ascertain the absolutely basic, indefinable entities and the absolutely fundamental indemonstrable propositions of mathematics. It might seem to you that the basic entities of mathematics are numbers and that the absolutely fundamental propositions are propositions of arithmetic such as 2 + 2 = 4. Russell, however, believed that propositions about numbers are only *apparently* or *grammatically* about numbers (just as the proposition we presented was only apparently or grammatically about square circles) and that arithmetical propositions are logically derivable from even more basic propositions.

The theory that the concepts of mathematics can be defined in terms of concepts of logic, and that all mathematical truths can be proved from principles of formal logic, is known as **logicism.** The first part of the theory (that mathematical concepts can be defined in terms of logical concepts) involves our friend analysis: propositions involving numbers must be analyzed into propositions involving logical concepts—just like we analyzed a proposition about squares and nonexistent things into a proposition about squares and their properties. The details of this analysis, and the derivation of mathematical truths from principles of formal logic, are too technical to be examined in a text like this.

Russell was not the only proponent of logicism. Somewhat earlier the German mathematician **Gottlob Frege** [FRAY-guh] (1848–1925) had devised a "language"—a series of symbols—in which logical properties could be stated precisely and without the ambiguities of ordinary language. Modern symbolic logic is derived from Frege's language—the importance of which Russell may have been the first person other than Frege himself to understand. Frege was concerned not only with the logical foundations of arithmetic but also with the issue of how words have meanings—an issue that was central throughout twentieth-century philosophy. For these reasons, many historians credit Frege even more than Russell for being the "founder" of analytic philosophy. However, Russell's writings were more widely read in English-speaking countries during at least the first half of the century, and in English-speaking countries Russell and Alfred North Whitehead's collaborative work, *Principia Mathematica* (final volume published in 1913), was considered the culminating work of logicism—and was a stunning intellectual achievement in any event.

Under the influence of his friend and colleague at Cambridge University, G. E. Moore (1873–1958), Russell began to conceive of the analytic method as *the* method of philosophy in general, a method that promised to deliver the same apparently indisputable results in other areas of philosophy as it had in the philosophy of mathematics. Around 1910 he began trying to do for epistemology exactly what he had attempted for mathematics: trying to determine the absolutely basic, indefinable entities and absolutely fundamental indemonstrable types of propositions of our knowledge of the external, physical world.

Moore, too, was concerned with our knowledge of the external world and devoted considerable energy to the analysis of some commonsense beliefs about physical objects. Moore also extended the analytic approach to propositions in moral philosophy (more on this in Part Two). Somewhat later, Gilbert Ryle (1900–1976), another important practitioner of analytic techniques, conceived of traditional philosophical problems as resting on "linguistic confusions." He achieved impressive apparent resolutions of several perennial knotty philosophical problems by using analytic techniques. Ludwig Wittgenstein (1889–1951), Russell's student and later a colleague, thought that by using analysis philosophy could actually disclose the ultimate logical constituents of reality, their interrelations, and their relationship to the world of experience. Wittgenstein thought the goal of analysis was to reduce all complex descriptive propositions to their ultimately simple constituent propositions. These latter propositions would consist of "names" in combination, which would represent the ultimate simple constituents of reality.

In the 1920s, Moritz Schlick (1882–1936), a philosopher at the University of Vienna, formed a group known as the **Vienna Circle,** the members of which were much impressed by the work of Russell and Wittgenstein. Referring to their philosophy as **logical positivism,** the group held that philosophy is not a theory but an activity whose business is the logical clarification of thought. The logical positivists proclaimed a "**verifiability criterion of meaning.**" According to this criterion, suppose you say something, but nobody knows what observations would verify what you are trying to say. Then you haven't really made a meaningful empirical statement at all. And thus, the logical positivists held, traditional metaphysical utterances are not meaningful empirical statements. Take, for example, Hegel's thesis that reason is the substance of the universe. How could this be verified? Well, it just could not be. So it is not a genuine factual proposition; it is not empirically meaningful. In a reading selection at the end of the chapter, A. J. Ayer (1910–1989), who was the most famous English member of the Vienna Circle, explains the verifiability criterion of meaning in more detail.

Moral and value statements, the logical positivists said, are likewise empirically meaningless. At best they are expressions of emotions rather than legitimate statements. Philosophy, they said, has as its only useful function the analysis of both everyday language and scientific language — it has no legitimate concern with the world apart from language, for that is the concern of scientists.

The Vienna Circle dissolved when the Nazis took control of Austria in the late 1930s, but to this day many people still equate analytic philosophy with logical positivism. This is true despite the fact that nowadays very few philosophers who refer to themselves as analysts subscribe to the verifiability criterion of meaning or accept many other of the basic assumptions of logical positivism.

In fact, today it is extremely doubtful whether many of those who would call themselves analytic philosophers would even describe analysis as the only proper method of philosophy. Indeed, few would even describe their daily philosophical task as primarily one of analysis. There are other philosophical tasks one might undertake than analysis, and some who would still not hesitate to call themselves analysts have simply lost interest in analysis in favor of these other tasks. Others, like Wittgenstein, have explicitly repudiated analysis as the proper method of philosophy. Wittgenstein's about-face was published in 1953 in his enormously influential *Philosophical Investigations.*

Further, it is now widely held that many philosophically interesting claims and expressions cannot intelligibly be regarded as complexes subject to resolution into simpler and less misleading expressions. Certainly, the intent to recast the meaning of an expression into a less misleading form can be carried out only if its "real" or "true" meaning can be ascertained by the analyst. But concerns have been raised, perhaps most notably by W. V. O. Quine (1908–2000), about whether it is ever possible to say in some absolute, nonrelativistic sense what the meaning of an expression is. And for many expressions it seems inappropriate in the first place to speak of their "meaning." Clearer understanding of many expressions seems to be achieved when we ask how the expression is used or what it is used to do rather than what it means, unless the latter question is taken as being equivalent to the two former questions, as it often is.

So it has become accepted that there are many useful philosophical methods and techniques other than the analysis of language, and it is pretty widely thought that good, substantial philosophical work is by no means always the result of analysis of some sort. Many of today's analytic philosophers would deny being directly concerned with language (though most are concerned with expressing themselves in clear language). Nor could it be said that all analytic philosophers mean the same thing when they speak of analysis. In its broadest sense, a call for "analysis" today is simply a call for clarification, and certainly today's analytic philosophers exhibit (or hope they exhibit) a concern for clarity of thought and expression as well as a great appreciation for detail. Most, too, would be inclined to say that at least some opinions expressed by earlier philosophers reflect linguistic confusions if not outright logical errors, but beyond this it is not the case that all analytic philosophers use some common unique method of philosophizing or have the same interests or share an identifiable approach to philosophical problems. In today's world, philosophers are apt to call themselves "analytic" to indicate that they do not have much training or interest in existentialism or phenomenology as much as for any other reason.

So, then, a history of analytic philosophy is, for all intents and purposes, a history of a predominant strain of twentieth-century philosophy in English-speaking countries that has evolved from the philosophical writings and discussions of Russell, Moore, Wittgenstein, and others.

## Language and Science

Frege's interest in the foundations of mathematics and the proper understanding of arithmetical terminology led Frege, and Russell after him, to reflect on broader questions about the nature of language and how language has meaning. Following the lead of Frege and Russell, many twentieth-century analytic philosophers were fascinated with questions of language — how words and sentences can have meaning, what it is for them to have meaning, and how they connect with the world. Many analytic philosophers indeed consider philosophy of language (which is concerned with such questions rather than with providing specific analyses of interesting or important propositions) to be more fundamental and important than metaphysics or epistemology. It is easy to understand why they might take this view. For example, according to the verifiability theory of meaning propounded by the logical positivists, an assertion purporting to be about reality can have meaning only if it is possible to verify it through observation. This theory led the positivists to reject metaphysical assertions as meaningless.

What is it for a word or phrase to have a meaning? If you had to answer this question, you would perhaps begin with the simplest kinds of words or phrases, words or phrases like the name "Mark Twain" or the naming phrase "the author of *Roughing It*" that simply designate things (in this case, a person). This was exactly the starting point of many philosophers of language, and a large literature was generated throughout the twentieth century on the problem of what it is for a name or naming phrase to have a meaning. A large literature was generated not only because such words and phrases are the simplest and most fundamental linguistic units but also because it wasn't clear what it is for such words and phrases to have a meaning. The starting point turned out to be located in rather deep water.

We cannot go into those matters here, but to give you an idea of only elementary difficulties, consider the apparently innocent question, What is the meaning of "Mark Twain"? The apparently obvious answer is that the meaning of "Mark Twain" is the person designated by that name, that is, Mark Twain. This answer will not do, of course: Mark Twain (the person) no longer exists, but "Mark Twain" (the name) still has a meaning. Further, since "Mark Twain" and "Samuel Clemens" designate the same person, according to the theory we are considering, the two names mean the same thing. Hence the theory we are considering absurdly entails that the sentence "Mark Twain was Samuel Clemens" means the same as the sentence "Mark Twain was Mark Twain." If what the theory entails is absurd, the theory itself must be defective.

It seems, therefore, that there is more to the meaning of a name than the thing it designates; but what more? Frege called this additional element the "sense" of the name, and he and Russell said that the sense of a name is given by a "definite description" associated with the name; in the case of "Mark Twain," this definite description might be "the American author who wrote *Tom Sawyer.*" Russell then proposed a theory of how definite descriptions can have a reference — a theory that he once said was his most important contribution to philosophy. However, these are technical issues; suffice it to say that the question of how even such elementary linguistic items as names have meaning has not been resolved.

Another seemingly easy question — that also turns out to be quite difficult — is, What is it for a sentence to have a meaning? Take the sentence "Our cockatoo is in its cage"; apparently the sentence must in some way "represent" the fact that our cockatoo is in its cage. But what, then, should we make of a sentence like "Our cockatoo is not in the refrigerator"? Does that sentence represent the "negative" fact of *not* being in the refrigerator? What kind of fact is that? For that matter, what is it for a sentence to "represent" a fact in the first place? And, incidentally, what *are* facts? As we shall see in a moment, Wittgenstein believed that a sentence "pictures" a fact — a belief from which he derived an imposing metaphysical system.

Further, as pointed out earlier, for many expressions meaning seems fixed by how the expression is used more than by what the words in it refer to. A threat or a promise might clearly fall into this category, for example. Some writers, accordingly, have been much concerned with the "pragmatics," or social aspects and uses, of language. All in all, questions of language, meaning, and the connection between language and the world still remain among the most actively discussed in contemporary analytic philosophy.

Another subject of interest for many analytic philosophers has been science. Many of the issues in the philosophy of science were first raised by the philosophers of the Vienna Circle — the logical positivists — who included not only philosophers but scientists and mathematicians as well. What might philosophers think about when they think about science? They might wonder whether and in what sense "scientific entities" (such as genes, molecules, and quarks) are "real" or what relation they bear to sensory experience. They may inquire as to the nature of a scientific explanation, theory, or law and what distinguishes one from the other. Are scientific observations ever free from theoretical assumptions? they might inquire. They may wonder what it is that marks off science from other kinds of inquiry, including philosophy and religion (do they perhaps at some level all accept something "on faith"?)—and from pseudoscience. In a similar vein, they may wonder what kind of reasoning, if any, characterizes science. They may consider the extent to which the natural sciences (if not all the individual sciences) are "reducible" to physics.

An issue that the logical positivists were concerned with was the relation of statements about theoretical scientific entities such as neutrons and protons to statements that record our observations. After all, protons cannot be observed, and according to the verifiability criterion of meaning, a statement that cannot be verified by observations is meaningless. Thus, some of the positivists felt that statements about protons (for example) must be logically equivalent to statements about observations; if they were not, they too would have to be thrown out as meaningless gibberish along with metaphysical utterances. Unfortunately, this "translatability thesis" turned out to be doubtful, and the question of the precise relationship between theory and observation is still very much under discussion.

The positivists assumed in any case that statements that report observations are directly confirmed or disconfirmed by experience and, in this respect, are unlike theoretical statements. But more recently some philosophers of science, such as notably H. R. Hanson, have suggested that what one observes depends on the theoretical beliefs one holds so that the distinction between theory and observation is very weak, if it exists at all. Indeed, some theorists have questioned whether there are theory-independent "facts" at all.

One contemporary philosopher of science, Thomas Kuhn, has been especially concerned with scientific activity conceived not as the verification of theories but, rather, as the solving of puzzles presented within a given scientific "paradigm"—a scientific tradition or perspective like Newtonian mechanics or Ptolemaic astronomy or genetic theory. Because, in Kuhn's view, observations are imbued with theoretical assumptions, we cannot confirm one theoretical paradigm over some other theoretical paradigm simply by appeal to some common and neutral set of observational data; alternative paradigms are incommensurable. As you will see, there are affinities between this view and what is called *antirepresentationalism,* which we discuss later.

One other point deserves mention in this overview of analytic philosophy. It used to be that the history of philosophy was largely the history of the philosophies of specific individuals—Plato's philosophy, Aristotle's philosophy, Kant's philosophy, and so forth. But this changed after Russell, Moore, and Wittgenstein. Twentieth-century philosophy, especially perhaps philosophy in the analytic tradition, tends to be treated as a history of specific ideas, such as those mentioned in this chapter. Historians of twentieth-century philosophy often mention specific individuals only to give examples of people who subscribe to the idea at hand. It is the idea, rather than the philosopher, that is more important.

In addition, although the views of some specific "big-name" philosophers have been enormously influential within analytic philosophy, the course of analytic philosophy has been determined primarily by the journal articles published by the large rank and file of professional philosophers. These papers are undeniably technical, are directed at other professionals within the field, and usually deal with a fairly limited aspect of a larger problem. Articles and books that deal in wholesale fashion with large issues (e.g., What is the mind? Is there knowledge? What is the meaning of life? What is the ideal state? What is truth?) are comparatively rare. For this reason, and perhaps for others, the work of analytic philosophers strikes outsiders as narrow, theoretical, irrelevant, inaccessible, and tedious. The work of twentieth-century mathematicians is doubtlessly equally incomprehensible to laypersons, but the public's expectations are different for philosophers.

## Experience, Language, and the World

Analytic epistemology and metaphysics is a maze of crossing paths, but it has focused primarily on two broad areas of concern. The first of these is the interrelationship of experience, language, and the world. The second broad concern is the nature of the mind. In this section we consider a specific metaphysical and epistemological theory that resulted from concern with experience, language, and the world.

Analytic philosophy's first major metaphysical theory, **logical atomism,** is associated primarily with Bertrand Russell and his student and colleague **Ludwig Wittgenstein** [VITT-ghen-shtine] (1889–1951). Russell connected to it an epistemological theory known as phenomenalism. Atomists (Russell, Wittgenstein, and others who subscribed to their views) believed that the world is not an all-encompassing Oneness, as Hegelians would have it, but a collection of "atomic facts." To say the world consists ultimately of *facts* is to say it does not consist only of *things* but, rather, of *things having properties and standing in various relations to one another.* Your study area, for example, has a chair and a desk and a lamp and so on standing in a certain arrangement; their being in this arrangement is not a thing, it is a fact.

The most basic facts, atomists like Russell and Wittgenstein believed, are *atomic,* which means they are components of more complicated facts but are not themselves composed of simpler or more basic facts; and it means they are logically independent of every other fact. (Logically independent here means that any basic or atomic fact could remain the same even if all other facts were different.)

Now, the atomists believed that profound metaphysical implications follow from the truism that we can form true propositions about the world, some of which are complexes of other propositions, for a complex proposition must in principle be resolvable into simpler propositions. As an example, the proposition "The United States elected a Republican as president" is resolvable, in principle, into propositions about individual people and their actions. But when people vote, they are really just doing certain things with their bodies. So a proposition about a person voting is resolvable, in principle, into propositions about these doings — about

## PROFILE: Ludwig Wittgenstein (1889–1951)

So many discussions of Wittgenstein's philosophy were submitted to philosophy journals in the 1950s and 1960s that for a while some journals declined to accept further manuscripts on his ideas. No other philosopher of the twentieth century, save perhaps Bertrand Russell, had as great an impact on philosophy in Great Britain and the United States.

Wittgenstein was born in Vienna into a wealthy family and studied to become an engineer. From engineering, his interests led him to pure mathematics and then to the philosophical foundations of mathematics. He soon gave up engineering to study philosophy with Russell at Cambridge in 1912–1913. The following year he studied philosophy alone and in seclusion in Norway, partly because he perceived himself as irritating others by his nervous personality. During World War I he served in the Austrian army; it was in this period that he completed the first of his two major works, the *Tractatus Logico-Philosophicus* (1921), which sets forth logical atomism, explained in the text.

Wittgenstein's father had left Wittgenstein a large fortune, which after the war Wittgenstein simply handed over to two of his sisters, and he became an elementary school teacher. Next, in 1926, he be-

came a gardener's assistant, perhaps a surprising walk of life for one of the most profound thinkers of all time. He did, however, return to Cambridge in 1929 and there received his doctorate, the *Tractatus* serving as his dissertation. In 1937 he succeeded G. E. Moore in his chair of philosophy.

During World War II Wittgenstein found himself unable to sit idly by, so he worked for two years as a hospital orderly and for another as an assistant in a medical lab. Time and again Wittgenstein, an heir to a great fortune and a genius, placed himself in the humblest of positions.

In 1944 Wittgenstein resumed his post at Cambridge, but, troubled by what he thought was his harmful effect on students and disturbed by their apparent poor comprehension of his ideas, he resigned in 1947. His second major work, the *Philosophical Investigations*, was published in 1953, two years after his death.

Reportedly, when he became seriously ill in April 1951 and was told by his physician that he was about to die, his response was, simply, "Good." When he died a few days later, his last words were, "Tell them I've had a wonderful life."

going into an enclosed booth, picking up a marking pen, marking a piece of paper, and so forth. Even a proposition such as "John Smith picked up a marking pen" is theoretically resolvable into propositions about John Smith's bodily motions and a piece of plastic that has certain properties; and indeed we are still quite far from reaching the end of this theoretical process of resolving complex propositions into more elementary ones.

Because complex propositions must in principle be resolvable into simpler propositions by analysis, theoretically there must be fundamental and absolutely uncomplex (i.e., simple) propositions that cannot be resolved further. Corresponding to these absolutely simple "atomic" propositions are the fundamental or atomic facts. (The precise nature of the "correspondence" between proposition and fact turned out to be a difficult matter. Wittgenstein thought the proposition *pictured* the fact.) Because every atomic fact is logically independent of every other, idealists were thought to be mistaken in believing that All is One. Further, because atomic facts are logically independent of one another, the propositions that corresponded to them are logically independent of one another.

Now, you may want an example or two of an atomic fact. Just what *is* a basic fact? Are these facts about minds or matter or neutrons or quarks or what? you will ask.

Well, the logical atomists, remember, were *logical* atomists, and this means that not all of those who subscribed to logical atomism were concerned with what *actually are* the atomic facts. Some of them, most famously Wittgenstein, were concerned with setting forth what logically must be the basic structure of reality and left it to others to determine the actual content of the universe. Determining the logical structure of reality was enough, no little task in its own right, they thought.

As for Russell: he was always somewhat less concerned about what *actually* exists than with what we must *suppose* exists. For all he knew, he said, all the gods of Olympus exist. But the essential point is that we have no reason whatsoever to suppose that this is so.

As for what we must suppose exists, Russell changed his mind over the course of his long life. But generally he believed that the bare minimum that must be supposed to exist does *not* include many of the things that "common sense" is inclined to say exist, such as physical objects and atoms and subatomic particles. Russell's view was that what we say and think and believe about such things as these—let's call them the objects of common sense and science—can in theory be expressed in propositions that refer only to *awarenesses,* or **sense-data.** His position was that philosophically we do not have to believe in the existence of chairs or rocks or planets or atoms, say, as a type of entity that in some sense is more than just sense-data. Here, on one hand, he said in effect, are "data" actually given to us in sensation; there, on the other, are the external objects we strongly believe are out there and that science tells us so much about. How do we get from knowledge of our sense-data to knowledge of the objects? What we truly *know,* Russell said, are the data of immediate experience, our sense-data. Therefore, he said, what we *believe* exists (physical objects and scientific entities like atoms and electrons) must be definable in terms of sense-data if our belief in physical objects and scientific entities is to be philosophically secure. The affinities of this view with those of the logical positivists discussed earlier will be clear.

This idea—that physical and scientific objects are "definable" in terms of sense-data, or, more precisely, the idea that propositions about such objects in theory are expressible in propositions that refer only to sense-data—is known as **phenomenalism.** During the first forty or so years of the twentieth century, phenomenalism seemed plausible to many analytic philosophers as a way of certifying our supposed knowledge of external objects. Think once again of the quarter that we talked about in connection with Hume. At first glance it seems that you could, in a variety of ways, be mistaken when you think that there before you is a quarter. But it is easy to suppose that, even though your belief that you are seeing a quarter might be mistaken, you could not possibly be mistaken about your sense-data. That is, it is easy to suppose that a proposition that refers to your present sense-data, a proposition such as "This seems to me to be a round silverish expanse" is **incorrigible**—that is, *incapable* of being false if you believe it is true. (After all, could you possibly be mistaken about the way things *seem* to you?) Therefore, if

When you think you see a quarter, you might be mistaken. What you see might, for example, be made out of plastic and painted to look like a quarter. It might be a hologram projected to the space immediately in front of you. You might even just be hallucinating. However, you could not possibly be mistaken about what it *seems* to you you are seeing.

the empirical meaning of a physical-object proposition, a proposition such as "There is a quarter," could in fact be captured by an incorrigible sense-data proposition, or set of such propositions, then the nagging skepticism about physical objects would have been answered, once and for all, finally.

So phenomenalism was interesting as a possible way around skepticism about the external world. It was interesting to epistemologists also simply because the precise nature of the *relationship* between our beliefs about the objects of everyday experience and science (i.e., physical objects and their constituents) and the *sensory information* that constitutes the stream of experience has always been of interest to epistemologists. Phenomenalism is a theory about this relationship.

Whether phenomenalism is sound rests on whether our supposed knowledge of an external world can be understood in purely sensory terms. It is the question, loosely speaking, of whether "reality" reduces to "appearances." The alternative — that reality does not reduce, that it is somehow *inferred* from the appearances — seems to leave the mind uncomfortably severed from the world. So, among analytic philosophers through the first forty years of the twentieth century, phenomenalism almost qualified as the "official theory" of the relationship between sensory experience, language, and the world.

But today few philosophers are phenomenalists. There was strong adverse criticism of the theory around the middle of the twentieth century for a number of reasons. First, it became generally accepted that there is no set of sense-data, the having of which logically entails that you are experiencing any given physical object. Second, it was unclear that physical-object propositions that mention specific times and places could find their equivalents in propositions that refer only to sense-data. And finally, it was thought that phenomenalists had to believe in the possibility of what is called a **private language,** and the idea of whether such a language is coherent was questioned (see the box "Private Languages?").

Now, consider the history of epistemology and metaphysics from Descartes onward. One way of characterizing this history is that it has been an extended

## Private Languages?

"What I mean by 'book' or 'blue' might be entirely different from what you mean by those words, and you and I cannot really understand one another."

This same thought may have occurred to you. The empiricist in you may well think that all words ultimately derive their meaning from sense-impressions and that, because one person cannot have another person's sense-impressions, I cannot really know what your words mean and vice versa. In short, we all speak private languages, right?

Let's pretend you are discussing the issue with a philosopher who is arguing that a private language is an impossibility. You begin with the obvious question.

*You:* And just why is it an impossibility?

*Philosopher:* Well, for something to be a word, you have to be able to tell whether you have used it consistently. If you have no way of telling whether you are using some sound to denote the same kind of thing each time you use it, then the sound would just be a noise, not a word.

*Y:* So what follows from that?

*P:* Well, if no one else knew what you meant by your words, then *you* could not know if you had used them consistently. So then they would not *be* words. They would just be noises.

*Y:* Yes, well, but *why* couldn't I know if I had used a word consistently under those circumstances?

*P:* Because you would have only your own memory to rely on. There would be no independent check for your belief that you used a sound like *book* to apply to the same thing today as you applied it to yesterday. Thus, you would, in effect, be using *book* in any way you pleased. And

a sound that you use as you please is not a word.

In this little discussion, the philosopher is interpreting a sketchy argument against "private languages" laid out in Ludwig Wittgenstein's (1889–1951) *Philosophical Investigations* (published in 1953 and regarded by many as one of the most important philosophical works of the twentieth century). As mentioned in the text, phenomenalists were thought to be logically committed to the possibility of private languages. If, as was thought, Wittgenstein had shown a private language to be impossible, then phenomenalism was defective.

The question of whether a private language is impossible is interesting apart from its connection to phenomenalism, for the idea that one person really *does not* know what another person means by a given word is an idea that — thanks to the influence of the British empiricists on our thinking — most people find quite plausible, once they think about it. What we tend to believe is that a word stands for an idea, or some other sort of mental entity, which we think is the meaning of the word. And therefore, we think, because a word's meaning is locked up inside the mind, what each of us means by our words is private to each of us.

What Wittgenstein argued is that the whole notion of a "private language," and the theory of meaning on which it rests, is pure bunkum. The meanings of words lie not inside the mind, he said, but in their *uses*, and these uses are governed by rules. As these rules are not our own private rules, other people can check the correctness of our usage of a given word. We do not have private languages, and could not possibly have them, for in such "languages" the correctness of our usage of words is not subject to a public check. In a "private language," the "words" would just be *sounds* that one could use any way one pleased.

search for metaphysical truth derived from *incorrigible foundations of knowledge.* (An incorrigible proposition is one that is incapable of being false if you believe it is true.) For that matter, philosophers from before Socrates to the present have searched incessantly for these incorrigible foundations. They have looked everywhere for an unshakable bedrock on which the entire structure of knowledge, especially metaphysical knowledge, might be built. Augustine found the bedrock in revealed truth. Descartes thought he had found it in the certainty of his own existence. Empiricists believed the foundational bedrock of knowledge must somehow or other lie in immediate sensory experience. Kant found the foundation in principles supplied by the mind in the very act of experiencing the world.

But must a belief really rest on *incorrigible* foundations if it is to qualify as knowledge? More fundamentally, must it even rest on *foundations*? Recently philosophers have begun to question whether knowledge requires foundations at all. Thus, they have begun to question an assumption on which much of traditional epistemology rests.

**Foundationalism** holds that a belief qualifies as knowledge only if it logically follows from propositions that are incorrigible (incapable of being false if you believe that they are true). For example, take for one last time my belief that this before me is a quarter. According to a foundationalist from the empiricist tradition, I *know* that this before me is a quarter only if my belief that it is absolutely follows from the propositions that describe my present sense-data, because these propositions alone are incorrigible. But, the antifoundationalist argues, why not say that my belief that there is a quarter before me *automatically* qualifies as knowledge, unless there is some definite and special reason to think that it is mistaken?

The question of whether knowledge requires foundations is currently under wide discussion among epistemologists. It is too early to predict what the results of this discussion may be.

Many of those who attack the foundationalist position have been inclined, recently, to endorse what is called **naturalized epistemology.** This is the view that traditional epistemological inquiries should be replaced by psychological inquiries into the processes actually involved in the acquisition and revision of beliefs. This view, which in its strongest form amounts to saying that epistemology should be phased out in favor of psychology, is highly controversial. Nevertheless, much recent writing in epistemology has reflected a deep interest in developments in psychology.

## Antirepresentationalism

In the first half of the twentieth century, many philosophers (within the analytic tradition, at any rate) *assumed* that the natural sciences give us (or will eventually give us) the correct account of reality. They assumed, in other words, that natural science — and the commonsense beliefs that incorporate science — is the true metaphysics. The task for philosophy, it was thought, was to *certify* scientific knowledge epistemologically. This was to be done, it was supposed, by "reducing" the propositions of science — propositions about physical objects and their atomic constituents — to propositions that refer to sense-data, that is, by analyzing the propositions of science in the language of sensory experience. Just as mathematics was shown to reduce to a foundation of logic, or at any rate to logic and set theory, scientific knowledge was thought to be reducible to an epistemological foundation, namely, the incorrigible knowledge of sense-data.

Eventually, though, as we have seen, philosophers became doubtful that this grand reduction could be carried out even in principle, and likewise many began to question the idea that knowledge requires foundations anyway.

In epistemology in the past couple of decades a leading alternative to foundationalism has been naturalized epistemology, which is the scientific study of the various processes involved in coming to have knowledge—perception, language acquisition, learning, and so forth. Now, in metaphysics during the past few decades, an alternative to the view that physical objects are constructs of sense-data has become widely held. According to this alternative to phenomenalism, physical objects are **theoretical posits,** entities whose existence we in effect hypothesize to explain our sensory experience. This nonreductionist view of physical objects as posited entities is also, like naturalized epistemology, associated with the work of W. V. O. Quine.

From a commonsense and scientific standpoint, physical objects are independent of the perceiving and knowing mind, independent in the sense that they are what they are regardless of what the mind thinks about them. The thesis that reality consists of such independent objects is known as **realism.** From a realist perspective, there are two epistemological possibilities: (1) we can know this independent reality; (2) we cannot know it: what is actually true may be different from what is thought to be true. The second view is skepticism, and phenomenalism was thought to be the answer to skepticism. But even if true, phenomenalism would refute skepticism only by denying realism; it would refute skepticism, that is to say, only by denying that objects are independent of the mind, or at least independent of our sense-data. The Quinean view of objects as theoretical posits is consistent with realism; however, it is also consistent with skepticism because (the skeptic would say) theoretical posits may not exist in fact.

Now it would seem that either objects exist outside the mind or they are some sort of constructs of the mind: it would seem that either realism is true or some form of idealism is true. But there is another possibility that some philosophers recently have been considering. To understand this third possibility, let's just consider what underlies the realist's conception. What underlies it is the idea that the mind, when it is thinking correctly about the world outside the mind, accurately conceives of this world. Alternatively put, what underlies realism is the idea that true beliefs accurately portray or *represent* reality: what makes them true is the states of affairs to which they "correspond" or that they "mirror" or "depict" or "portray." This view—that beliefs about reality represent reality (either correctly, if they are true, or incorrectly, if they are false)—is called **representationalism.** From the representationalist point of view, a belief counts as knowledge only if it is a true belief, and a belief is true only if it is an accurate representation of the state of affairs that it is about. Representationalism underlay Russell's philosophy, and the *magnus opus* of representationalism was Wittgenstein's *Tractatus Logico-Philosophicus,* commented upon in an earlier box.

But now it is possible to question the whole premise of representationalism, and that is exactly what several contemporary analytic philosophers, including most famously Richard Rorty (see Chapter 8), are doing. **Antirepresentationalism** takes several forms, but basically it denies that mind or language contains, or is a representation of, reality. According to the "old" picture, the representationalist picture, there is, on one hand, the mind and its beliefs and, on the other, the world or "reality"; and if our beliefs represent reality *as it really is*—that is, as it is "in itself" independent of any perspective or point of view—the beliefs are true. Antirepresentationalists, by contrast, dismiss this picture as unintelligible. They find no significance in the notion that beliefs represent reality (or in the notion that they fail to represent reality, if they are false beliefs); and they find no sense in the idea of the world "as it really is"—that is, as it is independent of this or that perspective or viewpoint. According to antirepresentationalists, truth is not a matter of a belief's corresponding to or accurately representing the "actual" state of affairs that obtains outside the mind. When we describe a belief as true, they hold, we are simply praising that belief as having been proven relative to our standards of rationality. And when we say that some belief is "absolutely true," we just mean that its acceptance is so fully justified, given our standards, that we cannot presently imagine how any further justification could even be possible.

This conception of truth seems to imply that different and perhaps even apparently conflicting beliefs could equally well be true—as long as they are fully justified relative to alternative standards of rationality. Perhaps you, by contrast, would maintain that although two conflicting beliefs could be *thought* to be true, they could not actually both *be* true. But if you hold this, then it may be because you are a representationalist and think that truth is a matter of a belief's correctly representing reality—reality as it is in itself, independent of any person's or society's perspective. But antirepresentationalists do not understand, or profess not to understand, what this business about a belief's correctly representing the world "as it really is" comes to. They say that nobody can climb outside his or her own perspective, and they say that this talk about the world "as it really is independent of perspective or viewpoint" is just mumbo jumbo.

Many of the themes of Rorty's antirepresentationalism were, of course, anticipated in the philosophy of the pragmatists. Dewey, who is probably still the most famous American philosopher outside of philosophy, and the other pragmatists are not part of the analytic tradition. But the ideas of the pragmatists have entered into analytic philosophy through Quine, Hilary Putnam, and other contemporary American analytic philosophers, and especially Rorty, who at any rate began as an analytic philosopher. Rorty frequently refers to himself as a "Deweyian" and a "pragmatist." Like Dewey, Rorty recommends just forgetting about trying to discover metaphysical absolutes or attempting "to get in touch with mind-independent and language-independent reality."

## Wittgenstein's Turnaround

Before we turn to the philosophy of mind, it is appropriate to say a bit more about Ludwig Wittgenstein, whom many consider to be the most important philosopher of the twentieth century. Wittgenstein's philosophy divides into two phases. Both had a great influence on his contemporaries, yet the philosophy of the second phase, that of the *Philosophical Investigations* (1953), is largely a rejection of the central ideas of the first, that of the *Tractatus* (1921). This is an unusual but not a unique occurrence in the history of philosophy, for other philosophers have come to reject their earlier positions as well.

In both works, Wittgenstein was concerned with the relationships between language and the world. The *Tractatus* assumes a single, essential relationship; the *Investigations* denies this assumption. In the *Tractatus,* Wittgenstein portrays the

According to Wittgenstein (subject to qualifications discussed in the text), a proposition like "the dog is on the surfboard" pictures a fact much as the photograph pictures that fact.

function of language as that of describing the world and is concerned with making it clear just how language and thought hook onto reality in the first place.

Well, just how does language hook onto reality? According to Wittgenstein, as we have seen, a proposition (or a thought) *pictures* the fact it represents. It can picture it, he said, because both it and the fact share the same *logical form,* a form that can be exhibited by philosophical analysis. All genuine propositions, he held, are reducible to logically elementary propositions, which, he said, are composed of *names* of absolutely simple objects. A combination of these names (i.e., a proposition) pictures a combination of *objects* in the world (i.e., a fact). The *Tractatus* is devoted in large measure to explaining and working out the implications of this *picture theory of meaning* across a range of philosophical topics. The result is logical atomism, as explained earlier.

But in the *Investigations,* Wittgenstein casts off completely this picture theory of meaning and the underlying assumption of the *Tractatus* that there is some universal function of language. After all, he notes in the later work, how a picture is *used* determines what it is a picture of — one and the same picture could be a picture of a man holding a guitar, or of how to hold a guitar, or of what a guitar looks like, or of what Bill Jones's fingers look like, and so on. Similarly, what a sentence means is determined by the use to which it is put within a given context or **language game.** Further, says the later Wittgenstein, there is nothing that the various uses of language have in common, and there is certainly no set of ideal elementary propositions to which all other propositions are reducible. In short, according to the later work, the earlier work is completely wrongheaded.

When philosophers ignore the "game" in which language is used, Wittgenstein says in the *Investigations*—when they take language "on a holiday" and try to straitjacket it into conformity with some idealized and preconceived notion of what its essence must be—the result is the unnecessary confusion known as a philosophical problem. From this perspective, the history of philosophy is a catalogue of confusions that result from taking language on a holiday.

No better illustration of how taking language on a holiday leads to strange results can perhaps be found than the paradox that lies at the end of Wittgenstein's earlier work, *Tractatus Logico-Philosophicus*. In that work, Wittgenstein had been held captive by a theory of how language links itself to the world, and his discussion of how language links itself to the world was expressed in language. This placed Wittgenstein in the paradoxical situation of having used language to represent how language represents the world. And this, he concluded, could not be done—despite the fact that he had just done it. Language, he said, may be used to represent the world but cannot be used to represent how language represents the world. "What expresses itself in language, we cannot express by means of language."

Thus, Wittgenstein concluded the *Tractatus* with an outrageous paradox: "My propositions serve as elucidations in the following way," he wrote. "Anyone who understands me eventually recognizes them as nonsensical, when he has used them—as steps—to climb up beyond them. (He must, so to speak, throw away the ladder after he has climbed up it.)" The later Wittgenstein just threw away the entire *Tractatus*.

## THE PHILOSOPHY OF MIND

To this point we have considered one of two main concerns in analytic epistemology and metaphysics; namely, the interrelationship between sensory experience, language, and the physical world. The other main concern has been with the mind.

The philosophy of mind is a vast area of analytic philosophy that deals not with a single problem but, rather, with a host of interrelated issues and concerns. These issues and concerns have become so numerous, complicated, and involved that many philosophers now treat the philosophy of mind as a separate major philosophical area in its own right, like epistemology and the philosophy of religion. What follows is only a brief overview.

The **philosophy of mind** is concerned primarily with the nature of consciousness, mental states (or psychological states, these being the same), and the mind. The approach usually taken (as you might expect from what we have said about analytic philosophy) is to look at everyday psychological vocabulary—with its reference to mental states of various sorts, including beliefs, desires, fears, suspicions, hopes, ideas, preferences, choices, thoughts, motives, urges, and so forth—and ask what this psychological vocabulary means or how it is to be analyzed. In the past twenty or so years, these inquiries have broadened to encompass the research and findings of psychologists, neuroscientists, computer scientists, linguists, artificial intelligence researchers, and other specialists. The philosophy of mind is no longer the preserve of the professional philosopher.

A good approach to this large subject is to ask whether the mind is physical (material), nonphysical, or both, or neither.

Let's begin by noting that many — perhaps most — members of Western societies take the position that a person has a nonmaterial or nonphysical mind or soul or spirit associated with his or her physical body. *You* may well take this position, a position known as *dualism* and associated forever with René Descartes (though see the box on Oliva Sabuco in Chapter 6).

## Dualism

According to the dualist, every existing thing (except for abstract items, e.g., geometric points, numbers, and brotherhood) is either *physical* (or material, these terms being used interchangeably here) or *nonphysical* (or immaterial or incorporeal, these terms also being interchangeable).

Physical things possess physical properties (like density, velocity, charge, temperature, mass, and, most fundamentally, spatial occupancy), and nonphysical things possess nonphysical properties. These latter properties are difficult to specify, though dualists would say that only nonphysical entities can have conscious states or exercise volition. Both physical and nonphysical things can have neutral properties. For example, physical and nonphysical things both have temporal properties, both may be numerous, both belong to groups, and so forth.

A human being, according to the dualist, has (or is) both a physical body and a nonphysical mind (or soul or spirit). Further, according to the dualist, a person's nonphysical and physical components are *interactive:* if someone comes along and gives you a shove, you may become angry. In other words, the shoving of your physical body causes anger to arise in your nonphysical mind. Or — to run this in reverse — when you decide to do something, your body normally follows through; that is, your nonphysical mind causes your physical body to walk or run or speak or whatever it is you want your body to do.

Actually, a dualist does not have to believe that the immaterial mind and the material body interact, but most dualists do, so when we talk about *dualism* here, we mean **interactionist dualism.**

Now, to the extent that many people have ever thought about it, it seems pretty nearly self-evident that a human being has a nonphysical component of some sort, be it called a mind, soul, spirit, or something else. But the difficulties in dualism have led many analytic philosophers to doubt whether dualism is a viable theory at all, and they have cast about for more attractive alternatives. The most heavily subscribed alternatives have all been physicalist. They are *behaviorism, identity theory,* and *functionalism.*

## Behaviorism

The word *behaviorism* is notoriously ambiguous. **Behaviorism** in one sense is a *methodological principle of psychology,* according to which fruitful psychological investigation confines itself to such psychological phenomena as can be behaviorally defined. *Philosophical behaviorism* is the doctrine we will now explain, which we are attributing to Gilbert Ryle. Ryle denied being a behaviorist, incidentally. Still, *The Concept of Mind* (1949) is regarded as one of the most powerful expositions of (philosophical) behaviorism ever written. (Hereafter, when we refer to behaviorism, we will mean *philosophical* behaviorism.)

According to Ryle, when we refer to someone's mental states (and this someone might be oneself), when we refer, for example, to a person's beliefs or thoughts or wishes, we are *not*, contrary to what is ordinarily supposed, referring to the immaterial states of a nonphysical mind. There is indeed no such thing as a nonphysical mind. There is, Ryle says, *no ghost within the machine.* A person is only a complicated—a very highly complicated—physical organism, one capable of doing the amazing sorts of things that people are capable of doing. When we attribute a so-called mental state to a person, we are in fact attributing to him or her a *propensity* or *disposition* to act or behave in a certain way.

For example, when you attribute to your friend the belief that it is going to rain, it might *seem* that you view her as having or possessing a nonphysical thing of some sort, termed a *belief,* a nonphysical, intangible, and unobservable entity that exists within her mind. But in fact, argues Ryle, to say that someone believes it is going to rain is merely to attribute to her a propensity or disposition to do things like close the windows and cover the barbecue and say things like "It's going to rain" and not to do certain other sorts of things like wash the car and hang out the sheets.

It is likewise when we credit someone with a thought or an idea. Thoughts and ideas, like beliefs, are not nonmaterial things, says Ryle. They are not even *things* at all. To be sure, "thought," "idea," and "belief" are words for things, that is, *thing-words.* But these thing-words are (to borrow an expression Ryle used in a different context) *systematically misleading.* Because they are thing-words, they mislead or tempt us into thinking that there must be things for which they stand. And because there seem to be no physical things for which they stand, we are tempted to conclude that they stand for nonphysical things.

In fact, however, when we say that someone has a specific thought, all we can really be doing is attributing to him or her a propensity to say or do certain things, a propensity to behave in certain ways. It is rather like what we mean when we say that someone has mechanical knowledge. "Mechanical knowledge" is a thing-word too. But we really do not think that someone who has mechanical knowledge possesses a *thing* that is out there in the toolbox alongside the screwdriver and adjustable crescent; nor do we think that mechanical knowledge is a ghostly nonphysical thing that is hidden away in the person's "mind." When we say that someone has mechanical knowledge, all we mean is that he or she is able, and apt, to do certain things in certain situations.

In short, references to someone's beliefs, ideas, thoughts, knowledge, motives, and other mental "things" must be analyzed or understood as references to the ways the person is apt to behave given certain conditions.

Might not Ryle strengthen his case by providing an *actual analysis* of a mental-state expression, a translation into behavioral language of a simple mental-state proposition such as "She believes that it is time to go home"? Indeed, Ryle could *not* strengthen his case in this way, for it is not his position that such translations could be made. According to behaviorists, there is no definite and finite list of

behaviors and behavioral propensities that we are attributing to someone when we say, "She believes it is time to go home." Instead, we are referring in an *oblique and loose way* to an indefinite and open set of behaviors and behavioral tendencies.

This, then, is **philosophical behaviorism:**

- There is no such thing as a nonphysical mind.
- Mental-state thing-words do not really denote things at all. A statement in which such words appear is a kind of loose shorthand reference to behaviors (including verbal behaviors) and behavioral propensities.
- Statements about a person's mental states cannot actually be translated into some set of statements about the person's behavior and behavioral propensities, because the sets of behaviors and behavioral propensities to which they in fact refer are indefinite and open and depend on the situations in which the person happens to be.

Behaviorism nicely accounts for another problem facing dualism, namely, explaining why it is that brain scientists and neuroscientists just never do have to postulate the existence of nonphysical mental states to explain the causes and origin of our behavior. The reason they never have to postulate such things, according to the behaviorist, is because there are no such things.

## Identity Theory

Another physicalist philosophy of the mind is **identity theory.** According to identity theory, so-called mental phenomena are all physical phenomena within the brain and central nervous system. A thought, for example, according to identity theory, is in fact some sort of occurrence within the brain/nervous system, though we do not yet know enough about the brain or central nervous system to stipulate which particular occurrence it is. Among the many adherents of identity theory is the Australian philosopher J. J. C. Smart (1920– ), who explains a version of identity theory at the end of this chapter.

Notice that the identity theorist does not say merely that thinking (or any other mental occurrence) is *correlated* with or *involves* a neural process of some sort. The claim is rather that thinking *is* a neural process. Just as light *is* electromagnetic radiation (and is not just "involved in" or "correlated with" electromagnetic radiation), and just as heat *is* movement of molecules, thinking and all other mental phenomena, according to identity theory, *are* physical states and happenings within the brain and central nervous system.

Beginning philosophy students sometimes have a difficult time distinguishing behaviorism from identity theory, usually, we think, for two reasons.

First, behaviorism and identity theory are both physicalistic (materialist) theories in the sense that, according to both, you and we and all other people are completely physical organisms: neither theory countenances the existence of the nonmaterial or nonphysical soul, spirit, or mind; and neither theory thinks that mental-state thing-words denote nonmaterial or nonphysical things.

Second, few theorists are *pure* behaviorists or identity theorists. Most philosophers who call themselves identity theorists do in fact accept a behavioristic analysis of at least some assertions about mental states, and most behaviorists do likewise accept identity theory with respect to some mental states.

But the two theories really should not be confused. *Identity theory* holds that mind-states are brain-states, that when we speak of a person's beliefs, thoughts, hopes, ideas, and the like, we are in fact referring to events and processes and states within his or her brain and nervous system. *Philosophical behaviorism* holds that when we use our everyday psychological vocabulary to describe someone, we are really just talking in a shorthand way about her or his behavioral propensities.

## Functionalism

Physicalist philosophers do not believe that people have nonphysical minds, and they deny that mental-state thing-words stand for states or processes of a nonphysical variety. But many physicalists question the identity theory, according to which each distinct mental state or process equates with one and only one brain state or process. It is possible, these physicalists say, that the selfsame psychological (mental) state could be correctly ascribed to quite different physiological systems.

For example, there may be beings in a far distant galaxy whose brains and nervous systems are radically different from our own but who nevertheless have thoughts and beliefs and desires and motives and other mental states. This is not a terribly far-fetched possibility. Now, if there are such beings, it is possible that when they believe something, what goes on in their "brains" and "nervous systems" may not be the same thing at all as what goes on in ours when we believe something. (They might not even have what we would call brains!)

For that matter, the belief process in a brain-damaged *human* may not be the same as in a normal human. And some day, thinking robots may be created (at least physicalists must admit that this is theoretically possible) with "brains" made out

# Monkeys Control Robotic Arm with Brain Implants

WASHINGTON POST

Scientists in North Carolina have built a brain implant that lets monkeys control a robotic arm with their thoughts, marking the first time that mental intentions have been harnessed to move a mechanical object.

The technology could someday allow people with paralyzing spinal cord injuries to operate machines or tools with their thoughts as naturally as others today do with their hands. It might even allow some paralyzed people to move their arms or legs again, by transmitting the brain's directions not to a machine but directly to the muscles in those latent limbs....

In the new experiments, monkeys with wires running from their brains to a robotic arm were able to use their thoughts to make the arm perform tasks. Before long, scientists said they will upgrade the monkeys' devices so they can transmit their mental commands to machines wirelessly.

The experiments, led by Miguel A. L. Nicolelis of Duke University in Durham and published today in the journal PLoS Biology, are the latest in a progression of increasingly science fictionlike studies in which animals—and in a few cases people—have learned to use the brain's subtle electrical signals to operate simple devices.

Until now, those achievements have been limited to "virtual" actions, such as making a cursor move across a computer screen, or to small actions such as flipping a little lever.

The new work is the first in which any animal has learned to use its brain to move a robotic device in all directions in space and to perform several interrelated movements—such as reaching toward an object, grasping it and adjusting the grip strength depending on the object's weight.

The device relies on tiny electrodes, each one resembling a wire thinner than a human hair. After removing patches of skull from two monkeys to expose the outer surface of their brains, Nicolelis and his colleagues stuck 96 of those tiny wires about a millimeter deep in one monkey's brain and 320 of them in the other animal's brain.

The monkeys were unaffected by the surgery, Nicolelis said. But now they had tufts of wires protruding from their heads, which could be hooked up to other wires that ran through a computer and on to a large mechanical arm.

Then came the training, with the monkeys first learning to move the robot arm with a joystick. The arm was kept in a separate room—"If you put a 50-kilogram robot in front of them, they get very nervous," Nicolelis said—but the monkeys could track their progress by watching a representation of the arm and its motions on a video screen.

The monkeys quickly learned how to use the joystick to make the arm reach and grasp for objects, and how to adjust their grip on the joystick to vary the robotic hand's grip strength. They could see on the monitor when they missed their target or dropped it from having too light a grip, and they were rewarded with sips of juice when they performed their tasks successfully.

While the monkeys trained, a computer tracked the patterns of bioelectrical activity in the animals' brains. The computer figured out that certain patterns amounted to "reach." Others, it became clear, meant "grasp." Gradually, the computer learned to "read" the monkeys' minds.

Then the researchers unplugged the joystick so the robotic arm's movements depended completely on a monkey's brain activity. In effect, the computer that had been studying the animal's neural firing patterns was now an interpreter, decoding the brain signals according to what it had learned from the joystick games and sending instruc-tions to the robot arm.

At first, Nicolelis said, the monkey kept moving the joystick, not realizing her brain was now solely in charge of the arm's movements. Then, he said, an amazing thing happened.

"She stops moving her arm," he said, "but the cursor keeps playing the game, and the robot arm is moving around."

The animal was controlling the robot with its thoughts.

---

Experiments like these, in which monkeys control a robotic arm with their thoughts, seem utterly mysterious and incomprehensible from the standpoint of dualism.

---

of silicon and plastic. Though these robots will think, in all probability somewhat different physical processes will be involved when they do than are involved when we think.

In light of such examples it seems unwise to say that each distinct mental phenomenon equates with one and only one brain/nervous-system phenomenon, as does identity theory. It seems sounder philosophically to say that a given mental state is identical with *some* brain/nervous-system phenomenon *or other.*

This is what so-called functionalists say. According to **functionalism,** a mental state is defined by its *function.* For example, you may believe it is going to rain. If you do, your belief will have been caused by certain sensory stimuli in conjunction with other beliefs that you have, and it (your belief that it is going to rain) will in turn have an effect on your behavior and other beliefs. In short, the belief will interact with your other mental states (including sensations) and your behavior in a way that is unique to just that belief. To play just that causal role it does play in this network of relationships is the *function* of that belief.

Thus, according to the functionalist, *any* physical process (regardless of what type of organism or physical system it occurs in) that has that precise function *is* that belief.

For the functionalist, therefore, a mental state is analogous to a mousetrap or a garage door opener or a word processor or anything else that is *defined by its function*. Mousetraps (or garage door openers or word processors) are not defined by what they are made of or how they are put together. Mousetraps may actually be made of *most anything* and put together in indefinitely many ways. Hence, they are not defined by what they are made of or how they are assembled but, rather, by their functions, that is, by what they do. Anything that has the function of a mousetrap, no matter how it is assembled and what it is made out of, is a mousetrap. The same holds true for garage door openers and word processors, and, according to the functionalist, the same holds for beliefs, thoughts, ideas, and other mental states and processes. Beliefs and the like, they say, are defined by their *function*—the role they play in affecting behavior and in affecting and being affected by other mental states.

Therefore, according to the functionalist, beliefs and other mental phenomena must be analyzed functionally, *not reductively*. You cannot *reduce* talk about mousetraps to talk about what they are made of. If someone were to ask what a mousetrap *is*, you would explain what a mousetrap *does*—what its unique function is. Beliefs and other mental phenomena, according to the functionalist, are likewise to be explained in terms of their unique functions—the specific roles they play relative to sensory data and other mental states and to behavioral output.

Thus, says the functionalist, though it is true that nothing nonphysical happens to you when you have a belief, that does not mean that we could somehow "translate" statements about your beliefs into statements about neurological processes. And conversely, the fact that we cannot translate talk about your beliefs into talk about neurological processes does not mean that beliefs are nonphysical.

So you can see that functionalism explains nicely why psychology—whether of the commonsense ("folk") or the scientific variety—has resisted reduction to neurology. It has been resistant not because psychological states are nonphysical but because they are functional. Functionalism is therefore thought to provide a conceptual framework for psychological research that, on one hand, does not commit the researcher to murky and questionable dualistic metaphysical notions and, on the other, also does not commit the researcher to the implausible idea that psychology, just like chemistry, "reduces" to physics.

A brief comment seems in order here. It has been the fond thought of many a philosopher that anything that happens could, in principle, be expressed in the language of physics. Let's call this thought **straightforward reductivist physicalism** or, for short, **physicalist reductivism.** The thought is this: just as chemistry is really just a matter of physics—that is, is reducible to physics—biology and neurophysiology are reducible to chemistry and physics and hence ultimately are reducible just to physics. Further (according to physicalist reductivism), because psychology is really just a matter of neurophysiology, ultimately it, too, reduces to physics. Sociology and the other social sciences (according to physicalist reductivism) likewise ultimately reduce to the psychology of groups; hence, ultimately, they too reduce to physics. And hence, if the Grand Reduction of physics itself to a single force or particle is achieved, as some physicists apparently believe it will be, everything from human thoughts and political elections to interactions of leptons and quarks will be reduced to and explained by a single physical factor (the physical version, perhaps, of God). If functionalism is correct, however, though everything that happens may indeed be physical, a thoroughgoing reduction of *everything* to physics is most unlikely.

Behaviorism, identity theory, and functionalism, then, are nondualist theories of mind that have been developed by analytic philosophers in the twentieth century. As we said earlier, these days perhaps most analytic philosophers of mind (not to mention cognitive psychologists and artificial intelligence researchers) accept some physicalist theory of the mind (usually functionalism). Nevertheless, they are aware of several philosophical problems that physicalist theories encounter.

Where will philosophy go in the English-speaking world in the twenty-first century? Almost certainly the philosophy of mind will continue to be an area of importance, but whether the pragmatist perspective reintroduced by Rorty and others will have lasting impact is not yet clear.

---

SELECTION 9.1
## The Elimination of Metaphysics *

*A. J. Ayer*

---

[*A. J. Ayer was the most famous British exponent of logical positivism. In this selection, Ayer sets forth and elaborates on the verifiability criterion of meaning.*]

The traditional disputes of philosophers are, for the most part, as unwarranted as they are unfruitful. The surest way to end them is to establish beyond question what should be the purpose and method of a philosophical inquiry. And this is by no means so difficult a task as the history of philosophy would lead one to suppose. For if there are any questions which science leaves it to philosophy to answer, a straightforward process of elimination must lead to their discovery.

We may begin by criticizing the metaphysical thesis that philosophy affords us knowledge of a reality transcending the world of science and common sense. Later on, when we come to define metaphysics and account for its existence, we shall find that it is possible to be a metaphysician without believing in a transcendent reality; for we shall see that many metaphysical utterances are due to the commission of logical errors, rather than to a conscious desire on the part of their authors to go beyond the

limits of experience. But it is convenient for us to take the case of those who believe that it is possible to have knowledge of a transcendent reality as a starting-point for our discussion. The arguments which we use to refute them will subsequently be found to apply to the whole of metaphysics.

One way of attacking a metaphysician who claimed to have knowledge of a reality which transcended the phenomenal world would be to inquire from what premises his propositions were deduced. Must he not begin, as other men do, with the evidence of his senses? And if so, what valid process of reasoning can possibly lead him to the conception of a transcendent reality? Surely from empirical premises nothing whatsoever concerning the properties, or even the existence, of anything superempirical can legitimately be inferred. But this objection would be met by a denial on the part of the metaphysician that his assertions were ultimately based on the evidence of his senses. He would say that he was endowed with a faculty of intellectual intuition which enabled him to know facts that could not be known through sense-experience. And even if it could be shown that he was relying on empirical premises, and that his venture into a nonempirical world was therefore logically unjustified, it would not follow that the assertions which he made concerning this nonempirical world could not

---

*From A. J. Ayer, *Language, Truth, and Logic,* 2nd ed. (London: Victor Gollancz, 1946). Reprinted by permission of Victor Gollancz, a division of the Orion Publishing Group.

be true. For the fact that a conclusion does not follow from its putative premise is not sufficient to show that it is false. Consequently one cannot overthrow a system of transcendent metaphysics merely by criticizing the way in which it comes into being. What is required is rather a criticism of the nature of the actual statements which comprise it. And this is the line of argument which we shall, in fact, pursue. For we shall maintain that no statement which refers to a "reality" transcending the limits of all possible sense-experience can possibly have any literal significance; from which it must follow that the labors of those who have striven to describe such a reality have all been devoted to the production of nonsense.

It may be suggested that this is a proposition which has already been proved by Kant. But although Kant also condemned transcendent metaphysics, he did so on different grounds. For he said that the human understanding was so constituted that it lost itself in contradictions when it ventured out beyond the limits of possible experience and attempted to deal with things in themselves. And thus he made the impossibility of a transcendent metaphysic not, as we do, a matter of logic, but a matter of fact. He asserted, not that our minds could not conceivably have had the power of penetrating beyond the phenomenal world, but merely that they were in fact devoid of it. And this leads the critic to ask how, if it is possible to know only what lies within the bounds of sense-experience, the author can be justified in asserting that real things do exist beyond, and how he can tell what are the boundaries beyond which the human understanding may not venture, unless he succeeds in passing them himself. As Wittgenstein says, "in order to draw a limit to thinking, we should have to think both sides of this limit,"[1] a truth to which Bradley gives a special twist in maintaining that the man who is ready to prove that metaphysics is impossible is a brother metaphysician with a rival theory of his own.[2]

Whatever force these objections may have against the Kantian doctrine, they have none whatsoever against the thesis that I am about to set forth. It cannot here be said that the author is himself overstepping the barrier he maintains to be impassable. For the fruitlessness of attempting to transcend the limits of possible sense-experience will be deduced, not from a psychological hypothesis concerning the actual constitution of the human mind, but from the rule which determines the literal significance of language. Our charge against the metaphysician is not that he attempts to employ the understanding in a field where it cannot profitably venture, but that he produces sentences which fail to conform to the conditions under which alone a sentence can be literally significant. Nor are we ourselves obliged to talk nonsense in order to show that all sentences of a certain type are necessarily devoid of literal significance. We need only formulate the criterion which enables us to test whether a sentence expresses a genuine proposition about a matter of fact, and then point out that the sentences under consideration fail to satisfy it. And this we shall now proceed to do. We shall first of all formulate the criterion in somewhat vague terms, and then give the explanations which are necessary to render it precise.

The criterion which we use to test the genuineness of apparent statements of fact is the criterion of verifiability. We say that a sentence is factually significant to any given person, if, and only if, he knows how to verify the proposition which it purports to express — that is, if he knows what observations would lead him, under certain conditions, to accept the proposition as being true, or reject it as being false. If, on the other hand, the putative proposition is of such a character that the assumption of its truth, or falsehood, is consistent with any assumption whatsoever concerning the nature of his future experience, then, as far as he is concerned, it is, if not a tautology, a mere pseudo-proposition. The sentence expressing it may be emotionally significant to him; but it is not literally significant. And with regard to questions the procedure is the same. We inquire in every case what observations would lead us to answer the question, one way or the other; and, if none can be discovered, we must conclude that the sentence under consideration does not, as far as we are concerned, express a genuine question, however strongly its grammatical appearance may suggest that it does.

As the adoption of this procedure is an essential factor in the argument of this book, it needs to be examined in detail.

In the first place, it is necessary to draw a distinction between practical verifiability, and verifiability in principle. Plainly we all understand, in many cases believe, propositions which we have not in fact

---

[1] *Tractatus Logico-Philosophicus,* Preface.

[2] Bradley, *Appearance and Reality,* 2nd ed., p. 1.

taken steps to verify. Many of these are propositions which we could verify if we took enough trouble. But there remain a number of significant propositions, concerning matters of fact, which we could not verify even if we chose; simply because we lack the practical means of placing ourselves in the situation where the relevant observations could be made. A simple and familiar example of such a proposition is the proposition that there are mountains on the farther side of the moon.[3] No rocket has yet been invented which would enable me to go and look at the farther side of the moon, so that I am unable to decide the matter by actual observation. But I do know what observations would decide it for me, if, as is theoretically conceivable, I were once in a position to make them. And therefore I say that the proposition is verifiable in principle, if not in practice, and is accordingly significant. On the other hand, such a metaphysical pseudo-proposition as "the Absolute enters into, but is itself incapable of, evolution and progress,"[4] is not even in principle verifiable. For one cannot conceive of an observation which would enable one to determine whether the Absolute did, or did not, enter into evolution and progress. Of course it is possible that the author of such a remark is using English words in a way in which they are not commonly used by English-speaking people, and that he does, in fact, intend to assert something which could be empirically verified. But until he makes us understand how the proposition that he wishes to express would be verified, he fails to communicate anything to us. And if he admits, as I think the author of the remark in question would have admitted, that his words were not intended to express either a tautology or a proposition which was capable, at least in principle, of being verified, then it follows that he has made an utterance which has no literal significance for himself.

A further distinction which we must make is the distinction between the "strong" and the "weak" sense of the term "verifiable." A proposition is said to be verifiable, in the strong sense of the term, if, and only if, its truth could be conclusively established in experience. But it is verifiable, in the weak sense, if it is possible for experience to render it probable. In which sense are we using the term

when we say that a putative proposition is genuine only if it is verifiable?

It seems to me that if we adopt conclusive verifiability as our criterion of significance, as some positivists have proposed,[5] our argument will prove too much. Consider, for example, the case of general propositions of law—such propositions, namely, as "arsenic is poisonous"; "all men are mortal"; "a body tends to expand when it is heated." It is of the very nature of these propositions that their truth cannot be established with certainty by any finite series of observations. But if it is recognized that such general propositions of law are designed to cover an infinite number of cases, then it must be admitted that they cannot, even in principle, be verified conclusively. And then, if we adopt conclusive verifiability as our criterion of significance, we are logically obliged to treat these general propositions of law in the same fashion as we treat the statements of the metaphysician.

In face of this difficulty, some positivists[6] have adopted the heroic course of saying that these general propositions are indeed pieces of nonsense, albeit an essentially important type of nonsense. But here the introduction of the term "important" is simply an attempt to hedge. It serves only to mark the authors' recognition that their view is somewhat too paradoxical, without in any way removing the paradox. Besides, the difficulty is not confined to the case of general propositions of law, though it is there revealed most plainly. It is hardly less obvious in the case of propositions about the remote past. For it must surely be admitted that, however strong the evidence in favor of historical statements may be, their truth can never become more than highly probable. And to maintain that they also constituted an important, or unimportant, type of nonsense would be unplausible, to say the very least. Indeed, it will be our contention that no proposition, other than a tautology, can possibly be anything more than a probable hypothesis. And if this is correct, the principle that a sentence can be factually significant only if it expresses what is conclusively verifiable is self-stultifying as a criterion of significance. For it leads to the conclusion that it is impossible to make a significant statement of fact at all.

---

[3] This example has been used by Professor Schlick to illustrate the same point.

[4] A remark taken at random from *Appearance and Reality*, by F. H. Bradley.

[5] E.g., M. Schlick, "Positivismus and Realismus," *Erkenntnis*, Vol. I, 1930. F. Waismann, "Logische Analyse des Warscheinlichkeitsbegriffs," *Erkenntnis*, Vol. I, 1930.

[6] E.g., M. Schlick, "Die Kausalität in der gegenwärtigen Physik," *Naturwissenschaft*, Vol. 19, 1931.

SELECTION 9.2

# Sensations and Brain Processes*

*J. J. C. Smart*

[*Here, J. J. C. Smart, an early and influential adherent of identity theory, presents and then rebuts objections to identity theory.*]

It seems to me that science is increasingly giving us a viewpoint whereby organisms are able to be seen as physico-chemical mechanisms: it seems that even the behavior of man himself will one day be explicable in mechanistic terms. There does seem to be, so far as science is concerned, nothing in the world but increasingly complex arrangements of physical constituents. All except for one place: in consciousness. That is, for a full description of what is going on in a man you would have to mention not only the physical processes in his tissue, glands, nervous system, and so forth, but also his states of consciousness: his visual, auditory, and tactual sensations, his aches and pains. That these should be *correlated* with brain processes does not help, for to say that they are *correlated* is to say that they are something "over and above." You cannot correlate something with itself. You correlate footprints with burglars, but not Bill Sikes the burglar with Bill Sikes the burglar. So sensations, states of consciousness, do seem to be the one sort of thing left outside the physicalist picture, and for various reasons I just cannot believe that this can be so. That everything should be explicable in terms of physics (together of course with descriptions of the ways in which the parts are put together—roughly, biology is to physics as radio-engineering is to electromagnetism) except the occurrence of sensations seems to me to be frankly unbelievable. . . .

Why should not sensations just be brain processes of a certain sort? There are, of course, well-known (as well as lesser-known) philosophical objections to the view that reports of sensations are reports of brain-processes, but I shall try to argue that these arguments are by no means as cogent as is commonly thought to be the case.

Let me first try to state more accurately the thesis that sensations are brain processes. It is not the thesis that, for example, "after-image" or "ache" means the same as "brain process of sort X" (where "X" is replaced by a description of a certain sort of brain process). It is that, in so far as "after-image" or "ache" is a report of a process, it is a report of a process that *happens to be* a brain process. It follows that the thesis does not claim that sensation statements can be *translated* into statements about brain processes. Nor does it claim that the logic of a sensation statement is the same as that of a brain-process statement. All it claims is that in so far as a sensation statement is a report of something, that something is in fact a brain process. Sensations are nothing over and above brain processes. Nations are nothing "over and above" citizens, but this does not prevent the logic of nation statements being very different from the logic of citizen statements, nor does it insure the translatability of nation statements into citizen statements. . . .

*Remarks on identity.* When I say that a sensation is a brain process or that lightning is an electric discharge, I am using "is" in the sense of strict identity. (Just as in the—in this case necessary—proposition "7 is identical with the smallest prime number greater than 5.") . . .

I shall now discuss various possible objections to the view that the processes reported in sensation statements are in fact processes in the brain. Most of us have met some of these objections in our first year as philosophy students. All the more reason to take a good look at them. Others of the objections will be more recondite and subtle.

*Objection 1.* Any illiterate peasant can talk perfectly well about his after-images, or how things look or feel to him, or about his aches and pains, and yet he may know nothing whatever about neurophysiology. . . .

*Reply.* You might as well say that a nation of slugabeds, who never saw the morning star or knew of its existence, or who had never thought of the expression "the Morning Star," but who used the expression "the Evening Star" perfectly well, could not use

*From J. J. C. Smart, "Sensations and Brain Processes" *Philosophical Review* 68 (1959), pp. 141–156.

this expression to refer to the same entity as we refer to (and describe as) "the Morning Star." . . .

Consider lightning. Modern physical science tells us that lightning is a certain kind of electrical discharge due to ionization of clouds of water-vapor in the atmosphere. This, it is now believed, is what the true nature of lightning is. Note that there are not two things: a flash of lightning and an electrical discharge. There is one thing, a flash of lightning, which is described scientifically as an electrical discharge to the earth from a cloud of ionized water molecules. . . .

In short, the reply to Objection 1 is that there can be contingent statements of the form "A is identical with B," and a person may well know that something is an A without knowing that it is a B. An illiterate peasant might well be able to talk about his sensations without knowing about his brain processes, just as he can talk about lightning though he knows nothing of electricity.

*Objection 2.* It is only a contingent fact (if it is a fact) that when we have a certain kind of sensation there is a certain kind of process in our brain. Indeed it is possible, though perhaps in the highest degree unlikely, that our present physiological theories will be as out of date as the ancient theory connecting mental processes with goings-on in the heart. It follows that when we report a sensation we are not reporting a brain-process.

*Reply.* The objection certainly proves that when we say "I have an after-image" we cannot *mean* something of the form "I have such-and-such a brain-process." But this does not show that what we report (having an after-image) is not *in fact* a brain process. . . .

Now how do I get over the objection that a sensation can be identified with a brain process only if it has some phenomenal property, not possessed by brain processes, whereby one-half of the identification may be, so to speak, pinned down?

My suggestion is as follows. When a person says, "I see a yellowish-orange after-image," he is saying something like this: "*There is something going on which is like what is going on when* I have my eyes open, am awake, and there is an orange illuminated in good light in front of me, that is, when I really see an orange." . . .

*Objection 4.* The after-image is not in physical space. The brain-process is. So the after-image is not a brain-process.

*Reply.* This is an *ignoratio elenchi.* I am not arguing that the after-image is a brain-process, but

that the experience of having an after-image is a brain-process. It is the *experience* which is reported in the introspective report. Similarly, if it is objected that the after-image is yellowy-orange but that a surgeon looking into your brain would see nothing yellowy-orange, my reply is that it is the experience of seeing yellowy-orange that is being described, and this experience is not a yellowy-orange something. So to say that a brain-process cannot be yellowy-orange is not to say that a brain-process cannot in fact be the experience of having a yellowy-orange after-image. . . .

*Objection 5.* It would make sense to say of a molecular movement in the brain that it is swift or slow, straight or circular, but it makes no sense to say this of the experience of seeing something yellow.

*Reply.* So far we have not given sense to talk of experiences as swift or slow, straight or circular. But I am not claiming that "experience" and "brain-process" mean the same or even that they have the same logic. "Somebody" and "the doctor" do not have the same logic, but this does not lead us to suppose that talking about somebody telephoning is talking about someone over and above, say, the doctor. . . .

*Objection 6.* Sensations are private, brain processes are *public.* If I sincerely say, "I see a yellowish-orange after-image" and I am not making a verbal mistake, then I cannot be wrong. But I can be wrong about a brain-process. The scientist looking into my brain might be having an illusion. Moreover, it makes sense to say that two or more people are observing the same brain-process but not that two or more people are reporting the same inner experience.

*Reply.* This shows that the language of introspective reports has a different logic from the language of material processes. It is obvious that until the brain-process theory is much improved and widely accepted there will be no *criteria* for saying "Smith has an experience of such-and-such a sort" *except* Smith's introspective reports. So we have adopted a rule of language that (normally) what Smith says goes.

*Objection 7.* I can imagine myself turned to stone and yet having images, aches, pains, and so on.

*Reply.* . . . I can imagine that the Evening Star is not the Morning Star. But it is. All the objection shows is that "experience" and "brain-process" do not have the same meaning. It does not show that an experience is not in fact a brain process.

SELECTION 9.3

# Objectivity, Relativism, and Truth★

*Richard Rorty*

[*Here, Richard Rorty explains the doctrine known as "antirepresentationalism" and contrasts it with its opposite, "representationalism."*]

The antirepresentationalist is quite willing to grant that our language, like our bodies, has been shaped by the environment we live in. Indeed, he or she insists on this point — the point that our minds or our language could not (as the representationalist skeptic fears) be "out of touch with the reality" any more than our bodies could. What he or she denies is that it is explanatorily useful to pick and choose among the contents of our minds or our language and say that this or that item "corresponds to" or "represents" the environment in a way that some other item does not. . . .

Antirepresentationalists . . . see no way of formulating an *independent* test of accuracy of representation — of reference or correspondence to an "antecedently determinate" reality — no test distinct from the success which is supposedly explained by this accuracy. Representationalists offer us no way of deciding whether a certain linguistic item is usefully deployed because it stands in these relations, or whether its utility is due to some factors which have nothing to do with them — as the utility of a fulcrum or a thumb has nothing to do with its "representing" or "corresponding" to the weights lifted, or the objects manipulated, with its aid. . . .

This point that there is no independent test of the accuracy of correspondence is the heart of [Hilary] Putnam's argument that notions like "reference" — semantical notions which relate language to nonlanguage — are internal to our overall view of the world. The representationalists' attempt to explain the success of astrophysics and the failure of astrology is, Putnam thinks, bound to be merely an empty compliment unless we can attain what he calls a God's-eye standpoint — one which has somehow broken out of our language and our be-

liefs and tested them against something known without their aid. But we have no idea what it would be like to be at that standpoint. As Davidson puts it, "there is no chance that someone can take up a vantage point for comparing conceptual schemes [e.g., the astrologer's and the astrophysicist's] by temporarily shedding his own."[1]

From the standpoint of the representationalist, the fact that notions like representation, reference, and truth are deployed in ways which are internal to a language or a theory is no reason to drop them. The fact that we can never *know* whether a "mature" physical theory, one which seems to leave nothing to be desired, may not be entirely off the mark is, representationalists say, no reason to deprive ourselves of the notion of "being off the mark." To think otherwise, they add, is to be "verificationist," undesirably anthropocentric in the same way in which nineteenth-century idealism was undesirably anthropocentric. It is to fall under the influence of what Thomas Nagel calls "a significant strain of idealism in contemporary philosophy, according to which what there is and how things are cannot go beyond what we could in principle think about."[2] Nagel thinks that to deprive ourselves of such notions as "representation" and "correspondence" would be to stop "trying to climb outside of our own minds, an effort some would regard as insane and that I regard as philosophically fundamental."[3]

Antirepresentationalists do not think such efforts insane, but they do think that the history of philosophy shows them to have been fruitless and undesirable. They think that these efforts generate the sort of pseudoproblems which Wittgenstein hoped to avoid by abandoning the picture which held him captive when he wrote the *Tractatus*. Wittgenstein

---

[1] Donald Davidson, *Inquiries into Truth and Interpretation* (Oxford: Oxford University Press, 1984), p. 185.

[2] Thomas Nagel, *The View from Nowhere* (New York: Oxford University Press, 1986), p. 9.

[3] Ibid., p. 11.

was not insane when he wrote that book, but he was right when he later described himself as having been buzzing around inside a fly-bottle. His escape from the bottle was not . . . a matter of buzzing off in the direction of transcendental idealism, but rather of refusing any longer to be tempted to answer questions like "Is reality intrinsically determinate, or is its determinacy a result of our activity?" He was not suggesting that we determine the way reality is. He was suggesting that questions which we should have to climb out of our own minds to answer should not be asked. He was suggesting that both realism and idealism share representationalist presuppositions which we would be better off dropping.

## CHECKLIST

To help you review, here is a checklist of the key philosophers and terms and concepts of this chapter. The brief descriptive sentences summarize the philosophers' leading ideas. Keep in mind that some of these summary statements are oversimplifications of complex positions.

### Philosophers

- **C. S. Peirce** stated that "in order to ascertain the meaning of an intellectual conception one should consider what practical consequences might conceivably result by necessity from the truth of that conception, and the sum of these consequences will constitute the entire meaning of the conception."

- **William James** said that "the whole function of philosophy ought to be to find out what definite differences it will make to you and me, at definite instants of our life, if this world-formula or that world-formula be the true one."

- **John Dewey** was an instrumentalist who claimed thinking is not a search for "truth" but, rather, is aimed at solving practical problems. He thought of metaphysics as escapism.

- **Bertrand Russell** held that analysis is the key to metaphysical truth. He sought connection between "hard" data given in sensory experience and supposedly external physical objects.

- **Gottlob Frege,** a German mathematician and founder of modern mathematical logic, undertook to establish logicism independently of Russell. He is often said to have been the founder of analytic philosophy.

- **Ludwig Wittgenstein** derived a metaphysics of logical atomism from a consideration of the relationship of language and the world. He advanced the picture theory of meaning, then later rejected it.

### Key Terms and Concepts

| | |
|---|---|
| pragmatism | theoretical posits |
| instrumentalism | realism |
| spectator theory of knowledge | representationalism |
| | antirepresentationalism |
| analysis | language game |
| logicism | philosophy of mind |
| Vienna Circle | interactionist dualism |
| logical positivism | behaviorism |
| verifiability criterion of meaning | philosophical behaviorism |
| logical atomism | identity theory |
| sense-data | functionalism |
| phenomenalism | straightforward reductivist physicalism |
| incorrigible | |
| private language | |
| foundationalism | physicalist reductivism |
| naturalized epistemology | |

## QUESTIONS FOR DISCUSSION AND REVIEW

1. What does philosophical analysis do? In other words, define *philosophical analysis*.

2. What is accomplished by the use of philosophical analysis?

3. "Square circles are nonexistent things." "No squares are circles." Which of these two propositions is simpler, philosophically, and why?

4. What is the verifiability criterion of meaning?

5. "The first woman president of the United States is unmarried." Is this sentence true or false or neither? Explain why.

6. What does it mean to say there are "atomic" facts?

7. "If X might exist but we have no reason to suppose that it actually does exist, then as metaphysicians we should not concern ourselves with X." Is this true? Why or why not?

8. Apply the principle stated in the preceding question by letting X stand for God, ghosts, and space aliens.

9. Can you know that physical objects exist when no one is perceiving them?

10. Explain the logical positivists' reasons for holding that all metaphysics is meaningless.

11. "Everything doubled in size last night." Could this be true?

12. "At least in part, a thing is what is thought about it within the various contexts in which it is used." What does this mean?

13. Present some reasons for believing that a human being is not a purely physical thing.

14. If humans are purely physical things, can they have free will? Explain.

15. Does the fact that a person can have knowledge of nonmaterial things, such as the truths of mathematics, demonstrate that humans are not purely physical?

16. Assuming that it is possible to doubt the existence of physical things but not your own mental states, does that show that your mental states are not physical things?

17. "My mental states are knowable by introspection, but my brain states are not; therefore, my mental states are not brain states." Evaluate this argument.

18. Can a mind be characterized only "negatively," that is, as not divisible, as not existing in space, and so on?

19. Explain and try to resolve, in favor of dualism, the interaction problem.

20. Do mental states reduce to brain states, according to the functionalist? Explain. Do functionalists believe that the mind and mental states are nonphysical?

21. "A brain scientist could never tell from looking at my brain what I am thinking. Therefore, my thoughts are not brain states." Discuss this argument.

22. When all is said and done, which of the theories of mind discussed in this chapter do you think is the soundest, and why?

## SUGGESTED FURTHER READINGS

David Armstrong, *A Materialist Theory of the Mind* (London: Routledge & Kegan Paul, 1968). An important statement of a materialist position.

A. J. Ayer, *Language, Truth and Logic*, 2nd rev. ed. (New York: Dover, 1946). Stimulating. Ayer explains the basic positivist position in strong language.

A. J. Ayer, *Philosophy in the Twentieth Century* (London: Allen & Unwin, 1984). A partisan yet lucid account of developments in twentieth-century philosophy.

A. J. Ayer, ed., *Logical Positivism* (Glencoe, Ill.: Free Press, 1959). An important anthology that contains essays both sympathetic to and critical of analytic philosophy and positivism, as well as an excellent bibliography.

Michael Beaney, ed., *The Frege Reader* (Malden, Mass.: Blackwell, 1997). A single-volume translation of Frege's philosophical writings, with a comprehensive introduction by the editor.

David Bell and Neal Cooper, eds., *The Analytic Tradition* (Cambridge, Mass.: Blackwell, 1990). A series of essays on the nature of analytic philosophy and its place in current debate.

N. Block, *Readings in Philosophy of Psychology* (Cambridge, Mass.: Harvard University Press, 1980). A good collection of (not always easy-to-read) essays on the philosophy of mind.

C. D. Broad, *The Mind and Its Place in Nature* (New York: Humanities Press, 1951). You will not find a better introduction to the subject, though it was originally written in 1925.

Edwin A. Burtt, *The Metaphysical Foundations of Modern Physical Science: A Historical and Critical Essay* (London: Routledge & Kegan Paul, 1932). Many regard this as the most important philosophical treatise on science.

Keith Campbell, *Body and Mind* (London: Macmillan, 1970). This slender volume clearly sets forth the basic positions on this subject.

David J. Chalmers, *Philosophy of Mind* (New York: Oxford University Press, 2002). Classic reference work centering on analytic philosophy.

William Charlton, *The Analytic Ambition* (Cambridge, Mass.: Blackwell, 1991). A basic introduction for beginners to analytic philosophy.

Paul M. Churchland, *The Engine of Reason, The Seat of the Soul* (Cambridge, Mass.: Bradford, 1995). Covers the ongoing research of the neurobiological and connectionist communities and probes the social and ethical parameters of experimentation in consciousness.

Paul M. Churchland, *Matter and Consciousness* (Cambridge, Mass.: Bradford, 1984). Excellent critical introduction to philosophy of mind. Slightly more difficult than Campbell's *Body and Mind*.

Jack Stuart Crumley II, *Problems in Mind: Readings in Contemporary Philosophy of Mind* (New York: McGraw-Hill, 1999). An anthology focussing on the central issues in the current philosophy of mind.

Jonathan Dancy and Ernest Sosa, eds., *A Companion to Epistemology* (New York: Blackwell, 2001). Reference work centered on analytic philosophy.

Daniel Dennett, *Brainstorms* (Montgomery, Vt.: Bradford Books, 1978). A widely read collection that contains sometimes difficult, but always well-written and entertaining essays on the mind and psychology.

Daniel Dennett, *Consciousness Explained* (New York: Little, Brown, 1991). An important philosophical examination of consciousness. A fine piece of writing, the book can be understood by nonphilosophers.

Keith DeRose, ed., *Skepticism* (New York: Oxford University Press, 1999). A collection of contemporary thinkers on various aspects of the skeptical epistemological stance.

John Dewey, *The Quest for Certainty* (New York: Minton Balch & Company, 1929). One of Dewey's most popular works. Portrays metaphysics as a quest for certainty.

Cora Diamond, *Wittgenstein, Philosophy, and the Mind* (Cambridge, Mass.: Bradford, 1991). Considered by some to be one of the more important books on Wittgenstein in the past fifteen years.

Hans-Johann Glock, ed., *Wittgenstein, A Critical Reader* (Malden, Mass.: Blackwell, 1996). A collection of new essays on Wittgenstein. Not necessarily the easiest reading for introductory students.

J. A. C. Grayling, *Wittgenstein: A Very Short Introduction* (New York: Oxford University Press, 2001). A brief, accessible look at Wittgenstein's life as well as his early and later philosophies.

John Greco and Ernest Sosa, eds., *The Blackwell Guide to Epistemology* (New York: Blackwell, 2002). Survey articles on important topics in the theory of knowledge. Contemporary readings on the complex workings of the human mind.

Christopher Hookway, *Skepticism* (New York: Routledge, 1990). A review of the historical development of skepticism and its consequences for present-day thought and action.

John Hospers, *An Introduction to Philosophical Analysis* (Englewood Cliffs, N.J.: Prentice-Hall, 1953). This is what you should read as the next step in acquainting yourself with analytic philosophy.

Michael Huemer, *Epistemology, Contemporary Readings* (New York: Routledge, 2002). Classic and contemporary readings on major issues in epistemology.

E. D. Klemke, ed., *Contemporary Analytic and Linguistic Philosophies* (Amherst, N.Y.: Prometheus Press, 1983). An introduction to this influential twentieth-century school of thought.

Hilary Kornblith, *Naturalizing Epistemology*, 2nd ed. (Cambridge, Mass.: Bradford, 1993). An anthology of papers that consider the interaction between psychology and epistemology. Not always easy to read.

Bruce Kuklick, *A History of Philosophy in America* (New York: Oxford University Press, 2001). The interesting story of the growth of philosophy in the United States.

Jordan Lindberg, *Analytic Philosophy: Beginnings to the Present* (New York: McGraw-Hill, 2000). A well-selected anthology of readings including topics such as pragmatism, positivism, and ordinary language philosophy.

William G. Lycan, ed., *Mind and Cognition. An Anthology* (Malden, Mass.: Blackwell, 1999). A well-received collection of articles in the area of philosophy of mind.

Norman Malcolm, "Wittgenstein's Philosophical Investigations," *Philosophical Review* 47 (1956). A reasonably readable explication of important aspects of Wittgenstein's difficult work.

Louis Menard, *The Metaphysical Club* (New York: Farrar, Straus and Giroux, 2001). A readable tracing of the history of American pragmatism by way of its greatest thinkers.

Ray Monk and Anthony Palmer, *Bertrand Russell and the Origins of Analytical Philosophy* (Herndon, Va.: Thoemmes Press, 1996). A collection of essays on Russell's contributions to analytical philosophy.

P. K. Moser and A. vander Nat, *Human Knowledge: Classical and Contemporary Approaches* (New York: Oxford University Press, 1987). Excellent anthology of readings, both classical and recent.

Thomas Nagel, "What Is It Like to Be a Lot?" in *Mortal Questions* (Cambridge: Cambridge University Press, 1979). A famous essay that explains the irreducibility of conscious experiences.

V. H. Newton-Smith, *A Companion to the Philosophy of Science* (Malden, Mass.: Blackwell, 2001). A reference book covering a broad spectrum of issues concerning the philosophy of science.

John Passmore, *A Hundred Years of Philosophy* (New York: Basic Books, 1967). Excellent, readable general history from Mill on to mid-century.

D. F. Pears, *Bertrand Russell and the British Tradition in Philosophy* (New York: Random House, 1967). Traces the development of Russell's metaphysics from 1905 to 1919.

Hilary Putnam, *Realism and Reason. Philosophical Papers,* vol. 3 (London: Cambridge University Press, 1983). An important work that covers most of the current hot topics in metaphysics and epistemology, by an influential American philosopher. Putnam typically begins his essays in nontechnical language but also typically can become difficult.

Hilary Putnam, *Representation and Reality* (Cambridge, Mass.: MIT Press, 1988). The most important current controversies in the philosophy of mind are all carefully examined. Mostly very readable.

Nicholas Rescher, *American Philosophy Today and Other Philosophical Studies* (Lanham, Md.: Rowman & Littlefield, 1994). A collection of interesting essays on various topics.

Howard Robinson, ed., *Objections to Physicalism* (New York: Oxford University Press, 1993). A collection of papers, mostly nontechnical, but not introductory.

George D. Romanos, *Quine and Analytic Philosophy* (Cambridge, Mass.: Bradford, 1983). A good, brief history of analytic philosophy; fine bibliography.

Richard Rorty, *Objectivity, Relativism, and Truth, Philosophical Papers,* vol. 1 (New York: Cambridge University Press, 1991). Explains the antirepresentationalist/representationalist debate in language that will not entirely discourage a beginner in philosophy.

Bertrand Russell, *The Analysis of Mind* (London: George Allen & Unwin, 1921). From Russell's "neutral monist" phase.

Bertrand Russell, *Autobiography,* 3 vols. (London: George Allen & Unwin, 1967–1969). Candid and highly entertaining.

Bertrand Russell, "The Philosophy of Logical Atomism," in *Logic and Knowledge,* R. C. Marsh, ed. (London: George Allen & Unwin, 1956). Introductory students will find this difficult to read, but not impossible.

Gilbert Ryle, *The Concept of Mind* (New York: Barnes and Noble, 1949). An important work, very readable.

Theodore Schick, *Readings in the Philosophy of Science from Positivism to Postmodernism* (New York: McGraw-Hill, 1999). A well-selected collection of readings tracing the development of the philosophy of science.

John Searle, *Minds, Brains, and Science* (Cambridge: Harvard University Press, 1984). This short book raised hackles throughout cognitive science. Read it and find out why. The argument is very easy to follow.

John Searle, *The Rediscovery of the Mind* (Cambridge, Mass.: Bradford, 1992). A readable attack by Searle on current theories of mind.

Peter Smith and O. R. Jones, *The Philosophy of Mind* (Cambridge: Cambridge University Press, 1986). Another introductory text on this subject, with a fairly good bibliography.

Barry Stroud, *The Significance of Philosophical Scepticism* (Oxford: Clarendon Press, 1985). Sets forth some of the current issues related to skepticism.

Richard Taylor, *Metaphysics,* 3rd ed. (Englewood Cliffs, N.J.: Prentice-Hall, 1983). An easy introduction to popular metaphysical issues, including the mind–body problem and free will.

Paul Thagard, ed., *Mind Readings* (Cambridge, Mass.: Bradford Books, 1998). A selection of readings introducing important issues in cognitive science.

Mel Thompson, *Teach Yourself Philosophy of Mind* (New York: McGraw-Hill, 2002). Exploration of ideas about the mind and related topics such as memory, free will, and artistic creativity.

J. O. Urmson, *Philosophical Analysis* (London: Oxford University Press, 1956). Surveys logical atomism and logical positivism. Not easy reading for introductory students, but detailed and complete.

Geoffrey James Warnock, *English Philosophy since 1900* (New York: Oxford University Press, 1958). Only covers the first part of the twentieth century but is accurate and very easy to read.

John Weiner, *Frege* (New York: Oxford Universiy Press, 1999). A new introduction to Frege's mathematical philosophy.

Cornel West, *The American Evasion of Philosophy, a Genealogy of Pragmatism* (London: Macmillan, 1989). A critical review of American pragmatism, including such figures as James, Peirce, Dewey, Mills, Quine, and Rawls.

Michael Williams, *Groundless Belief: An Essay on the Possibility of Epistemology,* 2nd ed. (Princeton, N.J.: Princeton University Press, 1999). Written for philosophers, this book may be tough for the layperson.

But it sets forth in clear detail some of the difficulties in foundationalism.

Ludwig Wittgenstein, *Philosophical Investigations,* G. E. M. Anscombe, trans. (Malden, Mass.: Blackwell, 1998). The definitive translation of Wittgenstein's *Philosophical Investigations,* by the late G. E. M. Anscombe, another important contemporary English philosopher, a student of Wittgenstein's. Contains Wittgenstein's attack on private languages but is rather bewildering to the layperson (and to professional philosophers too). An easy introduction to Wittgenstein's philosophy is George Pitcher's *Wittgenstein, The Philosophical Investigations* (Garden City, N.Y.: Doubleday Anchor, 1966).

# Part Two
# Moral and Political Philosophy

# 10

# Moral Philosophy

Happiness, then, is something final and self-sufficient, and is the end of action. — Aristotle

Morality is not properly the doctrine how we should make ourselves happy, but how we should become worthy of happiness. — Immanuel Kant

Advice is something you never stop getting, although good, sound advice is perhaps not too common.

Most advice you get — and give — is of a practical nature: "If you want to live longer," someone will say, "you should stop smoking." Or: "If I were you, I would buy life insurance now while you are young."

But advice is not always intended to be merely practical. Sometimes it is moral advice. Someone — a friend, your minister, a relative — may suggest that you should do something not because it will be in your own best interest to do it but because doing it is *morally right*. "You should donate money to a charity," the person might say. Or: "You should be kind to animals." These suggestions express moral judgments.

**Ethics,** or moral philosophy, is the philosophical study of moral judgments — value judgments about what is virtuous or base, just or unjust, morally right or wrong, morally good or bad or evil, morally proper or improper. We say *morally* right and *morally* good and so on because terms like *right* and *good* and *proper* (and their negative correlates *wrong* and *bad* and *improper*) can be used in *nonmoral* value judgments, as when someone speaks of a bad wine or of the right or proper way to throw a pass.

Many questions can be asked about moral judgments, so ethical philosophers discuss a wide array of issues. One basic question they ask is, What *is* a moral judgment? In other words, exactly what does it mean to describe something as morally right or wrong, good or evil; what is it to say that one thing ought to be done and

## The Good Life

We view philosophy as valuable and applicable to real life. But then, we may be biased because we get paid to philosophize. Nevertheless, here is a case in favor of our view.

As you read about the moral philosophies of Plato, Aristotle, and almost every other thinker covered in Part Two, you might note their concern with the question *In what does human happiness or well-being or the good life consist?* Maybe this question is not the *central* question of ethics, but it is close to the center. Almost every philosopher we cover in this part of the book offers an alternative answer to this question. The question is also of considerable practical importance—and worth considering *now*. Ultimately, we all die, and sometimes, unfortunately, people die sooner, sometimes much sooner, than they expected. To get a clear focus on this question only to learn that it is too late to do anything about it could be a great tragedy.

Maybe you will find something in this and the next chapter to help you settle on your own definition of the good life.

another thing ought not be done? Or they might ask, What makes a moral judgment a *moral* judgment? How do moral judgments differ from other value judgments, factual assertions, and pieces of practical advice? What distinguishes reasoning about moral issues from reasoning about other things (from reasoning about the structure of matter, say, or about the qualities of good art)? These are some of the questions ethical philosophers ask.

The most important question of ethics, however, is simply, Which moral judgments are correct? That is, what is good and just and the morally right thing to do? What is the "moral law," anyway? This question is important because the answer to it tells us how we should conduct our affairs. Perhaps it is the most important question, not of ethics, but of philosophy. Perhaps it is the most important question, period.

A less obvious question of ethics, though logically more fundamental, is whether there is a moral law in the first place. In other words, do moral obligations even exist? Are there really such things as good and bad, right and wrong? And if there are, what is it that makes one thing right and another wrong? That is, what is the ultimate justification of moral standards?

In what follows we will examine some of these issues, and related questions, as they have been treated throughout the history of philosophy. However, before we begin, we need to discuss several concepts that have been important throughout the history of moral philosophy.

## SKEPTICISM, RELATIVISM, AND SUBJECTIVISM

Many beginning students in philosophy accept one or more of three important ideas about morals. The first, **ethical skepticism,** is the doctrine that moral knowledge is not possible. According to the skeptic, whether there are moral standards is not knowable, or, alternatively, if there are any moral standards, we cannot know what they are.

You should be aware that the beliefs that there is no right or wrong and that "everything is permissible" (which we encountered in the previous chapter) are not skeptical beliefs. A person who makes either of these claims implies that he or she does have moral knowledge.

Another popular idea about ethics is called **descriptive relativism,** according to which the moral standards people subscribe to are different from culture to culture. This idea might seem obviously true, but you must remember that different *practices* do not necessarily entail different *standards.* For example, it might seem that the pro-choice "culture" and the pro-life "culture" obviously have different moral standards, and perhaps they do. On the other hand, they might both accept the standard that it is wrong to kill a living person but just disagree about whether a fetus counts as a living person.

In any case, descriptive relativism is not an ethical doctrine. It says merely that people in different cultures have different *beliefs* about what is morally right and wrong. It says nothing about what *is* morally right and morally wrong. The idea that what a culture *believes* is morally right or wrong *is* morally right or wrong for people in that culture is known as **cultural relativism,** and it is a popular idea among beginning philosophy students. Many tend to think, for example, that whether or not you should act selfishly is entirely determined by whether or not your culture thinks you should act selfishly. Beginning philosophy students who are cultural relativists sometimes also advocate being accepting toward the practices of other cultures. However, it would be inconsistent for a cultural relativist to advocate being accepting toward another culture's practice if her or his own culture thought that practice was wrong.

Another relativist doctrine is known as **individual relativism,** according to which what is right or wrong is what each individual believes is right or wrong. If you hold this view, then you would have to say that nobody ever acts wrongly, provided he or she is doing what he or she thinks is right. Both individual relativism and cultural relativism are sometimes spoken of as **subjectivist** ethical philosophies, in that what is right or wrong depends entirely on what a person (i.e., a "subject") or a culture (i.e., a group of "subjects") thinks is right or wrong.

## EGOISM

**Egoism** is another popular ethical doctrine, but there are two types of egoism. First, there is **descriptive egoism,** the doctrine that in all conscious action you seek to promote your self-interest above all else. Then there is **prescriptive egoism,** the doctrine that in all conscious action you *ought* to seek your self-interest above all else. The Epicurean ethical philosophy, for example, was a version of prescriptive egoism.

Often, beginning philosophy students accept descriptive egoism as almost self-evidently true. Many also favor prescriptive egoism as an ethical philosophy. Of course we always act to further our own ends! And that is exactly what we *ought* to do, right?

Does acting ethically mean squelching devilish selfish interests in favor of more high-minded objectives? Prescriptive egoism is the idea that you ought to act in your own self-interest.

But some philosophers see a difficulty in accepting both prescriptive and descriptive egoism in that it seems *trivial* or *pointless* to tell people they *ought* to do what you think they are *going to do anyway.* That is like advising someone that she or he has a moral obligation to obey the laws of physics, or to remain visible at all times, or to occupy space, these philosophers say.

A further comment. If you find yourself subscribing to prescriptive egoism (one ought to seek one's self-interest above all else), as many do, then you should consider this: Does it make sense for you to *advocate* your own egoistic philosophy? If you ought to seek your own self-interest above all else (as prescriptive egoism says), then should you really go around telling others to seek *their* self-interest above all else? Is telling them that in *your* best interests? Might it not be better for your interests to urge others to promote the *common* good?

## HEDONISM

**Hedonism** is the pursuit of pleasure. Philosophers distinguish between the *descriptive* doctrine known as **psychological hedonism,** according to which the ultimate object of a person's desire *is* always pleasure, and the *ethical* doctrine known as **ethical hedonism,** according to which a person *ought* to seek pleasure over other things. You should remember these doctrines.

The descriptive doctrine may be plausible at first glance, but on closer inspection it appears somewhat doubtful. We do seem to seek things beside pleasure — for example, food, good health, relaxation, rest, rightness in our actions, success, friends, and many other things too. As the British moralist and clergyman Bishop Joseph Butler (1692–1752) observed, we could not seek pleasure at all unless we had desires for something other than pleasure, because pleasure consists in satisfying these desires. And then, too, "the pleasure of virtue," as Irish historian W. E. H. Lecky wrote, "is one which can only be obtained on the express condition of its not being the object sought." In other words, if your motive in acting virtuously is to obtain the pleasure that accompanies virtuous acts, then you are not being virtuous and will not get that pleasure.

As for ethical hedonism, there are two kinds: **egoistic ethical hedonism,** according to which one ought to seek his or her own pleasure over other things, and **universalistic ethical hedonism,** otherwise known as utilitarianism, according to which one ought to seek the greatest pleasure for the greatest number of people over other things.

One difficulty utilitarians face is in explaining why pleasure for *others* is something one should seek. One common answer is that only by seeking others' pleasure can you experience a full allotment of pleasure for yourself. But this answer seems to assume that one's primary ethical duty is to oneself after all.

## THE FIVE MAIN ETHICAL FRAMEWORKS

Moral philosophers these days often regard ethical or moral theories as falling into one of the five following ethical frameworks or perspectives as to what one fundamentally ought to do. We list them in no particular order and mention philosophers who provide good examples of each category, to help you understand those philosophers when you read about them in this chapter.

- First, **divine-command ethics:** What ought I to do? What God ordains I ought to do. Augustine and Aquinas are good examples.
- Second, **consequentialism:** What ought I to do? Whatever has the most desirable consequences. The Epicureans, Stoics, and utilitarians are good examples.
- Third, **deontological ethics:** What ought I to do? Whatever it is my moral duty to do (in at least some cases, regardless of consequences). Kant is a good example.
- Fourth, **virtue ethics:** What ought I to do? What the virtuous person would do. (For virtue ethics, the primary question is not, What ought I to do? but, rather, What kind of person ought I to be?) Plato and Aristotle are good examples.
- Fifth, **relativism:** What ought I to do? What my culture or society thinks I ought to do. None of the philosophers covered in this chapter are relativists (though many students are).

Sometimes *contractarianism* (or *contractualism*) is mentioned as a basic ethical theory. However, more often it is treated as a theory of social justice, the theory that principles of justice are best constructed through negotiations among impartial, informed, and rational agents. We'll discuss this idea in Chapter 11, which deals with political philosophy.

Let's now take a closer look at these five various ethical perspectives as they debuted in the history of moral philosophy.

## THE EARLY GREEKS

That moral judgments must be supported by reasons is an idea we owe to the **Sophists,** those professional teachers of fifth-century B.C.E. Greece, and to **Socrates** (c. 470–399 B.C.E.). The Sophists, who attacked the traditional moral values of the Greek aristocracy, demanded rational justification for rules of conduct, as did Socrates. Their demands, together with Socrates' skillful deployment of the dialectical method in moral discussions, mark the beginning of philosophical reasoning about moral issues.

Maybe it was not inevitable that a time came when someone would insist that moral claims be defended by reasons. When children ask why they should do something their parents think is right, they may be content to receive, and their parents content to give, the simple answer, "Because that is what is done." In some societies, evidently, values are accepted without much question and demands for justification of moral claims are not issued. In our society it is frequently otherwise, and this is the legacy of the Sophists and Socrates.

It was Socrates especially who championed the use of reason in moral deliberation and with it raised good questions about some still-popular ideas about morality, such as that good is what pleases, that might makes right, and that happiness comes only to the ruthless.

Socrates was also concerned with the meaning of words that signify moral virtues, words like *justice, piety,* and *courage.* Because a moral term can be correctly applied to various specific acts — many different types of deeds count as courageous deeds, for example — Socrates believed that all acts characterized by a given moral term *must have something in common.* He therefore sought to determine (without notable success, we are sorry to report) what the essential commonality is. Socrates' assumption that a virtue has an essential nature, an essence that may be disclosed through rational inquiry, is still made by many philosophers and is central to several famous ethical theories, including Plato's, as you will see shortly.

Socrates also assumed that any sane person who possessed knowledge of the essence of virtue could not fail to act virtuously. He thus believed that ignoble behavior, if not the result of utter insanity, is always the product of ignorance. This is also a view that Plato shared, and it has its adherents today.

### Plato

**Plato** accepted the Socratic idea that all things named by a given term, including any given moral term, share a common essential or "defining" feature. For example, what is common to all things called *chairs* (yes, we know *chair* is not a moral term, but it will illustrate the point) is that feature by virtue of which a thing qualifies as a chair. What is common to all brave deeds is that feature that qualifies them all as brave. This essential or defining characteristic Plato referred to as the **Form** of the things in question; and, for various plausible reasons, he regarded this Form as possessing more reality than the particular things that exemplified it.

For an object to be a chair, it must possess the Form *chairness.*

We talked about this in Chapter 3, but let's look into Plato's reasoning again, for this bears closely on Plato's ethics.

For a thing to be a chair, we think you must agree, it must possess that feature that qualifies a thing as a chair. That feature—let's call it *chairness*—is what Plato called the Form. And so, for a thing to qualify as a chair, it must possess chairness. Thus, the Form *chairness* must exist if anything at all is to qualify as a chair. So the Form is more fundamental and "real" than even the chair you are sitting on or any other chair.

Forms, Plato held, are not perceptible to the senses, for what the senses perceive are individual things: particular chairs, particular people, particular brave deeds, and so forth. We do not perceive the Forms through the senses. We cannot see chairness, and we cannot reach out and grasp bravery or humanity. Thus, Forms, he maintained, are known only through reason.

Further, according to Plato, the individual things that we perceive by sense are forever changing. Some things—rocks, for example—change very slowly. Other things, such as people, change a good bit more rapidly. That means that knowledge by sense perception is uncertain and unstable. Not so knowledge of the Forms. Knowledge of the Forms is certain and stable, for the objects known—the Forms—are eternal and unchanging.

Now the various Forms, Plato maintained (and here we will see what all of this has to do with ethics), constitute a *hierarchy* in terms of their inherent value or worth. It is easy enough to understand his point. For example, does not the Form *beauty* (i.e., the essence of beautiful things) seem to you to be inherently of more worth than the Form *wartness* (i.e., the essence of warts)?

At the apex of all Forms, Plato said, is the Form *goodness,* or (as it is often expressed) *the Good,* because it is the Form of highest value. Thus, for Plato, because

a. the Forms define true reality, and because
b. the Form of the Good is the uppermost of all Forms, it follows that
c. individual things are real only insofar as they partake of or exemplify this ultimate Form.

A corollary of (c) is that things are less "real" the less they partake of the Good. Another corollary is that evil is unreal. Make a mental note of this second idea. You will come across it again.

Because the Form of the Good is the source of all value and reality, Plato believed, we must strive to obtain knowledge and understanding of it. Therefore, he maintained, because (remember) Forms can be apprehended only by reason, we should govern ourselves by reason. Similarly, the state should be ruled by intellectuals, he said, but more of this in Chapter 11.

So, to summarize to this point, according to Plato, the true reality of individual things consists in the Forms they exemplify, Forms that are apprehended by reason and not by the senses, and the Form highest in value is the Form of the Good. One should, therefore, strive for knowledge of the Good and be ruled by reason.

But now consider this moral edict that Plato has in effect laid down: "Be governed by reason!" Is this not a little too abstract? Does it not fail to enjoin anything *specific* about what the individual should or should not do?

Plato would have answered "no" to both questions. The human soul, he said (a couple of thousand years before Freud proposed his analogous theory of the id, the ego, and the superego), has three different elements: an element consisting of raw appetites, an element consisting of drives (like anger and ambition), and an intellectual element (i.e., an element of thought or reason). For each of these elements there is an excellence or virtue that obtains when reason is in charge of that element, as is the case when you govern yourself by reason. When our *appetites* are ruled by reason, we exhibit the virtue of *temperance;* when our *drives* are governed by reason, we exhibit *courage;* and when the *intellect* itself is governed by reason, we exhibit *wisdom.*

Thus, Plato held, the well-governed person, the person ruled by reason, exhibits the four cardinal virtues of temperance, courage, wisdom, and "justice." How did justice get in the list? Justice is the virtue that obtains when all elements of the soul function as they should in obedience to reason.

Given Plato's understanding of the soul, the principle "Be governed by reason," which follows from the theory of Forms, dictates that you be temperate, courageous, wise, and "just." And what, in turn, *these* dictates mean more specifically was much discussed by Plato, though we will not go into the details. Further, he said, only by being virtuous—that is, by possessing these four virtues—can you have a *well-ordered soul* and thus have the psychological well-being that is true happiness. In this way Plato connected virtue with happiness, a connection we still acknowledge by saying, "Virtue is its own reward."

## Plato and Divine-Command Ethics

Plato examined the idea that what is morally right and good is determined by divine command, that is, by the edict or decree of God—a popular idea today in Western (and other) societies—and the result of that examination was a question: Is something right or good because the gods (or God) decree that it is, or is it decreed by the gods (or God) as right or good because it is right or good? (If the question interests you, you might wish to read Plato's very short dialogue *Euthyphro*.)

Some critics of "divine-command" theories of ethics argue that Plato's question puts the adherents of these theories in an awkward position. If you say that God decrees that something is good because it *is* good, then you seem to imply that God is not the ultimate authority or the ultimate source of goodness: you seem to imply that there is something beyond God that makes good things good things. But if you say that something is good because God decrees that it is good, you seem to imply that God's decrees are arbitrary; he could just as well have decreed that the thing was not good.

In short, the question implies—so it is argued—either that God's moral prescriptions are arbitrary or that God is not the ultimate source of goodness.

But is a well-ordered or "just" or virtuous soul really required for happiness? Plato did not just assert that it is and expect us to close our eyes and blindly swallow the assertion. He knew as well as anyone that exactly the opposite seems to be true: that the people who seem to be the best off often seem to be very unscrupulous. So Plato examined the matter rather carefully, especially in the *Republic*. In that dialogue, Plato has various characters explain and defend the view that the life of the person who cleverly and subtly promotes his own ends at the expense of other people is *preferable* to the life of the virtuous person. Plato (in the person of his Socrates character) does think that this view is mistaken and attempts (at considerable length) to explain what is wrong with it—this attempt actually is the main theme of the *Republic*. Whether he succeeds you may wish to consider for yourself at some point. In any case, a more powerful defense of being *unjust* and *unvirtuous* than the one Plato sets forth (and tries to refute) in the *Republic* has never been devised.

Sometimes beginning philosophy students have difficulty seeing how Plato's theories apply to their own lives. Here, though, there seems to be direct applicability. Chances are that from time to time you find yourself in situations in which, apparently, the right or proper or just or virtuous thing to do seems to conflict with the course of action you think would benefit you the most or make you the happiest. In such situations you may not be sure what to do. But Plato would say, if you think there is a conflict, you have not thought these situations through carefully enough. For Plato asserts that the virtuous course of action is the one most apt to produce your own well-being.

Of course, you may agree with Plato's conclusion, that the virtuous course of action is the one most apt to produce your own well-being, because you believe that God will reward you in an afterlife if you are virtuous here and now and punish you if you are not. Notice, though, what you are assuming if you accept this belief, namely, that virtuous activity does *not* promote its own reward (i.e., happiness) in

## The Go-for-It Philosophy of Aristippus

At about the time Plato lived in Athens, another Greek, Aristippus (435–350 B.C.E.), who lived in Cyrene, espoused an ethical doctrine quite different from Plato's. Aristippus said our lives should always be dedicated to the acquisition of as many pleasures, preferably as intense as possible, as we can possibly obtain. Even when intense pleasures lead to subsequent pain, they should still be sought, he said, for a life without pleasure or pain would be unredeemingly boring. Pleasures are best obtained, according to Aristippus, when one takes control of a situation and other people and uses them to one's own advantage.

Perhaps you know people who agree with Aristippus.

**Cyrenaicism,** which is the name of this hedonistic (pleasure-seeking) philosophy, was the historical antecedent of Epicureanism. As you can see from the text, Epicurus' pleasure-oriented philosophy is considerably more moderate than Aristippus'. Epicurus recommended avoiding intense pleasure as producing too much pain and disappointment over the long run.

*this* life. Plato, though, believed that your well-being in *this* life is best promoted by virtuous activity. (See the box "Plato and Divine-Command Ethics.")

Plato's moral philosophy is applicable in other ways. He was also very interested in such popular views (popular both then and now and perhaps forevermore) as that *goodness is the same thing as pleasure,* that *self-control is not the best way to get happiness,* and that *it is better to exploit others than to be exploited by them.* He found, when he considered these ideas carefully, that they are mistaken. So if you are tempted to agree with any of these ideas, we recommend that you read the *Republic* and another famous Platonic dialogue, the *Gorgias,* before arranging your affairs in the belief that they are true. You should also read the box "The Go-for-It Philosophy of Aristippus." We present a brief excerpt from the *Gorgias* at the end of the chapter.

### A Complete Ethical Theory

Plato's moral philosophy is often cited as a complete ethical theory.\* It

- Identifies an *ultimate source of all value* (the Form of the Good).
- Sets forth a *metaphysical justification for accepting this source as ultimate* (the theory of Forms).
- Stipulates a *fundamental moral principle* ("Be governed by reason!").
- Provides a *rationale for accepting the principle as universally binding* (the Form of the Good is the source of all that is real).
- Specifies *how knowledge of the supreme intrinsic good is obtained* (only through reasoning).

---

\*For the concept of a complete ethical theory and this analysis of Plato's ethics as a complete ethical theory, we are indebted to Professor Rollin Workman.

## Is the Objective World Value Neutral?

According to Plato, the Form of the Good is the source of all that is real. It is itself real, of course (according to Plato), and, moreover, has a reality independent of our minds. In other words, it has *objective* reality.

Many people these days are inclined to think of **objective reality**—reality as it exists outside our minds and perceptions—as morally neutral. So far as they have considered the issue at all, they regard values as subjective creations of the mind that the mind superimposes on events and objects, which things are themselves neither good nor bad, right nor wrong. It is very, very likely that this is your view.

Still, *if* it is a fact that the universe "as it is in itself" is value neutral, this is not a fact that we *discovered* in the same way that we discovered the principles of physics, chemistry, and biology. Rather, it seems to be something we just *believe*. Is this belief more correct than the view of Plato, who thought that what is good does not depend on our opinions but is set by, and is inherent in, a reality external to our minds?

If you think Plato is wrong, how would you establish that?

---

- Finally, holds that *obedience to the moral principle is motivated,* for in being governed by reason, you meet the conditions that are necessary and sufficient for the well-being of the soul and thus for true happiness. An additional motivation to accept the governance of reason, according to Plato, is that in doing so you may obtain knowledge of the Forms. This knowledge is desirable to have because the Forms are unchanging and hence eternal, which means that when you come to know them, you gain access to immortality.

For these reasons, then, Plato's ethics is said to have provided philosophers with a standard of completeness. Measure your own ethics by this standard. While you are doing so, you might wish to read the box "Is the Objective World Value Neutral?"

### Aesara, the Lucanian

A strong echo of Platonic ethical themes may be found in the work of **Aesara** [ai-SAH-ruh], a Greek philosopher from Lucania (in southern Italy), who probably lived around 350 B.C.E. Only a fragment of her original work survives. Aesara has been mentioned only rarely in textbooks in philosophy, perhaps because of the scanty remains of her work, perhaps due to other reasons. But she is interesting and worth reading.

Like Plato, Aesara was concerned with the nature of human well-being or the good life. And like Plato, she saw the key to this to be the well-ordered or virtuous or "just" soul—the balanced and harmoniously functioning psyche. Also like Plato, she saw that the well-functioning state replicates the balance and order that exists in the well-functioning soul.

Aesara's analysis of the human psyche or soul was very similar to Plato's. She thought the soul has three parts: the mind, spiritedness, and desire. The *mind* analyzes ideas and reaches decisions. *Spiritedness* is the part of the soul that gives a person the ability to carry out decisions; we might call it the will. The element of *desire* contains moral emotions such as love.

It is worth noting that the role of women in ancient Greek society was to stay at home and raise virtuous, rational offspring, the male versions of whom would run the world of government and the marketplace—the world outside the home. As a woman, Aesara was keenly aware that men, even men philosophers, sometimes tended to think that justice applies only to the world outside the home. Are two different approaches to moral philosophy needed?—one for inside the home and another for dealings with people outside the family and for public institutions? We will encounter this question again in the twentieth century, but it seems clear that Aesara's answer would be "no." All morally significant decisions, whether regarding our families or the state, should reflect the appropriate proportions of reason, willpower, and such positive affective emotions as love.

Only a fragment of Aesara's original work remains. Even though Aesara's influence on the history of philosophy was less than that of, say, Plato or Aristotle, we remain convinced of the value of including Aesara's thoughts here. A more elegant statement than Aesara's cannot be found for two ancient Greek ideas—the idea that from the well-ordered soul, the soul characterized by the harmonious functioning and proper proportioning of its elements, springs virtue, and the idea that the human soul is the model for society. If you understand the nature of the soul, you understand how society and social justice ought to be.

## Aristotle

The ultimate source of all value for Plato was the Form of the Good, an entity that is distinct from the particular things that populate the natural world, the world we perceive through our senses. This Platonic idea, that all value is grounded in a *nonnatural* source, is an element of Plato's philosophy that is found in many ethical systems and is quite recognizable in Christian ethics. But not every ethical system postulates a nonnatural source of value.

Those systems that do not are called *naturalistic ethical systems.* According to **ethical naturalism,** moral judgments are really judgments of fact about the natural world. Thus, **Aristotle,** for instance, who was the first great ethical naturalist, believed that the good for us is defined by our natural objective.

Now, what would you say is our principal or highest objective by nature? According to Aristotle, it is the attainment of happiness, for it is that alone that we seek for its own sake. And because the attainment of happiness is naturally our highest objective, it follows that happiness is our highest good.

In what does happiness, our highest good, consist? According to Aristotle, to answer we must consider the human being's function. To discover what goodness is for an ax or a chisel or anything whatsoever, we must consider its function, what it actually does. And when we consider what the human animal does, as a *human* animal, we see that, most essentially, it (a) lives and (b) reasons.

Thus, happiness consists of two things, Aristotle concluded: *enjoyment (pleasure)* and the *exercise and development of the capacity to reason.* It consists in part of enjoyment because the human being, as a living thing, has biological needs and impulses the satisfaction of which is pleasurable. And it consists in part of developing and exercising the capacity to reason, because only the human being, as distinct from other living things, has that capacity. Because this capacity differentiates humans from other living things, its exercise is stressed by Aristotle as the most important component of happiness. Pleasure alone does not constitute happiness, he insists.

The exercise of our unique and distinctive capacity to reason is termed by Aristotle *virtue*—thus Aristotle's famous phrase that happiness is activity in accordance with virtue. There are two different kinds of virtues. To exercise actively our reasoning abilities, as when we study nature or cogitate about something, is to be *intellectually* virtuous. But we also exercise our rational capacity by moderating our impulses and appetites, and when we do this, we are said by Aristotle to be *morally* virtuous.

The largest part of Aristotle's major ethical work, the *Nicomachean Ethics*, is devoted to analysis of specific moral virtues, which Aristotle held to be the **mean between extremes** (e.g., courage is the mean between fearing everything and fearing nothing). He emphasized as well that virtue is a matter of *habit:* just as an ax that is only occasionally sharp does not fulfill its function well, the human who exercises his rational capacities only occasionally does not fulfill his function, that is, is not virtuous.

Aristotle also had the important insight that a person's pleasures reveal his true moral character. "He who faces danger with pleasure, or, at any rate, without pain, is courageous," he observed, "but he to whom this is painful is a coward." Of course, we might object that he who is willing to face danger *despite* the pain it brings him is the most courageous, but this is a quibble.

Another distinction made by Aristotle is that between instrumental ends and intrinsic ends. An **instrumental end** is an act performed as a means to other ends. An **intrinsic end** is an act performed for its own sake.

For example, when we, Bruder and Moore, sat down to write this book, our end was to finish it. But that end was merely instrumental to another end—providing our readers with a better understanding of philosophy.

But now notice that the last goal, the goal of providing our readers with a better understanding of philosophy, is instrumental to a further end, namely, an enlightened society.

Notice, too, that when your teacher grades you and the other students in the class, that act is instrumental to your learning, and that end also is instrumental to an enlightened society.

As a matter of fact, all the activities in the university are aimed at producing an enlightened society. For example, your teacher may recently have received a promotion. Promotions are instrumental to effective teaching in your university, and effective teaching also is instrumental to an enlightened society.

But notice that that end, an enlightened society, is merely instrumental to another end, at least according to Aristotle, for why have an enlightened society? An enlightened society is good, Aristotle would say, because in such a society people will be able to fulfill their natural function as human beings. And therefore, he would say, when we understand what the natural function of people is, then we finally will know what is intrinsically good, good for its own sake. Then we will know what the "Good of Man" is.

So to sum up the main points, Aristotle's ethics were basically naturalistic: human good is defined by human nature. Plato's were nonnaturalistic: goodness in all its manifestations is defined by the Form of the Good. Despite these differences, Aristotle and Plato would doubtless have agreed to a great extent in their praise and condemnation of the activities of other people. Aristotle, too, deemed the cardinal moral virtues to be courage, temperance, justice, and wisdom, and both he and Plato advocated the intellectual life.

Notice, too, that Plato and Aristotle both conceive of ethics as focusing on good *character traits* of individuals—virtues—rather than on a set of *rules for actions* (such as "treat others as you would have others treat you"). In the last quarter of the twentieth century (as we shall see in Chapter 12), there was considerable interest among Anglo-American philosophers in this type of ethical theory, which is known as virtue ethics. From the point of view of virtue ethics, the fundamental ethical question is not so much, What ought one do? but, rather, What kind of person ought one be?

Despite these similarities, it must be kept in mind that the ultimate source of all moral value—that is, the Good—was for Plato a nonnatural "Form," whereas Aristotle sought to define the good for humans in terms of what the human organism in fact naturally seeks, namely, happiness.

Ever since Aristotle's time, ethical systems have tended to fall into one of two categories: those that find the supreme moral good as something that *transcends* nature and thus follow the lead of Plato, and those that follow Aristotle by grounding morality *in* human nature.

## EPICUREANISM AND STOICISM

In the Greek and Roman period following Aristotle, there were four main "schools" of philosophy: the Epicureans, the Stoics, the Skeptics, and the Neoplatonists. The Neoplatonists and the Skeptics were discussed in Part One.

The Skeptics denied the possibility of all knowledge, and this denial included moral knowledge. They said that no judgments can be established and that it does not matter if the judgments are factual judgments or value judgments (a value judgment assigns a value to something). Accordingly, they advocated tolerance toward others, detachment from the concerns of others, and caution in your own actions. Whether the Skeptics were *consistent* in advocating toleration, detachment, and caution while maintaining that no moral judgment can be established you might consider for yourself.

Epicureanism and Stoicism, which mainly concern us in this chapter, were both naturalistic ethical philosophies, and both had a lasting effect on philosophy and ethics. To this day, "taking things philosophically" means responding to disappointments as a Stoic would, and the word *epicure* has its own place in the everyday English found outside the philosophy classroom.

## Epicureanism

**Epicureanism,** the theory that personal pleasure is the highest good, began with **Epicurus** [ep-uh-KYUR-us] (341–270 B.C.E.), flourished in the second and first centuries B.C.E., spread to Rome, and survived as a school until almost the third century C.E. Though few today would call themselves Epicureans, there is no question that many people still subscribe to some of the central tenets of this philosophy. You may do so yourself. We do.

According to Epicurus, it is natural for us to seek a pleasant life above all other things; it follows, he reasoned (as perhaps you will too), that we ought to seek a pleasant life above all other things. In this sense, Epicurus was a naturalist in ethics.

The pleasant life, Epicurus said, comes to you when your desires are satisfied. And there are three kinds of desires, he maintained:

- Those that are *natural and must be satisfied* for one to have a pleasant life (such as the desire for food and shelter)
- Those that, *though natural, need not necessarily be satisfied* for a pleasant life (including, for example, the desire for sexual gratification)
- Those that are *neither natural nor necessary* to satisfy (such as the desire for wealth or fame)

The pleasant life is best achieved, Epicurus believed, by neglecting the third kind of desire and satisfying only desires of the first kind, although desires of the second kind may also be satisfied, he said, when doing so does not lead to discomfort or pain. It is *never* prudent to try to satisfy unnecessary/unnatural desires, he said, for in the long run trying to do so will produce disappointment, dissatisfaction, discomfort, or poor health. There is, surely, much that is reasonable in this philosophy, even though many people spend a good bit of time and energy trying to satisfy precisely those desires that, according to Epicurus, are both unnecessary and unnatural.

As is evident, Epicurus favored the *pleasant life* over momentary pleasures and attached great importance to the avoidance of pain as the prime ingredient in the pleasant life. It is one of the ironies of philosophy that the word *epicure* is often used to denote a fastidious person excessively fond of refined tastes—a snob. Epicurus was certainly not an epicure in this sense, for he recommended a life of relaxation, repose, and moderation, as well as avoidance of the pleasures of the flesh and passions. He would not have been fond of expensive champagne or caviar.

## The Stoics

If Epicurus was not exactly an epicure (at least in one meaning of the word), were the Stoics stoical? A stoic is a person who maintains a calm indifference to pain and suffering, and yes, the Stoics were stoical.

The school was founded by **Zeno** (334–262 B.C.E.; not the same Zeno mentioned in Chapter 2), who met his students on the *stoa* (Greek for "porch"). **Stoicism** spread to Rome and survived as a school until almost the third century C.E.

Athletes often subscribe to the idea that physical improvement requires stoical acceptance of physical discomfort.

Its most famous adherents, other than Zeno, were **Epictetus** [ep-ik-TEET-us] (60–117 c.e.), the Roman statesman Cicero (106–43 b.c.e.), and Marcus Aurelius (121–180 c.e.), the Roman emperor.

Like the Epicureans, the Stoics believed that it is only natural for a person to seek a pleasant life and that therefore a person ought to seek such a life. But the Stoics were much influenced by the Cynics (see the box on Diogenes), who went *out of their way* to find hardship. The Stoics saw that the Cynics, by actively pursuing hardship, acquired the ability to remain untroubled by the pains and disappointments of life. The Stoics thought there was some sense in this. It occurred to them that untroubledness or serenity is a desirable state indeed.

The Stoics, however, more than the Cynics, had a *metaphysical justification* for their ethics. All that occurs, the Stoics believed, occurs in accordance with natural law, which they equated with reason. **Natural law,** they said, is the vital force that activates or (as we might say) energizes all things. It follows that

1. Whatever happens is the inevitable outcome of the logic of the universe.
2. Whatever happens, happens with a reason and therefore is for the best.

So, according to the Stoic philosophy, you can do nothing to alter the course of events because they have been fixed by the law of nature. Do not struggle against the inevitable, the Stoics said. Instead, understand that what is happening is for the best, and accept it.

If you are wise, according to the Stoics, you will approach life as an actor approaches his or her part. You will realize that you have no control over the plot or assignment of roles, and therefore you will distance yourself psychologically from

## Diogenes the Cynic

According to the **Cynics,** who were fiercely individualistic, the wise person avoids even the most basic comforts and seeks total self-reliance by reducing all wants to a minimum and by forgoing any convenience or benefit offered by society. The most famous Cynic, the fourth-century B.C.E. philosopher **Diogenes** [dy-AH-juh-neez], is said to have dressed in rags and lived in an empty tub and even to have thrown out his drinking cup when he observed a child drinking from his hands. Alexander the Great, who admired Diogenes, is said to have made his way to the latter and announced that he would fill Diogenes' greatest need. Diogenes replied that he had a great need for Alexander to stop blocking his sunlight.

Diogenes is also reported to have masturbated in public while observing that it was too bad that hunger could not be relieved in similar fashion merely by rubbing your stomach. His point in part was simply to flout conventions, but it was apparently also to contrast sexual needs with the need for food.

According to another story, Diogenes visited the home of a wealthy man. The man asked Diogenes to avoid spitting on the floor or furnishings because the home was expensively appointed. Diogenes responded by spitting in the man's face and commented that it was the only worthless thing in the room.

Whether these stories are true or not, the indifference to material things that they portray was appreciated by the Stoics. Yet even though the Stoics saw the advantages to scaling back needs in the manner of the Cynics, they were not nearly so flamboyant in what they said and did. The Cynics were often willing to do or say something just to shock people.

Incidentally, as the word is most commonly used today, a cynic is one who sneers at sincerity, helpfulness, and other virtuous activity as inspired by ulterior motives. It is clear how the word acquired this meaning, given the contempt the Cynics had for traditional institutions and practices.

---

all that happens to the character you play. Does the character you play grow ill in the play? Well, you will *act* the part to the best of your ability, but you certainly will not permit yourself to suffer. Do your friends die in the play? Do you die? It is all for the best because it is dictated by the plot.

Now perhaps you are thinking, Well, if I cannot control what happens to me, then how on earth can I control my attitude about what happens? If what happens is inevitable, then what happens to my attitudes is inevitable, too, right? Nevertheless, this was the Stoics' doctrine: *You can control your attitude. Remain uninvolved emotionally in your fate, and your life will be untroubled.*

The Stoic philosophy also had a political ethic according to which the Stoic had a duty to serve other people and respect their inherent worth as equals under natural law. So the Stoics thought that, although you should seek the untroubled life for yourself, your ethical concerns are not limited to your own welfare. Whether this social component of Stoicism is consistent with a philosophy of emotional noninvolvement, acceptance of the natural order, and seeking tranquility for yourself may be questioned, of course. In fact, whether a philosophy of self-interest is compatible with concern for the common good is one of the most important questions of ethics, and you know quite well that this is a very live issue even today.

Let's summarize this section: According to the Epicureans, one's ultimate ethical objective is to lead the pleasant life through moderate living. According to the

Stoics, the objective is to obtain the serene or untroubled life through acceptance of the rational or natural order of things while remembering that one is obligated to be of service to one's fellow creatures. Stoicism in particular had an impact on Christian thought, primarily through the philosophy of St. Augustine, to whom we shall turn next.

One of the selections at the end of this chapter is from Epictetus, among the most famous of Stoics. Epictetus also is unusual among philosophers in that he was sold as a slave when a child but was given an education and later freed, thereafter becoming an influential teacher of philosophy. As you might expect from what we have said about Stoicism and Epicureanism, the two philosophies are very similar (even though Epictetus thought he was recommending a way of life quite different from that of the Epicureans).

## CHRISTIANIZING ETHICS

Let us next turn to the way the Christian religion shaped the ancient idea of ethics and to the figure most responsible for that transformation.

### St. Augustine

The greatness of **St. Augustine** (354–430 C.E.) lay in this: he helped give Christianity philosophical weight and substance.

Augustine found philosophical justification for Christianity in the metaphysics of Plato, as reinterpreted by the Neoplatonist Plotinus (204–270 C.E.). Christianity rests on the belief in a transcendent God, and with the assistance of Platonic metaphysics, St. Augustine was able to make philosophically intelligible to himself the concept of a *transcendent realm,* a realm of being beyond the spatiotemporal universe that contains (or is) the source of all that is real and good. He also saw in Platonic and Neoplatonic doctrines the solution to the *problem of evil.* This problem can be expressed in a very simple question: How could evil have arisen in a world created by a perfectly good God?

One solution to this problem that Augustine considered was that evil is the result of a creative force other than God, a *force of darkness,* so to speak. But isn't there supposed to be just one and only one Creator? That is what Augustine believed, so this solution was not acceptable.

For Plato, remember, the Form of the Good was the source of all reality, and from this principle it follows that all that is real is good. Thus, given Plato's principle, evil *is not real.* St. Augustine found this approach to the problem of evil entirely satisfactory. Because evil is not something, it was not created by God.

This theory of evil is plausible enough as long as you are thinking of certain "physical" evils, such as blindness or droughts (though others, such as pain, seem as real as can be). Blindness, after all, is the absence of sight, and droughts are the absence of water.

Unfortunately, however, the absence theory does not plausibly explain *moral* evil, the evil that is the wrongdoing of men and women. How did Augustine account for moral evil? His explanation of moral evil was a variation of another idea of Plato's, the idea that a person never knowingly does wrong, that evil actions are the result of ignorance of the good, of misdirected education, so to say. But Augustine added a new twist to this idea. Moral evil, he said, is not exactly a case of misdirected *education* but, instead, a case of misdirected *love*. This brings us to the heart of Augustine's ethics.

For Augustine, as for the Stoics, a natural law governs all morality, and human behavior must conform to it. But for Augustine this is not an impersonal rational principle that shapes the destiny of the cosmos. The Augustinian natural law is, rather, the eternal law of God as it is written in the heart of man and woman and is apprehended by them in their conscience; and the eternal law is the "reason and will of God."

Thus, the ultimate source of all that is good, for Augustine, is God, and God alone is intrinsically good. Our overriding moral imperative is therefore to love God. The individual virtues are simply different aspects of the love of God.

Augustine did not mean that you must love *only* God. He meant that, although there is nothing wrong with loving things other than God, you must not love them as if they were good in and of themselves, for *only God is intrinsically good.* To love things other than God as if they were inherently good — for example, to love money or success as if these things were good in and of themselves — is *disordered* love: it is to turn away from God, and moral evil consists in just this disordered love.

Now do not let any of this make you think that Augustine was unconcerned with happiness, for as a matter of fact he did indeed think we should seek happiness. But happiness, he argued, consists in having all you want and wanting no evil. This may seem to be an odd notion at first, but when you think about it, it is by no means absurd. In any event, the only conceivable way to have all you want and to want no evil, Augustine thought, is to make God the supreme object of your love.

So, for Augustine, moral evil arises when man or woman turns away from God. Thus, *God* is not the creator of moral evil; it is *we* who create evil. But does it not then follow that *we* can create good? No, for God, remember, is the source of all that is good. We can do good only *through* God, Augustine said.

In sum, Augustine borrowed a theme from Plato by maintaining that physical evil can always be explained as the absence of something, and his concept of moral evil as arising from misdirected love can be viewed as a variation of Plato's idea of moral evil as ignorance of the good. In this way, Augustine thought he had solved the problem of evil without doing damage to principles of Christian faith.

One other aspect of Augustine's moral philosophy must be emphasized. According to Augustine, our highest good, or virtue, consists in loving and having God. By contrast, sin is distorted or misdirected or disordered love. So virtue and sin, according to Augustine, are *conditions of the soul.* What counts, for Augustine, is living out of love for God; doing supposedly good deeds is of *secondary* importance. When it comes to appraising a person's moral worth, therefore, what matters is not the person's accomplishments but, rather, the *state of mind* from which the person acts. We shall see that this idea — that a person's intent is what matters morally — came to play an important role in moral philosophy.

## St. Hildegard of Bingen

Augustine was the last of the great late ancient philosophers. Between the sixth century and the eleventh, Europe went through the Dark Ages, as we discussed in Chapter 5. **Hildegard** (1098–1179) was a light at the end of the tunnel. Her ethical writings typify the beginning of a period of religious mysticism that never came to a complete end: religious mysticism just went out of fashion with the onslaught of rationalism beginning with Descartes (see Chapter 6). Mysticism, we perhaps should mention, is belief in (or experience of) a form of higher, spiritual, mystical realm often found in trances or dreams.

Hildegard was unquestionably an important figure in the history of philosophy (see the Profile on her). It is true that she and other religious mystical philosophers are usually called "theologians," but what they have to say is important for both ethics and moral epistemology. They provided theories of the nature of moral knowledge.

For mystical philosophers, mystical experience provides as certain a form of knowledge as pure rational introspection ever could. Their mystical experiences often take the form of visions and sometimes take the form of ideas, thoughts, and even whole books that seemingly are dictated directly from some divine source during these experiences. We are not going to assess the validity of such claims here; we are just going to reproduce and talk about their contents.

In one of her books, Hildegard listed thirty-five vices and their opposite virtues. This kind of list of opposites is a traditional format for talking about virtue and vice and dates back to Pythagoras. One vice, *Immoderation* (lack of moderate desires), is opposed to the virtue *Discretion* (keeping things within appropriate bounds). Hildegard describes Immoderation in the following allegory:

> This one is just like a wolf. She is furiously cunning, in hot pursuit of all evils, without distinction. With flexed legs, she crouches, looking in all directions, in such a way that she would devour anything she could snatch. She has a tendency to anything low-grade, following the worst habits of her peculiar mind. She considers every empty, worthless thing.

Now before you jump to conclusions about this medieval Benedictine nun, before you dismiss her views on virtue and vice as narrow and constricted, take a look at her accounts of human sexuality. In these excerpts from her philosophy of medicine in *Causa et Curae (Causes and Cures)*, she gives the following accounts of what she considered to be healthy male and female sexuality:

> There are some men showing much virility, and they have strong and solid brains. The wind also which is in their loins has two tents to its command, in which it blows as if into a chimney. And these tents surround the stem of all manly powers, and are helpers to it, just like small buildings placed next to a tower which they defend. Therefore, there are two, surrounding the stem, and they strengthen and direct it so that the more brave and allied, they would attract the wind and release it again, just like two bellows which blow into a fire. When likewise they erect the stem in its manliness, they hold it bravely and thus at a later time the stem blossoms into a fruit.

# PROFILE: St. Hildegard of Bingen (1098–1179)

Hildegard was born at the end of the eleventh century in the Rhine River valley in Germany. She was the tenth child and was therefore "tithed" to God; at age seven or eight, she was sent to live with a group of women in a hermitage that eventually became the Benedictine convent of Disibodenberg. Hildegard learned Latin and studied the Bible, and she read the philosophical works of early church fathers, including St. Jerome and St. Augustine.

Even as a child, Hildegard experienced mystical visions. By the time Hildegard had been head of the convent at Disibodenberg for three years, God commanded her, during one of these visions, to begin writing them down and to teach others their content. This put Hildegard in a difficult position because women were considered by the church as well as by society to have no religious, theological, or philosophical authority. But the Bishop of Mainz (Germany) was impressed by her writings and convinced Pope Eugene III to consider them. The Pope was convinced that the visions were genuine messages from God and had part of Hildegard's messages read to the bishops, who had come from all over Europe to attend a conference called the Synod of Trier during the winter of 1147–1148.

Hildegard and her little convent were now better known than the adjoining monastery. As Hildegard's fame spread, more and more women flocked to her convent. When the monks at the monastery refused to give the nuns the additional living quarters and library space they needed, Hildegard moved the convent. The monks, who controlled the dowries of the nuns, tried to retain the money and valuables. But Hildegard had some power now and effectively convinced the bishops that the monks were obligated to turn the sizable dowries over to her. These funds and artifacts were needed to finance the construction of the new convent at Bingen and to provide support for her nuns. She was a formidable champion for the education of women, which at that time meant establishing convents (she founded two) where ancient copies of philosophical and religious texts were hand-copied by nuns who had been taught to read Latin.

Hildegard was a prolific writer. She wrote books on natural science and on medicine (she is credited with developing the theory that disease can be transmitted by dirty water—resulting in the construction of massive sewage systems in Germany), wrote music (recently released on CD!), and wrote lengthy works of religious philosophy that she had lavishly illustrated with replications of the visions upon which they were based.

She was a very influential thinker and traveled and "preached" the meaning of her visions throughout Germany. She was regularly consulted by a succession of four popes, and her many correspondents included two emperors, a king, and two queens. Hildegard lived to a ripe old age despite a lifetime of recurrent illnesses and the hardships of extended preaching tours.

And:

> Pleasure in a woman is compared to the sun which caressingly, gently, and continuously fills the earth with its heat, so that it can bear fruits, since if it would heat the earth more harshly in its constancy, it would hurt the fruits more than it would produce them. And so pleasure in a woman caressingly and gently, but nevertheless continuously, would have heat so that she can conceive and produce fruit. For when pleasure surges forth in a woman, it is lighter in her than it is in a man.

Clearly, sexual pleasure is not on this nun's list of vices.

## Heloise and Abelard

An important thinker who lived at the same time as Hildegard was the French abbess **Heloise** [HEL-oh-eez] (1100–1163). Heloise, like Hildegard, was concerned with virtue and vice, although Heloise was especially concerned with a specific virtue.

For Heloise, philosophy was life. If you believed in the truth of a theory of morality, you lived according to its principles. End of story. Heloise's writings on moral philosophy are found in her *Problemata* (Problems) and *Epistolae* (Letters), written when Heloise was in her thirties and all addressed to **Peter Abelard** (1079–1142), another major figure in the history of ethical philosophy and the most important logician of his time. The famous love story of Abelard and Heloise is explained in the box "The Truth about Heloise and Abelard."

The ethics of Heloise has two primary components. The first component, adapted from the Roman Stoic philosopher Cicero, places high value on the virtue *Disinterested Love*. True love for another, whether or not sexual, is completely unselfish and asks nothing, Heloise believed. The lover loves the beloved for who the beloved is. A true lover supports the beloved in achieving his goals and realizing his highest moral potential. In an ideal loving relationship, the beloved has reciprocal feelings for the lover. He loves her for herself, for who she is. He aspires to help her realize her highest moral potential and the fulfillment of her goals. He has no selfish desires.

The other major component of Heloise's moral philosophy concerns the **morality of intent,** which she derived basically from Abelard's own teachings. Think back to the Augustinian theory: it is not *what you do* that matters but, rather, the *state of mind* with which you do it (virtue is essentially a matter of having a mind that is disposed to do right). This theory was accepted throughout the Dark Ages and into the Middle Ages. The one who explored this theory most carefully prior to St. Thomas Aquinas was Abelard.

Abelard drew a distinction between moral defects or imperfections and other defects or imperfections of the mind, such as being stupid or having a bad memory. Moral defects dispose you to do what you should not do — or not do what you should do. He also drew a distinction between moral defects and sin. Sin is "contempt of God" — failing to do or renounce what we should.

Armed with these distinctions, Abelard argued that sin does not consist in *acting* on evil desires. In fact, it does not even consist in *having* evil desires. Sin consists instead in *consenting* to act on evil desires. Further, a wrongful act — an act that ought not be done, such as killing someone — can be committed without an evil will, in which case, although the act is wrong, the person who acts is not morally reprehensible.

Thus, Abelard's position is that virtue consists not in having no evil desires but in not consenting to act on them. And "the evil will itself, when restrained, though it may not be quenched, procures the palmwreath for those who resist it."

Heloise, too, accepted this theory: "In a wicked deed, rectitude of action depends not on the effect of the thing but on the affections of the agent, not on what is done but with what dispositions it is done."

This conception of ethics certainly played an important role in the relationship between Abelard and Heloise. Heloise argued that by voluntarily marrying Abelard

# The Truth about Heloise and Abelard

Heloise (1100–1163) was a French philosopher and poet who received an early education at the Benedictine convent of Argenteuil. By the time she was sixteen years old, she was known as the most learned woman in France. Heloise's uncle Fulbert, who was her guardian and also a canon at Notre Dame, hired an unordained cleric named Pierre Abelard (1079–1142) to teach Heloise philosophy.

The traditional literature tends to describe Heloise and Abelard's relationship as one of the great love affairs of all time, right up there with Romeo and Juliet. Now, that is true to a certain extent. Heloise certainly fell in love with her philosophy teacher — but she refused to have sex with him.

Abelard acknowledged that Heloise verbally refused to have sex and physically fought him off. In his words, "I frequently forced your consent (for after all you were the weaker) by threats and blows." Or, as we might say today if he were brought up on charges: on some occasions he beat her and raped her, and on other occasions he threatened to beat her again if she did not stop resisting.

Heloise became pregnant. Abelard offered to marry her. Heloise refused. As usual, Abelard would not take no for an answer. As her due date came near, he took her to his sister's farm in the country, where she gave birth. They named their son Astrolabe (after an astronomical instrument). Abelard convinced Heloise to marry him so that their son would not be a bastard. You see, illegitimate children could not be baptized back then, so if Heloise had not married Abelard, she would have been condemning their son to an eternity in limbo.

Now, saving your baby from eternal limbo might well be enough to make you marry someone who, incidentally, had already become an important medieval philosopher. But it is important, if you are going to understand Heloise's moral philosophy, to know about the other sordid details of their personal life. (Unfortunately, there are more.)

When the happy couple returned to Paris (leaving the baby at the farm), they lied to Uncle Fulbert about having gotten married. If the story got out that Abelard was married, Heloise knew, he would not be permitted to continue studying for the priesthood. The Cathedral School of Notre Dame,

Abelard and Heloise.

where Abelard taught, was turning into the University of Paris. It would be the first institution of higher learning in France (the second in Europe) to accept students who were not studying to be priests.

Heloise thought it would be a waste of Abelard's talents for him to miss out on this new experiment in education: a university. Worse, Heloise would feel responsible for keeping Abelard from fulfilling his ambitions.

Fulbert, though, was no fool. He figured things out and announced that Abelard had gotten married. Heloise tried to protect Abelard by denying the marriage, so Uncle Fulbert started mistreating Heloise (who was living at his house). To make it appear as if Heloise were not lying, Abelard ordered her to return to the convent and become a nun, which she did. At this point, Uncle Fulbert, who evidently was not given to halfway measures, hired thugs to castrate Abelard. (Heloise, who was in Argenteuil at the convent, did not hear about this for years.) But now that having sex with Heloise was permanently out of the question, Abelard sought final ordination as a priest. He set up a convent called the Paraclete and made Heloise its abbess. For decades, she never knew why.

she would have been the cause of Abelard's being barred from final ordination to the priesthood. She did not want to be morally responsible for that outcome. She felt he forced and tricked her into marrying him and that this was a consequence of her pregnancy, for which she was not morally responsible. Abelard's *Historica Calamitatum* (Story of my calamities), as well as Heloise's letters to Abelard, insists that she never agreed to have sex with him: he beat and raped her. She would not accept moral responsibility for the pregnancy because she had no evil intent to seduce him.

But because they actually were married, Abelard could order Heloise to enter a convent. After she did so, Abelard had almost no contact with her. Heloise did not understand why Abelard ignored her letters nor why he ignored the physical and spiritual welfare of her nuns. Decades later, she read his book and learned about his castration. She put two and two together.

Heloise might have loved Abelard in this ideal, disinterested type of love, but it was a one-way street. Although she loved him for himself and expressed that love by helping him achieve his goals (priesthood and a job as a philosopher at the emerging university), his love for her was predominantly sexual. After he was no longer able to have sex, she realized, Abelard had made her head of her own convent. Heloise had obeyed Abelard (who was both her husband and her religious superior), running the convent and teaching the nuns. All those years, Heloise had lived according to the moral theory she thought Abelard shared, loving him unselfishly, for himself.

## St. Thomas Aquinas

Augustine fashioned a philosophical framework for Christian thought that was essentially Platonic. He found many Platonic and Neoplatonic themes that could be given a Christian interpretation and thus is sometimes said to have Christianized Plato. Eight centuries later, **St. Thomas Aquinas** [uh-QUINE-nuss] (1225–1274), in a somewhat different sense, Christianized the philosophy of Aristotle. Aquinas' task was perhaps the more difficult of the two, for the philosophy of Aristotle, with its this-worldly approach to things, was less congenial to a Christian interpretation. Thus, it is customary to speak of Aquinas as having *reconciled* Aristotelianism with Christianity. In Aquinas' ethical philosophy, this amounted by and large to accepting both Christianity and the philosophy of Aristotle wherever that could be done without absurdity.

Aristotle said that the good for each kind of thing is defined with reference to the function or the nature of that kind of thing and is in fact the goal or purpose of that kind of thing. In the case of humans, goodness is happiness. Aquinas agreed. The natural (moral) law, which is God's eternal law as it is applied to man on earth, is apprehended by us in the dictates of our conscience and practical reasoning, which guide us to our natural goal, happiness on earth.

But there is also, according to Aquinas, an eternal, atemporal good — namely, happiness everlasting. The law that directs us to that end is God's divine law, which the Creator reveals to us through his grace.

Thus, the natural law of Aquinas is the law of reason, which leads us to our natural end insofar as we follow it. The **divine law** is God's gift to us, revealed through his grace. Therefore, according to Aquinas, there are two sets of virtues: the "higher" virtues of faith, love, and hope; and the natural virtues, such as fortitude and prudence, which are achieved when the will, directed by the intellect, moderates our natural drives, impulses, and inclinations. And Aquinas, like Aristotle, thought of the virtues as matters of character or habit — in Aquinas' view, the habit of acting according to the provisions of natural law.

Although Aquinas' ethics are thus a type of virtue-ethics, he does treat the moral goodness of actions. When evaluating an act, and only voluntary acts are subject to moral evaluation, we must consider not only what was done but also why it was done and the circumstances under which it was done.

Now suppose someone does something, or refrains from doing it, because the person's conscience tells him or her that this would be the morally proper thing to do or refrain from doing. And suppose further that in this case the individual's conscience is mistaken. Yes, an erring conscience is possible, according to Aquinas, despite the fact that it is through conscience that we become aware of natural law. In such a case, if the person acts as he or she honestly thinks is morally right, and the mistake in thinking is due to involuntary ignorance on the person's part, the person has not really sinned, according to Aquinas.

Aquinas' ethical system is complete (in the sense explained earlier in this chapter with regard to Plato), detailed, and systematic, and it is difficult to convey this in this brief summary. Aquinas treats highly general and abstract principles such as the ultimate objective of human existence, the nature of goodness, and the sources of action and also applies these principles to specific and concrete moral questions.

## HOBBES AND HUME

You have seen that the naturalism found in Aristotle's ethics and the nonnaturalistic ethics of Plato, with its conception of a transcendental source of ultimate value, flowed in separate streams through the philosophy of the centuries until the time of Aquinas. If it is not quite true to say that Aquinas channeled the waters from each of these two streams into a common bed, it may at least be said that he contrived to have them flow side by side, though in separate channels.

But the next philosopher we wish to discuss, **Thomas Hobbes** (1588–1679), drew exclusively from the Aristotelian channel. This is not surprising, for Hobbes was one of the first philosophers of the modern period in philosophy, a period marked by the emergence of experimental science, in which once again nature itself was an object of study, just as it had been for Aristotle. (You should be aware, nevertheless, that Hobbes, reacting to the Aristotelianism of his Oxford tutors, had harsh things to say about Aristotle.)

### Hobbes

Hobbes's metaphysics was a relentless materialism. All that exists, he said, are material things in motion. Immaterial substance does not exist. There is no such thing as the nonphysical soul. Thoughts, emotions, feelings — all are motions of the mat-

## Hobbes and the Beggar

The story is told of Hobbes that he was asked by a clergyman why he was giving alms to a beggar.

"Is it because Jesus has commanded you to do so?" the latter asked.

"No," came Hobbes's answer.

"Then why?"

"The reason I help the man," said Hobbes, "is that by doing so I end my discomfort at seeing his discomfort."

One moral that might be drawn from the story is that even the most altruistic and benevolent actions can be given an egoistic interpretation. Why did Hobbes help the beggar? To relieve his own discomfort. Why do saints devote their lives to relieving the suffering of others? Because it brings them pleasure to do so. Why did the soldier sacrifice his life to save his comrades? To end the distress he felt at thinking of his friends' dying — or maybe even because it pleased him to think of others praising him after his demise.

In short, because those who act to relieve their own discomfort or to bring pleasure to themselves are acting for their own self-interest, all of these seemingly altruistic actions can be interpreted egoistically.

Are you convinced?

Well, if you are, you should know that many philosophers are uncomfortable with this egoistic analysis of altruistic behavior. After all (they argue), it brings the saint pleasure to help others only if the saint is genuinely motivated to help others, right? Thus, if egoism is equated with the doctrine that we are never motivated to help others, it is false. If it is equated with the doctrine that we only act as we are motivated to act, it is true, but not particularly interesting.

ter within the brain, caused by moving things outside the brain. Even our reasoning and volition are purely physical processes.

As for values, according to Hobbes the words *good* and *evil* simply denote that which a person desires or hates. And Hobbes, like Aristotle, the Epicureans, the Stoics, and Aquinas, believed that one has a natural "end" or objective toward which all activity is directed. Hobbes specified this object of desire as the preservation of one's life. One seeks personal survival above all other things, he held. Hobbes also said that one has a "natural right" to use all means necessary to defend oneself or otherwise ensure one's survival.

Thus, Hobbes was a descriptive egoist, in the sense we explained earlier in this chapter. That is, he believed that in all conscious action one seeks to promote one's self-interest (for Hobbes this meant seeking survival) above all else. A story is reported in the box "Hobbes and the Beggar" that Hobbes was asked by a clergyman why he was giving alms to a beggar; Hobbes reportedly said he did so to end his own discomfort at seeing the beggar's discomfort. Beginning students in philosophy often are tempted to give a similar "selfish" analysis of even the most apparently unselfish actions; a difficulty in that idea is explained in the box.

Was Hobbes also a prescriptive egoist? That is, did he also think that one *ought* to seek to promote one's self-interest above all else? In general, Hobbes did not attempt to determine how people ought to behave in some absolute sense; he seems intent on describing how they ought to behave *if* they want best to secure their natural objective. A question he left for subsequent philosophers, and one that has not been resolved to this day, is this: If the universe is material, can there really *be* absolute values? Do good and evil, justice and injustice, exist in some *absolute* sense, or must they be regarded, as Hobbes so regarded them, as expressions of desires or the products of human agreements?

## Cold-Blooded Murder

A fundamental principle of Hume's philosophy is that moral judgments are not the offspring of reason.

A consideration that might favor Hume's thesis is that we tend to think of particularly heinous deeds — execution-style murders, for example — as "cold-blooded" and "heartless," not as "irrational." This is an indication that we view the murderer as lacking in *feeling* rather than as deficient in *reason*.

Is it hard to believe that an absolutely brilliant mind could commit murder? We think not. But is it hard to believe that someone with normal sensibilities could commit murder? We think that it is. These considerations favor Hume's principle.

Hobbes's major work, *Leviathan,* is a classic in moral and political philosophy and encompasses as well metaphysics, epistemology, ethics, and psychology. It secured for Hobbes a prime-time place in all histories of Western thought.

## Hume

Hobbes maintained that the idea of incorporeal or immaterial substance was a contradiction in terms, but he denied being an atheist. Nevertheless, he certainly did not rest his ethics on the authority of the Church. And although most of the major philosophers of the modern period shrank from Hobbes's extreme materialism, they, too — most of them — sought to discover the basic principles of morality elsewhere than in Scripture. Some, such as Locke, though believing that these principles are decreed by God, held, like Hobbes, that they are discoverable — and provable — by reason.

But in the eighteenth century, **David Hume** (1711–1776) argued with some force that moral principles are neither divine edicts nor discoverable by reason. Hume's general position regarding God, as we shall see in Part Three, was that the order in the universe does offer some slight evidence that the universe has or had a creative force remotely analogous to human intelligence. But we certainly cannot affirm anything about the moral qualities of the creator, he held; and we cannot derive guidelines for our own actions from speculating about his (its) nature. Christianity Hume regarded as superstition.

### Value Judgments Are Based on Emotion, Not Reason

Hume held likewise that moral judgments are not the "offspring of reason." Scrutinize an act of murder as closely as you can, he said. Do you find anything in the *facts of the case* that reveal the act is morally wrong? The *facts*, he said, are simply that one person has terminated the life of another in a certain way at a particular time and place. Reasoning can disclose how long it took for death to occur, whether the victim suffered great pain, what the motives of the killer were, as well as the answers to many other factual questions such as these. But it will not show the *moral wrongfulness* of the act. The judgment that an act is immoral, Hume maintained, comes not from reason but from *emotion*. Perhaps this idea has occurred to you as well. For an example, see the box "Cold-Blooded Murder."

It is the same, Hume believed, with all value judgments. Is the judgment that a portrait is beautiful founded on reason? Of course not. Reason can disclose the chemical composition of the paints and canvas, the monetary value of the work, and many similar factual things. But whether the portrait is beautiful is an issue that cannot be settled by reason.

Thus, for Hume, moral judgments, and all value judgments, are based on emotion. Actions that we find morally praiseworthy or blameworthy create within us feelings of pleasure or displeasure, respectively. Now, obviously, these feelings are different in kind from aesthetic pleasures and pleasures of the palate. Humans clearly have a capacity for moral pleasure as well as for other types of pleasure: we are *morally sensitive creatures*. Behavior that pleases our moral sensibilities elicits our approval and is deemed good, right, just, virtuous, and noble. Behavior that offends our moral sense is deemed bad, wrong, unjust, base, and ignoble.

## Benevolence

But just what is it about behavior that elicits our moral approval? *What do virtuous, good, right, and noble acts have in common?* Hume's answer was that the type of act we deem morally praiseworthy is one taken by an agent *out of concern for others*. The act that pleases our moral sensibilities is one that reflects a *benevolent character* on the part of the agent, he said. By "agent," philosophers mean the person who did the act.

Why does benevolence bring pleasure to us when we witness or read about or contemplate it? A cynical answer is that we imagine ourselves as benefiting from the benevolent activity, and imagining this is pleasant. Do you get a warm glow when you read about someone coming to the aid of a fellow person? Well, according to the cynical view, that is because you picture yourself on the receiving end of the exchange.

But this cynical theory is unnecessarily complex, said Hume. The reason you get that pleasant feeling when you read about or see someone helping someone else is that you *sympathize* with others. It just plainly upsets a normal person to see others suffering, and it pleases a normal person to see others happy. True, there are people who suffer from the emotional equivalent of color blindness and lack the capacity to sympathize with others. But these people are not the norm. The normal human being is a sympathetic creature, maintained Hume.

This aspect of Hume's moral philosophy may well have some significance for us today. On one hand, we tend to believe that you should care for others but, on the other hand, that you must also certainly look out for yourself. And we are inclined to think that there is a problem in this because self-concern and other-concern seem mutually exclusive. But if Hume is correct, they are not. Looking out for your own interests includes doing what brings you pleasure. And if Hume is correct, caring for others will bring you an important kind of pleasure. Indeed, if Hume is correct, when you praise an action as good, it is precisely because it brings you this kind of pleasure.

It is important to notice, finally, the emphasis Hume placed on character. As we said, according to Hume, the act that pleases our moral sensibilities is one that reflects a benevolent *character* on the part of the agent. Hume believed that when we morally praise (or condemn) someone, it is the person's character we praise (or condemn) primarily: his or her actions we find praiseworthy (or condemnatory) mainly as an indication of character. This idea—that we apply moral attributes primarily to a person's character and secondarily to the person's actions—is common in the virtue-ethics tradition of Plato, Aristotle, and Aquinas. In this respect, Hume is part of that tradition.

## Can There Be Ethics after Hume?

"Morality," Hume said, "is more properly felt than judged of." Ethical standards are not fixed by reason, he held; further, even if there is a God, he maintained, it is impossible for us to gain moral guidance from him.

Loosely speaking, therefore, ethics after Hume seems generally to have had these options. First, it might seek to establish that, despite Hume, morality *can* be grounded on reason or God. As we shall see next, this was the option taken by Kant, who favored reason as the ultimate ground of morality. Or second, ethics might try to find objective sources of moral standards other than reason and God. This is what the utilitarians tried to do, as we shall see shortly. Or third, it might try to determine how one should conduct one's affairs given the absence of objective moral standards. This is a primary concern of contemporary existentialists, as we saw in Chapter 8. Or fourth, ethics might abandon the search for moral standards altogether and concentrate instead on such factual questions as: What do people believe is good and right? What does it mean to say that something is good or right? How do moral judgments differ from other kinds of judgments? What leads us to praise certain actions as moral and condemn others as immoral? These are some of the issues that have captured the attention of many twentieth-century philosophers, such as G. E. Moore and R. M. Hare, who we will encounter in Chapter 12.

## KANT

**Immanuel Kant** (1724–1804) disagreed entirely with Hume's discounting of the possibility that reason can settle whether an act is morally right. In Kant's opinion, reason and reason alone can settle this. Kant's argument, paraphrased and distilled, went like this:

1. *Scientific inquiry can never reveal to us principles that we know hold without exception.* Scientific inquiry is based on experience, and in the final analysis experience can show only how things have been to this point, not how they must be. For example, science reveals to us physical "laws" that hold true of the universe as it is now, but it cannot provide absolutely conclusive guarantees that these laws will forever hold true. (If you have difficulty understanding this point, rereading the section on Kant in Chapter 7 will help.)

## Breaking Promises

According to Kant, if a universal law allowed breach of promise, then there would be no such thing as a promise. Thus, if the maxim "Break promises!" were to become a universal law, it would "destroy itself."

But hold on. Suppose I promise to return your car at 4 o'clock. And suppose that shortly before 4 my wife becomes ill and must be rushed to the hospital—and the only transportation available is your car! Should I break my promise to you to save my wife's life? And if I did, which maxim would I be acting on, breaking promises or saving lives?

Perhaps a reasonable answer would be that the maxim I acted on is "Break promises when doing so is required to save lives." And perhaps there is no inconsistency in willing this maxim to be a universal law.

Perhaps, then, the maxim "Break promises!" cannot be universalized. But that may not mean that, on Kantian principles, you should never break a promise.

2. *Moral principles, however, hold without exception.* For example, if it is wrong to torture helpless animals, then it would be wrong for anyone, at any time, to do so.

Thus, from these two premises — that moral principles hold without exception and that scientific investigations cannot reveal what holds without exception — it follows that:

3. *Moral principles cannot be revealed through scientific investigation.* Because Kant believed that any principle that holds without exception is knowable only through reason, he maintained that *reason alone can ascertain principles of morality.* For an example of how reason can ascertain universal laws of morality, see the box "Breaking Promises."

### The Supreme Principle of Morality

Further, according to Kant, because a moral rule is something that holds without exception — that is, holds universally — you should act only on principles that could hold universally. For example, if you think you must cheat to pass an exam, then the principle on which you would act (if you were to cheat) would be this: *To obtain a passing grade, it is acceptable to cheat.* But now consider: If this principle were a universal law, then a passing grade would be meaningless, right? And in that case the principle itself would be meaningless. In short, the principle logically could not hold universally, and (this comes to the same thing) it would be irrational for anyone to want it to hold universally.

Now if it would be irrational for you to want the principle on which you act to be a universal law, then that principle is morally improper, and the act should not be done. Thus, for Kant, the supreme prescription of morality, which he calls the supreme **categorical imperative,** is *to act always in such a way that you could, rationally, will the principle on which you act to be a universal law.* In Kant's words: "Act

Königsburg as it looks today. The home of
Immanuel Kant.

only on that maxim whereby you can at the same time will that it should become a
universal law."

Because, in Kant's view, a universal law would in effect be a sort of law of nature, he offers a second formulation of the categorical imperative: "Act as if the
maxim of your action were to become by your will a Universal Law of Nature."

## Why You Should Do What You Should Do

Moral principles, Kant observed, may always be expressed in the imperative form:
Do not steal! Be kind to others! Further, because moral imperatives must hold without exception, they are different from **hypothetical imperatives,** which state, in
effect, that one ought to do something *if* such-and-such an end is desired.

For example, the imperatives "If you wish to be healthy, then live moderately!"
and "If you wish to secure your own survival, then surrender your rights to a sovereign power!" are both hypothetical imperatives. Neither is a **moral imperative,** for
a moral imperative holds unconditionally or *categorically.* This means that a moral
imperative commands obedience for the sake of no other end than its own rightness.

Thus, for Kant, what I should do I should do *because it is right.* Doing something for any other purpose—for the sake of happiness or the welfare of humankind, for example—is not to act morally. It is to act under the command of a

hypothetical imperative, which is not unconditional, as a moral imperative must be. According to Kant, you should do your moral duty simply because it is your moral duty. You should be aware that duty-based ethical systems, like Kant's, are known as **deontological** ethical systems.

Furthermore, according to Kant, it's not the *effects or consequences* of your act that determine whether your act is good, for these are not totally within your control. What is within your control is the *intent* with which you act. Thus, what determines whether your act is good or bad is the intent with which it is taken. He wrote: "Nothing can possibly be conceived in the world, or even out of it, which can be called good, without qualification, except a good will."

And because a morally good will is one that acts solely for the sake of doing what is right, it follows, in Kant's opinion, that *there is no moral worth* in, say, helping others because you are sympathetic or inclined to do so. There is moral worth in helping others only because it is right to do so.

Because to violate the supreme principle of morality, the supreme categorical imperative, is to be irrational, rationality may be said to be the source of all value. Hence, the rational will alone is deemed inherently good by Kant. Accordingly, Kant offers yet another formulation of the supreme categorical imperative: *Treat rational beings (i.e., humans) in every instance as ends and never just as means!*

That this is an alternative formulation of the same principle may be seen in the fact that if you were to violate the categorical imperative and do something that you could not rationally will to be a law for all, then in effect you would be treating the interests of others as subordinate to your own; that is, you would be treating others as means and not as ends. Kant, it is often said (for obvious reasons), was the first philosopher to provide a *rational basis* for the golden rule found in many religions: Do unto others as you would have them do unto you.

Did Kant provide a viable response to Hume's idea that reason cannot determine whether an act is morally right? You decide.

## THE UTILITARIANS

Kant, we have seen, may well have offered a sound refutation of Hume's idea that moral principles are not determined by reason. It is therefore perhaps strange that two of the most celebrated ethical philosophers of the nineteenth century, the Englishmen **Jeremy Bentham** (1748–1832) and **John Stuart Mill** (1806–1873), largely ignored the rationalistic ethics of Kant, Bentham perhaps more so than Mill. Bentham and Mill did not, however, ignore Hume. Instead, they developed further Hume's idea that traits and actions that are virtuous promote the welfare of people, the "general happiness."

Bentham and Mill were **utilitarians,** which means they believed that *the rightness of an action is identical with the happiness it produces as its consequence.* What is new or exciting about this? Didn't Aristotle and the Epicureans and Augustine and Aquinas also advocate pursuing happiness? The difference is that, according to those earlier philosophers, it is *your own happiness* that you should strive for.

By contrast, the utilitarians said that the morally best act is the one that produces the greatest amount of happiness *with everyone considered.* But this is ambiguous: should we aim at increasing the *average* happiness or the *total* happiness — even if this would reduce the happiness per person? Usually the utilitarians are interpreted as favoring increasing the average happiness. In any case, they believed that when you are trying to produce happiness, it is not just your own happiness you should aim for but, rather, the happiness of people in general.

It is common to attribute to the utilitarians the view that the right act is the one that produces "the greatest happiness for the greatest number." That phrase — the greatest happiness for the greatest number — is unfortunate, because it tells us to maximize two different things. (Just try to plot the great happiness for the greatest number as a single line on a graph, with happiness as one variable and number as a second variable!) You can say, "The more people that have a given amount of happiness, the better," and you can say, "The more happiness a given number of people have, the better." But it is not clear what you could mean by saying, "The more happiness the greater number of people have, the better." We will interpret the utilitarians as favoring the view that the more happiness a given number of people have, the better (i.e., the higher the average happiness, the better). And again, according to this philosophy, your own happiness is *not* more important morally than that of others.

Notice, too, that for the utilitarians, it is the *consequences* of an act that determine its rightness, a position that contrasts strongly with Kant's idea that the moral worth of an act depends on the *will* or *motive* with which it is taken.

## Bentham

Bentham, the earlier of the two utilitarians, equated happiness with pleasure. "Nature," he wrote, "has placed mankind under the governance of two sovereign masters, *pain* and *pleasure*. It is for them alone to point out what we ought to do, as well as determine what we shall do."

The words *ought, right, good,* and the like have meaning only when defined in terms of *pleasure*, Bentham said. This fact is evident, he argued, in that all other intelligible moral standards either must be interpreted in terms of the pleasure standard or are simply disguised versions of the pleasure standard in the first place.

For example, suppose you maintain that the right act is the one that is preferred by God. Well, said Bentham, unless we know God's preferences — that is, unless we know what, exactly, pleases God — what you maintain is pretty meaningless, is it not? And the only way "to know what is His pleasure," he said, is by "observing what is our own pleasure and pronouncing it to be His."

Or consider the theory that a moral obligation to obey the law stems from a "social contract" among members of society. That theory, said Bentham, is unnecessarily complicated. For when we have a moral obligation to obey the law, he said, that obligation is more simply explained by the fact that obedience to the law would result in more pleasure for more people than disobedience would.

Bentham believed that the pain and pleasure an act produces can be evaluated solely with reference to *quantitative* criteria. Which of two or more courses of action you should take should be determined by considering the probable consequences of each possible act with respect to the certainty, intensity, duration,

## PROFILE: Jeremy Bentham (1748–1832)

You will find it easy to identify with Jeremy Bentham — if, that is, you studied Latin when you were four, started college when you were twelve, graduated by age fifteen, and finished law school and were admitted to the bar all while you were still a teenager.

Yes, Bentham was a sharp youth. When he was fifteen, he went to hear Sir William Blackstone, the famous English jurist. Bentham said that he instantly spotted errors in Blackstone's reasoning, especially on natural rights. Bentham came to believe that the whole notion of natural rights, including that found in the American Declaration of Independence, was just "nonsense on stilts." In 1776 he published his first book, *Fragment on Government,* a critique of Blackstone.

For David Hume and Hume's *Treatise on Human Nature,* however, Bentham had more respect, and he claimed that the work made the scales fall from his eyes about ethics. Bentham's own ethical philosophy reflects the great influence of Hume.

Though qualified to do so, Bentham never actually practiced law. He was much more interested in legal and social reform and wrote daily commentaries on English law and society. He advocated a simplified and codified legal system and worked for prison and education reform and extension of voting rights. Bentham also published numerous pamphlets on such abuses as jury packing and extortionate legal fees, and his followers, the "Benthamites," were an effective political force that endured after his death.

Bentham was in the habit of not finishing books that he started to write, and the only major philosophical treatise that he published himself is the *Introduction to the Principles of Morals and Legislation* (1789). The title states exactly Bentham's main concern in life: applying sound principles of morality to the law.

If you want to know what Bentham looked like, do not stop with a picture. Bentham's embalmed body, complete with a wax head and dressed just as he liked to, is there for you to see at the University College, London.

---

immediacy, and extent (the number of persons affected) of the pleasure or pain it produces, and with respect to the other kinds of sensations it is likely to have as a result over the long run. This "calculus" of pleasure, as it is often called, represents a distinctive feature of Bentham's ethics. Bentham believed that by using these criteria, one could and should calculate which of alternative courses of action would produce the greatest amount of pleasure and which, therefore, ought morally to be taken.

Through all of this you should be asking: But why ought I seek the *general* happiness and not give higher priority to my own? Bentham's answer was that your own happiness *coincides* with the general happiness: what brings pleasure to you and what brings pleasure to others fortunately go together.

You may wish to consider whether this answer is fully satisfactory.

## Mill

John Stuart Mill, who claimed to have discovered in Bentham's ethical theory what he needed to give purpose to his own life, was also concerned with providing a philosophical justification for the utilitarian doctrine that it is the *general* happiness

The cartoon points up the foolishness of the notion that we can seek pleasure *by itself.* Such a search has no direction to it. What we seek is food, shelter, companionship, sex, and so forth—we do not, strictly speaking, seek pleasure per se. And if you tried to seek pleasure, you would not know how to go about finding it. Your seeking must always be for something, such as food, that is not *itself* pleasure.

that one should aim to promote. The justification, according to Mill, lies in the fact that a moral principle by its very nature singles out no one for preferential treatment. Thus, Mill wrote, "as between his own happiness and that of others," the utilitarian is required "to be as strictly impartial as a disinterested and benevolent spectator." Compare Mill's justification with that of Bentham. Mill's justification is sounder, is it not?

Probably the most important difference between Mill and Bentham is that Mill believed that some pleasures are *inherently better* than others and are to be preferred even over a greater amount of pleasure of an inferior grade.

That some pleasures are better than others can be seen, Mill argued, in the fact that few people would be willing to trade places with an animal or even with a more ignorant person than themselves, even if the exchange guaranteed their having the fullest measure of an animal's or an ignoramus's pleasure. Here is what he meant. Would you trade places with a pig or a lunkhead? Would you do it even if you knew that as a pig or a lunkhead you would have more pig or lunkhead pleasures than you now have pleasure as an intelligent human being?

Thus, for Mill, in determining the pleasure for which we should strive, we must consider the *quality* of the pleasure as well as the quantity. Choose the pleasure of the highest quality.

Now this is all very well, but what settles which of two pleasures is of higher quality? Mill's answer is quite simple: Of two pleasures, if there is one to which most who have experienced both give a decided preference, that is the more desirable pleasure.

Notice what this answer seems to entail. It seems to entail that the pleasures preferred by the *intellectual* will be found to be of superior quality, for nonintellectuals "only know their own side of the question. The other party to the comparison knows both sides," said Mill.

According to Mill, then, it is not simply the quantity of pleasure an act produces that determines its moral worth; the quality of the pleasure produced must also be taken into account. Mill is thus said to have recognized implicitly (though not in so many words) a factor other than pleasure by which the moral worth of actions should be compared: the factor of quality. In other words, he is said to have proposed, in effect, a standard of moral worth other than pleasure, a standard of "quality" by means of which pleasure itself is to be evaluated. So he sometimes is said not to be a "pure" utilitarian, if a utilitarian is one who believes that the pleasure an act produces is the only standard of good.

It is not unusual, therefore, to find philosophers who think of Bentham's philosophy as more consistently utilitarian than Mill's, though everyone refers to both Mill and Bentham as "the" utilitarians.

There is one other, sort of fuzzy, difference between Bentham and Mill. Bentham's utilitarianism is what today is called **act utilitarianism:** the rightness of an *act* is determined by its effect on the general happiness. Mill also subscribed to act utilitarianism in some passages, but in other places he seems to have advocated what is called **rule utilitarianism.** According to this version of utilitarianism, we are to evaluate the moral correctness of an action not with reference to its impact on the general happiness but, rather, with respect to the impact on the general happiness of the *rule* or principle the action exemplifies.

Take this case, for example: Suppose that by murdering us you would increase the general happiness (maybe unknown to anyone, we harbor some awful contagious disease). Act utilitarianism would say that you should murder us. But a rule utilitarian, as Mill in some places seems to be, would say that if society accepted murder as a rule of conduct, ultimately the general happiness would be diminished, so you should not murder us. Rule utilitarianism is, in a way, much more Kantian than is act utilitarianism.

## FRIEDRICH NIETZSCHE

Another important nineteenth-century philosopher, one who believed that all previous moral philosophy was tedious and soporific and who had no use at all for the utilitarians, was **Friedrich Nietzsche** (1844–1900). In Nietzsche's view, moralities are social institutions, and basically there are just two moralities: master morality and slave morality, the morality of the masses. Slave morality—for Nietzsche, epitomized by Christian ethics—emphasizes such virtues as compassion, humility, patience, warmheartedness, and turning the other cheek. These "virtues" glorify weakness. Master morality, by contrast, is the morality of noble individuals, who are egoistic, hard, intolerant, but bound by a code of honor to their peers. Noble individuals define harm entirely in terms of what is harmful to themselves and despise altruism and humility.

The Paradox of Hedonism. The British moralist Henry Sidgwick (1838–1900) noted the curious fact, which he called the *paradox of hedonism*, that the desire for pleasure, if too predominant, defeats its own aim. (Sidgwick also observed that "the pleasures of thought and study can only be enjoyed in the highest degree by those who have an ardour of curiosity which carries the mind temporarily away from self and its sensations.")

According to Nietzsche, the enhancement of the species is always the result of aristocratic societies, which, he held, are the ultimate justification of human social existence. The primal life force, for Nietzsche, is the will-to-power, whose essence is the overpowering and suppression of what is alien and weaker and which finds its highest expression in the nobleman, or *Übermensch* ("Superman" in German). The principle by which the *Übermensch* lives is "There is no god or human over me." He is the source of ethical truth.

Nietzsche followed the ancient Greek philosopher Heraclitus (Chapter 2) in holding that life is quintessentially strife or warfare. It is only within the dark eye of battle that human energies are truly stretched and fruit-bearing actions become possible. Battles make heroes, he thought; peace renders us weak and ineffectual. One of Nietzsche's most famous proverbs was "What doesn't kill us makes us stronger."

The ultimate battle, Nietzsche thought, takes place within the human frame and is the battle between two forces, the Apollonian and the Dionysian. The Greek god Apollo represents the force of measure, order, and harmony. The Greek god Dionysius (or Bacchus in the Roman world) represents the counterforce of excess, destruction, and creative power, the ecstatic rush and rave of the original, formless will. In the human soul these two forces contest each other for ascendancy. While both are necessary if one is to be fully and creatively alive, the creative Dionysian force has been lost almost entirely in the slave mentality, with its emphasis on humility, meekness, mediocrity, and the denial of life.

The selection from Nietzsche at the end of the chapter conveys many of these themes clearly and will make it obvious why attempts often are made to censor Nietzsche from schools and libraries.

SELECTION 10.1

# Gorgias*

*Plato*

[*You may know someone—or be someone—who thinks that one should fully indulge one's appetites, or that pleasure, whatever its nature, is the key to happiness. In this excerpt from the Dialogue* Gorgias, *Plato has the character "Callicles" advancing this view and "Socrates" rebutting it.*]

*Socrates:* You make a brave attack, Callicles, with so frank an outburst, for clearly you are now saying what others may think but are reluctant to express. I entreat you therefore on no account to weaken, in order that it may really be made plain how life should be lived. And tell me. You say we should not curb our appetites, if we are to be what we should be, but should allow them the fullest possible growth and procure satisfaction for them from whatever source, and this, you say, is virtue.

*Callicles:* That is what I say. . . .

*S:* Consider whether you would say this of each type of life, the temperate and the undisciplined. Imagine that each of the two men has several jars, in the one case in sound condition and filled, one with wine, another with honey, another with milk, and many others with a variety of liquids, but that the sources of these liquids are scanty and hard to come by, procured only with much hard labor. Imagine then that the one after filling his vessels does not trouble himself to draw in further supplies but as far as the jars are concerned is free from worry; in the case of the other man the sources, as in the first instance are procurable but difficult to come by, but his vessels are perforated and unsound and he is ever compelled to spend day and night in replenishing them, if he is not to suffer the greatest agony. If this is the character of each of the lives, do you still insist that the life of the uncontrolled man is happier than that

of the orderly? Do I or do I not persuade you with this image that the disciplined life is better than the intemperate?

*C:* You do not, Socrates. The man who has filled his vessels can no longer find any pleasure, but this is what I just now described as living the life of a stone. Once the vessels are filled, there is neither pleasure nor pain any more. But a life of pleasure demands the largest possible influx.

*S:* Then if there is a big influx, must there not also be a great outflow, and must not the holes for the outflow be large?

*C:* Certainly.

*S:* It is the life of a plover you mean, not that of a corpse or a stone. And now tell me. You are thinking of some such thing as being hungry and, when hungry, eating?

*C:* I am.

*S:* And being thirsty and, when thirsty, drinking?

*C:* Yes, and experiencing all the other appetites and being able to satisfy them and living happily in the enjoyment of them.

*S:* Good, my worthy friend, just continue as you began, and mind you do not falter through shame. And I too, it seems, must throw all shame aside. First of all then, tell me whether one who suffers from the itch and longs to scratch himself, if he can scratch himself to his heart's content and continue scratching all his life, can be said to live happily.

*C:* How absurd you are, Socrates, a regular mob orator!

*S:* That, Callicles, is why I frightened Polus and Gorgias and put them to shame, but you surely will not be dismayed or abashed, for you have courage. Only give me your answer.

*C:* Well then, I say that even one who scratches himself would live pleasantly.

---

*From *Socratic Dialogues*, translated and edited by W. D. Woodhead (Edinburgh: Thomas Nelson & Sons, 1953).

*S:* And if pleasantly, happily?

*C:* Certainly.

*S:* If it was only his head that he wanted to scratch — or can I push the question further? Think what you will answer, Callicles, if anyone should ask all the questions that naturally follow. And as a climax of all such cases, the life of a catamite — is not that shocking and shameful and miserable? Will you dare to say that such people are happy, if they have what they desire in abundance?

*C:* Are you not ashamed, Socrates, to drag our discussion into such topics?

*S:* Is it I who do this, my noble friend, or the man who says so unequivocally that pleasure, whatever its nature, is the key to happiness, and does not distinguish between pleasures good and evil? But enlighten me further as to whether you say that the pleasant and the good are identical, or that there are some pleasures which are not good.

*C:* To avoid inconsistency if I say they are different, I assert that they are the same. . . .

*S:* Tell me, do you not think that those who fare well experience the opposite of those who fare ill?

*C:* I do.

*S:* Then if these things are opposites, the same must hold true of them as of health and sickness. A man cannot be both in health and sick at the same time, nor be rid of both conditions at the same time.

*C:* How do you mean?

*S:* Take, for example, any part of the body separately and consider it. A man perhaps has trouble with his eyes, which is called ophthalmia.

*C:* Of course.

*S:* Then his eyes are not at the same time sound.

*C:* By no means.

*S:* And what of when he is rid of ophthalmia? Does he then get rid of the health of his eyes, and is he finally quit of both conditions?

*C:* Certainly not.

*S:* For that would be miraculous and irrational, would it not?

*C:* Very much so.

*S:* But, I suppose, he acquires and gets rid of each in turn.

*C:* I agree.

*S:* And is it not the same with strength and weakness?

*C:* Yes.

*S:* And swiftness and slowness?

*C:* Certainly.

*S:* And good things and happiness, and their opposites, evils and wretchedness — does he possess and get rid of each of these in turn?

*C:* Assuredly, I think.

*S:* Then if we discover certain things which a man possesses and gets rid of simultaneously, it is obvious that these cannot be the good and the evil. Do we agree on this? Do not answer until you have considered it carefully.

*C:* I am in the most complete possible accord.

*S:* Back then to our previous admissions. Did you say hunger was pleasant or painful? Actual hunger, I mean.

*C:* Painful, but to satisfy hunger by eating is pleasant.

*S:* I understand. But hunger itself at least is painful, is it not?

*C:* I agree.

*S:* And thirst too?

*C:* Most certainly.

*S:* Am I to ask any further then, or do you admit that every deficiency and desire is painful?

*C:* I admit it; you need not ask.

*S:* Very well then, but to drink when thirsty you say is pleasant?

*C:* I do.

*S:* Now in this statement the word 'thirsty' implies pain, I presume.

*C:* Yes.

*S:* And drinking is a satisfaction of the deficiency and a pleasure?

*C:* Yes.

*S:* Then you say that in drinking there is pleasure?

*C:* Certainly.

*S:* When one is thirsty?

*C:* I agree.

*S:* That is, when in pain?

*C:* Yes.

*S:* Then do you realize the result — that you say a man enjoys pleasure simultaneously with pain, when you say that he drinks when thirsty? Does not this happen at the same time and the same place, whether in body or soul? For I fancy it makes no difference. Is this so or not?

*C:* It is.

*S:* Yes, but you say also that when one is faring well it is impossible for him at the same time to fare ill.

*C:* I do.

*S:* But you have agreed it is possible to experience pleasure at the same time as pain.

*C:* Apparently.

*S:* Then pleasure is not the same as faring well, nor pain as faring ill, and so the pleasant is different from the good.

*C:* I do not understand what your quibbles mean, Socrates.

*S:* You understand, Callicles, but you are playing coy. But push on a little further, that you may realize how cunning you are, you who admonish me. Does not each one of us cease at the same time from thirsting and from his pleasure in drinking?

*C:* I do not know what you mean.

*S:* Do not behave so, Callicles, but answer for our sakes too, that the arguments may be concluded.

*C:* But Socrates is always the same, Gorgias. He asks these trivial and useless questions and then refutes.

*S:* What difference does that make to you? In any case you do not have to pay the price, Callicles, but suffer Socrates to cross-examine you as he will.

*C:* Well then, ask these petty little questions, since Gorgias so wishes.

*S:* You are lucky, Callicles, in having been initiated in the Great Mysteries before the Little; I did not think it was permitted. Answer then from where you left off, whether thirst and the pleasure of drinking do not cease for each of us at the same time.

*C:* I agree.

*S:* And does not one cease from hunger and other desires, and from pleasures at the same time?

*C:* That is so.

*S:* Does he not then cease from pains and pleasures at the same time?

*C:* Yes.

*S:* Yes, but he does not cease from experiencing the good and the ill simultaneously, as you yourself agreed. Do you not agree now?

*C:* I do. What of it?

*S:* Only this, that the good is not the same as the pleasant, my friend, nor the evil as the painful. For we cease from the one pair at the same time, but not from the other, because they are distinct. How then could the pleasant be the same as the good, or the painful as the evil? Let us look at it in a different way, if you like, for I think that even here you do not agree. But just consider. Do you not call good people by that name because of the presence in them of things good, just as you call beautiful those in whom beauty is present.

## SELECTION 10.2
# The Nicomachean Ethics *

*Aristotle*

[*This is an excerpt from one of the classics of Western philosophy. In it, Aristotle provides a "rough outline" of the good.*]

Let us again return to the good we are seeking, and ask what it can be. It seems different in different actions and arts; it is different in medicine, in strategy, and in the other arts likewise. What then is the good of each? Surely that for whose sake everything else is done. In medicine this is health, in strategy victory, in architecture a house, in any other sphere something else, and in every action and pursuit the end; for it is for the sake of this that all men do whatever else they do. Therefore, if there is an end for all that we do, this will be the good achievable by action, and if there are more than one, these will be the goods achievable by action.

So the argument has by a different course reached the same point; but we must try to state this even more clearly. Since there are evidently more than one end, and we choose some of these (e.g. wealth, flutes,[1] and in general instruments) for the sake of something else, clearly not all ends are final ends; but the chief good is evidently something final. Therefore, if there is only one final end, this will be what we are seeking, and if there are more than one, the most final of these will be what we are seeking. Now we call that which is in itself worthy of pursuit more final than that which is worthy of pursuit for the sake of something else, and that which is never desirable for the sake of something else more final than the things that are desirable both in themselves and for the sake of that other thing, and therefore we call final without qualification that which is always desirable in itself and never for the sake of something else.

Now such a thing happiness, above all else, is held to be; for this we choose always for itself and never for the sake of something else, but honour, pleasure, reason, and every virtue we choose indeed for themselves (for if nothing resulted from them we should still choose each of them), but we choose them also for the sake of happiness, judging that by means of them we shall be happy. Happiness, on the other hand, no one chooses for the sake of these, nor, in general, for anything other than itself.

From the point of view of self-sufficiency the same result seems to follow; for the final good is thought to be self-sufficient. Now by self-sufficient we do not mean that which is sufficient for a man by himself, for one who lives a solitary life, but also for parents, children, wife, and in general for his friends and fellow citizens, since man is born for citizenship. But some limit must be set to this; for if we extend our requirement to ancestors and descendants and friends' friends we are in for an infinite series. Let us examine this question, however, on another occasion;[1] the self-sufficient we now define as that which when isolated makes life desirable and lacking in nothing; and such we think happiness to be; and further we think it most desirable of all things, without being counted as one good thing among others — if it were so counted it would clearly be made more desirable by the addition of even the least of goods; for that which is added becomes an excess of goods, and of goods the greater is always more desirable. Happiness, then, is something final and self-sufficient, and is the end of action.

Presumably, however, to say that happiness is the chief good seems a platitude, and a clearer account of what it is is still desired. This might perhaps be given, if we could first ascertain the function of man. For just as for a flute-player, a sculptor, or any artist, and, in general, for all things that have a function or activity, the good and the 'well' is thought to reside in the function, so would it seem to be for man, if he has a function. Have the carpenter, then, and the tanner certain functions or activities, and has man none? Is he born without a function? Or as eye, hand, foot, and in general each of the parts evidently has a function, may one lay it down that man similarly has a function apart from all these? What

---

*The author's footnotes have been deleted. From "Ethica Nicomachea," translated by W. D. Ross, from *The Works of Aristotle,* translated into English under the editorship of W. D. Ross, Vol. IX (Oxford: Oxford University Press, 1925). By permission of Oxford University Press.

then can this be? Life seems to be common even to plants, but we are seeking what is peculiar to man. Let us exclude, therefore, the life of nutrition and growth.[1] Next there would be a life of perception, but *it* also seems to be common even to the horse, the ox, and every animal. There remains, then, an active life of the element that has a rational principle; of this, one part has such a principle in the sense of being obedient to one, the other in the sense of possessing one and exercising thought. And, as 'life of the rational element' also has two meanings, we must state that life in the sense of activity is what we mean; for this seems to be the more proper sense of the term. Now if the function of man is an activity of soul which follows or implies a rational principle, and if we say 'a so-and-so' and 'a good so-and-so' have a function which is the same in kind, e.g. a lyre-player and a good lyre-player, and so without qualification in all cases, eminence in respect of goodness being added to the name of the function

(for the function of a lyre-player is to play the lyre, and that of a good lyre-player is to do so well): if this is the case, [and we state the function of man to be a certain kind of life, and this to be an activity or actions of the soul implying a rational principle, and the function of a good man to be the good and noble performance of these, and if any action is well performed when it is performed in accordance with the appropriate excellence: if this is the case,] human good turns out to be activity of soul in accordance with virtue, and if there are more than one virtue, in accordance with the best and most complete.

But we must add 'in a complete life.' For one swallow does not make a summer, nor does one day; and so too one day, or a short time, does not make a man blessed and happy.

Let this serve as an outline of the good; for we must presumably first sketch it roughly, and then later fill in the details.

## SELECTION 10.3
# Epicurus to Menoeceus*

*Epicurus*

[*Epicurus, like Callicles in the preceding selection, advocates living a life devoted to acquiring pleasure. But when you read this selection, you will see that Epicurus's concept of pleasure is much more sophisticated than Callicles'.*]

The things which I [unceasingly] commend to you, these do and practice, considering them to be the first principles of the good life. . . .

Become accustomed to the belief that death is nothing to us. For all good and evil consists in sensation, but death is deprivation of sensation. And therefore a right understanding that death is nothing to us makes the mortality of life enjoyable, not because it adds to it an infinite span of time, but because it takes away the craving for immortality. For there is nothing terrible in life for the man who has

truly comprehended that there is nothing terrible in not living. . . . Death, the most terrifying of ills, is nothing to us, since so long as we exist, death is not with us; but when death comes, then we do not exist. It does not then concern either the living or the dead, since for the former, it is not, and the latter are no more. . . .

We must then bear in mind that the future is neither ours, nor yet wholly not ours, so that we may not altogether expect it as sure to come, nor abandon hope of it, as if it will certainly not come.

We must consider that of desires some are natural, others vain, and of the natural some are necessary and others merely natural; and of the necessary some are necessary for happiness, others for the repose of the body, and others for very life. The right understanding of these facts enables us to refer all choices and avoidance to the health of the body and the soul's freedom from disturbance, since this is the aim of the life of blessedness. For it is to obtain this end that we always act, namely, to avoid pain

*From *Epicurus: The Extant Remains,* translated by Cyril Bailey, (Oxford: Oxford University Press, 1929). By permission of Oxford University Press.

and fear. And when this is once secured for us, all the tempest of the soul is dispersed, since the living creature has not to wander as though in search of something that is missing, and to look for some other thing by which he can fulfill the good of the soul and the good of the body. For it is then that we have need of pleasure, when we feel pain owing to the absence of pleasure; but when we do not feel pain, we no longer need pleasure. And for this cause we call pleasure the beginning and end of the blessed life. For we recognize pleasure as the first good innate in us, and from pleasure we begin every act of choice and avoidance, and to pleasure we return again, using the feeling as the standard by which we judge every good.

And since pleasure is the first good and natural to us, for this very reason we do not choose every pleasure, but sometimes we pass over many pleasures, when greater discomfort accrues to us as the result of them: and similarly we think many pains better than pleasures, since a greater pleasure comes to us when we have endured pains for a long time. Every pleasure then because of its natural kinship to us is good, yet not every pleasure is to be chosen: even as every pain also is an evil, yet not all are always of a nature to be avoided. Yet by a scale of comparison and by the consideration of advantages and disadvantages we must form our judgment on all these matters. For the good on certain occasions we treat as bad, and conversely the bad as good.

And again independence of desire we think a great good — not that we may at all times enjoy but a few things, but that, if we do not possess many, we may enjoy the few in the genuine persuasion that those have the sweetest pleasure in luxury who least need it, and that all that is natural is easy to be obtained, but that which is superfluous is hard. And so plain savours bring us a pleasure equal to a luxurious diet, when all the pain due to want is removed; and bread and water produce the highest pleasure, when one who needs them puts them to his lips. To grow accustomed therefore to simple and not luxurious diet gives us health to the full, and makes a man alert for the needful employments of life, and when after long intervals we approach luxuries disposes us better towards them, and fits us to be fearless of fortune.

When, therefore, we maintain that pleasure is the end, we do not mean the pleasures of profligates and those that consist in sensuality, as is supposed by some who are either ignorant or disagree with us or do not understand, but freedom from pain in the body and from trouble in the mind. For it is not continuous drinkings and revellings, nor the satisfaction of lusts, nor the enjoyment of fish and other luxuries of the wealthy table, which produce a pleasant life, but sober reasoning, searching out the motives for all choice and avoidance, and banishing mere opinions, to which are due the greatest disturbance of the spirit.

Of all this the beginning and the greatest good is prudence. Wherefore prudence is a more precious thing even than philosophy: for from prudence are sprung all the other virtues; and it teaches us that it is not possible to live pleasantly without living prudently and honourably and justly, not, again, to live a life of prudence, honour and justice without living pleasantly. For the virtues are by nature bound up with the pleasant life, and the pleasant life is inseparable from them. For indeed who, think you, is a better man than he who holds reverent opinions concerning the gods, and is at all times free from fear of death, and has reasoned out the end ordained by nature?

## SELECTION 10.4

# The Encheiridion*

*Epictetus*

[*Epictetus, like Epicurus and Callicles, advocates a life of pleasure. Epictetus advises us to get straight on what things are under our control and what things aren't. What happens isn't under our control, but our attitudes are. Therefore, the key to happiness is, when something bad happens, to take a stoical attitude.*]

1. Some things are under our control, while others are not under our control. Under our control are conception, choice, desire, aversion, and, in a word, everything that is our own doing; not under our control are our body, our property, reputation, office, and in a word, everything that is not our own doing. Furthermore, things under our control are by nature free, unhindered, and unimpeded; while the things not under our control are weak, servile, subject to hindrance, and not our own. Remember, therefore, that if what is naturally slavish you think to be free, and what is not your own to be your own, you will be hampered, will grieve, will be in turmoil, and will blame both gods and men; while if you think only what is your own to be your own, and what is not your own to be, as it really is, not your own, then no one will ever be able to exert compulsion upon you, no one will hinder you, you will blame no one, will find fault with no one, will do absolutely nothing against your will, you will have no personal enemy, no one will harm you, for neither is there any harm that can touch you. . . .

Make it, therefore, your study at the very outset to say to every harsh external impression, "You are an external impression and not at all what you appear to be." After that examine it and test it by these rules which you have, the first and most important of which is this: Whether the impression has to do with the things which are under our control, or with those which are not under our control; and, if it has to do with some one of the things not under our control, have ready to hand the answer, "It is nothing to me."

2. Remember that the promise of desire is the attainment of what you desire, that of aversion is not to fall into what is avoided, and that he who fails in his desire is unfortunate, while he who falls into what he would avoid experiences misfortune. If, then, you avoid only what is unnatural among those things which are under your control, you will fall into none of the things which you avoid; but if you try to avoid disease, or death, or poverty, you will experience misfortune. Withdraw, therefore, your aversion from all the matters that are not under our control, and transfer it to what is unnatural among those which are under our control. But for the time being remove utterly your desire; for if you desire some one of the things that are not under our control you are bound to be unfortunate; and, at the same time, not one of the things that are under our control, which it would be excellent for you to desire, is within your grasp. But employ only choice and refusal, and these too but lightly, and with reservations, and without straining. . . .

5. It is not the things themselves that disturb men, but their judgments about these things. For example, death is nothing dreadful, or else Socrates too would have thought so, but the judgment that death is dreadful, this is the dreadful thing. When, therefore, we are hindered, or disturbed, or grieved, let us never blame anyone but ourselves, that means, our own judgments. It is the part of an uneducated person to blame others where he himself fares ill; to blame himself is the part of one whose education has begun; to blame neither another nor his own self is the part of one whose education is already complete. . . .

8. Do not seek to have everything that happens happen as you wish, but wish for everything to happen as it actually does happen, and your life will be serene. . . .

*Reprinted by permission of the publishers and the Trustees of the Loeb Classical Library from *Epictetus*, Volume II, Loeb Classical Library Volume 218, translated by W. A. Oldfather, Cambridge, Mass.: Harvard University Press, 1928. The Loeb Classical Library® is a registered trademark of the President and Fellows of Harvard College.

11. Never say about anything, "I have lost it," but only "I have given it back." Is your child dead? It has been given back. Is your wife dead? She has been given back. "I have had my farm taken away." Very well, this too has been given back. "Yet it was a rascal who took it away." But what concern is it of yours by whose instrumentality the Giver called for its return? So long as He gives it to you, take care of it as of a thing that is not your own, as travellers treat their inn. . . .

15. Remember that you ought to behave in life as you would at a banquet. As something is being passed around it comes to you; stretch out your hand and take a portion of it politely. It passes on; do not detain it. Or it has not come to you yet; do not project your desire to meet it, but wait until it comes in front of you. So act toward children, so toward a wife, so toward office, so toward wealth; and then some day you will be worthy of the banquets of the gods. But if you do not take these things even when they are set before you, but despise them, then you will not only share the banquet of the gods, but share also their rule. For it was by so doing that Diogenes and Heraclitus, and men like them, were deservedly divine and deservedly so called.

16. When you see someone weeping in sorrow, either because a child has gone on a journey, or because he has lost his property, beware that you be not carried away by the impression that the man is in the midst of external ills, but straightway keep before you this thought: "It is not what has happened that distresses this man (for it does not distress another), but his judgment about it." Do not, however, hesitate to sympathize with him so far as words go, and, if occasion offers, even to groan with him; but be careful not to groan also in the centre of your being.

17. Remember that you are an actor in a play, the character of which is determined by the Playwright; if He wishes the play to be short, it is short; if long, it is long; if He wishes you to play the part of a beggar, remember to act even this role adroitly; and so if your role be that of a cripple, an official, or a layman. For this is your business, to play admirably the role assigned you; but the selection of that role is Another's. . . .

20. Bear in mind that it is not the man who reviles or strikes you that insults you, but it is your judgment that these men are insulting you. Therefore, when someone irritates you, be assured that it is your own opinion which has irritated you. And so make it your first endeavour not to be carried away by the external impression; for if once you gain time and delay, you will more easily become master of yourself.

21. Keep before your eyes by day death and exile, and everything that seems terrible, but most of all death; and then you will never have any abject thought, nor will you yearn for anything beyond measure. . . .

33. Lay down for yourself, at the outset, a certain stamp and type of character for yourself, which you are to maintain whether you are by yourself or are meeting with people. And be silent for the most part, or else make only the most necessary remarks, and express these in few words. But rarely, and when occasion requires you to talk, talk indeed, but about no ordinary topics. Do not talk about gladiators, or horse-races, or athletes, or things to eat or drink—topics that arise on all occasions; but above all, do not talk about people, either blaming, or praising, or comparing them. If, then, you can, by your own conversation bring over that of your companions to what is seemly. But if you happen to be left alone in the presence of aliens, keep silence.

Do not laugh much, nor at many things, nor boisterously.

Refuse, if you can, to take an oath at all, but if that is impossible, refuse as far as circumstances allow. . . .

In things that pertain to the body take only as much as your bare need requires, I mean such things as food, drink, clothing, shelter, and household slaves; but cut down everything which is for outward show or luxury.

In your sex-life preserve purity, as far as you can, before marriage, and if you indulge, take only those privileges which are lawful. However, do not make yourself offensive, or censorious, to those who do indulge, and do not make frequent mention of the fact that you do not yourself indulge.

If someone brings you word that So-and-so is speaking ill of you, do not defend yourself against what has been said; but answer: "Yes, indeed, for he did not know the rest of the faults that attach to me; if he had, these would not have been the only ones he mentioned." . . .

41. It is a mark of an ungifted man to spend a great deal of time in what concerns his body, as in

much exercise, much eating, much drinking, much evacuating of the bowels, much copulating. But these things are to be done in passing; and let your whole attention be devoted to the mind. . . .

44. The following statements constitute a non sequitur: "I am richer than you are, therefore I am superior to you"; or, "I am more eloquent than you are, therefore I am superior to you." But the following conclusions are better: "I am richer than you

are, therefore my property is superior to yours"; or "I am more eloquent than you are, therefore my elocution is superior to yours." But you are neither property nor elocution. . . .

46. On no occasion call yourself a philosopher, and do not, for the most part, talk among laymen about your philosophic principles, but do what follows from your own principles.

---

## SELECTION 10.5
# Foundations of the Metaphysics of Morals *

*Immanuel Kant*

---

[*In the first paragraph Kant states the "categorical imperative," the supreme principle of morality. He then illustrates the principle by examining four concrete and specific examples.*]

There is, therefore, only one categorical imperative. It is: Act only according to that maxim by which you can at the same time will that it should become a universal law.

Now if all imperatives of duty can be derived from this one imperative as a principle, we can at least show what we understand by the concept of duty and what it means, even though it remains undecided whether that which is called duty is an empty concept or not.

The universality of law according to which effects are produced constitutes what is properly called nature in the most general sense (as to form), i.e., the existence of things so far as it is determined by universal laws. [By analogy], then, the universal imperative of duty can be expressed as follows: Act as though the maxim of your action were by your will to become a universal law of nature.

We shall now enumerate some duties, adopting the usual division of them into duties to ourselves and to others and into perfect and imperfect duties.[1]

1. A man who is reduced to despair by a series of evils feels a weariness with life but is still in possession of his reason . . . sufficiently to ask whether it would not be contrary to his duty to himself to take his own life. Now he asks whether the maxim of his action could become a universal law of nature. His maxim, however, is: For love of myself, I make it my principle to shorten my life when by a longer duration it threatens more evil than satisfaction. But it is questionable whether this principle of self-love could become a universal law of nature. One immediately sees a contradiction in a system of nature whose law would be to destroy life by the feeling whose special office is to impel the improvement of life. In this case it would not exist as nature; hence that maxim cannot obtain as a law of nature, and thus it wholly contradicts the supreme principle of all duty.

2. Another man finds himself forced by need to borrow money. He well knows that he will not be able to repay it, but he also sees that nothing will be loaned him if he does not firmly promise to repay it at a certain time. He desires to make such a prom-

---

*From Beck, Lewis White, *Immanuel Kant: Foundations of the Metaphysics of Morals*, 2nd Edition. Copyright © 1990 Prentice-Hall, Inc. Used by permission of Random House, Inc.

[1] It must be noted here that I reserve the division of duties for a future *Metaphysics of Morals* and that the division here

stands as only an arbitrary one (chosen in order to arrange my examples). For the rest, by a perfect duty I here understand a duty which permits no exception in the interest of inclination; thus I have not merely outer but also inner perfect duties. This runs contrary to the usage adopted in the schools, but I am not disposed to defend it here because it is all one to my purpose whether this is conceded or not.

ise, but he has enough conscience to ask himself whether it is not improper and opposed to duty to relieve his distress in such a way. Now, assuming he does decide to do so, the maxim of his action would be as follows: When I believe myself to be in need of money, I will borrow money and promise to repay it, although I know I shall never do so. Now this principle of self-love or of his own benefit may very well be compatible with his whole future welfare, but the question is whether it is right. He changes the pretension of self-love into a universal law and then puts the question: How would it be if my maxim became a universal law? He immediately sees that it could never hold as a universal law of nature and be consistent with itself; rather, it must necessarily contradict itself. For the universality of a law which says that anyone who believes himself to be in need could promise what he pleased with the intention of not fulfilling it would make the promise itself and the end to be accomplished by it impossible; no one would believe what was promised to him but would only laugh at any such assertion as vain pretense.

3. A third finds in himself a talent which could, by means of some cultivation, make him in many respects a useful . . . man. But he finds himself in comfortable circumstances and prefers indulgence in pleasure to troubling himself with broadening and improving his fortunate natural gifts. Now, however, let him ask whether his maxim of neglecting his gifts, besides agreeing with his propensity to idle amusement, agrees also with what is called duty. He sees that a system of nature could indeed exist in accordance with such a law, even though man (like the inhabitants of the South Sea Islands) should let his talents rust and resolve to devote his life merely to idleness, indulgence, and propagation — in a word, to pleasure. But he cannot possibly will that this should become a universal law of nature or that it should be implanted in us by a natural instinct. For, as a rational being, he necessarily wills that all his faculties should be developed, inasmuch as they are given to him for all sorts of possible purposes.

4. A fourth man, for whom things are going well, sees that others (whom he could help) have to struggle with great hardships, and he asks, "What concern of mine is it? Let each one be as happy as heaven wills, or as he can make himself; I will not take anything from him or even envy him; but to his welfare or to his assistance in time of need I have no desire to contribute." If such a way of thinking were a universal law of nature, certainly the human race could exist, and without doubt even better than in a state where everyone talks of sympathy and good will, or even exerts himself occasionally to practice them while, on the other hand, he cheats when he can and betrays or otherwise violates the rights of man. Now although it is possible that a universal law of nature according to that maxim could exist, it is nevertheless impossible to will that such a principle should hold everywhere as a law of nature. For a will which resolved this would conflict with itself, since instances can often arise in which he would need the love and sympathy of others, and in which he would have robbed himself, by such a law of nature springing from his own will, of all hope of the aid he desires.

The foregoing are a few of the many actual duties, or at least of duties we hold to be actual, whose derivation from the one stated principle is clear. We must be able to will that . . . a maxim of our action become a universal law; this is the canon of the moral estimation of our action generally. Some actions are of such a nature that their maxim cannot even be *thought* as a universal law of nature without contradiction, far from it being possible that one could will that it should be such. In others this internal impossibility is not found, though it is still impossible to *will* that their maxim should be raised to the universality of a law of nature, because such a will would contradict itself. We easily see that the former maxim conflicts with the stricter or narrower (imprescriptible) duty, the latter with broader meritorious) duty. Thus all duties, so far as the kind of obligation (not the object of their action) is concerned, have been completely exhibited by these examples in their dependence on the one principle.

SELECTION 10.6

# Utilitarianism

*John Stuart Mill*

[*Here, John Stuart Mill states in plain English what utilitarianism is and corrects popular misconceptions of it.*]

## What Utilitarianism Is

. . . The creed which accepts as the foundation of morals "utility" or the "greatest happiness principle" holds that actions are right in proportion as they tend to promote happiness; wrong as they tend to produce the reverse of happiness. By happiness is intended pleasure and the absence of pain; by unhappiness, pain and the privation of pleasure. To give a clear view of the moral standard set up by the theory, much more requires to be said; in particular, what things it includes in the ideas of pain and pleasure, and to what extent this is left an open question. But these supplementary explanations do not affect the theory of life on which this theory of morality is grounded—namely, that pleasure and freedom from pain are the only things desirable as ends; and that all desirable things (which are as numerous in the utilitarian as in any other scheme) are desirable either for pleasure inherent in themselves or as means to the promotion of pleasure and the prevention of pain.

Now such a theory of life excites in many minds, and among them in some of the most estimable in feeling and purpose, inveterate dislike. To suppose that life has (as they express it) no higher end than pleasure—no better and nobler object of desire and pursuit—they designate as utterly mean and groveling, as a doctrine worthy only of swine, to whom the followers of Epicurus were, at a very early period, contemptuously likened; and modern holders of the doctrine are occasionally made the subject of equally polite comparisons by its German, French, and English assailants.

When thus attacked, the Epicureans have always answered that it is not they, but their accusers, who represent human nature in a degrading light, since the accusation supposes human beings to be capable of no pleasures except those of which swine are capable. If this supposition were true, the charge could not be gainsaid, but would then be no longer an imputation; for if the sources of pleasure were precisely the same to human beings and to swine, the rule of life which is good enough for the one would be good enough for the other. The comparison of the Epicurean life to that of beasts is felt as degrading, precisely because a beast's pleasures do not satisfy a human being's conceptions of happiness. Human beings have faculties more elevated than the animal appetites and, when once made conscious of them, do not regard anything as happiness which does not include their gratification. I do not, indeed, consider the Epicureans to have been by any means faultless in their drawing out their scheme of consequences from the utilitarian principle. To do this in any sufficient manner, many Stoic, as well as Christian, elements require to be included. But there is no known Epicurean theory of life which does not assign to the pleasures of the intellect, of the feelings and imagination, and of the moral sentiments a much higher value as pleasures than to those of mere sensation. It must be admitted, however, that utilitarian writers in general have placed the superiority of mental over bodily pleasures chiefly in the greater permanency, safety, uncostliness, etc., of the former—that is, in their circumstantial advantages rather than in their intrinsic nature. And on all these points utilitarians have fully proved their case; but they might have taken the other and, as it may be called, higher ground with entire consistency. It is quite compatible with the principle of utility to recognize the fact that some kinds of pleasure are more desirable and more valuable than others. It would be absurd that, while in estimating all other things quality is considered as well as quantity, the estimation of pleasure should be supposed to depend on quantity alone.

If I am asked what I mean by difference of quality in pleasures, or what makes one pleasure more valuable than another, merely as a pleasure, except its being greater in amount, there is but one possible answer. Of two pleasures, if there be one to which all or almost all of who have experience of both give a decided preference, irrespective of any feeling of moral obligation to prefer it, that is the more desirable pleasure. If one of the two is, by those who are competently acquainted with both, placed so far above the other that they prefer it, even though knowing it to be attended with a greater amount of discontent, and would not resign it for any quantity of the other pleasure which their nature is capable of, we are justified in ascribing to the preferred enjoyment a superiority in quality so far outweighing quantity as to render it, in comparison, of small amount.

Now it is an unquestionable fact that those who are equally acquainted with and equally capable of appreciating and enjoying both do give a most marked preference to the manner of existence which employs their higher faculties. Few human creatures would consent to be changed into any of the lower animals for a promise of the fullest allowance of a beast's pleasures; no intelligent human being would consent to be a fool, no instructed person would be an ignoramus, no person of feeling and conscience would be selfish and base, even though they should be persuaded that the fool, the dunce, or the rascal is better satisfied with his lot than they are with theirs. They would not resign what they possess more than he for the most complete satisfaction of all the desires which they have in common with him. If they ever fancy they would, it is only in cases of unhappiness so extreme that to escape from it they would exchange their lot for almost any other, however undesirable in their own eyes. A being of higher faculties requires more to make him happy, is capable probably of more acute suffering, and certainly accessible to it at more points, than one of an inferior type; but in spite of these liabilities, he can never really wish to sink into what he feels to be a lower grade of existence. We may give what explanation we please of this unwillingness; we may attribute it to pride, a name which is given indiscriminately to some of the most and to some of the least estimable feelings of which mankind are capable; we may refer it to the love of liberty and personal independence, an appeal to which was with the Stoics one of the most effective means for the inculcation of it; to the love of power or to the love of excitement, both of which do really enter into and contribute to it; but its most appropriate appellation is a sense of dignity, which all human beings possess in one form or other, and in some,

though by no means in exact, proportion to their higher faculties, and which is so essential a part of the happiness of those in whom it is strong that nothing which conflicts with it could be otherwise than momentarily an object of desire to them. Whoever supposes that this preference takes place at a sacrifice of happiness — that the superior being, in anything like equal circumstances, is not happier than the inferior — confounds the two very different ideas of happiness and content. It is indisputable that the being whose capacities of enjoyment are low has the greatest chance of having them fully satisfied; and a highly endowed being will always feel that any happiness which he can look for, as the world is constituted, is imperfect. But he can learn to bear its imperfections, if they are at all bearable; and they will not make him envy the being who is indeed unconscious of the imperfections, but only because he feels not at all the good which those imperfections qualify. It is better to be a human being dissatisfied than a pig satisfied; better to be Socrates dissatisfied than a fool satisfied. And if the fool, or the pig, are of a different opinion, it is because they only know their own side of the question. The other party to the comparison knows both sides.

It may be objected that many who are capable of the higher pleasures occasionally, under the influence of temptation, postpone them to the lower. But this is quite compatible with a full appreciation of the intrinsic superiority of the higher. Men often, from infirmity of character, make their election for the nearer good, though they know it to be the less valuable; and this is no less when the choice is between two bodily pleasures than when it is between bodily and mental. They pursue sensual indulgences to the injury of health, though perfectly aware that health is the greater good. It may be further objected that many who begin with youthful enthusiasm for everything noble, as they advance in years, sink into indolence and selfishness. But I do not believe that those who undergo this very common change voluntarily choose the lower description of pleasures in preference to the higher. I believe that, before they devote themselves exclusively to the one, they have already become incapable of the other. Capacity for the nobler feelings is in most natures a very tender plant, easily killed, not only by hostile influences, but by mere want of sustenance; and in the majority of young persons it speedily dies away if the occupations to which their position in life has devoted them, and the society into which it has thrown them, are not favorable to keeping that higher capacity in exercise. Men lose their high aspirations as they lose their intellectual tastes, because they have not the time or opportunity for indulging them; and they addict themselves to inferior pleasures, not because they deliberately prefer them, but because they are either the only ones to which they have access or the only ones which they are any longer capable of enjoying. It may be questioned whether anyone who has remained equally susceptible to both classes of pleasures ever knowingly and calmly preferred the lower, though many, in all ages, have broken down in an ineffectual attempt to combine both.

From this verdict of the only competent judges, I apprehend there can be no appeal. On a question which is the best worth having of two pleasures, or which of two modes of existence is the most grateful to the feelings, apart from its moral attributes and from its consequences, the judgment of those who are qualified by knowledge of both, or, if they differ, that of the majority among them, must be admitted as final. And there needs to be the less hesitation to accept this judgment respecting the quality of pleasures, since there is no other tribunal to be referred to even on the question of quantity. What means are there of determining which is the acutest of two pains, or the intensest of two pleasurable sensations, except the general suffrage of those who are familiar with both? Neither pains nor pleasures are homogeneous, and pain is always heterogeneous with pleasure. What is there to decide whether a particular pleasure is worth purchasing at the cost of a particular pain, except the feelings and judgment of the experienced? When, therefore, those feelings and judgment declare the pleasures derived from the higher faculties to be preferable *in kind,* apart from the question of intensity, to those of which the animal nature, disjoined from the higher faculties, is susceptible, they are entitled on this subject to the same regard.

I have dwelt on this point as being a necessary part of a perfectly just conception of utility or happiness considered as the directive rule of human conduct. But it is by no means an indispensable condition to the acceptance of the utilitarian standard; for that standard is not the agent's own greatest happiness, but the greatest amount of happiness altogether; and if it may possibly be doubted whether a noble character is always the happier for its nobleness, there can be no doubt that it makes other people happier, and that the world in general is immensely a gainer by it. Utilitarianism, therefore, could only attain its end by the general cultivation of nobleness of character, even if each individual were only benefited by the nobleness of others, and his own, so far as happiness is concerned, were a sheer deduction from the benefit. But the bare enunciation of such an absurdity as this last renders refutation superfluous.

According to the greatest happiness principle, as above explained, the ultimate end, with reference to and for the sake of which all other things are desirable — whether we are considering our own good or that of other people — is an existence exempt as far as possible from pain, and as rich as possible in enjoyments, both in point of quantity and quality; the test of quality and the rule for measuring it against quantity being the preference felt by those who, in their opportunities of experience, to which must be added their habits of self-consciousness and self-observation, are best furnished with the means of comparison. This, being according to the utilitarian opinion the end of human action, is necessarily also the standard of morality, which may accordingly be defined "the rules and precepts for human conduct," by the observance of which an existence such as has been described might be, to the greatest extent possible, secured to all mankind; and not to them only, but, so far as the nature of things admits, to the whole sentient creation.

. . . The utilitarian morality does recognize in human beings the power of sacrificing their own greatest good for the good of others. It only refuses to admit that the sacrifice itself is a good. A sacrifice which does not increase or tend to increase the sum total of happiness, it considers as wasted. The only self-renunciation which it applauds is devotion to the happiness, or to some of the means of happiness, of others, either of mankind collectively or of individuals within the limits imposed by the collective interests of mankind.

I must again repeat what the assailants of utilitarianism seldom have the justice to acknowledge, that the happiness which forms the utilitarian standard of what is right in conduct is not the agent's own happiness but that of all concerned. As between his own happiness and that of others, utilitarianism requires him to be as strictly impartial as a disinterested and benevolent spectator. In the golden rule of Jesus of Nazareth, we read the complete spirit of the ethics of utility. "To do as you would be done by," and "to love your neighbor as yourself," constitute the ideal perfection of utilitarian morality. As the means of making the nearest approach to this ideal, utility would enjoin, first, that laws and social arrangements should place the happiness, or (as, speaking practically, it may be called) the interest of every individual as nearly as possible in harmony with the interest of the whole; and, secondly, that education and opinion, which have so vast a power over human character, should so use that power as to establish in the mind of every individual as indissoluble association between his own happiness and the good of the whole, especially between his own happiness and the practice of such modes of conduct, negative and positive, as regard for the universal happiness prescribes; so that not only he may be unable to conceive the possibility of happiness to himself, consistently with conduct opposed to the general good, but also that of a direct impulse to promote the general good may be in every individual one of the habitual motives of action, and the sentiments connected therewith may fill a large and prominent place in every human being's sentient existence. If the impugners of the utilitarian morality represented it to their own minds in this its true character, I know not what recommendation possessed by any other morality they could possibly affirm to be wanting to it; what more beautiful or more exalted developments of human nature any other ethical system can be supposed to foster, or what springs of action, not accessible to the utilitarian, such systems rely on for giving effect to their mandates. . . .

---

SELECTION 10.7

## Beyond Good and Evil*

*Friedrich Nietzsche*

---

[*This passage contains a succinct, orderly, and easy-to-read statement by Friedrich Nietzsche of his conception of morality and the two types of morality (master morality and slave morality).*]

Every enhancement of the type "man" has so far been the work of an aristocratic society—and it will be so again and again—a society that believes in the long ladder of an order of rank and differences in value between man and man, and that needs slavery in some sense or other. . . . Let us admit to ourselves, without trying to be considerate, how every higher culture on earth so far has *begun*. Human beings whose nature was still natural, barbarians in every terrible sense of the word, men of prey who were still in possession of unbroken strength of will and lust for power, hurled themselves upon weaker, more civilized, more peaceful races, perhaps traders or cattle raisers, or upon mellow old cultures whose last vitality was even then flaring up in splendid fireworks of spirit and corruption. In the beginning, the noble caste was always the barbarian caste: their predominance did not lie mainly in physical strength or in strength of the soul—they were more whole human beings (which also means, at every level, "more whole beasts").

. . . The essential characteristic of a good and healthy aristocracy, however, is that it experiences itself *not* as a function (whether of the monarchy or the commonwealth) but as their *meaning* and highest justification—that it therefore accepts with a good conscience the sacrifice of untold human beings who, *for its sake,* must be reduced and lowered to incomplete human beings, to slaves, to instruments. Their fundamental faith simply has to be that society must *not* exist for society's sake but only as the foundation and scaffolding on which a choice type of being is able to raise itself to its higher task and to a higher state of *being*— comparable to those sun-seeking vines of Java—they called *Sipo Matador*—that so long and so often enclasp an oak tree with their tendrils until eventually, high above it but supported by it, they can unfold their crowns in the open light and display their happiness.

---

*From *Beyond Good and Evil* by Friedrich Nietzsche, translated by Walter Kaufmann. Copyright © 1966 by Random House, Inc. Used by permission of Random House, Inc.

Refraining mutually from injury, violence, and exploitation and placing one's will on a par with that of someone else — this may become, in a certain rough sense, good manners among individuals if the appropriate conditions are present (namely, if these men are actually similar in strength and value standards and belong together in *one* body). But as soon as this principle is extended, and possibly even accepted as the *fundamental principle of society,* it immediately proves to be what it really is — a will to the *denial* of life, a principle of disintegration and decay.

Here we must beware of superficiality and get to the bottom of the matter, resisting all sentimental weakness: life itself is *essentially* appropriation, injury, overpowering of what is alien and weaker; suppression, hardness, imposition of one's own forms, incorporation and at least, at its mildest, exploitation — but why should one always use those words in which a slanderous intent has been imprinted for ages?

Even the body within which individuals treat each other as equals, as suggested before — and this happens in every healthy aristocracy — if it is a living and not a dying body, has to do to other bodies what the individuals within it refrain from doing to each other: it will have to be an incarnate will to power, it will strive to grow, spread, seize, become predominant — not from any morality or immorality but because it is *living* and because life simply *is* will to power. But there is no point on which the ordinary consciousness of Europeans resists instruction as on this: everywhere people are now raving, even under scientific disguises, about coming conditions of society in which "the exploitative aspect" will be removed — which sounds to me as if they promised to invent a way of life that would dispense with all organic functions. "Exploitation" does not belong to a corrupt or imperfect and primitive society: it belongs to the *essence* of what lives, as a basic organic function; it is a consequence of the will to power, which is after all the will of life. . . .

Wandering through the many subtler and coarser moralities which have so far been prevalent on earth, or still are prevalent, I found that certain features recurred regularly together and were closely associated — until I finally discovered two basic types and one basic difference.

There are *master morality* and *slave morality* — I add immediately that in all the higher and more mixed cultures there also appear attempts at mediation between these two moralities, and yet more often the interpenetration and mutual misunderstanding of both, and at times they occur directly alongside each other — even in the same human being, with a *single* soul. The moral discrimination of values has originated either among a ruling group whose consciousness of its difference from the ruled group was accompanied by delight — or among the ruled, the slaves and dependents of every degree.

In the first case, when the ruling group determines what is "good," the exalted, proud states of the soul are experienced as conferring distinction and determining the order of rank. The noble human being separates from himself those in whom the opposite of such exalted, proud states finds expression: he despises them. It should be noted immediately that in this first type of morality the opposition of "good" and *"bad"* means approximately the same as "noble" and "contemptible." (The opposition of "good" and *"evil"* has a different origin.) One feels contempt for the cowardly, the anxious, the petty, those intent on narrow utility; also for the suspicious with their unfree glances, those who humble themselves, the doglike people who allow themselves to be maltreated, the begging flatterers, above all the liars; it is part of the fundamental faith of all aristocrats that the common people lie. "We truthful ones" — thus the nobility of ancient Greece referred to itself.

It is obvious that moral designations were everywhere first applied to *human beings* and only later, derivatively, to actions. Therefore it is a gross mistake when historians of morality start from such questions as: why was the compassionate act praised? The noble type of man experiences *itself* as determining values; it does not need approval; it judges, "what is harmful to me is harmful in itself"; it knows itself to be that which first accords honor to things; it is *value-creating.* Everything it knows as part of itself it honors: such a morality is self-glorification. In the foreground there is the feeling of fullness, of power that seeks to overflow, the happiness of high tension, the consciousness of wealth that would give and bestow: the noble human being, too, helps the unfortunate, but not, or almost not, from pity, but prompted more by an urge begotten by excess of power. The noble human being honors himself as one who is powerful, also as one who has power over himself, who knows how to speak and be silent, who delights in being severe and hard with himself and respects all severity and hardness. . . .

Noble and courageous human beings who think that way are furthest removed from that morality which finds the distinction of morality precisely in pity, or in acting for others . . . faith in oneself, pride in oneself, a fundamental hostility and irony against "selflessness" belong just as definitely to noble morality as does a slight disdain and caution regarding compassionate feelings and a "warm heart." . . .

A morality of the ruling group, however, is most alien and embarrassing to the present taste in the severity of its principle that one has duties only to one's peers; that against beings of a lower rank, against everything alien, one may behave as one pleases or "as the heart desires," and in any case "beyond good and evil." . . .

It is different with the second type of morality, *slave morality*. Suppose the violated, oppressed, suffering, unfree, who are uncertain of themselves and weary, moralize: what will their moral valuations have in common? Probably, a pessimistic suspicion about the whole condition of man will find expression, perhaps a condemnation of man along with his condition. The slave's eye is not favorable to the virtues of the powerful: he is skeptical and suspicious, *subtly* suspicious, of all the "good" that is honored there — he would like to persuade himself that even their happiness is not genuine. Conversely, those qualities are brought out and flooded with light which serve to ease existence for those who suffer: here pity, the complaisant and obliging hand, the warm heart, patience, industry, humility, and friendliness are honored — for these are the most useful qualities and almost the only means for enduring the pressure of existence. Slave morality is essentially a morality of utility.

Here is the place for the origin of that famous opposition of "good" and "evil": into evil one's feelings project power and dangerousness, a certain terribleness, subtlety, and strength that does not permit contempt to develop. According to slave morality, those who are "evil" thus inspire fear; according to master morality it is precisely those who are "good" that inspire, and wish to inspire, fear, while the "bad" are felt to be contemptible.

The opposition reaches its climax when, as a logical consequence of slave morality, a touch of disdain is associated also with the "good" of this morality — this may be slight and benevolent — because the good human being has to be *undangerous* in the slaves' way of thinking: he is good-natured, easy to deceive, a little stupid perhaps, *un bonhomme* [a "good person"]. Wherever slave morality becomes preponderant, language tends to bring the words "good" and "stupid" closer together.

One last fundamental difference: the longing for *freedom*, the instinct for happiness and the subtleties of the feeling of freedom belong just as necessarily to slave morality and morals as art and enthusiastic reverence and devotion are the regular symptom of an aristocratic way of thinking and evaluating. . . .

A *species* comes to be, a type becomes fixed and strong, through the long fight with essentially constant *unfavorable* conditions. Conversely, we know from the experience of breeders that species accorded superabundant nourishment and quite generally extra protection and care soon tend most strongly toward variations of the type and become rich in marvels and monstrosities (including monstrous vices).

Now look for once at an aristocratic commonwealth — say, an ancient Greek *polis,* or Venice — as an arrangement, whether voluntary or involuntary, for breeding: human beings are together there who are dependent on themselves and want their species to prevail, most often because they *have to* prevail or run the terrible risk of being exterminated. Here that boon, that excess, and that protection which favor variations are lacking; the species needs itself as a species, as something that can prevail and make itself durable by virtue of its very hardness, uniformity, and simplicity of form, in a constant fight with its neighbors or with the oppressed who are rebellious or threaten rebellion. Manifold experience teaches them to which qualities above all they owe the fact that, despite all gods and men, they are still there, that they have always triumphed: these qualities they call virtues, these virtues alone they cultivate. They do this with hardness, indeed they want hardness; ever aristocratic morality is intolerant — in the education of youth, in their arrangements for women, in their marriage customs, in the relations of old and young, in their penal laws (which take into account deviants only) — they consider intolerance itself a virtue, calling it "justice."

In this way a type with few but very strong traits, a species of severe, warlike, prudently taciturn men, closemouthed and closely linked (and as such possessed of the subtlest feeling for the charms and nuances of association), is fixed beyond the changing generations; the continual fight against ever constant *unfavorable* conditions is, as mentioned previously, the cause that fixes and hardens a type.

Eventually, however, a day arrives when conditions become more fortunate and the tremendous tension decreases; perhaps there are no longer any enemies among one's neighbors, and the means of life, even for the enjoyment of life, are superabundant. At one stroke the bond and constraint of the old discipline are torn: it no longer seems necessary, a condition of existence — if it persisted it would only be a form of *luxury,* an archaizing *taste.* Variation, whether as deviation (to something higher, subtler, rarer) or as degeneration and monstrosity, suddenly appears on the scene in the greatest abundance and magnificence; the individual dares to be individual and different.

At these turning points of history we behold beside one another, and often mutually involved and entangled, a splendid, manifold, junglelike growth and upward striving, a kind of *tropical* tempo in the competition to grow, and a tremendous ruin and self-ruination, as the savage egoisms that have turned, almost exploded, against one another wrestle "for sun and light" and can no longer derive any limit, restraint, or consideration from their previous morality. It was this morality itself that dammed up such enormous strength and bent the bow in such a threatening manner; now it is "outlived." The dangerous and uncanny point has been reached where the greater, more manifold, more comprehensive life transcends and *lives beyond* the old morality; the "individual" appears, obliged to give himself laws and to develop his own arts and wiles for self-preservation, self-enhancement, self-redemption.

All sorts of new what-fors and wherewithals; no shared formulas any longer; misunderstanding allied with disrespect; decay, corruption, and the highest desires gruesomely entangled; the genius of the race overflowing from all cornucopias of good and bad; a calamitous simultaneity of spring and fall, full of new charms and veils that characterize young, still unexhausted, still unwearied corruption. Again danger is there, the mother of morals, great danger, this time transposed into the individual, into the neighbor and friend, into the alley [*sic*], into one's own child, into one's own heart, into the most personal and secret recesses of wish and will: what may the moral philosophers emerging in this age have to preach now?

These acute observers and loiterers discover that the end is approaching fast, that everything around them is corrupted and corrupts, that nothing will stand the day after tomorrow, except *one* type of man, the incurably *mediocre.* The mediocre alone have a chance of continuing their type and propagating — they are the men of the future, the only survivors: "Be like them! Become mediocre!" is now the only morality that still makes sense, that still gets a hearing.

But this morality of mediocrity is hard to preach: after all, it may never admit what it is and what it wants. It must speak of measure and dignity and duty and neighbor love — it will find it difficult *to conceal its irony.*

---

## CHECKLIST

To help you review, here is a checklist of the key philosophers and terms and concepts of this chapter. The brief descriptive sentences summarize the philosophers' leading ideas. Keep in mind that some of these summary statements are oversimplifications of complex positions.

### Philosophers

- **Sophists**   were professional teachers of fifth-century B.C. Greece whose attack on traditional moral values marks the beginnings of ethical philosophy.

- **Socrates**   sought to discover the essences of moral virtues and championed the use of reason in moral deliberation.

- **Plato**   also sought the essences of moral virtues, identifying these with the unchanging Forms, the highest of which he held to be the Form of the Good, the ultimate source of all value and reality.

- **Aesara of Lucania**   was a Pythagorean philosopher from southern Italy who held that by introspecting about the nature and structure of the human soul we can identify a standard of personal and public morality.

- **Aristotle**   was an ethical naturalist who held that moral judgments are judgments of fact about the natural world. He said that happiness is our highest good.

- **Epicurus,**   an ethical egoist, held that one's highest objective is to lead the pleasant life through moderate living.

- **Zeno**   was the founder of Stoicism.
- **Epictetus,**   a leading Stoic, held that one's highest objective is to find a serene or untroubled life through acceptance of the rational natural order of things.
- **Diogenes**   was the most famous Cynic, who taught by shocking example that the wise person reduces all wants and avoids all comforts.
- **St. Augustine**   used Platonic concepts to solve "the problem of evil," held moral evil to be misdirected love, and identified God as the supreme moral authority and source of all goodness.
- **St. Hildegard of Bingen**   was a medieval German mystic philosopher who held that the moral powers of the soul come from its three faculties: understanding, insight, and execution.
- **Heloise**   was a medieval French philosopher who held that the morality or immorality of an action is determined by the intention with which it is done.
- **Peter Abelard**   set forth one of medieval philosophy's most careful analyses of the morality of intent.
- **St. Thomas Aquinas**   reconciled Aristotelian ethical naturalism with Christianity.
- **Thomas Hobbes**   held that "good" and "evil" denote what a person desires or hates; he maintained that our natural end is preservation of self.
- **David Hume**   held that moral principles are neither divine edicts nor discoverable by reason and that value judgments are based on emotion. He said that the act that pleases our moral sensibilities is one that reflects the agent's benevolent character.
- **Immanuel Kant**   held that the supreme prescription of morality is to act always in such a way that you could rationally will the principle on which you act to be a universal law. He believed that what you should do you should do not because it promotes some end but simply because it is right.
- **Jeremy Bentham,**   a utilitarian, held that the rightness of an action is identical with the pleasure it produces as its consequence and said that pleasure can be evaluated quantitatively.
- **John Stuart Mill,**   a utilitarian, held that the rightness of an action is identical with the happiness that it produces as its consequence and said that pleasure—a part of happiness—must be measured in terms of quality as well as quantity.
- **Friedrich Nietzsche**   distinguished between slave morality (the morality of the masses) and master morality (the morality of the nobleman). The former represents the denial of life; the latter represents the will-to-power.

## Key Terms and Concepts

| | |
|---|---|
| ethics | Form |
| ethical skepticism | Cyrenaicism |
| descriptive relativism | objective reality |
| cultural relativism | ethical naturalism |
| individual relativism | mean between |
| subjectivism | extremes |
| egoism | instrumental versus |
| descriptive egoism | intrinsic ends |
| prescriptive egoism | Epicureanism |
| hedonism | Stoicism |
| psychological | natural law |
| hedonism | Cynicism |
| ethical hedonism | morality of intent |
| egoistic ethical | divine law |
| hedonism | categorical imperative |
| universalistic ethical | hypothetical |
| hedonism | imperative |
| divine-command ethics | moral imperative |
| consequentialism | utilitarianism |
| deontological ethics | act utilitarianism |
| virtue ethics | rule utilitarianism |
| relativism | paradox of hedonism |

## QUESTIONS FOR DISCUSSION AND REVIEW

1. Is there some single thing that all morally good actions have in common? Defend your view.

2. "What is right is what you yourself believe is right." Critically evaluate this statement.

3. What is the connection between virtue and happiness in the philosophy of Plato?

4. Explain how Plato's theory may be regarded as "complete."

5. What is the connection among the structure of the soul, personal morality, and justice, according to Aesara of Lucania?

6. In what does happiness consist, according to Aristotle? When can we be said to be virtuous?

7. What is the connection between habit and moral character, for Aristotle?

8. Compare and contrast the ethical philosophies of Epicureanism and Stoicism. Which do you think is the superior philosophy, and why?

9. Is it a sound policy to reduce all wants to a minimum and to achieve utter self-reliance by avoiding all the comforts of society?

10. Can you control your attitude if you cannot control your fate?

11. What is Hildegard's concept of the structure and faculties of the soul? How does it compare to Aesara of Lucania's views on the soul?

12. Explain Heloise's view of the morality of intent and her view of the nature of disinterested love.

13. Explain Augustine's solution to the problem of evil, and determine whether it is sound.

14. Explain and evaluate Aquinas' reasons for believing that ultimate human happiness does not consist in wealth, worldly power, or anything in this life.

15. Do we seek personal survival above all other things?

16. Do we always act selfishly? Explain.

17. Explain and critically evaluate prescriptive egoism.

18. Does it make sense for a (prescriptive) egoist to advocate egoism?

19. Is altruism really disguised egoism?

20. Can reasoning disclose the moral wrongfulness of an act of murder?

21. Is Hume correct in saying that the type of act we deem morally praiseworthy is one done out of concern for others?

22. Is it abnormal not to have sympathy for others? Are selfish people really admired in today's society?

23. Is it true that moral principles hold without exception? Explain.

24. Is it true that moral principles cannot be revealed through scientific investigation?

25. Suppose you stole something that did not belong to you. Could you rationally will the principle on which you acted to be a universal law? Explain.

26. Explain the difference between a hypothetical imperative and a categorical imperative.

27. Which is it: Does the nature of an act or its consequences determine whether it is good, or is it the intent with which the act has been taken? Or is it something else altogether?

28. Kant held that there is no moral worth in helping others out of sympathy for them. What reasons are there for holding this view? Are they sound?

29. What does it mean to say that rational beings should be treated as ends and not as means? Give an example of treating another as a means.

30. Is your own happiness more important morally than that of others? ("It is to me" does not count as an answer.)

31. Was Bentham correct in saying that *ought, right, good,* and the like have meaning only when defined in terms of pleasure?

32. Explain the difference between psychological hedonism and ethical hedonism.

33. Is it true that the ultimate object of a person's desire is always pleasure? Explain.

34. Was Mill correct in saying that some pleasures are inherently better than others?

35. How does Mill propose to establish which of two pleasures is qualitatively better? Can you think of a better way of establishing this?

36. Leslie, who is in the Peace Corps, volunteers to aid starving Ethiopians. She travels to Ethiopia and, risking her own health and safety, works herself nearly to exhaustion for two years, caring for as many people as she can. Meanwhile, her father, Harold, dashes off a huge check for the Ethiopian relief fund. In fact, his check helps more people than Leslie's actions do. But, morally speaking, is Harold more praiseworthy than Leslie? What would Bentham say? Mill? You?

37. Explain the paradox of hedonism.

38. What does Nietzsche mean when he says life is the will to power?

39. "There cannot be moral values if there is no God." Critically evaluate this assertion.

## SUGGESTED FURTHER READINGS

Julia Annas, *The Morality of Happiness* (New York: Oxford University Press, 1993). An analysis of ancient ethical theory.

Julia Annas, *Platonic Ethics, Old and New* (Ithaca, N.Y.: Cornell University Press, 1999). A detailed and widely acclaimed analysis of Plato's ethical thought.

Aristotle, *The Nichomachean Ethics,* Martin Ostwald, ed. (Indianapolis: Bobbs-Merrill, 1962).

James Baillie, *Routledge Philosophy Guidebook to Hume on Morality* (New York: Routledge, 2000). A relatively clear presentation of Hume's thought on passions, taste, virtue, and other related topics.

Forrest E. Baird and Walter Kaufmann, *Nineteenth Century Philosophy* (Upper Saddle River, N.J.: Prentice-Hall, 1997). Important selections of philosophical writings from Bentham to Nietzsche.

Jeremy Bentham, *An Introduction to the Principles of Morals and Legislation,* J. J. Burns, H. L. A. Hart, and F. Rosen, eds. (New York: Oxford University Press, 1996). This is the edition you should own. Includes an important essay by Hart.

Simon Blackburn, *Ethics: A Very Short Introduction* (New York: Oxford University Press, 2003). A brief look at the basic issues and development in moral philosophy.

R. Bracht Branham and Marie-Odile Goulet-Cazé, eds., *The Cynics* (Berkeley: University of California Press, 1996). These essays provide a good overview of this movement and its significance.

R. Bracht Branham and Marie-Odile Goulet-Cazé, eds., *The Cynics: The Cynic Movement in Antiquity and Its Legacy* (Berkeley and Los Angeles: University of California Press, 1997). A collection examining Cynicism from every perspective — philosophical, historical, social, literary, and others.

Sarah Broadie, *Ethics with Aristotle* (New York: Oxford University Press, 1991). A respected treatment of the subject.

John Burnet, *Early Greek Philosophy,* 4th ed. (London: Macmillan, originally published in 1930). A standard work on early Greek philosophy.

Tom Butler-Bowdon, *50 Self-Help Classics* (London: Nicolas Brealey, 2003). Life-changing ideas from philosophers east and west, ancient and contemporary.

Chamfort, *Reflections on Life, Love and Society,* Douglas Parmée, trans. (London: Short Books, 2003). Excellent selection of the wise and witty comments on life by the French aphorist.

Thomas Cleary, trans., *Living a Good Life* (Boston: Shambhala, 1997). Practical advice on life in short quotations from Plato, Aristotle, Pythagoras, and Diogenes.

David E. Cooper, ed., *Ethics: The Classic Readings* (Malden, Mass.: Blackwell, 1997). A collection of critical texts concerning ethics, including contributions by Indian and Chinese philosophers.

F. C. Copleston, *Aquinas* (Baltimore: Penguin Books, 1955). See Chapter 5 of this text.

Robert Crisp and Michael Slote, eds., *Virtue Ethics* (New York: Oxford University Press, 1997). Some of the most significant work done on virtue ethics over the past forty years.

Arthur Dobrin, *Ethics for Everyone* (New York: John Wiley and Sons, 2002). An introductory guide in how to improve one's moral intelligence.

Epictetus, *Discourses, Book 1,* Robert F. Dobbin, trans. (New York: Oxford University Press, 1998). A new translation with background information.

Epictetus, *The Handbook of Epictetus,* Nicholas P. White, trans. (Indianapolis: Hackett, 1983). If you enjoyed the Epictetus selection, here is where you can find more.

Epicurus, *The Extant Remains,* C. Bailey, trans. (Oxford: Clarendon Press, 1962). For those who wish to read more from Epicurus.

Steven Estes, *History and Philosophy of Sport and Physical Education* (New York: McGraw-Hill, 2001). A history of the development of sport is complemented by an exploration of up-to-date issues such as the impact of politics and technology on sport.

Owen Flanagan and Amelie Oskenberg Rorty, eds., *Identity, Character and Morality* (Cambridge, Mass.: MIT Press, 1990). A group of essays relating contemporary ethics to psychology.

Philippa Foot, ed., *Theories of Ethics* (New York: Oxford University Press, 1990). A selection of papers relating to current issues in moral philosophy.

John Gaskin, ed., *The Epicurean Philosophers* (Rutland, Vt.: Charles Tuttle Co., 1995). A comprehensive collection of their surviving works.

E. Gilson, *The Christian Philosophy of St. Augustine* (New York: Random House, 1960). See the introduction and part 2 for relevant material.

J. Gould, *The Development of Plato's Ethics* (London: Cambridge University Press, 1955). Explains the important principles and concepts in Plato's ethics.

Baltasar Gracian, *The Art of Worldly Wisdom,* Joseph Jacobs, trans. (Boston: Shambhala, 2000). A good translation of the ultimate how-to-live book.

E. Hamilton and H. Cairns, eds., *The Collected Dialogues of Plato* (New York: Bollingen Foundation, 1961). This, as we said before, is what you need to acquaint yourself firsthand with Plato's dialogues. Be sure to read *The Republic.* The other dialogues especially relevant to ethics are *Gorgias, Meno,* and *Philebus.*

W. F. R. Hardie, *Aristotle's Ethical Theory* (Oxford: Clarendon Press, 1968). There are several reliable books on Aristotle's ethics. This is one of the most popular.

R. M. Hare, *The Language of Morals* (Oxford: Clarendon Press, 1952). An important treatise on the logic of moral discourse.

R. D. Hicks, *Stoic and Epicurean* (New York: Russell and Russell, 1962). Chapters 3, 4, and 5 are especially relevant to our discussion here.

Hildegard of Bingen, *Book of Divine Works,* Matthew Fox, ed. (Santa Fe, N.M.: Bear & Co., 1987).

Hildegard of Bingen, *Scivias,* Bruce Hozeki, trans. (Santa Fe, N.M.: Bear & Co., 1986).

Thomas Hobbes, *Leviathan,* J. C. A. Gaskin, ed. (New York: Oxford University Press, 1998). Includes annotations and an introduction by the editor.

David Hume, *An Enquiry Concerning the Principles of Morals,* Tom L. Beauchamp, ed. (New York: Oxford University Press, 1998). Hume's major work on ethics.

Terrence Irwin, *Plato's Ethics* (New York: Oxford University Press, 1995). An analysis.

Immanuel Kant, *Foundations of the Metaphysics of Morals,* R. P. Wolff, ed. (Indianapolis: Bobbs-Merrill, 1959). Contains Kant's most important moral philosophy together with commentary by Kant on assorted problems.

J. Kemp, *Ethical Naturalism: Hobbes and Hume* (London: Macmillan, 1970). See chapters 2 and 3. For original works, try F. J. E. Woodbridge, *Hobbes Selections* and C. W. Hendel, Jr., *Hume Selections,* both published by Scribner's in New York.

G. S. Kirk, J. E. Raven, and M. Schofield, *The Presocratic Philosophers: A Critical History with a Selection of Texts,* 2nd ed. (Cambridge: Cambridge University Press, 1983). This is a comprehensive treatment of the pre-Socratics.

S. Korner, *Kant* (Baltimore: Penguin Books, 1955). See chapters 6 and 7. A standard work on Kant.

Hugh La Folette, ed., *The Blackwell Guide to Ethical Theory* (New York: Blackwell, 2003). Survey of the major issues in contemporary moral philosophy.

Janet Lloyd, *The Great Sophists in Periclean Athens,* Jacqueline De Romilly, trans. (New York: Oxford University Press, 1998). An important interpretation.

A. A. Long, *Hellenistic Philosophy* (Berkeley: University of California Press, 1986). A readable account of Epicureanism, Skepticism, and Stoicism.

A. A. Long and P. N. Sedley, eds., *The Hellenistic Philosophers* (Cambridge: Cambridge University Press, 1987). Translations of texts from the Stoic, Epicurean, and Skeptic schools of thought.

J. S. Mill, *On Liberty and Other Essays,* John Gray, ed. (New York: Oxford University Press, 1998). The other essays include *Utilitarianism, Considerations on Representative Government,* and *The Subjection of Women.*

J. S. Mill, *Utilitarianism,* Roger Crisp, ed. (New York: Oxford University Press, 1998). Uses the 1871 edition of Mill's text, the last edition to be published in Mill's lifetime.

Friedrich Nietzsche, *Beyond Good and Evil,* Marion Faber and Robert C. Holub, eds. and trans. (New York: Oxford University Press, 1999). A new translation, with an introduction by an eminent Nietzsche scholar.

Louis P. Pojman, ed., *The Moral Life* (New York: Oxford University Press, 1999). Key moral issues are examined by both figures from the literary and philosophical worlds.

James Rachels, *The Right Thing to Do, Basic Readings in Moral Philosophy* (New York: McGraw-Hill, 2002). A selection of readings in moral philosophy from some of the great historical figures.

Betty Radice, trans., *The Letters of Abelard and Heloise* (New York: Penguin Books, 1974).

John Rawls, *Lectures on the History of Moral Philosophy,* Barbara Herman, ed. (Cambridge, Mass.: Harvard University Press, 2000). Lectures on the history of moral philosophy by one of the leading philosophers of our times.

Nina Rosenstand, *The Human Condition: An Introduction to the Philosophy of Human Nature* (New York: McGraw-Hill, 2001). Fiction and film are used as a way of understanding theories of human nature.

W. D. Ross, *Kant's Ethical Theory* (Oxford: Oxford University Press, 1954). Brief; excellent.

Samuel Scheffler, ed., *Consequentialism and Its Critics* (New York: Oxford University Press, 1991). Papers by Nozick, Nagel, and others regarding the consequentialist issue.

Nancy Sherman, *The Fabric of Character, Aristotle's Theory of Virtue* (New York: Oxford University Press, 1989). Explains and examines Aristotle's theory of virtue.

Henry Sidgwick, *Outlines of the History of Ethics* (Boston: Beacon, 1960) and *The Methods of Ethics* (New York: Dover, 1974). These are classic works in ethics.

Many standard ethical concepts, principles, and distinctions originated with Sidgwick, and his treatment of utilitarianism is complete and penetrating.

Mary Ellen Waithe, *A History of Women Philosophers*, vol. 2, *Medieval, Renaissance, and Enlightenment Women Philosophers: 500–1600* (Dordrecht: Kluwer Academic Publishers, 1989).

# 11

# Political Philosophy

Man, when perfected, is the best of all animals, but, when separated from law and justice, he is the worst of all. . . . Justice is the bond of men in states.
— Aristotle

That one human being will desire to render the person and property of another subservient to his pleasures, notwithstanding the pain or loss of pleasure which it may occasion to that individual, is the foundation of government.     — James Mill

While the state exists there is no freedom. Where there is freedom, there will be no state.     — Vladimir I. Lenin

Ethics is the philosophical study of moral judgments. But many moral judgments are at the same time political judgments.

Should goods be distributed equally? Or should they be distributed according to need? Or perhaps according to merit, or according to contribution to production, or to existing ownership, or to something else?

Is it justifiable for a government to restrict the liberty of its citizens and, if so, in what measure?

When, if ever, is fine or imprisonment legitimate? And what is the purpose of fine and imprisonment: punishment? deterrence? rehabilitation?

Are there natural rights that all governments must respect? What form of political society or state is best? Should there even be a state?

The answers to these questions are moral judgments of a political variety. Political philosophy considers such issues and the concepts that are involved in them.

More generally, **political philosophy** seeks to find the best form of political existence. It is concerned with determining the state's right to exist, its ethically legitimate functions and scope, and its proper organization. Political philosophy also seeks to describe and understand the nature of political relationships and political authority, though scholars whose inquiries are focused within the purely descriptive branch of political philosophy now usually call themselves political scientists.

## PLATO AND ARISTOTLE

Let's start with Plato and Aristotle because they were the first to try to build a political philosophy from the ground up.

### Plato

According to **Plato's** *Republic,* the human soul has three different elements, one consisting of raw appetites, another consisting of drives (such as anger and ambition), and a third consisting of thought or intellect. In the virtuous or "just" person, each of these three elements fulfills its own unique function and does so under the governance of reason. Likewise, according to Plato, in the ideal or "just" state there are also three elements, each of which fulfills its unique function and does so in accordance with the dictates of reason.

The lowest element in the soul — the appetitive element — corresponds in the well-ordered state to the class of *craftsmen.* The soul's drive element corresponds in the state to the class of *police-soldiers,* who are auxiliaries to the *governing class.* This last class, in the well-ordered state, corresponds to the intellectual, rational element of the soul.

The governing class, according to Plato, comprises a select few highly educated and profoundly rational individuals, including women so qualified. An individual becomes a member of a class by birth, but he or she will move to a higher or lower class according to aptitude.

In the healthy state, said Plato, as in the well-ordered soul, the rational element is in control. Thus, for Plato, the ideal state is a class-structured aristocracy ruled by **philosopher-kings.**

Unlike the craftsmen, the ruling elite and their auxiliaries, who jointly are the guardians of society, have neither private property nor even private families: property, wives, and children are all possessions held in common. Reproduction among the guardians is arranged always to improve the blood line of their posterity in intelligence, courage, and other qualities apt for leadership. The guardians not only must be trained appropriately for soldiering but also must be given a rigorous intellectual education that, for the few whose unique abilities allow it, prepares them for advanced work in mathematics and dialectic (that is, the Socratic method; see Chapter 3). These few, at age fifty and after many years of public service, advance to membership in the ruling aristocracy and to leadership of the state. Such is Plato's vision of the ideal political structure.

It is important to be aware that from Plato's perspective the state, like the person, is a *living organism* whose well-being must be sought by its subjects. Although he assumed that the healthy state is best for the individuals in it, Plato also believed that the health or well-being of the state is *desirable for its own sake*. And just as a person's health or well-being requires the proper functioning and coordination of the elements of the soul under the overarching rule of reason, the state's health or well-being lies in the proper functioning and coordination of its elements under the rule of the reasoning elite. The ideal state, according to Plato, is well ordered in this way, and its being well ordered in this way is something that is intrinsically desirable.

In Book VIII of the *Republic*, Plato identified five forms of government. The preferred form, of course, is an *aristocracy*, governed by rational philosopher-kings. According to Plato, however, even if this ideal state could be achieved, it would in time degenerate into a *timocracy*, in which the ruling class is motivated by love of honor rather than by love for the common good. A timocracy in turn gives way to a *plutocracy*, which is rule by men who primarily desire riches. Under a plutocracy, society becomes divided between two classes, the rich and the poor, Plato thought. Nevertheless, this form of government, Plato said, is preferable to the next degeneration, *democracy*, which results because "a society cannot hold wealth in honor and at the same time establish self-control in its citizens." (Perhaps we will eventually see if Plato is correct that a society that honors wealth cannot maintain self-control.) With Plato's democracy, people's impulses are unrestrained, and the result is lack of order and direction. "Mobocracy" is what we would call Plato's "democracy" today. *Tyranny*, the last form of government in Plato's classification, results when the democratic mob submits itself to a strongman, each person selfishly figuring to gain from the tyrant's rule and believing that the tyrant will end democracy's evil. In fact, Plato thought, the tyrant will acquire absolute power and enslave his subjects. Further, he, the tyrant, will himself become a slave to his wretched craving for power and self-indulgence. Plato was not always an optimist.

We, of course, are most likely to evaluate Plato's prescriptions solely according to what they would do for the general welfare — that is, the welfare of all the citizens or subjects of the state. And so it may occur to you that, if the citizens are satisfied with their class level and do not think that their natural abilities warrant higher placement, then they might like Plato's form of government. After all, the division of power, responsibility, and labor among classes as envisioned by Plato might maximize (as he thought it would) the productivity of the state; and the unavailability of private property to the ruling elite could conceivably remove acquisitive temptations so that members of the elite would devote their efforts to the public good rather than to personal gain. A state governed by wise and enlightened aristocracy that seeks the betterment of its citizens might well do much to enhance the public welfare and happiness, even if it sometimes might be difficult for a ruling aristocracy to understand the needs and desires of the populace. In short, you may be disposed to give Plato a passing grade on his state, at least with reference to what it would do for the welfare of its subjects. You would probably not be inclined to think of the state as an organism in its own right whose well-being is something desirable for its own sake.

## Aristotle, the Political Scientist

Aristotle was a keen observer of the world around him, including the political world. But he wasn't merely a describer of political systems. Aristotle did enunciate principles in terms of which various forms of government can be *evaluated*. Also, when he listed *monarchy, aristocracy,* and *polity* as proper forms of government and *tyranny, oligarchy,* and *democracy* as their corresponding improper forms, he was not merely describing these forms, as a modern-day political scientist might, but was also evaluating them, as a political philosopher will do.

Nor is Aristotle a historian of political systems. (You would have no inkling, from reading Aristotle's *Politics,* that the Greek city-state system of government went out of existence forever during his lifetime!)

The Platonic idea of the state as an organism whose well-being is desirable for its own sake has been exploited, as we will see, as justification for the more totalitarian premise that the individual must sacrifice his or her own well-being for that of the state. Plato himself, however, did not advocate tyrannical rule.

### Aristotle

**Aristotle,** too, regarded the state as an organism, as a living being that exists for some end, for some purpose. That purpose, he believed, is to promote the good life for humans. (The good life, for Aristotle, is one that gives you the highest human good—happiness.) Thus, Aristotle offered a standard of evaluation of the state different from Plato's. For Aristotle, a state is good only to the degree to which it enables its citizens themselves to achieve the good life, whereas for Plato a state is good to the extent that it is well ordered.

Aristotle, who had studied the constitutions, or basic political structures, of numerous Greek city- and other states, was a practical thinker. He insisted that the form of the ideal state depends on, and can change with, circumstances. Unlike Plato, Aristotle did not set forth a recipe for the ideal state. A state, he said, can be ruled properly by one person; but it can also be ruled properly by a few people or by many. When a state is properly ruled by one person, he said, it is a *monarchy;* improper rule by one is *tyranny.* Proper rule by the few is *aristocracy;* improper rule, *oligarchy.* Proper rule by the many is a *polity,* and improper rule by them is a *democracy.* Good forms of government tend to degenerate into bad, he thought, as Plato also did. Aristocracies become oligarchies, monarchies become tyrannies, polities become democracies. (Also see the box "Aristotle, the Political Scientist.")

Though Aristotle thought that states may be good or bad irrespective of their form, he observed that political societies always have three classes: a lower class of laborers and peasants; a middle class of craftsmen, farmers, and merchants; and an upper class of aristocrats. He further observed that political power rests in one or another of these social classes or is shared by them variously, irrespective of the form of the state.

Aristotle, like Plato, was no egalitarian. (An *egalitarian* believes that all humans are equal in their social, political, and economic rights and privileges.) But even though Plato's ideal state has no slaves, Aristotle held that some people are by nature suited for slavery, whereas others by nature are suited for freedom. Even freemen are not equals, Aristotle held. Those who, like laborers, do not have the aptitude (or time) to participate in governance should not be citizens. But, he said, beware: the desires of lesser men for equality are the "springs and fountains" of revolution and are to be so recognized by a properly functioning government, which takes precautions to avoid revolt.

## NATURAL LAW THEORY AND CONTRACTARIAN THEORY

Aristotle was an ethical naturalist (see previous chapter). For answers to questions about what *ought* to be the case, he looked around him (i.e., he turned to "nature") to see what *is* the case. To determine what the purpose of the state ought to be, he considered what the purpose of existing states actually is. Ought all people be equal in freedom? in citizenship? Aristotle's answers to these and other questions of political ethics were grounded on what he observed. In this instance, the apparent natural inequality of people he perceived prompted him to answer negatively.

Because of his naturalism, Aristotle is sometimes viewed as the source of **natural law political theory.** According to this theory, questions of political ethics are to be answered by reference to the so-called natural law, which alone supposedly determines what is right and wrong, good and bad, just and unjust, proper and improper.

As you saw in Chapter 10, however, the first relatively clear concept of natural law per se is probably found not in Aristotle's writings but later, in Stoic philosophy, in which the natural law is conceived as an impersonal principle of reason that governs the cosmos. But the Stoics were not primarily political philosophers. So it is to the celebrated Roman statesman Cicero that we turn for the classic expression of the Stoic concept of natural law as applied to political philosophy. "True law," wrote Cicero,

> is right reason in agreement with Nature; it is of universal application, unchanging and everlasting. . . . There will not be different laws at Rome and at Athens; or different laws now and in the future, but one eternal and unchangeable law will be valid for all nations and all times.

In other words, Cicero is proposing that there is only one valid law, the natural law of reason, which holds eternally and universally. This is a bold idea, and to a certain extent we still accept it today.

### Augustine and Aquinas

In the thought of **Augustine** (354–430) and **Aquinas** (1225–1274), the natural law as conceived by the Stoics, which according to Cicero was the only valid basis for human law, was *Christianized*. Natural law was conceived by these Church

The Roman statesman Cicero, who held there is but one valid law, the natural law of reason.

philosophers to be the eternal moral law of *God* as humans apprehend it through the dictates of their conscience and reason.

With Augustine and Aquinas, two vital questions were raised: the relationship of secular law to the natural law of God and, correspondingly, the relationship of state to church. According to both thinkers, the laws of the state must be just, which meant for them that the laws of the state must accord with God's natural law. If secular laws do not accord, they held, they are not truly laws, and there is no legitimate state. For Augustine, the purpose of the state is to take "the power to do hurt" from the wicked; for Aquinas, it is to attend to the common good (which, for Aquinas, meant much more than merely curbing human sinfulness). For both, the church provides for a person's spiritual needs, and, though the state does have rights and duties within its own sphere, it is subordinate to the church, just as its laws are subordinate to natural law.

Perhaps Aquinas' most distinctive contributions to political philosophy is his discussion of law. Aquinas distinguished among four kinds of law. Most fundamental is **eternal law,** which is, in effect, the divine reason of God that rules over all things at all times. Then there is **divine law,** which is God's gift to man, apprehended by us through revelation rather than through conscience or reason, and which directs us to our *supernatural* goal, eternal happiness. **Natural law** is God's eternal law as it applies to man on earth; in effect, it is the fundamental principles of morality, as apprehended by us in our conscience and practical reasoning. Natural law directs us to our *natural* goal, happiness on earth. Finally, **human law** is the laws and statutes of society that are derived from man's understanding of natural law. A rule or decree of a ruler or government must answer to a higher authority, said Aquinas; it must conform to natural law. Any rule or statute that does not, he said, should not be obeyed: "We ought to obey God rather than men." Aquinas' conception of law, especially of natural law and human law, bears widely on our own conceptions.

## Hobbes

Whereas Augustine, Aquinas, and other Christian thinkers conceived of the natural law as the moral law of God, **Thomas Hobbes** (1588–1679), whose ethical principles were discussed in Chapter 10, construed the natural law as neither the law of God nor moral law. In fact, Hobbes's conception of natural law amounts to discarding the older religious concept.

Hobbes did not speak of *the* natural law in the singular, as did the classical and church philosophers, but of natural *laws* in the plural. These, for Hobbes, are simply rational principles of prudent action, prescriptions for best preserving your own life. According to Hobbes, who was a naturalist and in this respect resembled Aristotle, there is no higher authority beyond nature that passes judgment on the morality or immorality of human deeds. You obey the laws of nature insofar as you act rationally, and insofar as you do not, you do not live long.

Hobbes's first law of nature is *to seek peace as far as you have any hope of obtaining it, and when you cannot obtain it to use any means you can to defend yourself.* As you can see, this "law" is indeed simply a prescription of rational self-interest.

It is easy to understand why Hobbes regarded this as the first law of nature. From Hobbes's perspective, the question of how best to prolong one's life was a pressing issue for most people. Historians emphasize the importance of the Scientific Revolution in the seventeenth century, which included the discoveries of Gilbert, Kepler, Galileo, Harvey, Boyle, Huygens, Newton, and others. The seventeenth century, in fact, reads like a *Who's Who* of scientific discoverers. But most seventeenth-century Europeans, plain folk and ruling aristocrats alike, had never even *heard* of these discoveries, and even if they had, they would have considered them uninteresting and irrelevant. That is because the seventeenth century was a century of political chaos and brutal warfare both in England and on the Continent. The Thirty Years' War, an ugly spectacle, happened during this century, and most Europeans were somewhat preoccupied with the safety of their skins. For most of them, the question of personal survival was of more than academic interest.

Hobbes's second law is *to be content, for the sake of peace and self-preservation, provided others are also content, with only so much liberty "against other men" as you would allow other men against yourself.* And the third law is *"that men perform the covenants they have made."* (A covenant is an agreement or contract, a compact.)

But nobody, Hobbes said, is so stupid as to live up to an agreement that turns out not to be in her or his own best interest. So, if you want people to live by their agreements, you have to make sure that they will *suffer* if they try to break them. This means you have to have some third power to enforce them. "Without the terror of some power to cause them to be observed," Hobbes wrote, covenants are only words.

In light of these considerations, Hobbes concluded, if you apply the three "laws of nature" listed here to real-life situations, what they mean is this: For their own welfare, people should transfer both their collective strength and their right to use whatever is necessary to defend themselves to a sovereign power that will use the acquired power to *compel* all citizens to honor their commitments to one another and to live together peacefully. This is the best road to peace and security, according to Hobbes. Without this central power to make them honor their

agreements and keep them in line, people live in a "state of nature," a state of unbridled war of each against all, a state of chaos, mistrust, deception, meanness, and violence in which each person stops at nothing to gain the upper hand, and life is "solitary, poor, nasty, brutish, and short."

The central **sovereign power** to which people will transfer their power and rights, if they are smart enough to see that it is in their own self-interest to do so, is called by Hobbes the **Leviathan.** (A leviathan is a sea monster often symbolizing evil in the Old Testament and Christian literature.) When people transfer their power and rights to the Leviathan, they in effect create a **social contract.** It is this contract that delivers people from the evils of the natural state to civil society and a state of peace.

The social contract is thus an agreement between individuals who, for the sake of peace, are willing to make this absolutely unconditional and irrevocable transfer of right and power to the sovereign or Leviathan.

According to Hobbes, only when people have contracted among themselves and created the Leviathan is there *law* or *justice,* and Hobbes was speaking of civil laws, not natural laws. *Justice* and *injustice* Hobbes defined as the keeping and the breaking of covenants. Because covenants and laws are meaningless unless there is a Leviathan to enforce them, law and justice can exist only under a Leviathan.

Now the original social covenant, or contract, that creates the Leviathan is not a contract *between* the Leviathan and its subjects, Hobbes stressed. It is a contract among the subjects themselves. There is not and cannot be any covenant *between* the Leviathan and its subjects. Here is why: because the Leviathan holds all the power, it would be free to break any pledge, promise, agreement, commitment, contract, or covenant that it made. And that means that a covenant between the Leviathan and its subjects would be unenforceable and hence would be empty words.

Therefore, because logically there cannot be any covenant between the Leviathan and its subjects, and because justice is defined by Hobbes as the keeping of a covenant, it is *impossible* for the Hobbesian sovereign or Leviathan to act unjustly toward its subjects. Likewise, the Leviathan's laws — and the Leviathan's laws are the only laws, for they alone can be enforced — cannot be unjust. The Leviathan,

## Power Politics: Niccolò Machiavelli

One of the most famous political treatises of all time, Machiavelli's *The Prince* (1532), explains how a prince best may gain and maintain power and is often regarded as the foundational treatise of modern political science.

Niccolò Machiavelli [mak-yah-VEL-ee] (1469–1527) did not mince words. He stated frankly that in the actions of princes the ends justify the means, and that princes who wish to survive had to learn how *not* to be good and how to be feared as well as loved. If the prince has to choose between the two, being feared or being loved, Machiavelli added, it is much safer for him to be feared. *The Prince* was a shocker when it was written and is still a shocker today. It established Machiavelli's reputation as a cold-blooded advocate of power politics.

Machiavelli, however, though recognizing the importance of power in politics and having but little belief in the intelligence or rationality of the common run of men, made a distinction between the virtuous leader and the villainous or ignoble one, finding little to admire in the latter type.

Further, his more expansive earlier political work, *Discourses on Livy* (1531), reveals his preference for free republics over monarchies as better means of securing liberty, order, stability, and the interests of all, though he thought that under the prevailing circumstances the only way to secure order was to establish an absolute power that could curb the excesses of the ambitious and avaricious.

In the Roman republic, people had been more devoted to liberty than in his time, he thought, and in general they had been stronger in character and less prone to become prey to evil-minded men. Why had people changed? Christianity, he perceived, in emphasizing humility, meekness, and contempt for worldly objects, had made men feeble and needy of the absolute rule of a prince.

according to Hobbes, has the right to lay down any laws it can enforce (although, as you will see shortly, it cannot require us to take our own lives), and we are not only physically but also morally obliged to obey them, for only through its laws are we kept from anarchy.

That no covenant exists between the Leviathan and its subjects means that the Leviathan has no legal or moral obligation to them. That it has no legal or moral obligation to its subjects means that they are *gambling* when they agree among themselves unconditionally to transfer all power and rights to it; they are gambling that life under its rule (conditions of "peace") will be better than it would be under the conditions of anarchy that otherwise would obtain. Perhaps a rational sovereign is likely to see that it is not in his own self-interest to destroy or abuse his subjects, but there is always a chance that he will not.

Hobbes, obviously, thought the gamble a wise one. Were people to live without a common power, he wrote, a power "to keep them all in awe," their innate viciousness would preclude development of any commerce, industry, or culture, and there would be "no knowledge on the face of the earth; no account of time; no arts; no letters; no society." There would be only, he wrote, "continual fear, and danger of violent death." In Hobbes's view, given the alternatives of anarchy and dictatorship (the Leviathan)—and these are the only alternatives—the most reasonable choice is dictatorship, even though it does involve the risk of despotism.

Hobbes did make the political establishment of the Leviathan subject to certain minimal safeguards for its subjects. If the Leviathan fails to provide security to its subjects, they may transfer their allegiance to another sovereign. Further, because no one has the right to take his own life, this right is not among those

## PROFILE: Thomas Hobbes (1588–1679)

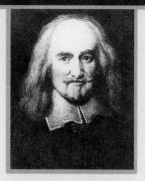

Scientific discovery, geometry, and the violence of civil war and anarchy—these were the major influences on Hobbes's philosophy.

A graduate of Oxford, Hobbes became a tutor in the influential Cavendish family, in which role he was able to meet many of the important intellectual figures of his day, including Galileo and Bacon. Through his acquaintance with the work of these and other early scientists, it occurred to him that everything that happens does so as the result of physical matter in motion. This perception became the basis of his entire philosophy, including his metaphysics and political thought.

Amazingly, it was not until his early forties that Hobbes chanced on a copy of Euclid's *Elements*. This work influenced him to think that all knowledge could be derived deductively from axioms based on observation. Consequently he devised a comprehensive plan, which he never fully com-

pleted, to apply the Euclidean deductive method to all questions of physical nature, human nature, and the nature of society.

Hobbes's political philosophy, however, has earned him his greatest fame. The basic themes of his political writings—that man is by nature violent, self-serving, and at war with all other men, and that for their own defense against their natural predaciousness, people must submit to a strong power capable of enforcing peace—are clear reflections of the political turbulence of the times. During Hobbes's lifetime, the Thirty Years' War on the European continent struck down half the population, and in England a state of anarchy followed the Civil War and the rule of Oliver Cromwell. Moreover, the plague ravaged England no fewer than four times during Hobbes's long life. Hobbes was no stranger to death, destruction, chaos, and the willingness of men to sacrifice others for their own ends.

transferred to the Leviathan at the time of the social contract of its subjects. Therefore, the Leviathan cannot rightfully compel a subject to take his or her own life.

Critics of Hobbes, not surprisingly, scoff at such "safeguards." As a practical matter, the Leviathan, having been given the collective power of its subjects, is able to do whatever it pleases with its subjects. As John Locke said, with Hobbes you trade the chance of being ravaged by a thousand men acting independently for the chance of suffering the same fate at the hands of one person who has a thousand men at his command.

One other important concept in Hobbes's political philosophy needs to be mentioned here: Hobbes uses the phrase "natural right" and asserts that when peace cannot be obtained we have a natural right to use all means to defend ourselves. Today we think of a natural right as something that it would be immoral for others to deprive us of. For example, when we say that a person has a natural right to life, we mean it would be wrong for others to act so as to deprive the person of life. For Hobbes the emphasis was slightly different. He meant that when peace cannot be obtained we suffer no moral restrictions whatsoever and that, if necessary for survival, each person can use any method he or she wants—including depriving another of his or her life. For Hobbes, one's natural right to life does not prohibit any activity.

We have spent some time here on Hobbes. This is because Hobbes, in basing the creation and power of the Leviathan on a social contract, is the first philosopher to enunciate systematically the concept that the state, and with it justice, is created through an agreement or "contract" among the people whom the state comprises. This is, of course, a familiar notion to Americans because the United States Constitution, about which more will be said later, is the social contract that brought this country into existence.

So Hobbes really did more than reject the principle of natural law as representing God's will and its corollary that the laws of the state, and the state itself, derive their *legitimacy* from their harmony with this divine natural law. According to Hobbes, the legitimacy of the state and its laws derives from an initial consent of those governed (though keep in mind that this consent is "required" by those principles of practical reason that Hobbes refers to as natural laws). With Hobbes begins an important tradition in Western political philosophy, so-called **contractualism.** Contractualism is the idea that the legitimacy of the state and/or the principles of sound justice derive their legitimacy from a societal agreement or social contract. *Contractarianism* is often used as a synonym. You will encounter other contractarian theories besides Hobbes's as we proceed, beginning with the philosophy of John Locke.

## TWO OTHER CONTRACTARIAN THEORISTS

Two other contractarian theorists from the modern period were very important to the history of political philosophy. Both influenced American political thought, especially the earlier of the two, John Locke.

## John Locke

Hobbes lived much of his life during a time of rather unpleasant turmoil, and he quite reasonably thought that civil peace should be a primary objective for people. **John Locke** (1632–1704), who was born some forty or so years later, responded in his writing to a threat other than that of anarchy and chaos — namely, the threat posed by a Roman Catholic monarch in Anglican England. To avoid getting lost in the maze known as English history, let's just say that this Catholic monarch, James II, was a blunderer of the first rank who not only suspended laws against fellow Catholics but also did his best to populate higher offices with them. In response, English aristocrats invited the Dutch head of state, the Protestant William of Orange, to take the throne (which, of course, he was happy to do). When William landed in England, James was forced to flee to France, and in 1688 the throne was offered jointly to William and his wife, Mary, who, incidentally, was James's daughter.

This switch was known as the Glorious Revolution, and its relationship to Locke's writings was this: Locke wished to define a right to resistance within a theoretical framework that would not at the same time undermine the state's power to govern effectively. Although Locke wrote his *Two Treatises of Government* before

## PROFILE: John Locke (1632–1704)

Locke, like Hobbes, was educated at Oxford. Though he became a lecturer there, he turned to the study of medicine, and as the physician, friend, and advisor of Lord Ashley (who later was the Earl of Shaftesbury and Lord Chancellor of the Realm), Locke became an influential man of state.

When Shaftesbury, who was involved in a plot to overthrow King Charles II, was forced to leave England, Locke found himself suspected by the king of disloyalty and went into exile in Holland in 1683. Five years later, when Prince William and Princess Mary of Orange were called to the throne in the Glorious Revolution, Locke returned to England as part of the entourage of the future Queen Mary.

Locke's two most important works, *Two Treatises of Government* and *An Essay Concerning Hu-*

*man Understanding,* were published in 1690, by which time Locke already was a famous philosopher and respected political advisor. In his last years he withdrew from political affairs and devoted himself to religious contemplation and study of the Epistles of St. Paul.

His contributions to epistemology and political theory were of major and lasting significance, and he is recognized as an articulate advocate of natural rights and religious freedom, as well as a strong opponent of the divine right of kings.

Locke's *Two Treatises of Government* were published anonymously. During his life, rumors correctly reported that Locke was the author of these works, but Locke always denied this.

the Glorious Revolution, he published them in 1690, and they were regarded as the philosophical justification of the Glorious Revolution.

Locke's treatises, and especially the *Second Treatise of Government,* are essentially an outline of the aims and purposes of the state. They have affected democratic theory at least as much as anything else that has ever been written. At the time of the American Revolution, Locke's political thought was well known to American political leaders and had become considerably incorporated in American popular political thought as well. It had a marked impact on the contents and wording of the Declaration of Independence, the Constitution, and the Bill of Rights and has had a continued substantial impact on American political thought and political institutions to this day. All Americans are directly or indirectly influenced by John Locke.

Locke, unlike Hobbes, believed there is a natural moral law that is more than a set of practical principles for survival. According to Locke, we are all made by God and are his "property." It logically follows that we are obliged to preserve ourselves and, as far as possible, the rest of humankind. Accordingly, except for the sake of just punishment, no person may take away or impair another's "life, liberty, health, limbs or goods," or anything on which these various items may depend.

That no person may destroy or impair another's life, liberty, or property requires, according to Locke, that each person has inalienable **natural rights** and duties. They are inalienable and natural in that their existence is entailed by the fact that we are God's creations. This conception of natural rights is more in accord with contemporary popular views than is the conception of Hobbes, discussed earlier.

## Catharine Trotter Cockburn and John Locke

Catharine Trotter Cockburn (1679–1749) was an Englishwoman who, with no apparent formal education, learned French, Latin, and Greek and read philosophy. Until very recently, her philosophical writings went unexamined by scholars. We mention her here in connection with Locke.

Trotter was an immensely successful playwright before she turned to writing philosophy. London's Drury Lane is the predecessor of New York's Broadway. When Trotter was a teenager, her first play, *Agnes de Castro*, was produced at Drury Lane. It was so popular that she was immediately able to get hundreds of subscribers to pay money in advance to support the writing of her next play. (The list of her subscribers reads like a *Who's Who* of England.) When she was twenty-one, she had three blockbuster plays on Drury Lane at the same time.

To connect this to Locke, Edward Stillingfleet, the Bishop of Wooster, was a subscriber to Trotter's plays. He was, in addition, a big-time critic of Locke's *Essay Concerning Human Understanding*, especially as to the consequences of it for morality and religion. He thought that Locke's views challenged the authority of divine revelations on the nature of morality and wrote several highly publicized (and unbelievably long) letters condemning Locke. An individual named Thomas Burnet of the Charterhouse anonymously pub-lished three sets of "Remarks" in support of Bishop Stillingfleet's criticism of Locke. Everyone ducked these broadsides, even Locke. Nobody would say a word against the powerful Bishop of Wooster.

Then Catharine Trotter anonymously published *A Defence of Mr. Locke's Essay of Human Understanding, Wherein Its Principles, with Reference to Morality, Revealed Religion, and the Immortality of the Soul, Are Considered and Justified: In Answer to Some Remarks on That Essay*. She published her defense of Locke anonymously because she was afraid that a defense of Locke by a woman would further inflame Bishop Stillingfleet. (How could a woman claim any religious or moral authority to give an opinion?) However, within six months, Catharine Trotter was identified as the author of the *Defence*, and her plays all closed, in an apparent blacklisting. Locke sought her out, and gave her some books and a large sum of money in gratitude.

Leibniz (see Chapter 6) was working on his own critique of Locke but put off finishing it until he could read Trotter's *Defence*. Several years after publishing *Defence*, Catharine Trotter married a clergyman named Cockburn [KO-burn] and continued to publish philosophical pamphlets defending Locke's philosophy from his religious critics until shortly before her death.

Locke was considerably less gloomy than Hobbes in his opinion of people and was not nearly so pessimistic about what they might do to one another in the absence of civil society (i.e., in a hypothetical "state of nature"). Nevertheless, he thought it plainly advantageous to individuals to contract among themselves to establish a state to govern them, because the state, chiefly through its laws, offers the means to protect the right to property and to ensure "the peace, safety, and public good of the people."

Thus Locke, like Hobbes, held that the state is created and acquires its legitimacy by an agreement or social compact on the part of its citizens and subjects. For both philosophers the purpose of the social compact is to ensure the "public good," but for Locke the purpose is also to protect natural rights. For Hobbes, each subject *gives up* his rights to the Leviathan in exchange for, or rather in hopes of

According to Locke, what is your property is what you mix your labor with (subject to certain provisos mentioned in the text). But here is a problem: Just *what* is the astronaut mixing his labor with?—the entire planet? Or just with what he has walked on? Or maybe just with the sign and the ground in which it is pounded? Also, *whose* labor is involved here, only the astronaut's?

obtaining, peace and security. For Locke, the subject *entrusts* his rights to the state for safeguarding.

For Locke, then, the legitimacy of the state and its governing of its citizens rests on their prior consent to the state's existence, authority, and power. Without that prior consent, it is a violation of a person's natural rights for the state to exercise political power over him. Because men are "by nature all free, equal and independent," he wrote, "no one can be . . . subjected to the political power of another without his consent."

It is plain, however, that most people in most states have never explicitly given their consent to be governed by the state. Do you recall ever having given such consent? Therefore, can it not be argued that existing states, by having laws and punishing lawbreakers, in effect violate the natural rights of their citizens?

Locke resolves this problem by maintaining that if we accept any of the advantages of citizenship—if, for instance, we own property or rely on the police or travel on a public highway—then we have given **tacit consent** to the state to make and enforce laws, and we are obliged to obey these laws. In this way, Locke can maintain that states do not violate the natural rights of citizens (and others subject to their authority) by exercise of governmental authority over them, even though these individuals have never explicitly expressed their consent to that authority.

***Locke and the Right to Property***   That people have a natural right to property Locke regarded as evident. Because all people are created by God and thus (as explained earlier) have a right to their body (their "limbs"), it follows, Locke reasoned, that they have a right to their body's labor and thus to whatever things they "mix their labor with." That is, they have a right to those things provided that the things do not already belong to or are not needed to sustain someone else, and provided that they do not exceed in amount what can be used before spoiling. Because money is durable, a person may "heap up as much of it" as he can, said Locke.

Locke's theory of property implies that *although all people equally have a right to property, they do not all have a right to equal property* because how much property a person lawfully has will depend on his ingenuity and industriousness. This distinction is important because it can go some way toward justifying an unequal distribution of wealth.

*Separation of Power*    When people agree to unite themselves in a state, Locke said, they consent to entrust to it the power to make and enforce laws and punish transgressors, and they consent to submit to the will of the majority. The majority must decide for itself what form of government is best — that is, whether it (the majority) will run the government itself or will delegate its ruling power to a select few, or even to one, or will adopt yet some other arrangement. The body to which the power is delegated (or the majority itself if the power is not delegated to anyone) is the *legislative* or lawmaking branch of the government.

Lawmaking is the central function of government, in Locke's opinion, for it is only through law that people are assured of equal, fair, and impartial treatment and are protected from the arbitrary exercise of power by the government.

But, Locke thought, the persons who make the laws should not themselves execute them, and so, he said, the government should have an *executive* branch as well. Further, in addition to the legislative and executive branches of government, there must, he believed, be a *federative* branch with the power to make war and peace. Though Locke believed it essential that there be a judiciary to settle disputes and fix the degree of punishment for lawbreakers, the idea that the judiciary should be a separate branch of government was not his but, rather, the influential French jurist Montesquieu's [MAHN-tes-kyu] (1689–1755).

Locke's political theory also contrasts sharply with Hobbes's in that, for Hobbes, political power is *surrendered* to an *executive authority,* whereas for Locke, political power is *delegated* to the *legislature.* Also, as we have seen, Locke, unlike Hobbes, called for a division of governmental authority.

Because, according to Locke, the power of the government is entrusted to it by the people of the state, the government is the *servant* of the people. Whenever in the view of the people the government acts contrarily to that trust, the people may dismiss their servant. In other words, when this violation of trust is perceived to have happened, rebellion is justified.

It is plain, then, that several basic concepts of the American democratic form of government are found in the political theory of John Locke. These include the ideas that people have natural rights that the government cannot infringe on, that the government is the servant of the people and its power is entrusted to it by them, that law rather than force is the basis of the government, that the will of the people is determined by majority vote, and that the government should be divided into separate branches.

## Jean-Jacques Rousseau

According to Hobbes and Locke, people are better off in the properly constituted state than they are or were in the "state of nature." Quite a different point of view was expressed by **Jean-Jacques Rousseau** [roo-SO] (1712–1778), at least in his early political writings.

## The General Will

Rousseau's concept of the general will is essentially the same as such familiar concepts as the "sentiment of a nation" and "the will of the people." The idea is that a group of people may *collectively* or *as a group* desire or wish or want something and that this collective desire, though it may coincide with the desires of the individuals in the group, is a metaphysically distinct entity.

Two questions about the general will, and all similar notions of a collective sentiment, are controversial to this day. First, what is it? Let us suppose, for example, that every member of a group of people believes that the federal deficit should be reduced. We may say, then, that the general will is that the federal deficit should be reduced. But can saying this possibly mean otherwise than simply that every individual in the group believes that it should be reduced? In this instance, that is, the general will seems no different from the wills of all individuals.

Let us suppose now that 60 percent of the group believes that the deficit should be reduced. If we now say that the general will is that the federal deficit should be reduced, can we mean anything other than that 60 percent believes that way? In this

instance, then, the general will seems no different from the individual wills of 60 percent.

Suppose, finally, that 50 percent believes in raising taxes to reduce the federal deficit and 50 percent believes in cutting taxes to reduce the federal deficit. If we ignore the differences about how the deficit should be reduced (these, Rousseau might say, are "pluses and minuses that cancel each other") and say that the general will is that the federal deficit should be reduced, do we mean anything other than what we did in the first instance, namely, that everyone believes that it should be reduced?

Thus, if the general will is supposedly something other than the will of all or the will of the majority — which clearly is Rousseau's view because he envisions circumstances in which the majority will and the will of all may actually run counter to the general will — the question is: What is it?

And the second question is: Even granting that a group may have a general will that is distinct from the will of all and the will of the majority, how is one to determine the specific propositions it endorses? Polls and elections disclose the will of all and the will of the majority; what discloses the general will?

In the state of nature, in which there was neither state nor civilization, people were essentially innocent, good, happy, and healthy, maintained Rousseau in his *Discourse on the Origin and Foundation of the Inequality among Men* (1754). Further, in the state of nature, he said, people enjoyed perfect freedom. But with the advent of private property, this all changed. "The first man who, having enclosed a piece of ground, bethought himself of saying *This is mine,* and found people simple enough to believe him, was the real founder of civil society," which brought with it the destruction of natural liberty and which, "for the advantage of a few ambitious individuals, subjected all mankind to perpetual labor, slavery and wretchedness."

To put this in some sort of perspective, Rousseau wrote this indictment of civilization in 1754. This was sixty-seven years after Newton had published his *Principia.* It was two years after Benjamin Franklin, with key and kite, had proved that lightning is electricity. Thirty years earlier, Fahrenheit had devised his thermometer. Bach had been dead four years, and it had been twenty-three years since he had completed the Brandenburg Concertos, a masterpiece of mathematical reasoning expressed in music. This, in short, was the eighteenth century, the Enlightenment, the age of light, the Age of Reason. Civilization was *stuffed* with benefits. Philosophers were (as always) critical, but *this* critical? Civilization a step backward? Rousseau was regarded as insane.

According to Rousseau, when you force a person to accept the general will, you are forcing him to be free.

But Rousseau later came to think that in the proper society people would surrender their individual liberty for a different and more important *collective* liberty. Through a social compact a people may agree, in effect, to unite into a collective whole, called "the state" or "the sovereign," and through the state or sovereign enact laws reflective of the *general will*. An important point to be aware of here is that, for Rousseau, the state or sovereign is *an entity in its own right,* a "moral person" (as Rousseau says), a nonbiological organism that has its own life and its own *will*. Rousseau's concept of the **general will**—that is, the will of a politically united people, the will of the state—is his most important contribution to political philosophy (for further discussion of the concept, see the box "The General Will").

If you have difficulty conceiving of a state as a person or an organic entity, remember that Plato also viewed the state as an organism. Or think of a football team, which can easily be regarded as something "over and beyond" the individual players that make it up, or of a corporation, which the law regards as a person.

The general will, according to Rousseau, defines what is to be the common good, and thus determines what is right and wrong and should and should not be done. And the state or sovereign (i.e., the people as a collective agent) expresses this general will by passing laws.

Further, the general will, the will of the people taken collectively, represents the *true* will of each person. Thus, insofar as the individual's actions coincide with the common will, he is acting as he "really" wants to act—and to act as you really want to act is to be free, said Rousseau. Compelling a person to accept the general will by obeying the laws of the state is *forcing him to be free,* Rousseau wrote in a famous passage. So we may lose individual or "natural" liberty when we unite to form a collective whole, but we gain this new type of "civil" liberty, "the freedom to obey a law which we prescribe for ourselves." Thus, Rousseau wrote, "it is to law alone that men owe justice and [civil] liberty."

## PROFILE: Jean-Jacques Rousseau (1712–1778)

*He [Rousseau] is surely the blackest and most atrocious villain, beyond comparison, that now exists in the world; and I am heartily ashamed of anything I ever wrote in his favor.*   —David Hume

Rousseau—philosopher, novelist, and composer—loved many women and eventually became paranoid to the point of madness. He was born a watchmaker's son in Geneva. In his early teens he was apprenticed to an engraver but ran away from his master. When he was about sixteen, he met Baroness Louise de Warens, who became his patroness and later his lover. With her he spent most of his time until he was thirty, attempting through wide reading to remedy the deficiencies in his education. In 1742 he went to Paris by himself to make his fortune, which he failed to do, with a new system of musical notation he had invented. There he became a close associate of several important literary figures of the time, including, most significantly, Denis Diderot (editor of the *Encyclopédie*, the crowning jewel of eighteenth-century rationalism). There he also met Thérèse Le Vasseur, an almost illiterate servant girl, who became his common-law wife.

In 1749 Rousseau won first prize in a contest sponsored by the Academy of Dijon for his essay on the question, Has the progress of the sciences and art contributed to the corruption or to the improvement of human conduct? His answer, startling to the sensibilities of the French Enlightenment, was an attack on the corrupting effects of civilization and instantly made him famous. A second essay, *Discourse on the Origin and Foundation of Inequality among Men* (1754), which again portrayed the evils brought to man by civilization, was also highly controversial. Voltaire, to whom Rousseau had sent a copy of the work, thanked him for his "new book against the human race."

At this time Rousseau, disillusioned with Paris, went briefly to Geneva to regain his Genevan citizenship, but he soon returned to Paris and retired to the estate of yet another woman, Madame d'Épinay. Always emotional, temperamental, suspicious, and unable to maintain constant friendships, he suspected his friends—Diderot, Mme. d'Épinay, and others—of conspiring to ruin him. He departed and became the guest of the Duc de Luxembourg, at whose chateau he finished the novel *La Nouvelle Heloise* (1761), written under the influence of his love for (yes!) the sister-in-law of Mme. d'Épinay.

*The Social Contract,* and his treatise on education, *Émile*, both published the following year, were so offensive to ecclesiastic authorities that Rousseau had to leave Paris. He fled to Neuchâtel and then to Bern. Finally, in 1766 he found a haven with David Hume in England. But after a year, Rousseau, who by this time had become deeply paranoid, quarreled with Hume, who he thought was plotting against him. In fact, Hume had been trying to procure a royal pension for Rousseau. (Hume's last opinion of Rousseau is stated at the beginning of this Profile.) Rousseau now returned to France, and eventually to Paris, even though he was in danger of arrest. He was left undisturbed, however, and spent his last years copying music, wandering about reading his *Confessions* out loud, and insulting the curious throngs who came to look at him.

Still, few philosophers have had as much impact as Rousseau on political philosophy, politics, education, or literature.

The question arises, of course: Just how do we know what the general will is? Rousseau's answer: If we, the citizens, are enlightened and are not allowed to influence one another, then a majority vote determines what the general will is.

The general will is found by counting votes. When, therefore, the opinion which is contrary to my own prevails, this proves neither more nor less than that I was mistaken, and that what I thought to be the general will was not so.

Rousseau, however, distinguished between the "will of all" and the general will. The former, Rousseau wrote,

> is indeed but a sum of private wills: but remove from these same wills the pluses and minuses that cancel each other, and then the general will remains as the sum of the differences.

According to Rousseau, it makes no sense to think of either delegating or dividing the general will. Therefore, he calculated, in the state there cannot validly be a division of powers (in contrast to what Locke thought), and though we may commission some person or persons to administer or enforce the law, these individuals act only as our *deputies,* not as our representatives.

Rousseau maintained that the citizens of the state have the right at any time to terminate the social contract. He also held that they have the right at any time to depose the officials of the state. The implication of the right of the citizenry to terminate the social contract at any time and of their right to remove officials of the state at any time is that the citizenry have a right of revolution and a right to resume anarchy at any time. Thus, Rousseau is thought to have provided a philosophical justification for anarchy and revolution.

Did Rousseau also unwittingly establish a philosophical basis for totalitarianism? Some think that is the case because he said that "the articles of the social contract [reduce] to this single point: the total alienation of each person, and all his rights, to the whole community." If the community is regarded not just as the sum total of its members but as an entity somehow over and above the individuals in it, an entity with its own life and will that can itself do no wrong and must always be obeyed, then Rousseau's words do have an ominous ring and invoke concepts that are incorporated wholesale in the philosophy of fascism. (Hitler's claim that the Führer instinctively knows the desires of the Volk [German for "the people"] and is therefore due absolute obedience is an appeal to the general will.) Also ominous is what Rousseau wrote near the end of *The Social Contract* (1762):

> If any one, after he has publicly subscribed to these dogmas [which dispose a person to love his duties and be a good citizen], shall conduct himself as if he did not believe them, he is to be punished by death.

## AMERICAN CONSTITUTIONAL THEORY

American constitutional political philosophy incorporates several of the concepts and ideas we have been examining. Before the American Constitution, philosophers had theorized about a social compact as the foundation of the state, but there had been few instances of written constitutions, and these were of no lasting importance. England was the only great power that had ever had a constitution, lasting a few months in the Cromwell period. Thus, the first significant experience with written constitutions was the U.S. Constitution.

The main trend in American political thought has been embodied in the development of theory pertaining to the Constitution. The trend relates essentially to *natural law* and *natural rights* and to incorporation in federal and state constitutions of a *social contract* to establish or control a political state. You now know something about the history of these concepts before the founding of the United States.

## Natural Law and Rights in the Declaration of Independence

In 1776, the Declaration of Independence proclaimed the doctrine of natural or divine law and of natural or God-given rights. The Declaration asserted that there are "Laws of Nature and of Nature's God," and the framers appealed "to the Supreme Judge of the World for the rectitude of our intentions." The Declaration also asserted that it is "self-evident" that "all men are created equal, that they are endowed by their Creator with certain unalienable rights, that among these are Life, Liberty and the pursuit of happiness." The framers of the Declaration also stated that "it is the Right of the People to alter or abolish" any form of government, whenever that form of government becomes destructive of "its ends to secure" the unalienable rights with which men are endowed by their creator.

In thus proclaiming the existence of natural or divine law and of natural and God-given rights, the Declaration of Independence incorporated what had become widespread political theory in the colonies by the time of the American Revolution, a theory that was prevalent among those who opposed the British king and Parliament. This political theory was rooted in (1) familiarity with the writings of European political theorists, particularly British, and in (2) the constant preaching of the clergy in the colonies, who had been dominant in civil and political as well as in religious matters, that the moral code reflected divine law and should determine civil law and rights.

But as for the philosophically vexing question of *who* should say what natural or divine law ordains and what God-given rights are in particular, it was no longer generally conceded, by the time of the Declaration, that this power belonged primarily in the clergy. Instead, it was recognized that the power lies ultimately in the people and mediately in the legislative branch of government subject (some people thought) to judicial review.

## Natural Law and Rights in the U.S. Constitution

The original Constitution itself, before adoption of the Bill of Rights constituted by the first ten amendments to the Constitution, makes scant allusion to natural law or divine rights. It does so implicitly only in its preamble, in stating its purpose to "establish Justice, insure domestic tranquillity, provide for the common defense, promote the General Welfare, and secure the Blessings of Liberty." Although it can plausibly be argued that these purposes are those of natural law and that the "Blessings of Liberty" include natural rights, nevertheless the original Constitution was directed toward establishing law and order and not toward guaranteeing natural rights. Nor is there any explicit reference to divine law or God-given rights in the original—or to God.

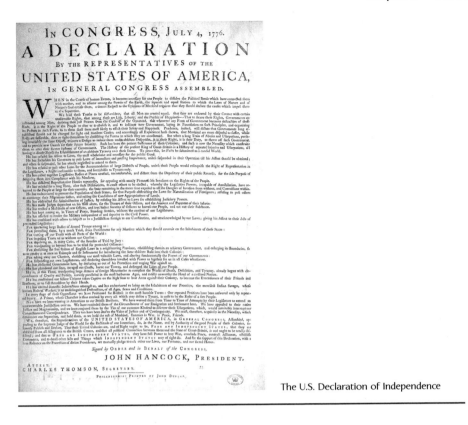

The U.S. Declaration of Independence

Ratification of the original Constitution was attained only by assurance that a Bill of Rights would immediately be adopted by amendment, which indeed occurred when the first ten amendments were ratified on 15 December 1791. This Bill of Rights arguably limits the federal government in ways dictated by natural law and arguably guarantees rights in ways dictated by the existence of natural rights. And, undoubtedly, the rights explicit (and implicit) in the Bill of Rights were regarded by the framers of the Constitution and by the American people in general as the unalienable rights to which the Declaration of Independence alluded.

Now in *Marbury v. Madison,* decided by the Supreme Court in 1803 under Chief Justice John Marshall, and in Supreme Court cases in its wake, it became firmly established that the Supreme Court has the power under the Constitution to declare void federal and state laws that violate it. Thus, the extent to which what may be called natural law and rights are incorporated in the Constitution is for the Supreme Court to determine.

Under Section 1 of the Fourteenth Amendment, ratified 9 July 1869, most of the limitations on government and guarantees of rights contained in the Bill of Rights became applicable to the states as well as to the federal government. The relationship of the authority of the states to the authority of the federal government has always been a central issue in American Constitutional philosophy.

## The Right to Privacy

Today there is much discussion about whether the Constitution protects a right to "privacy." Because it is the Supreme Court that decides such things, the views of potential (and actual) members of the Supreme Court on this important question are of widespread concern to the American people. In 1987, for instance, President Ronald Reagan's nominee to the Supreme Court, Robert H. Bork, was rejected by the U.S. Senate, mainly because of Bork's views on the question of whether there is a constitutional right to privacy. The question is especially controversial because in its landmark decision in *Roe v. Wade* the Supreme Court upheld a woman's right to abortion as included within the right to privacy.

Whether the U.S. Constitution protects a right to privacy is perhaps not a purely philosophical question. But it bears on the larger issue of the legitimate scope and authority of the state, and that issue is a philosophical one.

## CLASSIC LIBERALISM AND MARXISM

We turn now to the nineteenth century, the century ushered in by Romanticism in art, music, and literature; grandiose metaphysical speculations in philosophy; and (to mention something non-European for a change) the accession of Muhammad Ali (the pasha of Egypt, not the boxer). It was the century that saw spreading industrialization and nationalism, Darwin and Freud, the Suez Canal, civil war in America, the emergence of Italy and Germany as states, and the invention of photography and the automobile. The two major political philosophies were liberalism and Marxism. They still are, for the most part, despite the demise of Soviet communism. Marxism, of course, is the socialist philosophy of Karl Marx (1818–1883). **Liberalism** (from the Latin word for "liberty") is the philosophy well expressed by John Stuart Mill (1806–1873)—who will be discussed shortly—in his treatise *On Liberty:* "The sole end for which mankind are warranted, individually or collectively, in interfering with the liberty of action of any of their number, is . . . to prevent harm to others. His own good, either physical or moral, is not a sufficient warrant."

## Adam Smith

The most important classical liberal economic theorist was **Adam Smith** (1723–1790), a contemporary of David Hume. The principle of Smith's economic theory is that in a laissez-faire economy (one in which the government remains on the sidelines), each individual, in seeking her own gain, is led "by an invisible hand" to promote the common good, though doing so is not her intention. As an exponent of the benefits for everyone of **capitalism** (a system of private ownership of property and the means of production and distribution) and a **free-market economy** (in which individuals may pursue their own economic interests without governmental restrictions on their freedom), Smith advocated positions that resemble those of many contemporary American conservatives. His *An Inquiry into the Na-*

*ture and Causes of the Wealth of Nations* (1776) has become a classic among American political conservatives.

## Utilitarianism and Natural Rights

**Utilitarianism,** as you may recall from the preceding chapter, is the theory that the rightness of an act derives from the happiness or pleasure it produces as its consequences. You may also recall the name of **Jeremy Bentham** (1748–1832), the famous utilitarian. Here we mention him for his view that talk about natural rights is so much nonsense. And, indeed, utilitarian philosophy in general does not easily accommodate a belief in natural rights. Why? Well, consider a possible natural right—for example, the right to keep what you have honestly earned. If taking from you what you have honestly earned and distributing it to people who are poorer than you are increases the sum total of happiness, utilitarianism apparently requires that we do this, despite your "natural right." Utilitarianism seems to require violating any so-called natural right if doing so increases happiness.

Utilitarians often attempt to accommodate our intuitions about natural rights by maintaining that in civilized society more happiness results when what are called natural rights are respected than when they are not. They say that natural rights should be regarded as secondary rules of conduct that must be obeyed for the sake of the general happiness. However, in viewing natural rights as a system of moral rules that promote general happiness, utilitarians do not always explain why such rules should not be overridden when doing so better promotes the general happiness.

## Harriet Taylor

Like many women philosophers, **Harriet Taylor** (1807–1858) has been known to the public primarily through her association with a male philosopher; in Taylor's case the male philosopher was John Stuart Mill (coming up next). Taylor and Mill shared a long personal and professional intimacy, and each shaped and influenced the ideas of the other. However, Taylor was a published author of poetry before she even met Mill in 1831. Recently, a draft of an essay on toleration of nonconformity was discovered in Taylor's handwriting; it appears to have been written in 1832. She was a regular contributor of poetry, book reviews, and a literary piece to the radical, utilitarian, and feminist journal *The Monthly Repository*. Later, Mill too became a regular contributor, and eventually Taylor and Mill began writing together. However, their writings were published under Mill's name, partly because a man's name gave the work more legitimacy within a sexist culture, but also because Taylor's husband was unhappy with the idea of his wife's gaining notoriety. Nevertheless, from the evidence of their manuscripts and their personal correspondence, it is possible to piece together an idea of which works were primarily Taylor's and which were Mill's; she was a profound thinker in her own right.

Taylor was interested both in sweeping transformations of society and in specific legal reforms. One of her greatest concerns was the tendency of English society to stifle individuality, originality, and radical political and religious views. English society, in her opinion, was intolerant of opinions that failed to conform

## PROFILE: John Stuart Mill (1806–1873)

Many years ago, one of the authors came across a table of projected IQ scores for various historic "geniuses" in a psychology text. (Who knows how the scores were calculated?) At the top of the list, with some incredible score, was John Stuart Mill.

Mill began reading Greek at three and Latin at eight, and by adolescence had completed an extensive study of Greek and Latin literature, as well as of history, mathematics, and logic. Mill's education was administered by his father, who subjected young John to a rigorous regimen.

At fifteen Mill settled on his lifelong objective, to work for social and political reform, and it is as a reformer and ethical and political philosopher that he is most remembered. Mill championed individual rights and personal freedom and advocated emancipation of women and proportional representation. His most famous work, *On Liberty* (1859), is thought by many to be the definitive defense of freedom of thought and discussion.

In ethics Mill was a utilitarian, concerning which we have much to say in Chapter 10. He published *Utilitarianism* in 1863.

Mill's interests also ranged over a broad variety of topics in epistemology, metaphysics, and logic. His *System of Logic* (1843), which was actually read at the time by the person in the street, represented an empiricist approach to logic, abstraction, psychology, sociology, and morality. Mill's *methods of induction* are still standard fare in university courses in beginning logic.

When Mill was twenty-five, he met Harriet Taylor, a merchant's wife, and this was the beginning of one of the most celebrated love affairs of all time. Twenty years later, and three years after her husband died, Mrs. Taylor married Mill, on whose thought she had a profound influence. *On Liberty* was perhaps jointly written with her and, in any case, was dedicated to her.

Harriet Taylor died in 1858. Mill spent his remaining years in Avignon, France, where she had died, to be near her grave.

Mill's *Autobiography*, widely read, appeared in the year of his death. Mill still is the most celebrated English philosopher of his century.

to the mainstream. She considered the intolerance of nonconformity to be morally wrong and ultimately dangerous to human progress. Taylor's essay on such intolerance is a stirring statement of the theory that "the opinion of society — majority opinion — is the root of all intolerance." Her defense of minority viewpoints and individuality predated by twenty-seven years Mill's famous treatise *On Liberty* (see excerpt from this work at the end of the chapter).

### John Stuart Mill

Like Locke and Rousseau, **John Stuart Mill** (1806–1873) was much concerned with liberty. Mill, you will recall from the previous chapter, was a utilitarian. He believed that happiness not only is good but also is *the* good, the ultimate end of all action and desire. "Actions are right in proportion as they tend to promote happiness, wrong as they tend to produce the reverse of happiness," he wrote. But remember that utilitarians are not egoists, and Mill believed that it is not one's own

This idea comes straight from J. S. Mill, who observed that "no instructed person" would consent to become an ignoramus even if he were persuaded that as an ignoramus he would be happier than he presently is. Plato had a similar thing in mind when he said that a person who had found knowledge would rather be the slave of the poorest master than be ignorant.

happiness that one should seek but, instead, the greatest amount of happiness altogether — that is, the general happiness.

Unlike Rousseau, Mill does not view a community, a society, a people, or a state as an organic entity separate and distinct from the sum of the people in it. When Mill says that one should seek the general happiness, he is not referring to the happiness of the community as some kind of organic whole. For Mill, the general happiness is just the total happiness of the individuals in the group.

Now Mill, following Bentham and Hume, and like Rousseau, rejected Locke's theory that people have God-given natural rights. But he maintained that the general happiness requires that all individuals enjoy personal liberty to the fullest extent consistent with the liberties of others. "The only part of the conduct of anyone, for which he is amenable to society, is that which concerns others. In the part which merely concerns himself, his independence is . . . absolute." Mill regarded personal liberty, including freedom of thought and speech, as essential to the general happiness. It is essential, he argued, because truth and the development of the individual's character and abilities are essential to the general happiness, and only if there is personal liberty can truth be ascertained and each individual's capacities developed. It therefore follows that an individual should enjoy unrestrained personal liberty up to the point where his or her activities may harm others.

Of course, it is difficult to identify *when* an action may be said to harm others. Liberalism places the burden of proof on the person who claims that harm to others will be done. That the burden must be so placed is Mill's position.

The best form of government, according to Mill, is that which, among all realistic and practical alternatives, produces the greatest benefit. The form of government best suited to do this, he maintained, is representative democracy. But Mill was especially sensitive to the threat to liberty posed in democracies by the tyranny of public opinion as well as by the suppression by the majority of minority points of view. For this reason he emphasized the importance of safeguards such as proportional representation, universal suffrage, and enforcement of education by the state.

Now, promoting the general happiness would seem sometimes to justify (if not explicitly to require) restrictions on personal liberty. Zoning ordinances, antitrust laws, and motorcycle helmet laws, to take modern examples, are, arguably, restrictions of this sort. Mill recognized the dilemma that potentially confronts anyone who wishes both to promote the general happiness and to protect personal liberty. His general position is this: The government should not do anything that could be done more effectively by private individuals themselves; and even if something could be done more effectively by the government, if the government's doing it would deprive individuals of an opportunity for development or education, the government should not do it. In short, Mill was opposed to enlarging the power of the government unnecessarily.

## Georg Hegel

Georg Hegel (1770–1831), whose metaphysics we considered in Chapter 7, offered a social/political theory as part of his metaphysics. When you read about Karl Marx in the next section, you will see parallels with Hegel, though stripped of the metaphysical trappings.

Hegel believed that (in his words), "the human is nothing other than the series of his acts." Humans, he observed, have consciousness and speech. With these assets, they constitute the becoming that, in his metaphysics, is time and history.

Humans are restless and active, and their actions arise from their desires. Lower desires — animal desires — stem from a vague feeling of selfhood rather than from consciousness of self. This is not a difficult idea to grasp. Think of your pet dog, Smokey, let us say. Smokey cannot transcend his body or his feelings, and, although he barks, he does not truly speak. Most important, Smokey does not think of himself as an "I." Still, Smokey's desires make him superior to plant life — which, incidentally, explains why animals consume plants and not vice versa, according to Hegel. But you and I — we are humans and rise above mere animal desires — if we are to achieve true freedom and autonomy.

Now, according to Hegel, to desire only the present, immediate being (a la Smokey) is to be *enslaved* by it. Liberation to one's true self begins with desire for what is not *yet* — and this desire necessarily is the desire for nonbeing. All becoming, all time and all history, arises out of an ongoing annihilation of the present, that is, immediate being. The annihilating process can take the form of fighting — and it can take the form of working. Fighting and working both are processes by means of which the self is "transcended," and true being and liberation are found. We can sum it up this way: the human being for Hegel, is an *active process of becoming*, whose actions are driven by desires.

What is your deepest desire? According to Hegel, the deepest of human desires is the need for *recognition*. The human being longs not merely for recognition by others but for universal recognition through actions arising out of the nonbiological "I." Only universal recognition provides true and lasting satisfaction. Since this desire is the universal condition of the species, humans are in continuous "life and death fights" with each other, Hegel reasoned. Each person wants to override, negate, and destroy all others. For Hegel, if you do not enter into this fight, then you are not truly a human being.

By equating human satisfaction with "immortal" fame, Hegel resurrected an ancient Greek idea (though not endorsed by Plato) of personal immortality as fame. You could also think of Hegel as basing human action on the idea from Heraclitus that war is the father of all.

The victor in war is lord and master. What makes the master victorious is a willingness to go all the way in battle. He would rather die rather than submit and be dominated. Remember that the victor is fighting for a nonbiological goal, namely, for prestige and for recognition. The master is a fighter who demands to be recognized by others, namely, those whom he has defeated: his slaves. The master's keenest pleasure consists in knowing that his slaves recognize his superiority — though he is not adverse to booty or the physical goods that his slaves produce for him.

However, there are limitations in being a lord and master. First is the frustration of not being recognized by equals, but only by inferior slaves. Second is the master's static, nonevolving status. The master cannot grow and will eventually be outstripped by the very slaves he now owns and exploits. Let us consider how this happens.

The slave, according to Hegel, *begins* in a subordinate position — because of his unwillingness to fight to the death for recognition. Facing the possibility of death and experiencing the dread of ultimate nothingness, the slave opted for subservience rather than annihilation. As a result, he works for the master's ends and not his own. His life is in service to another. His master is free; he is not. He, the slave, is an object for the master's use and pleasure.

Nevertheless, his suffering, alienation, and coerced work eventually provide the slave with an intuition of his ideal or free self — and an intuition, as well, of the means eventually to achieve it. Consider the issue closely: The master attained freedom and domination by overcoming the instinct to live. The slave gradually, though his work and the accompanying thoughts of self-regard that arise out of it, comes to an idea that he likewise can come to dominate Nature. But the slave's form of domination is creative; it modifies and shapes Nature to thought and ideals, giving rise to a *science* of the natural world.

So the work and service of the slave lead to a transformation of Nature through science. Likewise, work and servitude transform and ultimately free the slave to a higher self. He gradually achieves self-regard based on his accomplishment of transforming Nature; to put it in Hegelian terminology, he becomes the incarnation or embodiment of the Absolute Idea and the realization of Absolute Knowledge. The ultimate result is that the slave has weapons not only to overcome the fear of death but also to escape the yoke of the master. Moreover, through this struggle, the slave provides the changes that determine the evolution of history. This fact provides the slave with an ultimate prestige as well as with freedom and autonomy. The slave is a slave no more but has risen above the master and Nature alike.

Now, this process that the slave undergoes to become free is a hard and enduring struggle. Furthermore, not all labor is freeing, Hegel believed. The all-important labor lies in *Bildung,* or self-building education. This shapes and humanizes the slave, bringing him ever closer to his own idea of selfhood. At the same time, it shapes and transforms the world, bringing it closer to its ideal realization. This dual process yields the "world historical individual," one who shapes the course of history. For Hegel, history is determined by historical individuals who understand instinctively what must be done and have the drive to do it. Their work *is* the progress of the world.

The struggle between master and slave has many stages, according to Hegel. One important stage is Christian ideology, in which the slave ceases to struggle for freedom. Instead, he commits to absolute slavehood under an absolute master. He equates freedom and happiness with the Hereafter, which he thinks begins with death. Consequently, he finds no reason to fight for freedom, and self-denial is considered a virtue. For Hegel, this phase of history expresses the ultimate domination of the slave's fear of death. He believed that freedom and self-realization occur only by surmounting this absolute enslavement to death.

The final stage of human development occurs in the demise of the master–slave dialectic. This happens when we accept our finitude and learn to live in this world as autonomous and free individuals. The key is to overcome fear of death. Through work and *Bildung,* as explained earlier, the individual is gradually formed and becomes self-conscious; he leaves the static, empty, boring stage of sheer being and become a particular, progressive, conscious realization of the Universal or Absolute Idea. This stage of human development represents for Hegel the actualization of the idea of the god-man. This god-man is immanent, present reality as Absolute Self-Consciousness. Here Hegel is following Spinoza's equation of Nature and God (*Natura sive deus*). Hegel claimed that after Spinoza, all philosophy would be Spinozism.

Heinrich Heine, a famous German poet, once heard Hegel lecture in Berlin. He put it as follows: "I was young and proud, and it flattered my presumption to learn from Hegel that the dear God did not really live in heaven as my grandmother supposed, but rather that I myself was the dear God down here on earth."

Hegel saw this final development of the human spirit in Napoleon, or, to put it more precisely, he saw it in the person of Napoleon as infused with Hegelian self-consciousness. The idea of a transcendental god having evolved into an immanent Universal existing in the world was, for Hegel, the Ideal State realized in history. Only in such a state can a person find ultimate satisfaction and total autonomy. Only in such a state can true individuality be achieved as a unique synthesis of Particularity and Universality. The evolution to this Ideal State involves not only human consciousness of the Absolute Idea but also its concrete realization in history.

## Marxism

The utilitarians pursued social and political reform. **Karl Marx** (1818–1883) went even further. Marx wanted not merely to reform society but to transform it.

Marx, who is famous for (among other things) his remark that philosophers have tried only to understand the world, whereas the real point is to change it, did not regard his work as philosophy. This must be kept in mind in the following discussion of Marx's thought. Marx offers a description and analysis of the human social and political condition, but he did not himself present this understanding as the absolute and final truth.

## PROFILE: Karl Marx (1818–1883)

When one of the authors was in high school, his civics teacher, Mr. Benson, listed the most important figures in history as (alphabetically) Einstein, Freud, Jesus, and Marx. His Western bias notwithstanding, Mr. Benson was certainly right about the preeminence of these four, especially Jesus and Marx. Of course, the followers of Marx probably outnumber even the followers of Jesus (and by a good margin). Some people, moreover, regard themselves as both Marxists and Christians.

Marx was the son of a Jewish lawyer who converted to Lutheranism despite having descended from generations of rabbis; Marx was thus raised as a Protestant. He studied at German universities in Bonn, Berlin, and Jena, first in law and then in philosophy. His Ph.D. at Jena (received when he was only twenty-three) was based on a completely ordinary dissertation on Democritus and Epicurus.

While in Berlin, Marx had come under the sway of Hegelianism (see Chapter 7) and a group of radical Hegelians. But later, strongly influenced by the philosophy of Ludwig Feuerbach, he rejected idealism for materialism and his own theory of history as the outworking of economic factors.

Marx's radical views prevented him from occupying an academic post. In 1842 he became editor of a Cologne newspaper that during his tenure became much too radical for the authorities and was suppressed. The twenty-five-year-old Marx then went to Paris, where he mingled with many famous radicals and established another radical periodical. In Paris he also met his future collaborator, Friedrich Engels.

In about a year Marx was expelled from Paris, and from 1845 to 1848 he lived in Brussels.

While there, he helped form a worker's union that together with other similar groups became known as the Communist League. It was for this organization that he and Engels wrote their famous and stirring *Communist Manifesto* (1848). Marx spent a brief period again in Paris and then in Cologne, participating in both the French and the German revolutions of 1848. He was, however, expelled once again from both countries. In 1849 he went to London and stayed there for the rest of his life.

In London, Marx required financial help from Engels, for just as some are addicted to gambling, Marx was addicted to reading and writing, and these activities did not produce much of an income. Despite Engels's help and the small amount of money he received for articles he wrote for the New York *Tribune,* he lived in poverty, illness, and—when his children and wife died one by one—immense sadness.

During this period Marx wrote the *Critique of Political Economy* (1859) and, more important, the work destined to become the primary document of international communism, *Capital* (vol. 1, 1867; vols. 2 and 3, edited by Engels, 1885 and 1894). In 1864 he helped create the International Workingmen's Association (the so-called First International), which he later led. A famous clash between Marx and the anarchist Mikhail Bakunin, however, led to its dissolution within about ten years (for more on anarchism, see the section by that title, later in this chapter). Marx died in London when he was sixty-five, of pleurisy.

*Means of Production versus Productive Relations*    For Marx the ideal society has no economic classes, no wages, no money, no private property, and no exploitation. Each person will not only be provided a fully adequate material existence but will also be given the opportunity to develop freely and completely all physical and mental faculties. The alienation (estrangement) of the individual from the world around will be minimal.

## Marxism and Liberalism Compared

"Classical" liberalism and "orthodox" Marxism both drew from the Enlightenment (eighteenth century) belief that the natural order produces perfection. Both looked forward to a future of ever-increasing human freedom and happiness and placed great faith in human goodness.

To highlight some of the similarities and differences between these philosophies, here is a list of ten doctrines that many orthodox Marxists accept, together with comments on how a group of classical liberals might respond to them. (Note that we said "classical" liberals. Contemporary so-called liberals share some but not all the values of classical liberals, and contemporary so-called conservatives do so as well. You will read more about contemporary usage of the term *liberal* in Chapter 12.)

1. *Ideally, society should provide for human beings as much happiness, liberty, opportunity for self-development, and dignity as possible.*

Liberals would agree to this claim, and who would not? Utilitarian liberals, however, would emphasize the importance of happiness over the other three values, or would regard the others as part of happiness.

2. *The only society that can provide these ends is a socialized society—that is, one in which both ownership and production are socialized.*

Many nineteenth- (and twentieth-) century liberals would not have denied that their ultimate ethical objectives could be achieved within a socialist society, but most would have denied that socialism *alone* could accommodate these objectives. Most also thought that these objectives are more likely to be achieved within a constitutionally based representative democracy with a market economy.

3. *In nonsocialist societies, the function of the state is to serve and protect the interests of the powerful.*

Liberals maintained that in nonsocialist societies it is possible for the state to serve and protect the interests and rights of all its subjects, both strong and weak, even though few states, if any, were thought effectively to have done so.

4. *A group's interests can be protected only through exercise of its power.*

A common liberal response is that a group's interests can be and are best protected through *law*. Marxists would say in rejoinder that, ever since Locke, the "rule of law" has been slanted toward protecting property and the propertied class.

5. *Human essence is defined historically, and economic factors largely determine history.*

Liberals also emphasized the importance of economics to social history and evolution but stressed

---

Furthermore, according to Marx, this type of society will ultimately arise as the result of the historical process. Here is why.

Humans, Marx believed, are social animals with physical needs, needs that are satisfied when we develop the means to satisfy them. These means of producing the satisfaction of needs are called the **means, or forces of production.** The utilization of any one set of means of production leads to fresh needs and therefore to further means of production. For example, the invention of iron tools (a new means of production) for the cultivation of needed crops leads to still a newer need—for iron—and therewith to the means for satisfying this newer need.

Thus, human history consists of successive stages of development of various means of production.

Furthermore, the utilization of any given means of production, whether it is a simple iron tool or a complex machine, necessarily involves certain social relationships, especially those involving property. These social relationships (or, as we might say, institutions or practices) are called the **productive relations.** Thus, the social relationships (the productive relations) depend on the stage of evolution of the forces of production.

that certain fundamental human characteristics (e.g., having rights, desiring pleasure) are unalterable by history.

6. *The value of a commodity is determined by the amount of labor required for its production.*

Liberals regarded this thesis as an oversimplification and maintained that many factors affect the value of a commodity.

7. *Capitalist societies necessarily are exploitative of a laboring class.*

Private ownership, many liberals believed (and still do), is not inherently or necessarily exploitative, though individual capitalists may exploit their workers. Exploitation, they say, may be eliminated through appropriately formulated laws, and a society in which a great unevenness in the distribution of wealth exists may nevertheless permit equal freedom and opportunity for all.

8. *A capitalist state cannot be reformed for two reasons: (a) It is inherently exploitative. (b) True reforms are not in the interest of the ruling class, which therefore will not permit them. Because such a state cannot be reformed, it must be replaced.*

Liberals thought (and still think) that, through reform, many states, including most capitalist states, can gradually be improved. They did not deny the appropriateness of revolutionary overthrow of dictatorships. Contemporary Marxists insist that liberal reforms in the United States are made possible through exploitation of Third World nations.

9. *The redistribution of goods through welfare, taxation, and similar means is mere tokenism serving only to pacify the exploited classes in order to protect the exploiting class from uprising and revolt.*

Liberals thought (and still think) that measures like these, if they benefit the less well off, are required by principles of fairness, justice, or utilitarian considerations.

10. *The philosophy of liberalism, with all its talk of fairness and justice, is merely an attempt to rationalize and legitimize capitalist oppression.*

Liberals regard this as an *argumentum ad hominem* (an attack on them rather than a refutation of their position). Liberal claims must be evaluated on their own merits, they say.

The forces of production at a given stage, however, develop to the point where they come into conflict with the existing social relationships, which are then destroyed and replaced by new social relationships. For example, the need at the end of the Middle Ages to supply the new markets in the Far East and the colonies in the New World required new methods of manufacture and commerce, which brought with their development societal changes incompatible with the feudal social structure of the Middle Ages.

The new social relationships then endure until new needs arise and a new stage is reached in the evolution of the forces of production.

This **dialectical process** repeats itself over and over again and is the history of people, economics, and society. To put this another way, *history is the result of productive activity in interplay with social relationships.* According to Marx, this interplay accounts not only for all socioeconomic-political situations but also for morality, law, religion, and, to a greater or lesser extent, even philosophy and art.

*Class Struggle*   As already stated, according to Marx the critical social relationships involve property. With the advent of private property, society became divided into two classes: those with property and those without.

Hostility between the two classes was, and is, inevitable, Marx said. Those with property, of course, are the dominant class, and government and morality are always the instruments of the dominant class. When the forces of production create conflict with the existing social relationships, class struggle becomes acute, revolution results, and a new dominant class seizes control of the organs of state and imposes its ethic. This dialectical process repeats itself until private property and the division of society into opposed classes disappears.

**Capitalism and Its Consequences**    In modern capitalist societies, what has happened, according to Marx, is that the means of production are primarily concentrated in large factories and workshops in which a group of individual workers cooperatively produces a product. They collectively "mix their labor with the product," as Locke would say. But the product they mix their labor with is not owned by them. Rather, it is appropriated by the owners of the factories, who thus in effect also own the workers. Out of this circumstance comes the fundamental conflict of capitalist society: *production is socialized, but ownership is not.*

Furthermore, Marx argued, capitalists obviously must sell what their workers produce for more than they pay the workers to make it. The laborers thus produce goods that are worth more than their wages. This exploitation of the workers is inevitable as long as the conflict between socialized means of production and nonsocialized ownership continues. It is a necessary part of the capitalist system and is not a result of wickedness or inhumanity on the part of the capitalist.

There are two further unavoidable consequences of continuing capitalism, in Marx's opinion. First, the longer the capitalist system continues, the smaller and wealthier the possessing class becomes. This is simply the result of the fact that the surplus value of products — that is, the value of a product less its "true" cost, which is the cost of the labor put into it — continues to accrue to the capitalists. Further, as smaller capitalists cannot compete, and as a result fail in their enterprise and sink into the ranks of the workers, society's wealth becomes increasingly concentrated: fewer and fewer people control more and more of it.

**Alienation**    The second consequence of continued capitalism, according to Marx, is the increasing alienation of the workers. The more wealth the workers produce, the poorer they become, relatively speaking, for it is not they who retain this wealth. So the result of increased productivity for the workers is, paradoxically (but inevitably), their *devaluation* in their own eyes and in fact. They have become mere commodities.

In addition, because workers produce through their labor what belongs to others, neither the workers' labor nor the products they make are their own. Both labor and products are as alien things that dominate them. Thus, workers feel at home with themselves only during their leisure time and in eating, drinking, and having sex. Workers' presence at work is not voluntary but imposed and, whenever possible, avoided. Because they have put their lives into what belongs to others, workers are abject, debased, physically exhausted, and overcome with malaise. And, because the relation of people to themselves is first realized and expressed in the relationship between each person and another, workers are alienated from their fellows.

*Capitalism Is Self-Liquidating*    The situation Marx describes is, in his view, self-liquidating. The capitalist system of property ownership is incompatible with the socialized conditions of production and ultimately destined to failure. Inevitable overproduction will result in economic crises, a falling rate of profit, and increased exploitation of the working class, which will increasingly become conscious of itself and its own intolerable condition, the inadequacy of capitalism, and the inevitability of history. The revolution of the **proletariat** (working class), leading to a dictatorship of the proletariat, will follow. In this instance, however, the overturning of the existing social order will eventually result in the classless society just described, for property, as well as the means of production, will have become socialized. The disappearance of classes will mark the end of class struggle and also, therefore, the end of political power because the sole function of political power is the suppression of one class at the expense of another.

## Marxism and Communism

By the end of the nineteenth century most European socialist parties were committed to Marxism, but a split developed between the *revolutionists,* those who believed (as for the most part had Marx) that a violent revolution was necessary to set in place the collective ownership of the means of production and distribution of goods, and the *revisionists* or *evolutionary socialists,* those who thought that these ends could be achieved through peaceful (and piecemeal) reform.

Although evolutionary socialism became strong in Great Britain and survives in the socialist parties of many nations to the present day, the revolutionists gained ascendancy in the Second International, the successor to Marx's International Working-men's Association or the First International (though the "revolutionists" were not particularly revolutionary). Under the leadership of Lenin, the revolutionist Bolsheviks came to control the Russian Social Democratic Labor Party and seized control of Russia itself in the Revolution of 1917, becoming in 1918 the Communist Party of the USSR.

Although the Russian Communists withdrew from the Second International and founded the Third International or Comintern in 1919 to gain leadership of the world socialist movement, most European Socialist parties disassociated themselves from the Communists. The term **Communism,** with a capital C, today still denotes the Marxist-Leninist ideology of the parties founded under the banner of the Comintern and is to be distinguished from lowercase-c **communism,** which denotes any form of society in which property or other important goods are held in common by the community.

## Anarchism

Anarchists deny that the state is necessary for peace, justice, equality, the optimum development of human capacities, or, indeed, for any other worthwhile pursuit. In the nineteenth century, **anarchism** was the main philosophical alternative to liberalism and Marxism.

Pierre Joseph Proudhon [prew-DOHn] (1809–1865), the so-called father of anarchism, was among the first in modern times to call himself an anarchist. Proudhon believed that all authoritarian political institutions hinder human development and should be replaced by social organizations founded on the free and voluntary agreement of individuals, organizations in which no person has power over another. The existence of private property, he argued, creates social inequalities and injustice and gives rise to government; both it and government should be eliminated, though not through violent means. Communists were much influenced by Proudhon's attack on the idea of private property.

The famous Russian anarchist Communists Mikhail Bakunin [ba-KOO-nin] (1814–1876) and Prince Piotr Kropotkin [krah-POT-kin] (1842–1921) both emphasized the intrinsic goodness of the individual and viewed law and government as the instruments of the privileged classes and the true source of human corruption (both Bakunin and Kropotkin were aristocrats, incidentally). Kropotkin, much influenced by Charles Darwin, held that humans have a biologically grounded propensity to cooperate that will hold society together even in the absence of government. Bakunin — who, unlike Proudhon and Kropotkin, advocated the violent overthrow of all government — was active in the Communist First International. A clash between Marx and Bakunin, and more generally between Marxist Communists and anarchist Communists concerning the necessity of a transitional dictatorship of the proletariat, led to the demise of that organization.

The slogan "From each according to his means, to each according to his needs" came from the anarchist Communists.

---

SELECTION 11.1

# Crito★

*Plato*

---

[*In this dialogue, Plato portrays "Socrates" in prison the day before his execution. Socrates' friend Crito has come to help Socrates escape, but Socrates refuses. In this excerpt, Socrates explains why it is wrong for him to try to escape: because doing so would violate an implicit agreement with the state.*]

*Socrates:*  Then consider the matter in this way — imagine I am about to escape, and the Laws and the State come and interrogate me: "Tell us, Socrates," they say, "what are you doing? Are you going to overturn us — the Laws and the State, as far as you are able? Do you imagine that a State can continue and not be overthrown, in which the decisions of Law have no power, but are set aside and overthrown by individuals?"

What will be our answer, Crito, to these and similar words? Anyone, and especially a clever orator, will have a good deal to say about the evil of setting aside the Law which requires a sentence to be carried out. We might reply, "Yes, but the State has injured us and given an unjust sentence." Suppose I say that?

*Crito:*  Very good, Socrates.

★From Christopher Biffle, *A Guided Tour of Five Works by Plato*, 3rd Edition, Mountain View, CA: Mayfield, 2001, pp. 66–69. Based on the Nineteenth Century translation by Benjamin Jowett. Reprinted with permission from The McGraw-Hill Companies.

S: "And was that our agreement with you?" the Law would say, "Or were you to abide by the sentence of the State?" And if I were surprised at their saying this, the Law would probably add: "Answer, Socrates, instead of opening your eyes: you are in the habit of asking and answering questions. Tell us what complaint you have against us which justifies you in attempting to destroy us and the State? In the first place did we not bring you into existence? Your father married your mother by our aid and conceived you. Say whether you have any objection against those of us who regulate marriage?" None, I should reply. "Or against those of us who regulate the system of care and education of children in which you were trained? Were not the Laws, who have the charge of this, right in commanding your father to train you in the arts and exercise?" Yes, I should reply.

"Well then, since you were brought into the world, nurtured and educated by us, can you deny in the first place that you are our child and slave, as your fathers were before you? And if this is true you are not on equal terms with us. Nor can you think you have a right to do to us what we are doing to you. Would you have any right to strike or do any other evil to a father or to your master, if you had one, when you have been struck or received some other evil at his hands? And because we think it is right to destroy you, do you think that you have any right to destroy us in return, and your country so far as you are able? And will you, O expounder of virtue, say you are justified in this? Has a philosopher like you failed to discover your country is more to be valued and higher and holier by far than mother and father or any ancestor, and more regarded in the eyes of the gods and of men of understanding? It should be soothed and gently and reverently entreated when angry, even more than a father, and if not persuaded, it should be obeyed. And when we are punished by the State, whether with imprisonment or whipping, the punishment is to be endured in silence. If the State leads us to wounds or death in battle, we follow as is right; no one can yield or leave his rank, but whether in battle or in a court of law, or in any other place, he must do what his city and his country order him. Or, he must change their view of what is just. If he may do no violence to his father or mother, much less may he do violence to his country," What answer shall we make to this, Crito? Do the Laws speak truly, or do they not?

C: I think that they do.

S: Then the Laws will say: "Consider, Socrates, if this is true, that in your present attempt you are going to do us wrong. For, after having brought you into the world, nurtured and educated you, and given you and every other citizen a share in every good we had to give, we further give the right to every Athenian, if he does not like us when he has come of age and has seen the ways of the city, he may go wherever else he pleases and take his goods with him. None of us Laws will forbid or interfere with him. Any of you who does not like us and the city, and who wants to go to a colony or to any other city, may go where he likes, and take his possessions with him. But he who has experience of the way we order justice and administer the State, and still remains, has entered into an implied contract to do as we command him. He who disobeys us is, as we maintain, triply wrong; first, because in disobeying us he is disobeying his parents; second, because we are the authors of his education; third, because he has made an agreement with us that he will duly obey our commands. He neither obeys them nor convinces us our commands are wrong. We do not rudely impose our commands but give each person the alternative of obeying or convincing us. That is what we offer and he does neither. These are the sort of accusations to which, as we were saying, Socrates, you will be exposed if you do as you were intending; you, above all other Athenians."

Suppose I ask, why is this? They will justly answer that I above all other men have acknowledged the agreement.

"There is clear proof," they will say, "Socrates, that we and the city were not displeasing to you. Of all Athenians you have been the most constant resident in the city, which, as you never leave, you appear to love. You never went out of the city either to see the games, except once when you went to the Isthmus, or to any other place unless you were on military service; nor did you travel as other men do. Nor had you any curiosity to know other States or their Laws: Your affections did not go beyond us and our State; we were your special favorites and you agreed in our government of you. This is the State in which you conceived your children, which is a proof of your satisfaction. Moreover, you might, if you wished, have fixed the penalty at banishment in the course of the trial — the State which refuses to let you go now would have let you go then. You pretended you preferred death to exile and that you were not grieved at death. And now you have forgotten these fine sentiments and pay no respect to us, the Laws, whom you destroy. You are doing what only a miserable slave would do, running away and turning your back upon the agreements which you made as a citizen. First of all, answer this very question: Are we right in saying you agreed to be governed according to us in deed, and not in word only? Is that true or not?"

How shall we answer that, Crito? Must we not agree?

*C:* We must, Socrates.

*S:* Then will the Laws say: "You, Socrates, are breaking the agreements which you made with us at your leisure, not in any haste or under any compulsion or deception, but having had 70 years to think of them, during which time you were at liberty to leave the city, if we were not to your liking or if our covenants appeared to you to be unfair. You might have gone either to Lacedaemon or Crete, which you often praise for their good government, or to some other Hellenic or foreign state. You, above all other Athenians, seemed to be so fond of the State and of us, her Laws, that you never left her. The lame, the blind, the maimed were not more stationary in the State than you were. Now you run away and forsake your agreements. Not, Socrates, if you will take our advice; do not make yourself ridiculous by escaping out of the city.

"Just consider, if you do evil in this way, what good will you do either yourself or your friends? That your friends will be driven into exile and lose their citizenship, or will lose their property, is reasonably certain. You yourself, if you fly to one of the neighboring cities, like Thebes or Megara, both of which are well-governed cities, will come to them as an enemy, Socrates. Their government will be against you and all patriotic citizens will cast suspicious eye

upon you as a destroyer of the Laws. You will confirm in the minds of the judges the justice of their own condemnation of you. For he who is a corruptor of the Laws is more than likely to be corruptor of the young. Will you then flee from well-ordered cities and virtuous men? Is existence worth having on these terms? Or will you go to these cities without shame and talk to them, Socrates? And what will you say to them? Will you say what you say here about virtue, justice, institutions, and laws being the best things among men. Would that be decent of you? Surely not.

"If you go away from well-governed states to Crito's friends in Thessaly, where there is a great disorder and immorality, they will be charmed to have the tale of your escape from prison, set off with ludicrous particulars of the manner in which you were wrapped in a goatskin or some other disguise and metamorphosed as the fashion of runaways is — that is very likely. But will there be no one to remind you in your old age you violated the most sacred laws from a miserable desire of a little more life? Perhaps not, if you keep them in a good temper. But if they are angry you will hear many degrading things; you will live, but how? As the flatterer of all men and the servant of all men. And doing what? Eating and drinking in Thessaly, having gone abroad in order that you may get a dinner. Where will your fine sentiments about justice and virtue be then? Say that you wish to live for the sake of your children, that you may bring them up and educate them — will you take them into Thessaly and deprive them of Athenian citizenship? Is that the benefit which you would confer upon them? Or are you under the impression that they will be better cared for and educated here if you are still alive, although absent from them because your friends will take care of them? Do you think if you are an inhabitant of Thessaly they will take care of them, and if you are an inhabitant of the other world they will not take care of them? No, if they who call themselves friends are truly friends, they surely will.

"Listen, then, Socrates, to us who have brought you up. Think not of life and children first, and of justice afterwards, but of justice first, that you may be justified before the rulers of the other world. For neither will you nor your children be happier or holier in this life, or happier in another, if you do as Crito bids. Now you depart in innocence, a sufferer and not a doer of evil; a victim, not of the Laws, but of men. But if you escape, returning evil for evil and injury for injury, breaking the agreements which have made with us, and wronging those whom you ought least to wrong, that is to say, yourself, your friends, your country, and us, we shall be angry with you while you live. Our brethren, the Laws in the other world, will receive you as an enemy because they will know you have done your best to destroy us. Listen, then, to us and not to Crito."

This is the voice which I seem to hear murmuring in my ears, like the sound of a divine flute in the ears of the mystic. That voice, I say, is humming in my ears and prevents me from hearing any other. I know anything more which you may say will be useless. Yet speak, if you have anything to say.

*C:* I have nothing to say, Socrates.

*S:* Then let me follow what seems to be the will of the god.

---

SELECTION 11.2

# Leviathan*

*Thomas Hobbes*

---

[*This is one of the most widely read passages in the history of political philosophy, in which Hobbes explains why people in the state of nature are always in a condition of war and puts forth the only way this condition can be avoided.*]

## Of the Natural Condition of Mankind As Concerning Their Felicity and Misery

Nature has made men so equal, in the faculties of the body, and mind; as that though there be found one man sometimes manifestly stronger in body, or of quicker mind than another; yet when all is reckoned together, the difference between man, and man, is not so considerable, as that one man can thereupon claim to himself any benefit, to which another may not pretend, as well as he. For as to the strength of body, the weakest has strength enough to kill the strongest, either by secret machination, or by confederacy with others, that are in the same danger with himself.

And as to the faculties of the mind . . . I find yet a greater equality amongst men, than that of strength. . . . That which may perhaps make such equality incredible, is but a vain conceit of one's own wisdom, which almost all men think they have in a greater degree, than the vulgar; that is, than all men but themselves, and a few others, whom by fame, or for concurring with themselves, they approve. For such is the nature of men, that howsoever they may acknowledge many others to be more witty, or more eloquent or more learned; yet they will hardly believe there be many so wise as themselves; for they set their own wit at hand, and other men's at a distance. But this proves rather that men are in that point equal, than unequal. For there is not ordinarily a greater sign of the equal distribution of any thing, than that every man is contented with his share.

From this equality of ability, arises equality of hope in the attaining of our ends. And therefore if any two men desire the same thing, which nevertheless they cannot both enjoy, they become enemies; and in the way to their end, which is principally their own conservation, and sometimes their delectation only, endeavour to destroy, or subdue one another. And from hence it comes to pass, that where an invader has no more to fear, than another man's single power; if one plant, sow, build, or possess a convenient seat, others may probably be expected to come prepared with forces united, to dispossess, and deprive him, not only of the fruit of

---

*Edited slightly for the modern reader.

his labour, but also of his life, or liberty. And the invader again is in the like danger of another.

And from this diffidence of one another, there is no way for any man to secure himself, so reasonable, as anticipation; that is, by force, or wiles, to master the persons of all men he can, so long, till he see no other power great enough to endanger him: and this is no more than his own conservation requires, and is generally allowed. . . .

Again, men have no pleasure, but on the contrary a great deal of grief, in keeping company where there is no power able to over-awe them all. For every man looks that his companion should value him, at the same rate he sets upon himself: and upon all signs of contempt, or undervaluing, naturally endeavours, as far as he dares, (which amongst them that have no common power to keep them in quiet, is far enough to make them destroy each other), to extort a greater value from his condemners, by damage; and from others, by the example.

So that in the nature of man, we find three principal causes of quarrel. First, competition; secondly, diffidence; thirdly, glory.

The first, makes men invade for gain; the second, for safety; and the third for reputation. The first use violence, to make themselves masters of other men's persons, wives, children, and cattle; the second, to defend them; the third for trifles, as a word, a smile, a different opinion, and any other sign of undervalue, either direct in their persons, or by reflection in their kindred, their friends, their nation, their profession, or their name.

Hereby it is manifest, that during the time men live without a common power to keep them all in awe, they are in that condition which is called war; and such a war, as is of every man, against every man. For WAR, consists not in battle only, or the act of fighting; but in a tract of time, wherein the will to contend by battle is sufficiently known: and therefore the notion of *time*, is to be considered in the nature of war; as it is the nature of weather. For as the nature of foul weather, lies not in a shower or two of rain; but in an inclination thereto of many days together; so the nature of war, consists not in actual fighting; but in the known disposition thereto, during all the time there is no assurance to the contrary. All other time is PEACE.

Whatsoever therefore is consequent to a time of war, where every man is enemy to every man; the same is consequent to the time, wherein men live without other security, than what their own strength, and their own invention shall furnish them withal. In such condition, there is no place for industry; because the fruit thereof is uncertain: and consequently no culture of the earth; no navigation, nor use of the commodities that may be imported by sea; no commodious building; no instruments of moving, and removing, such things as require much force; no knowledge of the face of the earth; no account of time; no arts; no letters, no society; and which is worst of all, continual fear, and danger of violent death; and the life of man, solitary, poor, nasty, brutish, and short.

It may seem strange to some man, that has not well weighed these things; that nature should thus dissociate, and render men apt to invade, and destroy one another; and he may therefore, not trusting to this inference, made from the passions, desire perhaps to have the same confirmed by experience. Let him therefore consider with himself, when taking a journey, he arms himself, and seeks to go well accompanied; when going to sleep, he locks his doors; when even in his house he locks his chests; and this when he knows there be laws, and public officers, armed, to revenge all injuries shall be done him; what opinion he has of his fellow-subjects, when he rides armed; of his fellow citizens, when he locks his doors; and of his children, and servants, when he locks his chests. Does he not there as much accuse mankind by his actions, as I do by my words? But neither of us accuse man's nature in it. The desires, and other passions of man, are in themselves no sin. No more are the actions, that proceed from those passions, till they know a law that forbids them: which till laws be made they cannot know: nor can any law be made, till they have agreed upon the person that shall make it. . . .

To this war of every man, against every man, this also is consequent; that nothing can be unjust. The notions of right and wrong, justice and injustice have there no place. Where there is no common power, there is no law: where no law, no injustice. Force, and fraud, are in war the two cardinal virtues. Justice and injustice are none of the faculties neither of the body, nor mind. If they were, they might be in a man that were alone in the world, as well as his senses, and passions. They are qualities that relate to men in society, not in solitude. It is consequent also to the same condition, that there be no propriety, no dominion, no *mine* and *thine* distinct; but only that to be every man's, that he can get; and for so long, as he can keep it. And thus much for the ill condition, which man by mere nature is actually placed in; though with a possibility to come out of it, consisting partly in the passions, partly in his reason.

The passions that incline men to peace, are fear of death, desire of such things as are necessary to commodious living; and a hope by their industry to obtain them. And reason suggests convenient articles of peace, upon which men may be drawn to agreement. These articles, are they, which otherwise are called the Laws of Nature: whereof I shall speak more particularly, in the two following chapters.

### Of the Interior Beginnings of Voluntary Motions; Commonly Called the Passions. And the Speeches by Which They Are Expressed.

. . . Whatever is the object of any man's appetite or desire, that is what he calls *good;* and the object of his hate and aversion, *evil;* and of his contempt, *vile* and *inconsiderable.* For these words are always used with relation to the person using them, there being nothing simply and absolutely so. Nor is there any common rule of good and evil, to be taken from the nature of objects themselves, but from the person of the man (where there is no commonwealth); or (in a commonwealth), from the person who represents it; or from an arbitrator, whom men disagreeing shall by consent agree to make his sentence their rule.

### Of the First and Second Natural Laws, and of Contracts

THE RIGHT OF NATURE, which writers commonly called *Jus Naturale,* is the liberty each man has to use his own power as he will himself, for the preservation . . . of his own life; and consequently of doing anything which in his own judgment and reason he shall conceive to be apt.

By LIBERTY is understood, according to the proper significance of the word, the absence of external impediments: which impediments may often take away part of a man's power to do what he would, but cannot hinder him from using the power left him, according as his judgment and reason shall dictate to him.

A LAW OF NATURE (*Lex Naturalis*), is a precept or general rule, found out by reason, by which a man is forbidden to do that which is destructive of his life or takes away the means of preserving the same; and to omit that by which he thinks it may be best preserved. For though they that speak of this subject confound *Jus* and *Lex,* right and law; yet

they ought to be distinguished; because right consists in liberty to do or to forbear; whereas law determines and binds to one of them: so that law and right differ as much as obligation and liberty; which in one and the same matter are inconsistent.

And because the condition of man (as has been declared in the preceding chapter) is a condition of war of everyone against everyone; in which case everyone is governed by his own reason; and there is nothing he can make use of, that may not be a help to him, in preserving his life against his enemies; it follows that in such a condition every man has a right to everything; even to one another's body. And therefore, as long as this natural right of man to everything endures, there can be no security to any man (how strong or wise he is) of living out the time which nature ordinarily allows men to live. And consequently it is a precept or general rule of reason, *that every man ought to endeavor peace, as far as he has hope of obtaining it; and when he cannot obtain it he may seek and use all helps and advantages of war.* The first branch of which rule contains the first and fundamental law of nature; which is *to seek peace and follow it.* The second, the sum of the Right of Nature; which is, *by all means we can, to defend ourselves.*

From this fundamental law of nature, by which men are commanded to endeavor peace, is derived this second law; *that a man be willing, when others are also, as far as for peace, and defense of himself he shall think it necessary, to lay down this right to all things; and be contented with so much liberty against other men, as he would allow other men against himself.* For as long as every man holds this right of doing anything he likes; so long are all men in the condition of war. But if other men will not lay down their right, as well as he; then there is not reason for anyone to divest himself of his: For that would be to expose himself to prey (which no man is bound to) rather than to dispose himself to peace. This is that law of the gospel; *whatsoever you require that others should do to you, that do to them. . . .*

To lay down a man's right to anything, is to divest himself of the liberty of hindering another of the benefit of his own right to the same. For he that renounces or passes away his right, gives not to any other man a right which he had not before; because there is nothing to which every man had not right by nature: but only stands out of his way that he may enjoy his own original right without hindrance from him; not without hindrance from another. So that the effect which reverberates to one man by another man's defect of right, is but so much diminution of impediments to the use of his own right original.

Right is laid aside, either by simply renouncing it; or by transferring it to another. By simply RENOUNCING; when he cares not to whom the benefit thereof reverberates. By TRANSFERRING; when he intends the benefit thereof to some certain person or persons. And when a man has in either manner abandoned or granted away his right; then is he said to be OBLIGED or BOUND not to hinder those to whom such right is granted or abandoned, from the benefit of it: and that he ought, and it is his DUTY, not to make void that involuntary act of his own: and that such hindrance is INJUSTICE and INJURY, as being *sine jure;* the right being before renounced or transferred. . . .

When a man transfers right or renounces it; it is either in consideration of some right reciprocally transferred to himself; or for some good he hopes for. For it is a voluntary act: and of the voluntary acts of every man, the object is good to himself. And therefore there are some rights which no man can be understood by any words or other signs to have abandoned or transferred. As first: a man cannot lay down the right of resisting them that assault him by force to take away his life; because he cannot be understood to aim thereby at good to himself. The same may be said of wounds and chains and imprisonment; both because there is no benefit consequent to such patience; as there is to the patience of suffering another to be wounded or imprisoned: as also because a man cannot tell, when he sees men proceeding against him by violence, when they intend his death or not. And the motive and end for which this renouncing and transferring of right is introduced is nothing else but the security of a man's person, in his life and in the means of so preserving life as not to be weary of it. And therefore if a man by words or other signs seems to rob himself of the end for which those signs were intended; he is not to be understood as if he meant it or that it was his will; but that he was ignorant of how such words and actions were to be interpreted.

The mutual transferring of right, is that which men call CONTRACT. . . .

### Of the Causes, Generation, and Definition of a Commonwealth

The final cause, end, or design of men (who naturally love liberty and dominion over others) in the introduction of that restraint upon themselves (in which we see them live in commonwealths) is the foresight of their own preservation and of a more contented life; that is to say, of getting themselves out from that miserable condition of war, which is necessarily consequent (as has been shown) to the natural passions of men, when there is no visible power to keep them in awe, and tie them by fear of punishment to the performance of their covenants, and observation of those laws of nature set down in the fourteenth and fifteenth chapters.

For the laws of nature (as justice, equity, modesty, mercy, and, in sum, doing to others as we would be done to) of themselves, without the terror of some power to cause them to be observed, are contrary to our natural passions, that carry us to partiality, pride, revenge, and the like. And covenants, without the sword, are but words, and of no strength to secure a man at all. Therefore notwithstanding the laws of nature (which everyone has then kept, when he has the will to keep them, when he can do it safely) if there be no power erected, or not great enough for our security; every man will, and may lawfully rely on his own strength and art, for caution against all other men. . . .

The only way to erect such a common power as may be able to defend them from the invasion of foreigners and the injuries of one another and thereby to secure them in such a way as that by their own industry, and by the fruits of the earth, they may nourish themselves and live contentedly; is to confer all their power and strength upon one man or upon one assembly of men, that may reduce all their wills, by plurality of voices, unto one will: which is as much as to say, to appoint one man or assembly of men to bear their person. . . .

This is more than consent or concord; it is a real unity of them all in one and the same person, made by covenant of every man with every man, in such manner as if every man should say to every man, I authorize and give up my right of governing myself to this man or to this assembly of men, on this condition that you give up the right to him and authorize all his actions in like manner. This done, the multitude so united in one person, is called a COMMONWEALTH, in Latin, *Civitas*. This is the generation of that great LEVIATHAN, or rather (to speak more reverently) of that mortal God to which we owe under the immortal God our peace and defense. For by this authority, given him by every particular man in the commonwealth, he has the use of so much power and strength conferred on him, by terror thereof, he is enabled to form the wills of them all, to peace at home, and mutual aid against their enemies abroad. And in him consists the essence of the commonwealth; which (to define it) is *one person, of whose acts a great multitude by mutual covenants one with another have made themselves every one the author, to the end he may use the strength and means of them all, as he shall think expedient, for their peace and common defense.*

And he that carries this person, is called SOVEREIGN, and said to have sovereign power; and everyone besides, his SUBJECT.

The attaining to this sovereign power, is by two ways. One, by natural force; as when a man makes his children submit themselves and their children to his government, as being able to destroy them if they refuse; or by war subdues his enemies to his will, giving them their lives on that condition. The other is when men agree amongst themselves, to submit to some man, or assembly of men, voluntarily on confidence to be protected by him against all others. This latter may be called a political commonwealth, or commonwealth by institution; and the former a commonwealth by acquisition.

---

SELECTION 11.3

# On Liberty

*John Stuart Mill*

---

[*The first sentence of this famous passage states clearly what Mill intends to accomplish in his essay.*]

## Chapter 1. Introductory

The object of this Essay is to assert one very simple principle, as entitled to govern absolutely the dealings of society with the individual in the way of compulsion and control, whether the means used be physical force in the form of legal penalties or the moral coercion of public opinion. That principle is, that the sole end for which mankind are warranted, individually or collectively, in interfering with the liberty of action of any of their number, is self-protection. That the only purpose for which power can be rightfully exercised over any member of a civilized community, against his will, is to prevent harm to others. His own good, either physical or moral, is not a sufficient warrant. He cannot rightfully be compelled to do or forbear because it will be better for him to do so, because it will make him happier, because, in the opinions of others, to do so would be wise, or even right. There are good reasons for remonstrating with him, or reasoning with him, or persuading him, or entreating him, but not for compelling him, or visiting him with any evil, in case he do otherwise. To justify that, the conduct from which it is desired to deter him must be calculated to produce evil to some one else. The only part of the conduct of any one, for which he is amenable to society, is that which concerns others. In the part which merely concerns himself, his independence is, of right, absolute. Over himself, over his own body and mind, the individual is sovereign.

It is, perhaps, hardly necessary to say that this doctrine is meant to apply only to human beings in the maturity of their faculties. We are not speaking of children, or of young persons below the age which the law may fix as that of manhood or womanhood. Those who are still in a state to require being taken care of by others, must be protected against their own actions as well as against external injury. For the same reason, we may leave out of consideration those backward states of society in which the race itself may be considered as in its nonage. The early difficulties in the way of spontaneous progress are so great, that there is seldom any choice of means for overcoming them; and a ruler full of the spirit of improvement is warranted in the use of any expedients that will attain an end, perhaps otherwise unattainable. Despotism is a legitimate mode of government in dealing with barbarians, provided the end be their improvement, and the means justified by actually effecting that end. Liberty as a principle, has no application to any state of things anterior to the time when mankind have become capable of being improved by free and equal discussion. Until then there is nothing for them but implicit obedience to an Akbar or a Charlemagne, if they are so fortunate as to find one. But as soon as mankind have attained the capacity of being guided to their own improvement by conviction or persuasion (a period long since reached in all nations with whom we need here concern ourselves), compulsion, either in the direct form or in that of pains and penalties for noncompliance, is no longer admissible as a means to their own good, and justifiable only for the security of others.

It is proper to state that I forgo any advantage which could be derived to my argument from the idea of abstract right, as a thing independent of utility. I regard utility as the ultimate appeal on all ethical questions; but it must be utility in the largest sense, grounded on the permanent interests of man as a progressive being. Those interests, I contend, authorize the subjection of individual spontaneity to external control, only in respect to those actions of each, which concern the interest of other people. If any one does an act hurtful to others, there is a prima facie case for punishing him, by law, or, where legal penalties are not safely applicable, by general disapprobation. There are also many positive acts for the benefit of others, which he may rightfully be compelled to perform; such as, to give evidence in a court of justice; to bear his fair share in the common defence, or in any other joint work necessary to the interest of the society of which he enjoys the protection; and to perform certain acts of individual beneficence, such as saving a fellow creature's life, or interposing to protect the defenceless against ill-usage, things which whenever it is obviously a man's duty to do, he may rightfully be made responsible to society for not doing. A person my cause evil to others not only by his actions but by his inaction, and in either case he is justly accountable to them for the injury. The latter case, it is true, requires a much more cautious exercise of compulsion than the former. To make any one answerable for doing evil to others, is the rule; to make him answerable for not preventing evil, is comparatively speaking, the exception. Yet there are many cases clear enough and grave enough to justify that exception. In all things which regard the external relations of the individual, he is *de jure* amenable to those whose interests are concerned, and if need be, to society as their protector. There are often good reasons for not holding him to the responsibility; but these reasons must arise from the special expediencies of the case: either because it is a kind of case in which he is on the whole likely to act better,

when left to his own discretion, than when controlled in any way in which society have it in their power to control him, or because the attempt to exercise control would produce other evils, greater than those which it would prevent. When such reasons as these preclude the enforcement of responsibility, the conscience of the agent himself should step into the vacant judgment-seat, and protect those interests of others which have no external protection; judging himself all the more rigidly, because the case does not admit of his being made accountable to the judgment of his fellow-creatures.

But there is a sphere of action in which society, as distinguished from the individual, has, if any, only an indirect interest; comprehending all that portion of a person's life and conduct which affects only himself, or, if it also affects others, only with their free, voluntary, and undeceived consent and participation. When I say only himself, I mean directly, and in the first instance: for whatever affects himself, may affect others *through* himself; and the objection which may be grounded on this contingency, will receive consideration in the sequel. This, then, is the appropriate region of human liberty. It comprises, first, the inward domain of consciousness, demanding liberty of conscience, in the most comprehensive sense; liberty of thought and feeling; absolute freedom of opinion and sentiment on all subjects, practical or speculative, scientific, moral, or theological. The liberty of expressing and publishing opinions may seem to fall under a different principle, since it belongs to that part of the conduct of an individual which concerns other people; but, being almost of as much importance as the liberty of thought itself, and resting in great part on the same reasons, is practically inseparable from it. Secondly, the principle requires liberty of tastes and pursuits; of framing the plan of our life to suit our own character; of doing as we like, subject to such consequences as may follow; without impediment from our fellow-creatures, so long as what we do does not harm them, even though they should think our conduct foolish, perverse, or wrong. Thirdly, from this liberty of each individual, follows the liberty, within the same limits, of combination among individuals; freedom to unite, for any purpose not involving harm to others: the persons combining being supposed to be of full age, and not forced or deceived.

No society in which these liberties are not, on the whole, respected, is free, whatever may be its form of government; and none is completely free in which they do not exist absolute and unqualified. The only freedom which deserves the name, is that of pursuing our own good in our own way, so long as we do not attempt to deprive others of theirs, or impede their efforts to obtain it. Each is the proper guardian of his own health, whether bodily, or mental and spiritual. Mankind are greater gainers by suffering each other to live as seems good to themselves, than by compelling each to live as seems good to the rest.

---

## SELECTION 11.4
# Communist Manifesto *
### *Karl Marx and Friedrich Engels*

---

[*Marx and Engels's* Communist Manifesto *is one of the most famous political documents of all time. This selection includes the most important aspects of the Marxist analysis of economic history.*]

## 1. Bourgeois and Proletarians

The history of all hitherto existing society is the history of class struggles.

Freeman and slave, patrician and plebian, lord and serf, guild-master and journeyman, in a word, oppressor and oppressed, stood in constant opposition to one another, carried on an uninterrupted, now hidden, now open fight, a fight that each time ended either in a revolutionary reconstitution of society at large or in the common ruin of the contending classes.

In the earlier epochs of history we find almost everywhere a complicated arrangement of society into various orders, a manifold gradation of social rank. In ancient Rome we have patricians, knights, plebians, slaves; in the Middle Ages, feudal lords, vassals, guild-masters, journeymen, apprentices, serfs; in almost all of these classes, again, subordinate gradations.

The modern bourgeois society that has sprouted from the ruins of feudal society has not done away with class antagonisms. It has but established new classes, new conditions of oppression, new forms of struggle in place of the old ones.

Our epoch, the epoch of the bourgeoisie, possesses, however, this distinctive feature: it has simplified the class antagonisms. Society as a whole is splitting up more and more into two great hostile camps, into two great classes directly facing each other: Bourgeoisie and Proletariat.

From the serfs of the Middle Ages sprang the chartered burghers of the earliest towns. From these burgesses the first elements of the bourgeoisie were developed.

The discovery of America, the rounding of the Cape, opened up fresh ground for the rising Bourgeoisie. The East Indian and Chinese markets, the colonization of America, trade with the colonies, the increase in the means of exchange and in commodities generally, gave to commerce, to navigation, to industry, an impulse never before known, and thereby, to the revolutionary element in the tottering feudal society, a rapid development.

The feudal system of industry, under which industrial production was monopolized by closed guilds, now no longer sufficed for the growing wants of the new markets. The manufacturing system took its place. The guildmasters were pushed on one side by the manufacturing middle class; division of labor between the different corporate guilds vanished in the face of division of labor in each single workshop.

Meantime the markets kept ever growing, the demand ever rising. Even manufacture no longer sufficed. Thereupon, steam and machinery revolutionized industrial production. The place of manufacture was taken by the giant, Modern Industry, the place of the industrial middle class by industrial millionaires — the leaders of whole industrial armies, the modern bourgeois.

Modern industry has established the work market, for which the discovery of America paved the way. This market has given an immense development to commerce, to navigation, to communication by land. This development has, in its turn,

---

* The authors' footnotes have been omitted.

reacted on the extension of industry; and in proportion as industry, commerce, navigation, railways extended, in the same proportion the bourgeoisie developed, increased its capital, and pushed into the background every class handed down from the Middle Ages.

We see, therefore, how the modern bourgeoisie is itself the product of a long course of development, of a series of revolutions in the modes of production and of exchange.

Each step in the development of the bourgeoisie was accompanied by a corresponding political advance of that class. An oppressed class under the sway of the feudal nobility, an armed and self-governing association in the medieval commune, here independent urban republic (as in Italy and Germany), there taxable "third estate" of the monarchy (as in France), afterward, in the period of manufacture proper, serving either the semi-feudal or the absolute monarchy as a counterpoise against the nobility, and, in fact, cornerstone of the great monarchies in general, the bourgeoisie has at last, since the establishment of Modern Industry and of the world market, conquered for itself, in the modern representative State, exclusive political sway. The executive of the modern State is but a committee for managing the common affairs of the whole bourgeoisie.

The bourgeoisie, historically, has played a most revolutionary part.

The bourgeoisie, wherever it has got the upper hand, has put an end to all feudal, patriarchal, idyllic relations. It has pitilessly torn asunder the motley feudal ties that bound man to his "natural superiors," and has left remaining no other nexus between man and man than naked self-interest, than callous "cash payment." . . .

The bourgeoisie cannot exist without constantly revolutionizing the instruments of production, and thereby the relations of production, and with them the whole relations of society. . . .

The need of a constantly expanding market for its products chases the bourgeoisie over the whole surface of the globe. It must nestle everywhere, settle everywhere, establish connections everywhere.

In place of the old wants, satisfied by the production of the country, we find new wants, requiring for their satisfaction the products of distant lands and climes. In place of the old local and national seclusion and self-sufficiency, we have intercourse in every direction, universal interdependence of nations. . . .

The bourgeoisie, by the rapid improvement of all instruments of production, by the immensely facilitated means of communication, draws all, even the most barbarian, nations into civilization. The cheap prices of its commodities are the heavy artillery with which it batters down all Chinese walls, with which it forces the barbarians' intensely obstinate hatred of foreigners to capitulate. It compels all nations, on pain of extinction, to adopt the bourgeois mode of production; it compels them to introduce what it calls civilization into their midst, i.e., to become bourgeois themselves. In a word, it creates a world after its own image.

The bourgeoisie has subjected the country to the rule of the towns. It has created enormous cities, has greatly increased the urban population as compared with the rural, and has thus rescued a considerable part of the population from the idiocy of rural life. Just as it has made the country dependent on the towns, so it has made barbarian and semi-barbarian countries dependent on the civilized ones, nations of peasants on nations of bourgeois, the East on the West.

The bourgeoisie keeps doing away more and more with the scattered state of the population, of the means of production, and of property. It has agglomerated population, centralized means of production, and has concentrated property in a few hands. The necessary consequence of this was political centralization. . . .

The bourgeoisie during its rule of scarce one hundred years has created more massive and more colossal productive forces than have all preceding generations together. Subjection of nature's forces to man, machinery, application of chemistry to industry and agriculture, steam navigation, railways, electric telegraphs, clearing of whole continents for cultivation, canalization of rivers, whole populations conjured out of the ground—what earlier century had even a presentiment that such productive forces slumbered in the lap of social labor?

We see then: the means of production and of exchange, on the foundation of which the bourgeoisie built itself up, were generated in feudal society. At a certain stage in the development of these means of production and of exchange, the conditions under which feudal society produced and exchanged, the feudal organization of agriculture and manufacturing industry, in a word, the feudal relations of property became no longer compatible with the already developed productive forces; they became so many fetters. They had to be burst asunder; they were burst asunder.

Into their place stepped free competition, accompanied by a social and political constitution adapted to it and by the economic and political sway of the bourgeois class.

A similar movement is going on before our own eyes. Modern bourgeois society with its relations of production, of exchange and of property, a society that has conjured up such gigantic means of production and of exchange, is like the sorcerer who is no longer able to control the powers of the nether world whom he has called up by his spells. For many a decade past the history of industry and commerce is but the history of the revolt of modern productive forces against modern conditions of production, against the property relations that are the conditions for the existence of the bourgeoisie and of its rule. It is enough to mention the commercial crises that by their periodical return put on trial, each time more threateningly, the existence of the entire bourgeois society. In these crises a great part not only of the existing products, but also of the previously created productive forces, are periodically destroyed. In these crises there breaks out an epidemic that in all earlier epochs would have seemed an absurdity — the epidemic of overproduction. Society suddenly finds itself put back into a state of momentary barbarism; it appears as if a famine, a universal war of devastation had cut off the supply of every means of subsistence; industry and commerce seem to be destroyed; and why? Because there is too much civilization, too much means of subsistence, too much industry, too much commerce. The productive forces at the disposal of society no longer tend to further the development of the conditions of bourgeois property; on the contrary, they have become too powerful for these conditions, by which they are fettered, and as soon as they overcome these fetters, they bring disorder into the whole of bourgeois society, endanger the existence of bourgeois property. The conditions of bourgeois society are too narrow to comprise the wealth created by them. And how does the bourgeoisie get over these crises? On the one hand by enforced destruction of a mass of productive forces; on the other, by the conquest of new markets and by the more thorough exploitation of the old ones. That is to say, by paving the way for more extensive and more destructive crises and by diminishing the means whereby crises are prevented.

The weapons with which the bourgeoisie felled feudalism to the ground are now turned against the bourgeoisie itself.

But not only has the bourgeoisie forged the weapons that bring death to itself; it has also called into existence the men who are to wield those weapons — the modern working class, the proletarians.

## CHECKLIST

To help you review, here is a checklist of the key philosophers and terms and concepts of this chapter. The brief descriptive sentences summarize the philosophers' leading ideas. Keep in mind that some of these summary statements are oversimplifications of complex positions.

### Philosophers

- **Plato**   held that the best or "just" state is a class-structured aristocracy ruled by "philosopher-kings."

- **Aristotle**   held that a state is good to the degree to which it enables its citizens to achieve the good life and believed that the form of the ideal state depends on the circumstances.

- **St. Augustine and St. Thomas Aquinas** Christianized the concept of natural law. They were concerned with the relationship of secular law to natural law and of the state to the church. Aquinas distinguished four kinds of law; this was one of his most important contributions to political philosophy.

- **Thomas Hobbes**   was a contractarian theorist who held that civil society, civil laws, and justice come into existence when people contract among themselves to transfer their power and rights to a sovereign power who compels people to live in peace and honor their agreements. Hobbes believed the transfer is "commanded" by natural law, which he held to be a set of rational principles for best ensuring self-preservation.

- **John Locke**   held that people have God-given natural rights and that the state is created for the protection of those rights by mutual agreement among its citizens, who entrust their rights to the state for safeguarding.

- **Jean-Jacques Rousseau,**   another contractarian, held that through a social compact people may agree to unite into a state and through the state to enact laws reflective of the general will. He believed that people neither give up their rights to the state nor entrust them to it, for they *are* the state.

- **Adam Smith**   was a classical liberal economic theorist who was an exponent of capitalism and a laissez-faire economy.

- **Jeremy Bentham,**   a utilitarian philosopher, dismissed talk about natural rights as meaningless.

- **Harriet Taylor**   was a reformist philosopher who advocated the liberation of women and stressed the importance of political tolerance and individualism.

- **John Stuart Mill,**   a classical liberal theorist, held that the function of the state is to promote the general happiness (not to safeguard natural rights). He stipulated that a person's liberty may be interfered with only to prevent harm to others.

- **Georg Hegel**   explained the road to freedom via master and slave.

- **Karl Marx**   held that human history is a dialectical interplay between social relationships and economic productive activity that involves class warfare but ultimately leads to an ideal society lacking classes, wages, money, private property, or exploitation.

## Key Terms and Concepts

| | |
|---|---|
| political philosophy | tacit consent |
| philosopher-king | general will |
| aristocracy | *Marbury v. Madison* |
| timocracy | *Roe v. Wade* |
| plutocracy | liberalism |
| democracy | capitalism |
| tyranny | free-market economy |
| monarchy | utilitarianism |
| oligarchy | means (forces) of |
| polity |     production |
| egalitarian | productive relations |

| | |
|---|---|
| natural law political | dialectical process |
|     theory | class struggle |
| eternal law | alienation |
| divine law | proletariat |
| natural law | revolutionists |
| human law | revisionists/ |
| sovereign power |     evolutionary |
| Leviathan |     socialists |
| social contract/ | Communism |
|     contractualism | communism |
| natural rights | anarchism |

## QUESTIONS FOR DISCUSSION AND REVIEW

1. According to Plato, the ideal state consists of three classes. What are they, what are their functions, and how is class membership determined?

2. Is the well-being of the state desirable in its own right, apart from what it contributes to the welfare of its citizens?

3. Evaluate Aristotle's idea that people who do not have the aptitude or time to participate in governance should not be citizens.

4. Explain the four types of law distinguished by Aquinas.

5. In the absence of civil authority, would anyone live up to an agreement that turns out not to be in his or her own best interest?

6. Would it be wise for people, for their own good, to transfer their collective strength to a sovereign power? Explain.

7. Can a covenant between the Leviathan and its subjects be made? Why is it impossible for Hobbes's Leviathan to act unjustly toward its subjects?

8. Which is better, in your view, dictatorship or anarchy? Why?

9. Does the Leviathan have the right to take your life, according to Hobbes? Explain.

10. Compare and contrast the purpose of the state and the relationship between it and its subjects for Hobbes, Locke, and Rousseau.

11. What is Locke's argument for saying that each person has inalienable natural rights?

12. What is tacit consent?

13. "All people equally have a right to property, but they do not all have a right to equal property." What does this mean? Do you agree?

14. Explain Locke's concept of private property. Is this a realistic concept?

15. What is the general will, and how do we know what it is?

16. Can you think of any justification for the principle that people have natural rights other than that proposed by Locke?

17. Do people have a natural right to privacy? Explain.

18. Can you think of a sounder justification for abortion rights than the "right to privacy"? Explain.

19. If people have a right to privacy, do children have that right? Do infants? Explain.

20. Would people be better off without any government at all? Explain.

21. "The only part of the conduct of anyone, for which he is amenable to society, is that which concerns others. In the part which merely concerns himself, his independence is absolute." Do you agree? Why or why not?

22. What, for utilitarians, are "natural rights"?

23. What did Taylor think was so important about toleration? In what ways did she think English society was intolerant?

24. Compare and contrast classical liberalism and orthodox Marxism.

25. What, according to Marx, are the consequences of capitalism, and why are they consequences?

26. Does alienation exist? Defend your answer.

27. Would Rousseau have agreed with Socrates' explanation to Crito (Selection 1) about why he should not try to escape from prison? Why or why not?

## SUGGESTED FURTHER READINGS

George Anastaplo, *Liberty, Equality and Modern Constitutionalism* (Newburyport, Maine: Focus Publishing, 1999). A two-volume collection of important social and political texts from Plato to Winston Churchill.

Julia Annas, *An Introduction to Plato's "Republic"* (Oxford: Clarendon Press, 1981). A systematic introduction to Plato's most important work.

Aristotle, *Politics*, in *The Complete Works of Aristotle*, vol. 2, J. Barnes, ed. (Princeton: Princeton University Press, 1984).

E. Barker, *The Political Thought of Plato and Aristotle* (New York: Putnam, 1906). Old but still good.

Richard Bellamy and Angus Ross, *A Textual Introduction to Social and Political Theory* (New York: Manchester University Press, 1996). Extracts and essays on the leading political philosophers from Socrates to Mill and Weber.

Isaiah Berlin, *Karl Marx, His Life and Environment* (New York: Oxford University Press, 1996). A classic treatment of Marx.

Steven M. Cahn, *Classics of Modern Political Theory* (New York: Oxford University Press, 1996). A comprehensive anthology.

Cicero, *De re publica*, and *De legibus*, both translated by C. W. Keyes (and both London: Loeb Classical Library, 1928). See book III of each of these classic works.

Ian Craib, *Classical Social Theory* (New York: Oxford University Press, 1997). A study of the classic social thinkers including Marx, Weber, and Durkheim.

R. Gettell, *History of American Political Thought* (New York: The Century Co., 1928). Excellent, if you can find it.

R. Gettell, *History of Political Thought* (New York: The Century Co., 1924). One of the best single-volume histories of political theory available.

E. Gilson, *The Christian Philosophy of St. Thomas Aquinas*, L. Shook, trans. (New York: Random House, 1956). See part III, chap. 1, sect. 4 for Aquinas' concept of law.

Jack Lively and Andrew Reeve, eds., *Modern Political Theory from Hobbes to Marx, Key Debates* (New York: Routledge, 1989). Important essays on major political theorists—Hobbes, Locke, Rousseau, Burke, Bentham, Mill, and Marx.

J. Locke, *The Second Treatise of Government*, Thomas P. Peardon, ed. (Indianapolis: Bobbs-Merrill, 1952). Features a short and critical introduction by the editor.

Steven Luper, *Social Ideals and Policies, Readings in Social and Political Philosophy* (New York: McGraw-Hill, 1998). A collection of essays on social ideals, society, and international order.

N. Machiavelli, *The Prince*, C. Detmold, trans. (New York: Airmont, 1965). Required reading for political science students as well as philosophy students.

Karl Marx and Friedrich Engels, *The Communist Manifesto*, David McLellan, ed. (New York: Oxford University Press, 1998). The editor, who contributes an introduction and notes, is an important Marx scholar.

Janice McLaughlin, *Feminist Social and Political Theory* (New York: Macmillan, 2003). Introduction to the relationship between feminism and contemporary social and political thought.

D. McLellan, *The Thought of Karl Marx* (New York: Macmillan, 1977). Excellent analytic treatment of Marx's philosophy. For an authoritative biography of Marx, see McLellan's *Marx: His Life and Thought* (New York: Harper & Row, 1973). For Marx readings, see McLellan's *Selected Writings* (New York: Oxford University Press, 1977).

J. S. Mill, *On Liberty,* E. Rapaport, ed. (Indianapolis: Hackett, 1978). The statement of classic liberalism.

R. G. Mulgan, *Aristotle's Political Theory* (Oxford: Clarendon Press, 1991). An examination of Aristotle's political theory as a practical, applicable science.

Ellen Frankel Paul, Fred D. Miller Jr., and Jeffrey Paul, eds., *Property Rights* (Cambridge: Cambridge University Press, 1994). A collection of articles on ownership and property rights.

Plato, *Republic,* in *The Collected Dialogues of Plato,* E. Hamilton and H. Cairns, eds. (New York: Bollingen Foundation, 1961). Plato's classic.

Louis Pojman, *Global Political Philosophy* (New York: McGraw-Hill, 2002). A review of global political philosophy dealing emphasizing current issues of the day.

Louis Pojman, *Political Philosophy: Classic and Contemporary Readings* (New York: McGraw-Hill, 2001). Unique collection of readings from both ancient and current authors.

Anthony Quinton, ed., *Political Philosophy* (New York: Oxford University Press, 1991). Papers on political issues such as sovereignty, democracy, liberty, equality, and the common good.

J. J. Rousseau, *The Social Contract,* C. Frankel, trans. and ed. (New York: Hafner, 1966). Few political philosophers are easier to read and understand than is Rousseau.

Paul E. Sigmund, *St. Thomas Aquinas on Politics and Ethics* (New York: Norton, 1988). New translations of selections from the *Summa Contra Gentiles* and *Summa Theologica* that include Aquinas' views on government, law, war, property, sexual ethics, the proofs of God, the soul, the purpose of man, and the order of the universe.

Peter Singer, *Marx: A Very Short Introduction* (New York: Oxford University Press, 2000). A brief introduction to Marx by a very clear writer.

R. Stewart, *Readings in Social and Political Philosophy,* 2nd ed. (Oxford: Oxford University Press, 1996). An excellent anthology of classic and contemporary readings in social and political philosophy.

Harriet Taylor, "Enfranchisement of Women," in *Essays on Sex Equality,* Alice S. Rossi, ed. (Chicago: University of Chicago Press, 1970). Almost all the writings by Taylor and John Stuart Mill are contained in this volume.

R. Taylor, *Freedom, Anarchy, and the Law: An Introduction to Political Philosophy,* 2nd ed. (Buffalo: Prometheus Books, 1982). A general introduction to political philosophy.

Catharine Trotter, *The Works of Mrs. Catharine Cockburn,* 2 vols. (London: Routledge/Thoemmes Press, 1992). Her philosophical writings, plays, poetry, and correspondence.

Mary Ellen Waithe, ed., *A History of Women Philosophers,* vol. 3, *Modern Women Philosophers: 1600–1900* (Dordrecht: Kluwer Academic Press, 1991). Chapters about thirty-one women philosophers of the period.

E. Jonathan Wolfe and Michael Rosen, eds., *Political Thought* (New York: Oxford University Press, 1999). A selection of important writings concerning the prime questions of political philosophy from Plato to contemporary times.

R. P. Wolff, *In Defense of Anarchism* (New York: Harper & Row, 1970). Also contains critiques of Rousseau and Locke.

F. J. E. Woodbridge, ed., *Hobbes Selections* (New York: Scribner's, 1930). You may also wish to have a look at the complete *Leviathan.* There is a good edition by M. Oakeshott with an introduction by R. S. Peters (New York: Collier, 1962).

# 12

# Recent Moral and Political Philosophy

The moral order is just as much a part of the fundamental nature of the universe as is the spatial or numerical structure expressed in the axioms of geometry or arithmetic.   —W. D. Ross

Hamlet: There is nothing either good or bad, but thinking makes it so.   —William Shakespeare

Contemporary ethical theory begins with **G. E. Moore** (1873–1958). Moore opened up new issues for consideration and altered the focus of ethical discussion. Much of twentieth-century analytic ethics, at least until recently, treated issues that were raised either by Moore or by philosophers responding to him or to other respondents. Although analytic ethical philosophers discussed many questions that were not directly (or indirectly) considered by Moore, even these questions were raised along tributaries that can be traced back to the main waterway Moore opened. Some people regret the influence Moore had on ethics. You will have to draw your own conclusions.

## G. E. MOORE

Moore believed that the task of the ethical philosopher is to conduct a "general inquiry into what is good." This seems reasonably straightforward, down to earth, and useful. If you know what good or goodness is and if you know what things are

357

Contemporary moral philosophy began with G. E.
Moore.

good, then you also know what proper conduct is, right? This, at any rate, is what
Moore maintained, because he believed the morally right act is the one that produces the greatest amount of good.

Now good, or goodness, which is the same thing, is a *noncomplex* and *nonnatural* property of good things, Moore argued. Goodness is noncomplex in that it
cannot be broken down or "analyzed" into simpler constituents. It is not at all like
the property of being alive, for example. A thing's being alive consists in many
simpler things, like having a beating heart and a functioning brain (at least for humans and other animals). But a thing's being *good* is rather more like a person's being in pain, at least with respect to the question of complexity. Pain is pain, and that
is that. Pain cannot be broken down into simpler constituent parts. (How we come
to have pain can be *explained*, but that is a different matter.) Good, too, is simple,
according to Moore: it is a property that cannot be further analyzed or broken
down into simpler constituent parts. Thus, good is also *indefinable*, he said; at least
you cannot come up with a definition of good that states its constituent parts (because there are none). Good is good, and that is that.

Good is also a nonnatural property, Moore stated. This is what he meant. Suppose that you pronounce that something is good. Is what you are saying equivalent
to saying that it is a certain size or shape or color or is pleasant or worth a lot of
money? Of course not. Size, shape, color, pleasantness, and monetary value are all
natural properties: they are a part of nature, construed broadly. They can be perceived. But good is not equivalent to these or any other natural properties, or so
said Moore. Take something you regard as good, like an act of generosity, for in-

stance. Now list all the natural properties (that is, all the properties that can be apprehended by sense) of this act. Do you find goodness on the list? Not at all. What you find are items such as the duration, location, causes, and consequences of the generous act. The *goodness* of the act is not identical with any of these items. It is something quite different from the act's natural properties.

That goodness does not equate with any natural property is easily seen, Moore argued, in a passage that became one of the most famous in all of twentieth-century ethics. Think of any natural property, for instance, pleasantness. Now, it is certainly reasonable to ask if pleasantness is good. But if pleasantness were *equivalent* to good, then asking, Is pleasantness good? would be the same as asking, Is good good? and that is *not* a reasonable question. Because it is legitimate and intelligible to ask of any natural property whether that property is good, it follows that good is not equivalent to any natural property. You can see that Moore did not agree with the utilitarians, who equated the goodness of an act with the pleasure it produced as a consequence.

Moore wanted especially to know which "good" things we can really hope to obtain. His answer: personal affection and aesthetic enjoyments. He wrote: "Personal affection and aesthetic enjoyments include by far the greatest good with which we are acquainted." Note how different this answer is from any that would have been proposed by the other philosophers we have discussed.

But the remarkable thing is that it was not Moore's opinion about what things are good that interested other philosophers. Rather, it was his "metaethical" opinions that were most discussed. If you are new to philosophy, you may never have heard of "metaethics," and so we must digress for a moment from Moore to explain.

## NORMATIVE ETHICS AND METAETHICS

Let's go back to the concept of a moral value judgment, or, more succinctly, the concept of a **moral judgment,** a judgment that states or implies that something is good or bad, right or wrong, a judgment like "You should be more generous," or "It was wrong for the president not to speak out more vigorously for minorities when she had the chance to do so," or "Act so as to promote the greatest happiness." Making and defending (or criticizing) moral judgments is the business of **normative ethics.** It's called "normative" because when you make or defend (or criticize) a moral judgment, you are appealing to a moral standard, or "norm."

Many people assume that moral philosophy is concerned primarily with supplying moral judgments; in other words, many people assume that moral philosophy is normative. And, indeed, prior to Moore, moral philosophy was mainly normative. However, a moral philosopher need not be concerned only (or even at all) with *making* moral judgments. Instead, he or she may be concerned with such issues as how moral value judgments are verified or validated, or what sort of thing is goodness, or how goodness and rightness are related, or what sort of thing *is* a moral judgment. Notice that questions of this sort do not require a moral judgment as an answer. The attempt to find answers to questions of this sort, in other words, the attempt to understand the sources, criteria, meaning, verification, or validation of moral value judgments — rather than to make moral judgments — is known as **metaethics.**

It was Moore's metaethical views, not his normative claims about what actually is good, that provoked the most discussion in the professional philosophical literature. Most important, Moore had held that goodness is a simple, nonnatural, and indefinable property. Is this **antinaturalism** doctrine correct, as Moore had argued? Much contemporary analytic ethical philosophy, which has grown out of the issues raised by Moore and by those who in turn responded to Moore, has been concerned with this and related metaethical issues. Now, frankly, many people outside moral philosophy find this state of affairs just awful. Philosophers, they say, should propose theories about what people (and societies and governments) should do and about what things are good. They should recommend courses of action, offer ethical counseling, and take a stand on the issues of the day. In short, they should make moral judgments. But — until fairly recently — contemporary analytic moral philosophers haven't regarded the making of moral judgments as an important aspect of their professional work in philosophy. Further, contemporary analytic moral philosophers interested in metaethics regard their work as quite important, even if to others it may seem boring or even trivial. Take Moore's antinaturalist position, that goodness is a simple, nonnatural, and indefinable property. If this metaethical position is correct, then all who equate goodness with a natural property, as many have done for more than twenty centuries, have based their values on what, essentially, is a mistake.

## W. D. ROSS

In an influential book, *The Right and the Good* (1930), **W. D. Ross** (1877–1970) defined his purpose as "to examine the nature, relations, and implications of three conceptions which appear to be fundamental in ethics — those of 'right,' 'good' in general, and 'morally good.'" Ross's purpose, therefore, was to conduct a metaethical inquiry, and his work was devoted largely to criticism of certain metaethical ideas set forth by G. E. Moore. Let's consider Ross briefly to get the sense of what he, and metaethics generally, was about.

Moore, as we noted, believed that that which alone makes right actions right is that they produce more good than alternative actions do. This seems reasonable enough, does it not? If a course of action is right, it must be because it is more productive of good than are alternative courses of action. But Ross disagreed. Certainly, he wrote, it is right and morally obligatory and our duty (these expressions all mean the same, for Ross) to bring into existence as many good things as possible. But the production of maximum good is not the only thing that makes an act right: we have other duties than to bring about good results.

For example, it is your duty to keep promises, Ross said. What makes it right for you to do what you have promised to do is not that your doing it will produce more good, as Moore thought, but simply the fact that you promised to do it.

In short, according to Ross there exist **prima facie duties** — things it is our duty to do unless that duty is overridden by some other duty. Our prima facie duties include, for example, keeping promises, relieving distress, showing gratitude, improving ourselves, and being truthful. What makes it right to do these things is not that doing so produces the maximum good (though it may have this as a side benefit) but simply that it is right to do them.

According to Ross, our prima facie duties are not *absolute* duties — for example, though it is our duty to keep promises, we are justified in breaking a promise to save someone's life — but it *is* our duty to do them unless other moral considerations take precedence.

And further, according to Ross, that it is right to keep promises, return services rendered, and so forth, is *self-evident*, "just as a mathematical axiom or the validity of a form of inference, is self-evident." "The moral order expressed in these propositions," Ross asserted, "is just as much part of the fundamental nature of the universe . . . as is the spatial or numerical structure expressed in the axioms of geometry or arithmetic."

Ross's views are similar in this regard to those of Kant. Kant, too, proposed a duty-based moral philosophy and was committed to the idea that our moral duty is self-evident. A duty-based moral philosophy is known as a deontological moral philosophy. **Deontological ethics** are usually contrasted with consequentialist ethics and virtue ethics, as explained in Chapter 10.

Now Ross recognized not only prima facie duties but also *intrinsic goods*, specifically, virtue, knowledge, and (with certain limitations) pleasure. We do indeed have a prima facie duty to produce as much of these good things as possible, Ross maintained. But what other philosophers mainly discussed was *not* Ross's thoughts about what things actually are good or about what our duties actually are but, rather, his *metaethical* theories. Philosophers explored Ross's ideas that *right is not reducible to good*, that *some true moral propositions are self-evident*, and that *some duties are "prima facie."*

## EMOTIVISM AND BEYOND

The utilitarians defined the rightness of an action in terms of the happiness it produces as a consequence. Accordingly, moral judgments in effect are a type of *factual judgment*, a judgment about how much happiness some action produces.

Moore and Ross denied that the rightness of an act or the goodness of an end can be defined in terms of happiness or any other natural property or thing. (They disagreed between themselves about the relationship between rightness and goodness.) But like the utilitarians, they believed that moral judgments are a type of factual judgment. To say that an end is good or that an act is right, for Moore and Ross both, is to state a fact. It is to attribute a property to the thing in question, a "nonnatural" property. Whether a certain type of act possesses the property of rightness and whether a certain end possesses the property of goodness are questions of fact, even though the fact is nonempirical. That it is right to keep a promise, Moore and Ross would agree, is a *fact:* it is *true* that you should keep your promises and *false* that you should break them.

A radically different view of moral judgments was set forth by the emotivists, a group of analytic philosophers who had read Moore and Ross and disagreed with them both.

The **emotivists** maintained that *moral judgments have no factual meaning whatsoever.* Such judgments, according to the emotivists, *are not even genuine propositions.* In their view, the judgment "It is right to keep your promises" is neither true nor false: the utterance is not really a proposition at all.

Thus, according to the emotivists, there is no question about what we are saying if, for example, we state, "Abortion is wrong." Because we are not really asserting a genuine proposition, we are not really *saying* anything at all. The question there is only what we *are doing* when we open our mouths and voice an expression like "Abortion is wrong."

And what we are doing, they said, is *expressing our distaste* for abortion and also, sometimes, *encouraging others to feel the same way.* Thus, C. L. Stevenson (1908–1979), an influential emotivist, maintained that an ethical judgment like "Abortion is wrong" is a linguistic act by which the speaker expresses her or his attitude toward abortion and seeks to influence the attitude, and in turn the conduct, of the listener.

Emotivism had some strong adherents within analytic philosophy, but it seemed to many other analytic philosophers that the emotivist analysis of ethical judgments was not essentially correct. The contemporary British linguistic philosopher R. M. Hare (1919–2002) said that the function of moral discourse is not to express or influence attitudes but, rather, to *guide conduct.*

A moral judgment, according to Hare, is a kind of **prescriptive judgment** that is "universalizable": when I make a moral judgment such as "You ought to give Smith back the book you borrowed," I am prescribing a course of conduct, and my prescription is general and exceptionless (i.e., I believe that anyone else in the same or relevantly similar situation ought to conduct himself or herself similarly).

That emotivism misrepresents, or indeed trivializes, moral discourse is now fairly widely accepted by contemporary philosophers.

Despite their differences, Moore, Ross, and the emotivists all agreed that descriptive statements and value judgments are logically distinct. If you say that (1) I did not do what I promised you I would do, you are making a purely descriptive statement. If you say that (2) I did not do what I ought to have done, you are making a value judgment. Most of the philosophers of the first half of the twentieth century accepted Hume's opinion that "you cannot deduce an 'ought' from an 'is'" and held that it is a mistake to think that any moral value judgment is logically entailed by any descriptive statement. This mistake was called the **naturalist fallacy.** Thus, for example, it would be committing the naturalist fallacy to suppose that (2) is logically deducible from (1).

## Environmental Philosophy

Frequently, philosophy departments offer courses in environmental ethics, one of the three main areas of **applied ethics.** The other two are business ethics and biomedical ethics. There is an extensive literature in environmental ethics, but, generally, discussion seems to fall under these two headings:

1. What, if any, are the root *philosophical* causes of ecological crises? Some see ecological problems as primarily due to *shallow* factors including near-sightedness, ignorance, and greed. Others seek a more basic explanation of ecological maladies, and discussion seems to have focused on three possible candidates. Some, deep ecologists, think the fundamental explanation of ecological crises is anthropocentrism, the view that humans are the central value of the universe. Others, known as ecofeminists, think the root problem is patriarchalism, or the oppression and exploitation of women—and nature—as subservient to men. Still others, social ecologists, think the fundamental causes are deep-seated authoritarian social structures based on domination and exploitation by privileged groups. Although there is considerable controversy among these groups, other environmental philosophers view their distinctions as irrelevant to such pressing problems as overconsumption and militarization.

2. What entities have moral standing and intrinsic values? For example, do nonhuman animals have rights or interests? Do plants? Do species? Do biotic communities, ecosystems, wilderness, or the planetary biosphere? And, closely related, what properties or characteristics must a thing have to have moral standing? For example, must it be able to experience sensation? Or must it just be alive? Must it simply have an end or goal or good of its own?

Writings on animal rights constitute a large literature in their own right, independent of environmental ethics.

---

But is the naturalist fallacy really a fallacy? The issue is important because if you hold that moral evaluations are logically independent of descriptive premises, it would then seem that you could commend morally any state of affairs you please—and would not logically have to accept as evidence for a moral evaluation the empirical evidence that most people accept as evidence. Eventually, philosophers began to consider this issue carefully—among the first to do so were Oxford's Phillipa Foot (1920– ) and University of California, Berkeley's, John Searle (1932– )—and now many philosophers do not accept the idea that moral evaluations are logically independent of the descriptive premises on which, in everyday conversation, they are often based. Instead, they maintain there are empirical criteria for ascribing moral predicates to actions, people, and states of affairs.

Now, these two related developments—the rejection of emotivism and the emerging idea that there are empirical criteria for moral evaluations—are important. Here is why. If it is assumed that moral judgments are just expressions of taste and are logically independent of any empirical facts about the world, then why bother discussing concrete moral issues? Given these assumptions, there would seem to be little room for reasoned deliberation in ethical matters. Consequently, as these assumptions were called into question, there was a renewal of interest in concrete ethical issues by moral philosophers. Much discussed in recent years, for example, have been issues of sexual morality, affirmative action, biomedical ethics, business ethics, and treatment of the environment. For an example, see the box "Environmental Philosophy."

But now a word of caution: that there has been a recent widespread and apparently growing interest in concrete moral questions should not lead you to conclude that metaethics is dead. It is probably true, as we move forward in the twenty-first century, that many professors of ethics focus their courses on concrete moral dilemmas such as abortion, equal rights, pornography, and so on. Nevertheless, several issues in metaethics are currently in controversy. Included are these:

- What makes a principle a *moral* principle? Can moral principles be about just anything? Or do they have some essential type of content?

- A *morally obligatory act* is one you ought to do, other things being equal. A *supererogatory act* is one that is morally commendable but beyond the call of duty. Is this a legitimate distinction? Can traditional philosophical theories of ethics accommodate this distinction, if it is legitimate?

- Is ethical truth relative to the ethical beliefs of a society or culture? That is, is ethical relativism true?

- How is the question, Why should I be moral? to be understood? Is it a legitimate question?

- Is there a necessary connection between believing that something is morally obligatory and being motivated to choose to do it? (So-called *internalists* assert that there is such a connection; *externalists* deny that there is.)

- What gives a being moral standing?

- Do some beings have a higher moral standing than others?

- How are moral judgments about institutions and other collectives to be understood? Groups are sometimes said to be morally responsible for their actions. Is this responsibility something over and above the responsibility of the individuals in the group?

- Is there a moral difference between doing something that you know will have certain undesirable consequences and doing it with the intention of producing those consequences?

On the other hand, a good example of a contemporary essay in moral philosophy that is *not* a piece of metaethics is included among the readings at the end of the chapter, the piece by James Rachels (1941–2003). In the article, Rachels discusses whether it is true that letting people die of starvation is as bad as killing them (the idea that the two are equally bad is known as the **Equivalence Thesis**). Although Rachels does not try to prove that the two are equally bad, he does try to show that letting people die is considerably worse than we usually think it is.

Further, at the same time that emotivism and antinaturalism were being examined, an independent development in political philosophy occurred, one that has also had a terrific impact on current moral philosophy. This development stems from the work of John Rawls, who, as we shall see shortly, set forth a contractarian theory of distributive justice—a theory for determining the appropriate distribution of the benefits and burdens of social cooperation. As a result of Rawls's work, there has been widespread discussion of the soundness of contractarianism itself and considerable interest in applying contractarian principles toward the resolution of specific moral issues. Therefore, Rawls's work also served to reinforce the current interest in "real-life" moral issues.

## JOHN RAWLS, A CONTEMPORARY LIBERAL

Perhaps the single most influential publication in moral philosophy in the twentieth century was *A Theory of Justice* (1971), by Harvard professor **John Rawls** (1921–2002). The work heralded a renewed concern in philosophy with justice; further, virtually every philosophical writer on justice subsequent to the publication of this work identified his or her position with reference to it. One recent commentator, Professor Charles Larmore of the University of Chicago, believes that Rawls is one of the three most important philosophers of the twentieth century, the other two being Wittgenstein (Chapter 9) and Heidegger (Chapter 8).

Rawls writes from within the liberal tradition, but he had grown dissatisfied with the utilitarianism on which liberalism was often based. He was also dissatisfied with attempts merely to circumscribe utilitarianism with ad hoc "self-evident" principles about our duties (see material on W. D. Ross earlier in this chapter). Rawls said that in writing *A Theory of Justice* he wanted to "carry to a higher order of abstraction the traditional doctrine of the social contract." The result was a lengthy and systematic attempt to establish, interpret, and illuminate the fundamental principles of justice; to apply them to various central issues in social ethics; to use them for appraising social, political, and economic institutions; and to examine their implications for duty and obligation. We will focus our discussion on the principles themselves.

### The Fundamental Requirements of the Just Society

According to Rawls, because society is typically characterized by a conflict as well as an identity of interests, it must have a set of principles for assigning basic rights and duties and for determining the appropriate distribution of the benefits and burdens of social cooperation. These are the *principles of distributive or social justice*. They specify the kinds of social cooperation that can be entered into and the forms of government that can be established. (It is here that Rawls's theory of justice intersects with traditional philosophical questions about the ethically legitimate functions and organization of the state.) For Rawls, a society (or a state) is not well ordered unless (1) its members know and accept the same principles of social justice and (2) the basic social institutions generally satisfy and are generally known to satisfy these principles.

If a society is to be well ordered, its members must determine by rational reflection what are to be their principles of justice, says Rawls. If the principles selected are to be reasonable and justifiable, they must be selected through a procedure that is *fair*. (Rawls's book is an elaboration on a 1958 paper he wrote titled "Justice As Fairness.")

John Rawls

## The Veil of Ignorance and the Original Position

Now, if the selection of principles of justice is to be fair, the possibility of bias operating in their selection must be removed, correct? Ideally, therefore, in our selection of the principles, none of us should have insider's knowledge. We should all be ignorant of one another's — and our own — wealth, status, abilities, intelligence, inclinations, aspirations, and even beliefs about goodness.

Of course, no group of people ever were or could be in such a state of ignorance. Therefore, says Rawls, we must select the principles *as if* we were behind a **veil of ignorance.** This is to ensure that nobody is advantaged or disadvantaged in the choice of principles by her or his own unique circumstances.

If from behind a veil of ignorance we were to deliberate on what principles of justice we would adopt, we would be in what Rawls calls the **original position** (or sometimes the *initial situation*). Like Locke and Rousseau's state of nature, the original position is an entirely hypothetical condition. (As noted, people never were and never could be in such a condition of ignorance.) Rawls's concepts of a veil of ignorance and an original position are intended "simply to make vivid to ourselves the restrictions that it seems reasonable to impose on arguments for principles of justice, and therefore on these principles themselves." Determining our principles of justice by imagining ourselves in the original position simply ensures that we do not tailor our conception of justice to our own case.

In short, according to Rawls, the basic principles of justice are those to which we will agree if we are thinking rationally and in our own self-interest and if we eliminate irrelevant considerations. Because the basic principles of justice are those to which we will agree, Rawls's theory of justice is said to be a *contractarian* theory, as were the theories of Hobbes, Locke, and Rousseau.

## The Two Principles of Social Justice

The principles we would select in the original position, if we are thinking rationally and attending to our own self-interest, are two, Rawls says.

The first, which takes precedence over the second when questions of priority arise, requires that *each person has an equal right to "the most extensive basic liberty compatible with a similar liberty for others."*

The second requires that *social and economic inequalities be arranged "so that they are both (a) reasonably expected to be to everyone's advantage and (b) attached to positions and offices open to all."*

These two principles, writes Rawls, are a special case of a more general conception of justice to the effect that *all social goods (e.g., liberty, opportunity, income) are to be distributed equally unless an unequal distribution is to everyone's advantage.*

We are led to this concept, Rawls writes, when we decide to find a concept of justice that "nullifies the accidents of natural endowment and the contingencies of social circumstances as counters in quest for political and economic advantage."

It follows from these principles, of course, that an unequal distribution of the various assets of society—wealth, for instance—*can be just,* as long as these inequalities are to everyone's benefit. (For example, it may be to everyone's benefit that physicians are paid more than, say, concrete workers.)

It also follows from the priority of the first principle over the second that, contrary to what utilitarian theory seems to require, someone's personal liberty *cannot* be sacrificed for the sake of the common good. Does the pleasure of owning slaves bring more happiness to the slave owners than it brings unhappiness to the slaves? If so, then the total happiness of society may be greater with slavery than without it. Thus, slavery would be to the common good, and utilitarianism would require that it should be instituted. Of course, utilitarians may maintain that slavery or other restrictions of liberties will *as a matter of fact* diminish the sum total of happiness in a society and for this reason cannot be condoned, but they must nevertheless admit that, *as a matter of principle,* violations of liberty would be justified for the sake of the happiness of the many. According to Rawls's principles, such violations for the sake of the general happiness are not justified.

## The Rights of Individuals

Although Rawls does not explicitly discuss the "rights" of individuals as a major topic, his theory obviously can be interpreted as securing such rights (see, for example, Rex Martin's 1985 book, *Rawls and Rights*). Many have believed that without God, talk of rights is pretty much nonsense; Rawls does not discuss God, and it seems plain that he does not need to do so to speak meaningfully of a person's rights. According to Rawls, a just society guarantees persons the right to pursue their own ends so long as they do not interfere with the right of others to pursue their own ends. It is not acceptable to restrict this "right" for some supposed higher good. Rawls, in effect, attempts to derive social ethics from a basis in rational self-interest rather than from God, natural law, human nature, utility, or other ground.

## Why Should I Accept Rawls's Provisions?

If Rawls's theory is correct, he has spelled out in plain language the fundamental requirements of the just society. Furthermore, if his theory is correct, these are the requirements that self-interested but rational people would, on reflection, accept. This means that Rawls's theory provides a strong answer to the person who asks of any provision entailed by one or the other of the two principles just stated, "Why should *I* accept this provision?"

Let's say, for example, that you want to know what is wrong with enslaving another person. The answer is that the wrongfulness of slavery logically follows from the two principles of social justice. But why *should you agree* to those principles? The answer is that you *would* agree to them. Why? Because they are the principles that would be selected by self-interested but rational people playing on a level playing field — one, that is, on which no one has an unfair advantage. They are the principles that would be selected by self-interested but rational people if the procedure through which they were selected was unbiased by anyone having insider's knowledge of his or her or anyone else's unique circumstances. They are, in short, the principles that self-interested but rational people would select if the procedure by which they were selected was a *fair* one. So, then, the reason you *should* accept that slavery is wrongful is because you *would* accept the principles from which the wrongfulness of slavery logically follows.

Few philosophical works by analytic philosophers have received such widespread attention and acclaim outside the circles of professional philosophers as did Rawls's *A Theory of Justice*. Though uncompromisingly analytical, it dealt with current issues of undeniable importance and interest and did so in light of recent work in economics and the social sciences. The book was reviewed not merely in philosophical journals but also in the professional literature of other disciplines and very widely in the popular press and in magazines of opinion and social commentary. It also became the focal point of numerous conferences, many of them interdisciplinary.

In a recent work, *Political Liberalism* (1993), Rawls considers more carefully how his conception of justice as fairness can be endorsed by the diverse array of incompatible religious and philosophical doctrines that exist over time in a modern democratic society like ours. To answer this question, he finds that he must characterize justice more narrowly than he did earlier, as a freestanding *political conception* rather than as a *comprehensive value system* (like Christianity) that governs all aspects of one's life, both public and private. Political justice becomes the focus of an overlapping consensus of comprehensive value systems and thus can still be embraced by all in a pluralistic democratic society. This change in Rawls's theory marks a change in Rawls's own theoretical understanding of justice as fairness. As a practical matter, though, the two principles of justice mentioned earlier still con-

---

### Self-Respect

The most important good, according to John Rawls, is self-respect.

*Self-respect?* Yes.

Self-respect, says Rawls, has two aspects: first, a conviction that one's plans and aspirations are worthwhile, and second, confidence in one's ability to accomplish these objectives.

Without self-respect, therefore, our plans have little or no value to us, and we cannot continue in our endeavors if we are plagued by self-doubt. Thus, self-respect is essential for any activity at all. When we lack it, it seems pointless to do anything, and even if some activity did seem to have a point, we would lack the will to do it. "All desire and activity become empty and vain, and we sink into apathy and cynicism."

---

stitute the best conception of political cooperation required for stability in a democratic regime, in Rawls's view.

## ROBERT NOZICK'S LIBERTARIANISM

If any other book by an analytic philosopher attracted as much attention as *A Theory of Justice*, it was *Anarchy, State, and Utopia*, published three years later (1974) by **Robert Nozick** [NO-zik] (1938–2002). By this time (thanks largely to Rawls) it was not unusual to find analytic philosophers speaking to "big" issues, and Nozick certainly did that.

The reaction to *Anarchy, State, and Utopia* was more mixed than that to Rawls's book, and, though many reviewers acclaimed it enthusiastically, others condemned it, often vehemently. These negative reactions are easily understandable in view of Nozick's vigorous espousal of principles of political philosophy that are not very popular with many contemporary liberal political theorists.

The basic question asked in *Anarchy, State, and Utopia* is, simply: Should there even be a political state and, if so, why? Nozick's answer is worked out in elaborate detail through the course of his book, but it consists essentially of three claims:

1. A minimal state, limited to the narrow functions of protection against force, theft, fraud, breach of contracts, and so on, is justified.
2. Any more extensive state will violate persons' rights not to be forced to do certain things, and is unjustified.
3. The minimal state is inspiring as well as right.

To each of these three claims Nozick devotes one part of his book. The first two parts are the most important.

### A Minimal State Is Justified

The first claim, that a minimal state is justified, will seem so obvious to many as hardly to require lengthy argument. The basic idea accepted by political theorists in the liberal political tradition, from John Locke through Mill and up to and

## Invisible-Hand Explanations

Often an action intended for a certain purpose generates unforeseen indirect consequences. According to Adam Smith, people, in intending only their own gain, are "led by an invisible hand to promote an end" that was not part of their intention, namely, the general good.

Nozick, after Adam Smith, calls an **invisible-hand explanation** one that explains the seemingly direct result of what someone has intended or desired to happen as not being brought about by such intentions or desires at all.

For example, it *looks* as if the state is the result of people's desire to live under a common government, and this is indeed what Locke — and many philosophers, political scientists, economists, and others — thought. But Nozick attempts to provide an invisible-hand explanation of the state as the by-product of certain *other* propensities and desires that people would have within a state of nature. Nozick's explanation is intended to show how a minimal state can arise without violating people's rights.

Another famous invisible-hand explanation presents the institution of money as the outcome of people's propensity to exchange their goods for something they perceive to be more generally desired than what they have. Another describes the characteristics and traits of organisms as the result of natural selection rather than God's wishes.

including Rawls, is that the political state — as compared with a state of anarchy or "the state of nature" — "advances the good of those taking part of it" (to quote Rawls). But *does* it?

If, as Nozick believes, "individuals have rights, and there are things no person or group may do to them (without violating their rights)," then it may well be true, as anarchists believe, that "any state necessarily violates people's moral rights and hence is intrinsically immoral." In the first part of his book, Nozick considers carefully whether this anarchist belief is true. His conclusion is that it is not. To establish this conclusion, he attempts to show that a minimal state can arise by the mechanism of an "invisible hand" (see box) from a hypothetical state of nature without violating any natural rights. As intuitively plausible as Nozick's conclusion is on its face, his defense of it is controversial, and the issue turns out to be difficult.

### Only the "Night-Watchman" State Does Not Violate Rights

The main claim advanced by Nozick in the second part of his book, and by far the most controversial claim of the work as a whole, is that any state more powerful or extensive than the minimal **night-watchman state** that protects its citizens from force and fraud and like things impinges on the individual's natural rights to his or her holdings and therefore is not legitimate or justifiable. It is further a corollary to this claim that concepts of justice that mandate the distribution of assets in accordance with a formula (e.g., "to each according to his ____") or in accordance with a goal or objective (e.g., to promote the general happiness) always require *re*distributing the goods of society and thus require taking from some individuals the goods that are rightfully theirs. Such concepts of justice are therefore illegitimate, according to Nozick.

Nozick's own concept of justice rests on an idea that comes naturally to many people (at least until they imagine themselves in Rawls's "initial situation" behind a "veil of ignorance" about their own assets and abilities). The idea is that *what is yours is yours:* redistributing your income or goods against your wishes for the sake of the general happiness or to achieve any other objective is unjust. Nozick defends this idea. *A person is entitled to what he or she has rightfully acquired, and justice consists in each person's retaining control over his or her rightful acquisitions.* This is Nozick's **entitlement concept of social justice.**

Nozick does not clarify or attempt to defend his entitlement concept of social justice to the extent some critics would like (he basically accepts a refined version of Locke's theory of property acquisition, according to which, you will remember, what is yours is what you mix your labor with). Instead, he mainly seeks to show that alternative conception of social justice, conceptions that ignore what a person is entitled to by virtue of rightful acquisition, are defective. According to Nozick, social justice, that is, justice in the distribution of goods, is not achieved by redistributing these goods to achieve some objective but, rather, by permitting them to remain in the hands of those who have legitimately acquired them:

> Your being forced to contribute to another's welfare violates your rights, whereas someone else's not providing you with things you need greatly, including things essential to the protection of your rights, does not *itself* violate your rights, even though it avoids making it more difficult for someone else to violate them.

According to Nozick's view of social justice, taking from the rich without compensation and giving to the poor is never just (assuming the rich did not become rich through force or fraud, etc.). This would also be Locke's view. According to the strict utilitarian view, by contrast, doing so *is* just if it is to the greater good of the aggregate of people (as would be the case, for example, if through progressive taxation you removed from a rich person's income an amount that he or she would miss but little and used it to prevent ten people from starving). Finally, according to Rawls's view of justice, taking from the rich and giving to the poor is just if it is to the greater good of the aggregate, *provided* it does not compromise anyone's liberty (which, in the case just envisioned, it arguably would not).

## The Rights of Individuals

In the opening sentence of his book, Nozick asserts that individuals have rights, and indeed his entire argument rests on that supposition, especially those many aspects that pertain to property rights. Unfortunately, Nozick's theoretical justification of the supposition is very obscure: it has something to do, evidently, with a presumed inviolability of individuals that prohibits their being used as means to ends and perhaps also with the necessary conditions for allowing them to give meaning to their lives. If Nozick has not made his thought entirely clear in this area, he has set forth very plainly the implications for social theory, as he sees them, of assuming that natural rights exist. In addition, his work contains many interesting and provocative side discussions, including critical discussions of Marx's theory of exploitation.

## Animals and Morality

One interesting side discussion in Nozick's *Anarchy, State, and Utopia* concerns the moral status of animals.

Animals are not mere objects, Nozick says: the same moral constraints apply to what one may do to animals as to what one may do to people. Even a modern utilitarian, who holds that the pleasure, happiness, pain, and suffering that an action produces determine its moral worth, must count animals in moral calculations to the extent they have the capacities for these feelings, Nozick suggests.

Furthermore, he argues, utilitarianism is not adequate as a moral theory concerning animals (or humans) to begin with. In his view, neither humans nor animals may be used or sacrificed against their will for the benefit of others; that is, neither may be treated as means (to use Kant's terminology) but only as ends. Nozick's argument for this view is a negative argument that challenges a reader to find an acceptable ethical principle that would prohibit the killing, hurting, sacrificing, or eating of humans for the sake of other ends that would not equally pertain to animals. Can you think of one?

Here is a good place to mention that the question of animal rights has been widely discussed by contemporary philosophers—and the animal rights movement of recent years, which frequently makes headlines, has received strong theoretical support from several of them. Others do not think that animals have rights in the same sense in which humans have them, and they are not philosophically opposed to medical experimentation involving animals or to eating them. (As far as we know, Nozick was not an activist in the animal rights movement.)

## COMMUNITARIAN RESPONSES TO RAWLS

According to Rawls, in a just society individuals are guaranteed the right to pursue their own ends to the extent that they do not interfere with the right of others to pursue their own ends. Compromising this basic right to individual liberty for the sake of any so-called higher good is not acceptable, in the Rawlsian view, and any

Modern-day members of "militias" complain about the government usurping the rights of its citizens (especially the right to bear arms). Who would they sympathize more with, Nozick or Rawls?

such "good" is not really a good thing at all. You could put the point by saying that for Rawls the right to personal liberty is more basic or fundamental than goodness. This is a view widely held by liberals.

However, some recent critics of Rawls say there exists a common good whose attainment has priority over individual liberty. Some of these critics are known as **communitarians,** for they hold that this common good is defined by one's society or "community." Important communitarian critics of Rawls include Michael Sandel (*Liberalism and the Limits of Justice,* 1982), Michael Walzer (*Spheres of Justice,* 1983, and *Thick and Thin,* 1994), and Alasdair MacIntyre (most widely known work: *After Virtue,* 1984).

Sandel believes that the community is an intersubjective or collective self because self-understanding comprehends more than just an individual human being: it comprehends one's family or tribe or class or nation or people — in short, one's community with its shared ends and common vocabulary and mutual understandings. The Rawlsian principle of equal liberty is subordinate to the good of this social organism for Sandel.

Walzer (also famous for his theorizing on just and unjust wars — see the box "War!") contrasts "thick" or particularist moral argument, which is internal to and framed within a specific political association or "culture," with "thin" moral argument, which is abstract and general and philosophical. Political philosophers, according to Walzer, seek an abstract, universal (thin) point of view and are concerned with the appropriate structure of political association in general. But any full account of how social goods ought to be distributed, he says, will be thick; it "will

# War!

The philosophical literature on war — its legality, morality, causes, and significance — is pretty expansive and we simply do not have space to go there, except briefly.

One important ethical issue pertains to the justness of war: When is a war just, and when is a war fought justly? The classical theory of the justness of a war comes from Augustine and, especially, Aquinas. Augustine said that just wars are those that avenge injuries: a state should be punished if it fails to right a wrong done by its citizens. Aquinas held that there are three conditions for a just war: (1) The ruler leading the war must have the authority to do so, (2) a just cause is required, and (3) right intention is required: those making the war must intend to achieve good and avoid evil.

A landmark discussion of justness in war was the 1977 book, *Just and Unjust Wars,* by Michael Walzer. Walzer covered many important issues that were later widely talked about in connection with the U.S. invasion of Iraq in 2003: preventive war and preemptive war, noncombatant immunity versus military necessity, terrorism, the right to neutrality, war crimes, and nuclear deterrence. Here we will say a few words about Walzer's view on when a war is just, as an example of philosophical discussion of the subject.

Walzer held that states have rights, including the right to political sovereignty, territorial integrity, and self-determination. He did not just throw this thesis out as a talk-radio host might but attempted to derive the rights of states from the rights of individual people, arguing that states' rights are simply the collective form of individual rights. States, like people, have duties to one another (as well as to their citizens) and can commit and suffer crimes (just as people can). Any use of military force by one state against another constitutes criminal aggression and justifies forceful resistance. However, the use of military force by one state on another can be justified only as a response to aggression and (except for a few unusual cases) not for any other end. For Walzer, democratic governments are not the only ones that have a right to political sovereignty; undemocratic and even tyrannical governments may have such a right as well. "Though states are founded for the sake of life and liberty," he wrote, "they cannot be challenged in the name of life and liberty by any other states."

These same themes were discussed, of course, when the United States went to war with Iraq in 2003. They will be discussed again, of that you can be sure.

be idiomatic in its language, particularist in its cultural reference, and historically detailed." For Walzer, a society is just if its way of life is faithful to the shared understanding of its members. There "are no eternal or universal principles" that can replace a "local account" of justice. All such principles are abstractions and simplifications that nevertheless still reflect particular cultural viewpoints. (Notice how Walzer's political philosophy echoes some of the relativistic themes discussed in current epistemology and metaphysics — see Chapter 9).

## Alasdair MacIntyre and Virtue Ethics

**Alasdair MacIntyre's** famous book *After Virtue* (2nd ed., 1984) was the major impetus behind a recent surge in interest, by philosophers, in **virtue ethics.**

Prior to MacIntyre, the theories most influential in contemporary moral philosophy were those from the utilitarians and from Kant. Moral philosophy (excluding metaethics) usually took the form of rules or principles of conduct: *act so as to promote the most happiness possible; social and economic inequalities should be arranged so that they are to everyone's advantage;* and so forth. But after MacIntyre, there's been much interest in the virtues, those beneficial traits of character — courage, compassion, generosity, truthfulness, justness, and the like — that enable individuals to *flourish* as human beings. The idea is that traits of character are in many ways morally more fundamental than rules for action. A cowardly act, for example, seems less commendable than a courageous one, even if the cowardly act happens to have better consequences. Whether acts count as moral or immoral seems to depend less on their consequences or on the intent of the person acting and more on the type of character they reflect. Other philosophers in the virtue-ethics tradition include Plato, Aristotle, Aquinas, Nietzsche, and (in certain respects) Hume.

In *After Virtue,* MacIntyre wrote that "there is no way to possess the virtues except as part of a tradition in which we inherit them and our understanding of them from a series of predecessors." The first in this series of predecessors, according to MacIntyre, were the "heroic societies" typified in Homer's *Iliad.* Here, "every individual has a given role and status within a well-defined and highly determinate system of roles and statuses." Consequently, moral duties are known and understood, and affairs lack ethical ambiguity.

MacIntyre went on to trace the evolution of ethical thought through the Sophists, Plato, Aristotle, the Stoics, the Middle Ages, and the Enlightenment, right up to Nietzsche. For MacIntyre, it is from Aristotle and the Aristotelian tradition that we have the most to learn. Among other lessons, MacIntyre accepted Aristotle's view that human nature cannot be specified merely by stating the average human's characteristics; instead, we must conceive of human nature in terms of its potentialities. Virtues, from this perspective, are traits that promote human flourishing and, thus, naturally produce pleasure.

For MacIntyre, Nietzsche represents the ultimate alternative to Aristotle. For with Nietzsche, the person must "raze to the ground the structures of inherited moral belief and argument." Nietzsche or Aristotle? For MacIntyre the choice is clear.

In addition to these themes, MacIntyre emphasized the "concept of a self whose unity resides in the unity of a narrative which links birth to life to death as narrative beginning to middle to end." That is, according to MacIntyre, the only way to make sense of decisions and actions is in their context in the person's story in which they happen. An action viewed in and of itself, independent of its place in the story that is this person's life, is unintelligible. This does not mean that your life can follow just any old story line. Your life story must be the search for attainment of your potential as human; that is, it must be the search for your excellence or good. The virtues, MacIntyre wrote, sustain us in a relevant kind of quest for the good.

However, each person's own quest for her or his own good or excellence must be undertaken from within that person's moral tradition. "The notion of escaping . . . into a realm of entirely universal maxims which belong to man as such, whether in its eighteenth-century Kantian form or in the presentation of some modern analytical moral philosophies, is an illusion."

How do we find the good? MacIntyre distinguishes between the excellences or goods that are internal to a practice and those that are external to it. For example, a good internal to the practice of medicine is patients' health; an external good is wealth. To attain a good internal to a practice, you must operate within a certain social context, abiding by the rules of the practice, which have arisen through the history of the practice. A virtue, for MacIntyre, may be analyzed as a quality required to attain a good internal to a practice. Unless some of the practitioners are virtuous, the practice will decay. Entire moral traditions are also subject to degeneration unless they have their virtuous practitioners.

Further, to understand the human good we can begin with the goods internal to human practices, noting how they are ordered in comparison with each other. For example, the good internal to one practice, medicine let's say, stands at a higher level than the good internal to another practice, playing football, perhaps. As we try to rank goods and to order our own affairs accordingly, we come to have a clearer understanding of the human good and ourselves.

Putting this complex understanding of virtue together, MacIntyre concluded:

> The virtues find their point and purpose not only in sustaining the relationships necessary if the goods internal to practices are to be achieved and not only in sustaining the form of an individual life in which that individual may seek out his or her good as the good of his or her whole life, but also in sustaining those traditions which provide both practices and individual lives with their necessary historical context.

## HERBERT MARCUSE, A CONTEMPORARY MARXIST

The thought of Karl Marx has been interpreted, expanded, and amended by his many followers, conspicuously so, of course, by the Communist Party. Today Marxism, like Christianity (as philosopher and social historian Sidney Hook has said), is a *family* of doctrines that is continually being renewed and revived. It is more appropriate to treat the details of the further evolution of Marxism in a text

Offstage music at Woodstock, 1969.

on political history than in this summary overview of political philosophy. Still, because Marxism has been very important in contemporary political philosophy, we shall describe briefly the views of a contemporary Marxist.

In the late 1960s the most famous philosopher in the United States was **Herbert Marcuse** [mar-KOO-zeh] (1898–1979). This was the era of tumultuous social and political unrest, the era of the New Left, Vietnam War protest, "people power," militant black and feminist disaffection, hippies, acid, four-letter words, and Woodstock. Marcuse was in. (See the box on Marcuse.)

Marcuse's reputation on the street arose from his book *One-Dimensional Man* (1964), a Marxist-oriented appraisal of contemporary industrial society. For the New Left the book was a clear statement of deficiencies in American society.

As we have seen, it is a Marxist doctrine (or, at any rate, a doctrine of orthodox Marxists) that a disenfranchised working class is the inevitable instrument of social change. But according to Marcuse, the working class has been *integrated* into advanced capitalist society. Indeed, it has been integrated so well that it "can actually be characterized as a pillar of the establishment," he said. This integration has been effected, he believed, through the overwhelming efficiency of technology in improving the standard of living. Because today's workers share so largely in the comforts of consumer society, they are far less critical of the status quo than if they had been indoctrinated through propaganda or even brainwashed.

In fact, Marcuse said, today's workers do not merely share these comforts, they actually *"recognize themselves* in their commodities." "They find their soul in their automobile, hi-fi set, split-level home, kitchen equipment." Their needs have been

## Marcuse in Southern California

What may sometimes be the penalty for advocating an unpopular political philosophy is illustrated by the treatment Herbert Marcuse received during his stay in Southern California in the late 1960s.

Marcuse left Germany after Hitler's rise to power and became a U.S. citizen in 1940. He obtained work with the Office of Strategic Services and the State Department and thereafter held positions at Harvard, Columbia, and Brandeis. Later, in 1965, he accepted a postretirement appointment at the University of California, San Diego, where he was a quiet but popular professor. Although he had acquired by then a worldwide reputation among leftists and radicals for his social criticism, in San Diego he was not widely known beyond the campus.

In 1968, however, it was reported in the national media that Marcuse had invited "Red Rudi" Dutschke, a notorious West German student radical, to visit him in San Diego. After this, the local populace quickly informed itself about Marcuse. The outcry against any possible Dutschke visit and against the perceived radicalism of Marcuse in that conservative naval community was vigorous and strident. In thundering editorials, the *San Diego*

*Union* denounced Marcuse and called for his ouster. Thirty-two American Legion posts in San Diego County demanded termination of his contract and offered the regents of the University of California the money to buy it out. Marcuse began receiving death threats and hate mail, and his student followers armed themselves with guns to protect him.

When his appointment neared its end in 1969, the question of reappointment arose and attracted nationwide attention. With the strong support of the faculty but in the face of strenuous opposition from the *Union*, the Legion, and other powerful groups, university chancellor John McGill decided to offer Marcuse a one-year contract of reappointment. When the regents of the University of California met to discuss McGill's decision, they had to do so under the protection of the San Francisco Police Department's Tactical Force. Though a substantial number strongly dissented, the majority supported McGill. Marcuse was reappointed.

By the expiration of the reappointment contract, Marcuse had passed the age of mandatory retirement. Nevertheless, he was permitted to keep his office and to teach informally.

determined by what are, in effect, new forms of social control, such as advertising, consumerism, the mass media, and the entertainment industry, all of which produce and enforce conformity in what people desire, think, and do.

Thus, according to Marcuse, in the West, with its advanced capitalist societies, the workers have lost their individual autonomy, their capacity to choose and act for themselves, to refuse and to dissent and to create. Yes, needs are satisfied, but the price the workers pay for satisfaction of need is loss of ability to think for themselves. Further, the perceived needs that are satisfied, in Marcuse's opinion, are *false* needs, needs stimulated artificially by producers to sell new products, needs whose satisfaction promotes insane wastefulness and does not lead to true fulfillment of the individual or release from domination.

Marcuse emphasized that the integration of the working class into the advanced capitalist society by the satisfaction of false needs created by advertising, television, movies, music, and other forms of consumerism does not mean that society has become classless. Despite the fact that their "needs" are satisfied, members of the working class are still in effect slaves because they remain mere instruments of production that capitalists use for their own purposes. Further, he wrote in *One-Dimensional Man,* if the worker and his boss enjoy the same television program and visit the same resorts, if the typist is as attractively made up as the daughter of her employer . . . if they all read the same newspaper, then this assimilation indicates not the disappearance of classes, but the extent to which the needs and satisfactions that serve the preservation of the Establishment are shared by the underlying population.

Thus, the working class in advanced capitalist societies, according to Marcuse, has been transformed from a force for radical change into a force for conservatism and the status quo.

The neutralizing of possible sources of radical social change through the integration of the working class into a one-dimensional society is visible everywhere to Marcuse. In the political sphere, the one-dimensionalization of society is apparent in the unification of labor and capital against communism in a "welfare and warfare state," in which the cold war and arms race unite all against the Communist threat while simultaneously stimulating the economy through the production of weapons.

Likewise, he said, a one-dimensional quality pervades contemporary art, language, philosophy, science, and all of contemporary culture. Thus, for example, art has lost its power to criticize, challenge, and transcend society and has been integrated as mere entertainment mass-produced in paperbacks, records, and television shows. As such, art now serves to promote conformity in thought, aspiration, and deed. The same is true of philosophy and science, he believed. The elite classes can tolerate free speech simply because such conformity of thought in art, philosophy, science, and politics is present.

Thus, as Marcuse saw it, advanced capitalist society has managed to assimilate and integrate into itself the forces that oppose it and to "defeat or refute all protest in the name of the historical prospects of freedom from toil and domination." Still, at the very end of *One-Dimensional Man* Marcuse acknowledged that there is a slim chance of revolutionary change at the hands of a substratum of the outcasts of society, such as persecuted ethnic minorities and the unemployed and unemployable.

In his later thought, moreover, Marcuse perceived a weakening of the integration of the working classes into society and a growing awareness on the part of workers, students, and the middle class that consumer prosperity has been purchased at too high a price and that a society without war, exploitation, repression, poverty, or waste is possible. The revolution that will produce this society, Marcuse said — and only through revolution can it be created, he maintained — will be born not of privation but of "disgust at the waste and excess of the so-called consumer society."

## THE OBJECTIVISM OF AYN RAND

Ayn Rand, born Alissa Rosenbaum, graduated from the University of Petrograd (Leningrad) in 1924, moved to the United States the following year, eventually becoming a Hollywood screenwriter. She achieved renown with the publication of two novels, *The Fountainhead* (1943) and *Atlas Shrugged* (1957). Rand founded a philosophical movement called objectivism, based on her interpretation of Aristotle. She saw Aristotle as a realist who established ethics on an objective understanding of human behavior rooted in knowable principles. Unlike Aristotle, however, she thought certainty in morality was possible. Rand's philosophy has not attracted quite as much interest among academic philosophers as have some of the others we have mentioned in this chapter, but it has been a source of widespread popular discussion.

Rand's early writings were based on her understanding of Nietzsche, and she followed his contempt for the ignorance of most humans. She has Kira, her protagonist in *We the Living* (1936), say: "What are your masses but millions of dull, shriveled, helpless souls that have no thoughts of their own, no dreams of their own, no will of their own, who eat and sleep and chew helplessly the words that others put into their brains? . . . I loathe most of them." Nietzsche scorned having pity on such herd animals, and Rand thought there was no worse injustice than giving to the undeserving. This is because she thought that true evil lay in the refusal to think, as do (in her view) the unthinking masses that place a drag on civilization. She thought of pity as a sign of a dangerous weakness that, historically, has led to the "sanctioning of the victim" that has allowed the weak, ignorant, and undeserving to become parasites on the strong and productive.

Likewise, Rand thought that progress is made by the brilliant few who affirm life and pleasure, who think for themselves, and who are the creative artists of life. These are the heroic, larger-than-life figures that change the world for the better.

Rand, still following Nietzsche, saw human fulfillment as the struggle of the individual to improve into something higher. However, she added to this concept the idea that the maximally fulfilled life involved productivity and moneymaking. She embraced a form of laissez-faire capitalism so pure it alienated her from conservatives and libertarians, whom she came to despise. She talked of an ideal society based on a "utopia of greed," where the government is so noninterventionist as to be invisible. In this utopia the ideas and action of the brilliant would provide the basis for the just state via her moral principles. Essentially, for Rand, morality meant creating something and then making money out of it. Her coffin, it is said, was draped with a dollar sign. She considered inheritance, fraud, or any other kind of nonproductivity as looting. The dollar symbolized the victory of the creative mind over the state, over religion, and over the unthinking masses.

Rand believed that rights are vested in the individual, never in the group. The state exists to protect individual rights, to the exclusion of almost all else. The government certainly must not provide undeserved bonuses to the mediocre, mindless, and meaningless masses.

Targets of objectivists include feminism and environmentalism. Rand held that men are superior to woman, and she called her position "male chauvinism." She thought a woman should not become president of the United States, for example. But she did not want women to be dependent or obedient to men.

## "ISMS"

Liberalism, communism, socialism, capitalism, fascism, conservatism—these ill-defined terms are sometimes thought to denote mutually exclusive alternative forms of government. Actually, they do not stand for parallel alternatives at all. We shall conclude this chapter with a brief scan of some of these "isms."

Classical **liberalism** emphasized the rationality and goodness of humans, individual freedom, representative government, individual property rights, social progress through political reform, and laissez-faire economics, which, by the way, is the view that the government should not interfere in economic affairs beyond the minimum necessary to maintain peace and property rights. A guiding principle of liberalism was eloquently articulated by Mill: the sole end for which people are warranted in interfering with an individual's liberty is never the individual's own good but, rather, to prevent harm to others.

Contemporary liberals also subscribe to these assorted concepts, except they are not so wedded to the laissez-faire idea. They are willing to put up with (or even ask for) government involvement in economic affairs when such involvement is perceived to promote equality of opportunity or to protect people from exploitation or discrimination or to protect the environment, or is done even merely to raise the overall quality of life. Thus, contemporary liberals tend to support social welfare programs paid for through taxation, as well as civil rights, women's rights, gay rights, affirmative action, and environmentalism. But contemporary liberals tend to oppose militarism, imperialism, exploitation of Third World countries, censorship, governmental support of religion, and anti-immigration crusades. American liberals are inclined to interpret the Bill of Rights very, well, liberally.

**Conservatism** was originally a reaction to the social and political upheaval of the French Revolution. Conservatives, as the word suggests, desire to conserve past social and political traditions and practices as representing the wisdom of a society's experience and are opposed to widespread social reform or experimentalism. Even so, Edmund Burke (1729–1797), the most eloquent and influential conservative writer of the eighteenth century, if not of all time, advocated many liberal and reform causes. Burke considered "society" as a contract among the dead, the living, and those to be born, and each social contract of each state but a clause in the great primeval contract of eternal society.

Contemporary American conservatism is in large measure a defense of private enterprise, laissez-faire economic policies, and a narrow or literal interpretation of the Bill of Rights. Conservatives are reluctant to enlist the power of government, especially its power to tax, to remedy social ills. Critics (liberals, mostly) charge that conservatives give mere lip service to the importance of individual liberty and consider it of lesser importance than a free-market economy. Conservatives respond that individual liberty is best protected by limiting the scope of government, especially in economic matters, and by dispersing its power. In emphasizing both personal freedom and free-market economics and in distrusting centralized power, modern conservatism is similar to nineteenth-century laissez-faire liberalism.

**Communists** (with a capital C), as explained in Chapter 11, accept the social, political, and economic ideology of the Communist Party, including the idea that the dictatorship of the proletariat will come about only through revolution; **communism** (lowercase c) is simply a form of economic organization in which the primary goods (usually the means of production and distribution) are held in common by a community. The definitions of **socialism** and communism are essentially the same, and Communists, of course, are advocates of communism.

**Capitalism** is an economic system in which ownership of the means of production and distribution is maintained primarily by private individuals and corporations. Capitalism, therefore, is an opposite to socialism and communism.

**Fascism** is the totalitarian political philosophy espoused by the Mussolini government of Italy prior to and during World War II, which emphasized the absolute primacy of the state and leadership by an elite who embody the will and intelligence of the people. Adolph Hitler and the National Socialists (Nazis) of Germany embraced elements of fascism; today "fascist" is used loosely to denounce any totalitarian regime.

Finally, another important political "ism" is **democratic socialism,** a term that denotes a popular political structure (especially in Western Europe) that many Americans have not heard of. Under democratic socialism there is a democratically elected executive and legislature, and there is no state ownership of business, though it permits considerable government intervention in the business sector. Yet this type of system provides guarantees of individual rights and freedom as well as a social safety net for the poor, the old, and the sick, as in Communist political arrangements.

Despite the myriad changes in the world political scene, one trend does appear fairly global: the preference for personal freedom and democratic government.

---

SELECTION 12.1

## Killing and Starving to Death *

*James Rachels*

---

[*Is it as bad, morally, to let a person die as it is to kill him or her? Many say no. In this selection, James Rachels challenges this view.*]

Although we do not know exactly how many people die each year of malnutrition or related health problems, the number is very high, in the millions. By giving money to support famine relief efforts, each of us could save at least some of them. By not giving, we let them die.

Some philosophers have argued that letting people die is not as bad as killing them, because in general our "positive duty" to give aid is weaker than our "negative duty" not to do harm. I maintain the opposite: letting die is just as bad as killing. At first this may seem wildly implausible. When reminded that people are dying of starvation while we spend money on trivial things, we may feel a bit guilty, but certainly we do not feel like murderers. Philippa Foot writes:

*From *Philosophy,* vol. 54, no. 208 (April 1979). Copyright © 1979 The Royal Institute of Philosophy. Reprinted with the permission of Cambridge University Press.

Most of us allow people to die of starvation in India and Africa, and there is surely something wrong with us that we do; it would be nonsense, however, to pretend that it is only in law that we make a distinction between allowing people in the underdeveloped countries to die of starvation and sending them poisoned food. There is worked into our moral system a distinction between what we owe people in the form of aid and what we owe them in the way of noninterference.

No doubt this would be correct if it were intended only as a description of what most people believe. Whether this feature of "our moral system" is rationally defensible is, however, another matter. I shall argue that we are wrong to take comfort in the fact that we *only* let these people die, because our duty not to let them die is equally as strong as our duty not to kill them, which, of course, is very strong indeed.

Obviously, the Equivalence Thesis is not morally neutral, as philosophical claims about ethics often are. It is a radical idea that, if true, would mean that some of our "intuitions" (our prereflective beliefs about what is right and wrong in particular cases) are mistaken and must be rejected. Neither is the view I oppose morally neutral. The idea that killing is worse than letting die is a relatively conservative thesis that would allow those same intuitions to be preserved. However, the Equivalence Thesis should not be dismissed merely because it does not conform to all our prereflective intuitions. Rather than being perceptions of the truth, our "intuitions" might sometimes signify nothing more than our prejudices or selfishness or cultural conditioning. Philosophers often admit that, in theory at least, some intuitions might be unreliable — but usually this possibility is not taken seriously, and conformity to prereflective intuition is used uncritically as a test of the acceptability of moral theory. In what follows I shall argue that many of our intuitions concerning killing and letting die *are* mistaken, and should not be trusted.

# I

We think that killing is worse than letting die, not because we overestimate how bad it is to kill, but because we underestimate how bad it is to let die. The following chain of reasoning is intended to show that letting people in foreign countries die of starvation is very much worse than we commonly assume.

Suppose there were a starving child in the room where you are now — hollow-eyed, belly bloated, and so on — and you have a sandwich at your elbow that you don't need. Of course you would be horrified; you would stop reading and give her the sandwich or, better, take her to a hospital. And you would not think this an act of supererogation; you would not expect any special praise for it, and you would expect criticism if you did not do it. Imagine what you would think of someone who simply ignored the child and continued reading, allowing her to die of starvation. Let us call the person who would do this Jack Palance, after the very nice man who plays such vile characters in movies. Jack Palance indifferently watches the starving child die; he cannot be bothered even to hand her the sandwich. There is ample reason for judging him very harshly; without putting too fine a point on it, he shows himself to be a moral monster.

When we allow people in faraway countries to die of starvation, we may think, as Mrs. Foot puts it, that "there is surely something wrong with us." But we most emphatically do not consider ourselves moral monsters. We think this, in spite of the striking similarity between Jack Palance's behavior and our own. He could easily save the child; he does not, and the child dies. We could easily save some of those starving people; we do not, and they die. If we are not monsters, there must be some important difference between him and us. But what is it?

One obvious difference between Jack Palance's position and ours is that the person he lets die is in the same room with him, while the people we let die are mostly far away. Yet the spatial location of the dying people hardly seems a relevant consideration. It is absurd to suppose that being located at a certain map coordinate entitles one to treatment that one would not merit if situated at a different longitude or latitude. Of course, if a dying person's location meant that we *could not* help, that would excuse us. But, since there are efficient famine relief agencies willing to carry our aid to the faraway countries, this excuse is not available. It would be almost as easy for us to send these agencies the price of the sandwich as for Palance to hand the sandwich to the child.

The location of the starving people does make a difference, psychologically, in how we feel. If there were a starving child in the same room with us, we could not avoid realizing, in a vivid and disturbing way, how it is suffering and that it is about to die. Faced with this realization our consciences probably would not allow us to ignore the child. But if the dying are far away, it is easy to think of them only abstractly, or to put them out of our thoughts altogether. This might explain why our conduct would be different if we were in Jack Palance's position, even though, from a moral point of view, the location of the dying is not relevant.

There are other differences between Jack Palance and us, which may seem important, having to do with the sheer numbers of people, both affluent and starving, that surround us. In our fictitious example Jack Palance is one person, confronted by the need of one other person. This makes his position relatively simple. In the real world our position is more complicated, in two ways: first, in that there are millions of people who need feeding, and none of us has the resources to care for all of them; and second, in that for any starving person we *could* help there are millions of other affluent people who could help as easily as we.

On the first point, not much needs to be said. We may feel, in a vague sort of way, that we are not monsters because no one of us could possibly save *all* the starving people — there are just too many of them, and none of us has the resources. This is fair enough, but all that follows is that, individually, none of us is responsible for saving everyone. We may still be responsible for saving someone, or as many as we can. This is so obvious that it hardly bears mentioning, yet it is easy to lose sight of, and philosophers have actually lost sight of it. In his article "Saving Life and Taking Life," Richard Trammell says that one morally important difference between killing and letting die is "dischargeability." By this he means that, while each of us can discharge completely a duty not to kill anyone, no one among us can discharge completely a duty to save everyone who needs it. Again, fair enough: but all that follows is that since we are only bound to save those we can, the class of people we have an obligation to save is much smaller than the class of people we have an obligation not to kill. It does *not* follow that our duty with respect to those we can save is any less stringent. Suppose Jack Palance were to say: "I needn't give this starving child the sandwich because, after all, I can't save everyone in the world who needs it." If this excuse will not work for him, neither will it work for us with respect to the children we could save in India or Africa.

The second point about numbers was that, for any starving person we *could* help, there are millions of other affluent people who could help as easily as we. Some are in an even better position to help since they are richer. But by and large these people are doing nothing. This also helps explain why we do not feel especially guilty for letting people starve. How guilty we feel about something depends, to some extent, on how we compare with those around us. If we were surrounded by people who regularly sacrificed to feed the starving and we did not, we would probably feel ashamed. But because our neighbors do not do any better than we, we are not so ashamed.

But again, this does not imply that we should not feel more guilty or ashamed than we do. A psychological explanation of our feelings is not a moral justification of our conduct. Suppose Jack Palance were only one of twenty people who watched the child die; would that decrease his guilt? Curiously, I think many people assume it would. Many people seem to feel that if twenty people do nothing to prevent a tragedy, each of them is only one-twentieth as guilty as he would have been if he had watched the tragedy alone. It is as though there is only a fixed amount of guilt, which divides. I suggest, rather, that guilt multiplies, so that each passive viewer is fully guilty, if he could have prevented the tragedy

but did not. Jack Palance watching the girl die alone would be a moral monster; but if he calls in a group of his friends to watch with him, he does not diminish his guilt by dividing it among them. Instead, they are all moral monsters. Once the point is made explicit, it seems obvious.

The fact that most other affluent people do nothing to relieve hunger may very well have implications for one's own obligations. But the implication may be that one's own obligations *increase* rather than decrease. Suppose Palance and a friend were faced with two starving children, so that, if each did his "fair share," Palance would only have to feed one of them. But the friend will do nothing. Because he is well-off, Palance could feed both of them. Should he not? What if he fed one and then watched the other die, announcing that he has done *his* duty and that the one who died was his friend's responsibility? This shows the fallacy of supposing that one's duty is only to do one's fair share, where this is determined by what would be sufficient *if* everyone else did likewise.

To summarize: Jack Palance, who refuses to hand a sandwich to a starving child, is a moral monster. But we feel intuitively that we are not so monstrous, even though we also let starving children die when we could feed them almost as easily. If this intuition is correct, there must be some important difference between him and us. But when we examine the most obvious differences between his conduct and ours — the location of the dying, the differences in numbers — we find no real basis for judging ourselves less harshly than we judge him. Perhaps there are some other grounds on which we might distinguish our moral position, with respect to actual starving people, from Jack Palance's position with respect to the child in my story. But I cannot think of what they might be. Therefore, I conclude that if he is a monster, then so are we — or at least, so are we after our *rationalizations* and thoughtlessness have been exposed.

This last qualification is important. We judge people, at least in part, according to whether they can be expected to realize how well or how badly they behave. We judge Palance harshly because the consequences of his indifference are so immediately apparent. By contrast, it requires an unusual effort for us to realize the consequences of our indifference. It is normal behavior for people in the affluent countries not to give to famine relief, or if they do give, to give very little. Decent people may go along with this normal behavior pattern unthinkingly, without realizing, or without comprehending in a clear way just what this means for the starving. Thus, even though those decent people may act monstrously, we do not judge them monsters. There is a curious sense, then, in which moral reflection can transform decent people into indecent ones; for if a person thinks things through, and realizes that he is, morally speaking, in Jack Palance's position, his continued indifference is more blameworthy than before.

The preceding is not intended to prove that letting people die of starvation is as bad as killing them. But it does provide strong evidence that letting die is much worse than we normally assume, and so that letting die is much *closer* to killing than we normally assume. These reflections also go some way towards showing just how fragile and unreliable our intuitions are in this area. They suggest that, if we want to discover the truth, we are better off looking at arguments that do not rely on unexamined intuitions.

SELECTION 12.2

# A Theory of Justice*

*John Rawls*

[*Here, Rawls explains his conception of justice as fairness, the original position, the veil of ignorance, and the two basic principles of social justice.*]

My aim is to present a conception of justice which generalizes and carries to a higher level of abstraction the familiar theory of the social contract as found, say, in Locke, Rousseau, and Kant. In order to do this we are not to think of the original contract as one to enter a particular society or to set up a particular form of government. Rather, the guiding idea is that the principles of justice for the basic structure of society are the object of the original agreement. They are the principles that free and rational persons concerned to further their own interests would accept in an initial position of equality as defining the fundamental terms of their association. These principles are to regulate all further agreements; they specify the kinds of social cooperation that can be entered into and the forms of government that can be established. This way of regarding the principles of justice I shall call justice as fairness.

Thus we are to imagine that those who engage in social cooperation choose together, in one joint act, the principles which are to assign basic rights and duties and to determine the division of social benefits. Men are to decide in advance how they are to regulate their claims against one another and what is to be the foundation charter of their society. Just as each person must decide by rational reflection what constitutes his good, that is, the system of ends which it is rational for him to pursue, so a group of persons must decide once and for all what is to count among them as just and unjust. The choice which rational men would make in this hypothetical situation of equal liberty, assuming for the present that this choice problem has a solution, determines the principles of justice.

In justice as fairness the original position of equality corresponds to the state of nature in the traditional theory of the social contract. This original position is not, of course, thought of as an actual historical state of affairs, much less as a primitive condition of culture. It is understood as a purely hypothetical situation characterized so as to lead to a certain conception of justice. Among the essential features of this situation is that no one knows his place in society, his class position or social status, nor does any one know his fortune in the distribution of natural assets and abilities, his intelligence, strength, and the like. I shall even assume that the parties do not know their conceptions of the good or their special psychological propensities. The principles of justice are chosen behind a veil of ignorance. This ensures that no one is advantaged or disadvantaged in the choice of principles by the outcome of natural chance or the contingency of social circumstances. Since all are similarly situated

*Rawls's footnotes have been omitted. Reprinted by permission of the publisher from *A Theory of Justice* by John Rawls, pp. 11–14, Cambridge, Mass.: The Belknap Press of Harvard University Press. Copyright © 1971, 1999 by the President and Fellows of Harvard College.

and no one is able to design principles to favor his particular condition, the principles of justice are the result of a fair agreement or bargain. For given the circumstances of the original position, the symmetry of everyone's relations to each other, this initial situation is fair between individuals as moral persons, that is, as rational beings with their own ends and capable, I shall assume, of a sense of justice. The original position is, one might say, the appropriate initial status quo, and thus the fundamental agreements reached in it are fair. This explains the propriety of the name "justice as fairness": it conveys the idea that the principles of justice are agreed to in an initial situation that is fair. The name does not mean that the concepts of justice and fairness are the same, any more than the phrase "poetry as metaphor" means that the concepts of poetry and metaphor are the same.

Justice as fairness begins, as I have said, with one of the most general of all choices which persons might make together, namely, with the choice of the first principles of a conception of justice which is to regulate all subsequent criticism and reform of institutions. Then, having chosen a conception of justice, we can suppose that they are to choose a constitution and a legislature to enact laws, and so on, all in accordance with the principles of justice initially agreed upon. Our social situation is just if it is such that by this sequence of hypothetical agreements we would have contracted into the general system of rules which defines it. . . .

I shall maintain . . . that the persons in the initial situation would choose two rather different principles: the first requires equality in the assignment of basic rights and duties, while the second holds that social and economic inequalities, for example inequalities of wealth and authority, are just only if they result in compensating benefits for everyone, and in particular for the least advantaged members of society. These principles rule out justifying institutions on the grounds that the hardships of some are offset by a greater good in the aggregate. It may be expedient but it is not just that some should have less in order that others may prosper. But there is no injustice in the greater benefits earned by a few provided that the situation of persons not so fortunate is thereby improved. The intuitive idea is that since everyone's well-being depends upon a scheme of cooperation without which no one could have a satisfactory life, the division of advantages should be such as to draw forth the willing cooperation of everyone taking part in it, including those less well situated. Yet this can be expected only if reasonable terms are proposed. The two principles mentioned seem to be a fair agreement on the basis of which those better endowed, or more fortunate in their social position, neither of which we can be said to deserve, could expect the willing cooperation of others when some workable scheme is a necessary condition of the welfare of all. Once we decide to look for a conception of justice that nullifies the accidents of natural endowment and the contingencies of social circumstance as counters in quest for political and economic advantage, we are led to these principles. They express the result of leaving aside those aspects of the social world that seem arbitrary from a moral point of view.

---

SELECTION 12.3

# Anarchy, State, and Utopia★

*Robert Nozick*

---

[*If the members of your society voluntarily limit their liberty for their mutual advantage, then are you obliged to limit your liberty if you benefit from the arrangement? Nozick says "no."*]

★Reprinted with permission of Perseus Books Group from *Anarchy, State, and Utopia* by Robert Nozick. Copyright © 1974 by Basic Books, Inc. Permission conveyed through Copyright Clearance Center, Inc.

A principle, suggested by Herbert Hart, which (following John Rawls) we shall call the *principle of fairness*, would be of service here if it were adequate. This principle holds that when a number of persons engage in a just, mutually advantageous, cooperative venture according to rules and thus restrain their liberty in ways necessary to yield advantages for all, those who have submitted to these restrictions have a right to similar acquiescence on the part of those who have benefited from their submission. Acceptance of benefits (even when this is not a giving of express or tacit undertaking to cooperate) is enough, according to this principle, to bind one. . . .

The principle of fairness, as we stated it following Hart and Rawls, is objectionable and unacceptable. Suppose some of the people in your neighborhood (there are 364 other adults) have found a public address system and decide to institute a system of public entertainment. They post a list of names, one for each day, yours among them. On his assigned day (one can easily switch days) a person is to run the public address system, play records over it, give news bulletins, tell amusing stories he has heard, and so on. After 138 days on which each person has done his part, your day arrives. Are you obligated to take your turn? You *have* benefited from it, occasionally opening your window to listen, enjoying some music or chuckling at someone's funny story. The other people *have* put themselves out. But must you answer the call when it is your turn to do so? As it stands, surely not. Though you benefit from the arrangement, you may know all along that 364 days of entertainment supplied by others will not be worth your giving up *one* day. You would rather not have any of it and not give up a day than have it all and spend one of your days at it. Given these preferences, how can it be that you are required to participate when your scheduled time comes? It would be nice to have philosophy readings on the radio to which one could tune in at any time, perhaps late at night when tired. But it may not be nice enough for you to want to give up one whole day of your own as a reader on the program. Whatever you want, can others create an obligation for you to do so by going ahead and starting the program themselves? In this case you can choose to forgo the benefit by not turning on the radio; in other cases the benefits may be unavoidable. If each day a different person on your street sweeps the entire street, must you do so when your time comes? Even if you don't care much about a clean street? Must you imagine dirt as you traverse the street, so as not to benefit as a free rider? Must you refrain from turning on the radio to hear the philosophy readings? Must you mow your front lawn as often as your neighbors mow theirs?

At the very least one wants to build into the principle of fairness the condition that the benefits to a person from the actions of the others are greater than the costs to him of doing his share. . . .

If the principle of fairness were modified so as to contain this very strong condition, it still would be objectionable. The benefits might only barely be worth the costs to you of doing your share, yet others might benefit from *this* institution much more than you do; they all treasure listening to the public broadcasts. As the person least benefited by the practice, are you obligated to do an equal amount for it? Or perhaps you would prefer that all cooperated in *another* venture, limiting their conduct and making sacrifices for *it*. It is true, *given* that they are not following your plan (and thus limiting what other options are available to you), that the benefits of their venture *are* worth to you the costs of your cooperation. However, you do not wish to cooperate, as part of your plan to focus their attention on your alternative proposal which they have ignored or not given, in your view at least, its proper due. (You want them, for example, to read the Talmud on the radio instead of the philosophy they are reading.) By lending the institution (their institution) the support of your cooperating in it, you will only make it harder to change or alter.

On the face of it, enforcing the principle of fairness is objectionable. You may not decide to give me something, for example a book, and then grab money from me to pay for it, even if I have nothing better to spend the money on. You have, if anything, even less reason to demand payment if your activity that gives me the book also benefits you; suppose that your best way of getting exercise is by throwing books into people's houses, or that some other activity of yours thrusts books into people's houses as an unavoidable side effect. Nor are things changed if your inability to collect money or payments for the books which unavoidably spill over into others' houses makes it inadvisable or too expensive for you to carry on the activity with this side effect. One cannot, whatever one's purposes, just act so as to give people benefits and then demand (or seize) payment. Nor can a group of persons do this. If you may not charge and collect for benefits you bestow without prior agreement, you certainly may not do so for benefits whose bestowal costs you nothing, and most certainly people need not repay you for costless-to-provide benefits which yet *others* provided them. So the fact that we partially are "social products" in that we benefit from current patterns and forms created by the multitudinous actions of a long string of long-forgotten people, forms which include institutions, ways of doing things, and language (whose social nature may involve our current use depending upon Wittgensteinian matching of the speech of others), does not create in us a general floating debt which the current society can collect and use as it will.

Perhaps a modified principle of fairness can be stated which would be free from these and similar difficulties. What seems certain is that any such principle, if possible, would be so complex and involuted that one could not combine it with a special principle legitimating *enforcement* within a state of nature of the obligations that have arisen under it. Hence, even if the principle could be formulated so that it was no longer open to objection, it would not serve to obviate the need for other persons' *consenting* to cooperate and limit their own activities.

## CHECKLIST

To help you review, here is a checklist of the key philosophers and terms and concepts of this chapter. The brief descriptive sentences summarize the philosophers' leading ideas. Keep in mind that some of these summary statements are oversimplifications of complex positions.

### *Philosophers*

- **G. E. Moore**  was the most important early figure in contemporary analytic ethics and metaethics. He held that goodness is an undefinable, noncomplex, and nonnatural property of good things. He said that what makes right actions right is that they produce more goodness than alternative actions.

- **W. D. Ross**  held that the production of maximum good is not the only thing that makes an act right; some things are just simply our moral duty to do.

- **John Rawls,**  an analytic (liberal) political philosopher, attempted to establish the fundamental principles of distributive justice through consideration of a hypothetical "original position" in which people's choice of principles is not biased by their individual unique circumstances. He held that all social goods are to be distributed equally unless an unequal distribution is to everyone's advantage.

- **Robert Nozick,**  an analytic (libertarian) political philosopher, held that a limited "night-watchman" state is ethically justified but that any more extensive state violates people's rights.

- **Alasdair MacIntyre**  was a leading twentieth-century exponent of virtue ethics.

- **Herbert Marcuse,**  a Marxist, held that the working class has been transformed from a force for radical change into a force for preserving the status quo because of the false needs created by consumerism and advertising.

- **Ayn Rand**  was the founder of "objectivism," a philosophy that championed the brilliant individual who rises to the top in an ideal society based on the freedom of the individual to create.

### *Key Terms and Concepts*

| | |
|---|---|
| moral judgment | entitlement concept |
| normative ethics | of social justice |
| metaethics | invisible-hand |
| antinaturalism | mechanism |
| prima facie duties | communitarian |
| deontological ethics | virtue ethics |
| emotivist | liberalism |
| prescriptive judgment | conservatism |
| naturalist fallacy | Communism |
| applied ethics | communism |
| Equivalence Thesis | socialism |
| veil of ignorance | capitalism |
| original position | fascism |
| night-watchman state | democratic socialism |

## QUESTIONS FOR DISCUSSION AND REVIEW

1. Is happiness identical with pleasure?

2. What does it mean to say that good is a nonnatural property? Explain in your own words Moore's reasons for saying that good is not equivalent to any natural property.

3. Are moral value judgments merely expression of taste? Explain.

4. Is it worse morally to send starving people poisoned food than to let them starve to death? Why?

5. Explain the differences among liberalism, communism, socialism, capitalism, fascism, and conservatism.

6. Is it true that a state is not "well ordered" unless both (a) its members know and accept the same principles of social justice and (b) the basic social institutions generally satisfy and are generally known to satisfy these principles? Does the United States meet these conditions?

7. Do you agree that the principles of justice stated by Rawls are those to which we will agree if we are thinking rationally and in our own self-interest and are not influenced by irrelevant considerations? Explain.

8. Can an unequal distribution of the various assets of society be just? Explain.

9. Would it be right and proper to legalize human slavery if that resulted in an increase in the overall happiness of society? Why or why not?

10. "Any state necessarily violates people's moral rights and hence is intrinsically immoral." Give some reasons for thinking that this is true. Then give some reasons for thinking that it is false.

11. Can you think of an ethical principle that would prohibit the killing, hurting, sacrificing, or eating of humans for the sake of other ends that would not equally pertain to animals?

12. Compare and contrast the concepts of social justice proposed by Rawls and Nozick.

13. Is self-respect the most important good, as Rawls says?

14. Which do you think is more important, the common good or individual freedom? Why?

15. Different cultures may have different conceptions of what is Good. Is the Good definable only in terms of some particular culture's standards?

16. Critically discuss Marcuse's theory that the needs satisfied by advanced capitalist societies are to a large extent false needs.

17. Are our needs determined by advertising, consumerism, the mass media, and the entertainment industry?

18. "A revolution will come, born of disgust at the waste and excess of the so-called consumer society." Is this very likely? Explain.

## SUGGESTED FURTHER READINGS

Susan J. Armstrong and Richard G. Botzler, *The Animal Ethics Reader* (New York: Routledge, 2003). A good anthology of readings on animal rights, laws, and other issues.

Norman P. Barry, *An Introduction to Modern Political Theory*, 2nd ed. (London: Macmillan, 1991). A review of some of the key issues, in current political parlance.

Alain de Botton, *The Consolations of Philosophy* (New York: Penguin, 2000). Entertaining and highly popular depiction of philosophy's possible application to daily life.

Alan Brown, *Modern Political Philosophy* (New York: Penguin Books, 1986). A survey of major trends in contemporary political theory, including Rawls, Nozick, and others.

Matthew Calarco and Peter Atterton, eds., *The Continental Ethics Reader* (New York: Routledge, 2003). Anthology of classical writings in ethics by Continental philosophers.

Anthony de Cresigny and Kenneth Minogue, eds., *Contemporary Political Philosophers* (London: Methuen, 1975). An overview of contemporary political philosophy, including figures not covered in this text.

Stephen Darwall, ed., *Virtue Ethics* (Malden, Mass.: Blackwell, 2003). Readings classical and contemporary on the approach to ethics based on virtue, personal development and character.

Robert Elliot and Arran Gare, *Environmental Philosophy* (Milton Keynes, UK: the Open University Press, 1983). Essays on geocentric issues.

Peter G. Filene, *In the Arms of Others. A Cultural History of the Right-to-Die in America* (Blue Ridge Summit, Pa.: Rowman & Littlefield, 1998). The book raises questions concerning the critical, contemporary issue as to when life support may be withdrawn and/or death hastened.

Owen Flanagan and Amelie Oksenberg Rorty, eds., *Identity, Character and Morality* (Cambridge, Mass.: MIT Press, 1990). A group of essays relating contemporary ethics to psychology.

Phillipa Foot, ed., *Theories of Ethics* (New York: Oxford University Press, 1990). A selection of papers relating to contemporary issues in moral philosophy.

Robert Frederick, W. Michael Hoffman, and Mark Schwartz, *Business Ethics: Readings and Cases in Corporate Morality* (New York: McGraw-Hill, 2000). The work deals with some of the complex issues involving corporate morality.

Robert E. Goodin and Philip Petit, eds., *Contemporary Political Philosophy* (Malden, Mass.: Blackwell, 1997). An anthology of articles on current political issues such as democracy, rights, liberty, equality, and oppression.

R. M. Hare, *The Language of Morals* (Oxford: Clarendon Press, 1952). An important treatise on the logic of moral discourse.

Gilbert Harman and Judith Jarvis Thomson, *Moral Relativism and Moral Objectivity* (Malden, Mass.: Blackwell, 1995). Do moral questions have objective answers? A debate by two influential contemporary philosophers.

John Harris, ed., *Bioethics* (New York: Oxford University Press, 2001). Recent writings in bioethics on such topics as the value of life, the sustaining of life, abortion, and professional ethics.

Dale Jamieson, ed., *Singer and His Critics* (Malden, Mass.: Blackwell, 1998). We haven't said much about the moral status of animals, but it is an important current topic. Singer is among the best known in this field and is one of the most important contributors to applied or "practical" ethics.

Frederik Kaufman, *Foundations of Environmental Philosophy* (New York: McGraw-Hill, 2002). A clear review of environmental concerns and issues with readings.

Alasdair MacIntyre, *After Virtue: A Study in Moral Theory*, 2nd ed. (London: Duckworth, 1981). Widely known to the general public, this is MacIntyre's most important work.

H. Marcuse, *One-Dimensional Man* (Boston: Beacon Press, 1964). Marcuse's searing indictment of advanced technological societies.

R. Martin, *Rawls and Rights* (Lawrence: University Press of Kansas, 1985). Rawls's theory of justice explained and interpreted in terms of rights.

Larry May, Angela Bolte, and Nancy E. Snow, *Philosophy of Law Multiple Perspectives* (New York: McGraw-Hill, 1999). Anthology into major areas of Anglo-American law from a variety of different perspectives.

G. E. Moore, *Principia Ethica* (New York: Cambridge University Press, 1903). A work of major importance in ethics. Not terribly difficult to read.

David S. Orderberg, *Applied Ethics* (Malden, Mass.: Blackwell, 1999). A consideration of a number of contemporary problems in the light of traditional ethical theory.

J. Paul, ed., *Reading Nozick: Essays on "Anarchy, State, and Utopia"* (Totowa, N.J.: Rowman & Littlefield,
1981). A collection of essays that explain and criticize Nozick's political philosophy.

Anthony Quinton, ed., *Political Philosophy* (New York: Oxford University Press, 1991). Papers on political issues such as sovereignty, democracy, liberty, equality, and the common good.

John Rawls, *Lectures on the History of Moral Philosophy*, Barbara Herman, ed. (Cambridge, Mass.: Harvard University Press, 2000). Lectures on the history of moral philosophy by one of the leading philosophers of our times.

John Rawls, *Political Liberalism* (New York: Columbia University Press, 1993). A series of lectures that makes adjustments in *A Theory of Justice* in light of criticism of the earlier work.

John Rawls, *A Theory of Justice* (Cambridge: Harvard University Press, 1971). An important work; very clearly written.

W. D. Ross, *The Right and the Good* (London: Oxford University Press, 1930). Clearly written. An important book; good example of metaethics.

Michael Sandel, *Liberalism and the Limits of Justice* (Cambridge: Cambridge University Press, 1982). An important work in communitarian political philosophy.

Sean Sayers and Peter Osborne, eds., *Socialism, Feminism, and Philosophy, a "Radical Philosophy" Reader* (New York: Routledge, 1990). An anthology of papers from *Radical Philosophy* on socialist, feminist, and environmental issues.

Samuel Scheffler, ed., *Consequentialism and Its Critics* (New York: Oxford University Press, 1991). Papers by Nozick, Nagel, and others regarding the consequentialist issue.

Samuel Scheffler, *The Rejection of Consequentialism*, Rev. ed. (New York: Oxford University Press, 1994). An important discussion of consequentialism (utilitarianism).

John Searle, "How to Derive 'Ought' from 'Is,'" *Philosophical Review* 73(1964): 43–58. This is technical academic philosophy, but laypersons will find it quite readable.

Thomas Simon, *Law and Philosophy* (New York: McGraw-Hill, 2000). An analytical anthology introduces subjects such as political philosophy, legal theory, and classic cases.

Peter Singer, *Practical Ethics* (New York: Cambridge University Press, 1999). A well-received introduction to applied ethics that considers many controversial social questions.

Peter Singer, ed., *Applied Ethics* (New York: Oxford University Press, 1990). A series of papers on diverse issues in applied ethics, such as overpopulation, abortion, and capital punishment.

Peter Singer, ed., *In Defense of Animals* (New York: Perennial Library, 1986). Singer is a leading exponent of animal rights.

Daniel Statman, *Virtue Ethics, A Critical Reader* (Edinburg: Edinburg University Press, 2003). Readings covering the whole range of virtue ethics and duty ethics.

C. L. Stevenson, *Ethics and Language* (New Haven: Yale University Press, 1944). The most influential emotivist analysis of ethics.

R. Stewart, *Readings in Social and Political Philosophy,* 2nd ed. (Oxford: Oxford University Press, 1996). An excellent anthology of classic and contemporary readings in social and political philosophy.

R. Taylor, *Freedom, Anarchy, and the Law: An Introduction to Political Philosophy,* 2nd ed. (Buffalo: Prometheus Books, 1982). A general introduction to political philosophy.

Suzanne Uniacke, *Permissible Killing: The Self-Defence Justification of Homicide* (Cambridge: Cambridge University Press, 1994). A good example of a book-length treatment of an interesting issue in applied ethics.

Jeremy Waldron, ed., *Theories of Right* (New York: Oxford University Press, 1990). Important essays concerning related topics such as rights, equality, and fairness.

Michael Walzer, *Spheres of Justice* (New York: Basic Books, 1983). Each society generates its own "sphere of justice."

Michael Walzer, *Thick and Thin, Moral Argument at Home and Abroad* (Notre Dame, Ind.: University of Notre Dame Press, 1994). An extension and revision of *Spheres of Justice.*

M. Warnock, *Ethics since 1900* (London: Oxford University Press, 1960). A brief but useful general treatment of analytic ethics in the first half of the twentieth century. Chapter 2 is a critical exposition of Moore's ethics. See also Warnock's *Existentialist Ethics* (London: Macmillan, 1967) for an introduction to existentialist ethics.

# *Part Three*
# Philosophy of Religion: Reason and Faith

# 13

# Philosophy and Belief in God

It is morally necessary to assume the existence of God.     —Immanuel Kant

God is dead.     —Friedrich Nietzsche

What is the difference between a theologian and a philosopher of religion? Let's back up about four steps and get a running start at the question.

If you subscribe to a religion, and the opinion polls say you most likely do, then you also accept certain purely philosophical doctrines. For example, if you believe in a nonmaterial God, then you believe that not all that exists is material, and that means you accept a metaphysics of immaterialism. If you believe that you should love your neighbor because God said you should, then you are taking sides in the debate among ethical philosophers concerning ethical naturalism. You have committed yourself to a stand against naturalism.

Your religious beliefs commit you as well to certain epistemological principles. A lot of people who make no claim to have seen, felt, tasted, smelled, or heard God still say they know that God exists. So they must maintain that humans can have knowledge not gained through sense experience. To maintain this is to take sides in an important epistemological issue, as you know from Part One.

These and many other metaphysical, ethical, and epistemological points of view and principles are assumed by, and incorporated in, religion, and it is the business of the philosophy of religion to understand and rationally evaluate them.

Of course, *theology* also seeks clear understanding and rational evaluation of the doctrines and principles found in religion, including those that are metaphysical, ethical, and epistemological. But, for the most part, theologians start from premises and assumptions that are themselves religious tenets. The philosopher of religion, in contrast, does not make religious assumptions in trying to understand and evaluate religious beliefs.

The religions of the world differ in their tenets, of course. Therefore, a philosopher of religion usually focuses on the beliefs of a specific religion or religious tradition, and in fact it is the beliefs of the Judaeo-Christian religious tradition that

## The Black Cat

An old saying goes that the difference between a metaphysician and a theologian is this: The metaphysician looks in a dark room for a black cat that is not there. The theologian looks in the same place for the same thing.

And finds it.

have received the most discussion by Western philosophers. Philosophers of religion may focus on the beliefs of a specific religion, but they will not proceed in their inquiries from the *assumption* that these beliefs are true, even though they may in fact accept them as a personal matter.

What are some of the metaphysical, ethical, and epistemological beliefs of the Judaeo-Christian tradition that philosophers have sought to understand and evaluate? Many of these beliefs have to do with *God:* that he exists, that he is good, that he created the universe and is the source of all that is real, that he is a personal deity, that he is a transcendent deity, and so forth. Many have to do with *humans:* that humans were created in the image of God, that they have free will, that they can have knowledge of God's will, that the human soul is immortal, and so on. Other beliefs have to do with *features of the universe:* for example, that there are miracles, that there is supernatural reality, that there is pain and suffering (a fact thought to require reconciliation with the belief in a good and all-powerful God). And still others have to do with *language:* that religious language is intelligible and meaningful, that religious utterances are (or are not) factual assertions or are (or are not) metaphorical or analogical, that terminology used in descriptions of God means the same (or does not mean the same) as when it is used in descriptions of other things.

This is a long list of issues. To simplify things, we will concentrate here on the philosophical consideration of the Christian belief in the existence of God. Let's begin with two Christian greats, St. Anselm and St. Aquinas.

## TWO CHRISTIAN GREATS

Other chapters have begun with discussions of ancient Greek philosophers, and we could have begun this chapter, too, with the ancient Greeks. Many modern religious beliefs contain ideas that were discussed by, and in some cases originated with, the Greeks. But we have narrowed the focus here to the philosophical consideration of the Judaeo-Christian belief in God's existence, and it is appropriate to begin with the man who was abbot of Bec and, later, archbishop of Canterbury.

## Anselm

**St. Anselm** (c. 1033–1109) was among the first to evaluate the belief in the Christian God from a purely philosophical perspective, that is, from a perspective that does not make religious assumptions from the outset. Nonetheless, Anselm never entertained the slightest doubt about whether God exists. Further, he made no distinction between philosophy and theology, and he thought it impossible for anyone to reason about God or God's existence without already believing in him.

Still, Anselm was willing to evaluate *on its own merit and independently of religious assumptions* the idea that God does *not* exist.

***The Ontological Argument***    This idea, that God does not exist, is attributed in Psalms 14:1 to the "fool," and Anselm thought it plain that anyone who would deny God's existence is *logically* mistaken and is indeed an utter fool. Anselm reasoned that the fool is in a self-contradictory position. The fool, Anselm thought, is in the position of saying *that he can conceive of a being greater than the greatest being conceivable.* This may sound like a new species of doubletalk, so we must consider Anselm's reasoning carefully. You may find it helpful to read the box "*Reductio Proofs*" before we begin.

Anselm began with the premise that by "God" is meant "the greatest being conceivable," or, in Anselm's exact words, "a being than which nothing greater can be conceived."

Now the fool who denies that God exists at least *understands* what he denies, said Anselm charitably. Thus, God at least exists in the fool's understanding. But, Anselm noted, a being that exists both in the understanding and outside in reality is greater than a being that exists only in the understanding. (That is why people prefer real houses and cars and clothes and vacations to those they just think about.)

But this means, Anselm said, that the fool's position is absurd. For his position is that God exists only in the understanding, but not in reality. So the fool's position, according to Anselm, is that "the very being, than which nothing greater can be conceived, is one, than which a greater can be conceived." And yes, this silliness is something like doubletalk, but Anselm's point is that the denial of God's existence leads to this silliness. Hence, God exists: to think otherwise is to be reduced to self-contradiction and mumbo jumbo.

This line of argument, according to which it follows from the very *concept* of God that God exists, is known as the **ontological argument.** It represents Anselm's most important contribution to the philosophy of religion. If Anselm's argument is valid, if Anselm did establish that it is self-contradictory to deny that God exists and hence established that God does exist, then he did so without invoking any religious premises or making any religious presuppositions. True, he made in effect an assumption about the *concept* of God, but even a non-Christian or an atheist, he thought, must concede that what is *meant* by "God" is "the greatest being conceivable." Thus, if the argument is valid, even those who are not moved by faith or are otherwise religious must accept its conclusion. Anselm in effect argued that the proposition "God exists" is *self-evident* and can no more be denied than can the proposition "A square has four sides," and anyone who thinks otherwise is either a fool or just does not grasp the concept of God.

Anselm gave another version of the ontological argument that goes like this: Because God is that than which nothing greater can be conceived, God's nonexistence is inconceivable. For anyone whose nonexistence *is* conceivable is not as great as anyone whose nonexistence is *not* conceivable, and thus is not God.

## *Reductio* Proofs

If a claim logically entails something that is absurd, nonsensical, or just plain false, you reject the claim, correct?

For example, if the claim that the butler killed Colonel Mustard in the kitchen means that the butler was in two different places at the same time (because it is known that he was in the library at the time of the murder), then you reject the claim that the butler killed Colonel Mustard in the kitchen.

This type of proof of a claim's denial is known as *reductio ad absurdum:* by demonstrating that a claim reduces to an absurdity or just to something false, you prove the denial of the claim. By showing that claim *C* entails falsehood *F,* you prove *not-C.*

Reductios, as they are called, are encountered frequently in philosophy and in real life. Anselm's ontological argument is a **reductio proof.** Here the claim, *C,* is that

*God does not exist.*

This claim, argued Anselm, entails the falsehood, *F,* that

*the very being than which nothing greater can be conceived is one than which a greater can be conceived.*

The conclusion of the argument is thus *not-C,* that

*God does exist.*

Are you convinced? Many are not. Many regard the ontological argument in any version as a cute little play on words that proves absolutely nothing.

*Gaunilo's Objection*   One who found the argument unconvincing was a Benedictine monk from the Abbey of Marmontier, a contemporary of Anselm whose name was **Gaunilo** [GO-nee-low]. One of Gaunilo's objections was to the first version of the argument, which, he argued, could be used to prove ridiculous things. For example, Gaunilo said, consider the most perfect island. Because it would be more perfect for an island to exist both in reality and in the understanding, the most perfect island must exist in reality, if Anselm's line of reasoning is sound. For if this island did not exist in reality, then (according to Anselm's reasoning) any island that did exist in reality would be more perfect than it — that is, would be more perfect than the most perfect island, which is impossible. In other words, Gaunilo used Anselm's reasoning to demonstrate the necessary existence of the most perfect island, implying that any pattern of reasoning that can be used to reach such an idiotic conclusion must obviously be defective.

Anselm, however, believed that his reasoning applied only to God: Because God is that than which a greater cannot be conceived, God's nonexistence is inconceivable; whereas, by contrast, the nonexistence of islands and all other things is conceivable.

As you will see in the selection from Anselm at the end of the chapter, which contains the first version of his ontological argument, Anselm was able to express his thought with elegant simplicity. You may find it a challenge to figure out what, if anything, is wrong with his reasoning.

Do not be confused when Anselm says that God is "something than which nothing greater can be thought." He just means, in plain English, "God is the being with the following characteristic. When you try to think of a greater or higher being, you cannot do it."

## Aquinas

About a century and a half after Anselm died, **St. Thomas Aquinas** (c. 1225–1274), whom we have discussed in earlier chapters, interpreted Aristotelian philosophy from a Christian perspective. Aristotle, as we have had occasion to mention, emphasized the importance to philosophy of direct observation of nature. In keeping with his empiricist, Aristotelian leanings, Aquinas regarded the ontological argument as invalid. You cannot prove that God exists, he said, merely by considering the word *God,* as the ontological argument in effect supposes. For that strategy to work, you would have to presume to know God's essence. The proposition "God exists," he said, unlike "A square has four sides," is not self-evident to us mere mortals. Although you can prove God's existence in several ways, he asserted, you cannot do it just by examining the concept of God. You have to consider what it is about nature that makes it manifest that it requires God as its original cause.

The ways in which the existence of God can be proved are in fact five, according to Aquinas. Although Aquinas' theological and philosophical writings fill many volumes and cover a vast range of topics, he is most famous for his **Five Ways** (but some philosophers — discussed later — do not regard Aquinas' proofs of God as his best philosophy). It would be surprising if you were not already familiar with one or another of Aquinas' Five Ways in some version. In any case, they are included as a reading selection at the end of the chapter.

***The First Way***    The *first way* to prove that God exists, according to Aquinas, is to consider the fact that natural things are in motion. As we look around the world and survey moving things, it becomes clear that they did not put themselves into motion. But if every moving thing were moved by another moving thing, then there would be no **first mover;** if no first mover exists, there would be no other mover, and nothing would be in motion. Because things are in motion, a first mover must therefore exist that is moved by no other, and this, of course, is God.

We should note here that Aquinas is usually understood as meaning something quite broad by "motion"— something more like *change in general*— and as including under the concept of movement the coming into, and passing out of, existence. Thus, when he says that things do not put themselves into motion, do not suppose that he thought that you cannot get up out of your chair and walk across the room. He means that things do not just bring themselves into existence.

***The Second Way***    Aquinas' *second way* of proving God's existence is very similar to the first. In the world of sensible things, nothing causes itself. But if everything were caused by something else, then there would be no first cause, and if no first cause exists, there would be no first effect. In fact, there would be no second, third, or fourth effect, either: if no first cause exists, there would be no effects, period. So we must admit a first cause, to wit, God. (This is a good time to read the box "The Big Bang," on page 427.)

Note that Aquinas did not say anything in either of the first two proofs about things being moved or caused by *earlier* motions or causes. The various motions and causes he is talking about are simultaneous in time. His argument is not the

## PROFILE: St. Thomas Aquinas (c. 1225–1274)

Aquinas, the son of a count of Aquino in Italy, studied for many years with Albertus Magnus (i.e., "Albert the Great"). Albertus, who had the unusual idea that Christian thinkers should be knowledgeable about philosophy and science, wished to make all of Aristotle's writings available in Latin. His fondness for Aristotle was a strong influence on his pupil, Aquinas.

Aquinas eventually received his doctorate from the University of Paris in his late twenties and soon acquired a substantial reputation as a scholar. For ten years in his thirties and early forties, he was a professor for the Papal Court and lectured in and around Rome.

Now the thirteenth century was a time of considerable intellectual controversy between the Platonists and the Aristotelians. Some theologians believed that the teachings of Aristotle could not be harmonized with Christian doctrines. This belief was in part a reaction to Averroes (1126–1198), a brilliant Arabian philosopher, and his followers, whose philosophy was built entirely around the thought of Aristotle. The Averroist philosophy conflicted with Church doctrine on creation and personal immortality, making Aristotle odious to some Christian theologians.

But Aquinas was no Averroist and defended his own version of Aristotle with inexorable logic. He returned to Paris in 1268 and became involved in a famous struggle with the Averroists, which he won. Although some factions within the Church voiced strong opposition to his philosophy, opposition that lasted for many years after his death, slowly but surely Aquinas' thinking became the dominant system of Christian thought. He was canonized (officially declared a saint) in 1323.

Aquinas was a stout fellow, slow and deliberate in manner. He was thus nicknamed the Dumb Ox. But he was a brilliant and forceful thinker, and his writings fill many volumes and cover a vast array of theological and philosophical topics. His most famous works are the *Summa Contra Gentiles* (1258–1260) and the *Summa Theologica* (1267–1273), a systematic theology grounded on philosophical principles. He was, in addition, a most humane and charitable man.

In 1879, Pope Leo XIII declared Aquinas' system to be the official Catholic philosophy.

common one you hear that things must be caused by something earlier, which must be caused by something earlier, and so on, and that because this chain of causes cannot go back infinitely, there must be a first cause, God. In Aquinas' opinion, there is no philosophical reason that the chain of causes could not go back infinitely. But there cannot be an infinite series of *simultaneous* causes or movers, he thought.

***The Third Way*** Aquinas' *third way* is easily the most complicated of the Five Ways. Many consider it his finest proof, though Aquinas himself seemed to prefer the first.

Many paraphrasings of the third proof are not faithful to what Aquinas actually said, which is essentially this: In nature some things are such that it is possible for them not to exist. Indeed, everything you can lay your hands on belongs to this "need-not-exist" category; whatever it is, despite the fact that it does exist, it need not have existed. Now that which need not exist, said Aquinas, at some time did not exist. Therefore, if everything belongs to this category, then at one time nothing existed, and then it would have been impossible for anything to have begun to exist—and thus even now nothing would exist. Thus, Aquinas reasoned, not everything is such that it need not exist: "There must exist something the existence of which is *necessary.*"

This is not quite the end of the third proof, however, for Aquinas believed that he had not yet ruled out the possibility that the necessity of this necessary being might be caused by another necessary being, whose necessity might be caused by another, and so on and so on. So, he asserted, "It is impossible to go on to infinity in necessary things which have their necessity caused by another." Conclusion: There must be some necessary being that has its own necessity, and this is God.

We said the third way was complicated.

***The Fourth and Fifth Ways***    Aquinas' *fourth way* to prove God is to consider the fact that all natural things possess degrees of goodness, truth, nobility, and all other perfections. Therefore, there must be that which is the source of these perfections, namely, pure goodness and truth, and so on, and this is what we call God.

And the *fifth way* or proof of God's existence is predicated on the observation that natural things act for an end or purpose. That is, they function in accordance with a plan or design. Accordingly, an intelligent being exists by which things are directed toward their end, and this intelligent being is God.

Aquinas' first three proofs of God's existence are versions of what today is called the **cosmological argument.** The cosmological argument is actually not one argument but a type of argument. Proponents of arguments of this type think that the existence of *contingent* things, things that could possibly not have existed, points to the existence of a noncontingent or *necessary* being, God, as their ultimate cause, creator, ground, energizer, or source of being. Note the difference between the cosmological argument and ontological arguments, which endeavor to establish the existence of God just by considering his nature or analyzing the concept of God, as we saw attempted by Anselm.

Aquinas' fourth proof, which cites the existence of goodness or good things, is called the **moral argument.** Here again, the term does not refer to just one argument but, rather, to a type of argument, and, as we will see, some of the "versions" of the moral argument resemble one another only vaguely.

Arguments like Aquinas' fifth proof, according to which the apparent purposefulness or orderliness of the universe or its parts or structure points to the existence of a divine designer, are called **arguments from design,** or **teleological arguments.**

Let's summarize all of this. Between them, Anselm and Aquinas introduced what have turned out to be the four principal arguments for God's existence. These are

- the ontological argument
- the cosmological argument

Earth from outer space. The cosmological and teleological arguments suppose that Earth and its features could not have arisen by chance.

---

- the teleological or design argument
- the moral argument

Notice that none of these four arguments rests on any religious assumptions. They should therefore require the assent of every nonreligious person, if they are sound.

To a certain extent, the history of the philosophy of religion is a continuing discussion of various versions and aspects of these four arguments. Therefore, understanding each type of argument provides you with a good grasp of the basics of the philosophy of religion.

Now before we leave Aquinas, we should call your attention to the fact that the distinction we drew at the beginning of this chapter between theology and the philosophy of religion is pretty much the same as the distinction Aquinas drew between theology and philosophy.

According to Aquinas, if your thinking proceeds from principles that are revealed to you in religion and that you accept on religious faith, then your thinking is theological, though he did not often use the word *theology*. If your reasoning proceeds from what is evident in sensory experience, then your thinking is philosophical.

According to Aquinas, some theological truths, truths of revelation, are such that philosophy could never discover them. For example, philosophy cannot establish that the universe had a beginning and is not eternal. And not everything discovered by philosophy is important for salvation. But philosophy and theology, although separate disciplines, are not incompatible; in fact, they complement each other, he thought (in contrast to some other Christian thinkers who thought that philosophy can lead to religious errors).

From the standpoint of theology, that God exists is a given, a truth that you start out knowing. From the standpoint of philosophy, that God exists is not a given but may be inferred from your experience.

Thus, Aquinas' proofs of God's existence are philosophical proofs. They do not depend for their soundness on any religious principles.

## MYSTICISM

Quite a different approach to God may be found in the writings of the anchoress **Julian of Norwich** (1342–1414?), one of the great mystics of all time.

Anchoress? That is a person who had the great fortune to be anchored for life to a church. You will find more information on this in the nearby Profile on Julian.

Why do you believe in God, if you do? Perhaps at some point you had a "mystical experience"—you experienced God directly; God *came* to you. If you have had this type of experience, you may be unable to offer a justification or argument for your belief, and your inability to do so may not bother you in the slightest. If you have had a mystical experience of God, this whole business of debating the strengths and weaknesses of arguments about God may strike you as just so much mental exercise.

It is, however, one thing to say "God came to me" and quite another to explain why this mystical experience is a reliable form of knowledge. Before we go any further, let's be clear. We are not talking about *hunches*—as in when you have a hunch that something good or bad will happen and it does. We are talking about serious beliefs people hold on the basis of this peculiar form of experience, beliefs like "God is real" or "Jesus has touched me."

In a very rich mystical experience, one that comes with all the accessories, the mystic is often unconscious, appears to be delirious, or seems to be having what today is sometimes called an out-of-body experience. The mystic may be dreaming, awake, or in a trance. He or she may see visions or hear voices. Commonly, those who have such experiences report being told things by God. Sometimes they are told to write down what they experience or to teach others. Before the development of rationalism in the seventeenth century, back before philosophers mostly believed that reason was the premier tool for acquiring knowledge, mystical experiences like this were given more credence. Today there is something of a tendency, at least among sophisticates, to discount such experiences as malfunctions in brain chemistry or temporal lobe disturbances or the like.

Julian of Norwich was a mystic, but she also *analyzed* her mystical experiences or "showings," as she called them. Her analysis focused on the nature of personal religious and moral knowledge, as well as on whether it is possible to know God. She denied that there is any meaningful difference in the validity of mystical revelations made directly to our soul and knowledge derived through reason. She held, indeed, that it is mistaken to divorce reason from experience, especially from mystical experience.

Julian also emphasized the importance of the "not showns"—what logically should have been part of the vision but was missing. She believed God intended her to use insight and instinct and reason to figure out what was not being communicated directly and to piece together the missing parts of the puzzle.

# PROFILE: The Anchoress, Julian of Norwich (1342–1414?)

Her name was Julian, but sometimes she is called "Juliana." She lived in the English cathedral city of Norwich during a nasty time in history. The Hundred Years' War, the Great Schism in the Church, the ruthless suppression of the Peasant's Revolt in Norwich, and the condemnation of John Wycliffe for heresy made the mid–fourteenth century a rough time for Norwich. The fact that the Black Plague hit Norwich when Julian was six, again when she was nineteen, and again when she was twenty-seven did not exactly make Norwich a fun place to live in.

Julian became an anchoress. It was the custom at that time to "anchor" someone to a church. Anchoring was a kind of permanent grounding of a scholarly nun or priest (it was an honor, not a punishment). The lucky person, someone known for saintly behavior and devotion to theology, was walled up alive in a small cell within the outer wall of the church. Food, books, and other items would be passed through a window, and occasionally the anchoress would be allowed to talk through the window to important clergy and nobility. She spent her life there, and when she died, she was entombed in a crypt in the church.

Julian wrote two versions (one short and one long) of her *Booke of Showings* (revelations). The short version is a partial description of a series of visions she had in 1373 when she was seriously ill. She became an anchoress soon after that experience. That left her lots of time for study, thought, and religious discussion. Many theologians and philosophers visited her to discuss the "showings" she described in the short version. She spent the next twenty years revising the manuscript, including fuller details and much analysis of what she thought the revelations meant.

Back then, women were not supposed to claim to have any religious or philosophical authority (or

any other kind of authority, for that matter). To avoid criticism for having the crust to act as if she knew something, a woman writer typically began her text with a "humility formula." Here is Julian's as she wrote it:

*Botte god for bede that ʒe schulde saye or take it so that I am a techere, for I meene nouʒt soo, no I mente nevere so; for I am a womann, leued, febille and freylle.*

Some of Julian's words had special religious and philosophical meanings that her readers would have understood. What she is saying is: "God says do not you act like I am a teacher. I do not mean to claim to be, and I never meant so. For I am a woman, ordinary ('lewd'), morally weak ('feeble'), and likely to fall from virtue ('frail')." Having disclaimed any authority, Julian went on to write seven hundred pages of philosophy.

Julian's interests are in the nature and certainty of religious knowledge. She held that there were three sources of religious knowledge: natural reason, teachings of religious leaders, and visions given by God. As God gives visions to whomever God chooses, and God loves everyone, in theory everyone is a candidate for mystical revelations. Julian of Norwich lived during the Crusades, when heretics were claiming that the Catholic religion was based on false ideas. How can someone tell true religious claims from false ones? Might God make revelations to ordinary people? Julian and many other mystics, including Hildegard of Bingen, St. John of the Cross, and his teacher St. Teresa of Avila (all of whom are known as philosophers), thought so. To claim that only religious leaders have a direct line to God suggests that God has limited ability to communicate. Julian called God "Christ, Our Mother" and "God, our Father." In her mind, God was both male and female, mother and father. God made us and nurtures us through the hard times.

In Julian's view, God lives in us and we in God; we are one with God and are nurtured and fed knowledge of God and of ourselves by our divine parent. Thus, she believed we could know God only partly through revelation; further knowledge comes through loving God. In addition, she maintained we could come to love God by loving our own souls.

Thomas Aquinas (who had recently been made a saint) had analyzed visions as the language God uses to convey God's meaning. Julian went beyond analysis to attempt to make the experiences of visionaries relevant to others. She believed that ordinary people could learn from visionaries and find comfort and reason to hope in their visions. Hope, we can imagine, must have been a valuable commodity in mid-fourteenth-century England, faced with seemingly endless outbreaks of plague, war, and religious disputation.

## SEVENTEENTH-CENTURY PERSPECTIVES

For our purposes here, we can now pass lightly over some three hundred years from the Middle Ages through the Renaissance to the seventeenth century. This is not to suggest that the time was unimportant for the history of religion. Europe had seen a mixture not only of enlightenment and religious revolution but also of reaction and intolerance; it had brought forth not only printed books and open discussion but also gunpowder and the stake. Luther had challenged the very foundations of Catholic doctrine, and Protestantism had spread throughout Europe. In England, Henry VIII had forced creation of the Anglican Church so that he could marry young Anne Boleyn and then, through a liberal use of execution, secured a loyal following. A new disorder had been rung in by the time of Descartes's birth, and before his death modern science was offering its own challenge to the established orthodoxy.

But all of this, though of great significance to the history of religion, was only indirectly important to the history of the philosophy of religion. The main point for our purposes is that the seventeenth century was the age of scientific discovery amid intellectual uncertainty and political and religious instability, an age in which past authorities and institutions and truths were questioned and often rejected or discarded.

### Descartes

The next figure in the philosophy of religion you should be familiar with is **René Descartes** (1596–1650). Descartes, longing for an unshakable intellectual footing, made it his primary business to devise what he thought was a new method for attaining certainty in his turbulent age. When he employed his new method, however, it revealed to him the certain existence of God.

As we saw in Chapter 6, Descartes's method was to challenge every belief, no matter how plausible it seemed, to ascertain which of his beliefs, if any, were absolutely unassailable. Employing this method, Descartes found that he could not doubt his existence as a thing that thinks: *cogito, ergo sum* (I think, therefore I am). He also found that he could not doubt the existence of God, for basically three reasons. These three reasons are Descartes's proofs of God.

**Descartes's First Proof**   Having established as absolutely certain his own existence as a thinking thing, Descartes found within his mind the idea of God, the idea of an infinite and perfect being. Further, he reasoned, because there must be a cause for his idea, and because there must be as much reality or perfection in the cause of an idea as there is in the content of the idea, and because he himself therefore certainly could not be the cause of the idea, it follows, he concluded, that God exists.

Let's call this Descartes's first proof. It is a simple proof, although Descartes makes it seem somewhat complicated because he has to explain *why* his idea of God could not have arisen from a source other than God, and, of course, it is difficult to do this.

As you can see, Descartes's first proof is sort of a combination ontological-cosmological argument. It is ontological in that the mere idea of God is held by Descartes to entail that God exists. It is cosmological in that the existence of some contingent thing—Descartes's idea of God—is considered by Descartes to require God as its ultimate cause.

**Descartes's Second Proof**   Descartes had two other proofs of God's existence. His second proof is only subtly different from the first and is basically this:

1. I exist as a thing that has an idea of God.
2. Everything that exists has a cause that brought it into existence and that sustains it in existence.
3. The only thing adequate to cause and sustain me, a thing that has an idea of God, is God.
4. Therefore, God exists.

In this second proof, God is invoked by Descartes as the cause of *Descartes,* a being that has the idea of God; whereas in the first proof, God is invoked by Descartes as the cause of Descartes's *idea* of God. In the second proof, Descartes also utilizes the important notion that a thing needs a cause to *conserve* or *sustain* it in existence. You will encounter this idea again.

**Descartes's Third Proof**   In contrast with the first two, Descartes's third proof is a straightforward and streamlined version of the ontological argument:

1. My conception of God is the conception of a being that possesses all perfections.
2. Existence is a perfection.
3. Therefore, I cannot conceive of God as not existing.
4. Therefore, God exists.

According to Descartes, when you think it through, you see that you couldn't have an idea of God unless God exists.

Now, assuming that this argument successfully gets you to conclusion (3), how about that move from (3) to (4)? Descartes had no difficulty with that move and said simply, "From the fact that I cannot conceive God without existence, it follows that existence is inseparable from Him, and hence that He really exists." He also offered what he thought was a parallel argument to support the move, and it was to this effect: Just as the fact that you cannot conceive of a triangle whose angles do not equal 180° means that a triangle must have angles that equal 180°, the fact that you cannot conceive of God as not existing means that God must exist.

Descartes's three proofs may be novel, but certain objections instantly spring to mind. A common criticism made of the first two proofs is that it seems possible to devise plausible alternative explanations for one's having an idea of God, explanations other than that given by Descartes. Descartes himself anticipates this objection and endeavors to show why the most likely alternative explanations fail.

The third proof—Descartes's version of the ontological argument—is more difficult to criticize, but about one hundred fifty years later Immanuel Kant formulated what became the classic refutation of ontological arguments. More about this when we turn to Kant.

A different sort of objection to Descartes's proofs is that, given Descartes's method—according to which he vowed not to accept any claim that is in the least bit doubtable—Descartes should not have accepted without question either the principle that he and his ideas must be caused or the principle that there must be as much perfection and reality in the cause as in the effect. Although Descartes regarded his proofs of God as providing certainty, they seem to rest on principles that many people would think of as less than certain. Yet Descartes seems to accept these principles without hesitation.

Nevertheless, Descartes's proofs are important in the history of our subject, for they raise the important question—at least the first two proofs raise this question—just how *does* a person come to have the idea of an *infinite* being?

## Leibniz

You may recall the name of Gottfried Wilhelm, Baron von Leibniz, or at least the "Leibniz" part, from our discussion in Chapter 6. **Leibniz** (1646–1716) was one of the Continental rationalists of the seventeenth century (Descartes and Spinoza were the other two). He is remembered for developing calculus independently of Newton and for his metaphysical doctrine of **monads**—the individual nonphysical units of activity that, he said, are the ultimate constituents of reality. Remember also that the Leibnizian metaphysical system is, or so Leibniz believed, derivable logically from a few basic principles, including, perhaps most famously, the **principle of sufficient reason.** According to this principle, there is a sufficient reason why things are exactly as they are and are not otherwise.

The principle of sufficient reason is used by Leibniz as a proof of God. To see how the proof works, consider any occurrence whatsoever, say, the leaves falling from the trees in autumn. According to the principle in question, there must be a sufficient reason for that occurrence. Now a *partial* reason for any occurrence is that something else happened, or is happening, that caused or is causing the occurrence—in our example, the days turning cold. But that happening is only a *partial* reason for the occurrence in question because it too requires a sufficient reason for happening. Why did the days turn cold?

So it is plain, thought Leibniz, that as long as you seek the sufficient reason for an occurrence from within the sequence of happenings or events, you never get the complete, final, sufficient reason for the occurrence. You only get to some other event, and that itself needs a reason for having happened. (The days turned cold because of a shift southward in the jet stream. The jet stream shifted southward because of a reduction in solar radiation. The solar radiation was reduced because of changes in the earth's orientation relative to the sun. And so forth.) So, unless there is something *outside* the series of events, some reason for the *entire series itself,* there is no sufficient reason for *any* occurrence.

Therefore, reasoned Leibniz, because there is a sufficient reason for every occurrence, it follows that there is something outside the series of events that is its own sufficient reason. And this "something outside," of course, is God. Further, because God is a sufficient reason for God's own existence, God is a *necessary* being, argued Leibniz.

In this way, then, the principle of sufficient reason, coupled with the fact that something has occurred or is occurring, leads straightaway to a necessary being, God—at least according to Leibniz.

This proof is yet another cosmological argument, and it is very much like Aquinas' third way. In fact, there is a tendency in the literature to interpret Aquinas' third way in this Leibnizian mode. Further, Leibniz's "argument from sufficient reason" is thought by many contemporary philosophers to be the soundest cosmological argument, and soundest proof of God of any type, ever put forward. As you will see directly when we turn to David Hume, however, not everyone is impressed with the argument.

Later we will mention that Kant thought that the cosmological argument depends on the ontological argument. Kant thought this, apparently, because

If you are real, God, why
did you let the Republicans
win the election?

This, of course, is a variation of the problem of evil
(discussed in the text in the section on Leibniz) from
a Democrat's viewpoint.

Leibniz's version ends up seeming to prove the existence of a necessary being, and it is the concept of God as a necessary being that is the foundation of the ontological argument. But it does seem doubtful that Leibniz's argument *depends* on the ontological argument or in any way *assumes* the existence of a necessary being. Instead, the argument seems to *prove* the existence of a necessary being.

Leibniz thought other proofs of God were sound, including an amended version of Descartes's ontological argument and a couple of others that rest on Leibniz's metaphysics. Leibniz, however, is most noted for the cosmological argument we have explained here.

*Leibniz and the Problem of Evil*   Unfortunately, there is a great deal of pain and suffering in the world, not to mention disease, murder, torture, poverty, rape, child abuse, droughts, earthquakes, floods, wars, hijackings, and many other unpleasant things. Now, given that these things exist, it follows either that (1) God cannot do anything about them, which means that God is not all powerful, or that (2) God does not mind that they exist, which means that either (a) God is not good or (b) these things are really good things in disguise. One further option is (3) God does not exist.

If these are the only options and if you believe that God exists and is good and all powerful, you will choose option (2b) and say that these things are really good things in disguise. Of course, you might not put it exactly that way: you might say that these things are evil, all right, but the existence of some evil is required for the greater good. But that is saying that these things serve a purpose and to that extent are not *purely* evil.

**Theodicy** is the defense of God's goodness and omnipotence (all-powerfulness) in view of apparent evil. Many theologians and philosophers have written theodicies. But one of the most important theodicies was that of Leibniz. For Leibniz subscribed to the principle of sufficient reason, and that principle means that God exists. It also means that the reason this world, this state of affairs exists, and not some other world, some other state of affairs, is that this must be the best of all possible worlds (for otherwise God would not have chosen it for existence). So, according to Leibniz, this is the best or most perfect of all worlds possible, and he is thus especially obligated to explain how apparent evil fits into it.

Leibniz's explanation, briefly, is that for God to create things other than himself, the created things logically must be limited and imperfect. Thus, to the extent that creation is imperfect, it is not wholly good, and thus it is "evil."

Further, Leibniz argues, you have to look at the entire painting. You cannot pronounce it bad if you look at this or that small part, for if you do that, all you will see is a confused mass of colors. Likewise, you have to look at the world from a global perspective and not focus in on this or that unpleasant aspect of it.

Not everyone, of course, finds this explanation of evil satisfactory. The optimism expressed in Leibniz's dictum that this is the best of all possible worlds was skewered with dripping sarcasm by Voltaire (1694–1778) in his famous novel *Candide*. Leibniz was of the opinion that one must look at evil from a global perspective, from which unfortunate events might be perceived as part of a larger fabric that, taken as a whole, is a perfect creation. This notion, in Voltaire's opinion, is meaningless from the standpoint of the individual who suffers a dreadful misfortune, and Voltaire had no difficulty in ridiculing it. If you look at the events of the world with a sober eye, Voltaire suggested, you will see anything but a just, harmonious, and ordered place. What you are more likely to see is injustice, strife, and rampant disorder.

"When death crowns the ills of suffering man, what a fine consolation to be eaten by worms," he wrote. You get the idea.

## EIGHTEENTH-CENTURY PERSPECTIVES

Recall now Aquinas' fifth way, a version of the teleological argument, which also often is called the argument from design. The basic idea of this type of proof of God's existence is that the world and its components act for a purpose and thus exhibit design; therefore, the world was created by an intelligent designer. One of the most famous criticisms of the design argument was made by the British empiricist David Hume.

### Hume

**David Hume** (1711–1776) was born some sixty years after Descartes died, during a period of European history that saw the clear emergence of two rivals, science and religion. Between Descartes's *Meditations* and Hume's writings on religion, science had made strong advances, especially in 1687 with the publication of Sir Isaac

Newton's *Principia Mathematica*. Although Newton himself did not question God's existence, his system seemed to confirm scientifically what Hobbes earlier had concluded philosophically (see Chapter 6) and what Descartes seemed most to fear: the universe is an aggregate of matter in motion that has no need of, and leaves no room for, God. Hume's case-hardened doubts about religion made blood pressures soar, but by the time Hume put them in print they were by no means considered capital offenses.

Hume's empiricist epistemological principles (if valid) in fact rule out the possibility of any meaningful ontological argument. But this is complicated business and need not detain us because it is Hume's harsh criticisms of the cosmological and especially the teleological arguments that have been most influential in the philosophy of religion. The most important criticism of the ontological argument comes from Kant, anyway. (Hume's thinking on the subject of miracles has also been influential; we discuss it in the box "Miracles.")

Hume stated the teleological argument (that is, the argument from design) and then went on to criticize it severely. Here is his statement of the argument; then we will explain his criticism of it.

> Look round the world; contemplate the whole and every part of it: you will find it to be nothing but one great machine, subdivided into an infinite number of lesser machines, which again admit of subdivisions, to a degree beyond what human senses and faculties can trace and explain. All these various machines, and even their most minute parts, are adjusted to each other with an accuracy, which ravishes into admiration all men, who have ever contemplated them. The curious adapting of means to ends, throughout all nature, resembles exactly, though it much exceeds, the productions of human contrivance; of human design, thought, wisdom, and intelligence. Since therefore the effects resemble each other, we are led to infer, by all the rules of analogy, that the causes also resemble; and that the Author of Nature is somewhat similar to the mind of men; though possessed of much larger faculties, proportioned to the grandeur of the work, which he has executed. By this argument a posteriori, and by this argument alone, we do prove at once the existence of a Deity, and his similarity to human mind and intelligence.

Now note that in this proof of God, as stated by Hume, the reasoning is from an *effect* (the "world," i.e., the universe) and its parts to its *cause* (God). Further, this is an **argument by analogy,** in which the effect (the world or universe) is likened to a human contrivance, the cause is likened to a human creator, and the mechanism of creation is likened to human thought and intelligence. Hume's criticisms of the proof are mainly related to (1) the appropriateness of these analogies, and (2) the legitimacy of this particular instance of effect-to-cause reasoning.

Hume began his criticism by noticing that in an effect-to-cause proof we cannot attribute to the supposed cause any qualities over and beyond those required for the effect. For example, is the world absolutely perfect? Is it free from every error, mistake, or incoherence? No? Then you cannot say that its cause is absolutely perfect either. Does the world reflect infinite wisdom and intelligence? Hume's own opinion is that at best the world reflects these qualities to *some degree;* and, therefore, though we perhaps can infer that the cause has these qualities to a similar degree, we are unauthorized to attribute to it these qualities in a higher degree, and we certainly are not authorized to attribute to it these qualities in an *infinite* degree.

## Miracles

Some Christians regard miracles as evidence of divine action. Hume, however, was highly skeptical of reports of miracles.

A miracle, he reasoned, is a violation of a natural law, such as that water flows downhill or that fire consumes wood. Thus, before it is reasonable to accept a report of a miracle as true, the evidence that supports the report must be even stronger than that which has established the natural law.

Because the evidence that a natural law holds is the uniform experience of humankind, it is almost inconceivable that any report of a miracle could be true. Therefore, before it would be reasonable to accept such a report, it would have to be a miracle in its own right for the report to be false. In fact, the report's being false would have to be a *greater* miracle than the miracle it reports.

"No testimony," wrote Hume, "is sufficient to establish a miracle, unless the testimony be of such a kind, that its falsehood would be more miraculous than the fact that it endeavors to establish."

The famous American patriot Thomas Paine once asked which is more likely, that a person would lie or that a river would flow upstream? Hume's point is that before you accept some person's report of a river flowing upstream, it must be even more unlikely that the person would be mistaken than that a river would indeed flow upstream:

> When anyone tells me, that he saw a dead man restored to life, I immediately consider with myself, whether it be more probable that this person should either deceive or be deceived, or that the fact which he relates should really have happened. I weigh the one miracle against the other; and always reject the greater miracle. If the falsehood of his testimony would be more miraculous than the event which he relates; then, and not till then, can he pretend to command my belief or opinion.

We also are not authorized to attribute to it *other* qualities, such as pure goodness or infinite power. The existence of evil and misery, in Hume's opinion, certainly does *not* indicate that the cause of the world is pure goodness coupled with infinite power. His point was not that the existence of pain and misery necessarily means that the creator of the world is *not* good or omnipotent. Rather, his point was just that, given the existence of evil and misery in the world, we cannot legitimately try to prove that the creator is all-good and all-powerful *by looking at the world*. To do that is to attribute something other to the cause than is found in the effect.

Hume also questioned whether we even *know* how perfect or good the world is. Given the limitations of our position, given that we have no basis for a comparison, can we be sure that the world does not contain great faults? Are we entitled to say that the world deserves considerable praise? If an ignorant chucklehead pronounces the only poem he has ever heard to be artistically flawless, does his opinion count for much? And is not our experience with worlds as limited as this ignoramus's experience with poetry?

Further, he noted, in the design proof of God, a cause is inferred from a single effect, namely, the world. But, Hume asked, is it legitimate to infer a cause from a *single* effect? If I learn (to take a modern illustration of the point) that a certain weird kind of sound is caused by a new type of electronic instrument, then when I hear that kind of sound again, I can infer that it was caused by a similar instrument. But if it is the first time I hear the sound, I cannot say much at all about its cause, save perhaps that it was not made by a trombone or guitar. In other words, if we have experience of only a single instance of the effect, as seems to be the case with the world, then it is not clear "that we could form any conjecture or inference at all concerning its cause."

Of course, we have had experience with the building of machines and ships and houses and so forth. But can the world really be compared to any of these? Can we pretend to show much similarity between a house and the universe? To speak of the origin of *worlds,* wrote Hume, "It is not sufficient, surely, that we have seen ships and cities arise from human art and contrivance."

Hume laid a great deal of emphasis on the limitedness of our viewpoint. We, who are but a part of the universe, use our intelligence and thought to build cities and machines. And so we suppose that there must be a divine creator who used thought and intelligence to create the universe. But we and our creations are but a tiny aspect of the universe, and human thought and intelligence are just one of hundreds of known principles of activity. Is it legitimate, Hume asked, for us to suppose that the mechanism by which one small aspect of the universe rearranges little bits of wood and steel and dirt is the same mechanism by which *the entire universe* was originally created? We would be amused by an ignorant peasant supposing that the principles that govern the world economy are the same as those by which he runs his household. Yet we in effect suppose that the principles by which we build our houses and cities are those that govern the creation of the universe!

Further, even if we can liken the creation of the world to the building of a house or boat, there is this further problem, said Hume: If we survey a ship, we would be tempted to attribute a great deal of ingenuity to its builder, when in fact its builder may be a beef-brained clod who only copied an art that was perfected over the ages by hundreds of people working through a series of trials, mistakes, corrections, and gradual improvements. Can we be sure the world was not the result of a similar process of trial and error and even intermittent bungling, involving a multitude of lesser "creators"?

For that matter, Hume asked, is it even proper to liken the world to a ship or watch or machine or other human artifact? Is not the world arguably as much like a living organism as a machine? And are not living organisms produced by processes radically different from those by which human artifacts are made?

This, then, is the substance of Hume's complaints about the design argument. Given what seemed to him to be its several difficulties, Hume's own conclusion about the argument, and evidently about God, was just this: There is an apparent order in the universe, and this apparent order provides some slight evidence of a cause or causes bearing some remote analogy to human intelligence. But that is all the evidence warrants, Hume thought. The manifestation of order is no evidence whatsoever for the existence of the God worshiped by people.

A cosmological argument, in the version Hume examines, says that anything that exists must have a cause (or reason or explanation) that is different from itself. But because the series of causes cannot go to infinity, there must be a first uncaused cause, God. A variation of the basic argument allows that the causal series can go to infinity but still stands in need of an uncaused cause that causes the whole infinite series. In either case, the uncaused cause cannot *not* exist. Thus, the uncaused cause is a **necessary being.**

Hume's objections to these lines of argument are that, *first,* as far as we can make out, the universe may itself be "the necessarily existent being"; *second,* if you

Hume suggested that the atheists and true believers are not all that different in their views.

maintain that everything has a prior cause, it is *contradictory* also to maintain that there was a first cause; and *third,* if I explain the cause of each member of a series of things, there is no further need for an explanation of the *series itself* as if it were some *further* thing.

*A Verbal Dispute?*   Now, before leaving Hume, one other thought of his deserves mention. Hume had the startling idea that the dispute between theists and atheists might be only a verbal dispute. This was his reasoning:

Theists say that the universe was created by the divine will. But they concede that there is a great and immeasurable difference between the creative activity of the divine mind and mere human thought and its creative activity.

But what do atheists say? They concede that there is some original or fundamental principle of order in the universe, but they insist that this principle can bear only some remote analogy to everyday creative and generative processes, or to human intelligence.

Thus, atheist and theist are very close to saying the same thing!

The main difference between them seems to lie only in this, Hume said: The theist is most impressed by the necessity of there being or having been a fundamental principle of order and generation in the universe, whereas the atheist is most impressed by how wildly different such a principle must be from any creative activity with which we are familiar. But then the more pious the theist, the more he will emphasize the difference between divine intelligence and human intelligence; the more he will insist that the workings of God are incomprehensible to mere mortals. The more pious the theist, in short, the more he will be like the atheist!

## Kant

This brings us to **Immanuel Kant** (1724–1804), whose contribution to the philosophy of religion equals in importance his work in epistemology and ethics. Kant invented one of the most famous moral arguments for God's existence. But Kant's criticisms of traditional proofs of God have seemed to many commentators to be more cogent than his proof, and in any case they are among the most important criticisms in the literature.

According to Kant, there are only three (traditional) ways of proving God's existence, and none of them work.

***What Is Wrong with the Ontological Proof?***   First is the ontological argument. Remember that according to Anselm's version of the argument, God is the greatest being conceivable. Hence, if you suppose that God does not exist, you are supposing that the greatest being conceivable is not the greatest being conceivable, and that is nonsense. According to Descartes's version, God possesses all perfections, and because existence is a perfection, God exists.

Now we are sure that you will agree that there is something very sneaky about the ontological argument, in any version. It seems intuitively wrong, somehow; yet it is difficult to pin down exactly what the problem is.

Kant provided a criticism that withstood the test of time, though in recent years there have been challenges to it. What is wrong with the argument, Kant said, is that it assumes that *existence is a "predicate," that is, a characteristic or an attribute.* Because Anselm assumed that existence is a characteristic, he could argue that a being that lacked existence lacked an important characteristic and thus could not be the greatest being conceivable. Because Descartes assumed that existence is a characteristic, he could argue that God, who by definition possesses all perfections, necessarily possesses the characteristic of existence.

But existence, said Kant, is not a characteristic at all. Rather, it is a *precondition* of having characteristics. Is there any difference between a warm day and an *existing* warm day? If you state that the potato salad is salty, do you further characterize the salad if you state that it is salty *and exists*? If you tell the mechanic that your tire is flat, do you further enlighten him if you add that the tire also *exists*? The answer to all such questions, in Kant's view, is obviously "no." To say of something that it exists is not to characterize it: existence is not a predicate.

So to apply this lesson first to Descartes: Existence is *not* a perfection or any other kind of characteristic. Certainly, *if* there *is* a being that possesses all perfections, then God exists, for existence is a precondition of something's having any perfections at all. But this fact does not mean that God actually exists.

And to apply this lesson to Anselm: Existence is not a characteristic, and so it is not one that belongs to greatness. Certainly, *if* the greatest being conceivable exists, then God exists, because God by definition is that being, and something cannot possess any aspect of greatness without existing. But that fact does not mean that such a being exists.

If Kant had not written another word about God, what he said about the ontological argument would itself have secured his high rank in the philosophy of religion.

Our cars are all mechanically sound, come with a six-month written guarantee, and exist.

USED CARS

Kant argued that existence is not a characteristic and that you do not enlarge a description of a thing to say that it exists. Of course, you may wish to assert that something — God, say, or ghosts — exists, but that sort of assertion is not really a description, Kant would maintain.

***What Is Wrong with the Cosmological and Teleological Proofs?***   The second way of proving God's existence, according to Kant, is the cosmological argument, which, he asserts, reduces to this: If something exists, an absolutely necessary being must likewise exist. I, at least, exist. Therefore, an absolutely necessary being exists.

This is certainly a simple and streamlined version of the cosmological argument compared with the arguments set forth by Aquinas, Descartes, Leibniz, and Hume. Unfortunately, Kant, who generally did not try to make things easy for his reader, made up for this unusual lapse into simplicity and clarity by submitting the argument to several pages of exceedingly subtle and confusing analysis.

Kant's basic criticisms of the cosmological argument, however, are two: First, the argument really rests on the ontological argument. His explanation of why and how this is so is notoriously obscure, probably unsound, and let's just let it go. Second, and more important anyway, the argument employs a principle (that everything contingent has a cause) that has significance only in the *experienced* world. The argument then uses that principle, Kant maintained, to arrive at a conclusion that goes beyond experience. (Kant, as we tried to make clear in Chapter 7, believed that causality is a concept applicable only to things-as-experienced. Why Kant held this position is too complicated to repeat here, but his case against the cosmological argument rests on his being correct about causality, which some people are inclined to doubt.)

The third and final way of trying to prove God's existence, according to Kant, is the teleological argument, the argument that cites the purposiveness and harmonious adaptation of nature as proof of the divine designer. Kant's main criticism is that at best the argument proves only the existence of an *architect* who works with the matter of the world, and not a creator. A similar line of thinking was found in Hume, as we saw.

***Belief in God Rationally Justified***   Despite Kant's criticisms of the three traditional proofs for God's existence, Kant believed in God. Further, amazingly to some, he thought this belief is rationally justified for any moral agent. Here, as almost always, his thinking is complicated, but what he had in mind was this:

Although we do not have theoretical or metaphysical knowledge of God, although we cannot prove or demonstrate that God exists, we must view the world *as if* it were created by God. Why? Because, Kant said, only if we assume the existence of God can we believe that virtue will be rewarded with happiness. Virtue, Kant held, is worthiness to be happy and is the supreme good. But without believing in God, the virtuous individual cannot be certain that the happiness of which he is worthy will in fact be his or that, in general, a person's happiness will be proportionate to his moral worth.

Thus, in Kant's opinion, God's existence cannot be proved but can and must rationally be assumed by a moral agent. That God exists, Kant said, is a postulate of *practical* reason. This particular argument for assuming that God exists is another version of the moral argument that we first encountered with Aquinas.

## NINETEENTH-CENTURY PERSPECTIVES

In the nineteenth century we find striking departures from traditional thinking about God. Probably the least radical of these thinkers is the Anglican cardinal John Henry Newman.

## Newman

Few intellectuals have been as highly esteemed in their own time as **John Henry Newman** (1801–1890) was. Newman, deeply religious from his youth, had been ordained in the Church of England and was made vicar of St. Mary's, Oxford. But in early middle age he revised his views on Roman Catholicism and was received into the Roman Catholic Church, eventually becoming a cardinal and inspiring many other Anglicans to convert as well. Newman was a churchman, but he was also a philosopher.

Newman was much concerned with the differences between formal logic and actual real-life reasoning ("concrete" reasoning, he called it)—and especially with the principles that validate the latter. He came to believe that whenever we concern ourselves with concrete matters of fact, our conclusions may not have the status of logical certainties, but we can nevertheless attain certitude, as a state of mind, about them. In particular, he held, we can achieve certitude in our religious faith.

Now it is by virtue of our experience of *conscience,* according to Newman, that we find certitude about God. Conscience, he said, can be relied on exactly as much as we rely on memory or reason. And feelings of conscience lead us to affirm an intelligent being as their cause, he held. Conscience is a sense of responsibility and duty that points toward something beyond the realm of people, toward a Supreme Governor or Judge whose dictates we are ashamed or fear to violate and whose approval we seek. In short, in the experience of conscience we find ourselves undeniably *answerable* to an intelligence beyond ourselves.

Newman thus endorsed a moral argument for God, but it is rather unlike Kant's moral argument. According to Kant, to assume that one can act morally is to assume that there is justice; it is to assume, that is, that moral uprightness will be rewarded with happiness. And this in turn is to assume the existence of a God who ensures that there is justice. In other words, if what ought to be is, then God exists. The requirements of morality thus lead us to *postulate* God, according to Kant.

But according to Newman, we are simply unable to doubt God's existence, given the experience of conscience. Newman's proof is much more direct: That God exists is as indisputable as our awareness that we are answerable to him, and this awareness we find in the dictates of conscience.

## Kierkegaard

It is interesting to contrast Cardinal Newman's philosophy with that of the Danish philosopher **Søren Kierkegaard** (1813–1855), who lived about the same time. Neither philosopher thought that you could rationally prove that God exists. But the similarity between the two ends there.

For Kierkegaard, "to exist" is to be engaged in time and history. Because God is an eternal and immutable being, "existence" does not even apply to God. But God as Christ existed, for Kierkegaard. Christ, however, is a paradox that the human intellect cannot comprehend, for in Christ the immutable became changing, the eternal became temporal, and what is beyond history became historical.

In short, Kierkegaard thought that God is beyond the grasp of reason and that the idea that God came to us as a man in the person of Jesus is intellectually absurd. Yet, at the same time, Kierkegaard's primary mission was to show what it is to be a Christian, and he was himself totally committed to Christianity. How can this be?

First, the notion that we can sit back and weigh objectively the evidence about God's existence pro and contra, that we can conduct an impartial investigation of the issue and arrive at the "truth," is totally rejected by Kierkegaard. He would not have bothered reading this chapter.

In fact, Kierkegaard mocks the whole idea of objective truth as giving meaning to life. Truth, he said, is subjective. Truth lies not in *what* you believe, but in *how you live*. Truth is passionate commitment. For example, think of a person who worships the "true" God but does so merely as a matter of routine, without passion or commitment. Compare this person with one who worships a mere idol but does so with the infinite commitment of his soul. In fact, said Kierkegaard, "The one prays in truth to God though he worships an idol; the other prays falsely to the true God, and hence worships in fact an idol."

Second, Kierkegaard rejected completely the Aristotelian idea that the essential attribute of humans is their capacity to reason. For Kierkegaard, the most important attribute of man is not thought but *will*. Man is a being that *makes choices*.

But if truth is not objective, then there are no external principles or criteria that are objectively valid and against which one might judge one's choices. How, then, are we to choose, if there are no objective, rational criteria and we have only our own judgment to rely on? This problem—the problem of knowing how and what to choose in the absence of objective truth—became, after Kierkegaard, the central problem of existentialism.

## God's Foreknowledge and Free Will

God supposedly knows everything. So whatever you did, he knew before you did it that you would do it. Did you sleep late this morning? God knew that you would.

And that means that you could not have *not* slept late this morning because God knew that you would sleep late. And if you could not have not slept late, then in what sense did you sleep late of your own free will? See the problem? It seems that the view that God knows everything conflicts with the idea that you have free will.

This problem is sometimes dismissed by beginning philosophy students as "merely verbal" or as "easily solved." If this is true, it will come as news to the heavyweight philosophers and theologians who have grappled with it, including Paul, Augustine, Luther, Calvin, and others. It is because they saw the logical implications of crediting God with omniscience (all-knowingness) that Calvinists (followers of the great sixteenth-century Protestant theologian John Calvin), for example, believed that God must preordain who will be saved and who will be damned.

Kierkegaard's answer is that we must commit ourselves totally to God. Salvation can be had only through a **leap of faith,** through a nonintellectual, passionate, "infinite" commitment to Christianity. "Faith constitutes a sphere all by itself, and every misunderstanding of Christianity may at once be recognized by its transforming it into a doctrine, transferring it to the sphere of the intellectual."

What Kierkegaard said must not be confused with what earlier Christian thinkers had maintained. Earlier Christian thinkers had said that faith precedes understanding and had held that you must have faith in God before rational thought about him can begin. But thinkers such as Augustine and Anselm had still looked for, and had fully expected there to be, rational grounds for confirming what they already accepted by faith. Kierkegaard, in contrast, thought that no such rational grounds exist: God is an intellectual absurdity.

Further, he held that rational grounds for believing in God, if there were any, would actually be *incompatible* with having faith. "If I wish to preserve myself in faith I must constantly be intent upon holding fast to the *objective uncertainty* [of God]," he said. The objective uncertainty of God, for Kierkegaard, is thus *essential* to a true faith in him. Only if there is objective uncertainty, he wrote, can "[I] remain out upon the deep, over seventy thousand fathoms of water, still preserving my faith."

### Nietzsche

"God is dead," said Nietzsche. By this infamous remark, **Friedrich Nietzsche** (1844–1900) did not mean that God once existed and now no longer does. He meant that all people with an ounce of intelligence would now perceive that there is no intelligent plan to the universe or rational order in it: they would now understand that there is no reason why things happen one way and not another and that the harmony and order we imagine to exist in the universe is merely pasted on by the human mind.

Nietzsche, however, would have regarded very few people as having this required ounce of intelligence, and he in fact had a way of denigrating everyone in sight. For the mass of people, Nietzsche thought, God certainly is not dead. But these people, in Nietzsche's opinion, are pathetic wretches governed by a

## Religion: Illusion with a Future

Religion, according to the founder of psychoanalysis, Sigmund Freud (1856–1939), is an exercise in mass delusion and serves mainly to keep people in a state of psychological infantilism. Religion is wish-fulfillment; it offers up the "figure of an enormously exalted father" who reassures us as our own fathers did. The infallible and omnipotent father in heaven assures us that there is meaning and purpose in life and that all will be well in the end. However, although religion enables us to retain our status as children throughout our lives, it is a dangerous illusion. Religion intimidates intelligence with its demands for unconditional submission to inscrutable laws and keeps us from distinguishing between fact and wishful thinking. It does this even when philosophers and theologians try to salvage the illusion by redefining God as an "impersonal, shadowy and abstract principle."

Sometimes belief in religion is fostered by the psychological feeling of the oneness of everything. Such "oceanic feelings," according to Freud, are just a recurrence of the limitless narcissism typical of early childhood. Freud thought human beings would be happier if they retained a modicum of reality in their thinking and cultivated their own gardens, as Voltaire had suggested.

worldview inculcated by religion, science, and philosophy, a worldview that in Nietzsche's opinion makes them feeble losers who are motivated mainly by resentment. They view the world as a rational, law-governed place and adhere to a slave morality that praises the man who serves his fellow creatures with meekness and self-sacrifice.

In Nietzsche's opinion, the negative morality of these pitiful slaves—the mass of humankind, ordinary people—must be reevaluated and replaced by life-affirming values. The new morality will be based on the development of a new kind of human being, whom Nietzsche calls the "overman" or "superman" (*Übermensch*). Such a one not only accepts life in all its facets, including all its pain, but also makes living into an art. Among the forerunners of the overman, Nietzsche cites Alexander the Great and Napoleon.

Nietzsche's thesis that there is no God and its apparent corollary that there are no absolute and necessary criteria of right and wrong were accepted by such twentieth-century existentialist philosophers as Albert Camus and Jean-Paul Sartre. For these thinkers, *the* fundamental problem of philosophy is how to live one's life, given the absence of absolutely valid standards by which to evaluate one's choices and decisions.

Nietzsche, Kierkegaard, and some existentialists would all have agreed that the various rational discussions about God's existence to which this chapter is devoted are impotent and meaningless. (However, for an interesting alternative view, you might like to read the box "Religion: Illusion with a Future," which discusses the views of Sigmund Freud.)

## James

**William James** published his first major work, *The Will to Believe and Other Essays*, in 1897. By the year 1900 there was a marked increase in agnosticism and antagonism between the religious view of the world as a divinely created paradise planned for the sake of human spiritual growth and the supposedly scientific view of the cosmos as a blind churning of material particles in accordance with physical laws. For the past two hundred years the blind-churning view had become more and more congenial to Western intellectuals. Around mid-century, Darwin had explained how the origin of species need not be divine (see the box "Creation or Evolution?"), and Karl Marx had pronounced religion to be the opium of the people. If the power of Hume's and Kant's reasoning did not force philosophers to take seriously their criticisms of the old proofs of God, the spirit of the times did. Before the end of the century, Friedrich Nietzsche, as we have seen, could proclaim that God was dead.

But God was not, and is not, dead for everyone. In fact, the question of God's existence was at the time, and still is, for very many (1) a *live* issue and furthermore (2) a *momentous* one. For William James it is both. It is also, in addition, according to James, (3) *forced,* which means that you cannot suspend judgment in the matter. For James, to profess agnosticism and to pretend to suspend judgment is in fact "backing the field against the religious hypothesis" (that is, deciding against God).

James argued for deciding the issue of God's existence in favor of God. He began his argument, not a simple one, by noting that "*our nonintellectual nature does influence our convictions.*" Indeed, usually our convictions are *determined* by our nonintellectual nature, he maintained. Rarely does pure reason settle our opinion. What settles our opinion usually is our wishing and willing and sentimental preferences, our fears and hopes, prejudices and emotions, and even the pressure of our friends. It is our "passional nature" that settles our opinion, he said.

Sometimes we even deliberately will what we believe, James held. Need proof that he is correct? Probably you would prefer not to accept claims that are based on pitifully insufficient evidence (we hope). So when someone asserts something that is based on insufficient evidence, what do you do? You *try not to believe it.* And often you are successful in not accepting the poorly supported claim. When you are, then have you not in fact *willed* yourself not to accept what the person has asserted? Your will, your desire not to accept unsupported claims, has influenced your beliefs.

Of course, if you are like most of us, you may find yourself accepting what the person says anyway. But if you consider the matter carefully, is your acceptance not also a case of something other than cold reason influencing your beliefs? You may *hope* that what the person has said is true. You may simply *want* to believe it, *despite* its having been poorly supported. If so, your hope that what has been said is true has simply *overcome* your desire not to accept unsupported claims. So here again your "passional nature" has settled your opinion.

Having argued that our nonintellectual nature influences our opinions, James next distinguished between the *two commandments* of rational thinkers. These are

1. to believe the truth
2. to avoid errors

Some individuals, James noted, favor (2) over (1): they would rather avoid errors than find the truth. "Better go without belief forever than believe a falsehood" is the creed dictated to them by their passional nature: better dead than misled. But favoring (2) over (1) is not James's creed. There are worse things than falling into

# Creation or Evolution?

The publication in 1859 of Charles Darwin's *On the Origin of Species by Means of Natural Selection; or, the Preservation of Favoured Races in the Struggle for Life* (usually referred to as *On the Origin of Species*) provoked responses from within Catholicism and conservative Protestantism. Pope Pius IX in 1870 declared evolution a heresy (though in 1996, in a message to the Pontifical Academy of Sciences, Pope John Paul II observed that while the occurrence of evolution is more than a theory, "theories of evolution which, in accordance with the philosophies inspiring them, consider the mind as emerging from the forces of living matter . . . are incompatible with the truth about man"). In 1874 Princeton theologian Charles Hodge, a Presbyterian, asked, "What is Darwinism?" and answered, "It is atheism."

But another contemporary of Darwin's, American botanist Asa Gray (1810–1888), was not so certain. Gray, who described himself as both a Darwinian and a convinced Christian, found room in Darwin's depiction of natural selection for the view that God was the ultimate designer of nature; Hodge himself claimed Darwinism was contrary to the Christian faith only insofar as it denied the existence of purpose in the universe.

Historian George Marsden, writing in 1984, found that twenty years after the publication of *On the Origin of Species,* Bible-believing American Protestant scientists and even conservative theologians did not make opposition to all forms of evolution a necessary test of faith. But such reconciliationist positions began to lose favor in the evangelical community after the Scopes "monkey trial," July 10–21, 1925, in Dayton, Tennessee. Though high school teacher John Scopes was found guilty of teaching evolution in the classroom (and fined $100), defense attorney Clarence Darrow held up to public ridicule the religious views of William Jennings Bryan, the prosecutor.

Revolutionary changes were sweeping American culture: surging immigration meant a breakdown of a common worldview (if one ever existed), critical biblical studies from Germany undermined the perceived authority of the Christian Bible, and a growing secularism in society loosened the ties of science and faith. Many fundamentalists, betrayed by an academy that no longer acknowledged revealed truth, retreated to a Christian subculture. Bible schools flourished, and many taught human origins from a perspective dubbed "creation-science."

Contemporary defenders include John D. Morris of the Institute for Creation Research (ICR) in El Cajon, California, who wrote in a 1992 newsletter article that evolution "embraces strict naturalism, an anti-God philosophy, and results in a denial of the major doctrines of Scripture. . . . If no supernatural agency has been at work throughout history, then creation is dead. But if evolutionists even allow a spark of supernatural design in history, then evolution is dead, for evolution necessarily relies on solely natural processes."

In 1999 the Kansas State Board of Education, reflecting the views of a conservative majority, wrote new state science standards that ushered creationism back into mainstream debate. The board mandated the teaching of so-called microevolution (changes within species) as illustrative of the working of natural selection. But the teaching of macroevolution (the origin of new organs or species) was made optional at the district level. In the revised document, science was no longer defined as that human activity that seeks *natural* explanations of what can be observed but, rather, one that seeks *logical* explanations. Proponents of the changes claimed victory for the renewed practice of legitimate science unencumbered by naturalistic (that is, materialist and, by definition, antisupernatural) assumptions.

Two years later, however, on February 14, 2001, after an election that changed its composition, the Kansas School Board reversed its earlier course. Evolution was reinstated "as a broad, unifying theoretical framework in biology" and would likely have a prominent place in the development of future statewide science tests. (The new document did note that while students were required to understand evolution, they were not required to believe it.)

While the board's decision appeared to be a loss for creationists, another development in the 1990s brought to the wider culture a more sophisticated debate over the nature of explanation. That devel-

*(continued)*

# Creation or Evolution? *(continued)*

opment was the publication of three controversial books: *Darwin On Trial* (first published in 1991) by Phillip E. Johnson (a graduate of Harvard University who has taught law at University of California, Berkeley, for more than three decades); *Darwin's Black Box: The Biochemical Challenge to Evolution* (1996) by Lehigh University biochemist Michael J. Behe; and *Intelligent Design: The Bridge Between Science and Theology* (1999) by William A. Dembski, holder of a doctorate in mathematics from the University of Chicago and a doctorate in philosophy from the University of Illinois at Chicago, whose more technical treatment of the subject had been published by Cambridge University Press the year before.

Johnson, Behe, and Dembski, leaders of what has come to be called the Intelligent Design movement, rejected the "young earth" position of ICR in favor of a more academically engaged critique of Darwinian foundations. In an essay published in the *New York Times* in 1996, Behe wrote that the theory of evolution founders in explaining cellular development. "Many cellular systems are what I term 'irreducibly complex.' That means the system needs several components before it can work properly. An everyday example of irreducible complexity is a mousetrap, built of several pieces (platform, hammer, spring and so on). Such a system probably cannot be put together in a Darwinian manner, gradually improving its function. You can't catch a mouse with just the platform and then catch a few more by adding the spring. All the pieces have to be in place before you catch any mice."

For Dembski, irreducible complexity is a specific case of a more general understanding of how to detect intelligent, as opposed to mere natural, causes: "Whenever we infer design, we must establish three things: *contingency, complexity* and *specification.* Contingency ensures that the object in question is not the result of an automatic and therefore unintelligent process that had no choice in its production. Complexity ensures that the object is not so simple that it can readily be explained by chance. Finally, specification ensures that the object exhibits the type of pattern characteristic of intelligence."

This pattern, he adds, has to be "detachable" from the particular set of data. Given a set of scrambled numbers, any mathematician could develop a formula to generate those numbers. But the pattern, the formula, is not detachable; it uniquely applies only to that set of numbers. But a string of numbers such as 011011100 . . . can be broken into the binary pattern 0, 1, 10, 11, 100, . . . (that is, 1, 2, 3, 4 . . .) that exhibits a specifiable pattern that is meaningful apart from that set of numbers; if the set is complex enough, and not the result of an automatic generating process, one could infer design or intelligence produced the sequence. Dembski argues that the same procedure is used in the Search for Extraterrestrial Life project in its analysis of far distant electromagnetic emissions. Numbers aside, however, the question Dembski must answer is whether the genetic code itself meets his design inference criteria.

Evolutionary biologist Richard Dawkins, in *The Blind Watchmaker* (1986) and other works, argues that any appearance of purpose in biological systems is merely the result of time and chance. "To 'tame' chance means to break down the very improbable into less improbable small components arranged in series. No matter how improbable it is that an X could have arisen from a Y in a single step, it is always possible to conceive of a series of infinitesimally graded intermediates between them. However improbable a large-scale change may be, smaller changes are less improbable."

Johnson, ever the political scourge of the evolutionists, also focuses on a critique of evolutionism's materialist assumptions, what he calls "methodological naturalism." The chemical or physical laws of nature, he writes, "produce simple repetitive order, and chance produces meaningless disorder. When combined, law and chance work against each other to prevent the emergence of a meaningful sequence. In all human experience, only intelligent agency can write an encyclopedia or computer program." Dawkins's blind watchmaker (natural selection and mutation) cannot, Johnson insists, create complex *new* genetic information.

Yet the issue of complexity seems a red herring in the inference of intelligent design. Dembski's analysis requires the presence of complexity to eliminate chance occurrence; Dawkins counters that chance can produce marvelous complexities.

It is also the case that noncomplex patterns can carry meaning, such as a pile of rocks indicating a grave site, which Dembski's formula overlooks. The attempt by Dembski and Dawkins to find the presence or absence of purpose based solely on empirical examination seems a fruitless quest if the status of materialism has not first been established. And that's a philosophical question.

Johnson presents a version of the claim that naturalism is self-refuting. (The argument was popularized by the British writer C. S. Lewis and adopted by the American analytic philosopher Alvin Plantinga.) He asks sarcastically, "If unthinking matter causes the thoughts the materialists *don't* like, then what causes the thoughts they *do* like?" This takes us back to the problem of explanation. The materialist must explain human reason, and indeed the existence of anything at all, in terms of "unthinking matter." If for Dawkins the appearance of purpose in evolution is merely an illusion, then what is the status of purposive human reason? If that, too, is an illusion, then there is no good reason to accept the argument. If it is not illusion, how can Dawkins explain the rise of genuine purpose or meaning from a purposeless flow of cause and effect? For those in the intelligent design movement, the most important metaphysical question, "Why is there something rather than nothing?" must go unanswered by the scientific materialist.

The same point is made in a joke told about a group of super-scientists who probed the secrets of life. One day they challenged the Deity in a contest to make a human being. "We can make a human out of the dust of the earth, just like you did!" they said, as they began gathering their materials. "Hold on!" exclaimed the Deity. "Get your own dirt!"

—Dan Barnett

error, he said. In some cases, he argued, it is best to regard "the chase for truth as paramount, and the avoidance of error as secondary."

Consider moral questions where you must either act or not act and cannot wait for objective, definitive proof that one choice is right. In such cases, it is not possible to suspend judgment because *not* to act is itself to make a judgment. In such cases, you make the best decision you can. Furthermore, according to James, it is *legitimate* to do this, even though you have no guarantee that your decision is correct.

And it is the same in religious matters, he said. At least it is the same if religion for you is a live and momentous issue that you cannot resolve through intellect alone. If it is, you cannot escape the issue by remaining skeptical and waiting for more information. To remain skeptical, James said, is tantamount to saying that it is better to yield to the fear of being in error than to yield to the hope that religion is true.

In fact, James argued, when it comes to religion, the other way is better: it is better to yield to the hope that all of it may be true than to give way to the fear of being in error. If you permit the fear of error to rule you and say to yourself, "Avoid error at any cost!" then you will withhold assent to religious beliefs. Doing so will, of course, *protect* you from being in error — if the religious beliefs are incorrect. But if you withhold your assent to religious beliefs, then you will also *lose the benefits* that come from accepting those beliefs. And it is worse, James thought, to lose the benefits than to gain the protection from erring.

Further, if the religious beliefs are *true* but the evidence for them is insufficient, then the policy "Avoid error at any cost!" effectively cuts you off from an

## PROFILE: William James (1842–1910)

Few philosophers have been better writers than William James, whose catchy phrases gave life and succulence to even the driest philosophical subjects. James had a knack for words, and he was able to state complex ideas with easy elegance. This might be expected because James was the older brother of Henry James, the great American novelist.

The James children were raised by their wealthy and eccentric theologian father in an intellectually stimulating atmosphere that promoted their mental development. The Jameses benefited from diverse educational experiences in several schools both in America and in Europe and were largely free to pursue their own interests and develop their own capacities. They became refined and cosmopolitan.

William James had wide-ranging interests. Though fascinated with science, he decided, at age eighteen, to try to become a painter. But he was also wise enough to see very soon that his artistic urge exceeded his ability.

So James went off to Harvard and studied science. Then he entered the college's medical school, though he did not intend to practice medicine, and in his late twenties he received his medical degree. A few years later, he joined the Harvard faculty as a lecturer on anatomy and physiology and continued to teach at Harvard until 1907. From 1880 on, he was a member of the Harvard department of philosophy and psychology. You should not think that James got interested in philosophy all of a sudden. He had always been fond of the subject and tended to give a philosophical interpretation to scientific questions.

James suffered from emotional crises until he was able to resolve the question of free will and to answer the compelling arguments for determinism. Around 1870, he found in the ideas of the French philosopher Charles Renouvier philosophical justification for believing in free will, and with it, apparently, the cure to his episodes of emotional paralysis.

In 1890, James published his famous *Principles of Psychology*, thought by many to be his major work. Equally important, from a purely philosophical standpoint, was his *The Will to Believe and Other Essays in Popular Philosophy* (1897). In this work is James's solution to the problem of free will, in the essay, "The Dilemma of Determinism." Other important works include *The Varieties of Religious Experience* (1902), *Pragmatism* (1907), *A Pluralistic Universe* (1909), *The Meaning of Truth* (1909), *Some Problems in Philosophy* (1911), and *Essays in Radical Empiricism* (1912).

William James was perhaps the most famous American intellectual of his time. Yet today some philosophers think of him as a lightweight—a popularizer of philosophical issues who failed to make a substantial contribution to technical philosophy (whatever that is). He is thought to bear the same relation to Hume or Kant, say, that Tchaikovsky bears to Mozart or Bach, the philosophical equivalent of the composer who only cranks out pretty melodies. But this is all a mistake. The discerning reader will find in James a great depth of insight.

opportunity to make friends with God. Thus, in James's opinion, the policy "Avoid error at all cost!"—when applied to religion—is a policy that keeps you from accepting certain propositions even if those propositions are really true, and that means that it is an *irrational* policy.

In short, even as a rational thinker you will be influenced by your passional nature. Thus, you will be led to give way either to the hope that the belief in God, and associated religious beliefs, is true or to the fear that if you accept these beliefs, you will be in error. Because this is the case, it is better to give way to the hope.

James stressed that he was *not* saying that you should believe what, as he put it, "you know ain't true." His strategy applies, he said, only to *momentous* and *living* issues that cannot be resolved by the intellect itself. It applies only to issues like God's existence.

James's philosophy was a species of pragmatism, according to which, at least in its Jamesian version, the true is "only the expedient in our way of thinking." Confronted with competing views or theories, both of which are more or less equally supportable rationally, you choose the viewpoint that works most beneficially. Applying the same strategy to the question of whether we have free will, James focused not directly on the question itself but, rather, on the outcomes that attend acceptance of the alternative viewpoints. Acceptance of determinism is unworkable, James believed, because it entails never regretting what happens (what happened had to happen, according to determinism, so it is illogical to feel that it should not have happened). Thus, acceptance of determinism is inconsistent with the practices of moral beings, who perceive themselves as making genuine choices that can affect the world for better or for worse.

## TWENTIETH-CENTURY PERSPECTIVES

James's reasoning elicited much criticism. Skeptics and believers both took issue with it. Skeptics thought James had elevated wishful thinking to the status of proof, and believers questioned James's implicit assumption that God's existence cannot be established. Still others said that belief grounded in James's way was not the uncompromising and unqualified faith in God demanded by religion. From their perspective, James's belief in God amounted to a gamble akin to **Pascal's wager** (see box) rather than to true religious acceptance of God.

James in any event takes us into the twentieth century, and we shall now consider two twentieth-century discussions of God's existence. The first is something like an argument that God does not exist, but in actuality it is an argument that the whole issue is pretty meaningless to begin with.

### God and Logical Positivism

In the late 1920s a group of philosophers, mathematicians, and scientists, led by Moritz Schlick, a philosopher at the University of Vienna, set forth a group of ideas known as **logical positivism.** A central tenet of this **Vienna Circle,** and of logical positivism, as we saw in Chapter 9, is the **verifiability principle,** according to which the meaning of a proposition is the experience you would have to have to know that it is true. What does it mean to say, "The sprinkler is on"? Well, to find out if that proposition is true, you would have to look out the window or go out into the yard or otherwise do some checking. The experience required to do the checking is what the proposition means, according to the verifiability principle.

What this principle entails is that a pronouncement that is not verifiable has no factual meaning. Take the remark "The sprinkler stopped working due to fate."

## Pascal's Wager

The French mathematician and philosopher Blaise Pascal (1623–1662) is famous, among other reasons, for his wager-argument for God. Either God exists or he does not. By believing that he does exist, you lose nothing if he does not and you gain a lot, namely, happiness and eternal life, if he does. So believing that God exists is a prudent wager; you will not lose anything, and you might gain much.

James denied that he was offering a version of Pascal's wager in his argument for the existence of God. You may wish to consider whether his denial is warranted.

What kind of checking would you do to see if this is true? There is no experience a person might have that would verify this remark. Therefore, it is factually meaningless, the logical positivists would say.

Of course, some propositions are true by virtue of what their words mean: for example, "You are older than everyone who is younger than you." Such *analytic propositions,* as they are called, are rendered true by definition rather than by experience, according to the logical positivists. But the proposition "The sprinkler stopped working due to fate" is not like that. It is not an analytic proposition, so it has to be verifiable in experience if it is to have factual meaning. And because it is not, it does not.

So, according to the logical positivists, the good many philosophical assertions from metaphysics, epistemology, and ethics that are neither analytic nor verifiable are factually meaningless. These assertions may perhaps express emotional sentiments, but they are neither true nor false. Rudolph Carnap (1891–1970), one of the most famous members of the Vienna Circle, even declared, "We reject *all* philosophical questions, whether of Metaphysics, Ethics or Epistemology."

The verifiability principle has its difficulties, the most famous of which is that the principle itself is not verifiable and thus must either be factually meaningless or a mere analytic verbal truth. Perhaps more important, at least to the logical positivists, is that even assuming that the principle is not factually meaningless, what it actually says is unclear. Does it require that a proposition must be *conclusively* verifiable? But in that case, universal claims, such as those that state the laws of physics, would be factually meaningless. And if absolute verifiability is not required, to what extent is partial verifiability required?

Today few philosophers would call themselves logical positivists. But most philosophers would still maintain that *empirical* or *factual* propositions must in *some* sense and to *some* extent be verifiable by experience.

So what, then, about assertions such as "God exists" or "God loves us"? These look like factual propositions. But are they in any sense verifiable? A reading by Antony Flew at the end of the chapter addresses the issue from a positivist perspective. Logical positivists, who dismissed the utterance "God exists" as meaningless, were usually perceived as denying God's existence. But were they? A person who denies God exists believes God does not exist. But the positivist position was not that God does not exist. It was that the utterance "God exists" is *meaningless.* Equally, they held, the proposition "God does not exist" is meaningless too. The debate between believers and doubters, they maintained, cannot be settled by sense experience and is therefore stuff and nonsense.

## The Big Bang

The view now accepted by most scientists is that the universe is an explosion, known as the **Big Bang.** Unlike other explosions, the Big Bang does not expand outward into space, like a dynamite or bomb explosion, nor does it have a duration in external time, as do all other explosions, because all space and all time are located within it. The beginning of the Big Bang is the beginning of space and time and of matter and energy, and it is, in fact, the beginning of our expanding universe.

The most prevalent view among the qualified experts who have an opinion on the matter is that it is impossible to know what transpired in the Big Bang before $10^{-43}$ seconds after zero time, when the Big Bang began. But for various reasons that we need not go into here, most of these experts do apparently believe that there was a zero time, that the universe did have an absolute beginning, that there was a first physical event.

Now either the first physical event, assuming that such a thing did take place, is explainable or it is not. On one hand, it is difficult to believe that the first physical event has no explanation, for that amounts to saying that the entire universe, with its incredible size and complexity, was just a chance occurrence, a piece of good luck. But on the other hand, if the first physical event is explicable, then it would seem that the explanation must refer to some sort of nonphysical phenomenon, which certainly could be called "God."

Thus, the Big Bang theory, if true—and there seems to be much reason for supposing that it is true—may require philosophers to make a hard choice between an unexplainable universe and one explainable only by reference to something nonphysical.

## Mary Daly: The Unfolding of God

An entirely different line of thinking about God is evident in what contemporary feminist scholar **Mary Daly** said on the subject in *Beyond God the Father* (1973).

The biblical and popular image of God as a *great father in heaven,* Daly wrote, a father who rewards and punishes according to his mysterious and seemingly arbitrary will, arose in patriarchal societies. Furthermore, according to Daly, the image serves patriarchal society by making mechanisms for the oppression of women seem right and fitting. "If God in 'his' heaven is a father ruling 'his' people, then it is in the 'nature' of things and according to divine plan and the order of the universe that society be male-dominated." Given the biblical and popular image of God, "the husband dominating his wife represents God himself." "If God is male, then the male is God."

This image of God, as Lord and Father, which has been sustained "by the usual processes of producing plausibility such as preaching and religious indoctrination," perpetuates the artificial polarization of human qualities into the traditional sexual stereotypes, Daly maintained. This image of the person in authority and the popular understanding of "his" role continually renew the eternal masculine stereotypes. They also nourish and justify domination and manipulation, both toward persons and toward the environment. They perpetuate the eternal female stereotypes of emotionalism, passivity, self-abnegation, and the like.

Of course, a defender of the traditional image of God will probably protest that God is popularly conceived also as love. But, according to Mary Daly, the concept of God as love is split with the image of the "vengeful God who represents his chosen people." This split has perpetuated a double standard of behavior. God, she

Mary Daly

wrote, is like Vito Corleone of *The Godfather*, a "marriage of tenderness and vio-lence blended in the patriarchal ideal." Given this image, worshipers feel justified in being intolerant. Thus, we should not be surprised by the numerous examples of fanatical believers who cruelly persecute "those outside the sacred circle." Nor should we be surprised when those who are anointed by society—scientists and leaders, for example—are given the blessings of priests for inventing and using napalm and the like to perpetrate atrocities.

Daly conceded that the conception of the Supreme Being as controlling the world according to his plan and "keeping humans in a state of infantile subjuga-tion" has declined among more sophisticated thinkers. But the image of God as Superfather in heaven endures in and permeates the thought of even sophisticated thinkers who can speak of God as spirit and in the same breath refer to "him," using one-sex symbolism for the human relationship to God. With rare exception, she argued, god-language is fixated on maleness (see the box "God Is Coming, and She Is Furious").

Now when Daly's view is compacted as it is here, it seems like an angry and exaggerated diatribe. But Daly countered that it would surely be unrealistic *not* to believe that the instruments for symbolism and communication, which include the whole theological tradition in world religions, have been formulated by males un-der the conditions of patriarchy. It is therefore "inherent in these symbolic and lin-guistic structures that they serve the purposes of patriarchal social arrangements." If further proof is needed, one need merely consider (she said) the blatant misog-ynism of religious "authorities" from Augustine to Aquinas, Luther, Knox, and Barth, which has "simply been ignored or dismissed as trivial."

## God Is Coming, and She Is Furious

So says the bumper sticker.

We speak of God as "he," and there is no doubt that most people who believe in God think of God as, in some sense or another, a male.

But in what sense is God a male? Certainly not in the sense that he possesses male genetic or anatomic features. And it seems doubtful that the qualities we attribute to him are uniquely male. For example, God, it is said, is knowing, loving, caring. But these are not uniquely male characteristics.

Even the qualities associated with God when he is viewed as like an earthly king or emperor are not uniquely male qualities. Yes, all kings are males. But queens too can and have functioned as beneficent, just, powerful, and wise rulers. And the concept of God as the creator of the heavens and earth—that

concept seems to call to mind nonhuman properties as much as anything else.

So our custom of speaking of God in the masculine voice is largely honorific. We honor God by speaking and thinking of him as a male: God is the best there is; therefore, God is not female or neuter.

But if we think we honor God by referring to him as "he," then that fact implies that we think there is something inferior about not being a male. If God is defined as male, everything outside maleness is automatically inferior. For this reason, various feminist philosophers have been more than casually interested in the question, Why is God thought to be a male?—and in the possible harmful social consequences of our internalized ideas about **God's gender.**

---

The problem, then, Daly said, is how to transform "the collective imagination so that this distortion of the human aspiration to transcendence loses its credibility." The question is how to "cut away the Supreme Phallus": "God"—the word, the image—must be *castrated*.

This change, Daly thought, must and will be accomplished by the liberation in women's thought. The women's movement is destined to overthrow the oppressive elements in traditional theism; women are to be the bearers of existential courage in society, she argued. Women's confrontation with the "structured evil of patriarchy" implies the liberation of all human beings, a new phase in the quest for God.

However, this confrontation involves much more than simply tinkering with language, giving "God" a linguistic facelift or transsexual operation, changing "him" to "her." Eventually, in all probability, the movement will generate a new language of transcendence, a whole new semantic field, a whole new meaning context. Why, indeed, Daly wrote, must "God" even be a *noun*? Why not a verb—the "most active and dynamic verb of all," the "Verb of Verbs," the verb infinitely more personal than a mere static noun, the verb that conveys that God is "Be-ing"? "God," as an intransitive verb, she wrote, would not be conceived as an object—which implies limitation—for God as Be-ing is contrasted only with nonbeing.

Why must the confrontation with "the structured evil of patriarchy" go beyond mere tinkering with the language used to talk about God? To stop at that level, she wrote, would be to trivialize the "deep problem of human becoming in women."

And just what *is* the "deep problem of becoming"? It is a striving toward psychic wholeness, toward self-realization, toward self-transcendence—becoming who we really are. This becoming of women requires existential courage, Daly wrote, to confront the experience of *nothingness*. It is a "radical confrontation" with nothingness. We are all threatened by nonbeing, she wrote, and the only solution is self-actualization—not denial of self. An example of such denial of self provided by Daly is the woman who "singlemindedly accepts the role of housewife." This individual "may to some extent avoid the experience of nothingness, but she also avoids a fuller participation in being which would be her only real security." "Submerged in such a role, she cannot achieve a breakthrough to creativity."

Becoming who one really is means turning one's back on "the pseudo-reality offered by patriarchy" and, by that act, affirming "I am." It means facing the threat of nonbeing with the courage to be — facing the anxieties of losing job, friends, social approval, and health. It also involves a "profound interrelationship with other finite beings," as *all* finite beings participate in the power of being.

It might appear, Daly wrote, that the women's revolution should just go about its business without worrying about God. But doing this, she thought, would be a mistake. A sustained effort toward self-transcendence requires keeping alive in one's consciousness ultimate transcendence — that is, God. "Whatever authentic power we have is derived from participation in ultimate reality." The women's revolution must, therefore, ultimately be religious. It must reach "outward and inward toward the God beyond and beneath the gods who have stolen our identity."

According to Daly, three false "demons dressed as God" especially need expurgation: the God of "explanation," who legitimizes suffering as due to God's will; God the Judge, whose chief activity lies in issuing after-death rewards and promises compensation for women's subjugation in this life; and, closely related, God the Judge of Sin, who maintains "false consciences and self-destructive guilt feelings." This last god enforces the rules of the patriarchal game (and is most blatant in arch-conservative religions, Daly wrote).

In the absence of false gods, women are able to experience *presence*, Daly maintained, the presence of a power of being, "which both is and is not yet."

The widening of experience called for by Daly obviously is not merely a matter of becoming equal to men in "patriarchal space." Nor is it a struggle "over who will be forced into the position of It." "It is only when the subject is brought to a recognition of the other's damaged but never totally destroyed subjectivity as equal to his/her own, having basically the same potential and aspiration to transcendence, that a qualitatively new way of being in the world and toward God can emerge."

Does this seem angry? From Daly's perspective, women are dealing with "demonic power relationships" and "structured evil"; therefore, rage is *required* as a positive creative force. Anger, she wrote, "can trigger and sustain movement from the experience of nothingness to recognition of participation in being." According to Daly,

> When women take positive steps to move out of patriarchal space and time, there is a surge of new life. I would analyze this as participation in God the Verb who cannot be broken down simply into past, present, and future time, since God is form-destroying, form-creating, transforming power that makes all things new.

## Who Needs Reasons for Believing in God?

For a belief to be rational, must we have supporting evidence for its truth? Maybe not, if the belief is a **basic belief,** a belief that is not inferred from evidence or from other beliefs but, rather, itself provides the rational foundation from which other beliefs are derived. For example, it seems rational to believe that there is an external world, that the past existed, and that other people have minds. Yet do we believe these things on the basis of evidence? On the contrary (it might be argued), we accept these beliefs just straight out and without evidence. Further, it is because we accept these things that we can even talk of evidence and rational inference in the first place. For example, unless we assume there was a past, the "evidence" we have that the car *now* has a flat because it ran over a nail does not make any sense — because without a past, there was no past for the car to have done anything.

Contemporary analytic philosopher **Alvin Plantinga** [PLAN-tin-guh] (1932–   ) has argued that the theist may accept the belief in God as a "basic belief," a belief that it is rational to hold without supporting evidence and that is foundational for the entire system of the theist's beliefs. Rationally speaking, the theist has the right, Plantinga suggests, to *start from* belief in God. The belief need not be an *end product* of justification and inference.

Interested? An easy-to-read essay by Plantinga titled "Advice to Christian Philosophers" may be found in the journal *Faith and Philosophy*, vol. 1, no. 3 (July 1984), pp. 253–271.

---

SELECTION 13.1

# Proslogion★

*St. Anselm*

---

[*This passage is St. Anselm's famous ontological argument.*]

Lord, who gives understanding to faith give to me as much as you deem suitable, that I may understand that You are as we believe You to be, and that You are what we believe You to be. Now we believe that You are something than which nothing greater can be thought. But perhaps there is no such nature since "the fool hath said in his heart: There is no God"? But surely this very same fool, when he hears what I say: "something than which nothing greater can be thought," understands what he hears, and what he understands is in his mind, even if he does not understand that it exists. For it is one thing for a thing to be in the mind, but something else to understand that a thing exists. For when a painter pre-thinks what is about to be made, he has it in

mind but he does not yet understand that it exists because he has not yet made it. But when he has already painted it, he both has it in his mind and also understands that it exists because he has already made it. Hence, even the fool is convinced that something exists in the mind than which nothing greater can be thought, because when he hears this he understands and whatever is understood is in the mind. But surely that than which a greater cannot be thought cannot exist merely in the mind. For if it exists merely in the mind, it can be thought to exist also in reality which is greater. So if that than which a greater cannot be thought exists merely in the mind, that very same thing than which a greater cannot be thought is something than which a greater can be thought. But surely this cannot be. Hence, without doubt, something than which a greater cannot be thought exists both in the mind and in reality.

Indeed, it exists so truly that it cannot be thought not to be. For something can be thought to exist which cannot be thought not to exist, which is greater than what can be thought not to exist. So, if that than which a greater cannot be thought can be thought not to exist, that very thing than which a greater cannot be thought, is not that than which a greater cannot be thought; which is impossible.

So there exists so truly something than which a greater cannot be thought that it cannot be thought not to exist.

You are that very thing, Lord our God.

---

SELECTION 13.2

## Summa Theologica★

*St. Thomas Aquinas*

---

*[Aquinas' five proofs of God's existence are set forth here in his Five Ways.]*

The existence of God can be proved in five ways.

The first and more manifest way is the argument from motion. It is certain, and evident to our senses, that in the world some things are in motion. Now whatever is moved is moved by another, for nothing can be moved except it is in potentiality to that towards which it is moved; whereas a thing moves inasmuch as it is in act. For motion is nothing else than the reduction of something from potentiality to actuality. But nothing can be reduced from potentiality to actuality, except by something in a state of actuality. Thus that which is actually hot, as fire, makes wood, which is potentially hot, to be actually hot, and thereby moves and changes it. Now it is not possible that the same thing should be at once in actuality and potentiality in the same respect, but only in different respects. For what is actually hot cannot simultaneously be potentially hot; but it is simultaneously potentially cold. It is therefore impossible that in the same respect and in the same way a thing should be both mover and moved, *i.e.,* that it should move itself. Therefore, whatever is moved must be moved by another. If that by which it is moved be itself moved, then this also must needs be moved by another, and that by another again. But this cannot go on to infinity, because then there would be no first mover, and, consequently, no other mover, seeing that subsequent movers move only inasmuch as they are moved by the first mover; as the staff moves

only because it is moved by the hand. Therefore it is necessary to arrive at a first mover, moved by no other; and this everyone understands to be God.

The second way is from the nature of efficient cause. In the world of sensible things we find there is an order of efficient causes. There is no case known (neither is it, indeed, possible) in which a thing is found to be the efficient cause of itself; for so it would be prior to itself which is impossible. Now in efficient causes it is not possible to go on to infinity, because in all efficient causes following in order, the first is the cause of the intermediate cause, and the intermediate is the cause of the ultimate cause, whether the intermediate cause be several, or one only. Now to take away the cause is to take away the effect. Therefore, if there be no first cause among efficient causes, there will be no ultimate, nor any intermediate, cause. But if in efficient causes it is possible to go on to infinity, there will be no first efficient cause, neither will there be an ultimate effect, nor any intermediate efficient causes; all of which is plainly false. Therefore it is necessary to admit a first efficient cause, to which everyone gives the name of God.

The third way is taken from possibility and necessity, and runs thus. We find in nature things that are possible to be and not to be, since they are found to be generated, and to be corrupted, and consequently, it is possible for them to be and not to be. But it is impossible for these always to exist, for that which can not-be at some time is not. Therefore, if everything can not-be, then at one time there was nothing in existence. Now if this were true, even now there would be nothing in existence, because that which does not exist begins to exist only through something already existing. Therefore, if at one time nothing was in existence, it would have been impossible for anything to have begun to exist;

★From *Basic Writings of Saint Thomas Aquinas*, ed. Anton C. Pegis, Vol. 1. Copyright © 1945 by Random House, Inc. Copyright renewed 1973 by Random House, Inc. First Hackett Publishing Company edition 1997. Reprinted by permission of Hackett Publishing Company, Inc. All rights reserved.

and thus even now nothing would be in existence—which is absurd. Therefore, not all beings are merely possible, but there must exist something the existence of which is necessary. But every necessary thing either has its necessity caused by another, or not. Now it is impossible to go on to infinity in necessary things which have their necessity caused by another, as has been already proved in regard to efficient causes. Therefore we cannot but admit the existence of some being having of itself its own necessity, and not receiving it from another, but rather causing in others their necessity. This all men speak of as God.

The fourth way is taken from the gradation to be found in things. Among beings there are some more and some less good, true, noble, and the like. But *more* and *less* are predicated of different things according as they resemble in their different ways something which is the maximum, as a thing is said to be hotter according as it more nearly resembles that which is hottest; so that there is something which is truest, something best, something noblest,

and consequently, something which is most being, for those things that are greatest in truth are greatest in being. . . . Now the maximum in any genus is the cause of all in that genus, as fire, which is the maximum of heat, is the cause of all hot things, as is said in the same book. Therefore there must also be something which is to all beings the cause of their being, goodness, and every other perfection; and this we call God.

The fifth way is taken from the governance of the world. We see that things which lack knowledge, such as natural bodies, act for an end, and this is evident from their acting always, or nearly always, in the same way, so as to obtain the best result. Hence it is plain that they achieve their end, not fortuitously, but designedly. Now whatever lacks knowledge cannot move towards an end, unless it be directed by some being endowed with knowledge and intelligence; as the arrow is directed by the archer. Therefore some intelligent being exists by whom all natural things are directed to their end; and this being we call God.

---

SELECTION 13.3

# The Gay Science★

*Friedrich Nietzsche*

---

[*Nietzsche said, "God is dead." Here he elaborates.*]

### The Meaning of Our Cheerfulness
The greatest recent event—that "God is dead," that the belief in the Christian god has become unbelievable—is already beginning to cast its first shadows over Europe. For the few at least, whose eye—the *suspicion* in whose eyes is strong and subtle enough for this spectacle, some sun seems to have set and some ancient and profound trust has been turned into doubt; to them our old world must appear daily more like evening, more mistrustful, stranger, "older." But in the main one may say: The

event itself is far too great, too distant, too remote from the multitude's capacity for comprehension even for the tidings of it to be thought of as having *arrived* as yet. Much less may one suppose that many people know as yet *what* this event really means—and how much must collapse now that this faith has been undermined because it was built upon this faith, propped by it, grown into it; for example, the whole of our European morality. This long plenitude and sequence of breakdown, destruction, ruin, and cataclysm that is now impending—who could guess enough of it today to be compelled to play the teacher and advance proclaimer of this monstrous logic of terror, the prophet of a gloom and an eclipse of the sun whose like has probably never yet occurred on earth?

Even we born guessers of riddles who are, as it were, waiting on the mountains, posted between today and tomorrow, stretched in the contradiction between today and tomorrow, we firstlings and premature births of the coming century, to whom the shadows that must soon envelop Europe really *should* have appeared by now — why is it that even we look forward to the approaching gloom without any real sense of involvement and above all without any worry and fear for *ourselves*? Are we perhaps still too much under the impression of the *initial consequences* of this event — and these initial consequences, the consequences for *ourselves,* are quite the opposite of what one might perhaps expect: They are not at all sad and gloomy but rather like a new and scarcely describable kind of light, happiness, relief, exhilaration, encouragement, dawn.

Indeed, we philosophers and "free spirits" feel, when we hear the news that "the old god is dead," as if a new dawn shone on us; our heart overflows with gratitude, amazement, premonitions, expectation. At long last the horizon appears free to us again, even if it should not be bright; at long last our ships may venture out again, venture out to face any danger; all the daring of the lover of knowledge is permitted again; the sea, *our sea,* lies open again; perhaps there has never yet been such an "open sea."

---

SELECTION 13.4

# Theology and Falsification *

*Antony Flew*

---

[*In this famous selection, British philosopher Antony Flew challenges those who believe in God to specify what they would accept as evidence that God does not exist or does not love us. Why should a believer try to do this? Flew explains why.*]

Let us begin with a parable. It is a parable developed from a tale told by John Wisdom in his haunting and revelatory article "Gods." Once upon a time two explorers came upon a clearing in the jungle. In the clearing were growing many flowers and many weeds. One explorer says, "Some gardener must tend this plot." The other disagrees, "There is no gardener." So they pitch their tents and set a watch. No gardener is ever seen. "But perhaps he is an invisible gardener." So they set up a barbed-wire fence. They electrify it. They patrol with bloodhounds. (For they remember how H. G. Wells's "invisible man" could be both smelt and touched though he could not be seen.) But no shrieks ever suggest that some intruder has received a shock. No movements of the wire ever betray an invisible climber. The bloodhounds never give cry. Yet still the Believer is not convinced. "But there is a gar-

dener, invisible, intangible, insensible to electric shocks, a gardener who has no scent and makes no sound, a gardener who comes secretly to look after the garden which he loves." At last the Sceptic despairs, "But what remains of your original assertion? Just how does what you call an invisible, intangible, eternally elusive gardener differ from an imaginary gardener or even from no gardener at all?"

In this parable we can see how what starts as an assertion, that something exists or that there is some analogy between certain complexes of phenomena, may be reduced step by step to an altogether different status, to an expression perhaps of a "picture preference." The Sceptic says there is no gardener. The Believer says there is a gardener (but invisible, etc.). One man talks about sexual behavior. Another man prefers to talk of Aphrodite (but knows that there is not really a superhuman person additional to, and somehow responsible for, all sexual phenomena). The process of qualification may be checked at any point before the original assertion is completely withdrawn and something of that first assertion will remain (Tautology). Mr. Wells's invisible man could not, admittedly, be seen, but in all other respects he was a man like the rest of us. But though the process of qualification may be, and of course usually is, checked in time, it is not always judiciously so halted. Someone may dissipate his assertion completely without noticing that he has done so. A fine brash hypothesis may thus be killed by inches, the death by a thousand qualifications.

---

*Author's footnotes have been omitted. Reprinted with the permission of Scribner, an imprint of Simon & Schuster Adult Publishing Group, and SCM Press Ltd., from *New Essays in Philosophical Theology* by Antony Flew and Alasdair MacIntyre. Copyright © 1955 by Antony Flew and Alasdair MacIntyre; copyright renewed © 1983.

And in this, it seems to me, lies the peculiar danger, the endemic evil, of theological utterance. Take such utterances as "God has a plan," "God created the world," "God loves us as a father loves his children." They look at first sight very much like assertions, vast cosmological assertions. Of course, this is no sure sign that they either are, or are intended to be, assertions. But let us confine ourselves to the cases where those who utter such sentences intend them to express assertions. (Merely remarking parenthetically that those who intend or interpret such utterances as crypto-commands, expressions of wishes, disguised ejaculations, concealed ethics, or as anything else but assertions, are unlikely to succeed in making them either properly orthodox or practically effective.)

Now to assert that such and such is the case is necessarily equivalent to denying that such and such is not the case. Suppose then that we are in doubt as to what someone who gives vent to an utterance is asserting, or suppose that, more radically, we are sceptical as to whether he is really asserting anything at all, one way of trying to understand (or perhaps it will be to expose) his utterance is to attempt to find what he would regard as counting against, or as being incompatible with, its truth. For if the utterance is indeed an assertion, it will necessarily be equivalent to a denial of the negation of that assertion. And anything which would count against the assertion, or which would induce the speaker to withdraw it and to admit that it had been mistaken, must be part of (or the whole of) the meaning of the negation of that assertion. And to know the meaning of the negation of an assertion is, as near as makes no matter, to know the meaning of that assertion. And if there is nothing which a putative assertion denies then there is nothing which it asserts either: and so it is not really an assertion. When the Sceptic in the parable asked the Believer, "Just how does what you call an invisible, intangible, eternally elusive gardener differ from an imaginary gardener or even from no gardener at all?" he was suggesting that the Believer's earlier statement had been so eroded by qualification that it was no longer an assertion at all.

Now it often seems to people who are not religious as if there was no conceivable event or series of events the occurrence of which would be admitted by sophisticated religious people to be a sufficient reason for conceding "There wasn't a God after all" or "God does not really love us then." Someone tells us that God loves us as a father loves his children. We are reassured. But then we see a child dying of inoperable cancer of the throat. His earthly father is driven frantic in his efforts to help, but his Heavenly Father reveals no obvious sign of concern. Some qualification is made — God's love is "not a merely human love" or it is "an inscrutable love," perhaps — and we realize that such sufferings are quite compatible with the truth of the assertion that "God loves us as a father (but, of course . . .)." We are reassured again. But then perhaps we ask: what is this assurance of God's (appropriately qualified) love worth, what is this apparent guarantee really a guarantee against? Just what would have to happen not merely (morally and wrongly) to tempt but also (logically and rightly) to entitle us to say "God does not love us" or even "God does not exist?" I therefore put to the succeeding symposiasts the simple central question: "What would have to occur or to have occurred to constitute for you a disproof of the love of, or of the existence of, God?"

SELECTION 13.5

## After the Death of God the Father*

*Mary Daly*

[*How is "God" an instrument of oppression? How do religious texts dehumanize women? Mary Daly offers her arguments in* Beyond God the Father, *from which this brief passage is excerpted.*]

The biblical and popular image of God as a great patriarch in heaven, rewarding and punishing according to his mysterious and seemingly arbitrary will, has dominated the imagination of millions over thousands of years. The symbol of the Father God, spawned in the human imagination and sustained as plausible by patriarchy, has in turn rendered service to this type of society by making its mechanisms for the oppression of women appear right and fitting. If God in "his" heaven is a father ruling "his" people, then it is in the "nature" of things and according to divine plan and the order of the universe that society be male-dominated.

Within this context a mystification of roles takes place: the husband dominating his wife represents God "himself." The images and values of a given society have been projected into the realm of dogmas and "Articles of Faith," and these in turn justify the social structures which have given rise to them and which sustain their plausibility. The belief system becomes hardened and objectified, seeming to have an unchangeable independent existence and validity of its own. It resists social change that would rob it of its plausibility. Despite the vicious circle, however, change can occur in society, and ideologies can die, though they die hard.

As the women's movement begins to have its effect upon the fabric of society, transforming it from patriarchy into something that never existed before — into a diarchal situation that is radically new — it can become the greatest single challenge to the major religions of the world, Western and Eastern. Beliefs and values that have held sway for thousands of years will be questioned as never before. This revolution may well be also the greatest single hope for survival of spiritual consciousness on this planet.

## The Challenge: Emergence of Whole Human Beings

There are some who persist in claiming that the liberation of women will only mean that new characters will assume the same old roles, and that nothing will change essentially in structures, ideologies, and values. This supposition is often based on the observation that the very few women in "masculine" occupations often behave much as men do. This kind of reasoning is not at all to the point, for it fails to take into account the fact that tokenism does not change stereotypes or social systems but works to preserve them, since it dulls the revolutionary impulse. The minute proportion of women in the United States who occupy such roles (such as senators, judges, business executives, doctors, etc.) have been trained by men in institutions defined and

designed by men, and they have been pressured subtly to operate according to male rules. There are no alternate models. As sociologist Alice Rossi has suggested, this is not what the women's movement in its most revolutionary potential is all about.

What *is* to the point is an emergence of woman-consciousness such as has never before taken place. It is unimaginative and out of touch with what is happening in the women's movement to assume that the becoming of women will simply mean uncritical acceptance of structures, beliefs, symbols, norms, and patterns of behavior that have been given priority by society under male domination. Rather, this becoming will act as catalyst for radical change in our culture. It has been argued cogently by Piaget that structure is maintained by an interplay of transformation laws that never yield results beyond the system and never tend to employ elements external to the system. This is indicative of what *can* effect basic alteration in the system, that is, a potent influence *from without*. Women who reject patriarchy have this power and indeed *are* this power of transformation that is ultimately threatening to things as they are.

The roles and structures of patriarchy have been developed and sustained in accordance with an artificial polarization of human qualities into the traditional sexual stereotypes. The image of the person in authority and the accepted understanding of "his" role has corresponded to the eternal masculine stereotype, which implies hyper-rationality (in reality, frequently reducible to pseudo-rationality), "objectivity," aggressivity, the possession of dominating and manipulative attitudes toward persons and the environment, and the tendency to construct boundaries between the self (and those identified with the self) and "the Other." The caricature of human being which is represented by this stereotype depends for its existence upon the opposite caricature — the eternal feminine. This implies hyper-emotionalism, passivity, self-abnegation, etc. By becoming whole persons women can generate a counterforce to the stereotype of the leader, challenging the artificial polarization of human characteristics into sex-role identification. There is no reason to assume that women who have the support of each other to criticize not only the feminine stereotype but the masculine stereotype as well will simply adopt the latter as a model for ourselves. On the contrary, what is happening is that women are developing a wider range of qualities and skills. This is beginning to encourage and in fact demand a comparably liberating process in men — a phenomenon which has begun in men's liberation groups and which is taking place every day within the context of personal relationships. The becoming of androgynous human persons implies a radical change in the fabric of human consciousness and in styles of human behavior.

This change is already threatening the credibility of the religious symbols of our culture. Since many of these have been used to justify oppression, such a challenge should be seen as redemptive. Religious symbols fade and die when the cultural situation that gave rise to them and supported them ceases to give them plausibility. Such an event generates anxiety, but it is part of the risk involved in a faith which accepts the relativity of all symbols and recognizes that clinging to these as fixed and ultimate is self-destructive and idolatrous.

The becoming of new symbols is not a matter that can be decided arbitrarily around a conference table. Rather, symbols grow out of a changing communal situation and experience. This does not mean that we are confined to the role of passive spectators. The experience of the becoming of women cannot be understood merely conceptually and abstractly but through active participation in the overcoming of servitude. Both activism and creative thought flow from and feed into the evolving woman-consciousness. The cumulative effect is a surge of awareness beyond the symbols and doctrines of patriarchal religion. . . .

**Beyond the Inadequate God**
The various theologies that hypostatize transcendence, that is, those which in one way or another objectify "God" as *a being*, thereby attempt in a self-contradictory way to envisage transcendent reality as finite. "God" then functions to legitimate the existing social, economic, and political status quo, in which women and other victimized groups are subordinate.

"God" can be used oppressively against women in a number of ways. First, it occurs in an overt manner when theologians proclaim women's subordination to be God's will. This of course has been done throughout the centuries, and residues remain in varying degrees of subtlety and explicitness in the writings of twentieth-century thinkers such as Barth, Bonhoeffer, Reinhold Niebuhr, and Teilhard de Chardin.

Second, even in the absence of such explicitly oppressive justification, the phenomenon is present when one-sex symbolism for God and for the human relationship to God is used. The following passage illustrates the point:

> To believe that God is Father is to become aware of oneself not as a stranger, not as an outsider or an alienated person, but as a son who belongs or a person appointed to a marvelous destiny, which he shares with the whole community. To believe that God is Father means to be able to say "we" in regard to all men.

A woman whose consciousness has been aroused can say that such language makes her aware of herself as a stranger, as an outsider, as an alienated person, not as a daughter who belongs or who is appointed to a marvelous destiny. She cannot belong to *this* without assenting to her own lobotomy.

Third, even when the basic assumptions of God-language appear to be nonsexist, and when language is somewhat purified of fixation upon maleness, it is damaging and implicitly compatible with sexism if it encourages detachment from the reality of the human struggle against oppression in its concrete manifestations. That is, the lack of explicit relevance of intellection to the fact of oppression in its precise forms, such as sexual hierarchy, is itself oppressive. This is the case when theologians write long treatises on creative hope, political theology, or revolution without any specific acknowledgment of or application to the problem of sexism or other specific forms of injustice. Such irrelevance is conspicuous in the major works of "theologians of hope" such as Moltmann, Pannenberg, and Metz. This is not to say that the vision of creative eschatology is completely irrelevant, but that it lacks specific grounding in the concrete experiences of the oppressed. The theorizing then has a quality of unreality. Perhaps an obvious reason for this is that the theologians themselves have not shared in the experience of oppression and therefore write from the privileged distance of those who have at best a "knowledge about" the subject. . . .

**Women's Liberation and
Revelatory Courage**
I have already indicated that it would be unrealistic to dismiss the fact that the symbolic and linguistic instruments for communication — which include

essentially the whole theological tradition in world religions—have been formulated by males under the conditions of patriarchy. It is therefore inherent in these symbolic and linguistic structures that they serve the purposes of patriarchal social arrangements. Even the usual and accepted means of theological dissent have been restricted in such a way that only some questions have been allowed to arise. Many questions that are of burning importance to women now simply have not occurred in the past (and to a large extent in the present) to those with "credentials" to do theology. Others may have been voiced timidly but quickly squelched as stupid, irrelevant, or naïve. Therefore, attempts by women theologians now merely to "up-date" or to reform theology within acceptable patterns of question-asking are not likely to get very far.

Moreover, within the context of the prevailing social climate it has been possible for scholars to be aware of the most crudely dehumanizing texts concerning women in the writings of religious "authorities" and theologians—from Augustine to Aquinas, to Luther, to Knox, to Barth—and at the same time to treat their unverified opinions on far more imponderable matters with utmost reverence and respect. That is, the blatant misogynism of these men has not been the occasion of a serious

credibility gap even for those who have disagreed on this "point." It has simply been ignored or dismissed as trivial. By contrast, in the emerging consciousness of women this context is beginning to be perceived in its full significance and as deeply relevant to the worldview in which such "authorities" have seen other seemingly unrelated subjects, such as the problem of God. Hence the present awakening of the hitherto powerless sex demands an explosion of creative imagination that can withstand the disapproval of orthodoxy and overreach the boundaries cherished by conventional minds.

The driving revelatory force that is making it possible for women to speak—and to *hear* each other speak—more authentically about God is courage in the face of the risks that attend the liberation process. Since the projections of patriarchal religion have been blocking the dynamics of existential courage by offering the false security of alienation, that is, of self-reduction in sex roles, there is reason to hope for the emergence of a new religious consciousness in the confrontation with sexism that is now in its initial stages. The becoming of women may be not only the doorway to deliverance which secular humanism has passionately fought for—but also a doorway *to* something, that is, a new phase in the human spirit's quest for God.

---

## CHECKLIST

To help you review, here is a checklist of the key philosophers and terms and concepts of this chapter. The brief descriptive sentences summarize the philosophers' leading ideas. Keep in mind that some of these summary statements are oversimplifications of complex positions.

### Philosophers

- **St. Anselm**   was the author of the ontological argument.

- **Gaunilo,**   a Benedictine monk, was a contemporary of Anselm and a critic of the ontological argument.

- **St. Thomas Aquinas**   was the author of the Five Ways of proving God's existence.

- **Julian of Norwich,**   an English anchoress and mystic, argued that we are in God and God is

in us. We learn about God by learning about ourselves.

- **René Descartes**   offered three proofs of God, including a streamlined version of the ontological argument.

- **Gottfried Wilhelm, Baron von Leibniz,** proposed one of the most effective versions of the cosmological argument.

- **David Hume,**   a religious skeptic, provided classic criticisms of the teleological and cosmological arguments.

- **Immanuel Kant**   criticized the ontological, cosmological, and teleological proofs of God and thought that God's existence cannot be proved, yet he believed that God's existence must be assumed by the rational, moral individual.

- **John Henry Newman,**   a famous nineteenth-century religious thinker, held that God's existence is evidenced by the experience of conscience.

- **Søren Kierkegaard** held that God is beyond reason's grasp, that truth is subjective, and that salvation can be attained only through a leap of faith to Christianity.

- **Friedrich Nietzsche** believed that the masses are ruled by a slave morality inculcated by religion, science, and philosophy. His statement "God is dead" meant that there is no rational order, not that people do not believe in God.

- **William James** held that it is rationally justifiable to yield to your hope that a God exists.

- **Mary Daly** is a contemporary feminist analyst/critic of traditional conceptions of God.

- **Alvin Plantinga** holds that theists may accept the belief in God as a "basic belief," one that is rational to hold without supporting evidence and that is a foundation for the entire system of the theists' beliefs.

### Key Terms and Concepts

ontological argument
*reductio* proof
Five Ways
first mover
cosmological
  argument
moral argument
argument from
  design/teleological
  argument
monad
principle of sufficient
  reason

theodicy
argument by analogy
necessary being
leap of faith
Pascal's wager
logical positivism
Vienna Circle
verifiability principle
Big Bang
God's gender
basic belief

## QUESTIONS FOR DISCUSSION AND REVIEW

1. Explain in your own words Anselm's two ontological proofs of God.

2. What is a *reductio* proof? Give an example other than one mentioned in the text.

3. Summarize Gaunilo's objection to Anselm's argument. What is Anselm's response to that objection?

4. State, in your own words, Aquinas' first, second, and third ways. Which of these arguments seems to you the soundest, and why?

5. In your own words, state Julian of Norwich's arguments for knowing that God exists, for knowing what God's nature is, and for knowing what God wants of us.

6. Compare Descartes's version of the ontological argument with one of Anselm's. Which version is the sounder, and why?

7. In your own words, state Leibniz's proof of God's existence. Can you find anything wrong with it?

8. Critically evaluate Leibniz's solution to the problem of evil.

9. In your own words, summarize Hume's criticisms of the teleological argument. Are these criticisms sound? Why or why not?

10. Explain Hume's reasoning for remaining skeptical of reports of miracles. Is this reasoning sound?

11. Hume maintained that if you explain the cause of each event in a series by reference to earlier events in the series, there is no sense in then trying to find a single cause for the entire series of events. Is this right? What does it have to do with the question of God's existence?

12. Does the world/universe — or something in it — give evidence of divine design? Explain.

13. Does the theory of evolution undermine the design argument?

14. Is Newman correct in thinking that the existence of God is given to us in the experience of conscience? Explain.

15. Explain James's argument for God. Is it a version of Pascal's wager? Is it sound? Why?

16. Is James correct in saying that you cannot really suspend judgment about God's existence?

17. Is the question of God's existence live and momentous, as James says?

18. Is it rare for people to decide things on the basis of reasoned arguments? Is it possible for them to do so?

19. Which is "better," to doubt everything that is less than certain or highly probable, or to believe falsehoods?

20. "It is impossible for normal people to believe that free will does not exist. Therefore, it does exist." Evaluate this remark. "It is impossible for normal people to believe that free will does not exist. Therefore, it is reasonable to believe that it does exist." Evaluate this remark.

21. "Most people believe in God; therefore, God must exist." Evaluate this claim.

22. Is the fact that the world is intelligible evidence of divine design?

23. "He died because God called on him." "The sprinkler stopped working due to fate." Are these claims equally meaningless? Explain. Is the claim "God exists" verifiable or falsifiable? Are any (other) claims made about God verifiable?

24. Assuming that there is scientific evidence that the universe had an absolute beginning, does that evidence also prove the existence of God? Explain.

25. Is the belief that the proposition "God exists" is meaningless a form of atheism?

26. "The features of the world add to the probability that God exists but do not automatically make it probable that God exists." Explain this remark.

27. Can you logically believe both that God knows everything and that there is free will? Explain the difficulty.

28. How valid as proof of God's existence are purported eyewitness reports of miracles?

29. "Even assuming that the existence of God explains why there is a world, what explains why there is a God?" Does this question contain a valid criticism of the cosmological proof of God?

30. Would universal acceptance of atheism be morally disastrous for society?

31. In what sense is it legitimate rationally to think of God as male?

## SUGGESTED FURTHER READINGS

Anselm, *Basic Writings*, S. N. Deane, trans. (La Salle, Ill.: Open Court, 1974). This work contains Anselm's basic writings, though what we have already given you in this text may well be sufficient for most purposes.

Aquinas, *Basic Writings of Saint Thomas Aquinas*, 2 vols., A. C. Pegis, ed. (New York: Random House, 1945). You have read the Five Ways, but you might also wish to consult the sections of *Summa Theologica* that deal with the nature and attributes of God and also part 1, questions 48 and 49, and the first part of part 2, question 79, for the classical Christian discussion of evil.

Thomas Aquinas, *Selected Philosophical Writings*, Timothy McDermott, trans. (New York: Oxford University Press, 1998). A helpful anthology of writings by Aquinas.

D. R. Burrill, ed., *The Cosmological Argument* (Garden City, N.Y.: Doubleday Anchor, 1967). Selected readings on the cosmological arguments, for and against.

Mary Daly, *Beyond God the Father* (Boston: Beacon Press, 1973). A fiery examination of sexism in theology and religious belief.

A. Flew, *Hume's Philosophy of Belief: A Study of His First Inquiry* (London: Routledge & Kegan Paul, 1961). Contains an analysis of Hume's treatment of the "religious hypothesis."

A. Flew and A. MacIntyre, eds., *New Essays in Philosophical Theology* (New York: Macmillan, 1984). A popular anthology covering a range of topics. For a follow-up to the article by Flew (Selection 13.4), see the pieces in this anthology by R. Hare and B. Mitchell titled "Theology and Falsification."

Paul Helm, ed., *Faith and Reason* (New York: Oxford University Press, 1999). An introductory reader on the relation of faith and reason beginning with ancient Greek texts and extending to the present.

C. W. Hendel Jr., *Hume Selections* (New York: Scribner's, 1927). See especially pp. 143–282 and 284–401.

J. Hick, "Theology and Verification," in *Theology Today*, vol. 17, no. 1 (April 1960). A response to verificationist attacks on religious language.

W. James, *The Will to Believe and Other Essays in Popular Philosophy*, Frederick H. Burkhardt, ed. (Cambridge: Harvard University Press, 1979). James is among the most pleasurable of philosophers to read.

W. T. Jones, *A History of Western Philosophy*, 2nd ed., vol. 6 (New York: Harcourt Brace Jovanovich, 1975). See chapter 6 for a good discussion of Kierkegaard and Nietzsche.

Julian of Norwich, *A Book of Showings to the Anchoress Julian of Norwich*, 2 vols., Colledge and Walsh, eds.

(Toronto: Pontifical Institute of Medieval Studies, 1978). The early English version. You have to read it aloud to understand it.

Julian of Norwich, *Revelations of Divine Love,* Clifton Wolters, trans. (Harmondsworth, England: Penguin, 1966, 1985). A good, cheap paperback version of "Showings" in modern English.

I. Kant, *Critique of Practical Reason,* L. W. Beck, trans. (New York: Liberal Arts, 1956). See book II, chapter II, sect. V.

I. Kant, *Critique of Pure Reason,* N. K. Smith, trans. (New York: St. Martin's, 1965). Check the index under "God." The most important material is in the chapter "The Ideal of Pure Reason."

W. Kaufmann, *Nietzsche* (New York: Meridian, 1956). A good introduction to Nietzsche's philosophy.

A. Kenny, *Five Ways: St. Thomas Aquinas's Proofs of God's Existence* (London: Routledge & Kegan Paul, 1969). Good critical discussion of the Five Ways.

G. Leibniz, *Theodicy,* E. M. Huggard, trans., and A. Farrer, ed. (La Salle, Ill.: Open Court, 1952).

J. L. Mackie, *The Miracle of Theism: Arguments For and Against the Existence of God* (Oxford: Clarendon Press, 1982). Excellent commentary on all the traditional proofs of God's existence.

Basil Mitchell, ed., *The Philosophy of Religion* (New York: Oxford University Press, 1991). A collection of papers on various themes connected with God and religious belief.

R. J. Moore and B. N. Moore, *The Cosmos, God and Philosophy* (New York: Peter Lang, 1988). Contains discussion of modern science on traditional proofs of God.

Thomas V. Morris, ed., *The Concept of God* (New York: Oxford University Press, 1987). Writings on the existence and nature of God.

J. H. Newman, *A Grammar of Assent,* C. F. Harrold, ed. (New York: Longmans, Green and Co., 1947). Newman's most important book.

W. Paley, *Natural Theology: Selections,* Frederick Ferré, ed. (Indianapolis: Bobbs-Merrill, 1963). There is more to Paley than his famous stone and watch analogy, as the reader of this book will discover.

N. Pike, ed., *God and Evil: Readings on the Theological Problem of Evil* (Englewood Cliffs, N.J.: Prentice-Hall, 1964). A popular anthology on the subject.

Alvin Plantinga, "Advice to Christian Philosophers," *Faith and Philosophy,* vol. 1, no. 3 (July 1984), pp. 253–271. Plantinga sets forth the idea that a belief in God may be a "basic belief."

A. Plantinga, *The Ontological Argument from St. Anselm to Contemporary Philosophers* (New York: Doubleday Anchor, 1965). Contains relevant articles written mainly by analytic philosophers. Some are very tough.

Louis Pojman, *Philosophy of Religion* (New York: McGraw-Hill, 2000). Analytically rigorous interpretation concerning issues such as the traditional proofs for the existence of God, the problem of evil, miracles.

Philip L. Quinn and Charles Taliaferro, *A Companion to Philosophy of Religion* (Malden, Mass.: Blackwell, 2002). A survey of the main issues and standpoints regarding the philosophy of religion.

I. Ramsey, *Religious Language* (New York: Macmillan, 1963). A discussion of the questions surrounding the meaning of religious language.

B. Russell and F. C. Copleston, "The Existence of God: A Debate between Bertrand Russell and Father F. C. Copleston." This lively debate touches on several lines of proof of God, and Copleston's version of Leibniz's cosmological argument is pretty effectively worded. The debate has been anthologized in many places. See, e.g., E. L. Miller, *Philosophical and Religious Issues: Classical and Contemporary Statements* (Encino, Calif.: Dickenson, 1971).

David Schatz, *Philosophy and Faith: A Philosophy of Religion Reader* (New York: McGraw-Hill, 2001). Traditional issues are investigated as well as fresh topics such as religious imagery, the hiddenness of god and divine action.

Richard Swinburne, *The Existence of God* (New York: Oxford University Press, 1991). This edition contains a response to powerful criticisms by J. L. Mackie and considers the evidential force of recent scientific discoveries.

F. R. Tennant, *Philosophical Theology,* vol. 2 (New York: Cambridge University Press, 1928).

Anthony C. Thiselton, *A Concise Encyclopedia of the Philosophy of Religion* (Oxford: Oneworld Publications, 2002). Entries cover the issues and concepts relevant for religious philosophy.

J. Thompson, *Kierkegaard* (Garden City, N.Y.: Doubleday, 1972). A collection of essays on Kierkegaard that were selected "so as to give the reader some sense of the shape and direction of recent Kierkegaardian criticism."

Mary Ellen Waithe, *A History of Women Philosophers,* vol. 2, *Medieval Women Philosophers, 500–1600.* (Dordrecht, Boston and London: Kluwer Academic Publishers, 1989). Includes an article on Julian of Norwich by Elisabeth Evasdaughter.

# Part Four
# Other Voices

# 14

# Feminist Philosophy

Feminism is an entire world view or *Gestalt*, not just a laundry list of "women's issues."  — Charlotte Bunch

Girls and boys develop different relational capacities and senses of self as a result of growing up in a family in which women mother.
  — Nancy Chodorow

As nature [during the scientific revolution] came to seem more like a woman whom it is appropriate to rape and torture than like a nurturing mother, did rape and torture come to seem a more natural relation of men to women?  — Sandra Harding

Feminist thought is often divided into two waves. The first, from the late eighteenth century through the early part of the twentieth century, tended to focus on legal issues, especially women's enfranchisement, and included as a notable accomplishment in the United States the vote for women in 1922. The second wave, still happening, began in 1949 with the publication of Simone de Beauvoir's *The Second Sex*. The second wave has focused more on personal issues, especially the personal relations between men and women, and is often referred to nowadays as **feminism.**

## THE FIRST WAVE

One of the grandmothers of feminist thought was **Mary Wollstonecraft** (1759–1797), who wrote in response both to what she saw around her and to some of the views about women that the philosophers of the time were putting forward. Her mother and sister were both victims of domestic violence, which caused her to take

## PROFILE: Mary Wollstonecraft (1759–1797)

Mary Wollstonecraft's early years were not happy; her father was an unsuccessful gentleman farmer who squandered the family's assets and took out his frustrations on his wife and children. While still quite a young woman, Wollstonecraft struck out on her own to London to become a writer. After some early years of struggle, her work began to gain considerable acceptance among the intelligentsia of London society. She was fairly well known by the time she published "A Vindication of the Rights of Woman."

Her personal life was unconventional and tumultuous. An affair with an American led to the birth of her first daughter, Fanny. When Fanny was still very young, Wollstonecraft met William Godwin, the political anarchist. They were well matched intellectually and emotionally, and after Wollstonecraft became pregnant, they married. Their life together was cut short, however, when Wollstonecraft died from complications following the delivery of the child. Godwin was devastated at Wollstonecraft's death and wrote a tender book of memoirs about her. This book caused significant public scandal both for Wollstonecraft and for Godwin, since he made no effort to hide the illegitimacy of her first child or the fact that she was pregnant when they married.

Their daughter, Mary Godwin, married Percy Bysshe Shelley and went on to write the novel *Frankenstein*. Mary Shelley had no interest in women's rights and spent considerable energy trying to cover up the unconventionality of her parents' lives. It was not until the end of the nineteenth century that the scandal associated with Mary Wollstonecraft died down enough to permit later feminists to include her name in their lists of honorable forebears.

issue with the idealized view of marriage being put forth by her culture. As an intellectual, she was familiar with many of the high-minded views of womanhood her contemporaries perpetuated. She was particularly annoyed at Rousseau's view of women because he advocated that women's education should be designed entirely to make them pleasing to men. "To please, to be useful to us, to make us love and esteem them, to educate us when young and take care of us when grown up, to advise, to console us, to render our lives easy and agreeable—these are the duties of women at all times, and what they should be taught in their infancy," reflected Rousseau. Wollstonecraft employed several arguments against Rousseau and his allies.

First, she argued that educating women to be the ornaments to, and playthings of, men would have bad consequences for society. How could silly, vain creatures ever be expected to do an adequate job of raising a family? They would become "mere propagators of fools."

Second, she argued that raising women to be ornamental would have bad consequences for women. No matter how charming a woman might be, after a few years of daily contact, her husband would ultimately become somewhat bored and distracted. If women have no inner resources to fall back on, Wollstonecraft argued, they will then "grow languid, or become a spring of bitterness," and love will turn to jealousy or vanity.

Third, and perhaps most important, she argued that women were as capable as men of attaining the "masculine" virtues of wisdom and rationality, if only society would allow those virtues to be cultivated. She noted that the "virtues" of women — docility, dependence, and sensitivity — were commonly associated with weakness. She held that there should be no distinction between female excellence and human excellence. Like many intellectuals of the Enlightenment, Wollstonecraft gave pride of place to rationality and argued that women must develop their capacity for reason to its fullest extent if they were to become excellent examples of humanity.

Wollstonecraft painted an unflattering portrait of the "ideal" woman of her era. Imagine what women would be like, she said in effect, if they did nothing but read the equivalent of today's Harlequin romances and aspired to be like the passive, swooning heroines of these books. Some women might be successful at imitating such heroines, and might enjoy themselves for a while, but Wollstonecraft pointed out that once past age nineteen or so, there is little left for such women to do with their lives. She suggested that women who have no other ambition than to inflame passions will have no real strength of character, no true moral virtue, and no inner resources. It was time, Wollstonecraft argued, to restore women to their lost dignity by encouraging better ideas of womanhood.

Utopian philosophers were also important in the struggle for women's rights. Who were the utopian philosophers? They were utilitarian reformers — social reformers who subscribed to the philosophy of Jeremy Bentham (see Chapter 10) — who wished to structure society so as to produce the greatest happiness of the greatest number. They envisioned societies in which all members were social equals, where education was reformed to promote the development of "benevolent" or "humanistic" feelings of mutual care and concern, and where property was redistributed to the benefit of all members of society. Model utopian societies sprang up in Europe and the United States; the utopian movement culminated in the late nineteenth century. For utopians, societies should help people feel they are doing something important for themselves, their families, and their communities; in an ideal society, people would work only because they wanted to, and they would want to work because they would understand that their work helps make their community a great place to be. Yet at that time the largest and most exploited (because unpaid) labor force was women, a fact that did not escape the attention of **Anna Doyle Wheeler** (1765–1833), a utilitarian reformer.

Wheeler was an Irish feminist, a self-educated philosopher, and an avid utilitarian who published numerous articles (under various pseudonyms) and frequent translations of French socialist philosophical writings. Jeremy Bentham introduced to Wheeler the utopian/reformist philosopher and economist **William Thompson** (1775–1833); Wheeler and Thompson collaborated on a famous essay titled "The Appeal of One Half of the Human Race, Women, against the Pretensions of the Other Half, Men, to Restrain Them in Political, and Thence in Civil and Domestic, Slavery." In the essay, published in 1825, Wheeler and Thompson argued that denying rights to women is in fact contrary to the interests of the whole of society and, accordingly, is not consistent with the greatest happiness of the greatest number. They also argued that denying rights to women is just plain unjust; many commentators think a more stirring defense of equal rights for men and women has never been put forth.

Another important utilitarian was **Harriet Taylor** (c. 1807–1858), who until recently was most often remembered through her connection with John Stuart Mill.

Taylor also thought that the nonphysiological differences between men and women were socially constructed, to the detriment of women and of society in general. She was a vociferous proponent of women's suffrage and used several arguments from justice in support of her appeal. Everyone agreed there should be no taxation without representation; well, she pointed out, many unmarried women paid taxes on their property yet could not vote for the government that spent their money. She argued that we cannot make arbitrary distinctions between groups of people without giving good reasons for doing so, and no good reasons could be given for saying that men could vote and women could not. The burden of proof should be on those in favor of discrimination, not on those who oppose it. And, Taylor argued, the differential in freedom between men and women was so drastic—including not only political liberty but personal freedom as well—that no good reasons could possibly be advanced for the discrimination. Eventually, of course, the rest of the British public saw it her way and women were given the vote. Taylor also provided the classic answer to the question, Why should women have a voice in government? (See the box by that title.)

The first wave of feminism saw some dramatic results, including changes in the laws regarding women's property rights and the right to vote. After 1920, when women in the United States obtained the right to vote, active theoretical work on feminist issues subsided for a few decades. But the larger social problems did not go away, and theorists who had hoped that the right to vote and own property would resolve the problem of women's lower social and economic status saw those hopes vanish. Women were still educated differently, still viewed primarily as ornamental and nurturing, still paid less, and still seen as having a lower fundamental worth than men.

## THE SECOND WAVE

Philosopher and novelist **Simone de Beauvoir** [bow-VWAHR] (1908–1986) recognized the problem. The earlier feminists were primarily English and American. They had been steeped in the traditions of empiricism and utilitarianism. De Beauvoir came from the Continental traditions of existentialism and phenomenology, and her approach focused less on the public world of laws, rights, and educational opportunities and more on the cultural mechanisms of oppression, which left women in the role of **Other** to man's **Self**. She developed this notion of women's essential otherness in her book *The Second Sex*.

And what a book. De Beauvoir undertook a sweeping analysis of all the ideas and forces that conspired to keep women in a subordinate position relative to men. Her examination encompassed Freud, Marx, the evidence of biology, the evidence of history, representative novelists, and what we would call the evidence of sociology. There had not previously been anything like this systematic and sustained analysis of the condition of women; de Beauvoir's work was unique.

But its very scope makes it a difficult book to summarize or outline. De Beauvoir, like some of her existentialist colleagues, was more interested in the fascinating variety of theoretical approaches than in the project of making them—or her

# Why Should Women Have a Voice in Government?

The classic answer was provided by Harriet Taylor, who was discussed earlier.

Even those who do not look upon a voice in the government as a matter of personal right, nor profess principles which require that it should be extended to all, have usually traditional maxims of political justice with which it is impossible to reconcile the exclusion of all women from the common rights of citizenship. It is an axiom of English freedom that taxation and representation should be coextensive. Even under the laws which give the wife's property to the husband, there are many unmarried women who pay taxes. It is one of the fundamental doctrines of the British Constitution, that all persons should be tried by their peers: yet women, whenever tried, are tried by male judges and a male jury. To foreigners the law accords the privilege of claiming that half the jury should be composed of themselves; not so to women. Apart from maxims of detail, which represent local and national rather than universal ideas; it is an acknowledged dictate of justice to make no degrading distinctions without necessity. In all things the presumption ought to be on the side of equality. A reason must be given why anything should be permitted to one person and interdicted to another. But when that which is interdicted includes nearly every-

thing which those to whom it is permitted most prize, and to be deprived of which they feel to be most insulting; when not only political liberty but personal freedom of action is the prerogative of a caste; when even in the exercise of industry, almost all employments which task the higher faculties in an important field, which lead to distinction, riches, or even pecuniary independence, are fenced round as the exclusive domain of the predominant section, scarcely any doors being left open to the dependent class, except such as all who can enter elsewhere disdainfully pass by; the miserable expediencies which are advanced as excuses for so grossly partial a dispensation, would not be sufficient, even if they were real, to render it other than a flagrant injustice. While, far from being expedient, we are firmly convinced that the division of mankind into two castes, one born to rule over the other, is in this case, as in all cases, an unqualified mischief; a source of perversion and demoralization, both to the favoured class and to those at whose expense they are favoured; producing none of the good which it is the custom to ascribe to it, and forming a bar . . . to any really vital improvement, either in the character or in the social condition of the human race.

own views — completely consistent. Like other existentialists, she borrowed liberally from the insights of psychoanalysis and from Marxian perspectives but tended to ignore the deterministic conclusions of those approaches. No matter that we may be controlled by our own internal psychodynamics or by the forces of economic history; ultimately, we can always "transcend our own immanence," create ourselves anew, and overcome the straitjackets of history and culture. This view, as you can imagine, has important consequences for political action. Suppose you believe that culture shapes individuals and that it is very hard, or impossible, to overcome cultural conditioning. Then if you conclude that the condition of a particular group, such as women, is not what it should be, you should emphasize that society overall should change so that women will be changed. But if you think that the individual can always overcome his or her circumstances, then you might argue that individuals should focus on their own self-transformation. De Beauvoir argued that society should change, but if you are a thoroughgoing existentialist, it is not clear

## PROFILE: Simone de Beauvoir (1908–1986)

Simone de Beauvoir graduated from the Sorbonne second in her class, behind only Simone Weil, the Jewish writer and mystic. While at the university, she met Jean-Paul Sartre, Maurice Merleau-Ponty, and many other young intellectuals who would go on to prominence in twentieth-century French letters and politics. Some of these men and women formed the group that Sartre and de Beauvoir would call "The Family"—a collection of writers, actors, and activists who associated for intellectual stimulation and social support for more than sixty years.

De Beauvoir and Sartre formed a partnership while they were in their early twenties. Sartre decided that theirs was an "essential" love that would be most important in their lives—but that did not rule out "contingent" love affairs with other people. Indeed, Sartre went on to develop a reputation as one of France's most compulsive womanizers. De Beauvoir consistently claimed that Sartre's myriad one-night stands did not bother her at all. She herself formed several years-long liaisons with other men, most notably Nelson Algren, the American writer. Algren pressed for marriage, but de Beauvoir was opposed to the institution and unwilling to put anyone before Sartre. De Beauvoir remained active and involved with writing, traveling, and constant political work until close to the end of her life.

why you should not focus on your own personal transformation to overcome the culture.

What is a woman? de Beauvoir wondered. It cannot be a simple biological category, for there are people who have the relevant biological equipment who are nevertheless excluded from "womanhood." In one of her most famous passages, de Beauvoir argues that "one is not born, but rather becomes, a woman." The category of womanhood is imposed by civilization. And the fundamental social meaning of woman is Other. De Beauvoir held, "No group ever sets itself up as the One without at once setting up the Other over against itself." She argued that people in small towns do this to strangers, natives of one country will view natives of another country as Others, and members of one race will invariably set up the members of another race as Others. Others are mysterious and almost by definition need not be treated with the same consideration and respect that the members of one's own group must be accorded. Men set up women as Others, de Beauvoir observed, and since men have the political and social power, women come to *see themselves* as Others. They become alienated from themselves.

As she articulated what it was like to be the Other, de Beauvoir ridiculed certain popular myths, including that of "feminine mystery." Very handy concept, she pointed out. To paraphrase her, if you do not understand what another person is complaining about, well, you need not bother to listen sympathetically or place yourself imaginatively in that person's position. Just say, "Oh well, members of that group are just so mysterious!" and you are off the hook. If they want something different from what you want, you do not need to give equal weight to their preferences because everyone knows that their preferences are mysterious. De Beauvoir

## Liberal Feminism and Radical Feminism

Feminism comes in lots of varieties: socialist, psychoanalytic, postmodern, radical, and liberal. These last two are the kinds you have probably come across the most often when reading the papers and popular magazines. Learning the differences between the two can help you make sense of the next editorial you read on women's issues.

**Liberal feminism** has its roots in some very traditional American notions: freedom of choice and equality of opportunity. Liberal feminists insist that women can do everything men do if only they are given a fair chance. Liberal feminists do not generally ask whether the things men are doing are really *worth* doing. Nor do they challenge those women who are living out traditional roles. Their focus is on making sure there is freedom and opportunity for those who *do not* want to live out traditional roles. Liberal feminists tend to focus on changing restrictive laws and eliminating formal barriers to women's advancement.

**Radical feminists** think the problems run very deep and that the solutions must cut deep too. They argue that entrenched social attitudes do as much or more harm than restrictive laws. To change social attitudes so that women are taken seriously, they think drastic steps must be taken. In particular, they believe that reducing women to their sexuality is the worst thing the culture does; it fosters rape, violence, and general contempt for women. Thus, they target cultural phenomena such as pornography, advertising, and music videos that present women as nothing but sexual toys. Liberal feminists object that protesting these phenomena is too much like censorship and, hence, contrary to freedom. Radical feminists reply that until women are safe from violence in the street and in their own homes, they will never truly be free.

pointed out that men had conveniently argued not that women were mysterious *to men* — that might imply that men were stupid — but, rather, that they were mysterious *objectively*, absolutely.

One final consequence of de Beauvoir's existentialist perspective is that she does not emphasize freedom of choice to the same extent that the English writers do. Not all choices are okay. From de Beauvoir's perspective, if all you do is stay home and have babies, then you might as well be a brood mare. After all, *all* animals reproduce; there is nothing distinctively human about simple reproduction. Distinctively human activity is the activity of the mind, of culture, and of self-transcendence.

The publication of *The Second Sex* in 1949 created a furor, and de Beauvoir was startled at the vitriolic response that many critics had toward her work. But there was no turning back; the ideas were now rolling again, and over the next thirty years there would be a huge resurgence of feminist thought. The end of the socially turbulent 1960s was a particularly fertile time for feminist theory (it was also when the public began talking about "radical feminists"; see the box "Liberal Feminism and Radical Feminism" for one explanation of "radical feminism"). The five-year period from 1968 to 1973 saw publication of several classic feminist texts, including Robin Morgan's *Sisterhood Is Powerful* (1970) and **Kate Millett**'s *Sexual Politics* (1970). Influential in bringing feminist thinking to the attention of the larger public was **Gloria Steinem** (see Profile).

Kate Millett's work was inspiring to many writers because she gave a systematic analysis of how women are oppressed by patriarchal institutions. Her work was

## PROFILE: Gloria Steinem

One of the best-known contemporary feminists is Gloria Steinem. Steinem was born into a working-class family in Toledo, Ohio, in 1934. Her parents were divorced when she was relatively young, and she spent much of her youth and adolescence in relative poverty, caring for her emotionally unstable mother. She graduated from Smith College in 1956 and began her career as a journalist. In the 1960s she became involved in the women's movement and has remained one of feminism's most visible and recognizable activists. Probably her single most important accomplishment was helping to found the original *Ms.* magazine, which brought women's perspectives and issues to the attention of mainstream America.

Steinem has written insightfully on many issues, including the differences between male and female college students. Young men, she noted, are often at their most radical and rebellious during their college years. Young women often start out quite conservative in their early twenties and become more radical and politically oriented only later on. Steinem suggests that this difference stems from the divergence in men's and women's lives as they get older.

In college, all students, male and female, are more or less equally poor, have equal living situations in dorms or shared housing, and are generally equally rewarded by their professors for hard work. Thus, for many women college students, the feminist battles all seem to be won; men and women are equal. Not until young women get out into the working world and are faced with (for example) the fact that male high school graduates still earn, on average, more than female college graduates, do the differences between men's and women's situations become more apparent. Furthermore, women come to recognize that children are still largely considered the mother's responsibility, so the problems of combining career and parenthood rest more heavily on them than on men.

Finally, women in their late teens and early twenties are at the peak of their social power: still very sexually desirable, still full of potential as wives and childbearers. As women age, however, they lose this social power as their attractiveness fades, and this loss can be a very radicalizing experience — particularly when their gray-haired male contemporaries are still being called distinguished, instead of haggard.

inspiring to many because she challenged those who suggested that women actually had lots of power to look at the avenues of power. She ran through the list: industry, the military, technology, academia, science, politics, and finance. How many of these avenues of power had women at the top ranks? There might be women bank tellers, but how many large banks had women presidents or even vice presidents? How many women were in Congress? How many women were generals? How many women university presidents — or even tenured professors? Millett directed attention not to personal relationships but, rather, to the structure of society. She also looked at the socialization process and observed that the characteristics systematically encouraged in women — passivity, ignorance, docility, "virtue" — were those that made them convenient subordinates. Millett focused especially on the way the political, sociological, and psychological aspects of male–female relations were interrelated. If you have to take on a certain type of role in society, Millett maintained, it is to your advantage to develop the psychological characteristics that make that role easier. One of Millett's major contributions to the second wave of feminism was to make these links explicit.

Another classic text from this period was **Shulamith Firestone**'s *The Dialectic of Sex* (1970). Now the writers discussed in this chapter take it for granted that women's subordinate status is a social and political problem, not a biological one. Almost all feminists think that the biological differences between men and women, though real, are not in themselves anywhere near sufficient to explain the extremely different social roles men and women play. Conservative thinkers such as Freud, who argued that anatomy is destiny, are routinely dismissed by contemporary feminists and other social philosophers. Firestone argued that women's childbearing was at the root of their social oppression. Thus, she might be categorized as a *biological determinist*. She argued that reproductive technology was the route to women's freedom; developments that liberated women from having to bear and nurse children would free them to participate as equals in the new society.

Firestone was not an unguarded optimist, though. She argued that reproductive technology could be used against women as well as for them. Therefore, it would be necessary for women to seize control of the new fertility technology to make sure it was put to legitimate uses. Firestone suggested that if babies were born through artificial reproduction, they would be born to both sexes equally and that "the tyranny of the biological family would be broken."

## Androgyny as an Alternative

Suppose you have become convinced that de Beauvoir was right, that people have an unfortunate tendency to set themselves up as Self versus Other, or Us versus Them. One solution that might seem hopeful is to eliminate the differences between groups of people as much as possible so that there would be less reason to feel that the members of a different group were Others. This is the logic of the "melting pot" ideal of race relations. If there were no more distinct races but, rather, only one blended race, there would be no more basis for racism.

Well, if there were no obvious differences between the sexes, there would be no more basis for sexism either. There is, of course, no possibility (in the near future) of *completely* eliminating the biological differences between the sexes; our reproductive plumbing will probably remain different. But as almost all feminists have observed, there are very few other differences between men and women that are not socially constructed. Certainly it seems likely that men's and women's behaviors and interests are formed more by society than by biology. There is plenty of evidence for that claim from anthropology and biology. In some cultures women adorn their bodies, and in some cultures men do. In some cultures men are responsible for the finances, and in other cultures women are. For almost every behavior you can name, there has probably been at least one culture in which it was men's purview and another in which it was women's.

You may think that women are physically weaker than men, and they may be as a general rule, but think how different they might be if they were raised to develop their physical strength as a matter of course. After all, women athletes are hardly fragile flowers. And if you compare women who do manual labor for a living with men who sit behind desks pushing pencils, you will hardly conclude that women are naturally weaker than men. A lot of that strength difference is culturally imposed, as are the more subtle social differences between men and women.

So many feminists in the late 1960s and early 1970s concluded that perhaps **androgyny** (from *andros,* the Greek word for man, and *gyne,* the Greek word for woman) would be the ideal solution. No more setting up one group as the Other; instead, let's all be one homogeneous group. Since there will be no other set, one set of people will not be able to abuse the other set.

An androgynous culture could take several forms. First, you could have a culture in which everyone, girls and boys, are raised exactly the same: given the same education, the same games to play, the same challenges to face, the same rules to follow. You would probably end up with a culture where it was not immediately apparent which people were female and which were male. There would be no sex roles; no concept of masculine and feminine. There would be only one standard for everyone.

Or you might have a culture in which there are concepts of masculine and feminine, but they are not directly matched with males and females. So you could have "feminine" men and "masculine" women. For such a society to work and really be free, there could be no social stigma attached to being a "masculine" woman or a "feminine" man. All choices would be equally acceptable. A very free world, indeed.

The first possible society, called **monoandrogyny,** is endorsed by **Ann Ferguson.** In her influential essay "Androgyny as an Ideal for Human Development" (1977), Ferguson argues that since men and women are socially unequal, there can be no true love between them. Ideal love is the love between equals. Ferguson also suggests that because of this lack of ideal love, we are all unable to develop fully as human beings. She argues that a truly androgynous society would allow us all to develop fully as human beings.

What would an androgynous personality be like? Ferguson wondered. Well, both men and women need to be active, independent, creative, and productive. They both need meaningful involvement in their community. Ferguson believed that being active and assertive were rightly thought of as valuable human characteristics, not just valuable male characteristics. Active and assertive did not necessarily mean aggressive and competitive; if we eliminate the competitive, hierarchical aspects of the culture, we might produce assertive people who were also cooperative and supportive of one another. Androgynous men would be more sensitive to the needs and concerns of others than they are now. This would make them better parents, among other things. But equally important, men and women would be able to enjoy much richer relationships with each other because they would have more in common. Shared experiences and shared activities frequently lead to deeper bonds between people. If men and women were raised androgynously, they would have more communication, more companionship, and deeper love and understanding for each other. Ferguson's hope was that a monoandrogynous society would lead to more loving and deeply mutual relationships between people.

**Joyce Trebilcot,** in "Two Forms of Androgynism" (1977), argues for the second type of androgynous society. She suggests that we need not eliminate the categories of "masculine" and "feminine." Instead, we should just let individuals choose which type of role they wish to adopt. She calls this type of society *P,* for **polyandrogyny,** and contrasts it with hypothetical society *M,* for monoandrogyny, the type of society Ferguson was arguing for. Trebilcot argues that society *P* is better than society *M* because *P* allows individuals greater freedom of choice; but she ends by suggesting that if *M* is really the better society, then people will probably eventually freely choose it.

Trebilcot was more concerned with freedom of choice than with fostering loving and mutual relationships between people. She understood the persuasive force of Ferguson's argument and reflected on the characteristics that might be valuable for both sexes. From traditionally feminine traits, she thought that openness, responsiveness, compassion, expressiveness, and tenderness might be good qualities for all to have. From the traditionally male basket, she believed that being logical, objective, efficient, responsible, independent, and courageous would benefit everyone. But Trebilcot was concerned how one might prove that these traits were good for everyone. She argued that the best test would be to allow everyone to pick whatever traits he or she might like to have. Then, once everyone was fully informed and genuinely free to choose what type of person to be, perhaps everyone would in fact choose monoandrogyny. Trebilcot argued that polyandrogyny was the best strategy to adopt because it preserved freedom and would lead to monoandrogyny anyway if monoandrogyny were indeed the best type of society to have.

## Problems with Androgyny as an Ideal

Although the logic behind the push for androgyny seemed reasonable, after a while some feminist theorists began to see that it had some deep conceptual problems. It was all very well to say that there were good feminine qualities and good masculine qualities and that everybody should have some of each, but what if those qualities were really direct opposites? It would then be impossible to combine the two sets of qualities because they would simply cancel each other out. If the ideal for one set of people is to be rational, calm, and silent, and the ideal for the other set is to be emotional and expressive, it is difficult to see how those qualities could all be combined to make one whole, balanced human. Feminist philosopher Mary Daly, whose work is discussed further in Chapter 13, argued that androgyny as an ideal would not work because it would be like "two distorted halves of a human being stuck together [something like Jennifer Aniston and Brad Pitt (our example, not Daly's) scotch-taped together] as if two distorted 'halves' could make a whole." After all, one cannot expect to combine the concept of "master" and the concept of "slave" and get the concept of a free person. The original concepts are both too warped to be usable. According to Daly, we must completely transcend those original categories and start over from scratch.

More evidence for the view that the categories of "masculine" and "feminine" were too broken ever to be fixed came both from the social sciences and from literature and philosophy. At the beginning of the 1970s, it was often remarked that **gender roles** inhibited everyone, male and female alike. Men were out of touch with their feelings and were unable to cry or show affection publicly. But soon people began to realize that masculine behavior, though limiting, limited men *to* the positions of power that Kate Millett listed in her book *Sexual Politics*. If you are unable to cry and show emotion, by the standards of our culture, that makes you a very good candidate for being a CEO or high-level politician since we would not want them to fall apart emotionally at a crucial moment. Of course, being unemotional is not a *sufficient* condition for being a CEO, but it is a *necessary* one. Similarly, being ambitious and competitive—traits generally valued in men—keeps them from settling down to a nurturant family role, but it also "limits" them to a better economic position. Some people argue that it is a greater benefit to be able to be expressive and nurturing than to be able to earn in the six figures. It certainly is not bad to be expressive and nurturing, but ask yourself this: Would you rather be expressive and emotional while living just above the poverty line? Or would you rather be a little more closed off emotionally and earn a comfortable living? Those are too often the real alternatives that face men and women today.

In her important 1983 article, "Sexism," **Marilyn Frye** argues that the whole system of gender is really one of power. She implies that masculinity is about dominance and that femininity is about subordination. She notes that we go to a great deal of trouble to keep the sexes distinct; even products that have no inherent differences—like shampoos, deodorants, and razor blades—are packaged differently for men and women. Men and women talk, move, and sit differently from each other. In a myriad of unnecessary details, men and women are trained to keep themselves distinct from each other. This whole process contributes to the dominance/subordination dynamic, Frye argues.

Or consider clothing. Ever since feminism first got media attention in the 1960s, there has been a lot of fuss over the way some women who are feminists dress. Many people criticize feminists for looking sloppy and unfeminine. Actually, however, most political and social groups eventually develop a general style of dress that helps them form a sense of community and solidarity. But for feminism, the issue goes deeper. High heels, short skirts, fragile fabrics, and tight-fitting jeans literally hobble women; they keep women more confined and uncomfortable than do the styles men wear. Frye observed that "ladies' clothing is generally restrictive, binding, burdening and frail; it threatens to fall apart and/or to uncover something that is supposed to be covered if you bend, read, kick, punch, or run." (And because physical assault is an all-too-real possibility for most women, being unable to defend yourself is a genuine problem.)

For one group to oppress another, Frye reasoned, there must be (at least) two distinct groups. The more differences between the members of one group and the members of the other group, the better because then it will seem more rational to treat the two groups differently. So, Frye argues, those thousands of ways in which artificial differences between women and men are reinforced are all little acts of **sexism.** It may seem harmless to have men's colognes and women's colognes, women's deodorants and men's deodorants, and so on, but every time we reinforce the view that men and women are inherently different, we also reinforce the notion that they must inevitably be treated differently. Anything that contributes to the appearance of extreme natural dimorphism also contributes to the practice of male dominance and female subordination.

But there is a double bind here, which particularly harms women. If women are traditionally feminine, then they are participating in social practices that limit

Deodorants are sometimes packaged differently for men and women.

them to home and hearth, or to subordinate job positions. But if women act traditionally male and behave aggressively and competitively, they are often socially "punished," called dykes or ballbreakers, and are excluded from the kind of socially approved family life that competitive men freely engage in. So they are damned if they do behave subordinately and damned if they do not. To take a recent illustration of Frye's point (as well as the similar point made by Kate Millett that we mentioned earlier), Michael Eisner, the chairman of Disney, may not be able to cry in public, but he makes hundreds of millions of dollars annually, maintains a family life, and has considerable public respect (notwithstanding conservative Christians who condemn Disney for offering benefits to the partners of gay employees). Behaving femininely might have resulted in social punishment for him, but behaving masculinely did not. Thus, Frye concluded that the social constraints on women are different from the ones on men because only women are caught in the double-bind effect.

## Feminist Moral Theory

Moral theory is another area that has been recently reconceptualized by feminist perspectives. **Carol Gilligan,** a psychologist who worked with Lawrence Kohlberg on his research on the moral development of people, observed that women seemed not to score as highly as men on Kohlberg's moral development scale. Was this a failure in moral development on the part of women? Gilligan noticed that the research on *children's* moral development was actually research on *boys'* moral development; the original studies had been done in boys' schools and universities and then were just assumed to fit the case of little girls and young women. Little girls who did not fit the mold set by the research on little boys were judged to be inadequate or defective just because they were not like little boys.

Gilligan did her own research and concluded, in her famous book *In a Different Voice* (1982), that women develop differently from men and that their moral intuitions and perspectives are different as well. This fact had not been recognized because men and women speak different languages that they assume are the same, "using similar words to encode disparate experiences of self and social relationships. Because these languages share an overlapping moral vocabulary, they contain a propensity for systematic mistranslation, creating misunderstandings which impede communication and limit the potential for cooperation and care in relationships."

Gilligan found that when we look at the way women reason about moral dilemmas, we find they put more emphasis on care and on preserving personal relationships: *issues of abstract justice and rights are secondary in their moral deliberation.* Girls will place more weight than boys do on knowing the context of a moral dilemma before rendering judgment. Thus, *context* and *care for others* are central features in women's moral reasoning.

Much of Gilligan's research was grounded in the insights of psychoanalyst **Nancy Chodorow** [CHO-duh-row]. Chodorow argued that our contemporary child-rearing practices foster a strong need for connectedness in little girls and for separation and autonomy in little boys. Because mothers are the first people children get attached to and identify with, girls and boys must then go through substantially different processes in establishing their gender identities: the girls can continue to perceive themselves as continuous with their mothers, but the boys must make a shift to adopt the male gender identity.

Little girls and little boys thus learn very different lessons about how to relate to the world and others in it. Girls develop their sense of themselves as women by means of *personal identification* with their mothers. According to Chodorow, personal identification consists in "diffuse identification with someone else's general personality, behavioral traits, values, and attitudes." Boys, however, develop their identities by means of *positional identification:* "Positional identification consists, by contrast, in identification with specific aspects of another's role." In other words, boys learn that to be a man means to be away at work, whereas girls learn that to be a woman means to be just like mommy in her personality, values, and so forth.

Chodorow argued that this split in gender development has resulted in a great deal of grief for the culture: boys wind up not just isolated and separate but positively **misogynous** because of their efforts to establish themselves as "not-mom." Girls, in contrast, often suffer because they do not extricate themselves sufficiently from others in their milieu and wind up unable to distinguish their own needs from those of others and hence are more easily subject to exploitation. Chodorow concluded that these problems could be diminished if men and women took equal responsibility for child rearing and work outside the home, thereby allowing both boys and girls to participate in both positional and personal identification. Presumably, little girls would become more autonomous and little boys would become more "connected" and less misogynous.

Another important theorist, **Nel Noddings,** in *Caring, a Feminine Approach to Ethics and Moral Education* (1984), described an ethics of caring as arising out of the memory of natural caring, in which the one caring responds to the one cared for out of love and natural inclination. An **ethics of caring** is not a set of principles or maxims but a way of responding to people and situations.

The ethics of caring was contrasted by Gilligan and Noddings with the abstract ethics of rights, justice, fairness, rules, and blind impartiality. Noddings notes that in the ethics of rights and justice, one's thought, in considering a moral situation, "moves immediately to abstraction where thinking can take place clearly and logically in isolation from the complicating factors of particular persons, places, and circumstances," whereas within an ethics of caring, one's thought "moves to concretization where its feelings can be modified by the introduction of facts, the feeling of others, and personal histories." Noddings, unlike Gilligan, thought the ethics of caring preferable to an ethics of rights; Gilligan did not make this claim of superiority.

Another writer who has picked up on these themes and worked toward developing a moral theory in response to them is **Sara Ruddick.** In her 1986 essay, "Maternal Thinking," Ruddick discussed the concerns and perspectives of mothers in some patriarchal cultures and then considered how these concerns and perspectives can structure our moral responses to the world. Ruddick calls this approach to the world **maternal thinking.**

Ruddick describes the social reality of motherhood as expressed in the heterosexual nuclear family of white, middle-class, capitalist America. She invites women from other traditions to reflect on the ways in which their experiences of mothering and being mothered are both similar to and different from her own experiences. Mothers must preserve their children, must foster their children's development, and must shape them into people who are acceptable to the next generation. Mothers are typically held responsible for these three things, though they do not have anywhere near complete control over their children's environment. In response to the very real fragility of children, who can be killed or disabled in accidents, suffer through long, painful illnesses, or simply fail to thrive in an often hostile world, mothers can develop a metaphysical attitude called "holding." Ruddick says it is "an attitude elicited by the work of 'world-*protection*, world-*preservation*, world-*repair* . . . the invisible weaving of a frayed and threadbare family life.'" Since mothers recognize that they love very fragile beings, maternal thinking sees humility and resilient cheerfulness as virtues. Humility in this sense is the knowledge that one has sharp limits on what can be done to protect and preserve fragile beings in a harsh world. The resilient cheerfulness is the refusal to sink into melancholy about one's own limitations. Ruddick distinguishes this cheerfulness from "cheery denial"; the good humor she has in mind is not the simple refusal to see the world as it is. Rather, it is the much harder task of seeing the pain in the world but refusing to be paralyzed and overcome by it.

Ruddick suggests we might employ these virtues in dealing with the world at large, not merely with our own children. A morality that extends the metaphor of maternal thinking would be less self-centered and less prone to hyperindividualism than other paradigms of morality. It is important to note, too, that Ruddick believes that "maternal practice" is something anyone can do, regardless of gender. Men who adopt this attitude toward the world and toward others are maternal thinkers even though they are not biological mothers. Ruddick is not guilty of biological determinism here.

Feminist ethics is not an undifferentiated monolith speaking forth in single loud acclaim for an ethics of caring and in denigration of an ethics of rights and justice. Some feminist ethicists have noted that a care-centered ethic has perhaps not been freely chosen by women but, rather, has arisen to serve the needs of patriarchal society. Men, it might be said, would hardly object to being surrounded by caring attendants. Other feminist moral and political philosophers, including one we discuss next, have emphasized the utility of an ethics of rights and justice as a foundation for social institutions where the competing claims of persons who do not know each other must be balanced. We have seen how Harriet Taylor operated within this framework to advance the cause of women in the nineteenth century.

## Justice, Gender, and the Family: Susan Moller Okin

One of the most important concepts of feminist ethics, some say *the* most important concept, is that of **gender.** A person's gender is the person's biological sex *as constructed, understood, interpreted, and institutionalized by society.* That gender is real is what de Beauvoir meant by her famous remark that one is not born but, rather, becomes a woman. Feminist social theorists have observed that traditional moral and political philosophies have largely ignored issues related to gender — or have served to perpetuate the inequalities between the genders.

In her book *Justice, Gender, and the Family* (1989), **Susan Moller Okin** analyzed several of the contemporary works on justice from a feminist perspective. She argued that the theories of Rawls, Nozick, MacIntyre, Walzer, and others (discussed in Chapter 12) have been virtually blind to questions of justice raised by the facts of gender. "Almost all current theorists continue to assume that the 'individual' who is the basic subject of their theories is the male head of a fairly traditional household," she wrote. Their theories "are about men with wives at home." "Thus the application of principles of justice to relations between the sexes, or within the household, is frequently, though tacitly, ruled out from the start."

Okin was especially critical of the virtue ethics theory of MacIntyre and the libertarian philosophy of Nozick, which, she wrote, is reduced to nonsense when women are taken into account. Nozick's theory is based on the ideas that a person owns what he produces through his own efforts, capacities, talents, and the like, and that his entitlement to what he owns takes precedence over all other rights, even the right to subsistence. The theory is predicated, Okin wrote, on the belief that each person owns himself. And that assumption works, she argued, only if we ignore that persons are themselves products of specifically female capacities and female labor. Nozick's theory, she charged, is simply unable to explain away the implication of this fact — namely, "that women's entitlement rights to those they produce must take priority over persons' rights to themselves at birth." His theory is thus illogical and absurd: "If persons do not even 'own' themselves, in the sense of being entitled to their own persons, bodies, natural talents, abilities, and so on, then there would appear to be no basis for anyone's owning anything else." In short, a feminist analysis of the theory "leaves the core of his theory — the principle of acquisition — mired in self-contradiction."

Okin was also critical of the communitarian theories of justice, like those of MacIntyre, that ground justice in traditions or "shared understandings." "A number of feminist theorists and scholars of moral development have come to look on communitarianism as an ally in their struggle against what they see as a masculinist abstraction and emphasis on justice, impartiality, and universality," she wrote. However, she said, "Feminists need to be wary of such alliances." MacIntyre's ethical "traditions," which, according to him, give the best account of justice, not only exclude but also *depend* "upon the exclusion of the great majority of people, including all women." "It is by now obvious that many of 'our' traditions, and certainly those evaluated most highly by MacIntyre, are so permeated by the patriarchal power structure within which they evolved as to require nothing less than radical and intensive challenge if they are to meet truly humanist conceptions of the virtues." According to MacIntyre, traditions are to be tested by whether they help persons answer real moral questions. Thus, Okin imagines a young American woman considering MacIntyre's preferred traditions:

> To start with, these traditions have no comprehension of her need to be both family member and wage worker. Engaging in conversation with Aristotle will first tell her that her sex is "a deformity in nature," which exists only for the purpose of procreating the male sex, the original and true form of the human being. Engaging in conversation with MacIntyre on Aristotle's exclusion of women from all but domestic life will raise the possibility of Plato's solution: abolish the family. . . . Turning to Augustine, she may be comforted by his conviction that she is the spiritual equal to man, but his equally firm conviction that her physical sexuality makes her necessarily man's inferior is unlikely to help her. . . . Turning to Thomism — the tradition MacIntyre finds the best embodiment of rationality because of its ability to accommodate Augustinian insights with Aristotelian theorizing — she will encounter the . . . view that women are a deformity in nature [combined] with the Christian view that women's sexuality is to blame for men's sinful lust. In this tradition, she will find serious consideration being given to questions such as whether women were included in the original Creation and whether, in order to be resurrected, they must be reborn as men. . . . And the woman I have imagined presents the easiest female test of these traditions, being among the most advantaged of women. If she were poor, black, lesbian, old, disabled, a single parent, or some combination of these, she would surely be even less likely to find herself and her situation rendered more coherent by turning to MacIntyre's traditions. . . . She may indeed conclude, without looking much further into them, that there is something fundamentally incoherent about the traditions themselves and that she will have to look elsewhere for answers to questions about justice and rationality.

By contrast, the famous two principles of justice put forth by John Rawls (and discussed in Chapter 12), in the opinion of Okin, if applied consistently and wholeheartedly, "can lead us to challenge fundamentally the gender system of our society." Rawls's original position, with the veil of ignorance hiding from its participants their sex as well as their other characteristics, talents, and aims, is, she wrote, a powerful concept for challenging the gender structure. Indeed, in Okin's view, fulfilling Rawls's criteria for justice would require *abolition* of gender.

However, Okin faulted Rawls for not drawing out and developing this important implication of his theory. She also criticized him for seeming to bring only male heads of families to the table in the original position. However, the main problem with Rawls, in Okin's view, is that he simply *assumes* the family is a just institution, whereas, in fact, this assumption needs careful consideration.

Okin's own consideration of the family led her to conclude that it is far from being a just institution and that, consequently, it is poorly suited for the sort of moral development of children that is required for understanding and applying Rawls's principles of justice. "How, in hierarchical families in which sex roles are rigidly assigned, are we to learn, as Rawls's theory of moral development requires us, to 'put ourselves into another's place and find out what we would do in his position'? Unless they are parented equally by adults of both sexes, how will children of both sexes come to develop a sufficiently similar and well-founded moral psychology to enable them to engage in the kind of deliberation about justice that is exemplified in the original position? If both parents do not *share* in nurturing activities, are they both likely to maintain in adult life the capacity for empathy that underlies a sense of justice?"

That someone would indict the family — and call it unjust — may startle some readers, especially in light of the current political trend toward widespread worship at the shrine of "family values." The problem, Okin argued, is that the practices of family life in society today are structured by *gender,* and gender-structured marriage makes women *vulnerable.* Even though many women today are employed, they still are expected to do the largest portion of unpaid family work, including child care and housework. They are much more likely than their husbands to leave their jobs or to work part time because of family responsibilities, and they are much more likely to move because of their husbands' jobs or career opportunities. This means that they advance more slowly than do their husbands and gain less seniority. Thus, the difference between their wages and their husbands' wages *increases* over time. And therefore, because the husband earns more, it becomes *even less desirable* for the unpaid family work to be shared equally. In short, "the cycle of inequality is perpetuated." In most cases the law treats men and women as equals, but the heavy weight of tradition, together with the effects of socialization, reinforces gender roles deemed unequal in prestige or worth.

## Sexism and Language

Language has contributed to women's lower social status in quite varied ways. Many terms of the language that are supposed to be gender neutral are not; *man,* for example, is supposed to serve double duty, referring both to humanity as a whole and male human beings. Similarly, *he* is the pronoun used both when we know that the person being referred to is male and when we do not know the gender of the individual. This is not logical; either there should be one pronoun to refer to everybody, or there should be three pronouns: male, female, and as-yet-undetermined. Feminist theorists have argued that by making words like *man* and *he* serve both as gender-specific and gender-neutral terms, the net effect is to "erase" women from our conversational landscape. The actual psychology of human beings is such that when we hear *he*, we think "male," even if that was not the speaker's intention. Philosopher Janice Moulton gives a good example of this tendency to hear *man* and *he* as male even when the original use of the term was gender-neutral. She asks us to consider the familiar syllogism:

1. All men are mortal.
2. Socrates is a man.
3. Therefore, Socrates is mortal.

Now substitute the name Sophia for Socrates. Clearly, the "man" in the first line is supposed to be gender neutral; it is supposed to mean "all members of the human species." Yet when the name Sophia is substituted, the second term of the syllogism seems glaringly false. Thus, Moulton argues, to say we have two meanings for "man," one gender neutral and one gender specific, and we can always keep them clear and separate really does not hold water. Though we might like to believe there are two clearly differentiated uses of "man" and "he," in practice we hardly make that distinction at all. This point is all the clearer when we realize that generations of logic teachers have taught that syllogism without ever noticing that it is invalid, since the "man" in the first term and the "man" in the second term have different extensions and intentions.

Sometimes the causality seems to flow the other way. Many historians and anthropologists have noted that anything associated with women tends to get devalued over time. Occupations associated with women tend to pay less and have lower status than those associated with men. This holds true across cultures even when the occupation is objectively the same; for instance, in cultures where the women build the homes, that occupation is looked down on, but in our own culture being a contractor is a perfectly respectable thing to do and often is quite well paid.

The same phenomenon holds true of language. Words associated with women come to have lower status and can even degenerate into insults. Many slang expressions and metaphors are evidence of this. These metaphors and slang expressions are taken to be evidence of underlying cultural attitudes toward women. Sometimes words start out with perfectly legitimate, nonderogatory literal meanings and, through their association with women, come to have derogatory and insulting slang meanings. Consider the words *queen, dame, madam, mistress, hussy* (which originally meant *housewife*), and *spinster*. None of the male equivalents of those words have suffered the same kind of devaluation. Through slang, women also get unflatteringly allied to animals, as in *vixen, bitch, pussy, biddy,* and *cow.* And finally, the words we use to describe sexual intercourse are often extremely violent — and the violence is metaphorically directed toward the women, not the men. The word *fuck* has *strike* as its etymological ancestor; *ream* and *drill* do not require any arcane linguistic background to understand. The language use and the attitudes are thought to influence one another; hence, if we make an effort not to use such violent metaphors, perhaps the attitudes of violence will decrease a little as well. But for the present it seems painfully clear that our language at least partly reflects certain hostile dispositions.

**Stephanie Ross,** for example, in her 1981 article "How Words Hurt: Attitude, Metaphor, and Oppression," argues that *screw* is a usefully representative metaphor that tells us more than we wanted to know about certain cultural attitudes toward women: "A screw is hard and sharp; wood by contrast is soft and yielding; force is applied to make a screw penetrate wood; a screw can be unscrewed and reused but wood—wherever a screw has been embedded in it—is destroyed forever." Ross argues that if we acknowledge that the metaphors we use convey cultural attitudes, then we can see that the attitude toward sex is that women are permanently harmed by intercourse. Furthermore, there is an odd mechanical connotation in the word *screw*. It suggests that intercourse is something alienated from ordinary human flesh and behavior. It is an interesting exercise to list all the common slang terms for sexual intercourse and try to analyze all the meanings and connotations associated with the metaphors.

## Division of Labor Analysis

The division of labor along sex lines, including the bearing and raising of children, has been extensively analyzed and discussed, especially by Marxist and socialist feminists. According to Friedrich Engels, in *The Origin of the Family, Private Property and the State* (1884), "the worldwide defeat of the female" happened when wage labor created surplus value (roughly, more wealth than the individual or society needs for survival). Those who owned private property (through which surplus value is preserved) needed to control women's reproduction so that surplus value could be transmitted to descendants through inheritance. In short, the subjugation of women, according to early Marxist theory, emerged with private property and wage labor (see Chapter 11 for more details on Marxist theory).

However, scientific research of cultures (ethnography) seems to indicate that social inequality between men and women exists even in cultures where there is no private property or wage labor. For an example of a Marxist feminist response, we might consider **Marielouise Janssen-Jurreit,** who theorized that sexual domination arose in conjunction not with surplus value that was derived from wage labor but, rather, with surplus value that derived from women's services for the family or group, services like gathering firewood, carrying water, hauling loads, and most important, child rearing.

Underlying the drive to bear and rear children, according to Janssen-Jurreit, is not merely the biological drive for reproduction but straightforward cost/benefit considerations as well. The benefits of children range from having allies against dangers from beyond the family, clan, group, or nation to sources of old-age care. In general, the more children (within the limitations imposed by environmental factors), the greater the security (where environmental constraints are violated, impoverishment results). However, for women but not men, each pregnancy means an increase in workload and, correspondingly, diminished power. The ultimate and inevitable result is male control of reproduction, which is organized to maximize security for the male chieftain. (The details are set forth in the selection from Janssen-Jurreit at the end of this chapter.) As we have seen, Shulamith Firestone also argued that the division of reproductive labor underlies women's oppression, and psychoanalyst Nancy Chodorow believed that problems of gender development stem from child-rearing practices.

## French Feminism and Psychoanalysis

Two fundamental pillars of psychoanalysis as developed by Sigmund Freud (1859–1939) were the Oedipus complex and the castration complex. The notions were discovered by Freud in the process of his own self-analysis. Simply put, the Oedipus complex is the desire of the male child to possess the mother and kill the father as a hated rival for the attentions of the mother. The castration complex involves the male child's fear of being castrated by the father or a surrogate because of the child's relative powerlessness. A correlate of these theories is that the female child experiences penis envy when she discovers the male child has a penis and she doesn't.

Although these two central notions have remained in play in pschoanalytic practice, their role had been softened or played down over time, in part because of the number of female patients and psychoanalysts. The Freudian perspective had undergone critical reexamination for its patriarchal starting point based on the male child–mother relationship. The relationship of the male child and the mother had seemed to become almost all important, to the exclusion of the father and others. It is here that **Jacques Lacan** (1901–1981) stepped in to reestablish the importance of the father in the development of the child. In the process of doing this, he reinvigorated the importance of the Oedipus complex and the castration complex, making them, if possible, more central than ever in psychoanalytic theory.

Melanie Klein (1882–1960) had earlier theorized that the penis is a uniquely special object for the child. Lacan extended that idea in three directions. First, he theorized, the child is dependent upon the mother from birth and the child seeks to please the mother in order to get what it needs for survival. The child therefore tries to discover what the mother wants and tries to be that object for the mother. And thus, for example, neurotics seek to be the phallus that the mother lacks. The attempt usually ends badly because the father is much more powerful than the child and prevents the child's ascendency.

Second, according to Lacan, the child, having been blocked by the father, is frustrated in his relationship to the mother, which is based merely on "imaginary objects." The child is forced to leave the Oedipal situation with the mother and to enter into a wider network of relationships in the world. Lacan refers to this as a community based on symbolic rather than merely imaginary interactions. It is a network of relations that are not merely one way (mother to child) but based on trading or an exchange of gifts. The child is forced, in other words, to leave the relatively exclusive regulation of the mother in the Oedipal relationship via the intervention of the father. This, according to Lacan, is a vital step in the child's growing up and achieving an identity of its own. In this way the child begins to become a "subject" and eventually an adult who can consciously pursue his own desires.

Third (according to Lacan), the phallus, now symbolic as well as imaginary, becomes that which will be promised to the male child for future usage. The child will eventually replace the father without the necessity of killing him. This movement on the part of the child out of the Oedipal situation is called the *paternal metaphor*. Not only does the father separate the child from the mother, but he begins to lead the child from the realm of imaginary images into the realm of symbolic verbal integration. This eventually allows the young person to find a place in the world via a process of identification with ideals. In this way the child grows up and is able to avoid neurotic or psychotic disorders.

Luce Irigaray (1930– ) was born in Belgium and originally studied literature at the University of Louvain. She later studied philosophy, linguistics, and psychology in Paris and became a Lacanian psychoanalyst. Irigaray gradually developed a radical feminist critique of Lacan and Freud, viewing traditional psychoanalytical theory as part and parcel of patriarchal society and culture. Eventually expelled from the Lacanian School of Psychoanalysis at Vincennes, she has been connected since 1987 with the International College of Philosophy in Paris.

Irigaray realized that for Lacan, the woman was reduced to the presymbolic, imaginary realm of the child. The symbolic order is purely phallic because the phallus is the source of all signification. This meant, she believed, that women were excluded from language and reduced to silence. In other words, women could only be understood via the masculine "look," masculine language, and masculine symbolism. An added consequence of the dominance of the phallus is that the masculine represented fullness of being and the feminine represented absence or a lack, hence penis envy. Since language is irreducibly phallic, women are reduced to being the radically other, that is, castrated men.

Irigaray represented an important part of an anti-Oedipus campaign. She rejected the reduction of the woman to an object and sought to establish them as *subjects*— subjects who are radically different from men. For her, the subject in philosophy has always been masculine, even when couched in a seemingly neutral or universal or transcendental form. She saw Plato's cave, for example, as a womb and the escape out of the cave into the sunlight as male escape from the womb. This is a variation of Lacan's notion that male identity occurs via abandoning the mother for the father. And it is the father who represents Plato's Idea of the Highest Good.

This cultural male dominance for Irigaray carries over into religion — in particular, where God is represented as patriarchal, namely, God the Father. Irigaray searched for the divine feminine and believed that the maternal gods preceded the paternal gods. In addition to looking for a feminine god, Irigaray also looked for philosophical concepts that are uniquely feminine and spurned in the male-dominated history of western philosophy. Examples of these concepts included the ideas of multiplicity, difference, becoming and the notion of the beauty of the human body.

Irigaray sought a radical "discourse" with the feminine. She demanded not only a feminine God, but also a feminine language and a feminine way of thinking critically and philosophically. The feminine must be established as a paradigm of maternal otherness or difference. The feminine body and female sexuality must be rediscovered and celebrated in its uniqueness. Instead of carrying the label of "hysterics" and being reduced to objects for male exploitation, women must find their own identity rooted in their own language, their own symbolism, their own thinking. This process of femininization must extend over the entire spectrum of human existence from the human body to the divine. A vital part of this project is the establishing of positive rights for women that must find expression in laws, customs, and everyday practices. With Irigaray, the woman is back in philosophy and psychoanalysis; and the dialectic continues.

## Pornography

Feminist writers suggest, both directly and indirectly, that the relations between men and women are built on the model of domination and subordination. Of course, sexuality is one of the important features of the relationships between men and women. It should not surprise you, then, to learn that many feminist critics maintain that our current practices of heterosexual sex are also structured by domination and subordination. In particular, they focus on the issue of pornography. Pornography, they argue, both encapsulates and reinforces all the worst aspects of heterosexual sex. It tends to objectify women; that is, it tends to reduce women to nothing other than their sexuality and suggests that their sexuality is the only important thing about them. To view someone as an object is to treat her as if she had no ends or goals of her own. Thus, it is suggested that pornography reinforces certain other problems in the culture, notably rape and sexual harassment. If we grow up in a culture in which women are characteristically viewed as being reducible to their sexuality, it is hard to see why men should not grope them at work or even rape them on dates, since men are not taught to emphasize that women have feelings and plans and purposes — purposes that might not include having sex right at that instant. Objectification is always a moral problem because objects are the opposite of persons. Persons must be treated respectfully, but objects have no feelings or ideas; they are there to be used.

But an even more significant (though related) problem with pornography is the rapidly increasing level of violence present even in the so-called mainstream magazines and movies; pick up any issue of *Penthouse,* and you will probably be surprised to see the number of violent stories and photo spreads. This fact has led some theorists to define pornography as "any use of the media which equates sex and violence." Feminist writer Andrea Dworkin and University of Michigan law professor Catharine MacKinnon's definition of pornography includes reference to "women . . . presented as sexual objects who enjoy pain and humiliation . . . women . . . presented in scenarios of degradation, injury, torture, shown as filthy or inferior, bleeding, bruised, or hurt in a context that makes these conditions sexual." Violence and humiliation are the instruments of oppression and domination. Thus, the objection to pornography is that it endorses and reinforces the use of violence and humiliation in structuring the relations between the sexes and interferes with true freedom and equality in the relations (sexual and otherwise) between men and women.

The work of Dworkin and MacKinnon excites tremendous anger in many people, especially those who have not read it. Their research extends over a wide variety of topics of interest to feminists; MacKinnon's most well-known work concerns violent pornography: the two authored legislation in Minneapolis and Indianapolis to provide civil remedies for women who could prove they had been injured by pornography. The idea of the legislation was (roughly) to require producers of pornography to meet the kind of strict products liability that manufacturers of cars or hairspray have to meet. The legislation was instantly (misleadingly) branded as censorship, and any reasonable discussion of the merits and demerits of the law was largely swallowed up in the panic generated whenever the word "censorship" is invoked.

## The Importance of Recognizing Diversity

It is important to recognize that a variety of challenges has been made to feminist theory, some of them from women who are generally sympathetic to some of the claims of feminism. One of the most important of these challenges has come from women of color and women from working-class backgrounds. Feminism has been a largely white, middle-class phenomenon; starting with Mary Wollstonecraft, most of the women who have dominated feminist thinking have been white and middle-class. Women from other racial and class backgrounds have often felt excluded from the discussion. This is a particularly damaging charge against feminism since the theory emphasizes including the formerly excluded. Women who are not white and middle-class often point out that though they are oppressed as women, that oppression takes different forms when it is seen in context with racial and class oppression. Race, class, and gender are inextricably tied together; a working-class African American woman will be disadvantaged in different ways from a middle-class white woman. They will both have problems associated with being women, but the problems will be different.

Furthermore, women of color often feel torn between the competing claims of the members of their sex and the members of their ethnic groups. Women's groups claim that the fundamental form of oppression is sexism; other members of their ethnic groups claim that racism is the more primary problem. Since it is true that women of color are oppressed both as women and as members of a particular racial or ethnic group, they often feel pulled in many directions at once. They are also sometimes inclined to resist both groups since both seem to want them to deny at least one important feature of their identities. Feminism has slowly begun to listen to women from these different social situations and to learn from them how sexism can take many shapes. Although the theory still has a long way to go, more anthologies offering the work of feminists of color are available today than even five years ago, and more of the challenges to white middle-class feminism are being discussed in all venues of feminist philosophy. Maria Lugones, bell hooks, and Angela Davis are just a few of the different voices now widely heard in feminist philosophy. Feminist theory will not be complete until all groups are fairly represented.

## Feminist Epistemology

Many feminist writers have argued that the traditional postpositivist empiricist epistemology, which has dominated philosophy in the twentieth century, is a limited theoretical approach to human knowing. This mainstream epistemology has tended toward assuming that ideal knowers are disembodied, purely rational, fully informed, and completely objective entities. Although most philosophers admit that no human being ever approximates this ideal knower, since real people have bodies, personal histories, points of view, and so forth, most philosophers are reluctant to let go of that ideal.

Feminist epistemologists have made several challenges. First, they argue, it is troubling that the ideal *knower* resembles the ideal *male* since men are supposedly more rational, objective, and unemotional. Feminists suggest that this conveniently excludes the knowledge claims of women right off the bat. Lorraine Code, one of today's leading feminist epistemologists, points out that for feminists "the questions continually arise: Whose science — or whose knowledge — has been proved? Why has its veneration led Western societies to discount other findings, suppress other forms of experience, deny epistemic status to female . . . wisdom?"

Let us take one example of the way scientific knowledge can be biased. Lila Leibowitz cites a case in which E. O. Wilson, the sociobiologist, argues that mouse lemurs are "essentially solitary" except for certain periods in the mating cycle. It turns out that female mouse lemurs nest together; it is the males who are "essentially solitary," and this behavior is generalized over the entire species. "Dominant" males are those who manage to breed. But why should we suppose them to be dominant just for that simple reason? Perhaps those males are merely the ones the females like best, for some reason known only to the female lemurs. This "evidence" of dominant behavior is then quickly overgeneralized to provide support for Wilson's view that almost all males of almost all species are dominant over females. Scientists are not idealized objective observers. As the Wilson example shows, they import their own prejudices and biases into their observations and theories. Feminist epistemologists ask that this fact about all human beings — male and female — be acknowledged. They point out that knowledge is never gathered in a vacuum. People look for answers to specific questions, even — perhaps especially — in science. Knowledge-gathering is always done to serve human purposes, and those purposes shape the kind of knowledge that is gathered. (For a feminist perspective on the reporting of scientific studies, see the box "Backlash.")

This is not to say that feminist epistemologists want to denigrate or discount rationality or objectivity. But many are concerned that the rational/emotional, objective/subjective dichotomies are false and misleading. Most emotions are structured by rationality. Suppose, for example, you come across a friend who is obviously extremely angry. You might ask, "What's wrong? What are you angry about?" If the answer is, "Light blue shirts are back in style!" you would probably ask a few more questions since this seems too insignificant to be intensely angry about. Was your friend traumatized by light blue shirts as a child? Was he or she forced to wear them every day? If the answer is, "No, I just hate light blue shirts!" you might plausibly conclude that your friend is a little weird. Only emotions based on plausible reasons make sense to most of us. It is not true that people generally have emotional responses "for no reason at all"; if they do, they are often considered mentally unstable. Reason and emotion are more interconnected than that. Feminist epistemologists generally emphasize that knowledge-gathering is a human project and must be identified as such. Reason, emotion, social class, gender, and

## Backlash

Susan Faludi's book *Backlash* (1991) drew considerable public attention in the early 1990s. Though most people identify it as a feminist work, it is also an indictment of journalistic ethics. For example, Faludi traces the wide ripples caused by one or two inconclusive studies about women's health and happiness. These studies were grossly distorted by one or two newspapers and then picked up by television, radio, and magazines until the country was saturated with inaccurate and distorted information about women's lives. Nowhere along the line were the facts adequately checked or the conclusions challenged. Faludi also reports the myriad ways the media report half-truths, sensationalize minor, isolated events and portray them as "trends," and generally belie their claims to fairness and balance in their reporting. Faludi uses the example of their treatment of women to make her case, but the book leaves the reader wondering how many other topics receive such sloppy and biased treatment.

other factors play a role in what we can know. Any ideal that rules out the "human factor" in its characterization of knowledge is bound to be wrong and will unjustly privilege the group claiming that true knowledge is only obtainable by people who are just like them and have only their social characteristics.

In the reading selections at the end of this chapter, you will find one by **Sandra Harding,** a feminist philosopher of science, who believes that the epistemologies of scientists and philosophers of science are revealed by the metaphors they use; in the selection, she examines some of the apparently misogynous metaphors used by scientists and philosophers at the beginning of the Scientific Revolution.

## Ecofeminism

**Ecofeminism** is an emerging branch of environmental philosophy. Ecofeminists see a connection between the domination of women and the domination of nature. However, there is much healthy controversy about what the linkage is, exactly.

Two examples of ecofeminist thought are provided by the writings of Karen J. Warren and **Val Plumwood.** We include an excerpt from Warren at the end of the chapter and say something about Plumwood here, focusing on her essay "Nature, Self, and Gender: Feminism, Environmental Philosophy, and the Critique of Rationalism." The essay appeared in the 1991 issue of the journal *Hypatia*. Hypatia (370/375–415), you may recall from Chapter 4, was a mathematician, astronomer, and philosopher who became very famous when she was still a young woman living in Alexandria.

Plumwood views the "inferiorization" of both women and nature as linked. Both, she thinks, are grounded in the rationalist conception of human nature and the liberal-individualist conception of the human self, two conceptions that complement each other, according to Plumwood. They are so intimately related for her that often she treats them as pretty much the same thing.

Rationalism, or the "rationalist framework," as she sometimes calls it, is among other things a network of value dualisms, such as mind–body, reason–emotion, and masculine–feminine. These dualisms polarize and accentuate the differences between each of the paired items and construe the difference between each item and its match as one of superiority–inferiority. The first/superior item is defined in opposition to the second/inferior item, and the interests of the first/superior item always take priority over those of the second/inferior item.

One such dualism deeply entrenched in the rationalist framework, and thus in Western thought, is that of mind–body. Within the rationalist tradition we think of the mind as the *essential* part of the human self. We conceive of the mind as standing in opposition to and as of higher value than the body, which we think of as something like a servant to the mind. Further, just as the body, with its biological and animal functions, is a part of nature, nature too is conceived as of lesser importance, according to rationalism. In other words, the "characteristically and authentically human" in the rationalist tradition is defined against or in opposition to the natural, physical, or biological realm. This means that what is taken to be authentically and characteristically human is not to be found in what humans share with the natural and animal. It is found, instead, in reason and its offshoots. The human sphere and the natural sphere, seen from the framework of rationalism, are separate and distinct and cannot significantly overlap. "Nature is divided off, is alien, and usually hostile and inferior."

Another and closely related value dualism is masculine–feminine. The masculine belongs within the family of the other first items of the matched pairs, that is, with the mind and with reason. The feminine is associated with the opposite and inferior items. Thus, from the perspective of rationalism, exclusion of nature from the human sphere is just part of the rationalist story, for rationalism also rejects as inferior those parts of the human character thought of as feminine — emotion, caring, and the like.

The problem facing feminism is the inferiorization of women. The problem facing environmental philosophy is the inferiorization of nature. Careful analysis of the two problems discloses that the problems are inseparable. Both are part and parcel of rationalism and its assorted value dualisms. Therefore, according to Plumwood, both feminism and environmental philosophy face the general problem of "revaluing and reintegrating what rationalist culture has split apart and devalued."

Challenging the dualisms postulated by rationalism would involve reevaluating them and recognizing the secondary qualities as equally and fully human. This would mean, Plumwood writes, that "reproductivity, sensuality, and emotionality would be taken to be as fully and authentically human qualities as the capacity for abstract planning and calculation." Likewise, in the case of the human–nature distinction, reexamination of both the concept of the human and the contrasting concept of nature is called for. The concept of human must be freed from the legacy of rationalism, and so must the concept of nature. How, then, is nature conceived? Nature is the polarized opposite to what is human — it is conceived of as lacking those qualities that are purely human. In other words, it is conceived of, says Plumwood, as purely material and purely mechanistic. Thus, a reconceptualization of nature would involve "development of alternatives to mechanistic ways of viewing the world."

Now, complementing the rationalist conception of human nature is the liberal-individualist conception of the human self. This is the conception of the self as essentially egoistic. (It is the conception we found in moral philosophy from the Stoics through Rawls and excluding Plato, Nietzsche, and some of the communitarian critics of Rawls—see Chapter 12.) Liberal individualism, according to Plumwood, portrays the self as autonomous and separate from other individuals and as lacking essential connections to them. Its interests are distinct from the interests of others, and it utilizes others, and the world generally, as a means to meeting its own needs. Thus, because liberal individualism has permeated our thinking, we view nature as a *resource*. Other people too are resources from this perspective, and that is why the liberal-individualist tradition is so concerned with rights, duties, and fairness. We have to check one another's efforts to use others.

However, this conception of the self as autonomous and separate is not accurate, Plumwood argues, drawing on the findings and theories of feminist scholars. Humans are *social* beings, and their interests are interdependent. For example, the well-being of Brooke Moore *requires* the well-being of Moore's children—and friends and relatives. So, for Plumwood, the "relational view of self" seems much more accurate than the purely disconnected or egoistic view of self that we find in the liberal tradition in philosophy. Furthermore, this relational view of the self is a much-needed alternative to human-centered (anthropocentric) rationalism: it recognizes that nature is distinct from self but at the same time affirms our continuity with nature. For this reason, Plumwood thinks the relational view of self is a better theory of the relation of humans to nature than the theories of environmental philosophers who attempt to identify the self with nature.

Environmental philosophy in general, according to Plumwood, has failed to engage with rationalism. Environmental philosophy, she says, has tended to utilize the "ethical approach," but this approach is infected with rationalist assumptions that are in fact undesirable.

For example, in *Respect for Nature* (1986), philosopher Paul Taylor worked out an ethical position that takes living things as worthy of respect in their own right. But Taylor's theory, according to Plumwood, is embedded in the Kantian ethical framework and depends on the reason–emotion dualism Plumwood criticized. Morality is the domain of reason, according to Taylor, and only actions that are taken as a matter of principle are deemed truly moral. Actions taken out of inclination or desire or caring or love, by contrast, do not count morally. Thus, Taylor was buying into the rationalist framework, Plumwood argued. Taylor discounted caring or love for nature or for some particular part of it as belonging to an inferior domain that should be dominated by "superior, disinterested, reason." But according to Plumwood, as we have seen, such thinking implicitly discounts the emotional and feminine as inferior and lacking in virtue.

The ethical approach of Taylor and others emphasizes impartiality and objectivity and discounts special relationships, such as a person's relationship to a friend (or, for that matter, to a particular oak tree). According to Plumwood, special relationships should not be discounted. They form the basis for much of our moral life, providing a deep level of concern that is not reached through abstract reasoning. Deep respect for others, and for nature, cannot be reduced to one's duty any more than can friendship.

Plumwood is also critical of the theory of philosopher Tom Regan. In *The Case for Animal Rights* (1986), Regan extended the concepts of rights to nature. But according to Plumwood, rights philosophy too is part of the rationalist, liberal-individualist tradition, with its strong separation of autonomous selves. The concept of rights, Plumwood believes, produces absurd consequences when applied to natural ecosystems. A more promising approach, in her view, would be to "remove rights from the center of the moral stage and pay more attention to some other less dualistic moral concepts such as respect, sympathy, care, concern, compassion, gratitude, friendship, and responsibility." All of these concepts, she says, have been treated as peripheral by environmental ethics—rationalist philosophy because from the rationalist standpoint they are construed as feminine. However, these concepts, she points out, extend to the nonhuman world far more easily than do the impersonal concepts seen as central by much of environmental philosophy.

Plumwood does not think we should abandon ethics or the ethical approach to environmental issues entirely. What is needed, she says, is a richer moral stance, one that reevaluates reason—emotion and other dualistic contrasts, attaches importance to ethical concepts owing to emotionality and special relationships, and abandons the exclusive focus on the universal and the abstract.

---

SELECTION 14.1

## A Vindication of the Rights of Woman

*Mary Wollstonecraft*

---

[*In the following selection, Wollstonecraft defends the view that society should abandon the practice of enculturating women to weakness and depravity.*]

I love man as my fellow; but this sceptre, real, or usurped, extends not to me, unless the reason of man. In fact, the conduct of an accountable being must be regulated by the operations of its own reason; or on what foundation rests the throne of God?

It appears to me necessary to dwell on these obvious truths, because females have been insulated, as it were; and, while they have been stripped of the virtues that should clothe humanity, they have been decked with artificial graces that enable them to exercise a short-lived tyranny. Love, in their bosoms, taking the place of every nobler passion, their sole ambition is to be fair, to raise emotion instead of inspiring respect; and this ignoble desire, like the servility in absolute monarchies, destroys all strength of character. Liberty is the mother of virtue, and if women be, by their very constitution, slaves, and

not allowed to breathe the sharp invigorating air of freedom, they must ever languish like exotics, and be reckoned beautiful flaws in nature. . . .

But should it be proved that woman is naturally weaker than man, whence does it follow that it is natural for her to labour to become still weaker than nature intended her to be? Arguments of this cast are an insult to common sense, and savour of passion. The *divine right* of husbands, like the divine right of kings, may, it is to be hoped, in this enlightened age, be contested without danger, and though conviction may not silence many boisterous disputants, yet, when any prevailing prejudice is attacked, the wife will consider, and leave the narrow-minded to rail with thoughtless vehemence at innovation.

It is time to effect a revolution in female manners — time to restore to them their lost dignity — and make them, as a part of the human species, labour by reforming themselves to reform the world. It is time to separate unchangeable morals from local manners.

## SELECTION 14.2
# The Second Sex★

*Simone de Beauvoir*

[*The selection is from the introduction to* The Second Sex. *In it de Beauvoir asks, What is a woman? and answers that she is the Other. She then clarifies the concept of the Other, examines parallels between women and other social groupings, and explains how a woman could still be the Other despite male dependence on her. The selection leaves off as de Beauvoir begins to consider how woman's status as the Other began.*]

But first we must ask: what is a woman? . . .

To state the question is, to me, to suggest, at once, a preliminary answer. The fact that I ask it is in itself significant. A man would never get the notion of writing a book on the peculiar situation of the human male. But if I wish to define myself, I must first of all say: "I am a woman"; on this truth must be based all further discussion. A man never begins by presenting himself as an individual of a certain sex; it goes without saying that he is a man. The terms *masculine* and *feminine* are used symmetrically only as a matter of form, as on legal papers. In actuality the relation of the two sexes is not quite like that of two electrical poles, for man represents both the positive and the neutral, as is indicated by the common use of *man* to designate human beings in general; whereas woman represents only the negative, defined by limiting criteria, without reciprocity. In the midst of an abstract discussion it is vexing to hear a man say: "You think thus and so because you are a woman"; but I know that my only defense is to reply: "I think thus and so because it is true," thereby removing my subjective self from the argument. It would be out of the qu4estion to reply: "And you think the contrary because you are a man," for it is understood that the fact of being a man is no peculiarity. A man is in the right in being a man; it is the woman who is in the wrong. It amounts to this: just as for the ancients there was an absolute vertical with reference to which the oblique was defined, so there is an absolute human type, the masculine. Woman has ovaries, a uterus; these peculiarities imprison her in her subjectivity, circumscribe her within the limits of her own nature. It is often said that she thinks with her glands. Man superbly ignores the fact that his anatomy also includes glands, such as the testicles, and that they secrete hormones. He thinks of his body as a direct and normal connection with the world, which he believes he apprehends objectively, whereas he regards the body of woman as a hindrance, a prison, weighed down by everything peculiar to it. "The female is a female by virtue of a certain *lack* of qualities," said Aristotle; "we should regard the female nature as afflicted with a natural defectiveness." And St. Thomas for his part pronounced woman to be an "imperfect man," an "incidental" being. This is symbolized in Genesis where Eve is depicted as made from what Bossuet called "a supernumerary bone" of Adam.

Thus humanity is male and man defines woman not in herself but as relative to him; she is not regarded as an autonomous being. Michelet writes: "Woman, the relative being. . . ." And Benda is most positive in his *Rapport d' Uriel:* "The body of man makes sense in itself quite apart from that of woman, whereas the latter seems wanting in significance by itself. . . . Man can think of himself without woman. She cannot think of herself without man." And she is simply what man decrees; thus she is called "the sex," by which is meant that she appears essentially to the male as a sexual being. For him she is sex—absolute sex, no less. She is defined and differentiated with reference to man and not he with reference to her; she is the incidental, the inessential as opposed to the essential. He is the Subject, he is the Absolute—she is the Other.

The category of the *Other* is as primordial as consciousness itself. In the most primitive societies, in the most ancient mythologies, one finds the expression of a duality—that of the Self and the Other. This duality was not originally attached to the division of the sexes; it was not dependent upon any empirical facts. It is revealed in such works

★Author's footnotes omitted. From *The Second Sex* by Simone de Beauvoir, translated by H. M. Parshley, copyright © 1952 and renewed 1980 by Alfred A. Knopf, Inc., a division of Random House, Inc. Used by permission of Alfred A. Knopf, a division of Random House, Inc.

as that of Granet on Chinese thought and those of Dumézil on the East Indies and Rome. The feminine element was at first no more involved in such pairs as Varuna–Mitra, Uranus–Zeus, Sun–Moon, and Day–Night than it was in the contrasts between Good and Evil, lucky and unlucky auspices, right and left, God and Lucifer. Otherness is a fundamental category of human thought.

Thus it is that no group ever sets itself up as the One without at once setting up the Other over against itself. If three travelers chance to occupy the same compartment, that is enough to make vaguely hostile "others" out of all the rest of the passengers on the train. In small-town eyes all persons not belonging to the village are "strangers" and suspect; to the native of a country all who inhabit other countries are "foreigners"; Jews are "different" for the anti-Semite, Negroes are "inferior" for American racists, aborigines are "natives" for colonists, proletarians are the "lower class" for the privileged.

Lévi-Strauss, at the end of a profound work on the various forms of primitive societies, reaches the following conclusion: "Passage from the state of Nature to the state of Culture is marked by man's ability to view biological relations as a series of contrasts; duality, alternation, opposition, and symmetry, whether under definite or vague forms, constitute not so much phenomena to be explained as fundamental and immediately given data of social reality." These phenomena would be incomprehensible if in fact human society were simply a *Mitsein* or fellowship based on solidarity and friendliness. Things become clear, on the contrary, if, following Hegel, we find in consciousness itself a fundamental hostility toward every other consciousness; the subject can be posed only in being opposed—he sets himself up as the essential, as opposed to the other, the inessential, the object.

But the other consciousness, the other ego, sets up a reciprocal claim. The native traveling abroad is shocked to find himself in turn regarded as a "stranger" by the natives of neighboring countries. As a matter of fact, wars, festivals, trading, treaties, and contests among tribes, nations, and classes tend to deprive the concept *Other* of its absolute sense and to make manifest its relativity; willy-nilly, individuals and groups are forced to realize the reciprocity of their relations. How is it, then, that this reciprocity has not been recognized between the sexes, that one of the contrasting terms is set up as the sole essential, denying any relativity in regard to

its correlative and defining the latter as pure otherness? Why is it that women do not dispute male sovereignty? No subject will readily volunteer to become the object, the inessential; it is not the Other who, in defining himself as the Other, establishes the One. The Other is posed as such by the One in defining himself as the One. But if the Other is not to regain the status of being the One, he must be submissive enough to accept this alien point of view. Whence comes this submission in the case of woman?

There are, to be sure, other cases in which a certain category has been able to dominate another completely for a time. Very often this privilege depends upon inequality of numbers—the majority imposes its rule upon the minority or persecutes it. But women are not a minority, like the American Negroes or the Jews; there are as many women as men on earth. Again, the two groups concerned have often been originally independent; they may have been formerly unaware of each other's existence, or perhaps they recognized each other's autonomy. But a historical event has resulted in the subjugation of the weaker by the stronger. The scattering of the Jews, the introduction of slavery into America, the conquests of imperialism are examples in point. In these cases the oppressed retained at least the memory of former days; they possessed in common a past, a tradition, sometimes a religion or a culture.

The parallel drawn by Bebel between women and the proletariat is valid in that neither ever formed a minority or a separate collective unit of mankind. And instead of a single historical event it is in both cases a historical development that explains their status as a class and accounts for the membership of *particular individuals* in that class. But proletarians have not always existed, whereas there have always been women. They are women in virtue of their anatomy and physiology. Throughout history they have always been subordinated to men, and hence their dependency is not the result of a historical event or a social change—it was not something that *occurred*. The reason why otherness in this case seems to be an absolute is in part that it lacks the contingent or incidental nature of historical facts. A condition brought about at a certain time can be abolished at some other time, as the Negroes of Haiti and others have proved; but it might seem that a natural condition is beyond the possibility of change. In truth, however, the nature of things is no more immutably given, once for all, than is historical reality. If woman seems to be the inessential which never becomes the essential, it is because she herself fails to bring about this change. Proletarians say "We"; Negroes also. Regarding themselves as subjects, they transform the bourgeois, the whites, into "others." But women do not say "We," except at some congress of feminists or similar formal demonstration; men say "women," and women use the same word in referring to themselves. They do not authentically assume a subjective attitude. The proletarians have accomplished the revolution in Russia, the Negroes in Haiti, the Indo-Chinese are battling for it in Indo-China; but the women's effort has never been anything more than a symbolic agitation. They have gained only what men have been willing to grant; they have taken nothing, they have only received.

The reason for this is that women lack concrete means for organizing themselves into a unit which can stand face to face with the correlative unit. They have no past, no history, no religion of their own; and they have no such solidarity of work and interest as that of the proletariat. They are not even promiscuously herded together in the way that creates community feeling among the American Negroes, the ghetto Jews, the workers of Saint-Denis, or the factory hands of Renault. They live dispersed among the males, attached through residence, housework, economic condition, and social standing to certain men—fathers or husbands—more firmly than they are to other women. If they belong to the bourgeoisie, they feel solidarity with men of that class, not with proletarian women; if they are white, their allegiance is to white men, not to Negro women. The proletariat can propose to massacre the ruling class, and a sufficiently fanatical Jew or Negro might dream of getting sole possession of the atomic bomb and making humanity wholly Jewish or black; but woman cannot even dream of exterminating the males. The bond that unites her to her oppressors is not comparable to any other. The division of the sexes is a biological fact, not an event in human history. Male and female stand opposed within a primordial *Mitsein*, and woman has not broken it. The couple is a fundamental unity with its two halves riveted together, and the cleavage of society along the line of sex is impossible. Here is to be found the basic trait of woman: she is the Other in a totality of which the two components are necessary to one another.

One could suppose that this reciprocity might have facilitated the liberation of woman. When Hercules sat at the feet of Omphale and helped with her spinning, his desire for her held him captive; but why did she fail to gain a lasting power? To revenge herself on Jason, Medea killed their children; and this grim legend would seem to suggest that she might have obtained a formidable influence over him through his love for his offspring. In *Lysistrata* Aristophanes gaily depicts a band of women who joined forces to gain social ends through the sexual needs of their men; but this is only a play. In the legend of the Sabine women, the latter soon abandoned their plan of remaining sterile to punish their ravishers. In truth woman has not been socially emancipated through man's need—sexual desire and the desire for offspring—which makes the male dependent for satisfaction upon the female.

Master and slave, also, are united by a reciprocal need, in this case economic, which does not liberate the slave. In the relation of master to slave the master does not make a point of the need that he has for the other; he has in his grasp the power of satisfying this need through his own action; whereas the slave, in his dependent condition, his hope and fear, is quite conscious of the need he has for his master. Even if the need is at bottom equally urgent for both, it always works in favor of the oppressor and against the oppressed. That is why the liberation of the working class, for example, has been slow.

Now, woman has always been man's dependent, if not his slave; the two sexes have never shared the world in equality. And even today woman is heavily handicapped, though her situation is beginning to change. Almost nowhere is her legal status the same as man's, and frequently it is much to her disadvantage. Even when her rights are legally recognized in the abstract, long-standing custom prevents their full expression in the mores. In the economic sphere men and women can almost be said to make up two castes; other things being equal, the former hold the better jobs, get higher wages, and have more opportunity for success than their new competitors. In industry and politics men have a great many more positions and they monopolize the most important posts. In addition to all this, they enjoy a traditional prestige that the education of children tends in every way to support, for the present enshrines the past—and in the past all history has been made by men. At the present time, when women are beginning to take part in the affairs of the world, it is still a world that belongs to men—they have no doubt of it at all and women have scarcely any. To decline to be the Other, to refuse to be a party to the deal—this would be for women to renounce all the advantages conferred upon them by their alliance with the superior caste. Man-the-sovereign will provide woman-the-liege with material protection and will undertake the moral justification of her existence; thus she can evade at once both economic risk and the metaphysical risk of a liberty in which ends and aims must be contrived without assistance. Indeed, along with the ethical urge of each individual to affirm his subjective existence, there is also the temptation to forgo liberty and become a thing. This is an inauspicious road, for he who takes it—

passive, lost, ruined—becomes henceforth the creature of another's will, frustrated in his transcendence and deprived of every value. But it is an easy road; on it one avoids the strain involved in undertaking an authentic existence. When man makes of woman the *Other*, he may, then, expect her to manifest deep-seated tendencies toward complicity. Thus, woman may fail to lay claim to the status of subject because she lacks definite resources, because she feels the necessary bond that ties her to man regardless of reciprocity, and because she is often very well pleased with her role as the *Other*.

But it will be asked at once: how did all this begin? . . .

---

SELECTION 14.3

## Sexism: The Male Monopoly on History and Thought★

*Marielouise Janssen-Jurreit*

[*In this reading, Janssen-Jurreit hypothesizes that patriarchy is grounded in the facts of reproduction. She theorizes that childbearing is affected by considerations of costs and benefits and explains how patriarchy results from the automatic increase in women's workloads that accompanies child rearing. She also explores the motives men have for controlling women's generative capabilities and for overriding the natural bond between mother and child.*]

The following presentation will be an attempt to explain the "empowerment" of sexuality—which emerges even before class societies—by means of a hypothesis contending that the economic and ideological structures of patriarchy are grounded in the historical formation of conditions for reproduction . . .

Underlying child rearing is a conscious or unconscious reckoning of cost and benefit, which of course comes out different according to the prevailing mode of production. Children can be conditioned emotionally and intellectually, and therefore make the best allies against the dangers of the environment or of other groups. After six or seven years, they are already helpers who fit into the labor-sharing society. Through the control of their marriages, possible alliances between groups or families can be formed, and the children are the guarantors of old-age care.

The usefulness of children consists in the maximization of one's own security. In principle it holds true that the larger the family, the clan, the tribe, or the nation I belong to, and the more young members it has, the greater the security.

This is why men as well as women are interested in having the optimal number of children that can be brought up in the particular environmental conditions and state of technology. But even if the increase in existential security through more children is fundamentally in the interest of both sexes, the degree of the interest is unequal.

For the women each pregnancy—and the labor time related to the care of a small child—means an automatic increase in the amount of work they do. Up until the First World War there were hardly any chances of survival for babies who were not nursed, because, as a result of the ignorance of sterilization, the use of animal's milk was not very successful. The feeding of other foods, which is necessary after the sixth month, depends on the availability of soft foodstuffs and requires spoon feeding by the mother. A woman who nurses totally is committed for about one and a half to two hours of work a day and requires about a thousand additional calories. Because for the man the increase in the number of children does not mean the sort of extensive increase in work that it does for the woman, men, under the conditions of the majority of preindustrial societies, have a stronger interest than women in maximizing the number of children.

This difference in interest on the part of men and women toward the creation of the next generation is a basic constellation of all societies, which favors the development toward patriarchy.

The frequency of pregnancies and the birth rate among hunting and gathering people is low. Birth intervals of four to five years are common. Women are frequently able to decide on the life of the newborn child, although the men are thoroughly oriented to population increase. Their frequent insinuations that the women might kill their children are an indication of this.

In cattle-breeding and agrarian societies, however, the great demand for human labor power leads to a much higher birth rate and encourages the institutionalization of patriarchal structures. The greater the women's reproductive burden, the fewer their chances to acquire influence. The higher the frequency of pregnancies, the more gynecological accidents (mother and infant mortality), the more children are required, so that at least some survive. On account of the security needs of the peasant family to have at least enough surviving children to guarantee old-age care and the continuity of production (in all agrarian societies with a low level of technology) the tendency exists to produce a surplus population.

When Thomas Robert Malthus formulated his famous population principle, he ascribed to humans a powerful biological reproduction drive, a blind passion for procreation that leads to overpopulation. Every population has "the tendency to multiply beyond the limits of the means of support provided by the given economic and social organization." This was "the most invulnerable and important natural law of the entire political economy to date."

However, reproduction rate and sex drive are two different things. The use of contraceptives, coitus interruptus, abortion, sexual abstinence, and child exposure are methods of birth control that can be practiced anywhere. To be sure, modern development has enlarged the spectrum of contraceptives, but the majority of island societies (Japan, and in the Pacific), which were not able to export their population surplus to new territories without difficulty, have practiced contraception, abortion, and child exposure on a large scale even under patriarchal conditions.

The problem of population increase, for which Malthus preached only late marriage age and abstinence, was not a result of the sex drive but of reproduction ideologies and conceptions of morality which provided security for the economic foundations of patriarchy. Views on whether contraception, abortion, and child exposure ought to be used change with the mode of production and the different degrees of patriarchal socialization.

Where child exposure was official birth control, other ideas prevail on the point in time at which the soul enters the child, as in Tahiti, where the child was considered not to have a soul during the first hours after the birth.

Today some scientists are of the opinion that Malthus's population law holds true for agrarian societies, while others argue that the population density basically stays below the maximum environmental limit.

Again and again, however, population growth as the driving force of patriarchal socialization has evidently tended to test the environmental limit. Population increase led either to processes of impoverishment or to innovations in the organization of labor and to increase in productivity.

The quintessence of patriarchy is the male control of reproduction, which is oriented to maximize the security for the individual paterfamilias, the oldest member of the clan, the chieftain, or the men of the ruling social classes.

The only economic systems which favor low reproduction rates are those of hunters and gatherers and the highly industrialized ones. That is why in these societies there are at least chances and tendencies toward equality of the sexes.

From the point of view of the biological allotment of tasks, women are the actual subjects of history because they are the manufacturers of the next generation and have an immediate relationship to them. Because men lack this immediate access, they are able to integrate themselves into history only by establishing a relationship to offspring on a social level. But unlike the women, they can hardly create equivalent bonding mechanisms for this purpose. A woman's children, whether male or female, are basically her natural allies. The intimate bond that women and children achieve is based on nursing, feeding, carrying, verbal and nonverbal communication, and constant emotional interplay.

There exists a very strong motive for men to control the generative capability of the woman — her fertility — and her relationship to the next generation. If children and young people were to exhibit an attitude of solidarity toward the mothers only, or were to prefer them, the position of the old men would be in constant danger. From this social weakness and uncertainty of position on the part of the old men stem the strongest motives: to reinforce their position and authority toward the children.

The most important prerequisite for the development of patriarchal institutions in a society consists in the disintegration of the mutual solidarity of mother and child. If men want to win allies in the following generation, they must develop a sex-specific solidarity structure. The control of women requires the suspension of the natural, close relations between the mother and the male child. The boys, in other words, must be convinced above all of the insignificance of motherhood.

On entering puberty or even earlier, boys are subjected to initiation rites and drastic socialization measures. Among the Baruya of New Guinea the alienation of the boy from the mother is a process that lasts over ten years, until his initiation is completed. Not until after this time, when he is already married and has children, is he allowed to speak with his mother again and to eat in front of her. In the initiation of an Indian Brahman son, a last meal together by mother and son was a part of the rite before he became an initiate at about age eight.

The old men shape the identity of the boys by a system of communication and meaning from which they exclude the women. Many of their ceremonies are associated with acts of terror against women and smaller children. The membership in the men's associations, secret societies, or military organizations is dependent upon these initiations.

Puberty rites for girls are lacking in most societies, or they consist of a brief individual observance of the girl's first menstruation. In contrast, the maturity rites for boys are for the most part collective and last over a long period of time or extend over the whole of adult life. . . .

The spiritual control of fertility is the power that the old men offer the young ones. Actually, it is the women who are fertile. They have the children; they plant, weed, and harvest the main foodstuffs. However, through their secret knowledge and their rites, it is the men who control all manifestations of fertility, while the women appear only as the caretakers and attendants of plants, animals, and children. The old men achieve their authority toward the young ones through an ancestor cult that confirms the solidarity of all men with the preceding generation of men and through an interpretation of the relationship of the sexes connected with ideological devaluation of the woman.

Every kinship group possesses as a kind of spiritual property the knowledge of its ancestors. Not until central political institutions have formed is the historical memory tended by specialists of the privileged social class. The legitimacy of the claims to sovereignty are established with the exact knowledge of the family trees. Through the association of cosmological narratives (mythos) and ancestor genealogy (history), and with the help of religion and law, men obtain the exclusive right to explain the meaning of human existence. Thus, they become leaders in the interpretations of meaning for the entire society.

Even though women may not accept all male value judgments, these interpretations nevertheless affect their life through purity rules, taboos, and rituals of conduct toward men which express women's subordination.

The formation of political authorities and the rise of states coincide with the reformation of the systems of religious meaning. It is characteristic that a hierarchy of gods or one divinity stands in the center of the religion. Women are now tolerated as passive believers. However, they are excluded from offices of the cult or are permitted less influential cults of their own.

The structural elements that make solidarity between old men and young possible — to the disadvantage of women — hardly offer women the chance for collective resistance. Even when the bond between son and mother is broken when the son reaches a certain age, his new, superior status still applies to women in general. He dominates his future wife and his sisters. In strictly patriarchal cultures, a mother remains subservient to the son; because the son supports her, her bond to the son is the only possibility of maintaining her social existence. The future daughter-in-law is a stranger who, in a patriarchal system, is usually dominated by her husband's mother.

The early forms of organization of the state developed in areas where population pressure was already high. The class societies arose out of groups competing for the exploitation of a particular optimal environment, like the big river deltas in Babylonia, China, and Egypt. Systematic warfare and the private acquisition of means of production are only a further phase in the patriarchal socialization characterized by constant attempts at growth.

In order to stabilize class societies, the state became the guarantor of paternal power, and the paternal power of the state became the guarantor for the subordinate relations of the classes. The control of the sexual impulses of the individual and the fathers' total control over sons, daughters, and wives served to internally maintain the order of the state.

The stability of state order was dependent upon a rigorous hierarchization and the strict compliance to command and obedience. For this reason, the preindustrial states of patriarchal class lack all the permissive regulations characteristic of the early societies of hunters and gatherers, gardeners, and cattle breeders, in which after a certain time breaches of taboos and infractions of ordinances can once more lead to the deviants' integration. The women's right to divorce and extramarital relations, acceptance of out-of-wedlock children, marriages based on love, and deviant sexual conduct become impossible or are punished with maximum severity.

No family system has attained such complete paternal authority as the Chinese, in which the wife/husband relationship was secondary to the father/son and mother/daughter-in-law relationship. The Chinese peasant family frequently adopted a daughter-in-law when she was only a child. With jesuitic strategy her will was broken until she was assimilated into her father-in-law's family. According to Chinese law, she was not allowed to act independently or to possess property, or to become the head of a family. She had no legal status. In the Confucian and Hindu ideologies, the procreation of a son was a prime religious duty.

Associated with paternal authority were doctrines promoting population increase, recorded in the first assemblies of law in the Near East region long before the Christian era. Sumerian, Assyrian, and Babylonian codices made abortion a criminal offense. According to Hindu law, abortion was one of three crimes, including murdering a husband or a Brahman, that made outcasts of women. A devout Hindu made full use of his wife's fertility. The husband who did not have intercourse with his wife during her fertile period was described in religious literature as an embryo killer.

In the Jewish faith the waste of male semen was seen as delaying the arrival of the Messiah; the Son of David would not appear until all the souls of the unborn were born. A similar concept is found in medieval Christianity: increased fertility would increase the population of heaven.

---

SELECTION 14.4

## Should the History and Philosophy of Science Be X-Rated? *

*Sandra Harding*

[*Harding believes that how scientists and philosophers of science think we all should think about nature and scientific inquiry is revealed in the metaphors they use. Specifically, she argues that scientists and philosophers think that "the best scientific activity and philosophic thinking about science are to be modeled on men's most*

*misogynous relations to women — rape, torture. . . ." In this selection, Harding examines some of the metaphors incorporated in the new conception of nature and scientific inquiry that arose at the start of the Scientific Revolution.*]

One phenomenon feminist historians have focused on is the rape and torture metaphors in the writings of Sir Francis Bacon and others (e.g., Machiavelli) enthusiastic about the new scientific method. Traditional historians and philosophers have said that these metaphors are irrelevant to the *real* meanings and referents of scientific concepts held by those who used them and by the public for whom they wrote. But when it comes to regarding nature as a machine, they have quite a different analysis: here, we are told, the metaphor provides the interpretations of Newton's mathematical laws: it directs inquirers to fruitful ways to apply his theory and suggests the appropriate methods of inquiry and the kind of metaphysics the new theory supports. But if we are to believe that mechanistic metaphors were a fundamental component of the explanations the new science provided, why should we believe that the gender metaphors were not? A consistent analysis would lead to the conclusion that understanding nature as a woman indifferent to or even welcoming rape was equally fundamental to the interpretations of these new conceptions of nature and inquiry. Presumably these metaphors, too, had fruitful pragmatic, methodological, and metaphysical consequences for science. In that case, why is it not as illuminating and honest to refer to Newton's laws as "Newton's rape manual" as it is to call them "Newton's mechanics"?

We can now see that metaphors of gender politics were used to make morally and politically attractive the new conceptions of nature and inquiry required by experimental method and the emerging technologies of the period. The organicist conception of nature popular in the medieval period—nature as alive, as part of God's domain—was appropriate neither for the new experimental methods of science nor for the new technological applications of the results of inquiry. Carolyn Merchant identifies five changes in social thought and experience in Europe during the fifteenth to seventeenth centuries that contributed to the distinctive gender symbolism of the subsequent scientific world view.

First of all, when Copernican theory replaced the earth-centered universe with a sun-centered universe, it also replaced a woman-centered universe with a man-centered one. For Renaissance and earlier thought within an organic conception of nature, the sun was associated with manliness and the earth with two opposing aspects of womanliness. Nature, and especially the earth, was identified on the one hand with a nurturing mother—"a kindly, beneficent female who provided for the needs of mankind in an ordered, planned universe"—and on the other with the "wild and uncontrollable [female] nature that could render violence, storms, droughts,

and general chaos." In the new Copernican theory, the womanly earth, which had been God's special creation for man's nurturance, became just one tiny, externally moved planet circling in an insignificant orbit around the masculine sun.

Second, for the Platonic organicism, active power in the universe was associated with the alive, nurturing mother earth; for the Aristotelian organicism, activity was associated with masculinity and passivity with womanliness. Central to Aristotle's biological theory, this association was revived in sixteenth-century views of the cosmos, where "the marriage and impregnation of the 'material' female earth by the higher 'immaterial' celestial masculine heavens was a stock description of biological generation in nature." Copernicus himself draws on this metaphor: "Meanwhile, the earth conceives by the sun and becomes pregnant with annual offspring." Resistance to this shift in the social meaning of womanliness is evident in the sixteenth-century conflicts over whether it was morally proper to treat mother earth in the new ways called for by such commercial activities as mining. But as the experience of "violating the body" of earth became increasingly more common during the rise of modern science and its technologies, the moral sanctions against such activities provided by the older organic view slowly died away. Simultaneously, a criterion for distinguishing the animate from the inanimate was being created. (This distinction is a theoretical construct of modern science, not an observational given familiar to people before the emergence of science. And, as we shall see, it is one that increasingly ceases to reflect "common sense.") Thus a "womanly" earth must be only passive, inert matter and indifferent to explorations and exploitations of her insides.

Third, the new universe that science disclosed was one in which change—associated with "corruption," decay, and disorder—occurred not just on earth, as the Ptolemaic "two-world view" held, but also throughout the heavens. For Renaissance and Elizabethan writers, these discoveries of change in the heavens suggested that nature's order might break down, leaving man's fate in chaos. Thinkers of the period consistently perceived unruly, wild nature as rising up against man's attempts to control his fate. Machiavelli appealed to sexual metaphors in his proposition that the potential violence of fate could be mastered: "Fortune is a woman and it is necessary if you wish to master her to conquer her by force; and it can be seen that she lets herself be overcome by the bold rather than by those who proceed coldly, and therefore like a woman, she is always a friend to the young because they are less cautious, fiercer, and master her with greater audacity."

Fourth, man's fate seemed difficult to control because of disorder not only in the physical universe but also in social life. The breakdown of the ancient order of feudal society brought the experience of widespread social disorder during the period in which the scientific world view was developing. Particularly interesting is the possibility that women's increased visibility in public life during this period was perceived as threatening deep and widespread changes in social relations between the genders. Women were active in the Protestant reform movements of northern Europe, and Elizabeth I occupied England's throne for an unprecedentedly long reign. Prepared by the organic view's association of wild and violent nature with one aspect of the womanly, and by the absence of clear distinctions between the physical and the social, the Renaissance imagination required no great leap to associate all disorder, natural and social, with women. By the end of the fifteenth century, this association had been fully articulated in the witchcraft doctrines. To women was attributed a "method of revenge and control that could be used by persons both physically and socially powerless in a world believed by nearly everyone to be animate and organismic."

Fifth, the political and legal metaphors of scientific method originated at least in part in the witchcraft trials of Bacon's day. Bacon's mentor was James I of England, a strong supporter of antifeminist and antiwitchcraft legislation in both England and Scotland. An obsessive focus in the interrogations of alleged witches was their sexual practices, the purpose of various tortures being to reveal whether they had "carnally known" the Devil. In a passage addressed to his monarch, Bacon uses bold sexual imagery to explain key features of the experimental method as the inquisition of nature: "For you have but to follow and as it were hound nature in her wanderings, and you will be able when you like to lead and drive her afterward to the same place again. . . . Neither ought a man to make scruple of entering and penetrating into those holes and corners, when the inquisition of truth is his whole object—as your majesty has shown in your own example." It might not be immediately obvious to the modern reader that this is Bacon's way of explaining the necessity of aggressive and controlled experiments in order to make the results of research replicable!

As I indicated earlier, this kind of analysis raises a number of problems and challenges. . . . There does, however, appear to be reason to be concerned about the intellectual, moral, and political structures of modern science when we think about how, from its very beginning, misogynous and defensive gender politics and the abstraction we think of as scientific method have provided resources for each other. The severe testing of hypotheses through controlled manipulations of nature, and the necessity of such controlled manipulations if experiments are to be repeatable, are here formulated by the father of scientific method in clearly sexist metaphors. Both nature and inquiry appear conceptualized in ways modeled on rape and torture—on men's most violent and misogynous relationships to women—and this modeling is advanced as a reason to value science. It is certainly difficult to imagine women as an enthusiastic audience for these interpretations of the new scientific method.

If appeal to gender politics provides resources for science, does appeal to science provide resources for gender politics? Do not metaphors illuminate in both directions? As nature came to seem more like a machine, did not machines come to seem more natural? As nature came to seem more like a woman whom it is appropriate to rape and torture than like a nurturing mother, did rape and torture come to seem a more natural relation of men to women? Could the uses of science to create ecological disaster, support militarism, turn human labor into physically and mentally mutilating work, develop ways of controlling "others"—the colonized, women, the poor—be just misuses of applied science? Or does this kind of conceptualization of the character and purposes of experimental method ensure that what is called bad science or misused science will be a distinctively masculinist science-as-usual? Institutions, like individuals, often act out the repressed and unresolved dilemmas of their infancies. To what extent is the insistence by science today on a value-neutral, dispassionate objectivity in the service of progressive social relations an attempt by a guilty conscience to resolve some of these early but still living dilemmas?

SELECTION 14.5

## Justice, Gender, and the Family*

*Susan Moller Okin*

[*Here, Okin explains what she means by* gender *and what she means when she says that gender-structured marriage makes women vulnerable. She then sets forth her view that theories of justice have (amazingly) ignored the question "How just is gender?" and have neglected women, gender, and inequalities between the sexes. She believes that most justice theorists assume (and do not even discuss) the traditional, gender-structured family and employ gender-neutral language in a false way that disguises the fact that the theories are actually about justice for the male head of a fairly traditional household.*]

A central source of injustice for women these days is that the law, most noticeably in the event of divorce, treats more or less as equals those whom custom, workplace discrimination, and the still conventional division of labor within the family have made very unequal. Central to this socially created inequality are two commonly made but inconsistent presumptions: that women are primarily responsible for the rearing of children; and that serious and committed members of the work force (regardless of class) do not have primary responsibility, or even shared responsibility, for the rearing of children. The old assumption of the workplace, still implicit, is that workers have wives at home. It is built not only into the structure and expectations of the workplace but into other crucial social institutions, such as schools, which make no attempt to take account, in their scheduled hours or vacations, of the fact that parents are likely to hold jobs.

Now, of course, many wage workers do not have wives at home. Often, they *are* wives and mothers, or single, separated, or divorced mothers of small children. But neither the family nor the workplace has taken much account of this fact. Employed

wives still do by far the greatest proportion of unpaid family work, such as child care and housework. Women are far more likely to take time out of the workplace or to work part-time because of family responsibilities than are their husbands or male partners. And they are much more likely to move because of their husbands' employment needs or opportunities than their own. All these tendencies, which are due to a number of factors, including the sex segregation and discrimination of the workplace itself, tend to be cyclical in their effects: wives advance more slowly than their husbands at work and thus gain less seniority, and the discrepancy between their wages increases over time. Then, because both the power structure of the family and what is regarded as consensual "rational" family decision making reflect the fact that the husband usually earns more, it will become even less likely as time goes on that the unpaid work of the family will be shared between the spouses. Thus the cycle of inequality is perpetuated. Often hidden from view within a marriage, it is in the increasingly likely event of marital breakdown that the socially constructed inequality of married women is at its most visible.

This is what I mean when I say that gender-structured marriage *makes* women vulnerable. These are not matters of natural necessity, as some people would believe. Surely nothing in our nature dictates that men should not be equal participants in the rearing of their children. Nothing in the nature of work makes it impossible to adjust it to the fact that people are parents as well as workers. That these things have not happened is part of the historically, socially constructed differentiation between the sexes that feminists have come to call *gender*. We live in a society that has over the years regarded the innate characteristic of sex as one of the clearest legitimizers of different rights and restrictions, both formal and informal. While the legal sanctions that uphold male dominance have begun to be eroded in the past century, and more rapidly in the last twenty years, the heavy weight of tradition, combined with the effects of socialization, still works powerfully to reinforce sex roles that are commonly regarded as of unequal prestige and worth. The sexual division of labor has not only been a fundamental part of the marriage contract, but so deeply influences us in our formative years that feminists of both sexes who try to reject it can find themselves struggling against it with varying degrees of ambivalence. Based on this linchpin, "gender"—by which I mean *the deeply entrenched institutionalization of sexual difference*—still permeates our society.

**Theories of Justice and the Neglect of Gender**
. . . Political theory, which had been sparse for a period before the late 1960s except as an important branch of intellectual history, has become a flourishing field, with social justice as its central concern. Yet, remarkably, major contemporary theorists of justice have almost without exception ignored the situation I have just described. They have displayed little interest in or knowledge of the findings of feminism. They have largely bypassed the fact that the society to which their theories are supposed to pertain is heavily and deeply affected by gender, and faces difficult issues of justice stemming from its gendered past and present assumptions. Since theories of justice are centrally concerned with whether, how, and why persons should be treated differently from one another, this neglect seems inexplicable. These theories are *about* which initial or acquired characteristics or positions in society legitimize differential treatment of persons by social institutions, laws, and customs. They are *about* how and whether and to what extent beginnings should affect outcomes. The division of humanity into two sexes seems to provide an obvious subject for such inquiries. But, as we shall see, this does not strike most contemporary theorists of justice, and their theories suffer in both coherence and relevance because of it. This book is about this remarkable case of neglect. It is also an attempt to rectify it, to point the way toward a more fully humanist theory of justice by confronting the question, "How just is gender?"

Why is it that when we turn to contemporary theories of justice, we do not find illuminating and positive contributions to this question? How can theories of justice that are ostensibly about people in general neglect women, gender, and all the inequalities between the sexes? One reason is that most theorists *assume*, though they do not discuss, the traditional, gender-structured family. Another is

that they often employ gender-neutral language in a false, hollow way. Let us examine these two points.

*The Hidden Gender-Structured Family*  In the past, political theorists often used to distinguish clearly between "private" domestic life and the "public" life of politics and the marketplace, claiming explicitly that the two spheres operated in accordance with different principles. They separated out the family from what they deemed the subject matter of politics, and they made closely related, explicit claims about the nature of women and the appropriateness of excluding them from civil and political life. Men, the subjects of the theories, were able to make the transition back and forth from domestic to public life with ease, largely because of the functions performed by women in the family. When we turn to contemporary theories of justice, superficial appearances can easily lead to the impression that they are inclusive of women. In fact, they continue the same "separate spheres" tradition, by ignoring the family, its division of labor, and the related economic dependency and restricted opportunities of most women. The judgment that the family is "non-political" is implicit in the fact that it is simply not discussed in most works of political theory today. In one way or another . . . , almost all current theorists continue to assume that the "individual" who is the basic subject of their theories is the male head of a fairly traditional household. Thus the application of principles of justice to relations between the sexes, or within the household, is frequently, though tacitly, ruled out from the start. In the most influential of all twentieth-century theories of justice, that of John Rawls, family life is not only assumed, but is assumed to be just—and yet the prevalent gendered division of labor within the family is neglected, along with the associated distribution of power, responsibility, and privilege. . . .

*False Gender Neutrality*  Many academics in recent years have become aware of the objectionable nature of using the supposedly generic male forms of nouns and pronouns. As feminist scholars have demonstrated, these words have most often *not* been used, throughout history and the history of philosophy in particular, with the intent to include women. *Man, mankind,* and *he* are going out of style as universal representations, though they have by no means disappeared. But the gender-neutral alternatives that most contemporary theorists employ are often even more misleading than the blatantly sexist use of male terms of reference. For they serve to disguise the real and continuing failure of theorists to confront the fact that the human race consists of persons of two sexes. They are by this means able to ignore the fact that there are *some* socially relevant physical differences between women and men, and the even more important fact that the sexes have had very different histories, very different assigned social roles and "natures," and very different degrees of access to power and opportunity in all human societies up to and including the present.

False gender neutrality is not a new phenomenon. Aristotle, for example, used *anthropos*—"human being"—in discussions of "the human good" that turn out not only to exclude women but to depend on their subordination. Kant even wrote of "all rational beings as such" in making arguments that he did not mean to apply to women. But it was more readily apparent that such arguments or conceptions of the good were not about all of us, but only about male heads of families. For their authors usually gave at some point an explanation, no matter how inadequate, of why what they were saying did not apply to women and of the different characteristics and virtues, rights, and responsibilities they thought women ought to have. Nevertheless, their theories have often been read as though they pertain (or can easily be applied) to all of us. Feminist interpretations of the last fifteen years or so have revealed the falsity of this "add women and stir" method of reading the history of political thought.

The falseness of the gender-neutral language of contemporary political theorists is less readily apparent. Most, though not all, contemporary moral and political philosophers use "men and women," "he or she," "persons," or the increasingly ubiquitous "self." Sometimes they even get their computers to distribute masculine and feminine terms of reference randomly. Since they do not explicitly exclude or differentiate women, as most theorists in the past did, we may be tempted to read their theories as inclusive of all of us. But we cannot. Their merely terminological responses to feminist challenges, in spite of giving a superficial impression of tolerance and inclusiveness, often strain credulity and sometimes result in nonsense. They do this in two ways: by ignoring the irreducible biological differences between the sexes, and/or by ignoring their different assigned social roles and consequent power differentials, and the ideologies that have supported them. Thus gender-neutral terms frequently obscure the fact that so much of the real experience of "persons," so long as they live in gender-structured societies, *does* in fact depend on what sex they are. . . .

The combined effect of the omission of the family and the falsely gender-neutral language in recent political thought is that most theorists are continuing to ignore the highly political issue of gender. The language they use makes little difference to what they actually do, which is to write about men and about only those women who manage, in spite of the gendered structures and practices of the society in which they live, to adopt patterns of life that have been developed to suit the needs of men. The fact that human beings are born as helpless infants—not as the purportedly autonomous actors who populate political theories—is obscured by the implicit assumption of gendered families, operating outside the range of the theories. To a large extent, contemporary theories of justice, like those of the past, are about men with wives at home.

## Gender as an Issue of Justice

For three major reasons, this state of affairs is unacceptable. The first is the obvious point that women must be fully included in any satisfactory theory of justice. The second is that equality of opportunity, not only for women but for children of both sexes, is seriously undermined by the current gender injustices of our society. And the third reason is that, as has already been suggested, the family—currently the linchpin of the gender structure—must be just if we are to have a just society, since it is within the family that we first come to have that sense of ourselves and our relations with others that is at the root of moral development.

*Counting Women In*    . . . When we turn to contemporary theories of justice, however, we expect to find more illuminating and positive contributions to the subject of gender and justice. As the omission of the family and the falseness of their gender-neutral language suggest, however, mainstream contemporary theories of justice do not address the subject any better than those of the past. Theories of justice that apply to only half of us simply won't do; the inclusiveness falsely implied by the current use of gender-neutral terms must become real. Theories of justice must apply to all of us, and to all of human life, instead of *assuming* silently that half of us take care of whole areas of life that are considered outside the scope of social justice. In a just society, the structure and practices of families must afford women the same opportunities as men to develop their capacities, to participate in political power, to influence social choices, and to be economically as well as physically secure.

*Gender and Equality of Opportunity*   The family is a crucial determinant of our opportunities in life, of what we "become." It has frequently been acknowledged by those concerned with real equality of opportunity that the family presents a problem. But though they have discerned a serious problem, these theorists have underestimated it because they have seen only half of it. They have seen that the disparity among families in terms of the physical and emotional environment, motivation, and material advantages they can give their children has a tremendous effect upon children's opportunities in life. We are not born as isolated, equal individuals in our society, but into family situations: some in the social middle, some poor and homeless, and some superaffluent; some to a single or soon-to-be-separated parent, some to parents whose marriage is fraught with conflict, some to parents who will stay together in love and happiness. Any claims that equal opportunity exists are therefore completely unfounded. Decades of neglect of the poor, especially of poor black and Hispanic households, accentuated by the policies of the Reagan years, have brought us farther from the principles of equal opportunity. To come close to them would require, for example, a high and uniform standard of public education and the provision of equal social services—including health care, employment training, job opportunities, drug rehabilitation, and decent housing—for all who need them. In addition to redistributive taxation, only massive reallocations of resources from the military to social services could make these things possible.

But even if all these disparities were somehow eliminated, we would still not attain equal opportunity for all. This is because what has not been recognized as an equal opportunity problem, except in feminist literature and circles, is the disparity *within* the family, the fact that its gender structure is itself a major obstacle to equality of opportunity. This is very important in itself, since one of the factors with most influence on our opportunities in life is the so-cial significance attributed to our sex. The opportunities of girls and women are centrally affected by the structure and practices of family life, particularly by the fact that women are almost invariably primary parents. What nonfeminists who see in the family an obstacle to equal opportunity have *not* seen is that the extent to which a family is gender-structured can make the sex we belong to a relatively insignificant aspect of our identity and our life prospects or an all-pervading one. This is because so much of the social construction of gender takes place in the family, and particularly in the institution of female parenting.

Moreover, especially in recent years, with the increased rates of single motherhood, separation, and divorce, the inequalities between the sexes have *compounded* the first part of the problem. The disparity among families has grown largely because of the impoverishment of many women and children after separation or divorce. The division of labor in the typical family leaves most women far less capable than men of supporting themselves, and this disparity is accentuated by the fact that children of separated or divorced parents usually live with their mothers. The inadequacy—and frequent nonpayment—of child support has become recognized as a major social problem. Thus the inequalities of gender are now directly harming many children of both sexes as well as women themselves. Enhancing equal opportunity for women, important as it is in itself, is also a crucial way of improving the opportunities of many of the most disadvantaged children.

As there is a connection among the parts of this problem, so is there a connection among some of the solutions: must of what needs to be done to end the inequalities of gender, and to work in the direction of ending gender itself, will also help to equalize opportunity from one family to another. Subsidized, high-quality day care is obviously one such thing; another is the adaptation of the workplace to the needs of parents. . . .

*The Family as a School of Justice*   One of the things that theorists who have argued that families need not or cannot be just, or who have simply neglected them, have failed to explain is how, within a formative social environment that is *not* founded upon principles of justice, children can learn to develop that sense of justice they will require as citizens of a just society. Rather than being one among many co-equal institutions of a just society, a just family is its essential foundation.

It may seem uncontroversial, even obvious, that families must be just because of the vast influence they have on the moral development of children. But this is clearly not the case. I shall argue that unless the first and most formative example of adult interaction usually experienced by children is one of justice and reciprocity, rather than one of domination and manipulation or of unequal altruism and one-sided self-sacrifice, and unless they themselves are treated with concern and respect, they are likely to be considerably hindered in becoming people who are guided by principles of justice. Moreover, I claim, the sharing of roles by men and women, rather than the division of roles between them, would have a further positive impact because the experience of *being* a physical and psychological nurturer—whether of a child or of another adult— would increase that capacity to identify with and fully comprehend the viewpoints of others that is important to a sense of justice. In a society that minimized gender this would be more likely to be the experience of all of us.

Almost every person in our society starts life in a family of some sort or other. Fewer of these families now fit the usual, though by no means universal, standard of previous generations, that is, wage-working father, homemaking mother, and children. More families these days are headed by a single parent; lesbian and gay parenting is no longer so rare; many children have two wage-working parents, and receive at least some of their early care outside the home. While its forms are varied, the family in which a child is raised, especially in the earliest years, is clearly a crucial place for early moral development and for the formation of our basic attitudes to others. It is, potentially, a place where we can *learn to be just*. It is especially important for the development of a sense of justice that grows from sharing the experiences of others and becoming aware of the points of view of others who are different in some respects from ourselves, but with whom we clearly have some interests in common. . . .

Among major contemporary theorists of justice, John Rawls alone treats the family seriously as the earliest school of moral development. He argues that a just, well-ordered society will be stable only if its members continue to develop a sense of justice. And he argues that families play a fundamental role in the stages by which this sense of justice is ac-

quired. From the parents' love for their child, which comes to be reciprocated, comes the child's "sense of his own value and the desire to become the sort of person that they are." The family, too, is the first of that series of "associations" in which we participate, from which we acquire the capacity, crucial for a sense of justice, to see things from the perspectives of others. As I shall show, this capacity—the capacity for empathy—is essential for maintaining a sense of justice of the Rawlsian kind. For the perspective that is necessary for maintaining a sense of justice is not that of the egoistic or disembodied self, or of the dominant few who overdetermine "our" traditions or "shared understandings," or (to use Nagel's term) of "the view from nowhere," but rather the perspective of every person in the society for whom the principles of justice are being arrived at. As I shall argue, the problem with Rawls's rare and interesting discussion of moral development is that it rests on the unexplained *assumption* that family institutions are just. If gendered family institutions are *not* just, but are, rather, a relic of caste or feudal societies in which responsibilities, roles, and resources are distributed, not in accordance with the principles of justice he arrives at or with any other commonly respected values, but in accordance with innate differences that are imbued with enormous social significance, then Rawls's theory of moral development would seem to be built on uncertain ground. This problem is exacerbated by suggestions in some of Rawls's most recent work that families are "private institutions," to which it is not appropriate to apply standards of justice. But if families are to help form just individuals and citizens, surely they must be *just families*.

In a just society, the structure and practices of families must give women the same opportunities as men to develop their capacities, to participate in political power and influence social choices, and to be economically secure. But in addition to this, families must be just because of the vast influence that they have on the moral development of children. The family is the primary institution of formative moral development. And the structure and practices of the family must parallel those of the larger society if the sense of justice is to be fostered and maintained. While many theorists of justice, both past and present, appear to have denied the importance of at least one of these factors, my own view is that both are absolutely crucial. A society that is committed to equal respect for all of its members, and to justice in social distributions of benefits and responsibilities, can neither neglect the family nor accept family structures and practices that violate these norms, as do current gender-based structures and practices. It is essential that children who are to develop into adults with a strong sense of justice and commitment to just institutions spend their earliest and most formative years in an environment in which they are loved and nurtured, *and* in which principles of justice are abided by and respected. What is a child of either sex to learn about fairness in the average household with two full-time working parents, where the mother does, at the very least,

twice as much family work as the father? What is a child to learn about the value of nurturing and domestic work in a home with a traditional division of labor in which the father either subtly or not so subtly uses the fact that he is the wage earner to "pull rank" on or to abuse his wife? What is a child to learn about responsibility for others in a family in which, after many years of arranging her life around the needs of her husband and children, a woman is faced with having to provide for herself and her children but is totally ill-equipped for the task by the life she agreed to lead, has led, and expected to go on leading?

---

## SELECTION 14.6
# The Power and the Promise of Ecological Feminism★

*Karen J. Warren*

---

[*Here Warren explains eight requirements (she calls them "boundary conditions") for a feminist ethic. She then examines how ecofeminism provides the framework for a feminist an environment ethic.*]

### Ecofeminism As a Feminist and Environmental Ethic

A feminist ethic involves a twofold commitment to critique male bias in ethics wherever it occurs, and to develop ethics which are not male-biased. Sometimes this involves articulation of values (e.g., values of care, appropriate trust, kinship, friendship) often lost or underplayed in mainstream ethics. Sometimes it involves engaging in theory building by pioneering in new directions or by revamping old theories in gender sensitive ways. What makes the critique of old theories or conceptualizations of new ones "feminist" is that they emerge out of sex-gender analyses and reflect whatever those analyses reveal about gendered experience and gendered social reality.

As I conceive feminist ethics in the pre-feminist

★Author's footnotes omitted. Excerpts from Karen J. Warren, "The Power and the Promise of Ecological Feminism," *Environmental Ethics*, vol. 12, no. 2 (Spring 1990), pp. 125–146. Reprinted by permission of the author and the publisher.

present, it rejects attempts to conceive of ethical theory in terms of necessary and sufficient conditions, because it assumes that there is no essence (in the sense of some transhistorical, universal, absolute abstraction) of feminist ethics. While attempts to formulate joint necessary and sufficient conditions of a feminist ethic are unfruitful, nonetheless, there are some necessary conditions, what I prefer to call "boundary conditions," of a feminist ethic. These boundary conditions clarify some of the minimal conditions of a feminist ethic without suggesting that feminist ethics has some ahistorical essence. They are like the boundaries of a quilt or collage. They delimit the territory of the piece without dictating what the interior, the design, the actual pattern of the piece looks like. Because the actual design of the quilt emerges from the multiplicity of voices of women in a cross-cultural context, the design will change over time. It is not something static.

What are some of the boundary conditions of a feminist ethic? First, nothing can become part of a feminist ethic—can be part of the quilt—that promotes sexism, racism, classism, or any other "isms" of social domination. Of course, people may disagree about what counts as a sexist act, racist attitude, classist behavior. What counts as sexism, racism, or classism may vary cross-culturally. Still, because a feminist ethic aims at eliminating sexism and sexist bias, and . . . sexism is intimately connected in conceptualization and in practice to racism, classism, and naturism, a feminist ethic must be anti-sexist, anti-racist, anti-classist, anti-naturist and opposed to any "ism" which presupposes or advances a logic of domination.

Second, a feminist ethic is a *contextualist* ethic. A contextualist ethic is one which sees ethical discourse and practice as emerging from the voices of people located in different historical circumstances. A contextualist ethic is properly viewed as a *collage* or *mosaic*, a *tapestry* of voices that emerges out of felt experiences. Like any collage or mosaic, the point is not to have *one picture* based on a unity of voices, but a *pattern* which emerges out of the very different voices of people located in different circumstances. When a contextualist ethic is *feminist*, it gives central place to the voices of women.

Third, since a feminist ethic gives central significance to the diversity of women's voices, a feminist ethic must be structurally pluralistic rather than unitary or reductionistic. It rejects the assumption that there is "one voice" in terms of which ethical values, beliefs, attitudes, and conduct can be assessed.

Fourth, a feminist ethic reconceives ethical theory as theory in process which will change over time. Like all theory, a feminist ethic is based on some generalizations. Nevertheless, the generalizations associated with it are themselves a pattern of voices within which the different voices emerging out of concrete and alternative descriptions of ethical situations have meaning. The coherence of a feminist theory so conceived is given within a historical and conceptual context, i.e., within a set of historical, socioeconomic circumstances (including circumstances of race, class, age, and affectional orientation) and within a set of basic beliefs, values, attitudes, and assumptions about the world.

Fifth, because a feminist ethic is contextualist, structurally pluralistic, and "in-process," one way to evaluate the claims of a feminist ethic is in terms of their *inclusiveness:* those claims (voices, patterns of voices) are morally and epistemologically favored (preferred, better, less partial, less biased) which are more inclusive of the felt experiences and perspectives of oppressed persons. The condition of inclusiveness requires and ensures that the diverse voices of women (as oppressed persons) will be given le-

gitimacy in ethical theory building. It thereby helps to minimize empirical bias, e.g., bias rising from faulty or false generalizations based on stereotyping, too small a sample size, or a skewed sample. It does so by ensuring that any generalizations which are made about ethics and ethical decision making include—indeed cohere with—the patterned voices of women.

Sixth, a feminist ethic makes no attempt to provide an "objective" point of view, since it assumes that in contemporary culture there really is no such point of view. As such, it does not claim to be "unbiased" in the sense of "value-neutral" or "objective." However, it does assume that whatever bias it has as an ethic centralizing the voices of oppressed persons is a *better bias*—"better" because it is more inclusive and therefore less partial—than those which exclude those voices.

Seventh, a feminist ethic provides a central place for values typically unnoticed, underplayed, or misrepresented in traditional ethics, e.g., values of care, love, friendship, and appropriate trust. Again, it need not do this at the exclusion of considerations of rights, rules, or utility. There may be many contexts in which talk of rights or of utility is useful or appropriate. For instance, in contracts or property relationships, talk of rights may be useful and appropriate. In deciding what is cost-effective or advantageous to the most people, talk of utility may be useful and appropriate. In a feminist *qua* contextualist ethic, whether or not such talk is useful or appropriate depends on the context; *other values* (e.g., values of care, trust, friendship) are *not* viewed as reducible to or captured solely in terms of such talk.

Eighth, a feminist ethic also involves a reconception of what it is to be human and what it is for humans to engage in ethical decision making, since it rejects as either meaningless or currently untenable any gender-free or gender-neutral description of humans, ethics, and ethical decision making. It thereby rejects what Alison Jaggar calls "abstract individualism," i.e., the position that it is possible to identify a human essence or human nature that exists independently of any particular historical context. Humans and human moral conduct are properly understood essentially (and not merely accidentally) in terms of networks or webs of historical and concrete relationships.

All the props are now in place for seeing how ecofeminism provides the framework for a distinctively feminist and environmental ethic. It is a feminism that critiques male bias wherever it occurs in ethics (including environmental ethics) and aims at providing an ethic (including an environmental ethic) which is not male biased—and it does so in a way that satisfies the preliminary boundary conditions of a feminist ethic.

First, ecofeminism is quintessentially anti-naturist. Its anti-naturism consists in the rejection of any way of thinking about or acting toward nonhuman nature that reflects a logic, values, or attitude of domination. Its anti-naturist, anti-sexist, anti-racist, anti-classist (and so forth, for all other "isms" of social domination) stance forms the outer boundary of the quilt: nothing gets on the quilt which is naturist, sexist, racist, classist, and so forth.

Second, ecofeminism is a contextualistic ethic. It involves a shift *from* a conception of ethics as primarily a matter of rights, rules, or principles predetermined and applied in specific cases to entities viewed as competitors in the contest of moral standing, *to* a conception of ethics as growing out of what Jim Cheney calls "defining relationships," i.e., relationships conceived in some sense as defining who one is. As a contextualist ethic, it is not that rights, or rules, or principles are *not* relevant or important. Clearly they are in certain contexts and for certain purposes. It is just that what *makes* them relevant or important is that those to whom they apply are entities *in relationship with* others.

Ecofeminism also involves an ethical shift *from* granting moral consideration to nonhumans *exclusively* on the grounds of some similarity they share with humans (e.g., rationality, interests, moral agency, sentiency, right-holder status) *to* "a highly contextual account to see clearly what a human being is and what the nonhuman world might be, morally speaking, *for* human beings." For an ecofeminist, *how* a moral agent is in relationship to another becomes of central significance, not simply *that* a moral agent is a moral agent or is bound by rights, duties, virtue, or utility to act in a certain way.

Third, ecofeminism is structurally pluralistic in that it presupposes and maintains difference—difference among humans as well as between humans and at least some elements of nonhuman nature. Thus, while ecofeminism denies the "nature/culture" split, it affirms that humans are both members of an ecological community (in some respects) and different from it (in other respects). Ecofeminism's attention to relationships and community is not, therefore, an erasure of difference but a respectful acknowledgment of it.

Fourth, ecofeminism reconceives theory as theory in process. It focuses on patterns of meaning which emerge, for instance, from the storytelling and first-person narratives of women (and others) who deplore the twin dominations of women and nature. The use of narrative is one way to ensure that the content of the ethic—the pattern of the quilt—may/will change over time, as the historical and material realities of women's lives change and as more is learned about women-nature connections and the destruction of the nonhuman world.

Fifth, ecofeminism is inclusivist. It emerges from the voices of women who experience the harmful domination of nature and the way that domination is tied to their domination as women. It emerges from listening to the voices of indigenous peoples such as Native Americans who have been dislocated from their land and have witnessed the attendant undermining of such values as appropriate reciprocity, sharing, and kinship that characterize traditional Indian culture. It emerges from listening to voices of those who, like Nathan Hare, critique traditional approaches to environmental ethics as white and bourgeois, and as failing to address issues of "black ecology" and the "ecology" of the inner city and urban spaces. It also emerges out of the voices of Chipko women who see the destruction of "earth, soil, and water" as intimately connected with their own inability to survive economically. With its emphasis on inclusivity and difference, ecofeminism provides a framework for recognizing that what counts as ecology and what counts as appropriate conduct toward both human and nonhuman environments is largely a matter of context.

Sixth, as a feminism, ecofeminism makes no attempt to provide an "objective" point of view. It is a social ecology. It recognizes the twin dominations of women and nature as social problems rooted both in very concrete, historical, socioeconomic circumstances and in oppressive patriarchal conceptual frameworks which maintain and sanction these circumstances.

Seventh, ecofeminism makes a central place for values of care, love, friendship, trust, and appropriate reciprocity—values that presuppose that our relationships to others are central to our understanding of who we are. It thereby gives voice to the sensitivity that in climbing a mountain, one is doing something in relationship with an "other," an "other" whom one can come to care about and treat respectfully.

Lastly, an ecofeminist ethic involves a reconception of what it means to be human, and in what human ethical behavior consists. Ecofeminism denies abstract individualism. Humans are who we are in large part by virtue of the historical and social contexts and the relationships we are in, including our relationships with nonhuman nature. Relationships are not something extrinsic to who we are, not an "add on" feature of human nature; they play an essential role in shaping what it is to be human. Relationships of humans to the nonhuman environment are, in part, constitutive of what it is to be a human.

By making visible the interconnections among the dominations of women and nature, ecofeminism shows that both are feminist issues and that explicit acknowledgment of both is vital to any responsible environmental ethic. Feminism *must* embrace ecological feminism if it is to end the domination of women because the domination of women is tied conceptually and historically to the domination of nature.

A responsible environmental ethic also *must* embrace feminism. Otherwise, even the seemingly most revolutionary, liberational, and holistic ecological ethic will fail to take seriously the interconnected dominations of nature and women that are so much a part of the historical legacy and conceptual framework that sanctions the exploitation of nonhuman nature. Failure to make visible these interconnected, twin dominations results in an inaccurate account of how it is that nature has been and continues to be dominated and exploited and produces an environmental ethic that lacks the depth necessary to be truly *inclusive* of the realities of persons who at least in dominant Western culture have been intimately tied with that exploitation, viz., women. Whatever else can be said in favor of such holistic ethics, a failure to make visible ecofeminist insights into the common denominators of the twin oppressions of women and nature is to perpetuate, rather than overcome, the source of that oppression. . . .

## Conclusion

I have argued in this paper that ecofeminism provides a framework for a distinctively feminist and environmental ethic. Ecofeminism grows out of

the felt and theorized about connections between the domination of women and the domination of nature. As a contextualist ethic, ecofeminism refocuses environmental ethics on what nature might mean, morally speaking, *for* humans, and on how the relational attitudes of humans to others — humans as well as nonhumans — sculpt both what it is to be human and the nature and ground of human responsibilities to the nonhuman environment. Part of what this refocusing does is to take seriously the voices of women and other oppressed persons in the construction of that ethic.

A Sioux elder once told me a story about his son. He sent his seven-year-old son to live with the child's grandparents on a Sioux reservation so that he could "learn the Indian ways." Part of what the grandparents taught the son was how to hunt the four leggeds of the forest. As I heard the story, the boy was taught, "to shoot your four-legged brother in his hind area, slowing it down but not killing it. Then, take the four legged's head in your hands, and look into his eyes. The eyes are where all the suffering is. Look into your brother's eyes and feel his pain. Then, take your knife and cut the four-legged under his chin, here, on his neck, so that he dies quickly. And as you do, ask your brother, the four-legged, for forgiveness for what you do. Offer also a prayer of thanks to your four-legged kin for offering his body to you just now, when you need food to eat and clothing to wear. And promise the four-legged that you will put yourself back into the earth when you die, to become nourishment for the earth, and for the sister flowers, and for the brother deer. It is appropriate that you should offer this blessing for the four-legged and, in due time, reciprocate in turn with your body in this way, as the four-legged gives life to you for your survival." As I reflect upon that story, I am struck by the power of the environmental ethic that grows out of and takes seriously narrative, context, and such values and relational attitudes as care, loving perception, and appropriate reciprocity, and doing what is appropriate in a given situation — however that notion of appropriateness eventually gets filled out. I am also struck by what one is able to see, once one begins to explore some of the historical and conceptual connections between the dominations of women and of nature. A *re-conceiving* and *re-visioning* of both feminism and environmental ethics, is, I think, the power and promise of ecofeminism.

## CHECKLIST

To help you review, here is a checklist of the key philosophers and terms and concepts of this chapter. The brief descriptive sentences summarize the philosophers' leading ideas. Keep in mind that some of these summary statements are oversimplifications of complex positions.

### Philosophers

- **Mary Wollstonecraft,** a leading early feminist, held that males and females should be educated according to the same standards.

- **Anna Doyle Wheeler,** an Irish feminist and utilitarian, was a utopian.

- **William Thompson** was an English liberal, utilitarian, utopian, feminist. An economist, he argued for women's rights and the rights of workers.

- **Harriet Taylor,** a utilitarian philosopher, thought nonphysiological differences between men and women were socially constructed, to the detriment of women and society in general. She was a vociferous proponent of women's suffrage.

- **Simone de Beauvoir** was a feminist existentialist who extended the discussion of feminism into all areas of intellectual endeavor.

- **Kate Millett,** a contemporary American feminist, argues that patriarchy extends to all areas of life.

- **Gloria Steinem** helped found *Ms.* magazine and brought feminist issues to the public's attention.

- **Shulamith Firestone** argues that new reproductive technologies could free women from oppression.

- **Ann Ferguson** argues that we should pursue a monoandrogynous society to ensure that we are all fully human.

- **Joyce Trebilcot** holds that the androgynous society should include as many options as possible, including traditionally male types and traditionally female types.

- **Marilyn Frye** argues that the concepts of "masculine" and "feminine" are shaped by ideas of dominance and subordination.

- **Carol Gilligan** argues that men and women have characteristically different ways of reasoning about moral issues.

- **Nancy Chodorow** argues that the differences between men and women can be traced to the psychodynamics of the nuclear family.

- **Nel Noddings** is a leading exponent of ethics of care.

- **Sara Ruddick** holds that the experience of being a mother influences one's moral perceptions.

- **Susan Moller Okin** is an important feminist analyst and critic of traditional and recent themes of justice.

- **Stephanie Ross** suggests that the metaphors we use in ordinary speech can shape the way we think about women.

- **Marielouise Janssen-Jurreit,** a feminist philosopher in the Marxist tradition, sees women's services involved in childbearing as the first source of "surplus value."

- **Jacques Lacan** reemphasized the importance of Freud's Oedipus complex, giving the father the role of freeing the child from its presymbolic, imaginary world and introducing it into the adult world.

- **Luce Irigaray,** French feminist who thought women should find their own identity rooted in their own symbolism.

- **Sandra Harding,** a feminist epistemologist and philosopher of science, is noted for her feminist analysis of the metaphors of early scientists and philosophers of science.

- **Val Plumwood** finds the inferiorization of women and nature to be linked and grounded in the rationalist conception of human nature and the liberal concept of the individual.

### Key Terms and Concepts

| | |
|---|---|
| feminism | gender roles |
| Self/Other | sexism |
| liberal feminism | misogyny |
| radical feminism | ethics of caring |
| androgyny | maternal thinking |
| monoandrogyny | gender |
| polyandrogyny | ecofeminism |

## QUESTIONS FOR DISCUSSION AND REVIEW

1. Do all oppressed groups suffer? Are all groups that suffer oppressed?

2. How does sexism influence language use?

3. How much do you think the metaphors we use influence the way we look at the world? What reasons can you give for your view?

4. What is the main feminist criticism of pornography?

5. How are the feminist criticisms of pornography different from the more fundamentalist, right-wing criticisms of pornography on TV or in the papers?

6. How can white/Anglo women try to learn about the perspectives of women of color? Do you think it is possible for different groups to have true, empathetic understanding of each other?

7. Is there linkage between the inferiorization of women and nature?

8. Do you agree that the first items of the mind–body, reason–emotion, and masculine–feminine dualisms are conceived of as superior to the second items? If so, how do you explain that fact?

9. According to Plumwood, what is the connection between rationalism and the inferiorization of nature?

10. Are "reproductivity," "sensuality," and "emotionality" seen as characteristically feminine traits and "abstract planning" and "calculation" seen as characteristically masculine traits? Are the former traits seen as less authentically human than the latter?

11. What is Plumwood's argument against Taylor's position that only actions taken as a matter of principle are truly moral?

12. What does de Beauvoir mean by the Self–Other distinction? What examples of this kind of reasoning do you see in politics today (apart from the feminism debates)?

13. What would de Beauvoir say is required of women for them to become fully human? Do you think there should be different pictures of "full humanness" for men and women?

14. Do you think there would be a difference in the world if the "avenues of power" Millett mentions were in the hands of women? What evidence can you give for your view?

15. What is Ferguson's argument for the value of androgyny?

16. Is universal bisexuality a necessary consequence of an androgynous society? Why or why not?

17. How might it be argued that sex roles are more limiting for women than for men?

18. What social purpose is served by having "male" and "female" deodorants, razor blades, and so forth?

19. Why do boys and girls develop differently, according to Chodorow?

20. How does maternal practice shape women's moral concerns, according to Ruddick?

21. In what ways have you personally benefited from a sexist society? In what ways would you benefit from a nonsexist society?

22. Theories of justice assume that the "individual" who is the basic subject of the theories is the male head of a fairly traditional household. Does this claim seem true to you? Does it point to an important problem in such theories? Why?

## SUGGESTED FURTHER READINGS

Prudence Allen, *The Concept of Woman* (Grand Rapids, Mich.: William B. Erdman's Publishing Co., 1985).

Sonya Andermahr, Terry Lovell, and Carol Wolkowitz, *A Glossary of Feminist Theory* (New York: Oxford University Press, 2002). Reference work providing the definition of concepts in current feminist thought.

Chris Beasley, *What Is Feminism?* (Thousand Oaks, Calif.: Sage, 1999). A concise introduction to feminist theory.

Simone de Beauvoir, *The Second Sex*, H. M. Parshley, trans. (New York: Vintage Books, 1974). The book that started the second wave.

Claudia Card, ed., *Feminist Ethics* (Lawrence: University of Kansas Press, 1991).

Nancy Chodorow, *Femininities, Masculinities, Sexualities: Freud and Beyond* (Lexington: University Press of Kentucky, 1994).

Nancy Chodorow, *The Reproduction of Mothering: Psychoanalysis and the Sociology of Gender* (Berkeley: University of California Press, 1978).

Barbara A. Crow, *Radical Feminism* (New York: New York University Press, 2000). Readings representing primary sources of radical feminist thought.

Ann Ferguson, "Androgyny as an Ideal for Human Development," in *Feminism and Philosophy,* Mary Vetterling-Braggin, Frederick Elliston, and Jane English, eds. (Totowa, N.J.: Rowman and Little-field, 1977). Ferguson's important discussion of androgyny.

Ann Ferguson, *Blood at the Root: Motherhood, Sexuality, and Male Dominance* (London: Pandora, 1989).

Miranda Ficker and Jennifer Hornsby, *The Cambridge Companion to Feminism in Philosophy* (New York: Cambridge University Press, 2000). Essays reviewing feminism in relationship to different areas of philosophy such as language, mind, science, political philosophy, and psychoanalysis.

Stanley G. French, Wanda Teays, and Laura Purdy, eds., *Violence against Women* (Ithaca, N.Y.: Cornell University Press, 1998). A series of papers concerning issues such as domestic violence, pornography, genital mutilation, and rape.

Marilyn Frye, "Sexism," in *The Politics of Reality: Essays in Feminist Theory* (Freedom, Calif.: Crossing Press, 1983). A thorough philosophical analysis of the concept of sexism.

Marilyn Frye, *Willful Virgin* (Freedom, Calif.: Crossing Press, 1992).

Gabriele Griffin and Rosi Braidotti, *Thinking Differently: A Reader in European Women's Studies* (New York: Zed Books, 2002).

Alison Jaggar, *Feminist Frameworks* (New York: McGraw-Hill, 1984). A wide variety of feminist essays designed for the student reader.

Alison Jaggar, ed., *Living with Contradictions: Controversies in Feminist Social Ethics* (Boulder, Colo.: Westview Press, 1994).

Alison Jaggar and Iris Young, eds., *A Companion to Feminist Philosophy* (Malden, Mass.: Blackwell, 1998). Fifty articles on the advent and development of feminist philosophy.

Beverly LaBelle, "The Propaganda of Misogyny," in *Take Back the Night,* Laura Lederer, ed. (New York: William Morrow, 1980). This whole volume covers the subject of pornography and violence against women.

Genvieve Lloyd, ed., *Feminism and History of Philosophy,* Oxford Readings in Feminism (New York: Oxford University Press, 2002). Feminist critiques of the history of philosophy. European thinkers address leading social issues from a feminist perspective.

Maria Lugones and Elizabeth V. Spelman, "Have We Got a Theory for You! Feminist Theory, Cultural Imperialism, and the Demand for 'The Woman's Voice,'" in *Women and Values* (Belmont, Calif.: Wadsworth, 1986). A discussion and dialogue between a white/Anglo woman and a Hispanic woman.

Linda Lopez McAlister, ed., *Hypatia's Daughters* (Bloomington: Indiana University Press, 1996). An anthology of women philosophers extending over 1,500 years.

Kate Millett, *Sexual Politics* (Garden City, N.Y.: Doubleday, 1970). An in-depth analysis of the workings of patriarchy, with emphasis on examples from literature.

Nel Noddings, *Caring, A Feminine Approach to Ethics and Moral Education* (Berkeley: University of California Press, 1984).

Susan Moller Okin, *Justice, Gender, and the Family* (New York: Basic Books, 1989). The first feminist account of distributive justice.

Susan Frank Parsons, *The Ethics of Gender* (Malden, Mass.: Blackwell, 2002). Investigation of the influence of gender thinking on ethics.

Stephanie Ross, "How Words Hurt: Attitudes, Metaphor and Oppression," in *Sexist Language,* Mary Vetterling-Braggin, ed. (Totowa, N.J.: Littlefield, Adams, 1981). The book as a whole covers many perspectives on the relationship between language and sexism.

Sara Ruddick, *Maternal Thinking: Toward a Politics of Peace* (New York: Ballantine Books, 1990).

Elizabeth V. Spelman, *Inessential Woman* (Boston: Beacon Press, 1988).

Allesandra Tanesini, *An Introduction to Feminist Epistemologies* (Malden, Mass.: Blackwell, 1998). An introduction to feminist epistemologies.

Joyce Trebilcot, *Dyke Ideas: Process, Politics, and Daily Life* (Albany, N.Y.: SUNY Press, 1994).

Mary Ellen Waithe, ed., *A History of Women Philosophers,* vol. 3, *Modern Women Philosophers: 1600–1900* (Dordrecht: Kluwer Academic Press, 1991). Chapters about thirty-one women philosophers of the period.

# 15

# Eastern Influences

The tree that brushes the heavens grew from the tiniest sprout. The most elegant pagoda, nine stories high, rose from a small pile of earth. The journey of a thousand miles began with but a single step.    —Lao Tzu

Is there any point in studying Eastern thinkers, some of whom lived more than two thousand years ago? Can they possibly have anything to say to us?

The answer is yes, for the foreign enlightens the domestic in more than wine and cheeses. As the German poet Hölderlin suggested, we never understand our home until we have left it. The philosophy of another civilization provides a new vantage point from which to view our own thought; it offers us a different perspective, one from which we may reconsider and reevaluate what is important to us in our own philosophy. Besides, it is a potential source of fresh ideas and new concepts.

The study of ancient Eastern philosophers is, of course, more than a journey in distance. It is a travel back in time to periods in the history of thought that have left messages of perhaps telling importance to us today. For many of the Westerners who have studied it, the philosophy of ancient Eastern thinkers has offered secure guidance to the full and contented life.

In this chapter we will consider Hinduism and Buddhism in India; Taoism, Confucianism, and Ch'an Buddhism in China; as well as Zen Buddhism and the Samurai tradition in Japan. No effort will be made to present the history of these important traditions or to trace their evolution over the centuries. Our intent is merely to introduce these philosophies and their most important thinkers. Islamic philosophy, too, is given a brief overview in the box by that name on page 500.

Eastern philosophy and Eastern religions are closely intertwined. Both Confucianism and Taoism took on the trappings of religion, with priests, rituals, and moral codes. Some forms of Taoism also were influenced by Chinese popular religions and superstitions. Today in Taiwan, for example, there are six levels of Taoism, including two kinds of Taoist priests, the red and the black. Only the highest level reflects the Taoist philosophy in its purest form, free from religious and superstitious add-ons.

Buddhism in China was influenced not only by Confucianism and Taoism but by popular religions as well. In India, a similar interaction took place among the ancient Buddhist writings and various religious belief systems and practices.

## HINDUISM

The long history of Indian philosophy has given rise to two main schools of thought, Hinduism and Buddhism. Hinduism, for example, contains both monism and dualism. Both also have had a long list of great thinkers, such as Nagarjuna (on the foundations of Buddhism). But this text must limit itself to a brief sketch of these traditional movements. **Hinduism,** from the Urdu word for India, *Hind,* is the Western term for the religious beliefs and practices of the majority of the Indian people.

The origins of Hinduism stretch back into the unknown past. Unlike other religions, it had no founder, and there is no single religious body to judge orthodoxy. In fact, Hinduism does not even contain a unified set of doctrines — or, to the extent it does, they are given diversified interpretations. All of this makes it difficult to talk about Hinduism in a limited space. Speaking of Hinduism as a single belief system is something like speaking of philosophy in the same way. It is best to view it as a spiritual attitude that gives rise to a wide range of religious and philosophical beliefs and practices. These range from the worship of village and forest deities, which often take zoomorphic forms, to sophisticated metaphysical theories.

Common to all forms of Hinduism, however, is acceptance of the authority of the Vedic scriptures as the basis for understanding the true hidden nature of things. The **Vedas** are the most ancient religious texts of Hinduism — indeed, they are the oldest religious texts in an Indo-European language. The *Vedas* were the literature of the Aryans, who invaded northwest India around 1500 B.C.E. Many, if not most, Hindu writings are commentaries on the Vedic scriptures.

In terms of popular religion, three contemporary movements might be mentioned. *Saivism* worships Siva as the supreme being and source of the universe; *Saktism* worships Sakti, the female part of the universe and the wife of Siva. *Vaisnavism* worships the personal god **Vishnu.** Buddha, according to orthodox Hindus, was an incarnation (*avatar*) of Vishnu.

The basis of Hindu philosophy is the belief that reality is absolutely one, that there is only one ultimate reality-being-consciousness (see the box "Ommmmm"). Six classical philosophical schools or traditions, however, interpret this reality variously: these six "insights," as they are called, are *Nyāya, Vaiśesika, Sāmkhya, Yoga, Mīmāmsā,* and *Vedānta.* All are designed to lead the searcher to a knowledge of the Absolute and the liberation of the soul. Vedanta is tradition based on the *Upanishads* that is the best known in the West (*Vedanta* means "the end of the Veda").

Philosophically, the most important Vedic scripture is the last book, the **Upanishads.** The *Upanishads,* which date from about the eighth to the fifth

## Ommmmm

During the 1960s, Indian philosophy, or what passed for it, became popular in the American youth culture, thanks in part to the Beatles's interest in it and in the music of the Indian sitar master Ravi Shankar. In San Francisco and New York and Madison, Wisconsin, it was common to see hippies chanting "*Ommmmm, ommmmm, ommmmm*" in an effort to induce a mystical state of higher consciousness.

What is "*ommm*"? It is the sound of the letters *A, U,* and *M,* which are the symbols in Hindu writings for the three ordinary states of consciousness: waking experience, dreaming sleep, and deep sleep. There is in addition, according to Hinduism, a fourth state (in Vedanta philosophy, *moksa*), one of higher awareness, which is described in the *Mandukya Upanishad* as "the coming to peaceful rest of all differentiated existence." *Yoga* is the general term for the spiritual disciplines in Hinduism and Buddhism that aim at attainment of this higher state. It is also the name of one of the six orthodox systems of Hindu philosophy (see text).

centuries B.C.E., are the inspiration for the six systems of philosophy just mentioned. The *Upanishads* are best known for the theories of *brahman* (the ultimate cosmic principle or reality) and *atman* (the inner self), and the identification of *brahman* with *atman*. There are four great sayings (*mahavakya*) of the *Upanishads,* which are all ways of saying that *brahman* and *atman* are one:

1. Consciousness is *brahman.*
2. That art thou.
3. The self is *brahman.*
4. I am *brahman.*

*Brahman* is considered the ultimate reality or principle and the source and sustainer of all things, including people and gods. It is absolute and eternal spirit — the supreme consciousness, the One, the One-and-only-One. A lower manifestation of *brahman*—namely, *brahma*—may be thought of as an individual deity or personal god, but *brahman* itself is without attributes or qualities. This absolute remains the hidden, unknown, ultimate mystery.

*Atman* is the self, the soul, the principle of individual life. Ultimately, however, the individual must come to a realization, through meditation and contemplation, that *brahman* and *atman* are the same thing—*brahman-atman*. With the realization of this absolute oneness of all things comes recognition of the relative nonreality of the world and of the individual ego. The identification of *brahman* and *atman* is sometimes spoken of by commentators as a pantheism, but it goes beyond the claim that all things are God. In Hinduism, the gods are parts or symbolic personifications of the absolute principle, *brahman*.

Further, the identification of *brahman* and *atman* has been subject to various interpretations over the centuries. It has been looked on as both transcendent and immanent. Samkara, who is thought to have lived between 788 and 820 C.E. and who gave the most rigorous interpretation of the *Upanishads,* was a pure monist who thought that all things are one — only the ultimate principle exists, and all else is an illusion. But another way of looking at the ultimate principle or reality was introduced by Rāmānuja (b. 1027 C.E.). He believed in the ultimate principle, but he also believed that souls are real and that the world is not merely an illusion. For a time, at least, the souls and the world must be separate from the ultimate principle to be of service to it, he held.

Yet a third way of interpreting the underlying ultimate reality is represented by the outright dualism of Madhva (1199–1278), who believed that, although the ultimate principle is the cause of the world, the soul still has a separate and independent existence of its own. You can see that Hindu philosophy in fact admits a variety of viewpoints.

The metaphysical question as to what constitutes the ultimate reality is not the only philosophical concern within Hinduism. There is also the issue of the human being's relation to that ultimate principle. Human life is a journey. Humans, though basically good, are caught up in a cycle of desire and suffering that is the direct result of ignorance and ego. In short, they are miserable. The desires that torment them are many and diverse, including sensual lusts and the desire for existence. The end result is *samsara,* the cycle of being born, dying, and being reborn. The human being often goes through a series of rebirths in various forms until he or she can escape the treadmill.

That which keeps an individual imprisoned by the transmigratory cycle is **karma,** which means "action" or "deed" in Pali. It refers to the chain of causes and necessary consequences in the world of human actions. Every action inevitably has its effect, and traces of these effects can last over several lifetimes. A good action brings joy; a bad action brings sorrow. And the consequences of actions build up over a lifetime and through multiple lifetimes. It is these residues that will help determine the quality of the next **reincarnation.** Despite the fact that humans create their own limitations through their choices of actions and motives, they nonetheless have the power to continue to choose or to resist falling victim to selfish desires. Building up good karma and reducing bad karma may eventually lead a person to escape the bondage of karma altogether by surrender to God and the liberation of enlightenment.

It is through the renunciation of desires and the giving up of possessions and worldly attachments that can lead to **nirvana,** or permanent liberation from the cycle of birth, death, and rebirth. *Nirvana* is the Sanskrit word for "extinction," and it means the merging of the individual, transitory existence into the ultimate reality, namely, Brahman. This is a condition of bliss at the highest state of transcendent consciousness. As part of Brahman, we watch *lila,* or the entire history of the world and of our lives.

Human life, then, is a journey wherein we try to control both the mind and the senses and become God oriented in the hope of experiencing total fulfillment in oneness with God. This means going from the state of everyday, ordinary consciousness to the blissful contemplation of the divine being itself. The human being seeks God by eliminating the shadow between the two, that is, the illusion of duality and separation.

Much of the wisdom of Hinduism in all times lies in its sages. This certainly holds true for the twentieth century, whose wise men include Rabīndranāth Tagore (1861–1941), Aurobindo Ghose (1872–1950), and Mohandas K. Gandhi (1869–1948) (see Chapter 16). Tagore won the Nobel Prize in 1913 for his poetry, in which he expressed the human quest for freedom and the divine. Aurobindo, who was educated in the West, sought political freedom for India. After being accused of terrorism and violence, he withdrew from political life altogether and developed a theory of spiritual evolution according to which the individual through self-effort can rise to ever higher states of spiritual consciousness.

Gandhi, of course, is known everywhere for his use of nonviolence to help attain political freedom for India and for striving to instill a sense of self-respect in all human beings (he called the lowest caste, the "untouchables," the children of God). Through the example of his simple life and teachings, Gandhi tried to make the traditional values of Hinduism available to all.

## BUDDHISM

**Buddhism** arose in India in the person of a prince, **Siddhartha Gautama** [sid-HAR-tuh, GO-tuh-muh], later known as **Buddha** [BOO-duh] (563–483 B.C.E.), "the Enlightened One." Originally, Buddhism essentially was a philosophical response to what might be called the problem of suffering — and suffering is here to be understood in the broad sense as including not merely outright pain and misery but also sorrow, disappointment, frustration, discontent, disaffection, pessimism, and the sense of unfulfillment that so often grows with the passing of the years.

### Buddha

When he was twenty-nine, Siddhartha, tortured by the suffering he saw around him, abandoned a life of luxury as well as a wife and son to discover why it is that suffering exists and what its cure must be. After six years of wandering and meditation, he found enlightenment.

Buddha's answer to the problem of suffering was contained in his doctrine of the **Four Noble Truths:** (1) There is suffering; (2) suffering has specific and identifiable causes; (3) suffering can be ended; (4) the way to end suffering is through enlightened living, as expressed in the Eightfold Path.

Suffering is in part the result, according to Buddha, of the transience and hence uncertainty of the world: indeed, all human problems are rooted in the fact of change and the uncertainty, anxiety, and fear that it causes. Suffering is also in part the result of karma. Karma, as we have seen, is the doctrine that one's point of departure in this life is determined by one's decisions and deeds in past lives and that decisions and deeds in this life determine one's beginning points in future incarnations. *Karma,* to repeat, means action or deed. The intention of an action determines whether the action is morally good or bad. The effect of an action leaves a trace that extends over several lifetimes, thereby helping to determine the quality of the reincarnation.

But the most immediate causes of human suffering, according to Buddha, are ignorance, which closes the door to enlightenment, and selfish craving, which enslaves an individual to desires and passions. The individual who is ruled by desires cannot possibly be happy in an ever-changing, uncertain world, especially because

# PROFILE: Siddhartha Gautama Buddha (563–483 B.C.E.)

Siddhartha Gautama, the Buddha, was born in northeastern India. His father was a wealthy king or clan chieftain, Suddhodana by name; through his mother, Maya, he was related to the Shakya tribe of Nepal. The family enjoyed a luxurious lifestyle, and his father sought to keep Siddhartha sheltered from the dust and trouble of the outside world. The young Siddhartha was athletic, handsome, and highly intelligent. He was married at the age of sixteen to Yasodhara, who eventually gave birth to a son, Rahula.

One day on a visit to the city of Kapilavastu, Siddhartha became deeply disturbed by the sight of suffering in its various guises. First, he encountered an old man whose body showed the ravages of the years. Next he saw a man in the throes of a virulent disease. Finally, he passed a funeral with its corpse and attendant mourners, meeting the problem of death on one hand and anguish on the other. His last experience of that eventful day was to behold a monk deep in meditation. All of these sights had a profound effect on Siddhartha, and the problem of suffering became the central focus of his thoughts. At the age of twenty-nine, he slipped away from his family during the night and entered the forest to seek a solution to the conundrum of suffering, shaving his head and taking on the raiments of poverty.

Early on in his quest, Siddhartha studied under at least two Hindu ascetics. From them he learned a form of yoga, as well as the arts of breathing and motionless meditation. Later Siddhartha joined a small band of ascetics who begged for a living. Like them, Siddhartha performed many acts of self-abnegation and self-renunciation. He grew extremely thin from excessive fasting and one day fell unconscious from his attempts to control his senses. When he awoke, he was fed milk and gruel. From that moment, it was clear to Siddhartha that ascetic practices, in and of themselves, do not lead to enlightenment.

Siddhartha dwelt in the forest for about six years. Thereafter he is thought to have sought a *middle way* between sensual indulgence and ascetic self-denial, striving for enlightenment through concentrating his mind in deep meditation. Siddhartha achieved enlightenment one day while meditating under a fig tree near the present-day town of Gaya in northeastern India. He continued to meditate for seven days. Henceforth this tree was known as the bodhi tree — the tree of enlightenment.

For almost fifty years Siddhartha, now the Buddha or Enlightened One, went about teaching the way of dealing with suffering. He founded a group or order, to which his wife and son ultimately belonged. Before he died, his philosophy had already found a large following. For Western readers, perhaps the most affecting account of the life of Buddha is presented by Hermann Hesse in his novel *Siddhartha*.

what happens is so much beyond one's control. For even when life goes as is hoped for, there is no guarantee that it will continue that way, and inevitably anxiety and fear overwhelm temporary satisfaction.

According to Buddha, through meditation and self-abnegation, selfish craving can be stilled and ignorance overcome. The result of doing so is a cessation of suffering in nirvana, a permanent state of supreme enlightenment and serenity that brings the continuing cycle of reincarnation to an end for the individual.

But Buddha held that attainment of nirvana requires more than merely letting go of selfish desires. It requires understanding that what are ordinarily thought of as one's body and one's consciousness are not real, are not the true Self. This

## Islamic Philosophy

Muslim philosophy arose around the eighth century, a time when Western Europe was experiencing its Middle Ages. From the beginning, it took into account theological considerations such as the person of Mohammed, the Quran, and the schools of theology, but these were not the only sources of influence. Neoplatonism and Aristotle played important roles in shaping both the problems faced and their proposed solutions. Many translations from the Greek were made during the ninth century.

Among the concerns of the early Islamic philosophers were the nature of God (Allah), the hierarchy of creation, the nature of human beings and their place within the universe, as well as the relationship between theology and philosophy. **Al-Kindi** [el-KIN-dee] (d. after 870) developed the idea of God as an absolute and transcendent being, which was in accord with certain Muslim ideas of the time. His definition of God took elements from both Aristotle and the Neoplatonists. He developed a cosmology based on the Neoplatonist idea of emanation, where everything evolves out of God and in some way participates in God. Al-Kindi also added the Muslim notion that God created the first being out of nothing by force of will.

**Al-Fārābī** [el-fuh-RAHB-ee] (875–950) further elaborated on the notion of God in terms of Plotinus's notion of the One and also the notion that everything emanates out of the One. He added Aristotle's notion of God as the first cause of everything. Al-Fārābī looked to the prophet-philosopher to gain the philosophical illumination that would be of profound meaning to his society.

**Avicenna** [av-uh-SEN-uh] (Abū ʿAli ibn-Sīnā, 980–1037) produced the best-known medieval system of thought. He envisioned God as a Necessary Being who emanated the contingent, temporal world out of himself. Everything was dependent on God, and the ultimate goal of human activity was a prophetic mind that attains an intuitive knowledge of God and his creation. For Avicenna, there was a parallelism between philosophy and theology. During this time, philosophy, and especially the mystical identification of a thinker with God, were occasionally considered a threat to Muslim orthodoxy. For example, **Al-Ghazālī** [el-guh-ZAHL-ee] (1058–1111) in his *Incoherence of the Philosophers* attacked Avicenna. Among other things, he criticized Avicenna's notion of the eternity of the world as well as the lower status given to the religious law

understanding, this totally nonegoistic perspective, is itself freedom from egoistic thoughts and desires and brings with it as well freedom from all fear and anxiety. By rejecting the fetters of egoistic craving, the individual overcomes the false self and achieves "the unsurpassed state of security . . . and utter peace" that is nirvana.

The way to the cessation of suffering is the **Eightfold Path.** In effect, the Eightfold Path sets forth the means of proper living:

1. *Right View,* which implies having adequate knowledge about those things that make human life sick and unwholesome—ignorance, selfish craving and grasping, and so on.
2. *Right Aim,* which requires overcoming selfish passions and desires by an effort of will and thus having no resentment, envy, or reason to harm another person.
3. *Right Speech,* which means refraining from lies, deceptions, harmful gossip, idle chatter or speculation about others, and so on.
4. *Right Action,* which means not responding to improper desires and cravings, including those that are sexual, and above all means not taking a human life. Right Action also includes doing good deeds (described by Buddha as the "treasure" of the wise).

as a mere symbol of higher truths to be accessed through intuition.

The antagonism between mystical philosophy and Muslim orthodoxy represents an ongoing problem. **Averroës** [ah-VAIR-oh-eez] (1126–1198), for example, was interpreted as holding a theory of two separate truths, the truth of religion and the truth of philosophy. Averroës, who taught the idea of eternal creation, was trying to extricate Aristotle's thought from both Neoplatonic and Islamic derivations.

Perhaps what is most intriguing to modern-day Western thought is the development of Sufism. **Sufism** represents a mystical, theosophical, and ascetic strain of Muslim belief that seeks union with God (Allah). **Sadr al-Dīn als Shīrazī** (1571–1640), later known as Mulla Sadrā, sought a monistic return to the First Principle of Being. Sufism, perhaps to a greater degree than orthodox Islamic belief, was influenced by the mystical tendencies of Neoplatonism and gnosticism. There was a seeking after a direct communion with the Absolute Being, who likewise represented Absolute Beauty. Through ascetic practices and concentrated inwardness, a human being might experience a sudden illumination and a sense of ecstatic union with God (Allah). This intuition might reveal to the person his utter nothingness, on one hand, as well as his pantheistic immanence in God, on the other. It is hardly surprising that a number of Sufis during the medieval period were executed for the blasphemy of identifying themselves with God. This ongoing difficulty was to some degree mollified by Al-Ghazālī, who brought Sufism closer to orthodox Muslim belief by playing down the pantheistic elements of Sufism.

There have been four main periods of Sufism: the first period (c. 750–1050), the second period (c. 1050–1450), the modern period (c. 1450–1850), and the contemporary period (1850 to the present). There are about one hundred Sufi orders in the world today with several million adherents. The movement has produced a number of great mystical poets; **Kabir** [kuh-BEER] (1435–1518) from Benares, India, is one of the best known in the West thanks to Robert Bly's translations. The Sufi literature, Sufi poetry, and the whirling dervishes have continued to influence the West's own contemporary pantheistic and mystical traditions.

5. *Right Living,* which requires obtaining one's livelihood through proper means and living one's life free from selfish cravings and graspings.
6. *Right Effort,* which means struggling against immoral and corrupt conditions.
7. *Right Mindfulness,* which is the source of Right Effort. Right Mindfulness implies having a duty to attain enlightenment and to understand the nature and effects of selfish craving. The right-minded person, according to Buddha, has no sense of attachment toward body, feelings, perceptions, activities, and thought, and naturally controls all covetous longings and desires. Right Mindfulness likewise means to develop the noble principles of life, especially the six just listed. It develops a pure mind and a clear memory, which are necessary if our every action, no matter how seemingly trivial, is to be imbued with "mindfulness." It brings all human activities under conscious control and thoughtfulness.
8. *Right Contemplation,* which is the ultimate concentration of mind, integrates the aforementioned principles in dealing with all aspects of life. It is the liberating consciousness that frees the mind from the bonds of our cravings, inclinations, and desires. Any personal consciousness is replaced by an "invisible, infinite, all-penetrating consciousness" that brings lasting peace. It is pure

## Buddhism and the West

The parallel concern of Buddhists and Stoics (see Chapter 10) with the problem of suffering is intriguing, but it is difficult to say whether there was any reciprocal influence between Buddhism and the philosophies of ancient Greece and Rome. The first major modern Western philosopher to be influenced in a significant way by Buddhist thought was Arthur Schopenhauer (1788–1860). Schopenhauer believed that human life is basically not rational and that humans are driven by blind and insatiable will. Only by overcoming one's ego and desires can a state of calm bliss be achieved, according to Schopenhauer.

After Schopenhauer, Buddhist and other Asian ideas have increasingly come to the West, mostly via Indian and Japanese gurus, monks, and martial artists. Many of these ideas are now entering the mainstream of popular culture.

cognition, free from any selfishness. This way to liberation is achieved by the utter annihilation of craving and therefore ultimately of suffering. Buddha emphasizes that this way is achieved slowly. Deliverance is attained step by step by constant effort in building an unshakable concentration. Right concentration is uninterrupted, blissful thoughtfulness that purifies deeds, words, and thoughts.

As you can see, the first two stages of the Eightfold Path have to do with the initial mental outlook of the individual, the next four specify appropriate behavior, and the last two pertain to the higher mental and spiritual qualities involved in a total disattachment from self.

Two additional concepts traditionally believed to have been introduced by Gautama Buddha became important for later Buddhism. The first, Gautama Buddha identifies in his *Sayings* as "clinging to existence" (*upadana*). This clinging is an extreme form of egoistic craving or desire and must be "destroyed" if the human being is ever to reach a state of peace and imperturbability. This clinging can take different forms—a clinging to the body and its worldly pleasure, a clinging to views, a clinging to rules and rituals, and a clinging to ego beliefs. It is necessary to cultivate nonclinging or nonattachment but in such a way that there is not clinging to nonclinging.

The other important concept is silence (*moneyya*). Gautama Buddha sat and meditated under the bodhi tree to reach enlightenment. Such enlightenment requires going beyond the verbiage and logics of discursive reasoning. In the *Sayings,* Gautama Buddha is thought to have spoken of three kinds of silence: the silence of body, the silence of mind, and the silence of word. Only the person who is silent in all three ways can be said to be free of taint. It is not surprising, then, that silent meditation becomes a critical way to enlightenment in later developments of Buddhism.

Buddha believed that he had found the cause of suffering in the world and a way of escaping it as well. He set forth a strategy for eliminating unnecessary fear and specified a way of living that is calming for the person but that also allows the person to be of service to others. Buddha did not believe in a divine creator or in divine salvation; thus, in his thinking, the problem of suffering is one that humans must cope with themselves.

Buddhism was purportedly brought to China by the Indian monk Bodhi-dharma about 520 C.E. There it gradually mixed with Taoism, Confucianism, and other influences and underwent a rather marked transformation (see the box "Bud-dhism and the West").

## TAOISM

Chinese philosophy, like Indian philosophy, goes back into the prehistoric past, and its origins are somewhat nebulous. Three great systems of thought dominate Chinese civilization: Taoism, Confucianism, and Buddhism. Our knowledge of **Taoism** [DOW-ism] derives chiefly from **Lao Tzu** [LAO-tsuh] (c. seventh–sixth century B.C.E.) and his chief follower, Chuang Tzu (c. fourth century B.C.E.).

### Lao Tzu

In an oft-reported meeting between Confucius and Lao Tzu, Confucius expressed his admiration for the depth of Lao Tzu's thought. Lao Tzu, in turn, is said to have expressed doubts about the heroes of the past whom Confucius had chosen as models of behavior. Lao Tzu also tried to convince Confucius of the hopelessness of the latter's attempts to improve society by direct action.

This little story nicely illustrates an essential difference between Confucius and Lao Tzu and between Confucianism and Taoism. Confucius sought to become an advisor to a ruler and directly to change society for the better, using heroes of the past as models. Lao Tzu's vision of things and strategies for change are very different. Within the Taoist tradition, one strain of thought even uses Lao Tzu's ideas as a means cunningly to obtain and retain power (the military and political strategies of **Sun Tzu** [SWUN-tsuh] might be mentioned as an example). Our way of looking at Lao Tzu's ideas is thus not the only possible one, and there are also a variety of different ways of interpreting his thought within the long Taoist tradition.

Lao Tzu's view of humankind is in at least one respect like that of the Greek philosopher Socrates. Both thought that even the wisest of humans is still ignorant. And to act on that ignorance under the pretense that it is knowledge, both held, is folly that leads not to progress and betterment within the individual and society but to the opposite effect. It is especially here that Taoists like Lao Tzu and Chuang Tzu found Confucius wanting. They thought that he sought to impose solutions without knowledge or understanding.

According to Lao Tzu, what is needed is not interference with the world but, rather, humble understanding of the way it functions, namely, understanding of the Tao. Humans cannot force "change" on the world without injuring themselves. All arbitrary interventions using "models" of the past simply lead to further disorder. The sage, he maintained, is the one who knows enough to do nothing: instead of intervening, he simply follows the patterns of the universe, of the ineffable Tao that gives order and substance to all things.

## PROFILE: Lao Tzu

Almost nothing is known of Lao Tzu's life because he spent it trying to remain unknown and nameless. He is thought to have been born in the late seventh or early sixth century B.C.E. and to have worked in the archives at Loyang (present-day Hunan province). Confucius is thought to have visited the older man during one of his journeys. These quotations reveal some of Lao Tzu's insights on the **Tao,** or **Way.**

The Tao that can be told of is not the eternal Tao;
The name that can be named is not the eternal name.
The Nameless is the origin of Heaven and Earth.

Can you understand all and penetrate all without taking any action?
To produce and to rear them,
To produce, but not to take possession of them,
To act, but not to rely on one's own ability,
To lead them, but not to master them —
This is called profound and secret virtue.

Reversion is the action of Tao.
Weakness is the function of Tao.
All things in the world come from being.
And being comes from non-being.

Tao produced the One.
The One produced the two.
The two produced the three.
And the three produced the ten thousand things.
To know that you do not know is the best.

To pretend to know when you do not know is a disease.

The sage desires to have no desire . . . and returns to what the multitude has missed (Tao).
Thus he supports all things in their natural state, but does not take any action.

A good traveler leaves no track or trace.

Now the Tao, for Lao Tzu, is one, natural, and eternal (see the box "The Tao, Logos, and God"). It gives rise to the expansive forces (**yang**) in the universe, and it gives rise to the contractive forces (**yin**). The Tao is like an empty bowl that holds and yields the vital energy (*ch'i*) in all things. It is also the *means* by which things come to be, take shape, and reach fulfillment. In contrast to Confucius, who believed that the Tao can be improved on (note Confucius's remark that "it is man that can make the Way great"), Lao Tzu believed that the Tao cannot be improved on, for it *is* the natural order of things.

According to Lao Tzu, the wise person, the sage, cultivates tranquility and equilibrium in his life in order to recognize the Tao. He comes to recognize that the enduring foundation of life is peace, not strife. The harshest storm, the sage understands, can last only a short while. He frees himself of selfish desires and turns his attention to the deep-rooted Tao, where all is one, and by doing so, he acquires the secrets of both the quiet and the long-lasting life.

By following the Tao, Lao Tzu held, the behavior of the sage is natural and free, for he harbors no unfit desires and no unnatural expectations. He simply does what is appropriate in the present circumstances. Like water, he accepts the lowest

## The Tao, Logos, and God

Ancient Chinese and Western philosophy show a striking similarity in their identification of the first principle (beginning) of all being and truth. In ancient Chinese philosophy this first principle is the eternal Tao, the source of all necessity, meaning, order, and existence, the Way the universe functions. Yet the Tao itself, according to Taoism, remains hidden, its nature ineffable. Any attempt to define the Tao or even to describe it in words must fail. According to Lao Tzu, it is the sign of the truly wise man that he will not even try to name it. He only seeks to submit to it and follow it humbly.

In ancient Greek philosophy a like notion was posited as the root of all things. Heraclitus (c. 535– 475 B.C.E.) named it *logos* and regarded it as the source of all order, lawfulness, and justice. There is no consensus on how *logos* should be translated into English, and dictionaries provide many different meanings for the term, including "reason," "proportion," "word," and others.

*Logos,* as Heraclitus sees it, is almost entirely unknown by earthly mortals — in part because nature loves to hide. Humans, Heraclitus thought, see the world in terms of opposites and as full of strife. But the deeper reality is the *logos,* the unity of opposites in which all is one. Seeing this deeper reality is reserved only for the gods and for those few humans who can escape conventional modes of understanding, according to Heraclitus.

The concept of God as it evolved in traditional Christian philosophy is a variation of Heraclitus' notion of *logos* as developed by Plato and Aristotle and reinterpreted by St. Augustine, St. Thomas Aquinas, and others. In fact, the "Word" that was "in the beginning" in *John* was *logos* in the Greek text. (*John*'s contribution to the *Bible* may not have been originally composed in Greek, of course.)

---

places with contentment and without resistance. He deems valuable what others consider worthless and have discarded. And, because he is selfless, he seeks to care for all things and to benefit them rather than use them for his own ends.

The sage's way, maintained Lao Tzu, is modest, slow, and cautious (see the box "Lao Tzu on Virtuous Activity"). Again like water, the sage is **soft and supple** rather than hard, and (like water), while appearing to do nothing, he achieves lasting effects. To others, the results seem mysteriously produced, for they are produced without apparent effort. The sage is merely following the flow and letting events unfold at their proper time and in their own way. Further, in doing so, he seeks to remain hidden, and he takes no credit for what is achieved, for he seeks neither possession nor domination. This absence of selfish desire is his secret virtue.

Lao Tzu believed that all enduring change is brought about by weakness, not by strength; by submission, not by intervention. Like an infant, the sage conserves his vital force and progresses gradually day by day. His strength lies in his softness and flexibility. As he lives in accord with the Tao, he is preserved from harm.

Lao Tzu extended his philosophy of nonstriving to the political sphere (see the box "Lao Tzu on Government"). He recognized the disadvantages of coercion: the use of force brings retaliation, and mutual hostility quickly escalates to the detriment of both sides. As coercion and the use of force arise from greed, he advocated a political strategy of nonacquisitiveness, in which weapons are regarded as instruments of destruction and wars are to be fought only when absolutely necessary and then only with regret.

The wise ruler, Lao Tzu believed, understands that violence is a last resort and knows that it can often be avoided by anticipation, by reconciling potential enemies

## Lao Tzu on Virtuous Activity

Good words shall gain you honor in the marketplace, but good deeds shall gain you friends among men.

There is no guilt greater than
    to sanction unbridled
    ambition.
No calamity greater than to
    be dissatisfied with one's
    own lot.
No fault greater than to wish
    continually of receiving.

With the faithful I would keep faith; with the unfaithful I would also keep faith, in order that they may become faithful.

The ability to perceive the significance of the small things of the world is the secret of clear-sightedness; the guarding of what is soft and vulnerable is the secret of strength.

The superior man hoards nothing. The more he uses for the benefit of others, the more he possesses himself. The more he gives to his fellow men, the more he has of his own.

The superior man is skillful in dealing with men, and so does not cast away anyone from his doorway.

The superior man prizes three things. The first is gentleness, the second is frugality, the third is humility. By being gentle he can be bold; by being frugal he can be liberal, and by being humble he becomes a leader among men.

The superior man anticipates tasks that are difficult while they are still easy, and does things that would become great while they are small. Therefore, the superior man, while he never does what is great, is able on that account to accomplish the greatest of things.

The superior man diminishes his actions and diminishes them again until he arrives at doing nothing on purpose.

    Having arrived at this point of non-action, there is nothing that he does not do.

He who keeps his mouth open and spends his breath in the continual promotion of his affairs will never, in all his life, experience safety.

and resolving difficulties when they first arise. It is because such a ruler sidesteps problems by anticipation that his success is unfathomable to others. And because he recognizes that there is no safety in the use of force, he remains calm and unhurried in dealing with any problems that cannot be avoided. His preference is to yield rather than to attack. Gentleness brings him eventual victory with apparently no effort. His strategy is "not to advance an inch but rather to retreat a foot." Slowly he wins over the enemy without the use of weapons. And the gain is lasting because it is achieved without the destructiveness of war and therefore without the long memories of resentment.

To achieve peace and stability, the sage ruler has no wish to dominate or exploit others, Lao Tzu believed. Rather, the wise ruler encourages openness and broad-mindedness. Cognizant of the sometimes violent ways of the world, he is cautious and reserved. The very essence of his method lies in not requiting injury with injury, a practice that leads only into the endless cycle of revenge. He responds to injury with kindness. He remains faithful even to the unfaithful. In this way, he gradually and effortlessly turns people from that lower nature that tends to dominate in times of war and strife, away from aggressive ambition to thoughtfulness and the search for modest goals.

A kingdom, according to Lao Tzu, cannot be preserved by force or cunning. Further, he said, too much government only means confusion. Too many laws create disorder rather than prevent it. Too much activity upsets the balance within a

## Lao Tzu on Government

It is the way of Heaven to take from those who have too much and give to those who have too little. But the way of man is not so. He takes away from those who have too little, to add to his own superabundance.

He who assists the ruler with Tao does not dominate the world with force.
The use of force usually brings requital.
Wherever armies are stationed, briers and thorns grow . . .
Whatever is contrary to Tao will soon perish.

Weapons are the instruments of evil, not the instruments of a good ruler.
When he uses them unavoidably, he regards calm restraint as the best principle. Even when he is victorious, he does not regard it as praiseworthy.
For to praise victory is to delight in the slaughter of men.

Tao invariably takes no action, and yet there is nothing left undone.

If kings and barons can keep it, all things will transform spontaneously.
If, after transformation, they should desire to be active,
I would restrain them with simplicity, which has no name.
Simplicity, which has no name, is free of desires.
Being free of desires, it is tranquil.
And the world will be at peace of its own accord.

Violent and fierce people do not die a natural death.
I shall make this the father [basis or starting point] of my teaching.

Govern the state with correctness.
Operate the army with surprise tactics.
Administer the empire by engaging in no activity.

---

state, just as it does in the life of the individual. The wise ruler does only what is absolutely necessary; because his heart is calm and nonacquisitive, his subjects are not excited to hysteria either by fear or avarice. The state achieves a stability in which all things come to completion in accordance with the Way.

In sum, according to Lao Tzu, the way of life recommended by the Tao is one of simplicity, tranquility, weakness, unselfishness, patience, and, above all, nonstriving or nonaction—allowing the world to follow its natural course. For Lao Tzu, this way of life is its own reward. Lao Tzu was concerned with this world, the world of living people; he was concerned with the human condition and not with otherworldly or supernatural subjects. He did not believe that the Way can be improved on; therefore, he did not think the wise ruler would seek to impose his way of thinking on the state.

You may well think Lao Tzu's philosophy naive or idealistic. Lao Tzu was only too aware that a path of quiet nonstriving was one that few, if any, had chosen or would choose to tread. He made it quite clear that he did not expect rule by force to die out soon or quickly to be replaced by a policy of noninterference. He only drew up what he thought would be a superior way of living for any who might wish to consider his opinion in the matter.

## Chuang Tzu

---

**Chuang Tzu** [CHWANG-tsuh] (c. fourth century B.C.E.), the most important Taoist next to Lao Tzu, perceived that many people live their lives as "slaves of power and riches." Chained by ambition and greed, they are unable to rest and are

## PROFILE: Chuang Tzu

Chuang Tzu was born in the fourth century B.C.E. in the kingdom of Meng, which borders present-day Shantung. He had a wife, was poor, and worked for an office connected with the city of Tsi Yuan. Little else is known about him except that he enjoyed differing with the followers of Confucius. He was not interested in holding public office because doing so, he feared, might disturb his peace of mind. A few of his insights emerge in these quotations:

> The mind of a perfect man is like a mirror. It grasps nothing. It expects nothing. It reflects but does not hold. Therefore, the perfect man can act without effort.

> Proof that a man is holding fast to the beginning lies in the fact of his fearlessness.

> The still mind discovers the beautiful patterns in the universe.

> Flow with whatever may happen and let your mind be free: Stay centered by accepting whatever you are doing. This is the ultimate.

Only the intelligent know how to identify all things as one. Therefore he does not use [his own judgment] but abides in the common [principle]. The common means the useful and the useful means identification. Identification means being at ease with oneself. When one is at ease with himself, one is near Tao. This is to let [nature] take its own course.

Heaven and earth are one attribute; the ten thousand things [infinite things] are one horse.

When "this" or "that" have no opposites, there is the very axis of Tao.

He who knows the activities of Nature lives according to Nature. . . . How do we know that what I call Nature is not really man and what I call man is not really Nature?

Your master happened to come because it was his time, and he happened to leave because things follow along. If you are content with the time and willing to follow along, then grief and joy have no way to enter in.

in constant friction with the world around them. They often feel trapped and do not know how to change their situation. They seem blind to what is happening and why it is happening. Their lives are driven and hectic, and they are in constant warfare with an indifferent world, a world that does not acquiesce to their desires.

But the world has its own wisdom, Chuang Tzu believed, as did Lao Tzu before him, and things come to fruition only at their proper time. Nature cannot be forced or hurried because nature, Chuang Tzu believed, unfolds according to the Tao: a tree's fruit must be picked only when it is ripe, not before and not after. If people choose to impose their will on the world, the result is strife, disquietude, and disruption.

Chuang Tzu also believed, as did Lao Tzu, that there is no need for people to force things for the sake of ambition or in the pursuit of profit or, indeed, for any other objective. Because it is the Tao, and not the person, that determines what is possible and what will happen, the wise individual accepts the course of events as it unfolds, with neither hope nor regret, for the Tao brings all things to fulfillment in due time (see the box "Cook Ting"). Thus for Chuang Tzu, as for Lao Tzu, the secret of the sage — the key to freedom from fear and stress — is simply to follow the Way of things, responding to them appropriately and dwelling in nonaction. The sage is a mirror: he seeks to be utterly clear about what is before him, but he has no wish to change things.

## Cook Ting

Chuang Tzu gave this story of Cook Ting as an illustration of the secret of the sage—to follow the Way of things, responding to them appropriately and never with force.

Cook Ting was cutting up an ox for Lord Wen-hui. At every touch of his hand, every heave of his shoulder, every move of his feet, every thrust of his knee—zip! zoop! He slithered the knife along with a zing, and all was in perfect rhythm, as though he were performing the dance of the Mulberry Grove or keeping time to the Ching-shou music.

"Ah, this is marvelous!" said Lord Wen-hui. "Imagine skill reaching such heights!"

Cook Ting laid down his knife and replied, "What I care about is the Way, which goes beyond skill. When I first began cutting up oxen, all I could see was the ox itself. After three years I no longer saw the whole ox. And now—now I go at it by spirit and don't look with my eyes. Perception and understanding have come to a stop and spirit moves where it wants. I go along with the natural makeup, strike in the big hollows, guide the knife through the big openings, and follow things as they are. So I never touch the smallest ligament or tendon, much less a main joint.

"A good cook changes his knife once a year—because he cuts. A mediocre cook changes his knife once a month—because he hacks. I've had this knife of mine for nineteen years and I've cut up thousands of oxen with it, and yet the blade is as good as though it had just come from the grindstone. There are spaces between the joints, and the blade of the knife has really no thickness. If you insert what has no thickness into such spaces, then there's plenty of room—more than enough for the blade to play about it. That's why after nineteen years the blade of my knife is still as good as when it first came from the grindstone.

"However, whenever I come to a complicated place, I size up the difficulties, tell myself to watch out and be careful, keep my eyes on what I'm doing, work very slowly, and move the knife with the greatest subtlety, until—flop! the whole thing comes apart like a clod of earth crumbling to the ground. I stand there holding the knife and look all around me, completely satisfied and reluctant to move on, and then I wipe off the knife and put it away."

"Excellent!" said Lord Wen-hui. "I have heard the words of Cook Ting and learned how to care for life!"

Cook Ting does not wear himself out by trying to force things. This would mean unnecessary friction. Like water, he seeks the empty places. When things become knotted, he only slows down and proceeds carefully. Even then, there is no need for friction or confrontation. Cook Ting's task is done by following rather than disturbing the order of things. By anticipating problems, he solves them before they become major. Total satisfaction is his reward.

As was true for Lao Tzu, Chuang Tzu applied his principles to statecraft, though he placed somewhat less emphasis on political affairs than did Lao Tzu. The sage ruler, Chuang Tzu believed, first gains knowledge of himself and of his subjects—gains knowledge of his and their nature and destiny—then effortlessly "goes along with what is right for things." He permits nothing to disturb either his own inner harmony or the harmony within the state. Like a tiger trainer who anticipates the wildness of his charges, he knows how to deal with the violence of others before it arises, thus minimizing the need for force. In his fearless adherence to the Way, he remains free from selfish designs and preset goals. Because he puts forth no special effort, his success is unfathomable to others (see the box "Chuang Tzu on Virtuous Activity"). This philosophy is, of course, quite similar to that espoused by Lao Tzu. (And Chuang Tzu, like Tao Tzu before him, was quite aware that rulership in accordance with these principles would be a rare occurrence.)

## Chuang Tzu on Virtuous Activity

Chuang Tzu was fishing in the river Phu when the king of Khu sent two high officers to him with the message "I wish to trouble you with the charge of all within my territories."

Chuang Tzu kept holding his rod without looking around and said, "I have heard that in Khu there is a magnificent tortoise shell, the wearer of which died three thousand years ago, and which the king keeps in his ancestral temple. Was it better for the tortoise to die and leave its shell to be thus honored? Or would it have been better for it to live and drag its tail after it over the mud?"

The two officers replied, "It would have been better for it to live and drag its tail through the mud."

"Go your way," said Chuang Tzu. "I will keep on dragging my tail after me through the mud."

Public spirited, and with nothing of the partisan; easy and compliant, without any selfish tendencies; following in the wake of others, without a double mind; not easily distracted because of any anxious thoughts; not scheming in the exercise of one's wisdom; not choosing between parties, but going along with all—all such courses are the path to true enlightenment.

Vacuity, tranquility, mellowness, quietness, and taking no action are the roots of all things. . . . These are the virtue of rulers and emperors when they manage things above.

If one assumes office with them [scholars] to pacify the world, his achievements will be great . . . and the empire will become unified. In tranquility he becomes a sage, and in activity he becomes a king. He takes no action and is honored. He is simple and plain and none in the world can compete with him in excellence. For such a one understands this virtue of Heaven and Earth. He is called the great foundation and the great source of all being and is in harmony with nature. One who is in accord with the world is in harmony with men. To be in harmony with men means human happiness, and to be in harmony with Nature means the happiness of Nature.

Chuang Tzu, it is perhaps well to add, is famous for his principle of the "equality of things," according to which opposites—life and death, beauty and ugliness, and all the rest—are in fact equal as a single entity within the Tao. Thus, he reasoned, the wise individual, the sage, does not distinguish between himself and the world and thus finds oneness with Tao.

Chuang Tzu's philosophy is also distinctive for the emphasis he placed on the danger of usefulness. Useful trees, like fruit and nut trees, he explained, are constantly cut back, kept small, and soon stripped of their fruit. Only "useless" trees live out their full term of life unhindered and unsavaged—but then it is only these useless trees that are able to provide shade and beauty. Likewise, Chuang Tzu reasoned, the sage avoids becoming too useful, if he is to fulfill his destiny. These and other nuggets of Chuang Tzu's philosophy are set forth in nearby boxes.

## CONFUCIANISM

Three great systems of thought dominate Chinese civilization: **Confucianism,** Taoism, and Buddhism. The most dominant is the one founded by **Confucius** [kun-FYOO-shus] (551–479 B.C.E.). Confucian political philosophy has dominated Chinese life in a way unequaled by any similar philosophy in the West.

## Confucius

Confucius loved learning, and by age fifteen he had committed his life to a diligent study of the ancient wise men. In addition, he sought a better way and order of doing things. Learning and knowledge, Confucius believed, must be practical. They must transform life for the better. The result of his own learning was a system of moral, political, and social precepts bound together by what is best called a philosophy of nature and by a faith in the perfectibility of the human character. The switch in Chinese thought from concern for the diety to concern for human effort and excellence began hundreds of years before Confucius was born. Nonetheless, it was Confucius who made humanity (*jen*) a cornerstone of Chinese philosophy. "The measure of man," he said, "is man." The nature and duties of the human being must be studied diligently and cultivated, he insisted, and humanity is to be loved.

To help others, Confucius said, one must first establish one's own humane character, which is done by imitating models of superior men from the past. Once the individual has a character that contains nothing contrary to humanity, he can rely on his humanity in all his actions. Through humanistic thinking and acting, according to Confucius, the superior man makes the Way (Tao) great.

That the human person is perfectible was a central tenet of Confucius's thinking. The human person, Confucius believed, is not always good but can become better. Betterment, he thought, comes through learning and service to others. No one begins with wisdom, but with diligence and determined study, wisdom can be acquired. And once acquired, wisdom becomes an instrument for perfecting oneself, the family, and society. Even nature itself, Confucius believed, cannot resist the power of wisdom: "It is man that can make the Way great," he said, "and not the Way that can make man great."

The Way, as here mentioned by Confucius, is a key concept in his philosophy. For Confucius, as for the Taoists, the Way, or Tao, is basically the path taken by natural events. Confucius uses the word *Way* or *Tao* often and in different senses. There is a way of the good man, a way of music, a way of proper government, and a cosmological way. Confucius even speaks of "my *tao*." Although interpreters are not in total agreement about this, it would seem that the Tao, for Confucius, is not a fixed and eternal transcendental principle that stands outside and above events and determines them. Rather, it is affected in no small part by human thought and human action. One can study the practices of the wise ancients to learn how to make the Way great in one's own time. Essentially, this means knowing how best to regulate your life. Confucius set forth ideals of human behavior based on his understanding of the Way. He believed that once you have achieved a knowledge of the Tao or Way of things, you cannot die in vain.

For Confucius, everything "thrives according to its nature." One way in which heaven works, he thought, is through the principle of the **Mean,** which provides a standard of measure for all things. Human behavior should avoid extremes and seek moderation. In the philosophy of Confucius, when things function in accordance with this principle of the Mean, they stand in a relationship of mutual dependence. In other words, the principle essentially requires reciprocal cooperation among things—between people and between people and nature. And when the

# PROFILE: Confucius (551–479 B.C.E.)

Confucius, or, in Chinese, K'ung Fu Tzu (K'ung the Great Master), was born "without rank in humble circumstances" in the small Chinese kingdom of Lu. Information about his life is scanty and is derived chiefly from the ***Analects,*** a collection of his sayings assembled by his disciples. Because of his father's death, he had to work at an early age to help support his mother. He was largely self-taught, and his hunger for learning was insatiable. With the exception of a brief period in which he served as prime minister of Lu, he did not have many opportunities to put his principles about statecraft into practice.

Confucius's ideas have influenced Chinese and Asian ways of life like those of no other philosopher, although their impact has varied from period to period. From the third to the seventh century, Con-

fucianism was eclipsed by other philosophies, but under the T'ang dynasty (618–907) it became the state religion. Neoconfucianism (which incorporated both a more developed metaphysics and Taoist and Buddhist principles) emerged during the Sung dynasty (960–1279) and was the predominant stream of Chinese philosophy until its decline in the twentieth century, which was especially rapid after the Communist revolution in 1949. This was, in part, a consequence of the difference between Chinese communism and the more traditional worldviews. But it was also a side effect of the change in the system of state civil service examinations, which had formerly been based on the Chinese classic texts, including Confucius.

principle is followed, things flourish and nourish one another without conflict or injury.

Confucius formulated this principle of reciprocity in a general way as it applied to human affairs by saying, "Do not do to others what you would not want them to do to you." Likewise, according to Confucius, "A virtuous man wishing to establish himself seeks also to establish others, and wishing to enlighten himself, seeks also to enlighten others." Just as nature is built on a principle of reciprocal cooperation rather than strife, so reciprocal cooperation must reign in human affairs, he believed.

Confucius limited his investigation and concern to this changing world: his philosophy was this-worldly and not other-worldly. When he was asked about serving the spirits of the dead, he answered: "While you are not able to serve men, how can you serve their spirits?" And he said: "We don't know about life; how can we know about death?" It is in this world that the human being must live and with other people that he must associate, Confucius emphasized.

Nevertheless, Confucius understood the importance of religious ritual for the state and was fastidious in carrying out its mandates. To achieve a proper balance in this regard is the mark of a superior man, he said: "Devote yourself earnestly to the duties due to men, and respect spiritual beings but keep them at a distance. This may be called wisdom."

Another key concept in Confucius's thought is that of the **sage,** or superior man. The sage represents, in effect, an ethical ideal to which humans should aspire. To achieve the status of sage, Confucius believed, requires having intimate knowl-

## Confucius: Insight on Life

At fifteen, I began to be seriously interested in study; at thirty, I had formed my character; at forty, doubts ceased; at fifty, I understood the laws of Heavens; at sixty, nothing that I heard disturbed me; at seventy, I could do as my heart desired without breaking the moral law.

I never take a walk in the company of three persons without finding that one of them has something to teach me.

The superior man is distressed by his want of ability; he is not distressed by men's not knowing him.

The superior man understands righteousness; the inferior man understands profit.

What you do not want done to yourself, do not do to others.

A man who is strong, resolute, simple, and slow to speak is near to humanity.

The way of the superior man is threefold, but I have not been able to attain it. The man of wisdom has no perplexities; the man of humanity has no worry; the man of courage has no fear.

edge both of change and of the order of things; it requires, more specifically, having a correct understanding both of human relationships and of the workings of nature. A correct understanding, according to Confucius, involves, among other things, setting right in thought, or *rectifying,* what is distorted or confused, and it especially involves the correct use, or **rectification,** of names. (This meant knowing, for example, when it is legitimate to accord someone a title or rank.) The sage or superior person, according to Confucius, puts this correct understanding into action and seeks the mutual cooperation that enables others to fulfill their own destiny.

According to Confucius, the sage's actions are superior to those of other men because his model of behavior is superior. Specifically, he patterns his behavior on the great men of the past. In addition, he constantly learns from his own personal experience. (Confucius said that if he were able to study change for fifty years, he would finally be free of mistakes.) Wisdom requires constant learning, and constant learning allows the superior man better to know the measure of things and to perform his duty accordingly.

Thus, the sage, in the philosophy of Confucius, not only thinks correctly but also lives correctly. Indeed, according to Confucius, for the sage no discrepancy exists between thought (or speech) and action. The sage does not think (or say) one thing and do a different thing: he matches word with deed.

Further, according to Confucius, the superior man is an altruist who provides impartial and equitable service to others. He is kind and benevolent; he does not repay evil with evil but rather with uprightness. His concern is with reform, not revenge. And his virtuous behavior is a matter of habit that holds even in the direst crisis. For this reason, Confucius believed, the sage can be counted on at all times. His fairness makes him a figure of trust to all, including the rulers of state.

Now the rulers of the Chinese states of Confucius's time did not entrust their affairs to superior men; nor did the rulers themselves merit this title. Instead, these states were dominated by military regimes that ruled by force and were constantly at war with one another and whose subjects lived in a state of dread. In the opinion of Confucius, the ignoble policies of such inferior rulers were based on four

## Confucius on Government

To govern means to make right. If you lead the people uprightly, who will dare not to be upright? Employ the upright and put aside all the crooked; in this way the crooked can be made to be upright. Go before the people with your example, and spare yourself not in their affairs. He who exercises government by means of his virtue may be compared with the polar star, which keeps its place, and all the stars turn toward it.

According to the nature of man, government is the greatest thing for him. There is good government when those who are near are made happy and when those who are afar are attracted.

Remember this, my children: oppressive government is more terrible than tigers. A ruler has only to be careful of what he likes and dislikes. What the ruler likes, his ministers will practice; and what superiors do, their inferiors will follow.

Guide the people with government measures and control or regulate them by the threat of punishment, and the people will try to keep out of jail but will have no sense of honor or shame.

Guide the people by virtue and control and regulate them by respect, and the people will have a sense of honor and respect.

Do not enter a tottering state nor stay in a chaotic one.

When the Way prevails in the empire, then show yourself; when it does not prevail, then hide.

Tzu-kung asked about government. Confucius said, "Sufficient food, sufficient armament, and sufficient confidence of the people." Tzu-kung said, "Forced to give up one of these, which would you abandon first?" Confucius said, "I would abandon armament." Tzu-kung said, "Forced to give up one of the remaining two, which would you abandon first?" Confucius said, "I would abandon food. There have been deaths from time immemorial, but no state can exist without the confidence of the people."

root evils: greed, aggressiveness, pride, and resentment, which singly or together cause a ruler to rationalize and to excuse the most odious behavior on his part. Further, according to Confucius, a ruler is invariably the model for the behavior of his subjects, and, as a consequence, societies ruled by vicious men are themselves vicious societies (see the box "Confucius on Government").

By contrast, a state so fortunate as to be ruled by a superior man, Confucius believed, will be peaceful, secure, and prosperous. Because the superior man is governed by the principle of the Mean, as a ruler he will be just and impartial and will seek to establish a fair distribution of wealth, which in turn will promote security and peace. And because his behavior will be emulated by his subjects, he will rule through virtuous example rather than by force of arms. Further, because he is conscientious in his service to all, he will act without fear or sadness.

Confucius's philosophy touched not only on the state and the individual but also on the family. In fact, for Confucius, the well-ordered family is a model for the well-ordered state and ultimately the world as a whole. The family, Confucius believed, should, like the state, be patriarchal and authoritarian.

Thus, the proper functioning of the family depends on the obedience of the subordinate members and the responsible governance of the parents (and ultimately the father) in accordance with the principle of the Mean and on the fundamental virtues of filial piety and brotherly respect. Together, these two virtues, according to Confucius, allow an optimal functioning of the five primary human relationships generally: those between ruler and subject, between parent and child, between elder and younger brother, between husband and wife, and between one friend and another. In the well-ordered family, because relationships are clearly defined, life will be stable and will provide the means for all members of the family to develop their capacities to the fullest extent.

Confucius's ideal of the superior man, who is wise, humane, honest, and just and whose actions spring from morality and not greed or pride; his urging of a society built not on force or military power but on justice and fairness; his belief in the inherent worth, perfectibility, and goodness of humankind; and his overall concern for humanity and human relationships all represented a strong and influential new vision in Chinese thought.

## Mencius

The work of the great Confucian philosopher **Mencius** [MEN-shus] (371–289 B.C.E.) is regarded as second only to that of Confucius himself. Mencius, like Confucius, was very saddened by the quality of life during his time. He spoke of princes who were deaf and blind to the terrible events about them that "boom like thunder and flash like lightning." Nevertheless, a central tenet of his thought, as with Confucius, was that human beings are basically good (see the box "Mencius and Thomas Hobbes on Human Nature").

According to Mencius, the natural goodness of humans had become perverted by circumstances. Still, he said, each person has the potential for becoming perfect: doing so is a matter of recovering his lost mind and forgotten heart; it is a matter of thinking and feeling *naturally*, a matter of following intuition and conscience.

Mencius never lost his optimism about the possibility of human betterment. For him, if anything is tended properly, it will grow and thrive. Therefore, human beings should nourish the noble or superior part of themselves so that it will come to predominate. Each person, however, will decide for himself whether he will transform his life for the better.

For the person who has chosen to seek it, the way to self-betterment, the way to a noble existence and the upright life, according to Mencius, can be found only within oneself. Conscience, for Mencius, is "the mind that cannot bear suffering [on the part of others]." The pathway to the upright life, however, must include *self*-suffering and difficulty, he said. "When Heaven is about to confer a great office on any man," he said, "it first exercises his mind with suffering, and his sinews and bones with toil. It exposes his body to hunger and subjects him to extreme poverty. It confounds his undertakings. By all these methods, it stimulates his mind, hardens his nature, and supplies his incompetencies."

Difficulty and suffering, according to Mencius, are to be considered privileges and opportunities to develop independence, excellence, mental alertness, freedom from fear, and quietude of spirit. He goes so far as to imply that prudence and the other virtues are hardly possible for those who have not suffered deeply.

In the process of perfecting one's own life, Mencius said, one is put in a position of benefiting one's family and, through teaching and leadership, society as a whole (see the box "Mencius on Virtuous Activity"). Indeed, true happiness, he

## PROFILE: Mencius

Mencius, or Meng-tzu, was born in what is now the Shantung province of China. He purportedly was taught by Confucius' grandson. Like Confucius, he lived in a time of political turmoil; he spent forty years traveling and teaching. His works became part of the "Four Classics" of ancient China and are based on his belief in the original goodness of human nature. These quotations reveal some of his insights.

The great end of learning is nothing else but to seek for the lost mind.

To preserve one's mental and physical constitution and *nourish one's nature* is the way to serve Heaven.

If you let people follow their feelings (original nature), they will be able to do good. This is what is meant by saying that human nature is good. If man does evil, it is not the fault of his natural endowment.

Humanity, righteousness, propriety, and wisdom are not drilled into us from outside. We originally have them with us. Only we do not think [to find them]. Therefore, it is said, "Seek and you will find it, neglect and you will lose it."

With proper nourishment and care, everything grows, whereas without proper nourishment and care, everything decays.

Those who follow the greater qualities in their nature become great men and those who follow the smaller qualities in their nature become small men.

That whereby man differs from the lower animals is small. The mass of the people cast it away, while the superior men preserve it.

The disease of men is this — that they neglect their own fields and go weed the fields of others.

Thus it may be said that what they require from others is great, while what they lay upon themselves is light.

said, does not consist in ruling an empire merely for the sake of power, the desire for which is the driving ambition of the inferior mind, the mind that, like that of an animal, contains no notion of what is great or honorable. True happiness consists in seeing one's parents and family alive and free from anxiety and in helping one's society. Further, he maintained, whoever is happy in this way is happy in another way, for he need never feel shame for his actions.

Thus, it may be seen that Mencius, too, like Confucius, was concerned not only with the person but also with the state (see the box "Mencius on Government"). Disorder in a state, he believed, is often caused by a ruler who takes no notice of conditions within his own state, a ruler who — again like an animal — is indifferent to all but his own selfish interests and petty ambitions. This indifference and selfishness is a form of blindness, maintained Mencius, and a state governed without vision, he said, inevitably falls into ruin and death.

Further, according to Mencius, the subjects of the state ruled by the inferior person follow the example of their leader and also become like beasts set to devour each other. In this thought Mencius echoed Confucius. But, unlike Confucius, Mencius held that killing such a monarch is not murder, for the establishment of a humane government is not possible under such an individual.

## Mencius and Thomas Hobbes on Human Nature

Mencius was quite aware that, by and large, people in his time were violent, self-serving, inclined to stop short of the mark in everything they attempted, and successful only in bringing premature death on themselves. But for Mencius, this evil came on people because circumstances had not allowed them to cultivate their inherent nobility and to search out within themselves love, wisdom, virtue, a sense of duty, and self-perfection. Human nature, according to Mencius, is inherently good, and this goodness can be actualized if people would develop their potentiality — as would happen under a just and humane regime.

Among the many Western philosophers who have also viewed people as selfish and violent, Thomas Hobbes (1588–1679) is probably the most famous. In the state of nature, Hobbes wrote, the life of man is "solitary, poor, nasty, brutish, and short." But Hobbes, unlike Mencius, attributed the ugly ways of humankind to human nature. So Hobbes believed that only through force wielded by an absolute sovereign can humans be prevented from devouring one another: *Homo lupus homini,* said Hobbes, quoting the Roman poet Plautus (c. 254–184 B.C.E.): *Man is the wolf of man.* Mencius, in contrast, believed that a wise ruler will successfully call forth the goodness inherent in human nature through mild and benevolent leadership.

Whether their malevolent actions mean that human beings, although essentially good by nature, exist in a fallen state or whether they indicate that human nature is essentially bad is a question that has not been resolved. Perhaps it is not resolvable.

## Mencius on Virtuous Activity

It is said that the superior man has two things in which he delights, and to be ruler over the empire is not one of them.

That the father and mother are both alive and that the condition of his brothers affords no cause for anxiety, this is one delight.

That when looking up he has no occasion for shame before Heaven, and below he has no occasion to blush before men — this is the second delight.

In the view of a superior man as to the ways by which men seek for riches, honors, gain, and advancement, there are few of their wives who would not be ashamed and weep together on account of them.

Men must be decided on what they will not do, and then they are able to act with vigor on what they ought.

If on self-examination I find that I am not upright, shall I not be in fear even of a poor man in loose garments of hair cloth?

If on self-examination I find that I am upright, neither thousands nor tens of thousands will stand in my path.

I have not heard of one's principles being dependent for their manifestation on other men.

Benevolence is man's mind and righteousness is man's path.

How lamentable it is to neglect the path and not pursue it, to lose the mind and not know to seek it again.

Benevolence subdues its opposite just as water subdues fire.

Those, however, who nowadays practice benevolence do it as if with one cup of water they could save a whole wagon load of fuel which was on fire, and, when the flames were not extinguished, were to say that water cannot subdue fire. This conduct greatly encourages those who are not benevolent.

## Mencius on Government

If a man should love others and the emotion is not returned, let him turn inward and examine his own benevolence.

If a man is trying to rule others, and his government is unsuccessful, let him turn inward and examine his wisdom.

If he treats others politely and they do not return the politeness, let him turn inward and examine his own feelings of respect.

Only the benevolent ought to be in high stations. When a man destitute of benevolence is in a high station, he thereby disseminates his wickedness among all below him.

Virtue alone is not sufficient for the exercise of government; laws alone cannot carry themselves into practice.

[In a state] the people are the most important; the spirits of the land (guardians of territory) are the next; the ruler is of slight importance. Therefore to gain [the hearts of] the peasantry is the way to become emperor.

Killing a bad monarch is not murder.

If a ruler regards his ministers as hands and feet, then his ministers will regard him as their heart and mind. If the ruler regards his ministers as dogs and horses, his ministers will regard him as any other man. If a ruler regards his ministers as dirt and grass, his ministers will regard him as a bandit and an enemy.

To say that one cannot abide by humanity and follow righteousness is to throw oneself away. Humanity is the peaceful abode of man and righteousness is his straight path.

All men have the mind which cannot bear [to see the suffering of] others. . . . When a government that cannot bear to see the suffering of the people is conducted from a mind that cannot bear to see the suffering of others, the government of the empire will be as easy as making something go round in the palm.

Humanity, righteousness, loyalty, faithfulness, and the love of the good without getting tired of it constitute the nobility of Heaven, and to be a grand official, a great official, and a high official — this constitutes the nobility of man.

The good ruler, Mencius maintained, is benevolent toward his subjects as a father is toward his children and will seek to establish a good order and a just regime. He displays, in addition to benevolence, three other primary virtues or attributes: righteousness, propriety, and knowledge. Further, the good ruler is mild in manner and governs with mind and heart rather than with the strong arm. Because of his mild manner, he encounters no enemies, and because he is humane and his subjects accordingly have confidence in his goodness, he will have only little opposition.

In short, this superior ruler, who has himself suffered on the path to betterment, acquires the mind that cannot bear the suffering of others, and, because it is humane and just, his governance is the foundation of all present and future good within the state.

Mencius's philosophy exhibits the humanistic concerns and faith in human goodness and perfectibility that characterize Confucian philosophy in general. Both Mencius and Confucius were aware, however, that in practice humans are often self-seeking and that their potential for goodness must be cultivated or nurtured. As may be seen in the boxes, Mencius offers much advice and sets forth many telling maxims that, in effect, constitute a method for cultivating the better part of human nature.

## Hsün Tzu

Another important Confucian philosopher, who blended Taoism with Confucianism and added his own, rather more pessimistic conception of human nature, was **Hsün Tzu** [SHWIN-tsuh] (298–238 B.C.E.). He was rationalistic and realistic in his approach, believing that the hierarchical order of society was established by following unchanging moral principles. If moral practices, laws, and the rules of propriety were followed, then order, peace, and prosperity would inevitably be the result. If they were not followed, disorder and disaster would result.

Hsün Tzu's view of the basic nature of human beings is what makes him strikingly dissimilar to other major Confucian thinkers. He did not agree with Mencius that human beings are originally good and therefore naturally inclined to goodness. Hsün Tzu believed that human beings are basically bad but that they are impelled to compensate for and overcome this defectiveness, this badness, through education and moral training. Fortunately, the human being is perfectible. Through a study of past and present sages, a human being may develop a moral understanding based on the ultimate virtues of humanity and righteousness.

For Hsün Tzu, the state, like the individual, can lose itself in seeking profit. The result is strife, violence, lewdness, and rebellion. Such an inferior state must be reconstructed through moral principles, which must come to be embodied in the person of the ruler. Hsün Tzu's thought was the official creed during the Han period (c. 206–220), and it has continued to have an important influence on Asian societies to the present.

## ZEN BUDDHISM IN CHINA AND JAPAN

**Zen Buddhism** is one of the Buddhist sects of Japan and China. (Buddhism, it may be recalled, originated in India.) *Zen* is Japanese and *Ch'an* is Chinese, and both words derive from the Sanskrit word for meditation, *dhyana*. When Buddhism first came to China, it emphasized the importance of meditation, rather than any particular scripture or doctrine, as the key to ultimate reality.

Although the heading for this section is Zen Buddhism, we discuss both the Chinese and Japanese traditions, Zen and Ch'an. It should be noted that other forms of Buddhism developed as well, but the Zen tradition is the one that has awakened the most philosophical interest in the West.

The growth of **Ch'an Buddhism** (Chinese Zen Buddhism) was slow at first, and it always was numerically one of the smaller sects. But over the centuries this sect spread throughout China and into neighboring countries like Japan and Korea. In the last century it has taken root in the United States and Europe. Its current spread in the West seems to indicate that Ch'an Buddhism responds to a need in a highly complex, technological world.

Buddhism in China and Japan has a long and rich history. Here it will only be possible to look briefly at a few of its most original and profound thinkers, the sixth patriarch of Chinese Zen, Hui Neng, Murasaki Shikibu, and Dogen Kigen, the

founder of the Japanese Soto tradition. The philosophies of these thinkers complement one another and give an overall perspective on basic elements in the Zen Buddhist tradition.

## Hui Neng

**Hui Neng** [HWAY-nung] (638–713) lost his father in childhood and had to sell
firewood to keep his mother and himself alive. He was illiterate.

One day, while delivering firewood to a shop, Hui Neng heard the chanting of
the Buddhist *Diamond Sutra* (perhaps the most important scripture of Chinese
Buddhism, in which Buddha strips his student Subhuti of his coarse views and allows him to see the fundamental oneness of all things and the immutability of perceived phenomena; *sutra* means secret doctrines and sacred teachings). Hui Neng
immediately grasped the deep truth latent in its words. But not until some time later
did a gift of money enable him to confirm his perception of truth by seeking out
Master Hung-jen, the fifth Chinese patriarch of Ch'an Buddhism, at Huang-mei
Mountain in Hupei.

During the first meeting with the fifth patriarch, Hui Neng did not hesitate to
manifest the unshakable strength of his vision, and he was accordingly accepted in
the Huang-mei monastery. For eight months, however, he worked in the kitchen
without even entering the main temple.

At this time, the fifth patriarch was seeking a successor and asked the monks
to write a poem showing the depth of their insight into truth. Only the person who
has a direct intuition into the truth achieves peace of mind, the Ch'an Buddhists
believed, and they also thought that each person must discover this truth for himself. That all is ultimately one was a basic precept of the fifth patriarch. This one
reality was thought to be our true self-nature and was held to be immanent within
human beings from the beginning. To see this ever-present truth exactly as it is
would require going beyond the usual way of thinking, which breaks down ultimate
being into distinct entities and classifies and relates them so that they are understood only in terms of the categories to which they belong and their relationships to one another. Hence poetry rather than a normal form of discourse would
be required to express insight into this truth, for normal forms of thought and
language can express neither the uniqueness of the individual entity nor the underlying oneness of all things. Perhaps you are reminded here of Heidegger.

Shen-hsui, the senior monk at the monastery, was the only one who dared to
write the requested poem, and the other monks doubted their ability to surpass him
in depth of understanding. His contribution, however, according to tradition, only
showed that he had not seen the ultimate truth and had not escaped the confines of
normal thought. Hui Neng, though illiterate, is said immediately to have sensed the
inadequacy of the vision conveyed by this poem when he overheard it being recited
by another monk and to have composed a reply to the poem on the spot (see the
box "Hui Neng's Poem of Enlightenment").

The monks, it is said, were astounded by the words of this twenty-three-year-
old illiterate, who had not yet even been admitted into the meditation hall. The fifth

## Hui Neng's Poem of Enlightenment

Hui Neng's spontaneous poem in answer to the request by the fifth patriarch of Ch'an Buddhism revealed immediately that he saw the fundamental nature of truth:

Fundamentally no bodhi-tree exists
Nor the frame of a mirror bright.

Since all is voidness from the beginning
Where can the dust alight?

Hui Neng intimates here that the ultimate reality or truth is beyond all conceptualization.

patriarch was moved as well and immediately recognized Hui Neng as his successor. Perceiving the possibility of jealousy and anger among the monks, he is said to have had Hui Neng come to him in the middle of the night to receive the robe and bowl symbolic of his new status as sixth patriarch and to learn the wisdom of the *Diamond Sutra*. According to tradition, Hung-jen, the fifth patriarch, convinced that the truth of the *Buddha-Dharma* (ultimate reality) would ultimately prevail through Hui Neng, instructed Hui Neng to leave the monastery immediately and to remain in hiding until he was ready to teach.

What is the ultimate **Dharma** (reality/truth/law)? Hui Neng gave it a number of different titles: the Self-Nature, the Buddha-Dharma, the Real Nature, and the eternal and unchanging Tao (note the Taoist influence implicit in the last name). All things, he said, are in reality one: there are no "things." Human thought and understanding, to make sense of a totality that cannot be grasped at once, impose categories, contrasts, and distinctions on reality (including thirty-six basic pairs of contrasts or opposites, such as light and darkness, yin and yang, birth and death, good and bad, and so on). But in truth there is only one thing, the Real Nature, and, as it is in itself, it exists prior to any distinctions or categorizations; it is (so to speak) beyond good and evil, permanence and impermanence, content and form. It is an absolute state of "suchness" that neither comes nor goes, neither increases nor decreases, neither is born nor dies. It is exactly as it is: it is reality and truth (see the box "Hui Neng on Life and Truth").

According to Hui Neng, though this ultimate reality or truth is in principle accessible to all, it remains hidden to many of us because we are focused on false attachments and selfish interests: in short, we lack a balanced, objective outlook. And, as a result of this imbalance in our perspective, our efforts too are one-sided in pursuit of our goals. Hui Neng made it his purpose to free humans from selfish, one-sided visions of reality. His recommendation was for a state of "no-thought" or "mindlessness," in which the mind does not impose itself on the truth but, rather, remains open and spontaneous—a mirror reflecting the wisdom inherent in reality, one that reflects but does not impede the flow of events.

To deepen one's spirit, he said, is to live in harmony with the true or "self-nature" of all things. When the mind is right, it thinks without bias or partiality and is thus considerate of the needs of each and every thing.

The blend of Taoist, Confucian, and Buddhist precepts is very much in evidence in Hui Neng's thought.

# Hui Neng on Life and Truth

As mentioned in the text, Hui Neng sought out the fifth patriarch of Ch'an Buddhism, Master Hung-jen, who eventually confirmed Hui Neng's insight into the truth and appointed him his successor. On meeting the fifth patriarch, Hui Neng is said to have said: "I confess to Your Reverence that I feel wisdom constantly springing from my own heart and mind. So long as I do not stray from my nature, I carry within me the field of bliss."

Other interesting quotations of Hui Neng as to life and truth are as follows:

How could I expect that the self-nature is in and of itself so pure and quiet! How could I expect that the self-nature is in and of itself unborn and undying! How could I expect that the self-nature is in and of itself self-sufficient, with nothing lacking in it! How could I expect that the self-nature is in and of itself immutable and imperturbable! How could I expect that the self-nature is capable of giving birth to all dharmas [laws]!

The *Bodhi* or Wisdom, which constitutes our self-nature, is pure from the beginning. We need only use our mind to perceive it directly to attain Buddhahood.

One Reality is all Reality.

Our original nature is Buddha, and apart from this nature there is no other Buddha. Within, keep the mind in perfect harmony with the self-nature; without, respect all other men. This is surrender to and reliance of one's self.

Light and darkness are two different things in the eyes of the ordinary people. But the wise and understanding ones possess as penetrating insight that there can be no duality in the self-nature. The Non-dual nature is the Real Nature . . . both its [the Real Nature's] essence and its manifestations are in the absolute state of suchness. Eternal and unchanging, we call it the Tao.

## Buddhism in Japan

At this point we depart from China for Japan, where Zen was introduced from China. As you have seen, under Hui Neng, Zen emerged as a distinct and separate Buddhist sect that combined elements of Indian Buddhist and Chinese thought. When it traveled to Japan, the sect was influenced by Japanese culture as well.

Medieval Japan was like the U.S.A. of Asia: a melting pot of philosophical and religious views. For men, the mixture of Asian philosophies probably was good enough, but its effect on women was less fortunate. If there were a recipe for medieval Japanese philosophy, it would read as follows:

    1 cup Shinto animism
    4 Buddhist Noble Truths
    1 yin
    1 yang
    1 handful Confucian virtues
    1 Mahayana Buddhist doctrine of the void

Mix all ingredients well, apply liberally to everyone. Prepares men for salvation. Prepares women for reincarnation as men.

Such recipes can give a reader only a broad idea of some main elements in Japanese Buddhism at the time and must not be taken as an exclusive or exhaustive treatment. By the late ninth century, Japanese culture reflected an unequal mixture of Shinto, Confucianism, Taoism, and Zen Buddhism (and its Mahayana branch, and *its* branches, Tendai and Shigon). Why was this recipe so unfortunate for women? (See the section on Murasaki Shikibu, following.) What are these ingredients? You already are familiar with most of them, other than Shinto and Mahayana.

Shinto, an ancient native religion of Japan, related humans to the **kami,** or gods of nature, that created the universe. People were said to be just another part of the physical universe. The Japanese language did not even have a word for nature as something distinct from humans. People were regarded as "thinking reeds" completely identified with and part of the natural and divine universe. Such a view is called **animism.**

People's duties were derived through their blood relationships. You were connected to the gods of nature through your ancestor's clan and through the divine clan of the Mikado, who was both national high priest and head of state. The Japanese word for government, *matsuri-goto,* means "things pertaining to worship." So there was no conceptual difference between religion, ethics, and government. And there was no conceptual difference between people and other natural objects.

Mahayana Buddhism was just a twist on Zen. It was introduced into Japan in the late sixth century, when Japan lost its territory in Korea, and its ally, the Paekche Kingdom, suffered military defeat. Many Korean war refugees, most of them Buddhists, fled to Japan, where their religion gained acceptance among Japanese diplomats and aristocrats. Prince Shotoku (his name means "sovereign moral authority") made it the official religion of Japan, incorporating it into Shinto. Shinto connected you to your historical, anthropological past; Mahayana Buddhism connected you to the present and to the future eternity. It incorporated the Confucian virtues of filial piety, veneration of ancestors, duties based on rank and position, honesty, and so forth. (Taoism, too, fit in nicely, with its views about the oneness of humans and nature, spiritual freedom, and peace—not to mention yin/yang emphasis on orderliness and balance.)

Mahayana saw humanity unified through spiritual enlightenment, in the worship of one god, who, as luck would have it, turned out to be the Mikado, the greatest earthly *kami.* This was the form of Buddhism adopted by Japanese aristocracy. The higher up the sociopolitical aristocracy you were, the closer you were to god—and thus the theory did not displace aristocrats.

This brings us to Murasaki.

## Murasaki Shikibu

**Murasaki Shikibu** [MOO-ruh-sah-kee shih-kih-boo] (970–1031) lived at the height of the Mahayana Buddhist influence in Japan. And while all Japanese shared this philosophical heritage, not all shared social and political equality.

The Tendai sect of Mahayana Buddhism held that the closer you were to the Mikado, the greater was your potential for moral excellence and for admission to the Western Paradise (heaven). But in Buddhism, women generally were considered to be of lesser moral worth than men. Women could achieve salvation, or

## PROFILE: Murasaki Shikibu (970–1031)

Murasaki Shikibu, or Lady Murasaki, as she is sometimes called, is an important Japanese, Shinto, Buddhist, and feminist philosopher. Murasaki Shikibu is almost certainly not her real name, however. She was given the nickname "Murasaki" because the real author strongly resembled a character by that name in the book she wrote. Murasaki came from a literary family of the Fujiwara clan. In Japan at that time, it was forbidden for women to study Chinese characters (the original written form of Japanese language). Murasaki learned young how to read Chinese characters by hanging around when her brother was being tutored. She eventually entered court service in the entourage of the teenaged empress Joto-Mon'in Shoshi, to whom Murasaki secretly taught Chinese. Learning how to read gave Murasaki access to the forbidden literatures of religion and philosophy.

In addition to some poetry, Murasaki left two works: a diary, *Murasaki Shikibu Nikki,* and an epic philosophical novel, *Genji Monogatari.* Despite the fact that it was written centuries before the invention of the printing press, once it was printed, *Tale of Genji* (as it is also known) never went out of print. It has been translated into more than thirty languages. Murasaki's primary philosophical interest was with the moral status of women under Japanese Buddhist ethics.

reach the psychological state of nirvana that would prepare them to enter the Western Paradise, but only after reincarnation as a male.

The fact that you were a woman was evidence that in a past life you had been a male who was now making up for a past life lacking in virtue. In the Buddhist doctrine of reincarnation, a good woman can hope at best for reincarnation as a man. After a lifetime as a virtuous man, it would be possible to achieve salvation and enter heaven. Women, no matter their virtue, could not hope for salvation, as Murasaki says:

> But then someone with as much to atone for as myself may not qualify for salvation; there are so many things that serve to remind one of the transgressions of a former existence. Ah, the wretchedness of it all!

Murasaki's women characters illustrated just how hopeless life was for Japanese women, especially those who thought about things like self-identity, morality, free will and determinism, predestination and salvation. Judging from the popularity of her very long book, *Tale of Genji,* and the fact that it was initially circulated a chapter at a time among aristocratic women (obviously, many had learned how to read Chinese characters on the sly), a lot of Japanese women did care about these philosophical issues.

Murasaki kept the basic recipe we gave in the "Buddhism in Japan" section, but she changed the directions and added a few ingredients. Here is Murasaki's version of the recipe:

1 cup Shinto animism
4 Buddhist Noble Truths
1 yin

1 yang
1 handful Confucian virtues
1 Mahayana Buddhist doctrine of the void
1 lifetime of spiritual enlightenment

Mix all ingredients well with a strong, feminist hand. Contemplate for a lifetime with as much detachment from worldly distractions as possible. (Become a nun if you can.) Use as an antidote to determinist misogynist elements of Tendai. With lifelong use, women may achieve salvation.

Murasaki's version of the recipe added the importance of spiritual enlightenment and contemplation. She also emphasized the virtues of simplicity and detachment from worldly possessions.

In sharp contrast to the views of women present in Buddhism and reflected in Japanese culture, Murasaki's female characters struggled with the problem that in Japanese culture and Buddhist religion women existed only as predestined, natural objects.

Murasaki's main character, Ukifune (which means "loose boat," "loose woman," or "person with no direction and uncertain destination"—you get the idea), becomes so depressed following a rape that she attempts to commit suicide, but she is saved by a monk, against the advice of other monks who think she should be allowed to drown.

Everyone, especially other women, has told Ukifune that she cannot do anything about the rape and its social consequences; it is just her fate. There is no hope for her other than to become a prostitute. Ukifune rages against the double injustice: first, she is just an object to a man who forcibly rapes her; second, she is punished socially for having been wronged. Rather than accept her fate, she challenges her destiny through suicide, hoping for reincarnation as a man.

But her rescue, although also attributed by the monk to fate, leads her to a path of religious contemplation. Ultimately, she becomes a nun—but not an ordinary nun performing public service. Ukifune spends her life contemplating life's meaning and seeking enlightenment. Ultimately, a lifetime of contemplation will reveal to her that she can control her destiny through self-knowledge.

Murasaki's women characters struggle to become free, responsible moral agents who assert that they have natural rights. They also assume moral responsibilities to others. Although Murasaki rejected mainstream Buddhism's view of women, her philosophy represents a minority Buddhist view that women are moral agents who, instead of blaming fate, can assume moral responsibility for their actions. Murasaki held that women should challenge their *karma* (destiny) and take control of their own lives by engaging in what were then forbidden, illegal activities such as reading the *sutras* (secret doctrines and sacred teachings) of the great Buddhist monks.

Murasaki's personal decision to become a nun and to read the *sutras* was the product of a wager that was worthy of Pascal (see Chapter 13):

The time too is ripe. If I get much older my eyesight will surely weaken to the point that I shall be unable to read the sutras, and my spirits will fail. It may seem that I am merely going through the motions of being a true believer, but I assure you that I can think of little else at the present moment.

## Zen Buddhism in Japan

There are two major forms of Zen Buddhism in contemporary Japan: Rinzai Zen and Soto Zen. Over the centuries, each has mutually influenced the other. The difference between the two has more to do with method than with doctrine. Both seek enlightenment apart from the scriptures.

**Rinzai Zen,** named after the famous Zen monk Rinzai (785–867) seeks sudden enlightenment, as preached by Hui Neng. To achieve the *satori,* or enlightenment experience, *koans* are often used in addition to sitting in meditation (*zazen*). Koans are illogical, even nonsensical, puzzles that are designed to break the stranglehold of conceptual thought so that the absolute, indivisible truth or reality may be suddenly and utterly seen or intuited. Among the most famous of all *koans* is "What is the sound of one hand clapping?"

The **Soto Zen** tradition places less emphasis on sudden enlightenment and tends not to use *koans.* As exemplified by Dogen, enlightenment is to be found slowly through *zazen* (meditation) and also by performing all daily duties in the same state of awareness as when sitting in *zazen.* This tradition recognizes no single moment of *satori,* for enlightenment is believed to be possible in all moments.

By understanding and living according to what Murasaki argued was the true meaning of Buddhism, women could achieve a state of contemplation that is compatible with reaching nirvana. Under Murasaki's philosophy, women need not be content to wait until they have been reincarnated as males to begin the difficult and long process of philosophical enlightenment. They can begin that process in this life by living, as do men, according to the teachings of Shinto and Buddhism. It should be taken into account that there have been more positive developments regarding women's status in Japanese Buddhism, especially recently.

### Dogen Kigen

By age fourteen, **Dogen** [DOE-gen] (1200–1253) was already a monk. He eventually became dissatisfied with the decadent state of Tendai Buddhism, which, being egalitarian and anti-elitist in nature, adopted many popular rituals like chanting the name of Amitabba Buddha. **Tendai Buddhism** was a Japanese variation of the T'ien-t'ai School of Buddhism in China. It was introduced into Japan in the ninth century. Its basic notion is that all phenomena are expressions of the absolute oneness or suchness (*tathatā*). Dogen therefore sought out a Tendai monk, Eisei, who had twice traveled to China to study Ch'an Buddhism. Eisei died soon after the encounter with Dogen, but Dogen continued his studies for nine years under Eisei's successor, Myozen. Afterward, Dogen went to China himself to deepen his studies, and eventually he came under the tutelage of Ju-Ching, at T'ien T'ung Shan monastery. After five years, he returned to Japan in 1227.

Dogen continued to teach and write in monasteries in and around the old capital city of Kyoto until 1243. During this time, he came increasingly in conflict with the predominant Tendai tradition and eventually withdrew into the mountains to establish the Eikei monastery. To this day, Eikeiji is the principal monastery of the Soto branch of Japanese Zen Buddhism.

## Dogen's Prescriptions for Virtuous Activity

Dogen, a Zen monk since early youth who traveled to China for further studies, gained a reputation as a strict teacher. His writings have had a profound influence up to the present day. Many of his works have been translated into English and have played an important part in the growth of Zen Buddhism. The following are his prescriptions for virtuous activity.

> To plow deep but plant shallow is the way to a natural disaster. When you help yourself and harm others, how could there be no consequence?

> Everyone has the nature of Buddha; do not foolishly demean yourself.

> Even worldly people, rather than study many things at once without really becoming accomplished in any of them, should just do one thing well and study enough to be able to do it even in the presence of others.

> While simply having the appearance of an ordinary person of the world, one who goes on harmonizing the inner mind is a genuine aspirant to the Way. Therefore as an Ancient said, "Inside empty, outside accords." What this means is to have no selfish thought in the inner mind, while the outer appearance goes along with others.

> Emperor Wen of Sui said, "Secretly cultivate virtue, await fulfillment." . . . If one just cultivates the work of the Way, the virtues of the Way will appear outwardly of their own accord.

> To practice the appropriate activity and maintain bearing means to abandon selfish clinging. . . . The essential meaning of this is to have no greed or desire.

> Students of the Way, do not think of waiting for a later day to practice the Way. Without letting this day and this moment pass by, just work from day to day, moment to moment.

> It is written (in the *Vinaya*), "What is praised as pure in character is called good; what is scorned as impure in character is called bad." It is also said, "That which would incur pain is called bad; that which should bring about happiness is called good."
>
> In this way should one carefully discriminate; seeing real good, one should practice it, and seeing real evil, one should shun it.

> Jade becomes a vessel by carving and polishing. A man becomes humane by cultivation and polish. What gem has highlights to begin with? What person is clever at the outset? You must carve and polish, train and cultivate them. Humble yourselves and do not relax your study of the Way.

> There is a saying of Confucius: "You can't be apart from the Way for even a second. If you think you are apart from it, that's not the Way." He also said, "As the sages have no self, everything is themselves."

Many of life's numerous problems, Dogen realized, are not easily solvable. There is, for example, the problem of the impermanence of life. Life passes like the rush of a spring stream, flowing on, day after day, and then it is gone. Dogen therefore urged humans not to waste a single second. Time must be utilized in a worthy pursuit, a single objective that merits an all-out effort. The life goal must be nothing small, selfish, or narrow-minded. It must be chosen from a broad perspective and with an eye to benefiting others as well as oneself. Dogen's philosophy is, in essence, a prescription for an unwasted or noble life, a life of happiness here and now.

It is difficult, of course, Dogen realized, to choose how to live and equally difficult, if not more so, to carry out that choice. One lives in an uncertain and hurried world, and "our minds go racing about like horses running wild in the fields, while our emotions remain unmanageable like monkeys swinging in the trees." The rapidity of life and the uncertainty of its course makes people's lives full of torment and confusion. They do not understand its nature or how best to manage themselves.

Moreover, according to Dogen, the mind overwhelmed by a world not understood seeks safety in selfish and self-protective acts. Life is perceived as a succession of real and suspected dangers, and it is viewed in stark contrasts of good and bad, right and wrong, black and white. This perception of the world is what Dogen called the "Lesser Vehicle," and it arises out of ignorance and fear. The ignorant, fearful mind constructs a list of things deemed bad and to be avoided, and anger and resentment are felt toward perceived sources of danger. The individual caught in a dark and threatening world he does not understand finds little rest or peace, and doing violence to himself or others is a frequent consequence of his entrapment.

This state of malcontent, according to Dogen, in which the world is perceived in terms of stark and fearful divisions, remains with the individual until he or she achieves clarification about the true nature of things. But everyone, Dogen said, has the nature of Buddha. Everyone can see the truth and live calmly and peacefully in its presence. It is simply necessary to abandon the selfish and narrow perspective in favor of the broad and unbiased view, in which the mind is expanded beyond the limitations of divisive categories like good/bad and desirable/undesirable, in which greed gives way to generosity, self-serving to other-serving. It is necessary to see things as the ancient sages did, from the perspective of the universe or "Buddha-Dharma" or "universal Self." To do this is to practice the Great Way.

Understanding from this broad perspective, Dogen thought, also involves acceptance—going along with things, following the Way. This, he said, is the wisdom of emptiness—allowing things to be, without exercising any preference or desire whatsoever. The similarity to the philosophy of Chuang Tzu is evident.

How does one acquire this perspective of the universal Self? For Dogen, the answer is practice—seeking to help others without reward or praise, caring for others as a parent would. If one makes a continuous effort to do all things with a parental mind and without seeking profit or praise, then one's life will be suffused with the attitude of a "Joyful Mind," in which life takes on a buoyancy and lightness that cannot be diminished by any external event.

Dogen endeavored to set forth a way to achieve permanent joy in *this* life, a way of living that enables the human to achieve a majestic dignity, uncompromisable nobility of character, and peace. "No one or anything could ever make merit decay in any way," he said. In his precepts, Dogen continued the tradition begun by Chuang Tzu, Lao Tzu, and Hui Neng. Life does involve suffering, pain, and transience. But despite the presence of these and of evil too, life, if lived according to the Tao, should be a joyful and fulfilling event. Dogen urged, "Rejoice in your birth in the world." If one does not escape the fears and insecurities of the small self, life is a torment. But if one lives as would the Magnanimous Mind, then one is living out the truth of the Way itself—the Way of the Buddha-Dharma.

## THE PHILOSOPHY OF THE SAMURAI (c. 1100–1900)

Japan's warrior class, the **samurai,** were also the ruling class for long periods of time. Their wisdom was transmitted in the form of martial precepts, the earliest dating to the twelfth century or earlier. These precepts were handed down the generations within the class, and they were often used to train the samurai and to teach them the art of ***bushido,*** that is, the art of being a samurai warrior. According to William Scott Wilson's *Ideals of the Samurai,* the word *bushi* (samurai warrior) is first recorded in an early history of Japan, one dated 797 C.E. These educated warriors served at the time in close attendance to the nobility. The weakness of civil government, however, led to the practice of clans and private estates developing their own armies and to increasing involvement by samurai in government. The warrior class eventually replaced the court aristocracy, and the late twelfth century marked the beginning of warrior-class rule, which lasted seven hundred years.

The literature of the samurai tradition has influenced all areas of Japanese thought and behavior. Westerners who have wished to understand the basis of the Japanese economic "miracle" since World War II have looked to such samurai classics as Miyamoto Musashi's *A Book of Five Rings* and Yamamoto Tsunetomo's *Hagakure.* The writings concerning the samurai tradition have become popular and widely read among business executives and entrepreneurs in the West as well as being used in business graduate schools. A recent American film, *Ghost Dog,* has sought to apply the teachings of the samurai to American life. Also influential in determining the samurai worldview were the Chinese classical views, including the writings of Confucius, Lao Tzu, and Sun Tzu as well as the *I Ching* or *Book of Changes.* **Miyamoto Musashi** [mee-yuh-moh-toh mu-sah-shee] (1584–1645) was one of Japan's greatest swordsmen and military strategists. His ideas teach martial strategy, but they seem to lend themselves equally well to business methods and to life generally. **Yamamoto Tsunetomo** [yah-muh-moh-toh tsu-neh-toh-moh] (1659–1719) served only a short time as a retainer before his master died. Thereafter, he withdrew from the world and lived as a recluse studying Zen Buddhism. During the final years of his life, his thoughts on the essence of the samurai way of life were written down and preserved (see the box "Samurai Insights from Yamamoto Tsunetomo, *Hagakure*"). The ideals of the samurai tradition have endured and still determine to no small extent the life and thought of modern-day Japan.

The worldview expressed in Tsunetomo's *Hagakure* will be familiar to readers of the material on Dogen. Human life at best Tsunetomo sees as "a short affair." No time may be squandered without regret and loss. Yet brevity is not what makes life so difficult and painful; this effect comes rather from life's uncertainty. Humans exist in a world of constant and unpredictable change.

When these changes are not anticipated, the result is often disastrous. Therefore, a samurai must train himself to be ready at all times for anything that may happen. He must train to anticipate all eventualities and deal with them before they become a problem. A samurai precept is "Win beforehand."

According to Tsunetomo, not only the uncertainty of events is problematic, but also human beings themselves are often flawed, ignorant, selfish, and unreasonable.

## Samurai Insights from Yamamoto Tsunetomo, Hagakure

Everything in this world is a marionette show.

[The samurai] remains undistracted twenty-four hours a day.

A samurai's word is harder than metal.

The Way of the samurai is in desperateness. Ten or more men cannot kill such a man.

With an intense, fresh, and undelaying spirit, one will make his judgment within the space of seven breaths. It is a matter of being determined and having the spirit to break right through to the other side.

If one will do things for the benefit of others and meet even those whom he has met often before in a first-time manner, he will have no bad relationships.

A samurai's obstinacy should be excessive.

It is natural that one cannot understand deep and hidden things. Those things that are easily understood are rather shallow.

Courage is gritting one's teeth . . . and pushing ahead, paying no attention to the circumstances.

There is nothing other than the single purpose of the present moment.

I never knew about winning . . . but only about not being behind in a situation.

There is nothing that one should suppose cannot be done.

One must be resolved in advance.

Human life is a short affair. It is better to live doing the things that you like.

If one will rectify his mistakes, their traces will soon disappear.

At a glance, every individual's own measure of dignity is manifested just as it is.

One cannot accomplish things simply with cleverness.

By being impatient, matters are damaged and great works cannot be done. If one considers something not to be a matter of time, it will be done surprisingly quickly.

A man's life should be as toilsome as possible.

People become imbued with the idea that the world has come to an end and no longer put forth any effort. This is a shame. There is no fault in the times.

When I face the enemy, of course it is like being in the dark. But if at that time I tranquilize my mind, it becomes like a night lit by a pale moon. If I begin my attack from that point, I feel as though I will not be wounded.

It is the highest sort of victory to teach your opponent something that will be to his benefit.

Win first, fight later.

There is nothing so painful as regret.

Money is a thing that will be there when asked for. A good man is not so easily found.

Meditation on inevitable death should be performed daily. . . . It is to consider oneself as dead beforehand.

Accordingly, the samurai must learn to be self-reliant. He cannot and does not depend on others acting properly. He knows that human beings will not always act either reasonably or justly. He is prepared for treachery and cowardice and awaits their arrival. Only by practicing alertness and bravery can a samurai avoid wasting his life.

Because of the uncertainty of the world and the unreliability of the human character, the samurai must learn the arts of war as well as the arts of peace. Human beings, like states, must be able to defend themselves. Kuroda Nagamasa (1568–1623), known as a great military strategist, wrote: "The arts of peace and the arts of war are like the wheels of a cart which, lacking one, will have difficulty in standing."

The samurai strives to realize Confucius's notion of the complete man, who is both scholar and warrior. Life requires constant training and learning. Without learning, a person would be ignorant of what is necessary; without hard training, he would be unable to carry the necessary actions into effect quickly and efficiently. The samurai works hard to know where his duty lies and to carry it out "unflinchingly." To do this, he hardens himself to suffering. He welcomes death if it comes in pursuit of duty (see the box "Courage and Poetry"). He learns to abhor luxury and considerations of money in order not to be attached to them or to life generally.

An important part of the samurai's study is past traditions, particularly the Confucian and other classical Chinese philosophies, and Zen Buddhism. These determine and shape *bushi* and are in turn unified and synthesized by *bushi* into a single, effective way of life.

## The Influence of Confucius

The model of the perfect samurai closely shadows the Confucian idea of the complete man. He is a scholar warrior, literate yet deeply knowledgeable about practical affairs. He knows that life involves change and that survival depends on understanding the inner workings of change. Although a few samurai teachers emphasized the art of war and the ways of increasing courage, more usual is the view of the *Hagakure*. Here the samurai is called on to develop his knowledge of whatever might be useful, "querying every item night and day." Above all, he must understand the Confucian principle of the Mean: more than merely the middle way between two extremes, the Mean is the universal standard that determines what is right and appropriate. The wise samurai reads the sayings of the ancients as the best way to find out what the Mean recommends and how best to follow it.

For Confucius, the three basic and interrelated qualities to be pursued are humanity, wisdom, and courage. According to the samurai tradition, these virtues allow those who have them to enjoy a useful life of service as well as a life free from anxiety and fear.

As Confucius also prescribed, the samurai should be filial, making every effort to respect and honor his parents; he should be polite, discreet in manners and conduct, proper in dress and speech, and upright and sincere. He must not lie. There is the story, for example, of the samurai who refused to take an oath because the word of the samurai is more certain than any oath.

In historical Japan, those who possessed these qualities exhibited enormous dignity. The samurai's dignity displayed itself in every action and in every word. His solemn behavior and resoluteness frequently struck fear in the ordinary observer. The samurai code sought to create a character that was flawless in behavior and taut in spirit.

Another samurai virtue had its roots in the philosophy of Confucius: the samurai was to be economical and, as noted, to avoid luxury. He was to save what he could, but only with an eye to using it on campaign when it was needed.

Because of his virtues, the samurai could be expected to establish and maintain an ordered state in the midst of the most chaotic times. His own steady and un-

## Courage and Poetry

Samurai warriors often sought to discipline their spirit and free themselves from fear by training with Buddhist masters. At various times, samurai and Zen monks both used poetry, especially short forms of poetry like *haiku,* to test the strength and validity of their insight into truth. At a critical moment, just before death, for example, a trainee was expected spontaneously to write a poem that revealed his perfect freedom under all circumstances, as well as the depth of his insight. He was expected to remain calm, clear-headed, and imperturbable even at the point of a sword. There are stories of captured warriors being spared death if they were sufficiently intrepid and their poem manifested deep wisdom.

The greatest of all the Japanese *haiku* writers was **Basho** [bah-sho] (1644–1694). He was deeply involved with Zen, and his death poem is regarded as profound:

Sick from the journey,
Yet over withered fields
Dreams wander on.

Dogen also gives an example of the genre:

Scarecrow in the hillock
Paddyfield
How unaware! How useful!

Here are two more poems considered to reveal the deep insight and spontaneous expression of the truly free individual:

Coming and going, life and death:
A thousand hamlets, a million houses.
Don't you get the point?
Moon in the water, blossom in the sky.
— Gizan (1802–1878)

Fifty-four years I've entered [taught]
Horses, donkeys, saving limitless beings.
Now farewell, farewell!
And don't forget — apply yourselves.
— Jisso (1851–1904)

shakable behavior would then serve as a model to be trusted and followed by all others. This, of course, is a Confucian theme.

### The Influence of Zen Buddhism

It is slightly ironic that members of the warrior class in Japan went to Zen monks for training, for Zen monks dedicated their lives to saving all living beings. Kamakura, a Zen center that dates back as far as the thirteenth century, was especially noted for training samurai warriors. Perhaps the most famous instance of this relationship was the influence of the Zen monk Takuan (1573–1645) on two of Japan's greatest swordsmen and strategists, Miyamoto Musashi and Yagyu Munenori [YAH-gyu mu-neh-NOH-ree] (1571–1646). All three men produced classic works that were used in the training of samurai.

The samurai, recall, were warriors who trained themselves to be ready at any moment to fight to the death. The ability to fight, of course, is frequently hampered by fear; for fear, if it does not paralyze a fighter completely, may well prevent the lightning-fast response that may be the difference between winning and losing. Though samurai engaged in ceaseless martial arts training, a state of fearlessness sometimes escaped even the best of them. Some samurai, therefore, sought out Zen masters to free themselves of their own fear.

Fear, according to the Zen Buddhist, arises from an excessive attachment or clinging to things and to life generally, a perspective of possessiveness from which

## The Magnificent Seven

One of the most popular Hollywood movies of all time was the 1960 John Sturges western, *The Magnificent Seven,* a story about seven gunslingers hired by a Mexican village as protection against a band of cutthroat bandits who preyed on the helpless villagers. Unknown to many American audiences at the time, the film was a remake of Akira Kurosawa's *The Seven Samurai* (1954), which at one point had been titled *The Magnificent Seven* for release in the United States. Kurosawa's story about a sixteenth-century Japanese village that hires professional warriors to protect them depicts the martial skill, humaneness, and strict sense of justice and honor of the samurai, whose virtues enable them to confront adversity unflinchingly and victoriously. Sturges's movie helped focus attention in America on Kurosawa's film, which in turn led to much interest in the United States in the samurai tradition.

anything and everything is viewed as a threat. The remedy to fear—the samurai learned from the Zen masters—is to free oneself from attachments and personal preferences, to rid oneself of the desire to possess anything, including life itself. The samurai was taught to overcome himself, so to speak—to free himself from all thoughts of gain or loss. He was taught to accept what happens without joy or sadness, without complaint, and even without resignation. This hard lesson was thought to require constant meditation on death so that the warrior was ready to "die completely without hesitation or regret."

In this way Zen training sought to rid the samurai of the self-imposed paralysis of fear. Both the Zen and the samurai traditions shared the same ideal: to attain *an unobstructed state of instant, untainted response.* For the samurai this state of mind was the key to total preparedness.

The samurai tradition therefore emphasized that through a vigorous training of the body and the mind the individual can perfect his character to respond immediately to any situation. Such training can create a resolute single-mindedness, in which the present moment is all there is and the present action alone is real, that is both efficient and powerful.

The ultimate goal of both Zen Buddhist and samurai training is the state of **mushin,** that is, the state of no mind, no thought. This is a state of awareness beyond calculation in which one moves "no-mindedly" in the here and now, doing exactly what is appropriate without any hesitation. This mind is the "secret" of the great swordsmen like Musashi and Yagyu Munenori.

The samurai tradition, together with Confucianism and Zen Buddhism, provided the Japanese with a noble ideal of character, a context in which the efficiency of Japanese society, and much of what is good and successful in Japan, may perhaps be understood. Certainly the vision of the noble person who trains all his life to be of benefit to others seems a fulfillment of the ideal of humanity put forward by Confucius, Zen, and the samurai. However, the chauvinist nationalism of the Japanese in World War II, the unquestioning obedience to authority, and the glorification of death may also perhaps be explained by reference to these same influences. It is interesting to speculate what these traditions might have yielded, what their effect on Japanese society might have been, if they had been stripped of their authoritarian and excessively militaristic qualities. Confucius seeks to delineate his notion of humanity (*jen*) in terms of what constitutes a superior human being.

Early in its history, Taoism had a relatively strong influence on rulers in China. But as Confucianism replaced it as the dominant value system within society, beginning with the T'ang dynasty (618–906), it increasingly focused on religious functions, an area in which it eventually had to compete with Buddhism. More and more, Taoism came to encompass magic, soothsaying, and incantations for healing and for warding off evil spirits. To this day, Taoist priests perform ceremonies at funerals and on other important occasions. Reportedly, Taoist hermits are still living out the highest forms of Taoist practice in the mountains of China.

As Confucianism established itself as the dominant moral and political philosophy, the Confucian classics became the basis of civil service examination, and in this way Confucianism became even further embedded into Chinese thinking. Between the eleventh and eighteenth centuries, there was a significant Neoconfucian movement, one of whose major figures was Wang Yang-ming (1472–1529).

Confucianism received a severe blow from the Communist revolution in 1949, and Mao Tse-tung made it a repeated target for ridicule. This does not mean that Mao was not himself influenced by Confucius both in his style of writing and of ruling, nor does it mean that Mao was loathe to use Confucianism to his own ends — for example, in transferring the individual's family allegiance to state allegiance. In any case, after Mao, Confucian thought is again making itself apparent.

Chinese Buddhism developed a number of different schools from the fourth to the ninth centuries. Ch'an Buddhism was especially powerful and innovative during the seventh to ninth centuries. Chinese Buddhist temples have provided religious services for the people from that time even until the present day. Further, the influence of Ch'an Buddhism spread to Japan, where Zen Buddhism and other forms of Buddhism have endured until the present. Currently, Zen Buddhism especially enjoys growing popularity in the United States and the West generally.

SELECTION 15.1
# Analects

*Confucius*

## Book I
CHAPTER I. 1. The Master said, "Is it not pleasant to learn with a constant perseverance and application?

2. "Is it not delightful to have friends coming from distant quarters?

3. "Is he not a man of complete virtue, who feels no discomposure though men may take no note of him?"

CHAP. II. 1. The philosopher Yû said, "They are few who, being filial and fraternal, are fond of offending against their superiors. There have been none, who, not liking to offend against their superiors, have been fond of stirring up confusion.

2. "The superior man bends his attention to what is radical. That being established, all practical courses naturally grow up. Filial piety and fraternal submission!—are they not the root of all benevolent actions?"

CHAP. III. The Master said, "Fine words and an insinuating appearance are seldom associated with true virtue."

CHAP. IV. The philosopher Tsa˘ng said, "I daily examine myself on three points:—whether, in transacting business for others, I may have been not faithful;—whether, in intercourse with friends, I may have been not sincere;—whether I may have not mastered and practised the instructions of my teacher."

CHAP. V. The Master said, "To rule a country of a thousand chariots, there must be reverent attention to business, and sincerity; economy in expenditure, and love for men; and the employment of the people at the proper seasons."

CHAP. VI. The Master said, "A youth, when at home, should be filial, and, abroad, respectful to his elders. He should be earnest and truthful. He should overflow in love to all, and cultivate the friendship of the good. When he has time and opportunity, after the performance of these things, he should employ them in polite studies."

CHAP. VII. Tsze-hsiâ said, "If a man withdraws his mind from the love of beauty, and applies it as sincerely to the love of the virtuous; if, in serving his parents, he can exert his utmost strength; if, in serving his prince, he can devote his life; if, in his intercourse with his friends, his words are sincere:—although men say that he has not learned, I will certainly say that he has."

CHAP. VIII. 1. The Master said, "If the scholar be not grave, he will not call forth any veneration, and his learning will not be solid.

2. "Hold faithfulness and sincerity as first principles.

3. "Have no friends not equal to yourself.

4. "When you have faults, do not fear to abandon them."

CHAP. IX. The philosopher Tsăng said, "Let there be a careful attention *to perform the funeral rites* to parents, and let them be followed when long gone *with the ceremonies of sacrifice;*—then the virtue of the people will resume its proper excellence."

CHAP. X. 1. Tsze-ch'in asked Tsze-kung, saying, "When our master comes to any country, he does not fail to learn all about its government. Does he ask his information? Or is it given to him?"

2. Tsze-kung said, "Our master is benign, upright, courteous, temperate, and complaisant, and thus he gets his information. The master's mode of asking information!—is it not different from that of other men?"

CHAP. XI. The Master said, "While a man's father is alive, look at the bent of his will; when his father is dead, look at his conduct. If for three years he does not alter from the way of his father, he may be called filial."

CHAP. XII. 1. The philosopher Yû said, "In practising the rules of propriety, a natural ease is to be prized. In the ways prescribed by the ancient kings, this is the excellent quality, and in things small and great we follow them.

2. "Yet it is not to be observed in all cases. If one, knowing *how* such ease *should be prized*, manifests it, without regulating it by the rules of propriety, this likewise is not to be done."

CHAP. XIII. The philosopher Yû said, "When agreements are made according to what is right, what is spoken can be made good. When respect is shown according to what is proper, one keeps far from shame and disgrace. When the parties upon whom a man leans are proper persons to be intimate with, he can make them his guides and masters."

CHAP. XIV. The Master said, "He who aims to be a man of complete virtue in his food does not seek to gratify his appetite, nor in his dwelling-place does he seek the appliances of ease; he is earnest in what he is doing, and careful in his speech; he frequents the company of men of principle that he may

be rectified:— such a person may be said indeed to love to learn."

CHAP. XV. 1. Tsze-kung said, "What do you pronounce concerning the poor man who yet does not flatter, and the rich man who is not proud?" The Master replied, "They will do; but they are not equal to him, who, though poor, is yet cheerful, and to him, who, though rich, loves the rules of propriety."

2. Tsze-kung replied, "It is said in the Book of Poetry, 'As you cut and then file, as you carve and then polish.'— The meaning is the same, I apprehend, as that which you have just expressed."

3. The Master said, "With one like Ts'ze, I can begin to talk about the odes. I told him one point, and he knew its proper sequence."

CHAP. XVI. The Master said, "I will not be afflicted at men's not knowing me; I will be afflicted that I do not know men."

---

SELECTION 15.2

# The Eightfold Noble Path *

*Buddha*

---

[*The Eightfold Noble Path is at the heart of Buddhist practice, ranging from moral mandates as to how to live to the experience of the ultimate enlightenment and blissful rapture.*]

### The Fourth Truth
### The Noble Truth of the Path That
### Leads to the Extinction of Suffering

(S.56) To give oneself up to indulgence in *Sensual Pleasure,* the base, common, vulgar, unholy, unprofitable, and also to give oneself up to *Self-mortification,* the painful, unholy, unprofitable; both these two extremes the Perfect One has avoided and found out the *Middle Path* which makes one both to

see and to know, which leads to peace, to discernment, to enlightenment, to Nibbana.

It is the Noble Eightfold Path, the way that leads to the extinction of suffering, namely:

1. Right Understanding, *Samma-ditthi*
2. Right Mindedness, *Samma-sankappa*
3. Right Speech, *Samma-vaca*
4. Right Action, *Samma-kammanta*
5. Right Living, *Samma-ajiva*
6. Right Effort, *Samma-vayama*
7. Right Attentiveness, *Samma-sati*
8. Right Concentration, *Samma-samadhi*

This is the Middle Path which the Perfect One has found out, which makes one both to see and to know, which leads to peace, to discernment, to enlightenment, to Nibbana.

Free from pain and torture is this path, free from groaning and suffering, it is the perfect path.

---

* "The Eightfold Noble Path," from *A Buddhist Bible* edited by Dwight Goddard, copyright 1938, renewed © 1966 by E. P. Dutton. Used by permission of Dutton, a division of Penguin Group (USA) Inc.

(Dhp. 274–75) Truly, like this path there is no other path to the purity of insight. If you follow this path, you will put an end to suffering.

(Dhp. 276) But each one has to struggle for himself, the Perfect Ones have only pointed out the way.

(M. 26) Give ear then, for the Immortal is found. I reveal, I set forth the Truth. As I reveal it to you, so act! And that supreme goal of the holy life, for the sake of which sons of good families go forth from home to the homeless state: this you will, in no long time, in this very life, make known to yourself, realise and attain to it.

## First Step
### Right Understanding
(D. 22) What now is Right Understanding?

1. To understand suffering; 2. to understand the origin of suffering; 3. to understand the extinction of suffering; 4. to understand the path that leads to the extinction of suffering. This is called Right Understanding.

(M.9) Or, when the noble disciple understands, what demerit is and the root of demerit, what merit is and the root of merit, then he has Right Understanding.

What now is demerit?

1. Destruction of living beings is demerit.
2. Stealing is demerit.
3. Unlawful sexual intercourse is demerit.
4. Lying is demerit.
5. Tale-bearing is demerit.
6. Harsh language is demerit.
7. Frivolous talk is demerit.
8. Covetousness is demerit.
9. Ill-will is demerit.
10. Wrong views are demerit.

And what is the root of demerit? Greed is a root of demerit; Anger is a root of demerit; Delusion is a root of demerit.

(A.X.174) Therefore, I say, these demeritorious actions are of three kinds: either due to greed, or due to anger, or due to delusion.

(M.9) What now is merit (*kusala*)?

1. To abstain from killing is merit.
2. To abstain from stealing is merit.
3. To abstain from unlawful sexual intercourse is merit.
4. To abstain from lying is merit.

5. To abstain from tale-bearing is merit.
6. To abstain from harsh language is merit.
7. To abstain from frivolous talk is merit.
8. Absence of covetousness is merit.
9. Absence of ill-will is merit.
10. Right understanding is merit.

And what is the Root of Merit? Absence of greed is a root of merit; absence of anger is a root of merit; absence of delusion is a root of merit.

(S.21 (5)) Or, when one understands that form, feeling, perception, mental formations and consciousness are transient, (subject to suffering and without an Ego) also in that case one possesses Right Understanding. . . .

## Second Step
### Right Mindedness
(D.22) What now is Right Mindedness?

1. The thought free from lust.
2. The thought free from ill-will.
3. The thought free from cruelty.

This is called right mindedness.

(M.117) Now, right mindedness, let me tell you, is of two kinds:

1. The thoughts free from lust, from ill-will, and from cruelty:—this is called the Mundane Right Mindedness, which yields worldly fruits and brings good results.

2. But, whatsoever there is of thinking, considering, reasoning, thought, ratiocination, application—the mind being holy, being turned away from the world and conjoined with the path, the holy path being pursued:—these Verbal Operations of the mind are called the Ultramundane Right Mindedness, which is not of the world, but is ultramundane and conjoined with the paths.

Now, in understanding wrong-mindedness as wrong and right-mindedness as right, one practises Right Understanding; and in making efforts to overcome evil mindedness, and to arouse right mindedness, one practises Right Effort; and in overcoming evil-mindedness with attentive mind, and dwelling with attentive mind in possession of right mindedness, one practises Right Attentiveness. Hence, there are three things that accompany and follow upon right mindedness, namely: right understanding, right effort, and right attentiveness.

**Third Step**
**Right Speech**
(A.X. 176) What now is Right Speech?

1. There, someone avoids lying, and abstains from it. He speaks the truth, is devoted to the truth, reliable, worthy of confidence, is not a deceiver of men. Being at a meeting, or amongst people, or in the midst of his relatives, or in a society, or in the king's court, and called upon and asked as witness, to tell what he knows, he answers, if he knows nothing: I know nothing, and if he knows, he answers: I know; if he has seen nothing, he answers: I have seen nothing, and if he has seen, he answers: I have seen. Thus, he never knowingly speaks a lie, neither for the sake of his own advantage, nor for the sake of another person's advantage, nor for the sake of any advantage whatsoever.

2. He avoids tale-bearing, and abstains from it. What he has heard here, he does not repeat there, so as to cause dissension there; and what he has heard there, he does not repeat here, so as to cause dissension here. Thus he unites those that are divided, and those that are united he encourages. Concord gladdens him, he delights and rejoices in concord; and it is concord that he spreads by his words.

3. He avoids harsh language, and abstains from it. He speaks such words as are gentle, soothing to the ear, loving, going to the heart, courteous and dear, and agreeable to many.

4. He avoids vain talk, and abstains from it. He speaks at the right time, in accordance with facts, speaks what is useful, speaks about the law and the discipline; his speech is like a treasure, at the right moment accompanied by arguments, moderate and full of sense.

This is called right speech. . . .

**Fourth Step**
**Right Action**
What now is Right Action?

(A.X. 176) 1. There someone avoids the killing of living beings, and abstains from it. Without stick or sword, conscientious, full of sympathy, he is anxious for the welfare of all living beings.

2. He avoids stealing, and abstains from it; what another person possesses of goods and chattels in the village or in the wood, that he does not take away with thievish intent.

3. He avoids unlawful sexual intercourse, and abstains from it. He has no intercourse with such persons as are still under the protection of father, mother, brother, sister or relatives, nor with married women, nor female convicts, nor even with flower-decked (engaged) girls.

This is called right action.
(M. 117) Now right action, let me tell you, is of two kinds:

1. Abstaining from killing, from stealing, and from unlawful sexual intercourse:—this is called the Mundane Right Action, which yields worldly fruits and brings good results.

2. But the abhorrence of the practice of this three-fold wrong action, the abstaining, withholding, refraining therefrom—the mind being holy, being turned away from the world and conjoined with the path, the holy path being pursued:—this is called the Ultramundane Right Action, which is not of the world, but is ultramundane and conjoined with the paths.

Now, in understanding wrong action as wrong, and right action as right, one practises Right Understanding; and in making efforts to overcome wrong action, and to arouse right action, one practises Right Effort; and in overcoming wrong action with attentive mind, and dwelling with attentive mind in possession of right action, one practises Right Attentiveness. Hence, there are three things that accompany and follow upon right action, namely: right understanding, right effort, and right attentiveness.

**Fifth Step**
**Right Living**
(D. 22) What now is Right Living?
When the noble disciple, avoiding a wrong living, gets his livelihood by a right way of living, this is called right living.
(M. 117) Now, right living, let me tell you, is of two kinds:

1. When the noble disciple, avoiding wrong living, gets his livelihood by a right way of living:—this is called the Mundane Right Living, which yields worldly fruits and brings good results.

5. Evaluate Mencius's idea that difficulty and suffering are opportunities to develop independence and peace of mind.

6. Do the subjects of the state adopt the ethical standards of their leaders? Or is it the other way around?

7. "Benevolence subdues its opposite just as water subdues fire." Evaluate this claim.

8. Are Lao Tzu's prescriptions for behavior realistic and practical? Explain.

9. Are power and riches chains, or are they the keys to freedom and happiness?

10. What is the sound of one hand clapping? Is this an intelligible question?

11. Comment on Hui Neng's poem of enlightenment (see the box on page 521).

12. How did Mahayana Buddhism reinforce sexism and elitism?

13. Why would suicide help a woman achieve salvation under Mahayana Buddhism?

14. How did Murasaki Shikibu's philosophy challenge Buddhist doctrines of karma, enlightenment, and salvation?

15. How important is it to have a life goal?

16. Is it possible for a person completely to abandon selfish desires?

17. How important is it to be self-reliant? Is total self-reliance possible?

18. Should the complete person be both wise and brave? If you wished to improve your wisdom or free yourself from fear, what would you do? How would you know if you had succeeded?

## SUGGESTED FURTHER READINGS

John Blofield, *The Secret and Sublime* (New York: E. P. Dutton, 1973). A very readable presentation of the philosophy of Taoism, popular Taoism, Taoist mysticism, and the relationship of Taoism and yogic practices.

Daniel Bonevac, *Understanding Non-Western Philosophy* (New York: McGraw-Hill, 1993). A collection of readings from African, Asian, and southern Mediterranean philosophers.

Brian Carr and Indira Mahalingam, *Companion Encyclopedia of Asian Philosophy* (New York: Routledge, 2001). Reference work concerning the philosophical traditions of the East.

Wing-tsit Chan, *A Source Book in Chinese Philosophy* (Princeton: Princeton University Press, 1963). First-rate anthology of Chinese philosophical writings placed in historical and philosophical context.

Thomas Cleary, trans., *The Spirit of the Tao* (Boston: Shambhala, 1998). An accessible selection from the most popular Taoist classics.

Diane Collinson, Kathryn Plant, and Robert Wilkinson, *Fifty Eastern Thinkers* (New York: Routledge, 2001). A brief exposition of fifty major thinkers in Eastern philosophy.

Diane Collinson and Robert Wilkinson, *Thirty-Five Oriental Philosophers* (New York: Routledge, 1994). A comprehensive overview of Eastern philosophy.

Confucius, *The Analects,* D. C. Lau, trans. (New York: Penguin, 1979). A good, inexpensive, and readily available collection of Confucius' philosophical insights.

Confucius, *The Analects,* Chichung Huang, trans. (New York: Oxford University Press, 1997). A relatively new translation of a classic, giving an excellent introduction to Confucius; humanist philosophy.

Confucius, *The Analects,* Raymond Dawson, trans. (New York: Oxford University Press, 2000). Favorable reviews for this new translation.

Dogen and Kosho Uchiyama, *Refining Your Life,* Thomas Wright, trans. (New York: Weatherhill, 1983). Dogen in this short treatise on Zen cooking provides an extraordinary method of performing any activity well and of living life as a whole.

Aislee T. Embree, ed., *The Hindu Tradition* (New York: Vintage Books, 1972). Readings that review the development of Hindu thought from the beginnings to the present.

Sue Hamilton, *Indian Philosophy: A Very Short Introduction* (New York: Oxford University Press, 2001). A quick overview of the wisdom to be found in Indian thought.

Kenneth Kraft, ed., *Zen: Tradition and Transition* (New York: Grove Atlantic Press, 1989). A sourcebook that provides an introduction to a wide range of approaches and concerns.

Joel J. Kupperman, *Classic Asian Philosophy* (New York: Oxford University Press, 2000). Designed to give beginners a sense of the most important texts.

D. C. Lau, trans., *Mencius* (Harmondsworth, England: Penguin, 1970). A highly readable translation of Mencius's writings.

Oliver Leaman, *Key Concepts in Eastern Philosophy* (New York: Routledge, 1999). A glossary of main terms found in Eastern philosophy.

Trevor Leggett, *Zen and the Ways* (Rutland, Vt.: Charles E. Tuttle, 1987). Shows how the meditative calmness taught in Zen can be applied to the ways of the martial arts and of life generally.

Miyamoto Musashi, *A Book of Five Rings,* Victor Harris, trans. (New York: Bantam, 1982). Written by the most famous swordsman and samurai, this is the great book of Japanese strategy. It is a guide for making decisions and acting decisively in even the worst of times.

Sarvepalli Radhakrishnan and Charles A. Moore, *A Source Book in Indian Philosophy* (Princeton: Princeton University Press, 1957). A splendid historical selection of philosophical writings with background information.

Murasaki Shikibu, *Tale of Genji / Genji Monogatari.* Many, many editions available at most public libraries.

D. Howard Smith, *Confucius and Confucianism* (London: Paladin, 1973). Places the teachings of Confucius in historical context and treats the interaction of Confucianism with Taoism and Buddhism.

Mel Thompson, *Teach Yourself Eastern Philosophy* (New York: McGraw-Hill, 2003). An examination of key ideas in Eastern thought with their social and ethical implications.

Yamamoto Tsunetomo, *Hagakure* (Tokyo: Kodansha International, 1979). The seventeenth-century classic that encapsulates the ethics, strategies, and worldview of the samurai class. Enlightening in itself, the *Hagakure* can also be used to understand contemporary Japanese ways of thinking.

Chuang Tzu, *The Complete Works,* Burton Watson, trans. (New York: Columbia University Press, 1968). A highly regarded translation of Chuang Tzu that is said to retain the wit of the philosopher himself.

Lao Tzu, *Tao Te Ching* (New York: Penguin, 1973). A good and inexpensive translation of a classic.

Mary Ellen Waithe, *A History of Women Philosophers,* vol. 2, *Medieval Women Philosophers, 500–1600* (Dordrecht, Boston, and London: Kluwer Academic Publishers, 1989). Includes a chapter by Waithe on Murasaki Shikibu.

# 16

# Postcolonial Thought

Strength does not come from physical capacity. It comes from an indomitable
will.    — Mahatma Gandhi

. . . the true criterion of leadership is spiritual. Men are attracted by spirit.
By power, men are forced. Love is engendered by spirit. By power, anxieties
are created.    — Malcolm X (el-Hajj Malik el-Shabazz)

In this chapter we encounter some representatives of postcolonial thought in
Africa, the Americas, and Asia. Postcolonial thought is an essentially modern
phenomenon. Growing out of group experiences of colonialist domination on
every populated continent, postcolonial thinking is shaping new work in ethics,
metaphysics, epistemology, political philosophy, and every other subdiscipline of
philosophy. Some well-known postcolonial thinkers include Mohandas Gandhi,
Martin Luther King, Jr., Fidel Castro, Malcolm X, and Desmond Tutu.

These and other postcolonial thinkers have brought traditional and radical
ideas together in a uniquely modern synthesis that opens up new possibilities of
practical engagement for philosophy. Whether reflecting through a history of slavery, systematic marginalization, or overt repression, postcolonial thinkers do their
work in recollection of deep cultural traumas that have occurred in the histories of
their respective peoples, leaving indigenous traditions self-consciously compro-
mised and needful of imaginative reconstruction from within. Postcolonial thought
addresses this need by taking up problems of cultural dissolution and questioning
previously unquestioned worldviews just as any modern way of thinking must.
As is true of modern thought generally, postcolonial thought challenges the uncritical acceptance of the notion of progress; indeed, postcolonial thought prob-
lematizes the phenomenon of progress along the same lines as recent Continental
philosophy.

In the postcolonial world, there is no agreement on how to integrate indigenous tradition into a modern philosophical project. There is agreement, however, on the centrality of a good education to this effort. In the economically constrained circumstances of the Third World, it has been common for people to insist that education should be narrowly vocational and practical. But philosophy is not optional, claim the majority of postcolonial thinkers who write on the topic, because it is the best way to keep struggling nations conscious and aware of the implications of their decisions. The issue for these philosophers is not whether scarce resources should be devoted to teaching philosophy but, rather, what sort of philosophy is appropriate for their countries. Without an indigenous philosophical literature in many cases, philosophy in these nations needs to be invented almost from the ground up. Even in those countries with extensive philosophical literatures, however, revaluations of key concepts have led to the introduction of radically new ways of thinking that seek to recast entire traditional vocabularies.

Postcolonial thinkers have long since realized that direct appeals for justice, reasonable as they might be, generally are not sufficiently compelling to bring about change. This is why raising consciousness through philosophy has become such an important undertaking. It is one thing to affirm that justice is a social good and yet another to have an idea of what justice might be, what conditions might be prerequisite to it, and how the best intentions may be subverted by subtly conflicting ideological claims. Detailed analysis of these sorts of issues occurs frequently as postcolonial thought pursues the ideal of sustainable social justice.

Because the postcolonial style of analysis is closely tied to concrete historical conditions, the writing of history itself has become an issue for philosophical investigation. **Historiography,** which takes the writing of history as a matter to be studied and analyzed, typically begins with a preconception of causation in history, an overarching idea of why events happen as they do. Having such a preconception directs the search for facts and guides the selection of what is meaningful from the mass of data. Thus, individual elements can be assembled into a story with a definite logic and a point of view. Recognizing that there are no bare facts apart from a conceptual framework and that those who would report those facts would not have a "God's-eye-view" to reveal them even if the possibility of perfectly simple atoms of truth existed, many postcolonial thinkers who take up the task of understanding history begin by making the choice of a conceptual framework within which the writing of history can have sense and purpose. As nineteenth-century positivism fades from influence, perspectivism has become an accepted part of postcolonial writing. In the twentieth century, some flavor of Marxism was the overwhelming theoretical choice among Third World writers even as Marxism was overwhelmingly rejected by First World writers.

Among the topics most intensively developed in postcolonial studies of history and justice has been the matter of domination. This theme has been known to extend beyond easy intuitive understanding since Hegel's discussion early in the nineteenth century of master–slave dynamics, in which the powerlessness of the slave was shown to entail numerous unavoidable consequences for the master (see Chapter 11). As the postcolonial program began to require an analysis of justice that satisfied both experiential and critical needs, the nature of the links between subjective perceptions and the systemic conditions under which people live began to come into view. For many thinkers, the international market system was the major force for injustice through a form of domination that reduces everything to a dollar value. This analysis is not unique to postcolonial thinkers, of course, but is shared in greater or lesser part with a number of modern philosophers outside the Third World.

## HISTORICAL BACKGROUND

In the premodern world, geographic and linguistic barriers ensured that most of humanity's ideas and techniques would originate and initially develop in relative isolation within their own particular cultures. The result: even now we often find distinctly different mythologies and ethical norms in groups whose territories border each other. Although modern communications greatly facilitate the spread of ideas, we should recall that in the ancient world, such activities as trade, conquest, or itinerant teaching only rarely expanded the geographic distribution of any concept.

Occasionally, research turns up multiple instances of a concept arising apparently independently in several different, isolated places. Some examples are kinship concepts, ethical categories of right and wrong, certain logical relationships, and the psychological construct of the other. More typically in philosophy and religion, though, apparent similarities among concepts, worldviews, and schools of thought that arise independently in multiple cultures have only a coincidental, superficial relationship to each other; even so, it has not been unusual for those who detect resonances of their own views in other cultures to claim a common grounding in human universals. From anthropology we learn to be very careful in making comparisons of concepts across cultures or historical periods.

With the advent of postcolonial consciousness, though, true cross-cultural commonality has become a much more frequent occurrence than ever before. Now, the development of similar viewpoints in the work of thinkers in several different modern cultures has become less likely to be a matter of mere coincidence and more likely to derive from participation in those common social/cultural realities that began to emerge in the fifteenth century, when the Spanish and Portuguese shifted from thinking locally to thinking globally. This development in imperial thinking led the Iberian powers to pursue a comparatively simple strategy of colonization based on extracting traditionally valuable metals and other commodities from the areas under their control and taking them back to the mother country.

The Latin American pattern of colonialism was not precisely replicated in other colonial experiments. A different profile occurred when the British realized that their colonies could serve not only as sources of raw materials, exotic produce, and precious minerals but also as markets for manufactured goods. This changed everything. To support trade in manufactured goods, British colonies in the eighteenth century needed to be fully functioning economic entities. This plan determined that the social tone of eighteenth-century British colonies on the North American continent would be set by an unambiguously economic agenda that quickly supplanted the religious concerns that dominated in the seventeenth century. To a certain degree, the influences that shaped the self-understandings of the colonists worked similarly on Native Americans. The indigenous inhabitants of areas colonized by the British seem to have acquired their sense of Old World values less through religious missions than through trade and territorial expansion, though missionary activity certainly did occur on a significant scale. The colonial pattern of relationship between whites and Indians of North America, which was based primarily on economic exploitation, continued after the American colonies won their independence. According to most histories, colonialism came to an end in the United States with the surrender of the British at Yorktown, but from the Native American perspective nothing of the sort occurred.

Thus, colonial activity went beyond simple extraction of wealth to become linked to technological development for some imperial powers. At varying levels of integration, colonized peoples joined the world money economy whether they wanted to or not and had to face all the cultural changes that such a development implies. Among the most dramatic effects of these policies was the impoverishment of rural India, which most analysts attribute directly to British mercantilism. There, centuries-old patterns of labor and exchange vanished within a few decades, creating not only economic hardship but social dislocation as well. In Southeast Asia and some other areas where money economies could be sustained among the colonized population, the French instituted a colonial model that was midway between the Spanish strategy of simple transfer of valuable materials and the British strategy of constructing a dynamic trading system that had a reasonable chance of providing comparatively stable returns over the long term. Whatever the model, colonization entailed not only the violent physical subjugation of indigenous peoples but also the introduction of the colonizers' values and beliefs into traditional societies around the world. The reduction of existence to financial equivalences is a continuing theme in postcolonial metaphysical critiques.

During the intense colonial activity of the eighteenth and nineteenth centuries and the first part of the twentieth, huge populations were participating directly or indirectly in some sort of militarily enforced experience of cultural confrontation. Whether one was on the winning or the losing side, these events occurred on such a scale and with such intensity that reflective interpretation on all sides was virtually inevitable. The depth of this interpretation was not uniform by present standards, however. Some thinkers in the West, such as England's Herbert Spencer, pleased large followings in their own countries by celebrating successful military adventures as evidence of the natural superiority of the victorious imperial nation. Others, whose peoples had endured colonial domination, inclined to more critical efforts to come to terms with their experience. These latter reflections, which consciously situate themselves within a history of subjugation and revolutionary impulses, constitute the substance of postcolonial philosophy. In the colonial and former colonial powers, postcolonial thought has often been marginalized, summarily dismissed, or even totally ignored. Just the opposite has been the case among subjugated and formerly subjugated populations, however, for whom the analyses and calls to action of postcolonial thinkers have resonated powerfully, providing ethical and metaphysical understandings that ring true to lived experience. Frequently, postcolonial thinkers have become social and political leaders in their respective countries; the roster includes Mohandas Gandhi in India, Sun Yatsen in China, Léopold Sédar Senghor in Senegal, Ho Chi Minh in Vietnam, Kwame Nkrumah in Ghana, Paulin Hountondji in Benin, Vaclav Havel in the Czech Republic, and numerous others.

Postcolonial philosophy is a diverse genre, but its voices share an intentionally substantial engagement with the historical realities of Third World peoples or those who have been systematically excluded from power in their societies. For these populations, the shared experience of domination has helped to structure a general revolutionary consciousness that often resists not only the values and conceptualizations of the colonizers but the very methods of interpretation and decision of the oppressive culture. This critical commonality may be obscured at first glance by the variety of expression in postcolonial thought, a range of beliefs that includes advocacy of both violence and nonviolence, capitalism and utopian socialism, absolute standards and anarchic relativism, to touch on only a few of the categories. Further, postcolonial thinkers within their respective traditions frequently disagree among themselves in their valuations of events and situations; if one ever needed proof that radically different conclusions could be inferred from very similar historical facts, postcolonial philosophy would provide it.

In no small measure, though, postcolonial thought constitutes a distinctive category of endeavor because it consciously traces back to the ineluctable dislocations that ensued from encounters with conquerors whose imperialism aimed at nearly total domination. Although the invaders asserted both physical and philosophical superiority, their ideas have received at best a mixed reception in the lands they once controlled. Given the available historical and anthropological information, it seems most reasonable to believe that the commonalities of postcolonial thought around the world are not so much due to the conceptual similarities of the specific ideas introduced by different groups of colonizers as to the similarities among experiences of invasion and foreign domination. This is not a trivial claim in the analysis of postcolonial thought, for it locates postcolonial thought as a defining event in the history of subjugated peoples rather than as a minor footnote in the intellectual history of colonizing powers. Postcolonial thought includes articulations of value systems and critical analyses that challenge the adequacy of the colonizers' understandings at every turn; this is partly reaction to the past and partly creation of the future through imagination of new ways of being and thinking.

## AFRICA

Among the peoples of Africa and from there into the Western hemisphere, diverse languages and traditions have constructed richly variant worlds of thought and experience, each developing its own ways of speaking of the good, the true, and the real. In the philosophies of African cultures, as in the other major geographic groupings in world philosophy, certain themes tend to recur, although no single worldview or school of thought enjoys general acceptance. Very few universal claims apply accurately across the many expressions of the philosophical impulse

Africa, as seen from outer space.

in African cultures and their offshoots beyond Africa. Taken together, these expressions have come to be known as **Pan-African philosophy,** a term with a range of meanings in the early twenty-first century. Understood in this inclusive sense, Pan-African philosophy reveals itself to be many philosophies in both content and method, all united by a geographic reference point. The first step in appreciating Pan-African philosophy as a cross-cultural phenomenon is to survey its realization in Africa itself.

The study of contemporary African philosophy presents some unique opportunities because of the sharp contrasts that occur in its truly multicultural milleu. Existing virtually side by side with contributions to international conversations on technical issues in semantics or the impact of technology on society are statements of ancient tribal memories and understandings transmitted by oral tradition. Of special significance, the centuries-long encounter of African cultures with powerful influences from outside Africa has inspired efforts in African and African American communities to preserve and extend originally African intellectual and spiritual resources.

The many tensions and tragedies of colonialism and its aftermath constitute the complex origin of African postcolonial philosophy. In Africa, reconciliation of tradition and modernity is emerging as an increasingly important concern for the present generation of philosophers. Charting new directions in the last half of the twentieth century, they often constructed their discourse purposefully to contribute to a distinctively African articulation of the history of ideas and critical analysis. One point of agreement among most contemporary Pan-African philosophers is that both antecedent and contemporary energies must be taken up into thinking; with very few exceptions, neither pure traditionalism nor pure modernism is accepted as an adequate style of response to the issues that African philosophers and their societies face.

After centuries of contact between African and non-African cultures, it is difficult to isolate a set of purely traditional African philosophical positions today. Even employing complex strategies of textual analysis, this may be an impossible task, for in spite of the well-documented resistance of traditional cultures to new ideas, the transcultural movement of ideas has been the rule in the development of philosophy around the world. Some analysts maintain that when intellectual boundary-lines have been drawn in the past by non-Africans, they have been constructed to minimize the achievements of African cultures and transfer them elsewhere. In no small measure as a result of African critiques, the entire boundary-drawing enterprise — once commonplace in the history of ideas — has become seriously suspect. So now, when Africanists point out the high probability that Egyptian concepts figure prominently in the thinking of such European figures as Pythagoras and Plato, for example, they also serve to remind their readers of the broader point that over the centuries thinkers have always appropriated and reworked the ideas of others, regardless of whatever cultural boundaries might exist. They also obviously make the point that Africa is to be viewed as a source of a share of those ideas.

We recall in this connection that the division between Mediterranean Africa and sub-Saharan Africa, so obvious today, seems to have been much less distinct before the comparatively recent desertification of huge areas in the northern part of the continent, so contact among the peoples of Africa did not entail overcoming quite the same geographic barriers in earlier times as now. Similarly, the distinction between Africa and Europe, more pronounced today than the north-south split in Africa itself, was not a very prominent consideration to the peoples of the ancient world who settled the coast of the Mediterranean and whose sense of place was more strongly defined by their shared relation to the sea than by the modern world-geographic categorization of continents. Given these facts, the most promising preliminary question to guide an inquiry into Pan-African philosophy is not what a purely African philosophy precisely is but, rather, *how philosophy has been done* in Africa and in the places outside Africa where Africans have resettled, whether voluntarily or by force. With this sensibility, contemporary African philosophy comes into view as a modern development in thinking even as some of its exponents retrieve the most ancient traditional concepts extant on the continent where humanity originated.

## Oral and Traditional Philosophy

The search for wisdom and understanding occurs everywhere, but it must begin somewhere. Before any direct statement of abstract principles or any intentional construction of a rational system of thought comes the telling of stories of desire, of bravery, of ancestors, of trickery, of the unseen, and of all else that is important to people. In these narratives, which are often highly ambiguous, the world's cultures have developed their unique visions and voices over thousands of years. As thoroughly as in literate cultures, oral traditions have transmitted complex value systems and their rationales.

Exclusively oral traditions were fairly common until the middle of the twentieth century but are fast either disappearing entirely or being supplemented with literacy. We are among the last generations able to find the origins of philosophy right before our eyes in living oral traditions. Nigerian philosopher Olu Sodipo observes in this connection that "even if it is true that an idea or attitude needs to be reflective and critical in order to deserve being called philosophical, it does not follow that any idea or attitude that is not expressed in writing is *ipso facto* unphilosophical." Although continuing indigenous written traditions of philosophy exist only in the lineages of the Asia civilizations following China's lead and in the Indo-European civilizations ranging chronologically across northern Africa, India, Europe, and the European cultures of the New World, all cultures possess continuous oral and folk traditions.

*Person*   Physically, the distinction between self and other appears to be given in the biology of organisms. In virtually all cultures of the world, this distinction has psychological and philosophical reality as well. That such a distinction seems to exist across species lines certainly does not mean, however, that different organisms possess uniform or even logically compatible senses of their own individuality. The same holds true for cultures. From our knowledge of human beings, at least, the sense of what it means to be a human being is something that must be created as much as discovered. One way philosophers have approached the matter of individuality has been to develop the notion of **person.**

What a person is cannot be adequately determined simply by observation or experiment. It is, rather, a metaphysical question, that is, a question whose answer is more a matter of decision about the general nature or being of something than of empirical knowledge about it. In other words, the idea of person, which can seem so self-evident, is more an invention of human beings than an inherent fact of nature. As such, the notion of person might be expected to vary greatly from culture to culture, and indeed it does.

*Historiography*   Poet, philosopher, and president of his native Senegal, **Léopold Sédar Senghor** [SENG-ohr] (1906–2002) almost single-handedly determined the issues and methods of philosophy in French-speaking Africa in the mid-twentieth century. From his studies in France, Senghor acquired an intimate acquaintance with the thoughtways of Continental philosophy. This background, demonstrated in close readings of the texts he considered foundational, also clearly informs his political writings, in which Senghor establishes a discipline far removed from the colorful rhetorical assertions that often take the place of thinking in the lives of nations. Senghor's hope was that Africans would find a way to adapt socialist theory to the needs of their postcolonial societies. Adaptation was necessary, in his view, because European ways and values were inadequate to the depth and richness of African understandings of life. To this end, he attempted to create a methodology that would work for Africans.

His doctrine of **negritude,** a concept that remains widely misunderstood to this day, sought to outline a distinctively African epistemology to explain the claim that there was an African way of knowing that was different from the European. Senghor's own method was phenomenological, that is, aiming to be dispassionately descriptive, but his claim that African cultures evaluate metaphors differently from European ones was widely treated as a simple opinion. A selection from Senghor appears at the end of this chapter.

*The Nature of Philosophy*    A series of articles breaking with past practice and proposing a rigorous program for the future of African philosophy brought Paulin Hountondji [hoon-TON-jee] to the forefront of postcolonial thought in the late twentieth century. Hountondji has attacked *ethnophilosophy* (philosophy that takes into account ethnic factors), the concept of negritude, and other colonialist assumptions. Hountondji, whose career includes service as Minister of Education in his native Benin, brings techniques of French critical theory to bear on the question of the integrity of African philosophy, focusing especially on the task of deconstructing texts that, in his analysis, perpetuate a colonial mentality. He has been most concerned to dismantle what he sees as the destructive influence of two connected positions in the African intellectual milieu — namely, ethnophilosophy and the advocacy of the concept of negritude. Hountondji's claim is that both of these positions work against African interests by perpetuating related falsehoods. The problem with ethnophilosophy, which seeks to describe traditional beliefs, is that its practitioners violate the experience of those they describe by abstracting ideas from their practical contexts.

Ethnophilosophy's first offense, then, is that it imposes external categorizations on those it studies. Its second offense is more historical in that its practitioners have often justified their work in terms of its usefulness to those who would control African consciousness by the judicious manipulation of symbols and concepts. A critical view of ethnophilosophy sees that Africans who buy into the ethnophilosophic story, which does contain an element of fact, are prone to mistake these facts for truth and thus acquiesce to control strategies they would otherwise resist. The same problem afflicts the adherents of the negritude position, says Hountondji, when they valorize African soul and relinquish African intellect. Not only is this a bad trade, he claims, but it also is built on an ideological illusion that serves the purposes of the colonizing forces. The remedy Hountondji prescribes at this juncture in history is a sustained critical examination of the task of a postcolonial philosophy and, to avoid unconscious perpetuation of conservative traditionalist or colonialist assumptions, a renunciation of most notions of cultural pluralism.

*The Good Life*    The question of what constitutes the good life is one of the oldest in philosophy. It assumes particular poignancy when the conditions of life are as difficult as they have been under colonial rule. Among the most painful realizations of postcolonial thinkers is the fact that colonialist regulations that provide a comparatively small economic or political benefit to the ruling class may cause a great deal of suffering among the colonized population. Over time, the consciousness of the people may become distorted through sustained brutalization, and traditional values and virtues may fall into obscurity. Countering the tendency to give in to baser motivations, especially once independence has been achieved, requires constant vigilance and personal discipline. In addressing this issue, some

# PROFILE: Desmond Tutu (1931–    )

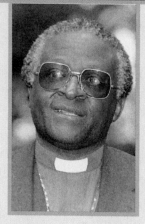

Desmond Tutu became prominent as a fighter against police brutality in South Africa in objecting to the massacre of children during the Soweto uprising. He pleaded with then President Vorster to dismantle apartheid for the future of the children. He also gave an impassioned speech at the gravesite of Steve Biko, a leader of the Black Consciousness movement who was murdered on September 12, 1977. Tutu became Secretary of the South African Council of Churches in 1978 and a leader in the fight against apartheid in South Africa. He called the South African government the most evil since the Nazis.

Apartheid for Tutu was "intrinsically evil" and had to be dismantled. He believed that no one could be neutral in this matter. "You are either on the side of the oppressed or on the side of the oppressor." To be fully free, Tutu believed, all must have freedom. He continually risked imprisonment traveling the world and condemning the brutal injustice of the apartheid system.

Tutu's method of fighting for liberation was through nonviolent action, a strategy with parallels to that of Martin Luther King, Jr. This was initially also the method of the African National Congress and Nelson Mandela. However, the strategy of that organization changed in 1961 after introduction of the stringent Security Laws, which were seen to interpret nonviolent resistance as weakness. The new method was to use force to resist force. Nelson Mandela immediately began to organize the armed resistance, was captured in 1962, and remained in prison until 1990. The question of the efficacy and necessity of armed resistance versus "nonviolent" resistance remains one of the central issues confronting the contemporary world. Archbishop Desmond Tutu was a vice-chairman of a group on "Christianity and the Social Order" at the 1988 Lambeth Conference, which adopted a resolution on South Africa stating that it "understands those who, after exhausting all other ways, choose the way of armed struggle as the only way to justice, whilst drawing attention to the dangers and injustices possible in such action itself."

Underlying the philosophy of Desmond Tutu is the concept of humaneness. Everyone must have the freedom to become fully human; apartheid prevented this both for whites and for blacks, he argued. "I lay great stress on humaneness and being truly human. In our African understanding, part of Ubantu — being human — is the rare gift of sharing. . . . Blacks are beginning to lose this wonderful attribute, because we are being inveigled by the excessive individualism of the West. I loathe Capitalism because it gives far too great play to our inherent selfishness."

---

postcolonial thinkers recommend socialism, some recommend democracy, some recommend religion. All, however, unite in recommending justice.

Archbishop **Desmond Tutu** (1931–    ) is widely credited with helping to maintain civility and minimize bloodshed as one of the architects of South Africa's revolutionary transition to representative democracy from an authoritarian regime characterized by apartheid's rigidly enforced subjugation of the mostly impoverished black majority. Speaking out frequently against economic exploitation, official brutality, and broad application of the death penalty, Archbishop Tutu not only helped focus the eyes of the world on injustice in his country, but he also articulated basic principles to guide his fellow citizens in what he saw as the inevitable shift to black control of the levers of power.

## THE AMERICAS

The history of colonialism and subjugation of native peoples in the Americas properly begins even before the arrival of Europeans in the fifteenth century. On both continents of the Western hemisphere, indigenous Americans from the Toltecs to the Onondagas engaged in vigorous campaigns of empire building. With the coming of the Europeans, however, imperial ambitions in the Americas were pursued from a position of technological superiority that the colonized native peoples could not match and with a sustained, single-minded acquisitiveness outside the experience of most tribes. Just as the numerically superior Dacians of Eastern Europe could not withstand the organized onslaught of Roman legions, so the Indians of the Americas were confronted by forces whose methods and ultimate objectives were utterly foreign to anything they had imagined in their mythology. Montezuma's destruction by a handful of Spaniards is just the most dramatic instance of a story line that played itself out numerous times on both continents of the Western hemisphere. The final episode of this centuries-long European conquest of the many native cultures of the Americas is being enacted today in the rain forests of South America.

With a few exceptions, especially in what is now Latin America, the evidence preserved in Indian oral histories suggests that both regularities and cataclysmic dislocations in the natural world could be grasped within the Indians' mythological and conceptual schemes. Upon the coming of the Europeans, however, history turned inscrutable for Native Americans and has largely remained a sequence of unwelcome surprises. Buffeted by centuries of broken agreements and destructive coercions, the Indian nations have tried to maintain their integrity by negotiation, by violent resistance, by legal process, and by plumbing the depths of their religious and philosophical traditions. In the worst cases, whole tribes have disappeared. With first-person accounts of genocidal aggression still part of the experience of many Native Americans, the postcolonial philosophical response has only begun to enter the literature.

The African diaspora has resulted in establishment of populations of African descent in many areas of the world, but only in the United States has there developed on a large scale a distinctive and continuous thread of critical and normative philosophy growing out of the transplanted group's unfolding historical-cultural experience. Thinking on these things has developed into a multifaceted effort to come to grips with the everyday realities of African American life, in which racial factors figure in some issues for virtually all writers and in virtually all issues for some of them. Some would argue that this material is not philosophy at all, but given the problematics of postcolonial thought, drawing more inclusive category boundaries for the field of philosophy makes good sense. Some conventional conceptions of philosophy are challenged in this categorization, for unlike most academic philosophy, African American postcolonial thinking occurs not only in self-identified philosophical texts but also in story and song—wherever propositions are presented and explicitly considered or justified. For most postcolonial thinkers, allowing the possibility of departures from the stylistic norms of philosophy is a strength, not a disqualification; the subtextual message is that any occasion may open up a space for philosophical reflection.

Hernán Cortés (1485–1547), Spanish conquistador and conqueror of Mexico.

In Latin America, the colonial order established in the fifteenth and sixteenth centuries did not evolve uniformly in all areas. Spain did not relinquish Cuba until the end of the nineteenth century, and Britain still maintains a tiny foothold on the Falkland Islands. After independence, most nations of Central and South America continued to be controlled by small, wealthy elites supporting authoritarian regimes. These regimes tended to attract the support of positivistic thinkers, although there has been variation from country to country. In this regard, Latin American philosophy roughly paralleled that of Western Europe. Beginning early in the twentieth century, however, positivism's influence began to decline in Latin America as in Europe, but for somewhat different reasons. Positivism's close identification in some places with discredited political factions was partly responsible, as was the vitality of competing currents in French and German philosophy. The introduction of Marxism to Latin America, which occurred mostly outside the traditional academic circles, provided the first serious challenge to the hegemony of Roman Catholic metaphysics, providing conceptual support for the still-vital commitment of Latin American thinkers to a discourse focused on the problematics of practical engagement (see the box "Colonialism and the Church"). Strongly influenced by intellectual advances made in Europe and, to a lesser extent, the United States, Latin American thinkers nonetheless avoided the style of European and American philosophizing. By the middle of the twentieth century, a major part of Latin American philosophical discourse had taken on a heavily religious cast; interestingly, this move, which has been studiously avoided by most philosophers in

## Colonialism and the Church

The Santa Barbara mission, founded in 1782 by Father Junipero Serra.

From the very beginning of colonial activity in the fifteenth century, heated debate occurred within the Roman Catholic Church about the motives and methods involved in the introduction of European cultural norms and religion to indigenous populations. With the subjection of native peoples to European colonial masters whose well-known cruelties actually differed from indigenous imperialistic practices only a little, some clergy became concerned about associations that would be made between these methods and Christianity's metaphysical and ethical teachings. Indeed, half a millennium later, many native groups, in the American West especially, still make a connection between colonial coercion and mission Christianity. The encounter of native peoples with Christianity cannot be categorized in purely negative terms, however, because in virtually all former colonies active indigenous Christian communities of varying size and demographics exist. Of special note, Latin American thinkers have taken the religious consequences of colonialism as a key issue and are actively debating the ambiguous legacy of Europe's highest ideals and most violent betrayals. The religious turbulence initiated by colonial adventurism has evolved into a dynamic set of spiritual and philosophical challenges on several continents.

Europe and North America, has been almost uniformly celebrated among postcolonial thinkers (see the box "Liberation Theology").

This fact points up a little-recognized commonality among the expressions of postcolonial thought: in virtually all cases, except those in which Marxist materialism has been consciously adopted, the line between religion and philosophy seems

## Liberation Theology

Postcolonial thought in Latin America is closely connected with Christian social activism. Seeking to show how adherence to Christian principles can lead to a better life, theologians of **liberation** have become especially well known for their work in ethics. Epistemology has also been an important concern, however, because it offers methodological resources with which to address prevailing prejudices. Theologians of liberation, as other postcolonial thinkers do, lay great emphasis on knowledge derived from experience as the first line of defense against illusion. One reason postcolonial thinkers so often privilege experience is that, for generations, religiously inspired otherworldly hopes and a quasimedieval hierarchical understanding of society preached by conservative clergy functioned to disarm revolutionary sentiments that might arise among the large numbers of peasants. These sorts of claims may have been spiritually beneficial, say thinkers who are inclined to give the Church the benefit of the doubt, but they did not lead to sufficient nurturing of the people. Moving beyond the straightforward social gospel school of preaching that was popular among North American Christians seeking a just society, liberation theology not only has delivered the homiletic message of social change through Christian love but also has developed a complex critical-theoretical infrastructure grounded in Continental philosophy.

very hard to draw. Whether the religion is the Christianity of Latin America, the pantheisms and myriad mythologies of Africa and the Americas, or the Hinduism of India, religiously metaphysical claims regularly serve as points of departure or elements of the presuppositional structures of postcolonial texts. In their own terms, this does not make them any less philosophical; instead, it is viewed as a technique to engage the whole person in the act of thinking and interpretation. As a larger methodological consideration, postcolonial thinkers contend, this mode of engagement seeks to overcome the kind of personal alienation that made colonialist brutality thinkable in the first place and that perpetuates its effects to this day.

### African American Thought

*Social Justice*    Decades after his assassination, the call for justice articulated in the writings of **Martin Luther King, Jr.** (1929–1968), remains the single most powerful determinant in the American civil rights movement. King's basic message was a simple one, stated memorably in the oft-quoted dedication to *Why We Can't Wait:* "To my children . . . for whom I dream that one day soon they will no longer be judged by the color of their skin but by the content of their character." How to turn vision into reality was, for King, not just a matter of the mass organizational strategies for which he is often remembered but of personal responsibility. King was strongly influenced by the example and writings of Mohandas Gandhi in both setting his agenda and deciding on the appropriate methods to achieve it. Like Gandhi, King did not separate the two, nor did he minimize the difficulties of this comprehensive project. It is no coincidence that King's background was religious, for as other thinkers in the postcolonial world found, commonly held religious sensibilities can provide a point of departure for ethical reasoning from a strong

## PROFILE: Martin Luther King, Jr. (1929–1968)

Martin Luther King, Jr., was America's most famous civil rights leader. He helped end racial segregation by organizing nonviolent resistance to unjust law.

The son of the pastor of the Ebenezer Baptist Church in Atlanta, Georgia, King was ordained in 1947 and in 1954 became the minister of a Baptist church in Montgomery, Alabama. He received his Ph.D. in 1955 from Boston University. In 1955 he led the boycott by Montgomery blacks against the segregated city bus lines; this landmark civil rights battle ended in 1956 with the desegregation of the city buses. King's passive resistance philosophy had won its first major victory, and King was catapulted to national prominence.

King organized the Southern Christian Leadership Conference, through which he fought for civil rights in the South and throughout the nation. Though he always advocated and used nonviolent methods, he was arrested and imprisoned many times and was, allegedly, the victim of a vendetta by FBI director J. Edgar Hoover.

In 1963 King organized the March on Washington. This, the largest demonstration in U.S. history, brought more than 200,000 people to the nation's capital. In 1964 King was awarded the Nobel Peace Prize.

By the mid-1960s, King's methods were being challenged by more militant civil rights leaders like H. Rap Brown ("Violence is as American as apple pie") and groups like the Student Nonviolent Coordinating Committee and the Black Panthers. At the same time, King's fight for justice was expanding; he became critical of the Vietnam War and concerned with poverty in general.

King was organizing a Poor People's March on Washington in 1968 when he made a side trip to Memphis, Tennessee, to support striking sanitation workers. There, standing on the balcony of a motel, he was slain by an assassin's bullet. James Earl Ray was convicted of the murder.

Martin Luther King, Jr., was a philosopher who made a difference.

---

set of broadly accepted premises. King believed that right behavior leads to right consequences.

*Feminism*   In the late twentieth century, beginning in France and the United States, the feminist movement pursued a thorough revaluation of the traditional themes and methods of philosophy. Feminism is sometimes caricatured as a movement of political reaction, but from a feminist perspective, this constitutes a rather transparent strategy to undermine the philosophical authenticity of feminist thinking. Within philosophical feminism, several schools of thought have emerged, each with its own profile of insights and emphases. In the African American community, awareness of the successes of the civil rights movement and the rise of feminism in the white middle class combined with firsthand knowledge of a mostly unwritten history of the particular difficulties of black women, including a high incidence of domestic violence, to produce a variant of feminism that is especially sensitive to the social-ethical problematics of marginalization. In the view of **bell hooks** (c. 1955–   ), whose writings range from general-audience essays in popular magazines to highly nuanced discourse most appreciated by academically trained minds, it is important to make some distinctions within the feminist movement.

# PROFILE: bell hooks (Gloria Watkins) (c. 1955– )

Acknowledged as one of the most provocative essayists in America today, bell hooks has devoted special attention to the suppression of the voices of black women. Writing under the name of her unlettered great-grandmother to symbolize this very problem, hooks often takes up controversial themes that other writers avoid by design or oversight. Her mordant analyses typically begin by calling attention to something that has been missed or covered over. Her interruptions of the conventional flow of cultural conversation have discomfited nearly every sort of reader in one way or another, and hooks does not spare herself as she searches for the examples that will inspire, edify, and (even) entertain.

Among the thorniest issues hooks has raised is that of class distinctions in the construction of American feminism; specifically, she has argued that a feminism that emphasizes the concerns of white, middle-class women with career plans does not do justice to minority women, many of whom must contend regularly with a very different set of economic realities.

bell hooks is the author of numerous books and articles, including *Ain't I a Woman: Black Women and Feminism* (1981), *Feminist Theory: From Margin to Center* (1984), *Breaking Bread: Insurgent Black Intellectual Life* (with Cornel West; 1991), and *Black Looks: Race and Representation* (1992). Her earlier writings are strongly flavored with Marxist ideology, but ideology seems to be less a concern for hooks than is finding ways to think and act inclusively. Thus, she advocates consensus decision making—and the redistribution of power that is implied by adoption of that way of thinking. Moreover, she valorizes the authentically collective action and liberation from repressive hierarchy that consensus can lead to. Adopting this set of values addresses the problem of the outsider, whose concerns are often submerged in the strong currents of majority views.

The writing of bell hooks attacks domination that is sometimes obvious and sometimes hidden. She does not stop at critique but instead ventures proposals that promise not only to benefit a narrow constituency but also to create a more just society generally.

Claims hooks, the feminism of the founders of the movement, at least in the United States, centered on careerism, a specifically middle-class concern. As such, it was liable to be coopted by the existing power structure to perpetuate a culture of competition and individualism, which she analyzes to be antithetical to the best, inclusive impulses of feminism. The problems of the more thoroughly disenfranchised require a more radical rethinking, hooks and others have argued.

*Afrocentrism* **Afrocentrism,** a school of thought primarily focused on investigating the heritage and influence of African cultures, derives primarily from the work of **Chaikh Anta Diop** (1923–1986). Diop, an Africanist, brought his acknowledged expertise in ancient Egyptian history and culture to bear in arguing for a set of theses that ran counter to ancient history as told by Europeans. Diop's history claimed among other things that black Africa was the origin of Egyptian civilization and that Europeans who were not purely Nordic traced their ancestry back to Africa. The matter remains hotly contested among historians at this writ-

## PROFILE: Cornel West (1953– )

There are some very deep questions confronting American culture, asserts Cornel West, and they cannot be addressed effectively if the society continues to think in conventional ways. Indeed, conventional thinking is precisely the barrier to a better quality of life. Lecturing and publishing frequently, West seeks to help chart the direction of genuinely beneficial change as he prophetically urges creation of a more compassionate society. Bringing about the necessary social reforms, he claims, requires changes in the way individuals live their lives, especially in the degree to which self-understanding develops. By living the examined life—here West sounds a perennial theme in the history of philosophy—one may progressively overcome the strictures of habit and prejudice. Now, says West, it is time to transcend the limits of Eurocentrism, multiculturalism, and all the other "isms" that keep people from perceiving the reali-

ties of life. This is not just a matter of intellectual clarity for West but also a challenge to a deeply personal commitment.

Always involved in the church throughout a career that has included appointments at Princeton and Harvard, West has consistently articulated philosophical positions that cannot be separated from religious insight. His major writings range topically from work in the critical history of ideas, represented by *The American Evasion of Philosophy: A Genealogy of Pragmatism* (1989), to the kind of personal statement represented by *Race Matters* (1993). In the realm of postcolonial thought, Cornel West occupies a position in the methodological mainstream by virtue of his explicit rootedness in social-historical experience, his use of religious tradition as a reference for thinking, and his critical analysis of current conditions and their causal antecedents.

ing. Whether Diop's case prevails in whole or in part is a matter for archaeologists and historians to decide, but whatever the eventual verdict, Diop has inspired a school of cultural interpretation that is pursuing a revaluation of virtually all things African. Afrocentric thinkers hold to a range of not necessarily compatible positions, but something of a mainstream constellation of ideas has been articulated by its chief architect, Molefi Kete Asante (1942– ), in numerous publications.

*Social Activism* **Cornel West** (1953– ), now at Princeton University, is among the most influential thinkers exploring the theological and philosophical vectors of social activism at the beginning of the twenty-first century. Although West's philosophical writings have dealt with a variety of issues, essays in which he combines trenchant analysis with positive recommendations for future action command his widest readership.

## Latin American Thought

Postcolonial Latin American thinkers work in a context that is at once strongly influenced by European philosophy and powerfully motivated to move out from under the shadow of European domination. One feature that importantly distinguishes

Latin American thought from most European philosophy is the sustained effort to explore the relevance of philosophy to problems of social justice. The concerns of Latin American philosophy encompass the full range of the philosophical spectrum, but its activity in postcolonial thought has concentrated on analysis of Marxist theses.

*Ontology*    Ontology is the branch of philosophy that concerns itself with the question of being. In the twentieth century, ontology was revived by the work of Martin Heidegger and Jean-Paul Sartre after centuries of dormancy. Although there is always a danger that orthodoxy will stifle thinking whenever the work of a philosopher is widely acknowledged, recent writings of Latin American philosophers demonstrate the possibility of interpreting Heidegger's work in ways that probably were not anticipated by either the politically conservative German philosopher or the politically progressive French philosopher. In an essay at the end of this chapter, Argentinian philosopher **Carlos Astrada** [uh-STRAH-duh] (1894–1970) takes Heidegger's thinking as evidence of the collapse of the bourgeois mentality that determined much of the course of colonial activity. Though Latin America's colonial pattern was more feudal than bourgeois, most historians agree that bourgeois influences from North America have played a great role in perpetuating unequal distributions of wealth inherited from colonial times. Postcolonial reality has brought with it the realization that surprises can overtake whole civilizations, including the awareness that longstanding patterns of wealth and poverty are not necessarily permanent fixtures in a society. Recent history, unfolding at the pace of technological change, plants doubts about the stability of existence. It should not be surprising, then, that a school of philosophy, existentialism, should arise that sees becoming as the fundamental fact of existence. For postcolonial thinkers, it is not surprising either that the wealthy would project the instability of their own power structures onto the existence of humanity itself. Astrada's essay demonstrates that works of existentialist ontology can be read as political-economic texts.

*Metaphysics of the Human*    For as long as we have been keeping records of our thoughts, human beings have sought a reliably firm foundation upon which to base ideas about ourselves, our laws, our destiny, and so on. Many promises of a final answer have been made, but outside of religious faith — a category of claims that arguably has its own distinct rules of discourse — no claims of foundational insight have stood the tests of time and philosophical investigation. In the sensibilities of postcolonial thinkers, though, the moral and metaphysical claims of the ruling elites of past and present demand constant vigilance and persistent critique. Marx called these dangerous claims **ideology,** meaning in his vocabulary a kind of self-interested delusion that infected the bourgeoisie and that they half-cynically, half-unconsciously passed on to the proletariat. Marx believed that the proletariat would eventually realize as he had that ideological claims were without necessity or merit and could, therefore, be contradicted. But, contends Peruvian philosopher **Francisco Miró Quesada** [keh-SAH-duh] (1918–   ), with the pragmatism that has become a trademark of recent Latin philosophy, contradicting the claims of one group with the claims of an alternative theory of reality does not solve the problem.

Instead, it creates conflict, and conflict creates suffering. Quesada continues on to argue that humanity itself must be reimagined. His argument consists of two main parts: first, a critique of the truth claims of theories, which concludes that theories cannot reliably deliver the truth, and second, a consequentialist argument centered on the suffering caused by people who take theories too seriously. The eventual proposal is to divide the human race into those who are willing to exploit people and those who are willing to defend them from exploitation.

*Gender Issues*   The phase of feminism as a movement of middle-class European and American women began in 1959. Analysis of the early rhetoric of the movement suggests an underlying assumption among that generation of feminists that all women shared common concerns. It was not long, however, before women in more traditional societies began to assert that the universal claims of most feminist literature did not speak well to the conditions of marginalized peoples. From both unreformed colonial and postcolonial perspectives, a certain myopia afflicted mainstream feminism.

Two major expansions of feminist intentionality have been suggested from outside the mainstream. The first calls for more attention to issues of class. In this connection the argument is made that commonalities based in shared gender become functionally irrelevant when class-based exploitation determines not only woman-to-woman relationships but also the circumstances of domestic relationships. A woman living in grinding poverty has few resources with which to overcome traditional strictures and inequities, Third World writers observe. The second major modification of feminist discourse suggested by several postcolonial writers was the abandonment of a black–white racial dichotomy. Because the majority of the women in the world are neither Euro-American white nor are they black, the reasoning goes, feminists who fall into a black–white polarization not only exclude a large ethnic segment, but, more ominously, they exclude a wide range of situations from analysis as well. Without analysis of diverse circumstances, the understanding of women's issues is truncated, and consciously constructed corrections are unlikely to be forthcoming. Sonia Saldívar-Hull addresses these problems in a selection at the end of the chapter.

## SOUTH ASIA

The history of European colonial rule in Asia began in the early sixteenth century and continues to this day. It included such developments as British domination of large areas of India and other parts of South Asia; French control of Vietnam, Cambodia, and Laos; the partitioning of Ch'ing China by multiple Western colonial powers; and much more. Although the vast inland deserts of Asia and the rugged Deccan plateau of India remained mostly outside the grip of invading powers, most of Asia's population centers experienced alien invasion at one time or another. The reactions of indigenous peoples to these events ranged from the pacifism of Gandhi to murderous secret societies from Afghanistan to China, with the Vietnam War marking the bloody culmination of an era of highly confrontational violence. According to the majority of contemporary analysts, colonialism has been economically and socially destructive in the former colonies. A few, however, claim that the legacy of specifically Northern European colonialism has been positive in terms of modern political infrastructure and value systems that facilitate success in a technological world. These sorts of determinations are hard to make at a distance, but one thing is certain: the formerly colonized peoples of Asia have documented their own ideas of what counts as good over thousands of years. Postcolonial thought in Asia draws sustenance from these cultural wellsprings.

Unlike the cultures of sub-Saharan Africa, the nations of Asia have traditions of written philosophy that stretch back more than three millennia, longer than in the West by at least a thousand years. The ancient *Vedas* of India and the Chinese classics anchor their respective cultures with unmistakable gravity, testifying to resources beyond the grasp of any colonizing power. The shock of colonialism to Asia was deep but not so comprehensive for these cultures that their philosophers have felt impelled to the kind of sustained reflection and cultural reconstruction that has been so prominent in Africa. Certainly, colonialism wrecked the economy of the Indian countryside and changed China's self-image forever, but the effect on the discourse of Indian and Chinese philosophy seems to have been a relatively small dislocation. This does not mean that no serious reflection occurred, only that Asian cultures already had so much internally generated philosophical momentum that outside influences, even outside influences with the intellectual resources of the West, could not effect a significant change of course. Instead, outside ideas and techniques, from British aesthetics to Marxist political-historiographical philosophy, were appropriated and reworked to conform to indigenous values.

From another angle, Asian thinkers in the colonial era could acknowledge Western technological superiority without the least impulse to generalize military and industrial might to philosophical capability. On the contrary, they frequently regarded Western thought as crude, simplistic, or just wrongheaded. Even so, the Western presence was hard to ignore. It prompted thoughtful efforts not only to develop an appropriate sense of history but also to project an appropriate relationship with the foreigners. The result included such disparate expressions as the highly reflective Young India school of thought in the waning years of the British Empire and the cynically manipulative, sloganeering rhetoric of Chairman Mao.

Our focus in these pages will be on India, which endured about two centuries of economic despoilment at the hands of the mercantilist-capitalist forces of Britain. It cannot be argued that the leaders of the independence movement relied on indigenous values to develop their notions of economic justice, for India had traditionally established rigid class lines that effectively excluded large numbers of people from the possibility of economic well-being. Ironically, the introduction of British values in India created the conceptual resources that Indians would use to remake their society — after figuring out how to expel the British. Gandhi looked to India's own traditions primarily in his quest for the contours of a future just society, but the majority of members of the dominant Congress party believed with

Jawaharlal Nehru, independent India's first prime minister, that the road to modernization also necessitated adoption of modern political-economic thinking.

The independence movement's greatest influence was certainly Gandhi, but many of its leading thinkers also mined the writings of modern socialists, including Marx. Drawing on Hindu psychology, which views grudging obedience to rules as a very serious problem, Nehru and his followers sought to avoid the imposition of socialism on a populace that was in part unwilling to engage in this transformation of Indian society. Though most of the early leaders of the Indian resistance to the British were convinced that socialism was the surest path to peace and justice, they also saw that domination of the minority by the majority, always possible in a democracy, had to be avoided. These thinkers consciously renounced the use of a colonialist style of coercion to achieve a postcolonial objective.

The topics taken up by Asian postcolonial thought are similar to those considered elsewhere in the world. As well, thinkers in the countries of Asia draw on indigenous thought forms to develop their inferences and expositions. Asian writers are the most likely of the postcolonial thinkers surveyed in this chapter to couch their discussions in terms of the abstract principles and linear inferences typical of Western philosophy. This stylistic similarity is not a borrowing from Western thought, however, but a continuation of local traditions of discourse.

## *Satyagraha*

*Satyagraha,* a concept closely identified with the social and political thinking of **Mohandas (Mahatma) Gandhi** [GAHN-dee] (1869–1948), has been translated as "clinging to truth." This definition immediately raises the question of the nature of truth. In traditional Indian philosophy, this issue had already received a great amount of attention. Thousands of years before Husserl's phenomenological method called for clearing the perceptions of prejudices, Indian philosophers were insisting on the same thing and developing a yoga, or discipline, to facilitate it. The discipline needed in the search for truth was not simply a matter of acquiring the tools of scientific investigation; one also had to practice such virtues as giving, nonattachment, and noninjury to develop mental purity. Without adjusting one's way of life to this task, they argued, truth would remain an empty abstraction no matter how much knowledge one accumulated. Gandhi is part of this tradition in his adoption of its rigorous demands for personal integrity.

Gandhi is also a modern figure, however, a student not only of the classical texts of India but also of Thoreau and Tolstoy. Seeking what was best in his tradition, he repudiated the claims of human inequality by circumstances of birth that underlay the caste system. Declaring freedom from ancient caste laws marked Gandhi as a modern figure despite his notable adherence to ancient ascetic forms. Gandhi's uncompromising concern for the welfare of the people of India and his courage in the struggle for independence from Britain established him as a political leader. His devotion to Hindu ideals and the simple life he lived made him a spiritual leader. Hailed as a saint in his own time and acknowledged as one of the

## PROFILE: Mohandas (Mahatma) Gandhi (1869–1948)

Mohandas Gandhi was the world's leading exponent of the strategy of passive resistance—the attempt to change unjust laws through nonviolent civil disobedience to them. This philosophy, which Gandhi used successfully time after time to produce legal and political change, was the inspiration and guiding light for protest movements throughout the world and was adopted by many American civil rights leaders, including Martin Luther King, Jr. Gandhi's life, like King's, was ended by an assassin— a Hindu fanatic upset by Gandhi's concern for Muslims.

Gandhi began his political activism not in India but in South Africa, where he was a successful lawyer and leader in the Indian community. While there, he gave up a Western mode of life and began living according to Hindu ideals of self-denial. It was there in South Africa, in 1907, that he organized his first campaign of civil disobedience, and this **satyagraha,** or "clinging to the truth," was so successful that the South African government agreed to alleviate anti-Indian discrimination.

In 1915 Gandhi returned to India a famous man. There he used *satyagraha* to advance numerous democratic reforms. He became known as Mahatma, or "great soul," and his influence was so considerable that he could exact concessions from the British government of India by merely threatening to fast to death. Not only was he the spiritual leader of the Indian people, but he was also a major political figure. He was the leader of the Indian National Congress and was a principal participant in the post–World War II conferences that led to India's independence and creation of a separate Muslim state, Pakistan (although he opposed the partition). When there was violence between Muslims and Hindus, Gandhi used his influence to help control it, often resorting to fasts and prayer meetings. It was during one such prayer meeting that he was assassinated.

Gandhi altered the courses of nations: his extraordinary power came not through guns but through his ability to bring out the best in people by setting the highest standards for his own life.

most influential thinkers of the modern age, Gandhi insisted that his way was open to any who would simply decide to follow it.

## Metaphysics

To this day, it is common for Indian thinkers to hold the view that India's role in the international community consists at least partly in promoting a spiritual understanding of the human race and the issues of the times. This orientation is not new to India, but there is novelty in the relatively recent need to adapt this thought to the problematics of colonialism and then modernity. Once Western cultures entered the Indian sphere of consciousness, they were evaluated to see not only how they met the standards of indigenous tradition but also how they might be recast to fit into the Hindu framework.

Around the turn of the twentieth century, while India was still a colony of Britain, **Rabindranath Tagore** [tuh-GORE] (1861–1941) developed in poetry

## PROFILE: Rabindranath Tagore (1861–1941)

Modern India's best-known poet was also in the vanguard of postcolonial thought. Rabindranath Tagore was not simply an advocate for an interest group but also a thinker who saw that philosophy and action must be unified in the life of the individual. Thus, his political claims were intentionally grounded in the traditions of Indian spirituality. As we have noted, postcolonial thought often makes use of traditional ideas and values in its critiques of the structures and methods of domination. It also tends to begin with concrete social situations; for Tagore, this translated into heartfelt advocacy of social reform as a task for Indians themselves, regardless of British policy. Tagore was himself inspired by the beauty and manifold possibilities of life, and he sought to share his vision as an artist through both the written word and the painted image.

Born to an upper-class family in Calcutta, Tagore's opportunities were broad, including a brief period of study in England. In later life, as he established a worldwide reputation, he traveled to Europe, the United States, and Japan. He began writing for periodicals while still very young and acquired a lifelong interest in education as a great hope for the betterment of the human condition. In 1901 he established a school in his native Bengal to put his ideas into practice. He continued to write and, in 1913, was awarded the Nobel Prize for literature. He promptly devoted the proceeds to his school. Knighted in 1915, Tagore resigned the title in 1919 in protest against the harshly repressive tactics employed by the British in maintaining their empire in India. Among his many works are *One Hundred Poems of Kabir* (1915), *Nationalism* (1917), *The Home and the World* (1919), *Broken Ties* (1925), and *The Religion of Man* (1931).

and essays his sense of a possible modern Indian consciousness. His approach to the issues of modernity was not a grand strategy but, rather, a path of individual cultivation. For Tagore a realistic consciousness of the challenges and opportunities of the time can come only if the true nature of human beings is acknowledged and actions are carried out accordingly. Indian tradition provides a guide to the complexities of human nature and the behaviors needed for a harmonious and enlightening life. The needed learning is not something that can be acquired once and then stored away for future reference. It must be examined and extended throughout one's life. In this way of thinking, human beings must devote themselves to living the examined life. Tagore's thoughts remind us of this most central theme in the history of world philosophy.

SELECTION 16.1

# On African Socialism*

*Léopold Sédar Senghor*

[*Senghor attempts to delineate the Negro African way of thinking, feeling, speaking. He differentiates it from the abstract European way of thinking based on the Latin ratio (reason).*]

Let us then consider the Negro African as he faces the object to be known, as he faces the Other: God, man, animal, tree or pebble, natural or social phenomenon. In contrast to the classic European, the Negro African does not draw a line between himself and the object; he does not hold it at a distance, nor does he merely look at it and analyze it. After holding it at a distance, after scanning it without analyzing it, he takes it vibrant in his hands, careful not to kill or fix it. He touches it, feels it, *smells* it. The Negro African is like one of those Third Day Worms,[1] a pure field of sensations. Subjectively, at the tips of his sensory organs, his insect antennas, he discovered the Other. Immediately he is moved, going centrifugally from subject to object on the waves of the Other. This is more than a simple metaphor; contemporary physics has discovered universal energy under matter: waves and radiations. Thus the Negro African *sympathizes*,[2] abandons his personality to become identified with the Other, dies to be reborn in the Other. He does not assimilate; he is assimilated. He lives a common life with the Other; he lives in a symbiosis. To use Paul Claudel's [French diplomat, poet, and dramatist] expression, he "knows[3] the Other." Subject and object are di-

alectically face to face in the very act of knowledge. It is a long caress in the night, an embrace of joined bodies, the act of love. "I want you to feel me," says a voter who wants you to know him well. "I think, therefore I am," Descartes writes. The observation has already been made that one always thinks something, and the logician's conjunction "therefore" is unnecessary. The Negro African could say, "I feel, I dance the Other; I am." To dance is to discover and to re-create, especially when it is a dance of love. In any event, it is the best way to know. Just as knowledge is at once discovery and creation—I mean, re-creation and recreation, after the model of God.

Young people have criticized me for reducing Negro-African knowledge to pure emotion, for denying that there is an African "reason" or African techniques. This is the hub of the problem; I should like to explain my thought once again. Obviously, there is a European civilization and a Negro-African civilization. Anyone who has not explained their differences and the reasons for them has explained nothing and has left the problem untouched.

Thus, I explain myself. However paradoxical it may seem, the vital force of the Negro African, his surrender to the object, is animated by reason. Let us understand each other clearly; it is not the *reasoning-eye* of Europe, it is the *reason of the touch*, better still, the *reasoning-embrace*, the sympathetic reason, more closely related to the Greek *logos* than to the Latin *ratio*. For *logos*, before Aristotle, meant both reason and the word. At any rate, Negro-African speech does not mold the object into rigid categories and concepts without touching it; it polishes things and restores their original color, with their texture, sound, and perfume; it perforates

---

*From Léopold Sédar Senghor, *On African Socialism*, translated by Mercer Cook (New York: Praeger, 1964). Used by permission of Mercer Cook, Jr. and Jacques Cook.

[1] An allusion to the Age of Reptiles. [Trans.]

[2] In the French text, *sym-pathise*, literally, "feels with." [Trans.]

[3] Here again the word is separated, *con-naît*, literally, "is born with." [Trans.]

See Arthur Koestler, *The Lotus and the Robot* (New York: The Macmillan Co., 1961), p. 43:

The traditional Eastern way of looking at things is to deny that there *are* things independently from the act of looking. The objects of consciousness cannot be separated from the conscious subject; observer and observed are a single, indivisible,

fluid reality, as they are at the dawn of consciousness in the child, and in the cultures dominated by magic. The external world has no existence in its own right; it is a function of the senses; but that function exists only in so far as it is registered by consciousness, and consequently has no existence in its own right.

them with its luminous rays to reach the essential surreality in its innate humidity — it would be more accurate to speak of subreality. European reasoning is analytical, discursive by utilization; Negro-African reasoning is intuitive by participation.

Young people in Black Africa are wrong to develop a complex and to believe the latter inferior to the former. "The most beautiful emotion that we can experience," wrote the great scientist Einstein, "is mystic emotion. It is the germ of all art and all true science." To return to Negro-African speech, I refer you to two significant articles. The first, "Ethnologie de la parole," is by Maurice Leenhardt, the second, "Introduction à l'étude de la musique africaine," is by Geneviève Calame-Griaule and Blaise Calame. Leenhardt studies the New Caledonians, who are blacks; he contends that the New Caledonian meaning of the *word* is related to that of Negro Africans; the Calame article confirms this. For him, therefore, the black word, "uttered

under the shock of *emotion*" (my italics) surpasses that emotion. Coinciding with the real, it is not only an expression of knowledge, but knowledge itself, ready for action, already action. "The word," he concludes, "is thought, speech, action." Now you will understand why, in my definition of Negro-African knowledge, I rejected abstract analysis on the European pattern, why I preferred to use analogous imagery, the metaphor, to make you *feel* the object of my speech. The metaphor, a symbolic short-cut in its sensitive, sensual qualities, is the method par excellence of Negro-African speech.

Today, it is also, quite often, the style of European speech. . . . So, our young people should not repudiate the Negro-African method of knowledge since, once again, it is the latest form of the European method. *Participation* and *communion* . . . are the very words that ethnologists specializing in the study of Negro-African civilizations have used for decades.

---

SELECTION 16.2

## The Sword That Heals*

*Martin Luther King, Jr.*

---

[*King explains the power of nonviolent resistance in bringing about political justice as well as giving dignity, courage, and heart to those who practice it.*]

The argument that nonviolence is a coward's refuge lost its force as its heroic and often perilous acts uttered their wordless but convincing rebuttal in Montgomery, in the sit-ins, on the freedom rides, and finally in Birmingham.

There is a powerful motivation when a suppressed people enlist in an army that marches under the banner of nonviolence. A nonviolent army has a magnificent universal quality. To join an army that trains its adherents in the methods of violence, you must be of a certain age. But in Birmingham, some

of the most valued foot soldiers were youngsters ranging from elementary pupils to teen-age high school and college students. For acceptance in the armies that maim and kill, one must be physically sound, possessed of straight limbs and accurate vision. But in Birmingham, the lame and the halt and the crippled could and did join up. Al Hibbler, the sightless singer, would never have been accepted in the United States Army or the army of any other nation, but he held a commanding position in our ranks.

In armies of violence, there is a caste of rank. In Birmingham, outside of the few generals and lieutenants who necessarily directed and coordinated operations, the regiments of the demonstrators marched in democratic phalanx. Doctors marched with window cleaners. Lawyers demonstrated with laundresses. Ph.D.'s and no-D's were treated with perfect equality by the registrars of the nonviolence movement.

As the broadcasting profession will confirm, no shows are so successful as those which allow for

---

audience participation. In order to be somebody, people must feel themselves part of something. In the nonviolent army, there is room for everyone who wants to join up. There is no color distinction. There is no examination, no pledge, except that, as a soldier in the armies of violence is expected to inspect his carbine and keep it clean, nonviolent soldiers are called upon to examine and burnish their greatest weapons — their heart, their conscience, their courage and their sense of justice.

Nonviolent resistance paralyzed and confused the power structures against which it was directed. The brutality with which officials would have quelled the black individual became impotent when it could not be pursued with stealth and remain unobserved. It was caught — as a fugitive from a penitentiary is often caught — in gigantic circling spotlights. It was imprisoned in a luminous glare revealing the naked truth to the whole world. It is true that some demonstrators suffered violence, and that a few paid the extreme penalty of death. They were the martyrs of last summer who laid down their lives to put an end to the brutalizing of thousands who had been beaten and bruised and killed in dark streets and back rooms of sheriffs' offices, day in and day out, in hundreds of summers past.

The striking thing about the nonviolent crusade of 1963 was that so few felt the sting of bullets or the clubbing of billies and nightsticks. Looking back, it becomes obvious that the oppressors were restrained not only because the world was looking but also because, standing before them, were hundreds, sometimes thousands, of Negroes who for the first time dared to look back at a white man, eye to eye. Whether through a decision to exercise wise restraint or the operation of a guilty conscience, many

a hand was stayed on a police club and many a fire hose was restrained from vomiting forth its pressure. That the Revolution was a comparatively bloodless one is explained by the fact that the Negro did not merely give lip service to nonviolence. The tactics the movement utilized, and that guided far-flung actions in cities dotted across the map, discouraged violence because one side would not resort to it and the other was so often immobilized by confusion, uncertainty and disunity.

Nonviolence had tremendous psychological importance to the Negro. He had to win and to vindicate his dignity in order to merit and enjoy his self-esteem. He had to let white men know that the picture of him as a clown — irresponsible, resigned and believing in his own inferiority — was a stereotype with no validity. This method was grasped by the Negro masses because it embodied the dignity of struggle, of moral conviction and self-sacrifice. The Negro was able to face his adversary, to concede to him a physical advantage and to defeat him because the superior force of the oppressor had become powerless.

To measure what this meant to the Negro may not be easy. But I am convinced that the courage and discipline with which Negro thousands accepted nonviolence healed the internal wounds of Negro millions who did not themselves march in the streets or sit in the jails of the South. One need not participate directly in order to be involved. For Negroes all over this nation, to identify with the movement, to have pride in those who were the principals, and to give moral, financial or spiritual support were to restore to them some of the pride and honor which had been stripped from them over the centuries.

SELECTION 16.3

# Existentialism and the Crisis of Philosophy*

*Carlos Astrada*

[*Astrada explains the death of the concept of modern man that has dominated Western thinking since the Renaissance. He looks to a new ideal of the "whole man," first proposed by Max Scheler, that contains a notion of full humanity more relevant to our current age.*]

## Toward a New Image of Man

The rationalist concept of man is dogmatically constructed on the peripheries of concrete humanity, of individual historic man, and of vital reality. Over against this rationalist concept, a real, living image of man is being raised, an image with blood and viscera, with earthly fluids and air to breathe.

A new image of man, man conceived according to other necessities and purposes, necessarily presupposes a new social order, a new hierarchical order of values to which the historical sensitivity of the age gives allegiance. The concept of man of rationalist humanism with its parallel postulate of progressivism is embedded in all the instances and sectors wherein it was able to gain preeminence, but even now, it is dead, though still hauled around on a declining verbal rather than mental plane on which are placed all the survivors of individual liberalism and its residual doctrinaire expressions.

This type of man, purely rational, antihistorical, and anonymous, is a ghostlike entity that eludes reality and struggles along a retreating front against the great events the future is preparing. It cannot be ignored, however, that this image of man has reigned for almost three centuries in the cultural and political life of the West, having shown that in the past it was an efficient reagent in the multiple aspects of this life. However, for the past three decades, this image of man is in obvious decline. It is barely a vanishing shadow that those adrift in the historical present vainly attempt to seize.

The completed man, conceptually constructed by rationalist humanism, that is to say, the isolated, completed, purely ideal man, without roots in a specific soil, with no vital ties to a nationality, with no connections to an instinctive and emotional repertoire of historically conditioned preferences—such a man does not exist. Neither is there an essential equality of all men based solely on universal reason as a constant and unalterable factor that would act independently in the psycho-vital, historical reality of national communities, classes, and racial constellations.

Having surpassed it, we are also far beyond the pseudoantinomy of *individualism* and *collectivism*. Our age no longer knows the individual as a social atom nor over against him the collectivity, considered as an aggregation of such atoms and billed as the leading actor of social and political history. It does recognize, however, opposing classes whose struggle, undoubtedly, is the crux of the economic-social process. There is also a growing awareness of the concrete historical man, the man who, without turning loose the bonds and surroundings in which he is implicated, stands out as a personal, psycho-vital unit, who affirms and gives life to his humanity as a function of his real goals, which are immanent in his particular becoming.

## The Extinction of Modern Man

The unbalanced society of our age, especially the capitalist and mercantile commanders who are the possessors of political power, attempt in vain to live off the remains of the rationalist idea of man embodied in so-called "modern man," an image already in a state of dessication. These commanders are the crusty bark oppressing and retarding the buds of a new idea of man of great historical significance that have been germinating rapidly in the deeper levels of contemporary life. Suppressed forces that are emotionally and historically articulated by a generation destined to place its seal on the future give added thrust and life to this idea of man with which the coming generation will impose a new *ethos*, affirming a particular political will and instituting also a different scale of evaluation for the culture, economy, and society.

---

*From *Latin American Philosophy in the Twentieth Century*, ed. Jorge J. E. Gracia (Buffalo, NY: Prometheus Books, 1986). Reprinted by permission of Jorge J. E. Gracia.

*Modern man* is a cadaver that senescent human groups, adrift in the storm of these days, attempt vainly to galvanize, appealing to slogans and incantations that no longer have meaning. In a letter to Dilthey,[1] Count Yorck von Wartenburg said: "Modern man, the man who began with the Renaissance and has endured until our time, is ready to be buried."

This type man, the man of individualistic liberalism, the ultimate, valedictory expression of "modern man," imbued with vestiges of the rationalist ideals of the nineteenth century is the corpse to be buried. The present age is responsible for carrying out this task so the new man can cover the whole surface of history and thus affirm and give full meaning to the spiritual and political orders now germinating.

History has no compassion for values in decline nor for human types that are repositories of endangered sensibilities and ideals, inanimate modules of a destiny that has made its rounds and can no longer swell history with new hope or give it new impetus. History takes into its flow only the vital ascending force, the *ethos* in which a new message for men is given form, the promise of accomplishment that is the incentive for renewed effort. History — the matrix of all possibilities — yields itself only to those generations capable of engendering the fullness of a new age, that is, to that type of man capable of implanting an ascending meaning in history and of proposing to it new and valuable goals. . . .

## Sameness, Otherness, and *Humanitas*

To be sure, there is a realm of ends, norms, and values structured on an objective plane that transcends individual consciousness. One may also conceive and accept the effectiveness of an objective spirit as a structured whole that has emerged from the historical process, but this process is a far cry from being the domain of pure contingency and subjective irrationality. For it is precisely man's ability to establish an objective realm of the spirit that permits him, in each moment of his becoming, to be himself, to apprehend his own self-sameness.

While man aspires to fulfill himself in his being, to affirm himself in his humanity, to feel identical

with himself in each moment of temporal transition, the personal identity to which he aspires leads him to postulate time, a transcendence in the sense of otherness, as a guarantee of his identity and as the goal of his efforts. Stating this problem as a function of the finite-infinite, historicity-eternity antinomy, Kierkegaard tells us that man in his sameness, in his desired self-existence, always finds something, the Absolute, before which he is his own self-sameness.

While the sameness of man lives and exists, in the proper sense of these terms, through his becoming this sameness is bound to a concrete self-consciousness that, because it is expressed in temporality, is also becoming and thus never crystallizes, since there is no crystallizing in the existing man. This concrete self-consciousness gathers man into the lived experience of its own identity, anchored to the temporal structures of existence. This is because man, in everything (ideals, values, objective norms of life) toward which he transcends and projects himself from his concrete historicity — which is the ineradicable moment of his being, of his being made in time — in all this transcending, man searches only for himself, he attempts only to seal his identity in the midst of mutations and change, shaping it into a consistent and stable image of himself, into an idea of his "humanitas."

He now strives toward a new actualization of his being, a new image of himself. He aspires to actualize and conceive himself in all his immanent possibilities, to integrate himself with his potentialities, to reencounter himself, at last, in the full concretion of his essential humanity.

Magnetizing its thrust, which is historically conditioned and limited, the ideal of the *full man* — as proposed by Max Scheler — is lifted up as the goal that at the same time that it transcends pure becoming, receives from it its meaning, which is latent, to the degree it is *existential,* in the immanence of the temporal structure. Although "this full-man, in an absolute sense, is far from us, . . . a relatively whole-man, a maximum of full humanity, is accessible to each age."

For the concrete, existing man, this ideal of the whole-man as a goal and model is an index of transcendence, a mediating synthesis of all objective structures. These structures represent *the other,* not in the sense of the naturalist idea of being or of an absolute conceived as a personal God, but of an *other* that, as a transcending instance toward which

---

[1] Wilhelm Dilthey (1833–1911) was a German philosopher noted for his work in textual analysis and the history of ideas.

what is human is projected, permits man in each moment and stage of his temporal passing to know his concrete sameness. It is the apparently fixed limit that as an ideal point of reference hovers above

historical becoming. Ultimately, however, existence activates and gives meaning to historical becoming, for existence historically determines and actualizes the humanity in man.

SELECTION 16.4

# Man without
# Theory★

*Francisco Miró Quesada*

[*Quesada reviews many of the pitfalls in trying to frame a theory as to what constitutes a human being. Nonetheless, he concludes that humans must voice their beliefs about the world and about human nature, albeit without presupposing any certain theoretical axioms.*]

The history of humanity is an impressive succession of complicated, yet false theories that man has woven around himself. Along the millennial pathway of history, theories lay semidestroyed and rusted like military equipment left behind by an army in retreat. Each great theoretical crisis, each great change, each new development marks the shift from one culture to another, from one age to another. In earlier days men were not sufficiently aware of what was happening, although they were aware that something was happening and expectantly waited the new. At times their desires were implemented in a conscious, more or less rapid manner. At other times, however, the restructuring process lasted centuries. Intuitively men grasped the significance of the situation, but the mechanism for restructuring was not grasped for two reasons: the lack of historical consciousness, that is, awareness of the relationship between their world view and historic era, and the lack of understanding of what a theory is. In the nineteenth century a great movement began that culminated in our day and overcame both limitations. For this reason, in the present, in this modern, troubled atomic era, the era of the machine and technology, we are aware nevertheless of what is really happening. We have a clear

understanding that history is a succession of ways of conceiving the world and man, of ways considered absolute by men of different ages but that today are no more than vague shadows, difficult to understand. Our civilization, therefore, is the most philosophical of all, because none has had as clear an awareness of its limitation and relativity. In truth, our age is characteristically an age of search, of disorientation, and of acute consciousness of its negative traits. Contemporary man is one who experiences in his own flesh the failure of a great theory concerning himself: European rationalism, in all its facets, from the liberalism of "laissez faire" to Nazism and Marxism. Ortega has said of our age that it is an "age of disillusioned living," but to be more precise we should say, "an age of disillusioned theorizing." Scheler begins one of his books, perhaps his best, with the celebrated phrase, "Never has man been such an enigma to himself."

Given this situation the inevitable question is "What shall we do?" The depth of the question does permit a dogmatic answer. Indeed, perhaps this essay should end here. However, to be human means to try unceasingly to overcome every "non plus ultra" and since we do not wish to deny our human condition, we have no alternative but to forge ahead. Yet, before continuing we wish to emphasize that what follows is no more than the point of view of a particular individual who, along with all other individuals in this age, is faced with an immense problem that by its very nature transcends any purely individual response.

The first thought that might come to mind, and perhaps a majority already favors it, is to commit our efforts to the reconstruction of the old theory, making it more comprehensive and adapting it to

★From *Latin American Philosophy in the Twentieth Century,* ed. Jorge J. E. Gracia (Buffalo, NY: Prometheus Books, 1986). Reprinted by permission of Jorge J. E. Gracia.

the demands of our modern circumstance. Or, should this not be possible, to elaborate a new theory that may or may not be related to the old or to earlier theories, but would constitute an organic system, capable of providing answers to the most pressing questions and have the scope and flexibility necessary to permit men of our day to work with the total range of their problems. In actual experience, the normal or spontaneous attitude always develops a theory. So we, although disillusioned by theories, in seeing ourselves in a bind, think of amplifying or creating theories, like men of other ages. In this day, however, there is a difference: men of previous ages were not aware of the relativity or limits of their theories, nor of the horrible dangers implicit in creating a complicated theory concerning man from which "unforeseeable and mortal consequences were derived. Furthermore, they did not suspect that their theories ran the same risks as all preceding theories. Therefore they created under illusion, but in faith, and so their theories had "vital force" and served to resolve human problems since men believed in them and were convinced that all previous ages had been in error whereas they were in the truth. In this day, however, we are not convinced our position is unique, true, or definitive. Indeed, we know that whatever we do, our theory about man will suffer the same end as the others.

Yet, instead of searching for a new theory and instinctively following the destiny of Sisyphus, what if we assume a completely different attitude? Instead of inventing a new and dangerous theory, why not simply give up formulating theories about ourselves? Now this proposal may well produce a scandal and for two good reasons. First, because man is so accustomed to formulating theories about himself, to taking for granted that he knows what he is, to feeling himself at the helm of a world of structures and hierarchies, to renounce theory leaves him with the impression that he is giving up the possibility of finding solutions, that he is spineless and morally decadent, that he has given up the struggle for good and against evil. Second, because it is believed, more for theoretical than practical considerations, that no matter what man does he is condemned to theorize and that he can give up everything except formulating a complete concept of the world, of things, and of himself. It is believed that man needs theory to live, that without it he flounders and does not know what to hold on to, he is a lost soul on a ship without a rudder. For, although he may deny theory, implicitly he is always constructing a system of concepts for clarifying the meaning of his life.

To be sure, this second argument is much more powerful than the first. Its strength, however, lies in its inclusive breadth, for its detailed analysis of situations is slipshod. For example, if one analyzes all the elements constituting the world within which man includes himself, one sees there are various dimensions. One dimension is the surrounding world. This dimension, naturally, is undeniable. If man does not possess a well-formulated theory concerning the surrounding world he is not even able to walk down the street. The simple act of dodging an automobile indicates the possession of a rather clear concept of the principles of causality and the laws of dynamics. Further, our cultural crisis is not a crisis in knowledge of the natural world. The cosmic world, our surrounding environment, is known with increasingly greater certainty and vigor. It is perhaps the only part of our general vision of the world that at present follows a linear evolution. We have reached such a comprehension of what physical theory is, that the elaboration of that type theory is carried out in the awareness that in time it will be surpassed, and that it will be necessary to amplify it to include new facts. For this reason, it is possible that the nuclear emphasis of the old theory may be preserved intact and that it may be possible to consider it as a special case of a new theory. Some might believe that this procedure is applicable to the theory about the nature of man. However, given the complexity of all anthropological theory, this is not possible. Physical as well as mathematical theories are very simple, since they are based on broad abstractive processes. Therefore, this approach is not adequate for anthropological theory. But if we do not make use of it, we encounter the earlier objection, namely, that every theory concerning the surrounding world presupposes an integrated theory of the human being. And here we come to the crux of the issue. For, if this affirmation is true, then we will never be able to free ourselves from a theory concerning ourselves and we will always return to that monotonous, well-beaten path. This, however, we believe to be false, because even though it is undeniable that every theory concerning the cosmos presupposes a theory concerning man, it does not presuppose necessarily that the theory of the cosmos is complete. In order to grant validity to a theory about the cosmos, we must presuppose certain epistemological postulates, certain beliefs concerning the structure and organization of our consciousness, but in no way does such a theory necessarily include hypotheses about the moral life or destiny of man. The most to be said is that from these epistemological presuppositions, one can derive many consequences as to the possibilities of knowing the world in general and even ourselves and that these consequences may be positive or negative in some or in many aspects. However, this does not invalidate our point of view because what we are specifically trying to do is place brackets around our cognitive faculties insofar as these are applied to ourselves.

However, man is so accustomed to living on the theoretical level that he does not conceive the possibility of refraining from decisions about his own nature and fundamental relationships with the surrounding world. Thus he always finds arguments that justify his use of theories. In the present case, those who deny the possibility of avoiding theory about man adduce that this avoidance is impossible because determining one's orientation in the world without language is impossible. To establish interhuman communication, whatever it may be, is impossible without speech, but speech is in itself a theory. The philosophical analysis of language shows unequivocally that every expressive system acquires its ultimate meaning from theoretical presuppositions about the nature of the world and of man. Thus the very possibility of language implies the immersion of the human being in a complete theory concerning himself, a theory that refers not only to his objective relationship with the environing world, but also to his norms of action and destiny. Philological analysis of the most trivial words reveals, in a surprising way at times, the immense background of cosmological, metaphysical, and ethical theory upon which all possible language rests. The argument, then, would seem to be definitive: man cannot live without an orientation in the world and to seek an orientation in the world requires a specific theory concerning the physical structure of the cosmos. This theory, however, cannot be elaborated without language, but language is the great, universal theory, the expression of what in the ultimate, collective, anonymous, and therefore inevitable sense man believes about the world and himself. Thus, it is impossible to live as a human being without presupposing certain theoretical axioms concerning our nature and our destiny.

## SELECTION 16.5

# Feminism on the Border: From Gender Politics to Geopolitics*

*Sonia Saldívar-Hull*

[*In this selection, Sonia Saldívar-Hull expresses her belief that feminism as found in First World countries oppresses and exploits Third World women. She also notes that, in her opinion, some "Third World feminists" are really agents of patriarch, capitalism, and imperialism.*]

Is it possible for Chicanas to consider ourselves part of this "sisterhood" called feminism? Can we assume that our specific interests and problems will

*Excerpts from Sonia Saldívar-Hull, "Feminism on the Border: From Gender Politics to Geopolitics," in *Criticism in the Borderlands: Studies in Chicano Literature, Culture, and Ideology,* ed. David Saldívar, pp. 203–220. Copyright © 1991 Duke University Press. All rights reserved. Used by permission of the publisher.

be taken care of by our Marxist compañeros? In her essay, "Feminism, Marxism, Method, and the State," Catherine MacKinnon decrees that "[s]exuality is to feminism what work is to marxism: that which is most one's own yet most taken away" (1982, 515). MacKinnon argues that while we can draw parallels between Marxist and feminist methodologies, we must remember not to conflate these two "theories of power and its distribution" (1982, 516), that one theory must not be subsumed into the other. . . .

But to the Chicana, a woman with a specific history under racial and sexual and class exploitation, it is essential that we further problematize the feminist/Marxist discussion by adding the complication of race and ethnicity. Our feminist sisters and

Marxist compañeros/as urge us to take care of gender and class issues first and race will naturally take care of itself. Even MacKinnon, as thorough as she is, constantly watching that she herself does not recreate a monolithic "woman," uses footnotes to qualify the difference between the white woman's and the black woman's situations. . . .

My project . . . does insist, however, that our white feminist "sisters" recognize their own blind spots. When MacKinnon uses the black woman as her sign for all dispossessed women, we see the extent to which Chicanas, Asian-American, Native American, or Puerto Rican women, for example, have been rendered invisible in a discourse whose explicit agenda is to expose ideological erasure. Chicana readings of color *blindness* instead of color consciousness in "politically correct" feminist essays indicate the extent to which the issues of race and ethnicity are ignored in feminist and Marxist theories. . . .

As Chicanas making our works public — publishing in marginalized journals and small, underfinanced presses and taking part in conferences and workshops — we realize that the "sisterhood" called feminism professes an ideology that at times comes dangerously close to the phallocentric ideologies of the white male power structure against which feminists struggle. In her essay, "Ethnicity, Ideology, and Academia," Rosaura Sánchez reminds us of the ideological strategies that the dominant culture manipulates in order to mystify "the relation between minority cultures and the dominant culture" (1987, 80). She points out that U.S. cultural imperialism extends beyond the geopolitical borders of the country, "but being affected, influenced, and exploited by a culture is one thing and sharing fully in that culture is another" (1987, 81). If we extend the analogy to feminism and the totalizing concept of sisterhood, we begin to understand how the specific interests of Anglo-American and other European feminists tend to erase the existence of Chicana, Puerto Rican, Native American, Asian-American, and other Third World feminists. Indeed, feminism affects and influences Chicana writers and critics, but feminism as practiced by women of the hegemonic culture oppresses and exploits the Chicana in both subtle and obvious ways.

When white feminists begin to categorize the different types of feminisms, we in turn can begin to trace the muting of issues of race and ethnicity under other feminist priorities. Elaine Showalter in *A Literature of Their Own* charts the "stages" of writing by women into the categories of "feminine, feminist, and female" (1977, 13). She first establishes that *all* "literary subcultures, such as black, Jewish, Canadian, Anglo-Indian, or even American," go through phases of imitation, internalization, protest, and finally self-discovery (1977, 13). In addition to the misrepresentation of what "literary subcultures" write, Showalter creates an ethnocentric, Eurocentric, middle-class history of women's writing. . . .

In our search for a feminist critical discourse that adequately takes into account our position as women under multiple oppressions we must turn to our own "organic intellectuals." But because our work has been ignored by the men and women in charge of the modes of cultural production, we must be innovative in our search. Hegemony has so constructed the idea of method and theory that often we cannot recognize anything that is different from what the dominant discourse constructs. We have to look in nontraditional places for our theories: in the prefaces to anthologies, in the interstices of autobiographies, in our cultural artifacts, our *cuentos,* and if we are fortunate to have access to a good library, in the essays published in marginalized journals not widely distributed by the dominant institutions. . . .

In the same way that we must break with traditional (hegemonic) concepts of genre to read Chicana feminist theory, working-class women of color in other Third World countries articulate their feminisms in nontraditional ways and forms. The Chicana feminist acknowledges the often vast historical, class, racial, and ethnic differences among women living on the border, but the nature of hegemony practiced by the united powers of patriarchy, capitalism, imperialism, and white supremacy promotes an illusion of an irreconcilable split between feminists confined within national borders. We must examine and question the First versus Third World dichotomy before we accept the opposition as an inevitable fissure that separates women politically committed in different ways from any common cause.

In her testimony, *Let Me Speak* (1978), Bolivian activist Domitila Barrios de Chungara acknowledges the separation between "First" and "Third" World feminists: "Our Position is not like the feminists' position. We think our liberation consists primarily in our country being freed forever from the yoke of imperialism and we want a worker like us to be in power and that the laws, education, everything, be controlled by this person. Then, yes, we'll have better conditions for reaching a complete liberation, including a liberation as women" (Barrios 1978, 41). Her statement, however, is problematized by her occasion for speaking. As a participant at the UN-sponsored International Year of the Woman Conference held in Mexico City in 1975, Barrios witnessed co-optation of "feminism" by governments which use women and women's issues to promote their own political agendas. Barrios observed Imelda Marcos, Princess Ashraf Pahlevi, and Jihan Sadat as some of the conference's "official" Third World representatives. We begin to reformulate the dichotomy when we no longer choose to see these representatives as "Third World feminists," but as agents of their respective governments: agents of patriarchy, capitalism, and imperialism. Suddenly the First World/Third World dichotomy emerges as the arena where the split between the ruling class and the working class, between those in power and the disenfranchised, is exposed.

## SELECTION 16.6
## *Satyagraha*★                         *Mohandas K. Gandhi*

[*Gandhi seeks to explain his principle of social change, namely,* satyagraha, *as a truth-force and love-force. It is more than mere passive resistance and nonviolence. Through patience and self-suffering, it is a vindication and an insistence upon the truth by way of civil disobedience.*]

### 3: Satyagraha

For the past thirty years I have been preaching and practicing Satyagraha. The principles of Satyagraha, as I know it today, constitute a gradual evolution.

Satyagraha differs from Passive Resistance as the North Pole from the South. The latter has been conceived as a weapon of the weak and does not exclude the use of physical force or violence for the purpose of gaining one's end, whereas the former has been conceived as a weapon of the strongest and excludes the use of violence in any shape or form.

The term *Satyagraha* was coined by me in South Africa to express the force that the Indians there used for full eight years and it was coined in order to distinguish it from the movement then going on in the United Kingdom and South Africa under the name of Passive Resistance.

Its root meaning is holding on to truth, hence truth-force. I have also called it Love-force or Soul-force. In the application of Satyagraha I discovered in the earliest stages that pursuit of truth did not admit of violence being inflicted on one's opponent but that he must be weaned from error by patience and sympathy. For what appears to be truth to the one may appear to be error to the other. And patience means self-suffering. So the doctrine came to mean vindication of truth not by infliction of suffering on the opponent but on one's self.

But on the political field the struggle on behalf of the people mostly consists in opposing error in the shape of unjust laws. When you have failed to bring the error home to the law-giver by way of petitions and the like, the only remedy open to you, if you do not wish to submit to error, is to compel him by physical force to yield to you or by suffering in your own person by inviting the penalty for the breach of the law. Hence Satyagraha largely appears to the public as Civil Disobedience or Civil Resistance. It is civil in the sense that it is not criminal.

The lawbreaker breaks the law surreptitiously and tries to avoid the penalty, not so the civil resister. He ever obeys the laws of the State to which he belongs, not out of fear of the sanctions but

★ From *Non-Violent Resistance* by M. K. Gandhi. Copyright © 1951 by The Navajivan Trust. Reprinted by permission of the Navajivan Trust.

because he considers them to be good for the welfare of society. But there come occasions, generally rare, when he considers certain laws to be so unjust as to render obedience to them a dishonour. He then openly and civilly breaks them and quietly suffers the penalty for their breach. And in order to register his protest against the action of the law givers, it is open to him to withdraw his co-operation from the State by disobeying such other laws whose breach does not involve moral turpitude.

In my opinion, the beauty and efficacy of Satyagraha are so great and the doctrine so simple that it can be preached even to children. It was preached by me to thousands of men, women and children commonly called indentured Indians with excellent results. . . .

### 7: The Theory and Practice of Satyagraha

Carried out to its utmost limit, Satyagraha is independent of pecuniary or other material assistance; certainly, even in its elementary form, of physical force or violence. Indeed, violence is the negation of this great spiritual force, which can only be cultivated or wielded by those who will entirely eschew violence. It is a force that may be used by individuals as well as by communities. It may be used as well in political as in domestic affairs. Its universal applicability is a demonstration of its permanence and invincibility. It can be used alike by men, women and children. It is totally untrue to say that it is a force to be used only by the weak so long as they are not capable of meeting violence by violence. This superstition arises from the incompleteness of the English expression, *passive resistance*. It is impossible for those who consider themselves to be weak to apply this force. Only those who realize that there is something in man which is superior to the brute nature in him and that the latter always yields to it, can effectively be Satyagrahis. This force is to violence, and, therefore, to all tyranny, all injustice, what light is to darkness. In politics, its use is based upon the immutable maxim, that government of the people is possible only so long as they consent either consciously or unconsciously to be governed. We did not want to be governed by the Asiatic Act of 1907 of the Transvaal, and it had to go before this mighty force. Two courses were open to us: to use violence when we were called upon to submit to the Act, or to suffer the penalties prescribed under the Act, and thus to draw out and exhibit the force of the soul within us for a period long enough to appeal to the sympathetic chord in the governors or the law-makers. We have taken long to achieve what we set about striving for. That was because our Satyagraha was not of the most complete type. All Satyagrahis do not understand the full value of the force, nor have we men who always from conviction refrain from violence. The use of this force requires the adoption of poverty, in the sense that we must be indifferent whether we have the wherewithal to feed or clothe ourselves. During the past struggle, all Satyagrahis, if any at all, were not prepared to go that length. Some again were only Satyagrahis so called. They came without any conviction, often with mixed motives, less often with impure motives. Some even, whilst engaged in the struggle, would gladly have resorted to violence but for most vigilant supervision. Thus it was that the struggle became prolonged; for the exercise of the purest soul-force, in its perfect form, brings about instantaneous relief. For this exercise, prolonged training of the individual soul is an absolute necessity, so that a perfect Satyagrahi has to be almost, if not entirely, a perfect man. We cannot all suddenly become such men, but if my proposition is correct — as I know it to be correct — the greater the spirit of Satyagraha in us, the better men will we become. Its use, therefore, is, I think, indisputable, and it is a force, which, if it became universal, would revolutionize social ideals and do away with despotisms and the ever-growing militarism under which the nations of the West are groaning and are being almost crushed to death, and which fairly promises to overwhelm even the nations of the East. If the past struggle has produced even a few Indians who would dedicate themselves to the task of becoming Satyagrahis as nearly perfect as possible, they would not only have served themselves in the truest sense of the term, they would also have served humanity at large. Thus viewed, Satyagraha is the noblest and best education. It should come, not after the ordinary education in letters, of children, but it should precede it. It will not be denied, that a child, before it begins to write its alphabet and to gain worldly knowledge, should know what the soul is, what truth is, what love is, what powers are latent in the soul. It should be an essential of real education that a child should learn, that in the struggle of life, it can easily conquer hate by love, untruth by truth, violence by self-suffering.

SELECTION 16.7

# Towards Universal Man*

*Rabindranath Tagore*

[*Tagore seeks an alternative view of the human being to the Western notion of the survival of the fittest. In its place he would put the notion that human life is a spiritual journey toward self-emancipation and a rebirth into the infinite.*]

The flesh is impure, the world is vanity, and stern renunciation is the way to salvation — that was the ideal of spiritual life held forth in medieval Europe. Modern Europe, however, considers it unwholesome to admit an everlasting feud between the human world of natural desires and social aims on one hand and the spiritual life with its aspirations and discipline on the other. According to her, we enfeeble the moral purpose of our existence if we put too much stress on the illusoriness of this world. To drop down dead in the race-course of life, while running at full speed — that is acclaimed as the most glorious death.

Europe, it is true, has gained a certain strength by pinning her faith onto the world, by refusing to dwell on its evanescence and condemning the preoccupation with death as morbid. Her children are trained up in the struggle which, as science says, is for the survival of the fittest. That, Europe seems to think, is the whole meaning of life. But then, whatever the practical value of such a philosophy of living, the fact remains that our connection with the world is far from permanent.

Nature, for its own biological purposes, has created in us a strong faith in life by keeping us unmindful of death. Nevertheless, not only does our physical existence end, but all that it had built up goes to pieces at the peak of achievement. The greatest prosperity dissolves into emptiness; the mightiest empire is overtaken by stupor amidst the flicker of its festive lights. We may be weary of this truism, but it is true none the less. Therefore, all our actions have to be judged according to their harmony with life's background, the background which is death.

And yet it is equally true that, though all our mortal relationships must end, we cannot ignore them while they last. If we behave as if they do not exist, merely because they will not persist, they will all the same exact their dues, with a great deal over by way of penalty. We cannot claim exemption from payment of fare because the railway train has not the permanence of the dwelling house. Trying to ignore bonds that are real even if temporary, only strengthens and prolongs the bondage.

That is why the spirit of attachment and that of detachment have to be reconciled in harmony, and then only will they lead us to fulfilment. Attachment is the force drawing us to truth in its finite aspect, the aspect of what is, while detachment leads us to freedom in the infinity of truth which is the ideal aspect. In the act of walking, attachment is in the step that the foot takes when it touches the earth; detachment is in the movement of the other foot when it raises itself. The harmony of bondage and freedom is the dance of creation. According to the symbolism of Indian thought, Shiva, the male principle of Truth, represents freedom of the spirit, while Shivani, the female principle, represents the bonds of the material. In their union dwells perfection.

In order to reconcile these opposites, we must come to a true understanding of man; that is, we must not reduce him to the requirements of any particular duty. To look on trees only as firewood, is not to know the tree in its entirety; and to look on man merely as the protector of his country or the producer of its wealth, is to reduce him to soldier or merchant or diplomat, to make his efficacy the measure of his manhood. Such a narrow view is hurtful; those whom we seek to invest with glory are in fact degraded.

How India once looked on man as greater than any purpose he could serve, is revealed in an ancient Sanskrit couplet which may be translated thus:

For the family, sacrifice the individual;
For the community, the family;

For the country, the community;
For the soul, all the world.

A question will be asked: "What is this soul?" Let us first try to answer a much simpler question: "What is life?" Certainly life is not merely the facts of living that are evident to us, the breathing, digesting and various other functions of the body; not even the principle of unity which comprehends them. In a mysterious manner it holds within itself a future which continually reaches from the envelopment of the present, dealing with unforeseen circumstances, experimenting with new variations. If dead materials choke the path of its ever-unfolding future, then life becomes a traitor that betrays its trust.

The soul is our spiritual life and it contains our infinity within it. It has an impulse that urges our consciousness to break through the dimly lighted walls of animal life where our turbulent passions fight to gain mastery in a narrow enclosure. Though, like animals, man is dominated by his self, he has an instinct that struggles against it, like the rebel life within a seed that breaks through the dark prison, bringing out its flag of freedom to the realm of light. Our sages in the East have always maintained that self-emancipation is the highest form of freedom for man, since it is his fulfilment in the heart of the Eternal, and not merely a reward won through some process of what is called salvation. . . .

Renounce we must, and through renunciation gain — that is the truth of the inner world. The flower must shed its petals for the sake of fruition, the fruit must drop off for the rebirth of the tree. The child leaves the refuge of the womb in order to achieve further growth of body and mind; next, he has to leave the self-centered security of a narrow world to enter a fuller life which has varied relations with the multitude; lastly comes the decline of the body, and enriched with experience man should now leave the narrower life for the universal life, to which he must dedicate his accumulated wisdom on the one hand and on the other, enter into relationship with the Life Eternal; so that, when finally the decaying body has come to the very end of its tether, the soul views its breaking away quite simply and without regret, in the expectation of its own rebirth into the infinite.

From individual body to community, from community to universe, from universe to Infinity — this is the soul's normal progress.

---

## CHECKLIST

To help you review, here is a checklist of the key philosophers and terms and concepts of this chapter. The brief descriptive sentences summarize the philosophers' leading ideas. Keep in mind that some of these summary statements are oversimplifications of complex positions.

### Philosophers

- **Léopold Sédar Senghor**   was president of Senegal, a poet, and a philosopher. He formulated the concept of negritude, which asserts an essential uniqueness in African cultures that explains certain historical phenomena and determines an African way of understanding.

- **Desmond Tutu**   is a South African Anglican bishop who provided significant spiritual and moral leadership in the successful struggle against apartheid.

- **Martin Luther King, Jr.,**   led the African American drive for equal civil rights. His non-violent methods were influenced by the teachings of Mohandas Gandhi and were embraced by a majority of his constituents.

- **bell hooks**   is a contemporary American essayist known for, among other things, her critical analysis of types of feminism that fail to do justice to the needs of minority women.

- **Chaikh Anta Diop**   was an important Africanist who argued that black Africa was the origin of Egyptian civilization.

- **Cornel West,**   an African American scholar active in theology and philosophy, is best known for his analysis of depth dimensions of racial issues.

- **Carlos Astrada**   is an Argentinian philosopher whose early work in existential phenomenology transitioned into a deeply felt commitment to Marxist politics.

- **Francisco Miró Quesada,**   a Peruvian philosopher with degrees in mathematics, philosophy, and law, is noted for his work in theory of knowledge and political theory, which avoids metaphysical solutions to problems.

- **Mohandas (Mahatma) Gandhi** was the twentieth century's greatest theorist of nonviolence and the architect of India's independence from Great Britain.

- **Rabindranath Tagore,** an Indian poet and essayist, winner of the 1913 Nobel Prize for literature, united a sense of Indian tradition with a vision of how India might adapt to the changing conditions of the modern world.

## *Key Terms and Concepts*

*Note:* Many of the terms listed below have a variety of meanings, but the authors of the readings use them in specific ways that you should be able to discuss.

| | |
|---|---|
| historiography | liberation |
| Pan-African | Afrocentrism |
|   philosophy | ideology |
| person | *satyagraha* |
| negritude | |

## QUESTIONS FOR DISCUSSION AND REVIEW

1. Is a person only a body? Can you think of two alternative understandings of what is essential to a person?

2. Does one need to appeal to a supernaturally determined standard to demonstrate that an act is good or at least permissible? Why or why not?

3. Should philosophy concern itself with practical matters?

4. What difference would it make for people in various disciplines to study epistemology along with their particular subjects?

5. Is it reasonable for a philosopher to hold to a particular ideology? Is it possible for anyone not to have an ideology?

6. Should philosophy be done the same way in all cultures?

7. Is truth simply a matter of personal belief? Why does the answer to this question matter at all?

8. If Country A invades Country B, do the inhabitants of Country B have the right (or even the responsibility) to harass or kill any citizen of Country A they encounter?

9. If you believed that establishing an American colonial government in some country in South America would benefit the native peoples and help save the rain forests, would you have a responsibility to support colonialism under those circumstances?

10. What does Senghor mean by the phrase "sympathetic reason"?

11. Can a set of explained but otherwise unargued claims about life count as philosophy? Why or why not?

12. It is sometimes said that people who live in different cultures live in different worlds. What philosophical issues arise when people from "different worlds" find themselves in the same physical space?

13. Why would a physically stronger adversary refrain from destroying a nonviolent opponent? Try to avoid purely strategic considerations; instead, specifically address philosophical issues such as personal identity (or being), ethics, political philosophy, and so forth.

14. Can there be experience without interpretation?

15. What might it mean to me if I were to learn that many people speak of me in categories that I would not use to speak of myself?

16. Is there such a thing as a fixed human nature? Or does human nature change with historical circumstances?

17. Can people live without theories and principles? If you say "yes," then what determines what one does at any moment? If you say "no," then what is the proper role of theories and abstract principles in the conduct of daily life?

18. Should people who believe in political organization as a way for their group to increase its power participate in empowering members of their group with whom they have serious disagreements? For example, should middle-class Anglo feminists, most of whom believe in the right to abortion, help to empower Chicanas,

many of whom probably do not believe in
such a right?

19. Can religious claims be the basis of a philosophical position?

20. Could traditional modes of spirituality be an
important or even essential element in overcoming colonialist reductionism that persists
in a culture even after a people has regained
its autonomy? Or should traditional ways of
thinking be avoided in postcolonial reconstruction because following them opened up
the people to conquest from the outside in the
first place?

## SUGGESTED FURTHER READINGS

Jacqueline Andall, *Gender and Ethnicity in Contemporary Europe* (New York: Berg, 2003). This reader
attempts to link ethnic issues with the process of
feminization.

Aurobindo Ghose (Sri Aurobindo), *The Essential
Aurobindo*, Robert A. McDermott, ed. (New York:
Schocken Books, 1973). Selected writings of a
thinker whose career began with radical political
activism and concluded as a worldwide spiritual
mission.

John A. A. Ayoade, "Time in Yoruba Thought," in
*African Philosophy: An Introduction*, Richard A.
Wright, ed. (Washington, D.C.: University Press of
America, 1984). Analysis of assumptions and impli-
cations relevant to Yoruba metaphysics.

James Baldwin, *No Name in the Street* (New York: Dial
Press, 1972). Analysis of social and philosophical is-
sues in late-twentieth-century America from an
African American perspective.

P. O. Bodunrin, ed., *Philosophy in Africa* (Ile-Ife, Nige-
ria: University of Ife Press, 1985). Collection of readings on various aspects of African philosophy.

Fidel Castro, *History Will Absolve Me*, Robert Taber,
trans. (New York: Lyle Stuart, 1961). The full text
of Castro's defense at his 1953 trial for conspiracy
and armed insurrection.

Chaikh Anta Diop, *The African Origin of Civilization*,
Mercer Cook, ed. and trans. (Westport, Conn.:
Lawrence Hill & Co., 1974). The most thorough
argument to date for the claim that a great portion
of European thought traces back to black Africa.

W. E. B. Du Bois, *The Souls of Black Folk* (Millwood,
N.Y.: Kraus-Thomson Organization, 1973).
Groundbreaking social analysis from early in the
twentieth century that has become a classic.

Emmanuel Chukwudi Eze, *African Philosophy* (Malden,
Mass.: Blackwell, 2000). An anthology of readings
from African thinkers on a broad range of subjects.

Emmanuel Chukwudi Eze, ed. *African Philosophy. An
Anthology* (Malden, Mass.: Blackwell, 1997). A selection of important philosophical writings from
African, African American, Afro-Caribbean, and
black European thinkers.

Gustavo Gutierrez, *Liberation and Change* (Atlanta, Ga.:
John Knox Press, 1977). A leading liberation theologian explains what sorts of spiritual and intellectual
changes are needed to translate the desire for social
justice into reality.

Kwame Gyekye, "Akan Concept of a Person," in *African
Philosophy*, Richard Wright, ed. (Lanham, Md.: University Press of America, 1984). A widely respected
voice in African philosophy uses analytic and comparative methods to explain a key metaphysical
category.

J. Newton Hill, "African Sculpture," in *Africa from the
Point of View of American Negro Scholars* (New York:
American Society of African Culture, 1963). Focused on examples of sculpture in a single collection,
this essay includes valuable insights into African
aesthetics.

Paulin J. Hountondji, *African Philosophy* (Bloomington:
Indiana University Press, 1983). Represents the position that African philosophy should be intentionally
situated as an element of a worldwide philosophical
conversation.

Homer A. Jack, *The Gandhi Reader* (Twin Lakes,
Wis.: Lotus Press, 1984). A collection of writings by
Gandhi on self-restraint, nonviolent resistance, education, the emancipation of women, and many other
subjects.

Miguel Jorrín and John D. Martz, *Latin American Political Thought and Ideology* (Chapel Hill: University
of North Carolina Press, 1970). Fleshes out the intellectual context of Latin American postcolonial
thought.

Lacinay Keita, "The African Philosophical Tradition,"
in *African Philosophy*, Richard Wright, ed. (Lanham,
Md.: University Press of America, 1984). Sketches
connections of African thought with European and
Islamic philosophical traditions from ancient to modern times.

Mao Tse-tung, *Selected Works* (New York: International
Publishing, 1954). Mao's early thinking on social and
political issues is presented without coloration from
the Cultural Revolution of his last decades.

John S. Mbiti, *African Religions and Philosophy* (London:
Heinemann, 1988). General survey of African

thought encompassing both traditional and more recent perspectives.

Jawaharlal Nehru, *India's Freedom* (New York: Barnes & Noble, 1962). Selections from the writings of the first prime minister of independent India, who was Gandhi's closest disciple.

Kwame Nkrumah, *Revolutionary Path* (New York: International Publishers, 1973). A collection of essays in which the former president of Ghana explains and justifies his plans for a Pan-African socialist program.

Arturo Andrés Roig, *The Actual Function of Philosophy,* C. Schofield, trans., excerpted in Jorge J. E. Gracia, ed., *Latin American Philosophy in the Twentieth Century* (Buffalo, N.Y.: Prometheus, 1986). Critical appraisal of major threads in twentieth-century Latin philosophy.

Henry Schwartz and Sangeeta Ray, eds., *A Companion to Postcolonial Studies* (Malden, Mass.: Blackwell, 2000). Original essays from leading thinkers of postcolonial study in the Americas, Europe, India, Africa, East and West Asia.

Tsenay Serequeberhan, *African Philosophy: The Essential Readings* (New York: Paragon House, 1991). General readings in modern African thought.

Gayatri Chakravorty Spivak, *The Post-Colonial Critic: Interviews, Strategies, Dialogues,* Sarah Harasym, ed. (New York: Routledge, Chapman, and Hall, 1990). Uses concepts from recent political and literature theory to enhance understanding of ethnic and gender issues in postcolonial thought.

Placide Tempels, *Bantu Philosophy* (Paris: Présence Africaine, 1969). Controversial groundbreaking attempt to situate the ideas of an African people typologically in the history of ideas.

Arnold Temu and Bonaventure Swai, *Historians and Africanist History: A Critique* (London: Zed Press, 1981). Detailed exposition of theoretical and critical issues in the construction of postcolonial historiography.

UNESCO, *Teaching and Research in Philosophy: Africa* (Paris: United Nations Scientific and Cultural Organization, 1984). A collection of essays surveying the organization and content of philosophy instruction in Africa and arguing for future emphases and directions.

Kwasi Wiredu, *Philosophy and an African Culture* (New York: Cambridge University Press, 1980). Discussion of traditional philosophical problems from an analytic perspective.

Malcolm X, *The Autobiography of Malcolm X* (New York: Ballantyne, 1964). Traces the development of a thinker who demonstrates the dynamic nature of critical consciousness through an account of his life from childhood up to his assassination.

# Appendix
## Philosophy of Art /Aesthetics

**Dominic McIver Lopes**
*University of British Columbia*

Dominic McIver Lopes teaches philosophy at the University of British Columbia, in Vancouver, Canada. He works in philosophy of mind and philosophy of art, specifically the interpretation and evaluation of pictures. He is the author of two forthcoming books, *Understanding Pictures* and *Sight and Sensibility*, and has coedited several collections of papers.

Unlike most other academic disciplines, philosophy is not confined to a specific subject matter. History concerns the past, biology concerns organisms, and education studies concern learning. In principle, it is possible to do the philosophy of X, where you may substitute anything you please for X. In practice, however, philosophers conserve their energies for topics of some importance. Philosophy of art, also called *aesthetics*, illustrates this process in two ways. First, artistic achievement is a life goal for some people and almost everyone values listening and dancing to music, reading stories, and looking at images. The value of art is obvious, but it is also puzzling. The point can be put abstractly: What sense could intelligent beings inhabiting an art-free environment make of our art? What could you tell them about the value of dancing, for example? The point also has a practical side: Why should public resources belonging either to the state or private foundations be used to support the arts, especially when other needs are pressing? Puzzlement about art is one reason to do philosophy of art, and you may wish to study the subject because you care about art. Second, art interests philosophers because philosophical questions about art connect to all the central areas of philosophy. Here is a sample. What is art (metaphysics)? What makes some art good (value theory)? How can we judge art good or bad (epistemology)? How is it possible to tell stories about things that do not exist (philosophy of language)? What is creativity (philosophy of mind)? Doing philosophy of art is one way of doing philosophy. You may be surprised to learn that some philosophers of art are not great art lovers, and you may wish to study aesthetics only because you are interested in some of the toughest problems in philosophy.

## WHAT IS ART?

This question is the first a philosopher of art might think to pose. After all, a prudent first step in any inquiry is to fix upon what it is you want to understand, keeping in mind that what you decide will have an impact on how you answer other questions. The task for the philosopher of art is especially tricky because art and ideas about art have changed rapidly and radically during the past century. "What is art?" is not merely a philosopher's question: it arises for every gallery visitor and every pop music fan.

At one time, "art" — or "fine art" — referred to the sorts of pictures housed in art galleries, music performed in concert halls, and novels found in the "Literature" department of the bookstore. During the past forty years, philosophers have embraced a more expansive conception of art that includes children's drawings, popular music, pulp fiction, B movies, and vernacular architecture. These items all fall within the extension of art — the class of things the term *art* picks out. Presumably philosophers and others noticed that comic books and television shows have certain features that qualify them as art.

One possibility is that these features define art. A definition is a statement of the features that are necessary and sufficient for anything to be art. A piece of writing, for instance, is art only if it has these features and if it has the features then it is art. Philosophers have devised several definitions of art. Plato thought that art is the imitation of objects and actions. Tolstoy thought that art is the expression of feelings that bind a community or culture. Clive Bell, an important early theorist of painting, thought that visual artworks express a special "aesthetic emotion" through arrangements of shapes and colors. None of these ideas is very convincing. Not all art is imitation (e.g., most instrumental music), and not every imitation is art. Not all art is expressive (e.g., Mondrian's grid paintings), and many expressions of feeling are not artistic.

Still, you may suspect that art must have something to do with imitation and expression. Sharing this hunch, some philosophers reject the assumption that the answer to "What is art?" should take the form of a definition (a statement of necessary and sufficient conditions for being art). Art is a cluster of items. Nothing is common to all works of art and nothing separates all art from all nonart. Some are imitative and not expressive; others are expressive and not imitative.

One day in 1964, the Columbia University philosopher Arthur Danto visited the Stable Gallery in New York, which was showing Andy Warhol's "sculptures"

Andy Warhol's work entitled "The Brillo Boxes."

of Brillo soap pad boxes. Danto later wrote that the "Warhol show raised a question which was intoxicating and immediately philosophical, namely why were his boxes works of art while the almost indistinguishable utilitarian cartons were merely containers for soap pads? Certainly the minor observable differences could not ground as grand a distinction as that between Art and Reality!"[1] Warhol showed that artworks can be perceptually indistinguishable from ordinary, nonart objects.

---

[1] Arthur Danto, "Art, Philosophy, and the Philosophy of Art," *Humanities* 4 (1983): 1–2.

The lesson is that art cannot be defined as long as we assume that its defining features must be perceivable—that we should always be able to tell art from non-art just by looking. *Brillo Boxes* are art but they look just like Brillo boxes. What makes them art is the way they are interpreted or the context in which they are made. Anything can be art if interpreted or made in the right conditions. In some contexts art is imitation, in others art is expression, and in others it is neither. Danto suggests a resilient definition of art. The features defining art have to do with interpretation and creation. The upshot is that we must find out what kinds of interpretations or creative contexts transform nonart into art. It means we must view art as a social phenomenon. Philosophers inspired by Danto's work have had a lot to say about this.

## A PARADOX OF FICTION

Knowing what art is does not tell us why we care about art or what its value is. The capacity of artworks to arouse emotions is one source of the value of many artworks. Consider movies. Some movies are good because they deliver a strong jolt of horror. Others are tear-jerkers. Strangely enough, tear-jerkers are often "feel-good" movies. Aristotle noticed that the "tear-jerker" tragedies of his day must somehow bring pleasure, though grief, anxiety, and the other emotions that tragedies arouse are far from pleasurable—they are not emotions we normally spend good money to endure. Painful art is pleasurable to experience: this is a paradox that philosophers such as Hume, Schopenhauer, and Nietzsche have tried to explain away. But there is another, more fundamental paradox about our emotional responses to artworks, a paradox that makes us wonder how it is possible to have emotional responses to many artworks.

The following three statements all seem to be true:

1. We often respond emotionally to fictional characters and their situations,
2. Emotional responses to objects typically presuppose beliefs in the existence of the objects, but
3. We do not believe in the existence of fictional objects.

The first statement is manifestly true. We are saddened by the fate of Anna Karenina and cheer Road Runner as he outwits Wile E. Coyote, but Anna, Wile E., and the Road Runner are fictional and, as (3) says, we do not believe in the existence of fictional objects. The second statement requires some explanation. Many philosophers hold that emotions are more than bodily feelings. Anger and frustration, for example, feel the same because both involve a rise in adrenalin and stepped-up heart rate, but they are different because one is a reaction to a situation that is believed to be unfair or wrong whereas the other involves a belief that one's efforts are obstructed. Likewise, fear involves a belief that the situation is dangerous and joy involves a belief that things are going well. Learning that the situation is not really dangerous dispels our fear and learning that Road Runner eventually falls prey to Wile E. Coyote deflates our cheer, as learning that we have not been wronged defuses our anger and learning that our efforts will succeed undoes our frustration. Emotions are not irrational; they are ways of thinking about and appraising our situation and the are revised as our beliefs change.

The paradox is that although (1) to (3) all seem true, at least one must be false. Suppose that feeling sad for somebody does involve a belief in her existence and suppose we do not believe in the existence of Anna. That means we cannot feel sad for Anna—(1) is false. Or suppose that we do feel sad for Anna and believe that she exists. That means either that we do not know she is fictional or else that we believe in the existence of fictional objects—(3) is false. Or suppose that we do not believe that Anna exists but nevertheless we feel sad for her. That means that emotions do not involve an element of belief—(2) is false. If any two of (1) to (3) are true, then the other is false.

How can we resolve the paradox? It is tempting to deny (3). Perhaps when you are reading or watching a fiction, you temporarily believe that what happens in the story is true and the characters in the story are real. The story evokes a kind of illusion (and the storyteller is a kind of Cartesian evil deceiver). This idea is problematic, however. We do not act, when we read the story, as we would act if we believed the story were true and Anna exists. For one thing, we quite properly take pleasure in her sadness, but we do not properly take pleasure in the sadness of real people. It is one thing to find a soap opera entertaining and another thing to be entertained by horrible things that befall the neighbors!

Another solution is presented in the most important recent book in aesthetics, *Mimesis as Make-Believe,* by Kendall Walton, a philosopher at the University of Michigan. Walton accepts (2) and (3) but amends them both slightly. We do not believe in the existence of fictional objects, but we do *imagine* them. Moreover, emotional responses typically presuppose beliefs, but sometimes imaginings will do instead of beliefs—particularly imaginings about the existence of fictional objects. Reading Tolstoy, you imagine Anna's suffering and so feel something like sadness for her. You do not *really* feel sad for her because sadness is dispelled by the realization that the object of your sadness does not exist. Instead, you feel quasisadness, which is like sadness except it involves imagination instead of belief. Since quasisadness is an emotion, (1) is true.

Notice how this problem in aesthetics touches on epistemology (which is about what we should believe) and metaphysics (which is about what exists) and philosophy of mind (which is about the nature of our mental lives). At the same time it touches on a mystery of everyday human life: we make artworks that engender emotional responses.

## THE PUZZLE OF MUSICAL EXPRESSION

We feel sad for Anna because Tolstoy's story represents her as desperate and distraught. The novel expresses what she feels by representing her as acting the way a person acts when they are desperate and distraught. Many artworks, such as novels and movies, express emotions by representing objects and events. What about music, though? Much music does not represent anything (set aside music with lyrics and so-called program music) and yet it is expressive of emotion. How is that possible? After all, emotions are mental states, so to think of something as expressing an emotion is to think of it as sentient; but music is just structured sound—it is not sentient and we do not normally think it is sentient.

This suggests we should find some sentient creature on whom we have good reason to pin the emotions expressed by the music. One ancient idea is that music expresses what the composer felt as she composed. The trouble with this idea is that the emotions we have good reason to attribute to the composer are not necessarily the emotions expressed by the music. While writing joyous music, a composer may only feel pride in her compositional cleverness or anxiety about meeting her publication deadline. Another popular idea is that music expresses feelings by arousing them in its listeners (we have just seen that artworks can arouse emotional reactions). This idea also faces difficulties. Some listeners all of the time, and most listeners some of the time, are "dry-eyed critics." Your unshakably morose mood need not render you incapable of detecting the joyfulness of a song—indeed, detecting its joyfulness while in a morose mood may simply annoy you.

Impressed by the difficulties facing these ancient and popular ideas, some philosophers propose that we attribute the emotions music expresses to a fictional *persona*. When we hear the music's expression of joy, we imagine that this fictional entity feels the joy. The proposal is especially compelling when applied to long stretches of serious classical music, where something like an emotional narrative unfolds (e.g., dread leading to grief leading to anger leading to resignation and finally hope) and it is natural to think of a fictional person as undergoing this emotional process. Do you imagine a fictional persona undergoing what is expressed by every jingle and ditty, however?

Other philosophers propose that we abandon the assumption that expression implies that someone has the emotion that is expressed. The suggestion gets some plausibility from the fact that it is possible for me or you to express an emotion though we do not feel it. My job interview smile hides my nervousness—it does not reveal inner happiness. Likewise, music may wear a sonic smile, which is an expression of happiness that nobody feels. Peter Kivy, a philosopher of music who teaches at Rutgers University, takes the metaphor of "sonic smiles" seriously. He suggests that the tonal structure, rhythms, and dynamics of a piece of music can mimic a human expression of sadness. Music sounds sad, for example, because its tempo mimics the slow gait of a sad person. The idea has some appeal for explaining expressions of garden variety emotions such as sadness, joy, and anger, but how can music mimic an expression of hope or determination?

Music is quite often emotionally expressive, and this is an important element of its value for us. Nothing could be clearer. Still, it is difficult to understand how music can be expressive in anything like the way people's faces and gestures are expressive.

## ENVOI

Theories of art, the paradox of fiction, musical expressiveness: this is a small sample of what interests philosophers of art. Like most topics in philosophy of art, they do two things: they go to the heart of our puzzlement about a unique human institution and they demand all the skills and resources that philosophy has to offer. Why is a perfect forgery of a painting not as valuable as the original painting it is a copy of? Why should our knowledge about an artist's life have any impact on our

## Boggs's Bills

J. S. G. Boggs makes exacting life-size drawings of currency. On one side of each drawing is a rendition of a bank note embellished by amusing giveaways, such as the replacement of "ONE" with "FUN" on the U.S. one-dollar bill. On the back is documentation of the drawing, including the artist's signature. Most artists sell their drawings; Boggs "spends" his. Presented with the tab at a bar, he offers the bartender a choice between cash payment or a Boggs Bill. The Boggs Bill is offered at "face value"—if a hundred-dollar Boggs Bill is offered in payment for a sixty-dollar bar tab, Boggs expects forty dollars in change. However, Boggs Bills are now reselling at substantially more than face value. You can see, print out, and "spend" a Boggs Bill at www.jsgboggs.com.

The U.S. government charged Boggs as a counterfeiter. Boggs insists he is an artist raising questions about art and value. Who is right? Boggs? The government? Neither? Both? If Boggs is right, what is his artwork, his masterful handicraft or his culture jamming transactions? Would you printout and "spend" a Boggs Bill, following the instructions at www.jsgboggs.com? Why or why not?

appreciation of their work? Does it matter that Leni Riefenstahl's acclaimed 1936 film, *Triumph of the Will,* is also a piece of Nazi propaganda? Does a work of music exist if nobody plays it or listens to it? Why bother to listen to it if you can read the score? The questions about art are seemingly endless, and that is where the philosophy begins.

## QUESTIONS FOR DISCUSSION AND REVIEW

1. What is a definition, and what is the purpose of a definition, of art?

2. There is some evidence that artists make objects specifically in order to agitate against current definitions of art. Is this a good reason to give up trying to define art?

3. What is the difference between emotional responses to fictional and true stories? Are there any advantages or disadvantages to using fiction to provoke emotional response?

4. Suppose a song expresses emotions that it never arouses in its listeners—we always remain "dry-eyed critics." Is this a failing of the song? Suppose a song is so emotionally powerful that it is impossible to remain a dry-eyed critic. Is this a failing of the song?

5. The Getty Foundation is promoting a program of "discipline based art education" for school children. One component of the program is philosophy of art. Is this a good idea? Why or why not?

## SUGGESTED FURTHER READINGS

Noël Carroll, *Philosophy of Art: A Contemporary Introduction* (London: Routledge, 1999).

———, *The Philosophy of Horror, Or Paradoxes of the Heart* (London: Routledge, 1990).

Arthur Danto, *Transfiguration of the Commonplace* (Cambridge: Harvard University Press, 1981).

Berys Gaut and Dominic McIver Lopes, eds., *Routledge Companion to Aesthetics* (London: Routledge, 2000).

Nelson Goodman, *Languages of Art,* 2nd ed. (Indianapolis: Hackett, 1976).

Gordon Graham, *Philosophy of the Arts: An Introduction to Aesthetics* (London: Routledge, 1997).

Eileen John and Dominic McIver Lopes, eds., *Philosophy of Literature: An Anthology* (Oxford: Blackwell, 2003).

Peter Kivy, *Introduction to a Philosophy of Music* (Oxford: Oxford University Press, 2002).

Peter Lamarque and Stein Haugom Olsen, eds., *Aesthetics and the Philosophy of Art: An Anthology* (Oxford: Blackwell, 2003).

Kendall Walton, *Mimesis as Make-Believe* (Cambridge: Harvard University Press, 1990).

# Credits

## Photo and Illustration Credits

Page 9: © Myron Jay Dorf/CORBIS. Page 21: © Bettmann/CORBIS. Page 24: © Mimmo Jodice/CORBIS. Page 26: The Granger Collection. Page 28: © Mike King/CORBIS. Page 30: © Archivo Iconografico, S.A./CORBIS. Pages 36 and 38: © Bettmann/CORBIS. Page 41: © Kim Sayer/CORBIS; AP Photo/Ed Bailey. Page 64: © Bettmann/CORBIS. Page 67: © Yahn Arthus-Bertrand/CORBIS. Page 69: © AFP/CORBIS. Page 76: © Chris Lisle/CORBIS. Page 78: © Avaldo de Luca/CORBIS. Page 79: © Bettmann/CORBIS. Page 85: © Bettmann/CORBIS. Page 87: AFP/Getty Images. Page 90: © David Michel Zimmerman/CORBIS. Pages 101 and 104: © Bettmann/CORBIS. Page 112: Detail from *Young Woman with a Letter,* Samuel Van Hoogstraeten (1627-1678), from the collection of the Mauritshuis, The Hague, the Netherlands. Reproduced in Peter Lopston, ed. The Principles of the Most Ancient and Modern Philosophy by Anne Conway. Pages 114 and 119: © Bettmann/CORBIS. Page 122: © Ted Streshinsky/CORBIS. Pages 135, 140, 144, and 145: © Bettmann/CORBIS. Page 147: Hulton Archive/Getty Images. Pages 162, 163, 168, and 171: © Bettmann/CORBIS. Page 176: © PAL/Topham/The Image Works. Page 182: © Gary Houlder/CORBIS. Page 186: © Bettmann/CORBIS. Page 188: Martine Franck/Magnum Photos. Page 192: Raymond Depardon/Magnum Photos. Page 195: Marty Katz/Time/Pix. Pages 213 and 217: © Bettmann/CORBIS. Page 223: Courtesy of The Master and Fellows of Trinity College. Page 225: David Young Wolff/PhotoEdit Inc. Page 230: © Julian Hirshowitz/CORBIS. Page 256: Felicia Martinez/PhotoEdit Inc. Page 265: AP Photo/Jeff Roberson. Page 270: Reprinted from *Hildegard of Bingen's Book of Divine Words,* edited by Matthew Fox, illustrations by Angela Werneke, © 1987 Bear and Company, Santa Fe, NM. Page 272: © Bettmann/CORBIS. Page 280: AP Photo. Page 283: © Bettmann/CORBIS. Page 314: © Araldo de Luca/CORBIS. Pages 318 and 320: © Bettmann/CORBIS. Page 321: © National Portrait Gallery Archive Engravings Collection no. 47398. Page 326: © Bettmann/CORBIS. Page 329: © Public Record Office/Tohpam-HIP/The Image Works. Pages 333 and 337: © Bettmann/CORBIS. Page 360: The Granger Collection. Page 366: Courtesy Harvard University News. Page 372: © Pat Doyle/CORBIS. Page 373: © Mark Peterson/Getty Images. Page 375: © Reuters New Media Inc./CORBIS. Page 377: © John Dominis/The Image Works. Page 399: © Bettmann/CORBIS. Page 401: © Bryan Allen/CORBIS. Page 403: © 1998 Lu Bro. Bridge Building Images, Inc., P.O. Box 1048, Burlington, VT 05402-1048, www. Bridge Building.com. Page 424: © Bettmann/CORBIS. Page 428: Courtesy of Mary Daly. Pages 445, 449, and 451: © Bettmann/CORBIS. Page 456: Amy Etra/PhotoEdit Inc. Page 499: © Bettmann/CORBIS. Page 504: The Granger Collection. Page 512: © Bettmann/CORBIS. Pages 515 and 524: The Granger Collection. Pages 533: © Bettmann/CORBIS. Page 548: © Topham/The Image Works. Pages 552 and 554: © Bettmann/CORBIS. Page 555: © Robert Galbraith/Reuters New Media Inc./CORBIS. Page 557: © Bettmann/CORBIS. Page 558: © Donna Dietrich. Page 559: Matrix. Pages 564 and 565: © Bettmann/CORBIS. Page A-3: Hulton Archive/Getty Images.

## Text Credits

p. 236: Excerpts from Rick Weiss, "Monkeys Control Robotic Arm with Brain Implants, *The Washington Post,* October 13, 2003, p. A1. © 2003, The Washington Post, reprinted with permission. p. 504; From Chan, Wing-tsit, *The Way of Lao Tzu,* 1st edition, © 1963. Reprinted by permission of Pearson Education, Inc., Upper Saddle River, NJ. p. 506: From Chan, Wing-Tsit: *A Source Book in Chinese Philosophy.* © 1963 Princeton University Press, 1991 renewed PUP. Reprinted by permission of Princeton University Press. p. 507: From Chan, Wing-tsit, *The Way of Lao Tzu,* 1st edition, © 1963. Reprinted by permission of Pearson Education, Inc., Upper Saddle River, NJ. p. 509: From *The Complete Works of Chuang Tzu,* translated by Burton Watson. © 1968 Columbia University Press. Reprinted with the permission of the publisher. p. 510: From *The Complete Works of Chuang Tzu,* translated by Burton Watson. © 1968 Columbia University Press. Reprinted with the permission of the publisher. p. 517: From Chan, Wing-Tsit: *A Source Book in Chinese Philosophy.* © 1963 Princeton University Press, 1991 renewed PUP. Reprinted by permission of Princeton University Press. p. 518: From Chan, Wing-Tsit: *A Source Book in Chinese Philosophy.* © 1963 Princeton University Press, 1991 renewed PUP. Reprinted by permission of Princeton University Press. p. 521: Hui Neng's Poem of Enlightenment from *The Three Pillars of Zen* by Philip Kapleau, copyright © 1989 by Roshi Philip Kapleau. Afterword © 2000 by Bodhin Kjolhede. Used by permission of Anchor Books, a division of Random House, Inc. p. 527: From *Record of Things Heard* by Dogen, translated by Thomas Cleary. Boston: Shambhala Publications, 1989. p. 530: from *Hagakure: The Book of the Samurai* by Yamamoto Tsunetomo, translated by William Scott Wilson. Copyright © 1979 by Kodansha International Ltd. Reprinted by permission of the publisher. p. 532: From *Zen Poems of China and Japan: The Crane's Bill,* translated by Lucien Stryk and Takashi Ikemoto, copyright © 1973 by Lucien Stryk, Takashi Ikemoto & Taigan Takayama. Used by permission of Doubleday, a division of Random House, Inc.

# Glossary/Index

Abandonment (Sartre), 170–172

Abbagnano, Nicola, 164

Abelard, Peter, 271–273

**Absolute, the:** That which is unconditioned and uncaused by anything else; it is frequently thought of as God, a perfect and solitary, self-caused eternal being that is the source or essence of all that exists but that is itself beyond the possibility of conceptualization or definition, 144

**Absolute Idealism:** The early-nineteenth-century school of philosophy that maintained that being is the transcendental unfolding or expression of thought or reason, 143, 159

Absolute Idealists, 142; Fichte, Johann Gottlieb, 143; Hegel, Georg Wilhelm Friedrich, 143–146; Russell, Bertrand on, 216; Schelling, Friedrich Wilhelm Joseph von, 143

Absurdity, 166–170, 172

**Academics:** Philosophers of the third and second centuries B.C.E. in what had been Plato's Academy; they had the reputation of maintaining that all things are inapprehensible, 82

Action at a distance, 116

Actuality (Aristotle), 66. *See also* Pure act/actuality

**Act-utilitarianism:** A form of utilitarianism (subscribed to by Bentham) in which the rightness of an act is determined by its effect on the general happiness, 285

Adorno, Theodor, 183

Aesara [ai-SAH-ruh], 260–261

**Aesthetics:** The philosophical study of art and of value judgments about art and of beauty in general, 10, A1–A7

Afrocentrism, 558–559

"After the Death of God the Father" (Daly), **435–438**

*After Virtue* (MacIntyre), 375–376

Age of Reason, The, 102. *See also* Enlightenment, The

Age of Technology, The, 102

*Agoge:* Way of living, 82

Albert the Great, 88

Alexander the Great, 63, 64, 75, 266, 419

Al-Farabi [el-fuh-RAHB-ee], 500

Al-Ghazali [el-guh-ZAHL-ee], 500–501

Alienation, 337, 340

Al-Kindi [el-KIN-dee], 500

Allah, 500–501

American constitutional theory, 327–330

Ames, Van Meter, 1

Amyntas II, 64

*Analects* (Confucius), 512, **535–536**

**Analysis:** Resolving a complex proposition or concept into simpler ones to gain better understanding of the original proposition or concept; *analysis* comes from a Greek word meaning to "unloosen" or "untie," 215

**Analytic philosophy:** The predominant twentieth-century philosophical tradition in English-speaking countries; analytic philosophy has its roots in British empiricism and holds that analysis is the proper

method of philosophy, 160, 214–238, 357–365 *See also* individual philosophers

Analytic proposition, 426–427

**Anarchism:** A utopian political theory that seeks to eliminate all authority and state rule in favor of a society based on voluntary cooperation and free association of individuals and groups, 337, 341–342, 370

*Anarchy, State, and Utopia* (Nozick), 369, **386–388**

Anaxagoras [an-ak-SAG-uh-rus], 27–28, 29

Anaximander [a-NAK-suh-MAN-der], 21–22

Anaximenes [an-nex-IM-in-eez], 22

**Androgyny:** Having both male and female characteristics; unisex, 452–456; critique of, 454–456

"Androgyny As an Ideal for Human Development" (Ferguson), 453

Animal rights, 363, 372

Animism, 523

Anselm, St., 395–397, 414; *Proslogion,* **431–432**

Anthropocentrism, 471

Anthropology, philosophical, 184

Antifoundationalism, 227

Antinaturalism, 360

**Antirepresentationalism:** A philosophy that denies that the mind or language contains or is a representation of reality, 221, 227–229, 243–244

Apartheid, 552

*Apology* (Plato), 36, 37, 38, **45–48**

**Appeals to emotion:** Flawed reasoning that tries to establish

the work of African thinkers and thinkers of African descent wherever they are located, 548–549

**Paradox of hedonism:** Henry Sidgwick's term for the fact that the desire for pleasure, if it is too strong, defeats its own aim, 286

**Parallelism:** The doctrine that there are two parallel and co-ordinated series of events, one mental and the other physical, and that apparent causal interaction between the mind and the body is to be explained as a manifestation of the correlation between the two series, 108

Parmenides [par-MEN-uh-deez], 24–26, 120

*Parole* (Saussure), 187

Pascal, Blaise, 426, 525

Paul, St. (Paul of Tarsus), 78, 81, 418

Peirce, C. S., 212–214; pragmatic theory of truth, 212–213

**Perception:** A modern word for what Thomas Hobbes called "sense," the basic mental activity from which all other mental phenomena are derived, 110–111

Peripatetics, 65

Person, 550

**Personal identity, problem of:** What are the criteria of sameness of person? 24

Perspectivism, 544

Phantasm (Hobbes), 110

**Phenomena:** In Kant's philosophy, objects as experienced and hence as organized and unified by the categories of the understanding and the forms of space and time, 142; things as they appear to us or, alternatively, the appearances themselves, 142, 174

**Phenomenalism:** The theory that we only know phenomena; in analytic philosophy, the theory that propositions referring to physical objects can, in principle, be expressed in

propositions referring only to sense-data, 224–225

**Phenomenological reduction:** A method of putting aside the ordinary attitude toward the world and its objects in order to see the objects of pure consciousness through intuition, 175

**Phenomenology:** A tradition of twentieth-century Continental philosophy based on the phenomenological method that seeks rigorous knowledge not of things-in-themselves but rather of the structures of consciousness and of things as they appear to consciousness, 160, 174–180

*Phenomenology of Mind* (Hegel), 144, 174

Philip of Macedonia, 64, 75

Philosopher-king (Plato), 310

*Philosophy and Social Hope* (Rorty), **206–207**

Philosophy of art. *See* Aesthetics

Philosophical anthropology, 184

Philosophical behaviorism. *See* Behaviorism

*Philosophical Investigations* (Wittgenstein), 218, 223, 226, 229–231

Philosophy and myth, 29

*Philosophy of History, The* (Hegel), **152**

**Philosophy of mind:** That area of analytic philosophy concerned with the nature of consciousness, mental states, the mind, and the proper analysis of everyday psychological vocabulary, 231–238; dualism, 232; behaviorism, philosophical, 232–234; functionalism, 235–237; identity theory, 234–235, 241–242 physicalist theories, 237–238

Philosophy of religion, 394–438. *See also* God; Anselm, St., 395–397, **431–432;** argument from design, 400, 410–412, 415; cosmological argument, 398–400, 405, 407–408, 412–413, 415; Daly, Mary, 427–430, **435–438,** 454; Descartes, René, 404–406;

Gaunilo, 397; James, William, 419–425; Julian of Norwich, 402–404; Kant, Immanuel, 414–416; Kierkegaard, Søren, 417–418; Leibniz, Gottfried Wilhelm, 407–409; logical positivism, 425–426; moral argument, 400; mysticism, 402–404; Newman, John Henry, 416–417; Nietzsche, Friedrich, 418–419, **433–434;** ontological argument, 396–397, 405, 407–408; Plantinga, Alvin, 423, 430–431; and theology, 394–395; Thomas Aquinas, St., **432–433**

Philosophy; benefits of studying, 11–13; misconceptions about, 5–7; the word, 2

Physicalism. *See* Materialism

Physicalist reductivism, 237–238

Picture theory of meaning (Wittgenstein), 232

Pirsig, Robert M., 166

*Plague, The* (Camus), 169

Plantinga [PLAN-tin-guh], Alvin, 423, 430–431

Plato, 34, 36, 37–45, 63,64, 66, 67, 84, 88, 90, 120, 191, 192, 267, 334, A2; *Apology,* 36, 37, 38, **45–61;** Aristotle, critique by, 68–70; and Augustine, St., 79–80; cave allegory, 29, 40, 42, 43, illustration, 42; *Cratylus,* 38; *Crito,* 36, **342–345;** Divided Line, 42; epistemology, 40–43; ethics, 255–260; *Euthyphro,* 258; *Gorgias,* 38, **287–289;** immortality of soul, 56; *Laws,* 38; Love and becoming, theory of, 43–45; *Meno,* 38, **56–61;** metaphysics, 37–40; and myth, 29; *Parmenides,* 38; *Phaedo,* 36; Phaedrus, 38; political philosophy, 310–312; philosopher-king, 310; profile, *38;* recollection, 56; *Republic,* 29, 37, 38, **48–55,** 258, 310; *Sophist,* 38; *Symposium,* 29, 38, 44; *Theaetetus,* 38, 42; *Timaeus,* 29, 38

**Platonic dualism,** 40

Platonic Form, see Form

Plato's Academy, 38, 64

Plato's Dialogues, 36, 37, 38

Plautus, 517

the laws of your state by continuing to live in it, 322

Tagore [tuh-GORE], Rabindranath, 497, 564–565; profile, *565; Towards Universal Man,* **540–541**

Takuan, 534

*Tale of the Genji* (Murasaki), 524

Tao: In Chinese philosophy, the Way: the ultimate and eternal principle of unity, meaning, and harmony in the universe, 504–505, 511. *See also* Taoism

Taoism: One of the great philosophical traditions in China, according to which the individual will find peace and tranquility through quietly following the Tao, 503–510; Chuang Tzu, 507–510; Lao Tzu, 503–507

Taylor, Harriet, 331–332, 446–447, 448

Taylor, Paul, 471

Teleological argument. *See* Argument from design

Teleological explanation: An explanation of a thing in terms of its ends, goals, purposes, or functions, 91

Tendai Buddhism, 526

Ten Tropes: A collection of ten arguments by the Skeptics against the possibility of knowledge, 81

Thales [THAY-leez], 20–21, 29, 65; on myth, 29; profile, *21*

*Theaetetus* (Plato), 38, 42

Theano [thee-AHN-o], 22–23

Theater of the absurd, 167

Theodicy: A defense of God's goodness and omnipotence in view of apparent evil, 408–409

"Theology and Falsification" (Flew), **434–435**

Theology and philosophy, 89, 394–395, 401

Theology, Christian, 81

Theoretical posits: Entities whose existence we hypothesize to explain our sensory experience, 228

Theory of Forms: Plato's central metaphysical concept, 37–40. *See also* Form

*Theory of Justice, A* (Rawls), 365–369, **385–386**

Thesis (Hegel), 144–145

*Thick and Thin* (Walzer), 373

Thing-in-itself: English for *Ding-an-sich:* a thing as it is independent of any consciousness of it, 142

Third Man argument: Aristotle's criticism of Plato's Theory of Forms, according to which there must be a third thing that ties together a Form with the particular things that exemplify it, 69

Thomas Aquinas [uh-QUINE-nuss], St., 79, 78–81, 88–91; and Aristotle, 88–91; epistemology, 91; essence and existence, 89–90; ethics, 271, 273–274, 275; metaphysics, 89–91; philosophy of religion, 398–402; political philosophy, 313–314; profile, *399; Summa Theologica,* **432–433**

Thompson, William, 446

Thoreau, Henry David, 165

Thought: According to Descartes, the essential attribute of mind, 107

*Timaeus* (Plato), 29, 38

Time and God, 80, 112–113

Timocracy, 311

Tolstoy, Leo, 167, A2, A5

Total skeptic: One who maintains nothing can be known or, alternatively, suspends judgment in all matters, 81

*Towards Universal Man* (Tagore), **540–541**

*Tractatus Logico-Philosophicus* (Wittgenstein), 223, 229–231, 239

Trakl, Georg, 165

Trammell, Richard, 384

Transcendental phenomenology: An epistemological method that seeks the certainty of a pure consciousness of objects in the transcendental ego, 175

*Treatise Concerning the Principles of Human Knowledge* (Berkeley), 119, **128–130**

*Treatise of Human Nature, A* (Hume), 135, 139, 241

Trebilcot, Joyce, 453–454

*Trial, The* (Kafka), 167

*Triumph of the Will* (Riefenstahl), A7

Trotter Cockburn, Catharine, 321

Truth, 196, 417, 563; antirepresentationalist, 221, 228–229, 243–244; pragmatic, 194–195, 212–214,

Truth, as relative, 6, 196

Tutu [too-too], Desmond, 552; profile, *552*

"Two Forms of Androgynism" (Trebilcot), 453–454

Two-realms concept (Plato), 37–40, 80, 101

*Two Treatises of Government* (Locke), 320

Tyranny, 311, 312

*Übermensch* (Nietzsche), 161, 286, 419

Unamuno, Miguel de, 164

Uncaused cause of existence, 90

Universal: That which is denoted by a general word, a word (such as "chair") that applies to more than a single thing, 69–70, 87, 88

Universalistic ethical hedonism: The doctrine that one ought to seek, over everything else, the greatest pleasure for the greatest number of people, 254. *See also* Utilitarianism

Universal phenomenology of consciousness: Attempts made by Hegel and Husserl to devise a pure science of knowing, 174–175

Universals, problem of, 87. *See also* Universal

*Upanishads,* 495–496

Utilitarianism: The doctrine that the rightness of an action is identical with the happiness it produces as its consequence, 281–285, **297–300,** 331–334, **349–351;** critique of, 367, 372

*Utilitarianism* (Mill, John Stuart), **297–300,** 332

Utopianism, 446

*Vaisesika,* 495

*Vaisnavism,* 495

**Part 1**
**Metaphysics and**
**Epistemology**

St. Thomas Aquinas (1225–1274)
Julian of Norwich (1342–1414)
Oliva Sabuco de Nantes (b. 1562) •
Thomas Hobbes (1588–1679)
René Descartes (1596–1650)
Anne Finch Conway (1631–1679)
Benedictus de Spinoza (1632–1677)
John Locke (1632–1704)
Gottfried Wilhelm, Baron von Leibniz (1646–1716)
Catharine Trotter Cockburn (1679
George Berkeley (1
Émile Du C
D

**Part 2**
**Moral and**
**Political Philosophy**
**and Postmodernism**

Hildegard von Bingen (1098–1179)
Heloise (1100/1–1163)
St. Thomas Aquinas (1225–1274)
Niccolò Machiavelli (1469–1527)
Thomas Hobbes (1588–1679)
John Locke (1632–1704)
Catharine Trotter Cockburn (1679
Charles Louis de Secondat, Baron Montesquieu (
Da
Jean-Jacques

**Part 3**
**Philosophy**
**of Religion**

• Gaunilo (eleventh century)
St. Anselm (c. 1033–1109)
St. Thomas Aquinas (1225–1274)
Julian of Norwich (1342–1414)
René Descartes (1596–1650)
Blaise Pascal (1623–1662)
Gottfried Wilhelm, Baron von Leibniz (1646–1716)
Da

**Part 4**
**Eastern and**
**Postcolonial**
**Voices**

Murasaki Shikibu (970–1031)
Avicenna (980–1037)
Al-Ghazālī (1058–1111)
Averroës (1126–1198)
Dogen Zenji (1200–1253)
Sadr al-Di
Yagyu
Miyamo

• Al-Kindi (d. after 870)
Al Fārābī (875–950)